INSTRUCTOR EDITION

WELCOME

At Course Technology our mission is to help people teach and learn about technology. This special Instructor Edition is all about helping YOU teach. We know you have a great deal to manage, and for this reason, we provide you with great tools and resources with every book. This Instructor Edition will save you time by helping you sort through all of this material, and choose the right combination of tools to help you teach the way you want to teach.

INSTRUCTOR EDITION CONTENTS AT A GLANCE

RESOURCES

We know you need more than great textbooks to effectively teach your class. That's why we take the next step in providing you with outstanding Instructor Resources—developed by educators and tested through our rigorous Quality Assurance process. Our goal is to make the teaching and learning experience in your classroom the best it can be. With Course Technology's resources, you'll spend less time prepping, and more time teaching.

INSTRUCTOR RESOURCES CD & WEB SITE: When preparing for your next class, the Instructor Resources CD-ROM is the best place to start. Most of the materials on the Instructor Resources CD-ROM are also available for download on course.com. Check the instructor download section at course.com before each semester for updates to the Instructor Resources for this title! The Instructor Resources CD-ROM (ISBN: 0-619-18758-1) for *Microsoft Office 2003—Illustrated Introductory* contains the following:

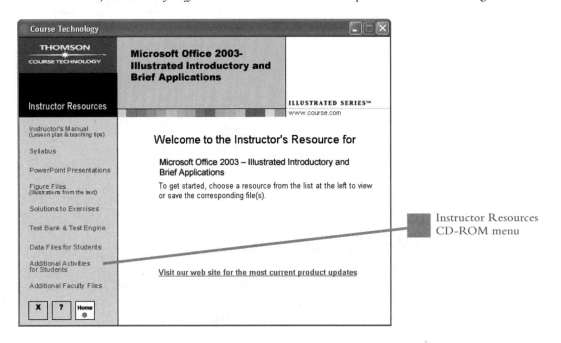

Instructor Resources CD-ROM menu

STUDENT DATA FILES: Many units in this book require that students have access to a set of data files, to bring the lessons being learned to life in realistic settings. While these files are available for your students to download from course.com on their own, many instructors prefer to download the data files from either the Web or the Instructor Resources CD and put them on a location on their school's network for easier student access.

Putting your data files on your own network? Write the location of the files for this book here, for easy reference: _____

And to make your life even easier, the student data files for this title are available in CD format for a small cost to the student (ISBN: 0-619-18783-2). Simply ask your Course Technology Sales representative to bundle this CD with your next shipment of books, and your students will be able to get their files themselves!

ADDITIONAL ACTIVITIES FOR STUDENTS: The Illustrated Series provides two Extra Independent Challenges for every unit in this book. Assign these for group projects, homework, in-class quizzes or as review for the final exam.

INSTRUCTOR'S MANUAL: Need to compile a lecture on Office 2003 for your class that's starting in an hour? Or looking for ways to challenge your students with classroom activities or quick quizzes? The electronic Instructor's Manual is a great place to look for solutions to all of these dilemmas. The Microsoft Word-formatted document for each unit is easily customized for your own notes, includes a Lecture Note for every lesson and is chock-full with great ideas from instructors like yourself.

EXAMVIEW TEST BANK: ExamView features a user-friendly testing environment that allows you to not only publish traditional paper and LAN-based tests, but also Web-deliverable exams. Utilize the ultra-efficient Quick Test Wizard to create an exam in less than five minutes, take advantage of the Course Technology question banks, or customize and create your own exams.

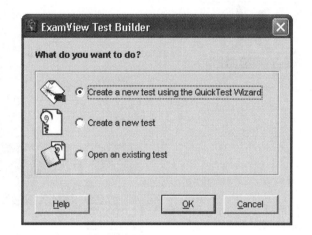

To create an exam in ExamView, open a question bank, click **File** and from the drop down menu select **Switch to Test Builder**.

Select what type of Test Builder you would like to use, click **OK** and then follow the instructions on your screen (will vary depending on what type you choose to create).

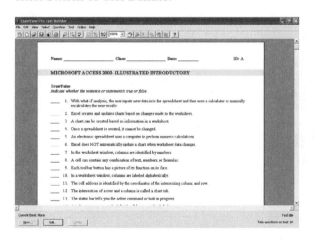

When you are finished, you will have a test ready to distribute to your class and an answer key for easy grading.

SOLUTION FILES: Make homework corrections a snap with all of the solutions right at your fingertips. The Illustrated Series provides you with every file the student is asked to create or modify in the lessons and End-of-Unit material. A Microsoft Word document also includes the answers for the Concepts Review and Skills Review in the End-of-Unit material. New for this edition are checklists for quickly grading the Independent Challenges and the Visual Workshop. The Extra Independent Challenge solution files are also located in this section of your Instructor Resource CD.

POWERPOINT FILES: Delivering engaging and visually impressive lectures is easy with the professionally-designed PowerPoint presentations available for each unit in this book. You can edit the files to fit your needs, post them to your network for students to review key concepts, or save them to the Web for your Distance Learning students.

FIGURE FILES: Looking for figures in the book that are not included in the PowerPoint Presentations? Illustrations for every figure in the textbook are available in electronic form. Use this ancillary to present a slide show in lecture or to print transparencies for use in lecture with an overhead projector.

WEBCT AND BLACKBOARD WebCT and Blackboard are the leading distance learning solutions available today. In the past few years, they've also become popular class-management platforms. Course Technology has partnered with WebCT and Blackboard to bring you online content that fits into both platforms. *Microsoft® Office 2003—Illustrated Introductory* is available with online content in WebCT e-Pack and Blackboard Course Cartridge-format, which includes the following components:

- Topic reviews
- Practice exams
- Case projects
- Custom syllabus
- Test banks
- PowerPoint Presentations

Click on these links in Blackboard to access the syllabus, Topic Reviews, Review Questions, Case Projects, PowerPoint Presentations, Test Bank, and more!

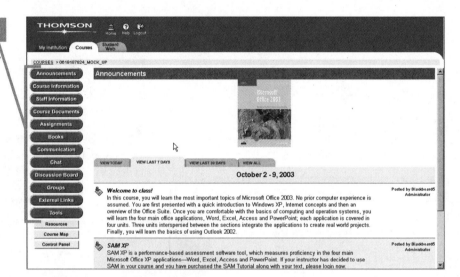

STUDENT ONLINE COMPANION Students also deserve a wealth of resources to reinforce their studies. This text's Student Online companion features links for End of Unit assignments.

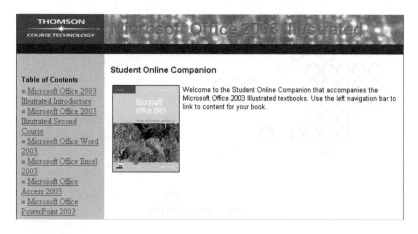

WWW.COURSE.COM

Course Technology is the world's leading IT publisher. Because we focus solely on the Information Technology area, we have the unique ability to address the needs of customers like you.

Find out about the latest technology trends, products, and courseware solutions on the Course Technology Web site, www.course.com.

Stop here before preparing for your class!

Visit often to:

- Connect with your peers through our Online forums
- Learn about the latest software releases and how they will impact you in the classroom
- Browse our online catalog
- Locate and contact your local sales representative
- Register for the next Conference for Information Technology Educators and our other educational events
- Download the files that are contained on this CD

SAM: SOFTWARE TO HELP YOU TEACH, TEST, AND TRAIN.

You can reinforce the lessons presented in this text with SAM Assessment and Training.

The SAM Assessment software allows you to administer hands-on performance exams that measure your students' skill in Microsoft Office applications, the Internet, computer concepts, and much more.

Each skill-based SAM Assessment task includes a corresponding SAM Training exercise. SAM Training enables your students to learn real-world computer tasks in a simulated environment, and helps them absorb these concepts in a variety of ways—through reading, observation, step-by-step practice, and hands-on application.

The SAM system puts you in control of how you deliver exams and training in your course. For example, after completing a given unit in this text you can:

- Schedule a SAM Training lesson that covers only the topics introduced in the unit, and end the lesson with a capstone SAM Assessment exam.
- Schedule an end-of-unit SAM Assessment exam that automatically generates a custom SAM Training pass based on tasks performed incorrectly.
- Allow your students to "skill and drill" on individual SAM Training topics through an interactive SAM Assessment study guide.

SAM ASSESSMENT & TRAINING ALLOWS YOU TO:

- Save time from creating and hand-grading pencil and paper based tests.
- Track students' testing and training progress through more than one dozen reports.
- Seamlessly integrate SAM results into your WebCT or Blackboard platform.
- Protect exams and training assignments with powerful security options.

In addition, you can build customized exams and training exercises from the ground up, allowing you to give pre-assessment tests, mid-terms, final exams, and more.

NOTE: *This Instructor Edition includes an annotated table of contents that lists the SAM skills included in each unit.*

For more information on how to make SAM work for you, please refer to the SAM instructor demonstration CD, which is bound into this Instructor Edition. You can also access the demonstration online at www.course.com/sam.

PASSWORDS AND SECURITY

INSTRUCTOR RESOURCES ON COURSE.COM

Depending on the type of Educational Institution you are, please call one of the support services teams to obtain your password to our online Instructor Resources.

For colleges and universities in the US:
Call Course Technology at **1.800.648.7450** and select option 3 for Support Services.

For Private Career Colleges:
Call Thomson Learning—Career at:
1.800.477.3692

For High Schools:
Call Thomson Learning—School at:
1.800.824.5179

For Corporations, IT Training Centers, and Federal Government Agencies:
Call Course Technology at **1.800.648.7450**

Ensuring students don't get their hands on the answers, test banks, or other resources that we provide you on course.com, password protection is at the forefront of our minds at all times. We monitor each and every caller requesting a password to our instructor resources by verifying with the school the caller indicates as their affiliation.

OTHER RESOURCES AND PASSWORDS

Course Technology knows that protecting these passwords from students is critical, but keeping track of all the passwords for all the tools you may adopt in a given course (one for your online instructor resources, another for SAM, another for your schools' servers...) can be quite a hassle. For your convenience, we're providing space below for you to keep track of all your login information (either literally or with your own code that students won't understand!) for this course.

RESOURCE	USERNAME	PASSWORD

ANNOTATED TABLE OF CONTENTS

Now that you have a better understanding of all the tools that come with *Microsoft® Office 2003—Illustrated Introductory*, how do you fit them all together? This annotated Table of Contents will help sort through the tools and what may be appropriate where. It is also available on your Instructor Resources CD and website in electronic format for easy incorporation into your syllabus.

WINDOWS XP UNIT A: GETTING STARTED WITH WINDOWS XP

This unit is an orientation to the Windows XP operating system covering how to start and properly shut down Windows, using a mouse, moving and resizing windows as well as starting and closing programs.

Assign End-of-Unit material to check student progress. This unit includes Concepts Review, Skills Review, four Independent Challenges and a Visual Workshop.

Independent Challenges are case problems requiring critical thinking and application of the skills learned in the unit. They progress in difficulty - the first having the most step-by-step detailed instructions while the second, third and fourth become more open-ended.

INSTRUCTOR'S MANUAL The Instructor's Manual for this Windows unit contains a preparation guide, teaching tips on Logging into Windows and understanding the variations in desktops, and a classroom activity on using Help.

 SAM The unit opener in this unit refers to an optional SAM assignment. You can assign SAM training for added reinforcement or extra credit. Or you could assign a quiz in SAM Assessment. Some of the topics in SAM that map to this unit include:

■ Keyboard Shortcuts

LABS The "Using Input Devices" and "Using Windows" Student Edition labs (by themselves or a part of SAM) are designed to give hands-on practice with important Windows skills. They provide a great opportunity for students to get more reinforcement of working with Windows.

NOTES:

_____

_____

_____

_____

_____

_____

Windows XP B covers working with multiple programs and understanding file management. Students learn to create, edit and save work in programs such a WordPad and Paint as well as how to work with My Computer and Windows Explorer. Searching for files, as well as deleting and restoring files is covered.

INSTRUCTOR'S MANUAL The Instructor's Manual includes a Quick Quiz to use after covering the lesson Viewing Files and Creating Folders with My Computer and a discussion topic on comparing My Computer and Windows Explorer.

There are Extra Independent Challenges for both Units A and B. Remember to also use the PowerPoint Presentation, ExamView Test Bank, and Distance Learning content for other ways to make preparing and teaching the course easier for you!

 SAM The unit opener in this unit refers to an optional SAM assignment. You can assign SAM training for added reinforcement or extra credit. Or you could assign a quiz in SAM

Assessment. Some of the topics in SAM that map to this unit include:

- Viewing Files and Folders with My Computer
- Creating a Folder
- Opening a File from Windows Explorer
- Restoring Files

LABS The "Managing Files" Student Edition lab (by itself or a part of SAM) is designed to give hands-on practice with important file management skills. They provide a great opportunity for students to get more reinforcement of managing files.

NOTES:

_____

_____

_____

_____

_____

This 4 page appendix focuses on formatting a floppy disk and includes a Clues to Use outlining more information on disks including Zip disks and CD drives. How students organize their Data Files is also covered in this appendix.

 SAM The unit opener in this unit refers to an optional SAM assignment. You can assign SAM training for added reinforcement or extra credit. Or you could assign a quiz in SAM Assessment. Topics in SAM that map to this unit include:

- Formatting a Disk

NOTES:

_____

_____

_____

_____

_____

_____

This unit provides students the chance to get out onto the Internet and learn about Web browsers, how to navigate Web pages, search for information and save and organize a Favorite Web Page. A Clues to Use on page Office-55 covers computer networks and intranets. On page Office-71, a Clues to Use covers using media players including RealOne and Windows Media Player. All four Independent Challenges in this unit are E-Quests.

INSTRUCTOR'S MANUAL The Instructor's Manual includes a discussion topic on the history of the World Wide Web, a quick quiz on terminology associated with the Internet and a classroom activity on using search engines. You can also integrate Extra Independent Challenges, PowerPoint Presentation, and the ExamView Test Bank into this unit.

 SAM The unit opener in this unit refers to an optional SAM assignment. You can assign SAM training for added reinforcement or extra credit. Or you could assign a quiz in SAM

Assessment. Some of the topics in SAM that map to this unit include:

- Starting Microsoft Internet Explorer
- Save a Web page
- Printing a Web Page
- Getting Help in Internet Explorer
- Exiting Internet Explorer

LABS The "Connecting to the Internet" and "Getting the Most out of the Internet" Student Edition labs (by themselves or a part of SAM) are designed to give hands-on practice with important Internet skills.

NOTES:

_____

_____

_____

_____

_____

_____

Before your students start Office 2003, have them read this 16 page unit defining the Office Suite and featuring a two page spread on each of the applications, Internet Explorer and how to integrate Office Information.

INSTRUCTOR'S MANUAL After this unit, use the Instructor's Manual to review the key terms and discuss topics such as integration to prepare students for working in each Office application.

NOTES:

_____

_____

_____

_____

_____

Word Unit A helps students understand Word 2003 as a word processing software and teaches basic skills such as planning a document, starting, saving and printing a document along with coverage of the revamped Help system for Office 2003. An introduction to the new Reading Layout view and Full Screen view are covered in a Clues to Use on page Office-97. A table on page Office-108 describing the function of each task pane used in Word.

Assign End-of-Unit material to check student progress. This unit includes four Independent Challenges which pose case problems for students to solve while increasing in difficulty. The Visual Workshop provides a great self-graded capstone project for the unit.

New to this edition—in many of the units, you will find Advanced Challenge Exercises (ACE) set within the Independent Challenges. These optional steps, set off by an ACE icon and blue bulleted steps, challenge students to explore other areas of the program. If a student chooses not to try them, they can skip over the bulleted tasks and continue on with the lettered steps to complete the project. Two solution files will be provided on the Instructor Resources CD—one if the ACE steps are completed and one if they are not.

INSTRUCTOR'S MANUAL Along with a Lecture Note for each lesson, the Instructor's Manual includes a discussion topic on Word's automatic features, quick quiz on the Save vs. Save As dialog box and also a

classroom activity on using Help. Two Extra Independent Challenges provide additional practice for students. The PowerPoint presentation and test-bank also provide additional content for this unit. Remember to use the grading checklist for the Independent Challenges.

 SAM The unit opener in this unit refers to an optional SAM assignment. You can assign SAM training for added reinforcement or extra credit. Or you could assign a quiz in SAM Assessment. Some of the topics in SAM that map to this unit include:

- Open a document
- Using Word Wrap
- Use Word Help
- Use Print Preview
- Close a document and Exit Word

NOTES:

_____

_____

_____

_____

_____

_____

New to this edition, the Spelling, grammar and Thesaurus lesson has been split into two lessons. The lesson on using the Thesaurus focuses on the Research task pane. This lesson also includes a Clues to Use on viewing and modifying the document properties.

On page Office-124, a Clues to Use has been added on copying and moving items in a long document.

Other topics in this unit include how to open a document, select text, cut and paste vs. copy and paste text, how to use the Office Clipboard, find and replace text and using wizards and templates.

INSTRUCTOR'S MANUAL The Instructor's Manual includes Lecture Notes on each lesson, a teaching tip on Scrolling a document, a classroom activity on techniques for selecting text and a discussion question on search options in the Find and Replace dialog box. Remember to use the PowerPoint Presentation, ExamView Test Bank, Student Online Companion, and Distance Learning content for other ways to make preparing this unit easier.

SAM The unit opener in this unit refers to an optional SAM assignment. You can assign SAM training for added reinforcement or extra credit. Or you could assign a quiz in SAM Assessment. Some of the topics in SAM that map to this unit include:

- Select text
- Cut and Paste text
- Copy and Paste text
- Collect and Paste using the Clipboard task pane
- Check Spelling
- Use the Thesaurus
- Check grammar

NOTES:

_____

_____

_____

_____

_____

_____

This unit covers how to format fonts and effects, work with tabs and indents, bullets and numbering as well as borders and shading.

New to this edition, we have added a Clue to Use on page Office-145 on adding a drop cap and a Clues to Use on page Office-151 on comparing formatting in a document using the Reveal Formatting task pane. We have removed the Clues to Use on Creating a Table from the previous edition and given it its own lesson in Unit D.

Assign End-of-Unit material to check student progress. This unit includes a Concepts Review, Skills Review, four Independent Challenges and a Visual Workshop.

New to this edition—you will find Advanced Challenge Exercises (ACE) set within Independent Challenges 2 and 3. These optional steps, set off by an ACE icon and blue bulleted steps, challenge students to explore Word. If a student chooses not to try them, they can skip over the bulleted tasks and continue on with the lettered steps to complete the project. Two solution files will be provided on the Instructor Resources CD—one if the ACE steps are completed and one if they are not.

INSTRUCTOR'S MANUAL Along with a Lecture Note for each lesson, there is a Quick Quiz on font styles and effects, a discussion topic on understanding the differences between tabs and indents as well as types of indents. For a classroom activity, assign

"Formatting Checklist." Remember to use the grading checklist, PowerPoint Presentation, ExamView Test Bank, Student Online Companion, and Distance Learning content for other ways to make preparing this unit easier.

 SAM The unit opener in this unit refers to an optional SAM assignment. You can assign SAM training for added reinforcement or extra credit. Or you could assign a quiz in SAM Assessment. Some of the topics in SAM that map to this unit include:

- Changing line spacing
- Indent paragraphs
- Add bullets
- Add numbering
- Apply a paragraph border
- Apply shading to paragraphs

NOTES:

_____

_____

_____

_____

_____

_____

Unit D includes topics on formatting Word documents. Lessons cover setting margins, inserting page breaks and page numbers, headers and footers, formatting columns, and inserting Clip Art.

Two new lessons have been added for this edition: one on inserting a table, page Office-182, and another on inserting WordArt, page Office-184.

A new Clues to Use on page Office-183 features the Document Map and moving around in a long document. More coverage of buttons on the Header and Footer toolbar has been added to Table D-3.

INSTRUCTOR'S MANUAL Along with a Lecture Note for every lesson, there is also a discussion topic on controlling the flow of text in a document, and a classroom activity on MLA Style. The PowerPoint Presentation, ExamView Test Bank, Student Online Companion, and Distance Learning material provide additional content for other ways to make preparing this unit easier.

SAM The unit opener in this unit refers to an optional SAM assignment. You can assign SAM training for added reinforcement or extra credit. Or you could assign a quiz in SAM Assessment. Some of the topics in SAM that map to this unit include:

- Modify page margins
- Insert Clip Art
- Create WordArt
- Change the page orientation
- Create tables

LABS The "Word Processing" Student Edition lab (by itself or a part of SAM) is designed to give hands-on practice with important word processing skills. Incorporate this lab after completing Units A-D of Word for students to get more reinforcement.

NOTES:

_____

_____

_____

_____

_____

_____

Excel Unit A gives an overview of using a spreadsheet program and teaches basic topics such as starting Excel, opening and saving a workbook, entering labels and values, previewing and printing a worksheet, getting Help and exiting Excel. Table A-2 familiarizes the student with commonly used pointers and a Clues to Use on page Office-213 covers using the Office Assistant.

Assign End-of-Unit material to check student progress. This unit includes four Independent Challenges which pose case problems for students to solve while increasing in difficulty. The Visual Workshop provides a great self-graded capstone project for the unit.

You will find Advanced Challenge Exercises (ACE) set within Independent Challenges 1 and 3 in this unit. These optional steps, set off by an ACE icon and blue bulleted steps, challenge students to explore areas of Excel. If a student chooses not to try them, they can skip over the bulleted tasks and continue on with the lettered steps to complete the project. Two solution files will be provided on the Instructor Resources CD—one if the ACE steps are completed and one if they are not.

INSTRUCTOR'S MANUAL The Instructor's Manual includes a Lecture Note on every lesson along with a discussion topic on the common uses for spreadsheets, a Quick Quiz on understanding the Excel

window, and a classroom activity on using Help. The PowerPoint Presentation, ExamView Test Bank, Student Online Companion, and Distance Learning material provide additional content for other ways to make preparing this unit easier.

 SAM The unit opener in this unit refers to an optional SAM assignment. You can assign SAM training for added reinforcement or extra credit. Or you could assign a quiz in SAM Assessment. Some topics in SAM that map to this unit include:

- Print preview a worksheet
- Print a worksheet
- Use Save

NOTES:

_____

_____

_____

_____

_____

This unit covers editing cell entries, entering formulas, using functions and understanding relative and absolute cell references. Covered in Clues to Use boxes are the "Order of precedence in Excel formulas" page Office-230, "Using the MIN and MAX function" on page Office-233, and a new Clues to Use on page Office-239 that covers printing worksheet formulas.

Assign End of Unit Material as homework or an in-class quiz. The Concepts Review outlines elements of the Excel worksheet and the Skills Review provides additional hands-on reinforcement. The Visual Workshop provides a practical project that requires independent thinking—perfect for a capstone project!

INSTRUCTOR'S MANUAL The Instructor's Manual includes a Quick Quiz on formulas and functions, a discussion topic on understanding cell references and a classroom activity on planning and designing a worksheet. There are also Lecture Notes for every lesson, two Extra Independent Challenges, a grading checklist, PowerPoint presentation and an ExamView test bank for this unit.

SAM The unit opener in this unit refers to an optional SAM assignment. You can assign SAM training for added reinforcement or extra credit. Or you could assign a quiz in SAM Assessment. Some of the topics in SAM that map to this unit include:

- Use absolute references
- Use relative references
- Create formulas using the SUM function

NOTES:

_____

_____

_____

_____

_____

_____

_____

EXCEL 2003 UNIT C: FORMATTING A WORKSHEET

Excel Unit C covers how to format a worksheet using fonts and font sizes, adjusting column widths, inserting and deleting rows and columns, applying colors, patterns, and borders and checking spelling. Clues to Use in this unit cover the Format Painter, page Office-253, inserting and adjusting clip art, page Office-255 and using email to send a workbook, Office-266.

INSTRUCTOR'S MANUAL The Instructor's Manual includes a Lecture Note for every lesson, a Quick Quiz on the formatting they have learned in the first three lessons, and a Classroom Activity on Formatting Choices. The PowerPoint Presentation, ExamView Test Bank, Student Online Companion, and Distance Learning material provide additional content for this unit.

SAM The unit opener in this unit refers to an optional SAM assignment. You can assign SAM training for added reinforcement or extra credit. Or you could assign a quiz in SAM Assessment. Some of the topics in SAM that map to this unit include:

- Change Fonts
- Apply bold, italics and underline
- Change the font color
- Add borders
- Email a workbook from within Excel

NOTES:

_____

_____

_____

_____

_____

_____

Excel Unit D covers working with charts, including how to plan and design a chart, create, move and resize a chart, format a chart, draw on a chart and preview and print a chart.

Table D-1 describes commonly used chart types and Clues to Use topics cover changing the location of a chart, page Office-283 and exploding a pie chart, page Office-291.

INSTRUCTOR'S MANUAL The Instructor's Manual for this unit includes a discussion topic on choosing the best chart and a classroom activity on chart comparisons. Lecture Notes for each lesson are available to integrate into your own notes and remember to look at the PowerPoint presentation, Extra Independent Challenges, ExamView testbank and Distance Learning material for additional content.

 SAM The unit opener in this unit refers to an optional SAM assignment. You can assign SAM training for added reinforcement or extra credit. Or you could assign a quiz in SAM

Assessment. Some of the topics in SAM that map to this unit include:

- Edit a Chart
- Position a Chart
- Print a Chart
- Format Charts
- Create Charts using the Pie Chart type

LABS The "Spreadsheets" Student Edition lab (by itself or a part of SAM) is designed to give hands-on practice with important skills used in Excel. Incorporate this lab after completing Units A-D of Excel for students to get more practice with spreadsheets.

NOTES:

_____

_____

_____

_____

_____

New to this edition are three units of Portfolio Projects. Each unit contains 2 projects which integrate the skills learned in each Office application. Assign these projects as tests, capstone projects or have students create a portfolio to show off these real-world documents!

Portfolio Project A integrates the skills students have learned in the Word and Excel units. Topics in Project 1 include creating charts in Excel, creating a report in Word and then linking the charts with the report. Project 2 covers creating a price list in Excel and then inserting that price list into a Word document.

INSTRUCTOR'S MANUAL The Instructor's Manual includes Lecture Notes and discussion topics. You can also integrate the PowerPoint presentation into your classroom lecture.

NOTES:

_____

_____

_____

_____

_____

_____

Access Unit A provides students with an overview of Access 2003 including understanding relational database, database terminology, starting Access and opening a database, navigating records, and printing a datasheet. To help get students familiarized with Access, Table A-3 describes elements of the database window.

INSTRUCTOR'S MANUAL Lectures Notes are available for every lesson to incorporate into your notes. A discussion topic on relational databases and a classroom activity on database examples are also included. The PowerPoint presentation, ExamView test bank and Distance Learning material all provide additional coverage of this unit. You can also assign the Extra Independent Challenges for homework or an in-class quiz.

 SAM The unit opener in this unit refers to an optional SAM assignment. You can assign SAM training for added reinforcement or extra

credit. Or you could assign a quiz in SAM Assessment. Some of the topics in SAM that map to this unit include:

- Start Access
- Use Access Help
- Close Access
- Open an existing database
- Preview a report

NOTES:

_____

_____

_____

_____

_____

_____

This unit covers using table and queries including organizing fields, creating a table, formatting a datasheet, understanding sorting, filtering and finding as well as creating and modifying a query. Clues to Use in this unit include using wildcards, page Office-352, searching for blank fields, page Office-357 and understanding And and Or criteria, page Office-361.

Assign End-of-Unit material to check student progress. This unit includes a Concepts Review, Skills Review, four Independent Challenges and a Visual Workshop.

New to this edition—you will find Advanced Challenge Exercises (ACE) set within Independent Challenges 2 and 3. These optional steps, set off by an ACE icon and blue bulleted steps, challenge students to explore areas of Access. If a student chooses not to try them, they can skip over the bulleted tasks and continue on with the lettered steps to complete the project. Two solution files will be provided on the Instructor Resources CD—one if the ACE steps are completed and one if they are not.

INSTRUCTOR'S MANUAL The Instructor's Manual includes a discussion topic on choosing data types and a classroom activity on reverse engineering of a database. There is also a quick quiz on the different tools in a database to find information. Each lesson

has a Lecture Note and there is also a PowerPoint presentation and ExamView testbank that contains more information to incorporate into your notes. Remember to look at the grading checklist for more information.

 SAM The unit opener in this unit refers to an optional SAM assignment. You can assign SAM training for added reinforcement or extra credit. Or you could assign a quiz in SAM Assessment. Some of the topics in SAM that map to this unit include:

- Create a table using the Table Wizard
- Create Select queries using the Simple Query Wizard
- Open a query

NOTES:

_____

_____

_____

_____

_____

_____

Unit C is about using form in Access. Content includes planning a form, creating a form, using text boxes for calculations, modify tab order, enter, edit and print records and inserting an image. Table C-1 lists all the form controls that students will use and also lists if they are bound or unbound.

INSTRUCTOR'S MANUAL The Instructor's Manual includes a Lecture Note for every lesson and has both a discussion topic and classroom activity on examining forms. You can use the Extra Independent Challenges for homework assignments. There is also PowerPoint presentations, an ExamView test bank and Distance Learning material for this unit.

 SAM The unit opener in this unit refers to an optional SAM assignment. You can assign SAM training for added reinforcement or extra

credit. Or you could assign a quiz in SAM Assessment. Some of the topics in SAM that map to this unit include:

- Create forms using the Form Wizard
- Modify labels
- Edit records from a table using a datasheet
- Modify labels

NOTES:

_____

_____

_____

_____

_____

_____

INSTRUCTOR EDITION

Access Unit D focuses on using reports and includes coverage of planning and creating a report, changing the sort order, aligning and formatting controls and changing the page layout.

Clues to Use in the unit include Why Reports should be based on Queries, page Office-399 and adding a field to a report, page Office-403.

INSTRUCTOR'S MANUAL The Instructor's Manual includes a discussion topic on grouping versus sorting and a classroom activity on examining reports as well as a Lecture Note for every lesson. There is also a PowerPoint presentation, ExamView test bank and Distance Learning content for this unit.

 SAM The unit opener in this unit refers to an optional SAM assignment. You can assign SAM training for added reinforcement or extra credit. Or you could assign a quiz in SAM Assessment. Some of the topics in SAM that map to this unit include:

- Create a report using Report Wizard
- Format controls

- Sort records in a database
- Format a report

LABS The "Database" Student Edition lab (by itself or a part of SAM) is designed to give hands-on practice with important skills used in Access. Incorporate this lab after completing Units A-D of Access for students to get more practice with databases.

NOTES:

_____

_____

_____

_____

_____

Portfolio Project B integrates the skills students have learned in the Word, Excel and Access units. Topics in Project 1 include creating a database, creating a cylinder chart in Excel and creating a profile in Word. Project 2 covers creating a database and analyzing the data and creating a memo in Word.

Assign these projects as tests, capstone projects or have students create a portfolio to show off their real-world documents!

INSTRUCTOR'S MANUAL The Instructor's Manual includes Lecture Notes and Discussion topics. Be sure to integrate the PowerPoint presentation into your classroom lecture.

NOTES:

_____

_____

_____

_____

_____

_____

PowerPoint Unit A gives an overview of presentation software that includes starting the application, using the AutoContent Wizard, viewing and saving a presentation, how to get Help and research information, and print, close and exit PowerPoint. A Clues to Use on page Office-437 explains how to create a shortcut on the desktop.

Assign End-of-Unit material to check student progress. This unit includes a Concepts Review, Skills Review, four Independent Challenges and a Visual Workshop.

New to this edition—you will find Advanced Challenge Exercises (ACE) set within Independent Challenges 1 and 4. These optional steps, set off by an ACE icon and blue bulleted steps, challenge students to explore areas of PowerPoint. If a student chooses not to try them, they can skip over the bulleted tasks and continue on with the lettered steps to complete the project. Two solution files will be provided on the Instructor Resources CD—one if the ACE steps are completed and one if they are not.

INSTRUCTOR'S MANUAL The Instructor's Manual includes a Lecture Note for every lesson in the unit. There is a discussion topic on giving presentations and a Classroom Activity on AutoContent Wizards.

The PowerPoint Presentation, ExamView Test Bank, Student Online Companion, and Distance Learning material provide additional content for this unit.

 SAM The unit opener in this unit refers to an optional SAM assignment. You can assign SAM training for added reinforcement or extra credit. Or you could assign a quiz in SAM Assessment. Some of the topics in SAM that map to this unit include:

- Create presentations from a blank presentation
- Using the Research Task Pane
- Print Handouts

NOTES:

_____

_____

_____

_____

_____

_____

PowerPoint Unit B outlines how to create a presentation and covers topics such as planning an effective presentation, enter slide text, adding slide headers and footers, choosing a look for a presentation, check the spelling in a presentation and how to evaluate a presentation. Clues to Use topics include using templates from the Web, page Office-463, using Speech Recognition, page Office-465 and entering and printing notes, page Office-471.

INSTRUCTOR'S MANUAL Along with a Lecture Note for every lesson that you can incorporate into your notes, there is a discussion topic on building an effective presentation, and a classroom activity on evaluating a presentation. Use the Extra Independent Challenges as homework or an in-class quiz. The PowerPoint presentation, ExamView text bank and Distance Learning material are also available for this unit.

SAM The unit opener in this unit refers to an optional SAM assignment. You can assign SAM training for added reinforcement or extra credit. Or you could assign a quiz in SAM Assessment. Some of the topics in SAM that map to this unit include:

- Add text to slide
- Check Spelling
- Add information to the Footer area of Slide Master

NOTES:

_____

_____

_____

_____

_____

_____

PowerPoint Unit C includes coverage of opening an existing presentation, drawing and modifying an object, aligning and grouping objects, formatting text and importing text from Microsoft Word. A Clues to Use on page Office-499 teaches students how to insert slides from other presentations.

End of Unit Material makes great homework or in-class assignments. Independent Challenges require critical thinking and increase in difficulty. The fourth Independent Challenge is an E-quest which is a case project with a web-focus. The Visual Workshop provides a great self-graded capstone project for the unit.

INSTRUCTOR'S MANUAL The Instructor's Manual includes a discussion topic on formatting text and a classroom activity on exploring formatting. Remember to use the Lecture Notes for every lesson as well as the grading checklist and PowerPoint presentation for this unit.

SAM The unit opener in this unit refers to an optional SAM assignment. You can assign SAM training for added reinforcement or extra credit. Or you could assign a quiz in SAM Assessment. Some of the topics in SAM that map to this unit include:

- Format text in slides
- Modify presentation templates

NOTES:

_____

_____

_____

_____

_____

PowerPoint Unit D focuses on enhancing a presentation. Students learn to insert clip art, embed a chart, create tables, use slide show commands and set slide show timings and transitions as well as slide animation effects. Be sure to review table D-2 which outlines the basic slide show keyboard controls. A Clues to Use on page Office-525 covers rehearsing slide show timing.

INSTRUCTOR'S MANUAL The Instructor's Manual has a Lecture Note for each lesson, a discussion topic on a presentation checklist and a Classroom activity where students give a presentation.

The PowerPoint presentation, ExamView test bank and Distance Learning content provide additional material for this unit that can be incorporated into your notes.

 SAM The unit opener in this unit refers to an optional SAM assignment. You can assign SAM training for added reinforcement or extra credit. Or you could assign a quiz in SAM

Assessment. Some of the topics in SAM that map to this unit include:

- Add Clip Art images to a slide
- Add Charts to slides
- Create tables on slides
- Apply an animation effect to a single slide

LABS The "Presentation software" Student Edition lab (by itself or a part of SAM) is designed to give hands-on practice with important skills used in PowerPoint. Incorporate this lab after completing Units A-D of PowerPoint for students to get more practice with presentation software.

NOTES:

_____

_____

_____

_____

_____

Portfolio Project C integrates the skills students have learned in the Word, Excel, Access and PowerPoint units. Topics in Project 1 include creating source materials and creating and updating a presentation. Project 2 covers creating a presentation and adding Excel and Word objects to that presentation.

Assign these projects as tests, capstone projects or have students create a portfolio to show off their real-world documents!

INSTRUCTOR'S MANUAL The Instructor's Manual includes Lecture Notes and Discussion topics. Be sure to integrate the PowerPoint presentation into your classroom lecture.

NOTES:

_____

_____

_____

_____

_____

This unit gives students an overview of working with Microsoft Outlook. Topics covered include understanding e-mail, starting Outlook 2003, add a contact to the Address Book, create and send a new message, reply to and forward messages, send a message with an attachment, create a distribution list and send a message to a distribution list. Clues to Use cover topics such as Email etiquette, page Office-551, flagging messages on page Office-561, and options when sending messages, page Office-563.

INSTRUCTOR'S MANUAL The Instructor's Manual includes Lecture Notes for every lesson and a discussion topic on email etiquette, a quick quiz on the different parts of the Outlook window, and a classroom activity on exploring Outlook tools. There is an Extra Independent Challenge for this unit that can be assigned as homework or a quiz. The PowerPoint presentation also provides additional content for these lessons.

LABS The "E-mail" Student Edition lab (by itself or a part of SAM) is designed to give hands-on practice with important skills used in e-mail applications. Incorporate this lab after completing Outlook for students to get more practice with e-mail.

NOTES:

_____

_____

_____

_____

_____

_____

OUTLOOK 2003 APPENDIX: MANAGING INFORMATION USING OUTLOOK

This appendix on managing information includes coverage of organizing your contacts, managing your appointments and tasks and using the Journal and Notes. A Clues to Use on page Office-578 covers using Outlook Today.

NOTES:

_____

_____

_____

_____

_____

Microsoft® Office 2003

ILLUSTRATED

INTRODUCTORY

(1 of 2)

Beskeen • Cram • Duffy • Friedrichsen • Reding

THOMSON
COURSE TECHNOLOGY

Australia • Canada • Mexico • Singapore • Spain • United Kingdom • United States

THOMSON

COURSE TECHNOLOGY

Microsoft® Office 2003 - Illustrated Introductory

Beskeen/Cram/Duffy/Friedrichsen/Reding

Executive Editor:
Nicole Jones Pinard

Production Editors:
Anne Valsangiacomo, Aimee Poirier, Philippa Lehar, Daphne Barbas, Melissa Panagos

QA Manuscript Reviewers:
Chris Carvalho, John Freitas, Chris Kunciw, Burt LaFontaine, Jeff Schwartz, Alex White

Product Manager:
Christina Kling Garrett

Developmental Editors:
Rachel Biheller Bunin, Pamela Conrad, Kim Crowley, Jeanne Herring, Jane Hosie-Bounar, Lisa Ruffolo

Text Designer:
Joseph Lee, Black Fish Design

Associate Product Manager:
Emilie Perreault

Editorial Assistant:
Abbey Reider

Composition House:
GEX Publishing Services

Contributing Author:
Rachel Biheller Bunin

The Illustrated Series Vision

Teaching and writing about computer applications can be extremely rewarding and challenging. How do we engage students and keep their interest? How do we teach them skills that they can easily apply on the job? As we set out to write this book, our goals were to develop a textbook that:

- works for a beginning student

- provides varied, flexible and meaningful exercises and projects to reinforce the skills

- serves as a reference tool

- makes your job as an educator easier, by providing resources above and beyond the textbook to help you teach your course

Our popular, streamlined format is based on advice from instructional designers and customers. This flexible design presents each lesson on a two-page spread, with step-by-step instructions on the left, and screen illustrations on the right. This signature style, coupled with high-caliber content, provides a comprehensive yet manageable introduction to Microsoft Office 2003 - it is a teaching package for the instructor and a learning experience for the student.

Author Acknowledgments

David Beskeen I would like to thank Rachel Biheller Bunin for her tireless efforts and editorial insights, which have made my work better. I would also like to thank Course Technology for all of their vision and support over the last 10 years; I look forward to many more!

Rachel Biheller Bunin I would like to thank Nicole Pinard for asking me, once again, to contribute to this terrific project and work with the Office Illustrated Team. I want to thank Christina Kling Garrett for her guidance, superb project management, and sense of humor during the project. I also want to thank Jeanne Herring, my Development Editor, for her skillful edits and creative suggestions; and Anne Valsangiacomo, our Production Editor for creating this gorgeous book. Special thanks to my husband David and my three wonderful children, Jennifer, Emily, and Michael for their support and enthusiasm during the long hours I spent working on this book.

Carol Cram A big thank you to developmental editors Jane Hosie-Bounar and Jeanne Herring for their patience, good humor, and insight! And, as always, everything I do is made possible by Gregg and Julia. They make everything worthwhile.

Jennifer Duffy Many talented people at Course Technology helped to shape this book — thank you all. I am especially indebted to Pam Conrad for her precision editing and endless good cheer throughout the many months of writing. On the home front, I am ever grateful to my family for their patience, and to Nancy Macalaster, who so lovingly cared for my babies during the long hours I needed to be at my desk.

Lisa Friedrichsen The Access portion is dedicated to my students, and all who are using this book to teach and learn about Access. Thank you. Also, thank you to all of the professionals who helped me create this book.

Elizabeth Eisner Reding Creating a book of this magnitude is a team effort. I would like to thank my husband, Michael, as well as Christina Kling Garrett, the project manager who experienced a true baptism-by-fire, Emilie Perreault, associate product manager, and my development editors, Kim Crowley and Jeanne Herring, for their suggestions and corrections. I would also like to thank the production and editorial staff for all their hard work that made this project a reality.

Preface

Welcome to *Microsoft® Office 2003–Illustrated Introductory*. Each lesson in this book contains elements pictured to the right.

How is the book organized?

The book is organized into sections, by application, illustrated by the brightly colored tabs on the sides of the pages: Windows XP, Internet Explorer, Introducing Office 2003, Word, Excel, Access, PowerPoint, and Outlook. Three units of integration projects follow the Excel, Access, and PowerPoint sections.

What kinds of assignments are included in the book? At what level of difficulty?

The lessons use MediaLoft, a fictional chain of bookstores, as the case study. The assignments on the light purple pages at the end of each unit increase in difficulty. Data files and case studies, with many international examples, provide a great variety of interesting and relevant business applications. Assignments include:

- **Concepts Reviews** include multiple choice, matching, and screen identification questions.

- **Skills Reviews** provide additional hands-on, step-by-step reinforcement.

- **Independent Challenges** are case projects requiring critical thinking and application of the unit skills. The Independent Challenges increase in difficulty, with the first one in each unit being the easiest (most step-by-step with detailed instructions). Independent Challenges 2 and 3 become increasingly open-ended, requiring more independent problem solving.

- **E-Quest Independent Challenges** are case projects with a Web focus. E-Quests require the use of the World Wide Web to conduct research to complete the project.

- **Advanced Challenge Exercises** set within the Independent Challenges provide optional steps for more advanced students.

- **Visual Workshops** are practical, self-graded capstone projects that require independent problem solving.

Each 2-page spread focuses on a single skill.

Concise text introduces the basic principles in the lesson and integrates a real-world case study.

UNIT A Word 2003

Saving a Document

To store a document permanently so you can open it and edit it in the future, you must save it as a **file**. When you **save** a document you give it a name, called a **filename**, and indicate the location where you want to store the file. Files can be saved to your computer's internal hard disk, to a floppy disk, or to a variety of other locations. You can save a document using the Save button on the Standard toolbar or the Save command on the File menu. Once you have saved a document for the first time, you should save it again every few minutes and always before printing so that the saved file is updated to reflect your latest changes. You save your memo with the filename Marketing Memo.

STEPS

TROUBLE
If you don't see the extension .doc on the filename in the Save As dialog box, don't worry. Windows can be set to display or not to display the file extensions.

1. **Click the Save button on the Standard toolbar**
   The first time you save a document, the Save As dialog box opens, as shown in Figure A-7. The default filename, Memorandum, appears in the File name text box. The default filename is based on the first few words of the document. The .doc extension is assigned automatically to all Word documents to distinguish them from files created in other software programs. To save the document with a different filename, type a new filename in the File name text box, and use the Save in list arrow to select where you want to store the document file. You do not need to type .doc when you type a new filename. Table A-3 describes the functions of the buttons in the Save As dialog box.

2. **Type Marketing Memo in the File name text box**
   The new filename replaces the default filename. It's a good idea to give your documents brief filenames that describe the contents.

TROUBLE
This book assumes your Data Files for Unit A are stored in a folder titled UnitA. Substitute the correct drive or folder if this is not the case.

3. **Click the Save in list arrow, then navigate to the drive or folder where your Data Files are located**
   The drive or folder where your Data Files are located appears in the Save in list box. Your Save As dialog box should resemble Figure A-8.

4. **Click Save**
   The document is saved to the location you specified in the Save As dialog box, and the title bar displays the new filename, "Marketing Memo.doc."

5. **Place the insertion point before August in the second sentence, type early, then press [Spacebar]**
   You can continue to work on a document after you have saved it with a new filename.

6. **Click **
   Your change to the memo is saved. Saving a document after you give it a filename saves the changes you make to the document. You also can click File on the menu bar, and then click Save to save a document.

Clues to Use

Recovering lost document files

Sometimes while you are working on a document, Word might freeze, making it impossible to continue working, or you might experience a power failure that shuts down your computer. Should this occur, Word has a built-in recovery feature that allows you to open and save the files that were open at the time of the interruption. When you restart Word after an interruption, the Document Recovery task pane opens on the left side of your screen and lists both the original and the recovered versions of the Word files. If you're not sure which file to open (original or recovered), it's usually better to open the recovered file because it includes your latest changes to the document. You can, however, open and review all the versions of the file that were recovered and select the best one to save. Each file listed in the Document Recovery task pane has a list arrow with options that allow you to open the file, save the file, delete the file, or show repairs made to the file.

WORD A-10 GETTING STARTED WITH WORD 2003

OFFICE-102

Hints as well as troubleshooting advice, right where you need it–next to the step itself.

Clues to Use boxes provide concise information that either expands on the major lesson skill or describes an independent task that in some way relates to the major lesson skill.

Special Office feature! Sequential page numbers 1–612.

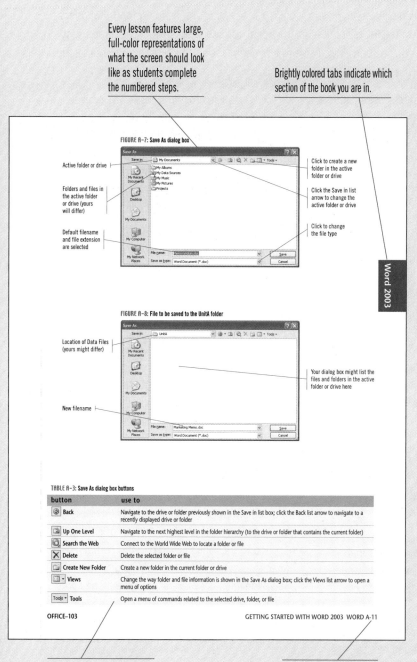

Every lesson features large, full-color representations of what the screen should look like as students complete the numbered steps.

Brightly colored tabs indicate which section of the book you are in.

FIGURE A-7: Save As dialog box

Active folder or drive

Folders and files in the active folder or drive (yours will differ)

Default filename and file extension are selected

Click to create a new folder in the active folder or drive

Click the Save in list arrow to change the active folder or drive

Click to change the file type

Word 2003

FIGURE A-8: File to be saved to the UnitA folder

Location of Data Files (yours might differ)

New filename

Your dialog box might list the files and folders in the active folder or drive here

TABLE A-3: Save As dialog box buttons

button	use to
Back	Navigate to the drive or folder previously shown in the Save in list box; click the Back list arrow to navigate to a recently displayed drive or folder
Up One Level	Navigate to the next highest level in the folder hierarchy (to the drive or folder that contains the current folder)
Search the Web	Connect to the World Wide Web to locate a folder or file
Delete	Delete the selected folder or file
Create New Folder	Create a new folder in the current folder or drive
Views	Change the way folder and file information is shown in the Save As dialog box; click the Views list arrow to open a menu of options
Tools	Open a menu of commands related to the selected drive, folder, or file

OFFICE-103

GETTING STARTED WITH WORD 2003 WORD A-11

Tables are quickly accessible summaries of key terms, toolbar buttons, or keyboard alternatives connected with the lesson material. Students can refer easily to this information when working on their own projects at a later time.

The pages are numbered according to section and unit. Word indicates the section, A indicates the unit, 11 indicates the page.

Is this book Microsoft Office Specialist Certified?

When used in conjunction with *Microsoft® Office 2003—Illustrated Second Course,* this book covers the Microsoft Office Specialist objectives for Word, Excel, Access, and PowerPoint. See the inside front cover for more information on other Illustrated titles meeting Microsoft Office Specialist certification.

The first page of each unit includes objectives set in red to indicate which skills covered in the unit are Microsoft Office Specialist skills. A grid on the Review Pack and the Instructor's Resource disk lists all the exam objectives and cross-references them with the lessons and exercises.

What online content solutions are available to accompany this book?

Visit www.course.com for more information on our online content for Illustrated titles. Options include:

MyCourse 2.0
Need a quick, simple tool to help you manage your course? Try MyCourse 2.0, the easiest to use, most flexible syllabus and content management tool available. MyCourse 2.0 offers you brand new content, including Topic Reviews, Extra Case Projects, and Quizzes, to accompany this book.

WebCT
Course Technology and WebCT have partnered to provide you with the highest quality online resources and Web-based tools for your class. Course Technology offers content for this book to help you create your WebCT class, such as a suggested Syllabus, Lecture Notes, Practice Test questions, and more.

Blackboard
Course Technology and Blackboard have also partnered to provide you with the highest quality online resources and Web-based tools for your class. Course Technology offers content for this book to help you create your Blackboard class, such as a suggested Syllabus, Lecture Notes, Practice Test questions, and more.

Instructor Resources

The Instructor Resources CD is Course Technology's way of putting the resources and information needed to teach and learn effectively into your hands. With an integrated array of teaching and learning tools that offers you and your students a broad range of technology-based instructional options, we believe this CD represents the highest quality and most cutting edge resources available to instructors today. Many of these resources are available at www.course.com. The resources available with this book are:

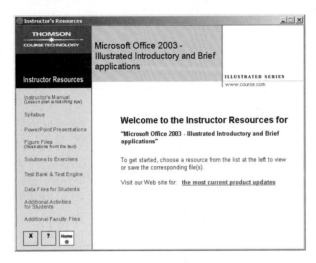

- **Data Files for Students**—To complete most of the units in this book, your students will need **Data Files**. Put them on a file server for students to copy. The Data Files are available on the Instructor Resources CD-ROM, the Review Pack, and can also be downloaded from www.course.com.

Instruct students to use the **Data Files List** included on the Review Pack and the Instructor Resources CD. This list gives instructions on copying and organizing files.

- **Solutions to Exercises**—Solutions to Exercises contains every file students are asked to create or modify in the lessons and End-of-Unit material. A Help file on the Instructor Resources CD includes information for using the Solution Files. There is also a document outlining the solutions for the End-of-Unit Concepts Review, Skills Review and Independent Challenges.

- **PowerPoint Presentations**—Each unit has a corresponding PowerPoint presentation that you can use in lecture, distribute to your students, or customize to suit your course.

- **Instructor's Manual**—Available as an electronic file, the Instructor's Manual is quality-assurance tested and includes unit overviews, detailed lecture topics with teaching tips for each unit.

- **Sample Syllabus**—Prepare and customize your course easily using this sample course outline.

- **Figure Files**—The figures in the text are provided on the Instructor Resources CD to help you illustrate key topics or concepts. You can create traditional overhead transparencies by printing the figure files. Or you can create electronic slide shows by using the figures in a presentation program such as PowerPoint.

- **ExamView**—ExamView is a powerful testing software package that allows you to create and administer printed, computer (LAN-based), and Internet exams. ExamView includes hundreds of questions that correspond to the topics covered in this text, enabling students to generate detailed study guides that include page references for further review. The computer-based and Internet testing components allow students to take exams at their computers, and also saves you time by grading each exam automatically.

SAM 2003 Assessment & Training

SAM 2003 helps you energize your class exams and training assignments by allowing students to learn and test important computer skills in an active, hands-on environment.

With SAM 2003 Assessment, you create powerful interactive exams on critical applications such as Word, Outlook, PowerPoint, Windows, the Internet, and much more. The exams simulate the application environment, allowing your students to demonstrate their knowledge and think through the skill by performing real-world tasks.

Designed to be used with the Illustrated series, SAM 2003 Assessment & Training includes built-in page references so students can create study guides that match the Illustrated textbooks you use in class. Powerful administrative options allow you to schedule exams and assignments, secure your tests, and run reports with almost limitless flexibility.

Contents

| WINDOWS XP | **Appendix: Formatting a Floppy Disk** | **49** |

| INTERNET | **Unit A: Getting Started with Internet Explorer** | **53** |

| OFFICE 2003 | **Unit A: Introducing Microsoft Office 2003** | **77** |

| EXCEL 2003 | Unit A: Getting Started with Excel 2003 | 197 |

| EXCEL 2003 | Unit B: Building and Editing Worksheets | 223 |

EXCEL 2003	Unit C: Formatting a Worksheet	251

EXCEL 2003	Unit D: Working with Charts	277

INTEGRATION

Unit A: Integrating Word and Excel   301

ACCESS 2003

Unit A: Getting Started with Access 2003   317

ACCESS 2003

Unit D: Using Reports   395

INTEGRATION

Unit B: Integrating Word, Excel, and Access   421

POWERPOINT 2003

Unit A: Getting Started with PowerPoint 2003   437

POWERPOINT 2003 **Unit B: Creating a Presentation** **461**

POWERPOINT 2003 **Unit C: Modifying a Presentation** **485**

POWERPOINT 2003

Unit D: Enhancing a Presentation   509

INTEGRATION

Unit C: Integrating Word, Excel, Access, and PowerPoint   533

OUTLOOK 2003   Unit A: Getting Started with Outlook 2003   549

OUTLOOK 2003   Appendix: Managing Information Using Outlook   573

Read This Before You Begin

Software Information and Required Installation

This book was written and tested using Microsoft Office 2003 - Professional Edition, with a typical installation on Microsoft Windows XP, including installation of the most recent Windows XP Service Pack, and with Internet Explorer 6.0 or higher. Some of the exercises in this book assume that your computer is connected to the Internet. If you are not connected to the Internet, see your instructor for information on how to complete the exercises.

Tips for Students

What are Data Files?

To complete many of the units in this book, you need to use Data Files. A Data File contains a partially completed database, so that you don't have to type in all the information in the database yourself. Your instructor will either provide you with copies of the Data Files or ask you to make your own copies. Your instructor can also give you detailed instructions on how to organize your files, as well as a complete listing of all the files you'll need and will create, or you can find the list and the instructions for organizing your files in the Review Pack. In addition, because Word has no Data Files for Unit A and PowerPoint has no Data Files for Units A and B, you will need to create those folders at the same level as the other unit folders so that you have a place to save the files you create. In addition, if you are using floppy disks for your Data Files, you'll need to consider the important information about Access Data Files on page XX as you organize your files for this book. You may also need to use multiple disks to complete some of the work in the Integration units, depending on the size of the graphics files you use in your projects.

Why is my screen different from the book?

Your desktop components and some dialog box options might be different if you are using an operating system other than Windows XP.

Depending on your computer hardware capabilities and the Windows XP Display settings on your computer, you may also notice the following differences even if you are using Windows XP:

- Your screen may look larger or smaller because of your screen resolution (the height and width of your screen).

- Your title bars and dialog boxes may not display file extensions. To display file extensions, click Start on the taskbar, click Control Panel, click Appearance and Themes, then click Folder Options. Click the View tab if necessary, click Hide extensions for known file types to deselect it, then click OK. Your Office dialog boxes and title bars should now display file extensions.

- The colors of the title bar in your screen may be a solid blue, and the cells in Excel may appear different from the orange and gray because of your color settings.

- Depending on your Office settings, your toolbars may be displayed on a single row and your menus may display a shortened list of frequently used commands. Office menus and toolbars can modify themselves to your working style by displaying only the most frequently used buttons and menu commands.

Toolbars in one row

Toolbars in two rows

To view buttons not currently displayed, click a Toolbar Options button ▪ at the end of either the Standard or Formatting toolbar. To view the full list of menu commands, click the double arrow at the bottom of the menu.

In order to have your toolbars displayed in two rows, showing all buttons, and to have the full menus displayed, you must turn off the personalized menus and toolbars feature. Click Tools on the menu bar, click Customize, select the show Standard and Formatting toolbars on two rows and Always show full menus check boxes on the Options tab, and then click Close. This book assumes you are displaying toolbars in two rows and displaying full menus.

Important Information for Access Units if you are using floppy disks

Compact on Close?

If you are storing your Access databases on floppy disks, *you should **not** use the Compact on Close option* (available from the Tools menu). While the Compact on Close feature works well if your database is stored on your hard drive or on another large storage device, it can cause problems if your database is stored on a floppy when the size of your database is greater than the available free space on the floppy. Here's why: When you close a database with the Compact on Close feature turned on, the process creates a temporary file that is just as large as the original database file. In a successful compact process, this temporary file is deleted after the compact procedure is completed. But if there is not enough available space on your floppy to create this temporary file, the compact process never finishes, which means that your original database is never closed properly. If you do not close an Access database properly before attempting to use it again, you can corrupt it beyond repair. *Therefore, if you use floppies to complete these exercises, please follow the Review Pack guidelines on how to organize your databases or ask your instructor for directions so that you do not run out of room on a floppy disk or corrupt your database.*

Closing a Database Properly

It is extremely important to close your databases properly before copying, moving, e-mailing the database file, or before ejecting the Data Files floppy disk from the disk drive. Access database files are inherently multi-user, which means that multiple people can work on the same database file at the same time. To accomplish this capability, Access creates temporary files to keep track of which record you are working on while the database is open. These temporary files must be closed properly before you attempt to copy, move, or e-mail the database. They must also be closed before you eject a floppy that contains the database. If these temporary files do not get closed properly, the database can be corrupted beyond repair. Fortunately, Access closes these temporary files automatically when you close the Access application window. So to be sure that you have properly closed a database that is stored on a floppy, *close not only the database window, but also **close the Access application** window before copying, moving, or e-mailing a database file, as well as before ejecting a floppy that stores the database.*

2000 vs. 2002/2003 File Format

New databases created in Access 2003 default to an Access 2000 file format, which is why "Access 2000 file format" is shown in the database window title bar for the figures in this book. This also means that Access databases now support seamless backward compatibility with prior versions of Access including Access 2000 and Access 2002, like other products in the Microsoft Office suite, such as Word and Excel.

But while the Data Files for this book can be opened and used in Access 2000 or Access 2002, the figures in this book present the Access 2003 application, use the Access 2003 menus and toolbars, and highlight the new features of Access 2003 including new smart tags, new error indicators, the ability to easily locate object dependencies, the ability to update properties automatically, a new backup tool, new themes for forms, and improvements to PivotTables and PivotCharts.

Microsoft Jet database engine Information

You may not have the latest version of the Microsoft Jet database engine. To obtain the latest update, follow the prompts in the dialog box that appears when you open a database. (This dialog box will only appear if you do not have the latest version of the Microsoft Jet database engine.)

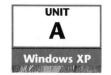

Getting Started with Windows XP

OBJECTIVES

Start Windows and view the desktop
Use the mouse
Start a program
Move and resize windows
Use menus, keyboard shortcuts, and toolbars
Use dialog boxes
Use scroll bars
Use Windows Help and Support Center
Close a program and shut down Windows

If you have a SAM user profile, you may have access to hands-on instruction, practice, and assessment of the skills covered in this unit. Log in to your SAM account and go to your assignments page to see what your instructor has assigned.

Microsoft Windows XP, or simply Windows, is an operating system. An **operating system** is a kind of computer program that controls how a computer carries out basic tasks such as displaying information on your computer screen and running other programs. Windows helps you save and organize the results of your work as **files**, which are electronic collections of data, with each collection having a unique name (called the **filename**). Windows also coordinates the flow of information among the programs, printers, storage devices, and other components of your computer system, as well as among other computers on a network. When you work with Windows, you use **icons**, small pictures intended to be meaningful symbols of the items they represent. You will also use rectangular-shaped work areas known as windows, thus the name of the operating system. This unit introduces you to basic skills that you can use in all Windows programs.

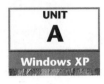

Starting Windows and Viewing the Desktop

When you turn on your computer, Windows XP automatically starts and the desktop appears (you may be prompted to select your user name and/or enter your password first). The desktop, shown in Figure A-1, is where you can organize all the information and tools you need to accomplish your computer tasks. On the desktop, you can access, store, share, and explore information seamlessly, whether it resides on your computer, a network, or on the **Internet**, a worldwide collection of over 40 million computers linked together to share information. When you start Windows for the first time, the desktop appears with the **default** settings, those preset by the operating system. For example, the default color of the desktop is blue. If any of the default settings have been changed on your computer, your desktop will look different from the one in the figures, but you should be able to locate the items you need. The bar at the bottom of the screen is the **taskbar**, which shows what programs are currently running. You click the **Start button** at the left end of the taskbar to perform such tasks as starting programs, finding and opening files, and accessing Windows Help. The **Quick Launch toolbar** often appears next to the Start button; it contains several buttons you can click to start Internet-related programs quickly, and another that you can click to show the desktop when it is not currently visible. Table A-1 identifies the icons and other elements you see on your desktop. If Windows XP is not currently running on your computer, follow the steps below to start it now.

STEPS

TROUBLE

If a Welcome to Microsoft Windows tour opens, move your mouse pointer over the Next button in the lower-right corner of the dialog box and click the left mouse button once; when you see the Do you want to activate Windows now? dialog box, click the No, remind me every few days option. See your instructor or technical support person for further assistance.

1. **Turn on your computer and monitor**

   When Windows starts, you may see an area where you can click your user name or a Log On to Windows dialog box. If so, continue to Step 2. If not, view Figure A-1, then continue on to the next lesson.

2. **Click the correct user name, if necessary, type your password, then press** [Enter]

   Once the password is accepted, the Windows desktop appears on your screen. See Figure A-1.

   If you don't know your password, see your instructor or technical support person.

Clues to Use

Accessing the Internet from the Desktop

Windows XP provides a seamless connection between your desktop and the Internet with Internet Explorer. Internet Explorer is an example of a **browser**, a program designed to access the **World Wide Web** (also known as the **WWW**, or simply the **Web**). Internet Explorer is included with the Windows XP operating system. You can access it on the Start menu or by clicking its icon if it appears on the desktop or on the Quick Launch toolbar. You can use it to access Web pages and to place Web content such as weather or stock updates on the desktop for instant viewing. This information is updated automatically whenever you connect to the Internet.

FIGURE A-1: Windows desktop

Icons (yours might be different)

Start button

Taskbar

Quick Launch toolbar

TABLE A-1: Elements of a typical Windows desktop

desktop element	icon	allows you to
My Computer		Work with different disk drives, folders, and files on your computer
My Documents folder		Store documents, graphics, video and sound clips, and other files
Internet Explorer		Start the Internet Explorer browser to access the Internet
Recycle Bin		Delete and restore files
My Network Places		Open files and folders on other computers and install network printers
My Briefcase		Synchronize files when you use two computers
Outlook Express		Send and receive e-mail and participate in newsgroups
Start button	start	Start programs, open documents, search for files, and more
Taskbar		Start programs and switch among open programs and files
Quick Launch toolbar		Display the desktop, start Internet Explorer, and start Outlook Express

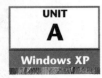

UNIT A Windows XP

Using the Mouse

A **mouse** is a handheld **input** or **pointing device** that you use to interact with your computer. Input or pointing devices come in many shapes and sizes; some, like a mouse, are directly attached to your computer with a cable; others function like a TV remote control and allow you to access your computer without being right next to it. Figure A-2 shows examples of common pointing devices. Because the most common pointing device is a mouse, this book uses that term. If you are using a different pointing device, substitute that device whenever you see the term "mouse." When you move the mouse, the **mouse pointer** on the screen moves in the same direction. You use the **mouse buttons** to select icons and commands, which is how you communicate with the computer. Table A-2 shows some common mouse pointer shapes that indicate different activities. Table A-3 lists the five basic mouse actions. ▰▰▰ Begin by experimenting with the mouse now.

STEPS

1. **Locate the mouse pointer on the desktop, then move the mouse across your desk or mouse pad**

   Watch how the mouse pointer moves on the desktop in response to your movements; practice moving the mouse pointer in circles, then back and forth in straight lines.

> **TROUBLE**
> If the Recycle Bin window opens during this step, your mouse isn't set with the Windows XP default mouse settings. See your instructor or technical support person for assistance. This book assumes your computer is set to all Windows XP default settings.

2. **Position the mouse pointer over the Recycle Bin icon**

   Positioning the mouse pointer over an item is called **pointing**.

3. **With the pointer over the , press and release the left mouse button**

   Pressing and releasing the left mouse button is called **clicking** (or single-clicking, to distinguish it from double-clicking, which you'll do in Step 7). When you position the mouse pointer over an icon or any item and click, you select that item. When an item is **selected**, it is **highlighted** (shaded differently from other items), and the next action you take will be performed on that item.

4. **With selected, press and hold down the left mouse button, move the mouse down and to the right, then release the mouse button**

   The icon becomes dimmed and moves with the mouse pointer; this is called **dragging**, which you do to move icons and other Windows elements. When you release the mouse button, the item is positioned at the new location (it may "snap" to another location, depending on the settings on your computer).

5. **Position the mouse pointer over the , then press and release the right mouse button**

   Clicking the right mouse button is known as **right-clicking**. Right-clicking an item on the desktop produces a **shortcut menu**, as shown in Figure A-3. This menu lists the commands most commonly used for the item you have clicked. A **command** is a directive that provides access to a program's features.

> **QUICK TIP**
> When a step tells you to "click," use the left mouse button. If it says "right-click," use the right mouse button.

6. **Click anywhere outside the menu to close the shortcut menu**

7. **Position the mouse pointer over the , then quickly press and release the left mouse button twice**

   Clicking the mouse button twice quickly is known as **double-clicking**; in this case, double-clicking the Recycle Bin icon opens the Recycle Bin window, which displays files that you have deleted.

8. **Click the Close button ⊠ in the upper-right corner of the Recycle Bin window**

FIGURE A-2: Common pointing devices

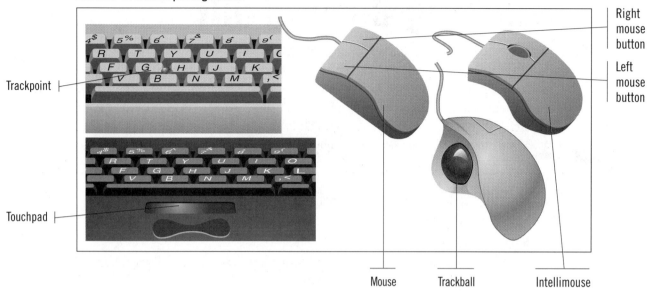

Trackpoint

Touchpad

Right mouse button

Left mouse button

Mouse   Trackball   Intellimouse

FIGURE A-3: Displaying a shortcut menu

Selected icon

Pointer positioned over icon

Shortcut menu

My Documents

My Computer

My Network Places

Recycle

Open
Explore
Empty Recycle Bin

Create Shortcut

Properties

Intern Explorer

TABLE A-2: Common mouse pointer shapes

shape	used to
⇖	Select items, choose commands, start programs, and work in programs
I	Position mouse pointer for editing or inserting text; called the insertion point or Text Select pointer
⧖	Indicate Windows is busy processing a command
↔	Change the size of a window; appears when mouse pointer is on the border of a window
⦥	Select and open Web-based data and other links

TABLE A-3: Basic mouse techniques

technique	what to do
Pointing	Move the mouse to position the mouse pointer over an item on the desktop
Clicking	Press and release the left mouse button
Double-clicking	Press and release the left mouse button twice quickly
Dragging	Point to an item, press and hold the left mouse button, move the mouse to a new location, then release the mouse button
Right-clicking	Point to an item, then press and release the right mouse button

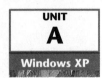

Starting a Program

Clicking the Start button on the taskbar opens the **Start menu**, which lists submenus for a variety of tasks described in Table A-4. As you become familiar with Windows, you might want to customize the Start menu to include additional items that you use most often. Windows XP comes with several built-in programs, called **accessories**. Although not as feature-rich as many programs sold separately, Windows accessories are useful for completing basic tasks. In this lesson, you start a Windows accessory called **WordPad**, which is a word-processing program you can use to create and edit simple documents.

STEPS

1. **Click the** Start button **on the taskbar**

   The Start menu opens.

2. **Point to** All Programs

   The All Programs submenu opens, listing the programs and categories for programs installed on your computer. WordPad is in the category called Accessories.

QUICK TIP

The left side of the Windows XP Start menu lists programs you've used recently, so the next time you want to open WordPad, most likely it will be handy in this list of recently opened programs.

---

3. **Point to** Accessories

   The Accessories menu, shown in Figure A-4, contains several programs to help you complete common tasks. You want to start WordPad.

4. **Click** WordPad

   WordPad starts and opens a blank document window, as shown in Figure A-5. Don't worry if your window does not fill the screen; you'll learn how to maximize it in the next lesson. Note that a program button appears on the taskbar and is highlighted, indicating that WordPad is open.

TABLE A-4: Start menu categories

category	description
Default	Displays the name of the current user; different users can customize the Start menu to fit their work habits
Internet Explorer / Outlook Express	The two programs many people use for a browser and e-mail program; you can add programs you use often to this list (called the "pinned items list")
Frequently used programs list	Located below Internet Explorer and Outlook Express, contains the last six programs used on your computer; you can change the number listed
All Programs	Displays a menu of most programs installed on your computer
My Documents, etc.	The five items in this list allow you to quickly access files you've saved in the three folders listed (My Documents, My Pictures, and My Music), as well as access My Computer, which you use to manage files, folders, and drives on your computer; the My Recent Documents list contains the last 15 files that have been opened on your computer
Control Panel / Connect To / Printers and Faxes	Control Panel displays tools for selecting settings on your computer; Connect To lists Internet connections that have been set up on your computer; and Printers and Faxes lists the printers and faxes connected to your computer
Help and Support / Search / Run	Help and Support provides access to Help topics and other support services; Search locates files, folders, computers on your network, and Web pages on the Internet; Run opens a program, file, or Web site by letting you type commands or names in a dialog box
Log Off / Turn Off Computer	End your Windows session; used when you are done using the computer and don't expect to use it again soon

FIGURE A-4: Cascading menus

Arrow indicates submenu

Submenu

Click to open WordPad

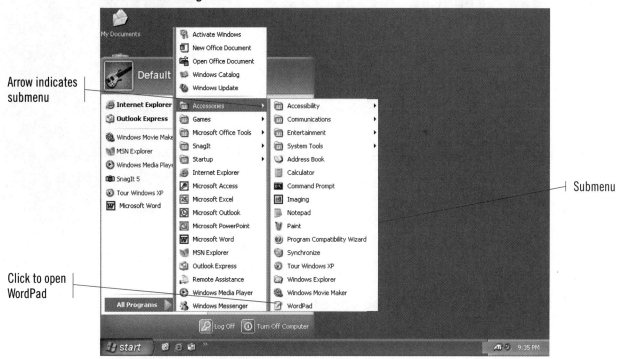

FIGURE A-5: WordPad program window

Document window

Program button indicates open program

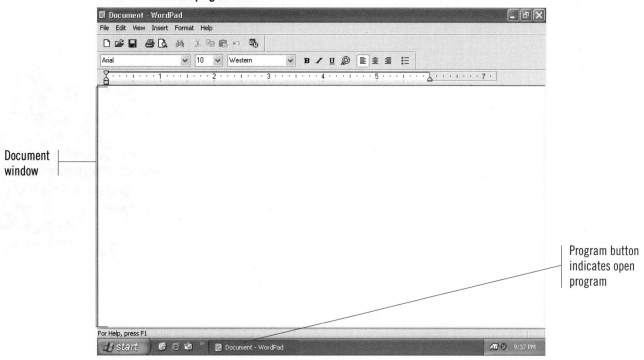

Clues to Use

Customizing the Start Menu

With Windows XP, you can change the way the Start menu looks and behaves by opening the Control Panel (click the Start button and then click Control Panel), switching to Classic view, if necessary, then double-clicking Taskbar and Start Menu. To get the look and feel of the classic Start menu from earlier versions of Windows, click the Start Menu tab and then click the Classic Start menu option button. You can then click the Customize button to add shortcuts to the Start menu for desired programs and documents, or change the order in which they appear. To preserve the Windows XP look of the Start menu but modify how it behaves, click the Customize button next to the Start menu and select the options you want.

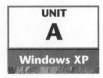

Moving and Resizing Windows

One of the powerful features of Windows is the ability to open more than one window or program at once. This means, however, that the desktop can get cluttered with the various programs and files you are using. You can keep your desktop organized by changing the size of a window or moving it. You can do this by clicking the sizing buttons in the upper-right corner of any window or by dragging a corner or border of any window that does not completely fill the screen. ▰▰▰▰▰ Practice sizing and moving the WordPad window now.

STEPS

1. **If the WordPad window does not already fill the screen, click the** Maximize button ▣ **in the WordPad window**

   When a window is **maximized**, it takes up the whole screen.

2. **Click the** Restore button ▣ **in the WordPad window**

   To **restore** a window is to return it to its previous size, as shown in Figure A-6. The Restore button only appears when a window is maximized.

3. **Position the pointer on the right edge of the WordPad window until the pointer changes to ↔, then drag the border to the right**

   The width of the window increases. You can change the height or width of a window by dragging any of the four sides.

   > **QUICK TIP**
   > You can resize windows by dragging any corner. You can also drag any border to make the window taller, shorter, wider, or narrower.

4. **Position the pointer in the lower-right corner of the WordPad window until the pointer changes to ↖, as shown in Figure A-6, then drag down and to the right**

   The height and width of the window increase proportionally when you drag a corner instead of a side. You can also position a restored window wherever you want on the desktop by dragging its title bar. The **title bar** is the area along the top of the window that displays the filename and program used to create it.

5. **Drag the** title bar **on the WordPad window up and to the left, as shown in Figure A-6**

   The window is repositioned on the desktop. At times, you might want to close a program window, yet keep the program running and easily accessible. You can accomplish this by minimizing a window.

   > **QUICK TIP**
   > If you have more than one window open and you want to quickly access something on the desktop, you can click the Show Desktop button ▣ on the Quick Launch toolbar. All open windows are minimized so the desktop is visible. If your Quick Launch toolbar isn't visible, right-click the taskbar, point to Toolbars, and then click Quick Launch.

6. **In the WordPad window, click the** Minimize button ▬

   When you **minimize** a window, it shrinks to a program button on the taskbar, as shown in Figure A-7. WordPad is still running, but it is out of your way.

7. **Click the** WordPad program button **on the taskbar to reopen the window**

   The WordPad program window reopens.

8. **Click the** Maximize button ▣ **in the upper-right corner of the WordPad window**

   The window fills the screen.

FIGURE A-6: Restored program window

Title bar

Sizing buttons

Drag to
resize height
and width
proportionally

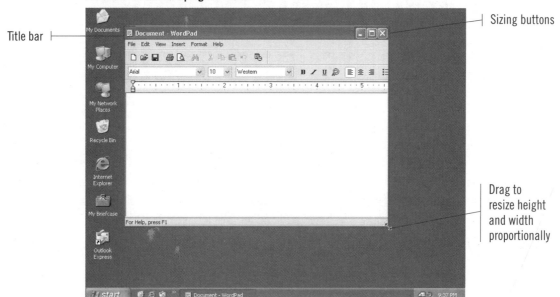

FIGURE A-7: Minimized program window

Indicates
program is
running but
not in use

Clues to Use

More about sizing windows

Keep in mind that some programs contain two sets of sizing buttons: one that controls the program window itself and another that controls the window for the file with which you are working. The program sizing buttons are located in the title bar and the file sizing buttons are located below them. See Figure A-8. When you minimize a file window within a program, the file window is reduced to an icon in the lower-left corner of the program window, but the size of the program window remains intact. (*Note:* WordPad does not use a second set of window sizing buttons.)

Also, to see the contents of more than one window at a time, you can open the desired windows, right-click a blank area on the taskbar, and then click either Tile Windows Vertically or Tile Windows

Horizontally. With the former, you see the windows side by side, and with the latter, the windows are stacked one above the other. You can also click Cascade Windows to layer any open windows in the upper-left corner of the desktop, with the title bar of each clearly visible.

FIGURE A-8: Program and file sizing buttons

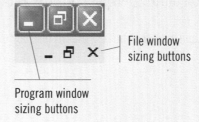

File window
sizing buttons

Program window
sizing buttons

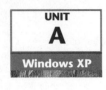

Using Menus, Keyboard Shortcuts, and Toolbars

A **menu** is a list of commands that you use to accomplish certain tasks. Each Windows program also has its own set of menus, which are located on the **menu bar** under the title bar. The menus organize commands into groups of related tasks. See Table A-5 for a description of items on a typical menu. **Toolbar buttons** offer another method for executing menu commands; instead of clicking the menu and then the menu command, you click the button for the command. A **toolbar** is a set of buttons usually positioned below the menu bar. You will open My Computer, use a menu and toolbar button to change how the contents of the window appear, and then add and remove a toolbar button.

STEPS

> **TROUBLE**
>
> If you don't see the My Computer icon on your desktop, right-click the desktop, click Properties, click the Desktop tab, click the Customize Desktop button, click the My Computer check box, then click OK twice.

1. **Minimize WordPad, if necessary, then double-click the** My Computer icon 🖥️ **on the desktop**

   The My Computer window opens. You now have two windows open: WordPad and My Computer. My Computer is the **active window** (or active program) because it is the one with which you are currently working. WordPad is **inactive** because it is open but you are not working with it.

2. **Click** View **on the menu bar**

   The View menu appears, listing the View commands, as shown in Figure A-9. On a menu, a **check mark** identifies a feature that is currently enabled or "on." To disable or turn "off" the feature, you click the command again to remove the check mark. A **bullet mark** can also indicate that an option is enabled.

3. **Click** List

   The icons are now listed one after the other rather than as larger icons.

> **TROUBLE**
>
> [Alt][V] means that you should press and hold down the Alt key, press the V key, and then release both simultaneously.

4. **Press** [Alt][V] **to open the View menu, then press** [T] **to open the Toolbars submenu**

   The View menu appears again, and then the Toolbars submenu appears, with check marks next to the selected commands. Notice that a letter in each command on the View menu is underlined. These are **keyboard navigation indicators**, indicating that you can press the underlined letter, known as a **keyboard shortcut**, instead of clicking to execute the command.

5. **Press** [C] **to execute the Customize command**

   The Customize Toolbar dialog box opens. A **dialog box** is a window in which you specify how you want to perform a task; you'll learn more about working in a dialog box shortly. In the Customize Toolbar dialog box, you can add toolbar buttons to the current toolbar, or remove buttons already on the toolbar. The list on the right shows which buttons are currently on the toolbar, and the list on the left shows which buttons are available to add.

6. **Click the** Home button **in the Available toolbar buttons section, then click the** Add button **(located between the two lists)**

   As shown in Figure A-10, the Home button is added to the Standard toolbar.

7. **Click the** Home button **in the Current toolbar buttons section, click the** Remove button, **then click** Close **on the Customize Toolbar dialog box**

   The Home button disappears from the Standard toolbar, and the Customize Toolbar dialog box closes.

> **QUICK TIP**
>
> When you rest the pointer over a button without clicking, a ScreenTip often appears with the button's name.

8. **On the My Computer toolbar, click the** Views button list arrow 🔲 ▾, **then click** Details

   Some toolbar buttons have an arrow, which indicates the button contains several choices. Clicking the button shows the choices. The Details view includes a description of each item in the My Computer window.

FIGURE A-9: Opening a menu

Menu bar

Check mark

Bullet

Commands in View menu

Arrow indicates submenu

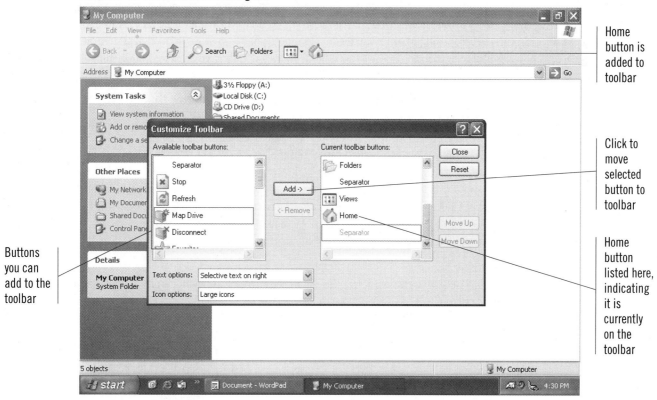

FIGURE A-10: Customize Toolbar dialog box

Home button is added to toolbar

Click to move selected button to toolbar

Home button listed here, indicating it is currently on the toolbar

Buttons you can add to the toolbar

TABLE A-5: Typical items on a menu

item	description	example
Dimmed command	Indicates the menu command is not currently available	Recent File
Ellipsis	Indicates that a dialog box will open that allows you to select additional options	Save As...
Triangle	Opens a cascading menu containing an additional list of commands	Toolbars ▸
Keyboard shortcut	Executes a command using the keyboard instead of the mouse	Print... Ctrl+P
Underlined letter	Indicates the letter to press for the keyboard shortcut	Exit

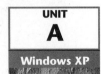

Using Dialog Boxes

A **dialog box** is a window that opens when you choose a menu command that needs more information before the program can carry out the command you selected. Dialog boxes open in other situations as well, such as when you open a program in the Control Panel. See Figure A-11 and Table A-6 for some of the typical elements of a dialog box. Practice using a dialog box to control your mouse settings.

STEPS

TROUBLE
If you don't see Printers and Other Hardware in the Control Panel window, you are using Classic view, not the default Category view. In the left pane, click Switch to Category view.

1. **In the left side of the My Computer window, click** Control Panel**; in the Control Panel window, click** Printers and Other Hardware**, then click the** Mouse icon

   The Mouse Properties dialog box opens, as shown in Figure A-12. **Properties** are characteristics of a computer element (in this case, the mouse) that you can customize. The options in this dialog box allow you to control the way the mouse buttons are configured, select the types of pointers that appear, choose the speed and behavior of the mouse movement on the screen, and specify what type of mouse you are using. **Tabs** at the top of the dialog box separate these options into related categories.

2. **Click the** Pointer Options tab **if necessary to make it the frontmost tab**

   This tab contains three options for controlling the way your mouse moves. Under Motion, you can set how fast the pointer moves on the screen in relation to how you move the mouse. You drag a **slider** to specify how fast the pointer moves. Under Snap To is a **check box**, which is a toggle for turning a feature on or off—in this case, for setting whether you want your mouse pointer to move to the default button in dialog boxes. Under Visibility, you can choose three options for easily finding your cursor and keeping it out of the way when you're typing.

3. **Under Motion, drag the** slider **all the way to the left for Slow, then move the mouse pointer across your screen**

   Notice how slowly the mouse pointer moves. After you select the options you want in a dialog box, you need to click a **command button**, which carries out the options you've selected. The two most common command buttons are OK and Cancel. Clicking OK accepts your changes and closes the dialog box; clicking Cancel leaves the original settings intact and closes the dialog box. The third command button in this dialog box is Apply. Clicking the Apply button accepts the changes you've made and keeps the dialog box open so that you can select additional options. Because you might share this computer with others, you should close the dialog box without making any permanent changes.

QUICK TIP
You can also use the keyboard to carry out commands in a dialog box. Pressing [Enter] is the same as clicking OK; pressing [Esc] is the same as clicking Cancel.

4. **Click** Cancel

   The original settings remain intact, the dialog box closes, and you return to the Printers and Other Hardware window.

FIGURE A-11: Elements of a typical dialog box

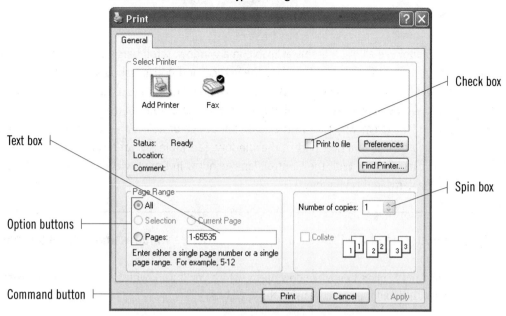

FIGURE A-12: Mouse Properties dialog box

TABLE A-6: Typical items in a dialog box

item	description
Tab	A place in a dialog box that organizes related commands and options
Check box	A box that turns an option on (when the box is checked) and off (when it is unchecked)
Command button	A rectangular button with the name of the command on it
List box	A box containing a list of items; to choose an item, click the list arrow, then click the desired item
Option button	A small circle that you click to select a single dialog box option; you cannot select more than one option button in a list
Text box	A box in which you type text
Slider	A shape that you drag to set the degree to which an option is in effect
Spin box	A box with two arrows and a text box; allows you to scroll in numerical increments or type a number

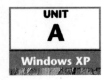

Using Scroll Bars

When you cannot see all of the items available in a window, scroll bars appear on the right and/or bottom edges of the window. **Scroll bars** are the vertical and horizontal bars along the right and bottom edges of a window and contain elements that you click and drag so you can view the additional contents of the window. When you need to scroll only a short distance, you can use the scroll arrows. To scroll the window in larger increments, click in the scroll bar above or below the scroll box. Dragging the scroll box moves you quickly to a new part of the window. See Table A-7 for a summary of the different ways to use scroll bars. ▓▓▓▓ With the Control Panel window in Details view, you can use the scroll bars to view all of the items in this window.

STEPS

TROUBLE
Your window might be called Printers and Faxes or something similar, and the Printing link may appear as Troubleshoot printing, but you should still be able to complete the steps.

1. **In the left side of the Printers and Other Hardware window, under Troubleshooters, click** Printing

   The Help and Support Center window opens, which you'll work with further in the next lesson. For now, you'll use the window to practice using the scroll bars.

2. **If the Help and Support Center window fills the screen, click the** Restore button ☐ **in the upper-right corner so the scroll bars appear, as shown in Figure A-13**

TROUBLE
If you don't see scroll bars, drag the lower-right corner of the Help and Support Center window up and to the left until scroll bars appear.

3. **Click the** down **scroll arrow, as shown in Figure A-13**

   Clicking this arrow moves the view down one line.

4. **Click the** up **scroll arrow in the vertical scroll bar**

   Clicking this arrow moves the view up one line.

5. **Click anywhere in the area below the scroll box in the vertical scroll bar**

   The view moves down one window's height. Similarly, you can click in the scroll bar above the scroll box to move up one window's height. The size of the scroll box changes to reflect how much information does not fit in the window. A larger scroll box indicates that a relatively small amount of the window's contents is not currently visible; you need to scroll only a short distance to see the remaining items. A smaller scroll box indicates that a relatively large amount of information is currently not visible.

6. **Drag the** scroll box **all the way up to the top of the vertical scroll bar**

   This view shows the items that appear at the top of the window.

7. **In the horizontal scroll bar, click the area to the right of the scroll box**

   The far right edge of the window comes into view. The horizontal scroll bar works the same as the vertical scroll bar.

8. **Click the area to the left of the scroll box in the horizontal scroll bar**

9. **Click the** Close button ☒ **to close the Help and Support Center window**

   You'll reopen the Help and Support Center window from the Start menu in the next lesson.

FIGURE A-13: Scroll bars

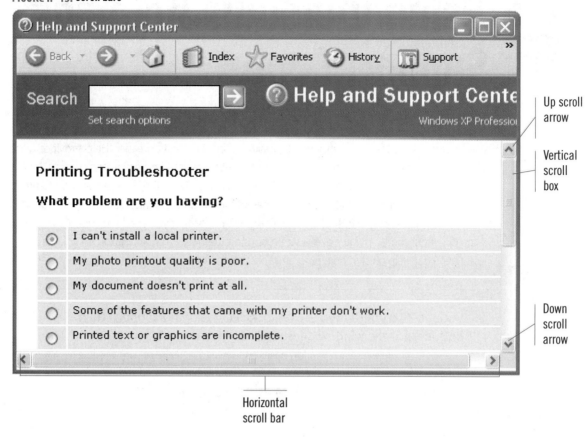

Up scroll arrow

Vertical scroll box

Down scroll arrow

Horizontal scroll bar

TABLE A-7: Using scroll bars

to	do this
Move down one line	Click the down arrow at the bottom of the vertical scroll bar
Move up one line	Click the up arrow at the top of the vertical scroll bar
Move down one window height	Click in the area below the scroll box in the vertical scroll bar
Move up one window height	Click in the area above the scroll box in the vertical scroll bar
Move up a large distance in the window	Drag the scroll box up in the vertical scroll bar
Move down a large distance in the window	Drag the scroll box down in the vertical scroll bar
Move a short distance side-to-side in a window	Click the left or right arrows in the horizontal scroll bar
Move to the right one window width	Click in the area to the right of the scroll box in the horizontal scroll bar
Move to the left one window width	Click in the area to the left of the scroll box in the horizontal scroll bar
Move left or right a large distance in the window	Drag the scroll box in the horizontal scroll bar

Using Windows Help and Support Center

When you have a question about how to do something in Windows XP, you can usually find the answer with a few clicks of your mouse. The Windows Help and Support Center works like a book stored on your computer, with a table of contents and an index to make finding information easier. Help provides guidance on many Windows features, including detailed steps for completing procedures, definitions of terms, lists of related topics, and search capabilities. You can browse or search for information in the Help and Support Center window, or you can connect to a Microsoft Web site on the Internet for the latest technical support on Windows XP. You can also access **context-sensitive help**, help specifically related to what you are doing, using a variety of methods such as holding your mouse pointer over an item or using the question mark button in a dialog box. 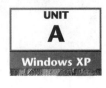 In this lesson, you get Help on starting a program. You also get information about the taskbar.

STEPS

1. **Click the Start button on the taskbar, click Help and Support, then click the Maximize button ▣ if the window doesn't fill the screen**

   The Help and Support Center window opens, as shown in Figure A-14. This window has a toolbar at the top of the window, a Search box below where you enter keywords having to do with your question, a left pane where the items matching your keywords are listed, and a right pane where the specific steps for a given item are listed.

   > **QUICK TIP**
   > Scroll down the left pane, if necessary, to view all the topics. You can also click Full-text Search Matches to view more topics containing the search text you typed or Microsoft Knowledge Base for relevant articles from the Microsoft Web site.

2. **Click in the Search text box, type start a program, press [Enter], then view the Help topics displayed in the left pane**

   The left pane contains a selection of topics related to starting a program. The Suggested Topics are the most likely matches for your search text.

3. **Click Start a program**

   Help information for this topic appears in the right pane, as shown in Figure A-15. At the bottom of the text in the right pane, you can click Related Topics to view a list of topics that are related to the current topic. Some Help topics also allow you to view additional information about important words; these words are underlined, indicating that you can click them to display a pop-up window with the additional information.

4. **Click the underlined word taskbar, read the definition, then click anywhere outside the pop-up window to close it**

   > **QUICK TIP**
   > You can click the Favorites button to view a list of Help pages that you've saved as you search for answers to your questions. You can click the History button to view a list of Help pages that you've viewed during the current Help session.

5. **On the toolbar at the top of the window, click the Index button**

   The Index provides an alphabetical list of all the available Help topics, like an index at the end of a book. You can type a topic in the text box at the top of the pane. You can also scroll down to the topic. In either case, you click the topic you're interested in and the details about that topic appear in the right pane.

6. **In the left pane, type tiling windows**

   As you type, the list of topics automatically scrolls to try to match the word or phrase you type.

7. **Double-click tiling windows in the list in the left pane and read the steps and notes in the right pane**

   You can also click the Related Topics link for more information.

8. **Click the Support button on the toolbar**

   Information on the Web sites for Windows XP Help appears in the right pane (a **Web site** is a document or related documents that contain highlighted words, phrases, and graphics that link to other sites on the Internet). To access online support or information, you would click one of the available options in the left pane.

9. **Click the Close button ☒ in the upper-right corner of the Help and Support Center window**

   The Help and Support Center window closes.

FIGURE A-14: **Windows Help and Support Center**

Help toolbar

Type keyword
or phrase
to search
for topics

Links for
popular
Help topics

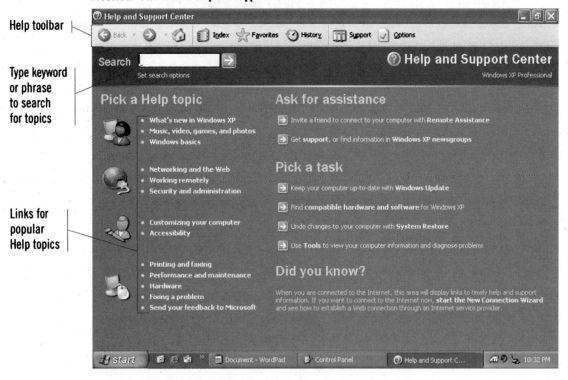

FIGURE A-15: **Viewing a Help topic**

Type search
text here

Left pane
contains
list of
Help topics
matching
your search
text

Click this
topic

Right pane
contains
information
on the topic
you select

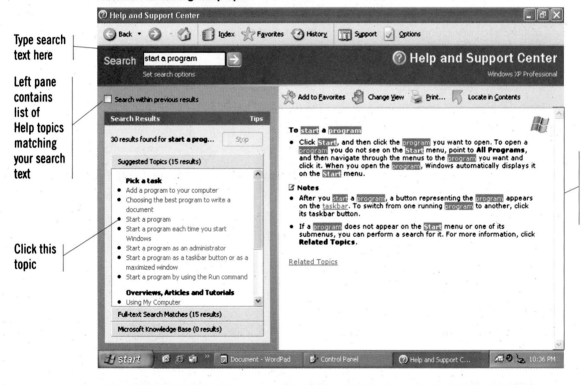

Clues to Use

Other forms of Help

The Help and Support Center offers information on Windows itself, not on all the other programs you can run on your computer. To get help on a specific Windows program, click Help on that program's menu bar. Also, to receive help in a dialog box (whether you are in Windows or another program), click the Help button [?] in the upper-right corner of the dialog box; the mouse pointer changes to ⌖?. Click any item in the dialog box that you want to learn more about. If information is available on that item, a pop-up window appears with a brief explanation of the selected feature.

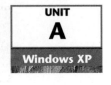
Closing a Program and Shutting Down Windows

When you are finished working on your computer, you need to make sure you shut it down properly. This involves several steps: saving and closing all open files, closing all the open programs and windows, shutting down Windows, and finally, turning off the computer. If you turn off the computer while Windows is running, you could lose important data. To **close** a program, you can click the Close button in the window's upper-right corner or click File on the menu bar and choose either Close or Exit. To shut down Windows after all your files and programs are closed, click Turn Off Computer on the Start menu, then select the desired option in the Turn off computer dialog box, shown in Figure A-16. See Table A-8 for a description of shut down options. ▰▰▰▰▰ Close all your open files, windows, and programs, then exit Windows.

1. **In the Control Panel window, click the Close button ⊠ in the upper-right corner of the window**
   The Control Panel window closes.

2. **Click File on the WordPad menu bar, then click Exit**
   If you have made any changes to the open file, you will be asked to save your changes before the program closes. Some programs also give you the option of choosing the Close command on the File menu in order to close the active file but leave the program open, so you can continue to work in it with a different file. Also, if there is a second set of sizing buttons in the window, the Close button on the menu bar will close the active file only, leaving the program open for continued use.

3. **If you see a message asking you to save changes to the document, click No**
   WordPad closes and you return to the desktop.

Complete the remaining steps to shut down Windows and your computer only if you have been told to do so by your instructor or technical support person. If you have been told to Log Off instead of exiting Windows, click Log Off instead of Turn Off Computer, and follow the directions from your instructor or technical support person.

4. **Click the Start button on the taskbar, then click Turn Off Computer**
   The Turn off computer dialog box opens, as shown in Figure A-16. In this dialog box, you have the option to stand by, turn off the computer, or restart the computer.

5. **If you are working in a lab, click Cancel to leave the computer running; if you are working on your own machine or if your instructor told you to shut down Windows, click Turn Off, then click OK**

6. **If you see the message "It is now safe to turn off your computer," turn off your computer and monitor**
   On some computers, the power shuts off automatically, so you may not see this message.

FIGURE A-16: Turn off computer dialog box

Click to leave Windows running but reduce computer's power mode

Click to exit Windows and automatically restart it

Click to exit Windows safely and turn off your computer

Click to return to the desktop without taking any action

Clues to Use

The Log Off command

To change users on the same computer quickly, you can choose the Log Off command from the Start menu. When you click this command, you can choose to switch users, so that the current user is logged off and another user can log on, or you can simply log off.

Windows XP shuts down partially, stopping at the point where you click your user name. When you or a new user clicks a user name (and enters a password, if necessary), Windows restarts and the desktop appears as usual.

TABLE A-8: Turn off options

Turn off option	function	when to use it
Stand By	Leaves Windows running but on minimal power	When you are finished working with Windows for a short time and plan to return before the end of the day
Turn Off	Exits Windows completely and safely	When you are finished working with Windows and want to shut off your computer for an extended time (such as overnight or longer)
Restart	Exits Windows safely, turns off the computer automatically, and then restarts the computer and Windows	When your programs might have frozen or stopped working correctly

Practice

▼ CONCEPTS REVIEW

Identify each of the items labeled in Figure A-17.

FIGURE A-17

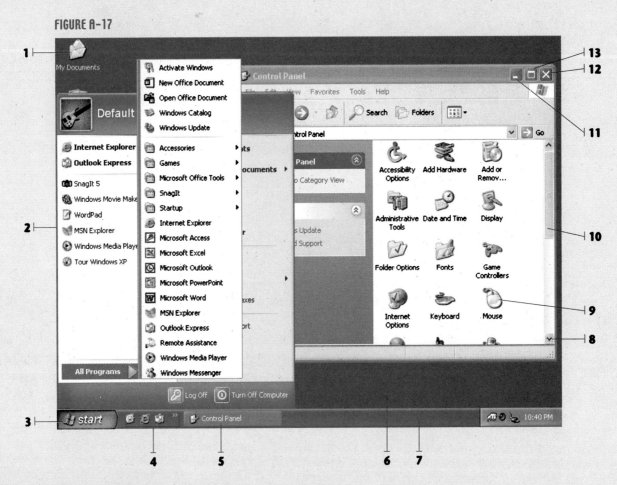

Match each of the statements with the term it describes.

14. Shrinks a window to a button on the taskbar
15. Shows the name of the window or program
16. The taskbar item you first click to start a program
17. Requests more information for you to supply before carrying out command
18. Shows the Start button, Quick Launch toolbar, and any currently open programs
19. An input device that lets you point to and make selections
20. Graphic representation of program

a. dialog box
b. program button
c. taskbar
d. Minimize button
e. icon
f. mouse
g. Start button

Select the best answer from the list of choices.

21. **The term "file" is best defined as**
    a. a set of instructions for a computer to carry out a task.   c. a collection of icons.
    b. an electronic collection of data.   d. an international collection of computers.

22. **Which of the following is NOT provided by Windows XP?**
    a. The ability to organize files
    b. Instructions to coordinate the flow of information among the programs, files, printers, storage devices, and other components of your computer system
    c. Programs that allow you to specify the operation of the mouse
    d. Spell checker for your documents

23. **All of the following are examples of using a mouse, EXCEPT**
    a. clicking the Maximize button.   c. double-clicking to start a program.
    b. pressing [Enter].   d. dragging the My Computer icon.

24. **The term for moving an item to a new location on the desktop is**
    a. pointing.   c. dragging.
    b. clicking.   d. restoring.

25. **The Maximize button is used to**
    a. return a window to its previous size.   c. scroll slowly through a window.
    b. expand a window to fill the computer screen.   d. run programs from the Start menu.

26. **What appears if a window contains more information than can be viewed in the window?**
    a. Program icon   c. Scroll bars
    b. Cascading menu   d. Check boxes

27. **A window is active when**
    a. you can only see its program button on the taskbar.   c. it is open and you are currently using it.
    b. its title bar is dimmed.   d. it is listed in the Programs submenu.

28. **You can exit Windows by**
    a. double-clicking the Control Panel application.
    b. double-clicking the Program Manager control menu box.
    c. clicking File, then clicking Exit.
    d. selecting the Turn Off Computer command from the Start menu.

▼ SKILLS REVIEW

1. **Start Windows and view the desktop.**
   a. Turn on the computer, select your user name, then enter a password, if necessary.
   b. After Windows starts, identify as many items on the desktop as you can, without referring to the lesson material.
   c. Compare your results to Figure A-1.

2. **Use the mouse.**
   a. Double-click the Recycle Bin icon, then click the Restore button if the window fills the screen.
   b. Drag the Recycle Bin window to the upper-right corner of the desktop.
   c. Right-click the title bar of the Recycle Bin, then click Close.

3. **Start a program.**
   a. Click the Start button on the taskbar, then point to All Programs.
   b. Point to Accessories, then click Calculator.
   c. Minimize the Calculator window.

4. **Move and resize windows.**
   a. Drag the Recycle Bin icon to the top of the desktop.
   b. Double-click the My Computer icon to open the My Computer window (if you don't see the My Computer icon, read the Trouble in the lesson on menus and toolbars for how to display it).
   c. Maximize the My Computer window, if it is not already maximized.

   d. Restore the window to its previous size.

   e. Resize the window until you see the vertical scroll bar.

   f. Minimize the My Computer window.

   g. Drag the Recycle Bin icon back to its original position.

5. Use menus, keyboard shortcuts, and toolbars.

   a. Click the Start button on the taskbar, then click Control Panel.

   b. Click View on the menu bar, point to Toolbars, then click Standard Buttons to deselect the option and hide the toolbar.

   c. Redisplay the toolbar.

   d. Press [Alt][V] to display the View menu, then press [B] to hide the status bar at the bottom of the window.

   e. Note the change, then use keyboard shortcuts to change the view back.

   f. Click the Up button to view My Computer.

   g. Click the Back button to return to the Control Panel.

   h. Click View, point to Toolbars, then click Customize.

   i. Add a button to the toolbar, remove it, then close the Customize Toolbar dialog box.

6. Use dialog boxes.

   a. With the Control Panel in Category view, click Appearance and Themes, click Display, then click the Screen Saver tab.

   b. Click the Screen saver list arrow, click any screen saver in the list, then view it in the preview monitor above the list.

   c. Click the Appearance tab in the Display Properties dialog box, then click the Effects button.

   d. In the Effects dialog box, click the Use large icons check box to select it, click the OK button to close the Effects dialog box, then click OK to close the Display Properties dialog box.

   e. Note the change in the icons on the desktop, minimizing windows if necessary.

   f. Right-click a blank area on the desktop, click Properties on the shortcut menu, click the Appearance tab, click the Effects button, click the Use large icons check box to deselect it, click OK, click the Screen Saver tab, return the screen saver to its original setting, then click Apply.

   g. Click the OK button in the Display Properties dialog box, but leave the Control Panel open and make it the active program.

7. Use scroll bars.

   a. In the left side of the Control Panel window, click Switch to Classic View, if necessary, click the Views button on the toolbar, then click Details.

   b. Drag the vertical scroll box down all the way.

   c. Click anywhere in the area above the vertical scroll box.

   d. Click the down scroll arrow until the scroll box is back at the bottom of the scroll bar.

   e. Click the right scroll arrow twice.

   f. Click in the area to the right of the horizontal scroll box.

   g. Drag the horizontal scroll box all the way back to the left.

8. Get Help.

   a. Click the Start button on the taskbar, then click Help and Support.

   b. Click Windows basics under Pick a Help topic, then click Tips for using Help in the left pane.

   c. In the right pane, click Add a Help topic or page to the Help and Support Center Favorites list.

   d. Read the topic contents, click Related Topics, click Print a Help topic or page, then read the contents. Leave the Help and Support Center open.

9. Close a program and shut down Windows.

   a. Click the Close button to close the Help and Support Center window.

   b. Click File on the menu bar, then click Close to close the Control Panel window.

   c. Click the Calculator program button on the taskbar to restore the window.

   d. Click the Close button in the Calculator window to close the Calculator program.

   e. If you are instructed to do so, shut down Windows and turn off your computer.

▼ INDEPENDENT CHALLENGE 1

You can use the Help and Support Center to learn more about Windows XP and explore Help on the Internet.

a. Open the Help and Support Center window and locate help topics on adjusting the double-click speed of your mouse and displaying Web content on your desktop.

If you have a printer, print a Help topic for each subject. Otherwise, write a summary of each topic.

b. Follow these steps below to access help on the Internet. If you don't have Internet access, you can't do this step.

i. Click a link under "Did you know?" in the right pane of the Help and Support Home page.

ii. In the left pane of the Microsoft Web page, click Using Windows XP, click How-to Articles, then click any link.

iii. Read the article, then write a summary of what you find.

iv. Click the browser's Close button, disconnect from the Internet, and close Help and Support Center.

▼ INDEPENDENT CHALLENGE 2

You can change the format and the actual time of the clock and date on your computer.

a. Open the Control Panel window; in Category view, click Date, Time, Language, and Regional Options; click Regional and Language Options; then click the Customize button under Standards and formats.

b. Click the Time tab, click the Time format list arrow, click H:mm:ss to change the time to show a 24-hour clock, then click the Apply button to view the changes, if any.

c. Click the Date tab, click the Short date format list arrow, click dd-MMM-yy, then click the Apply button.

d. Click the Cancel button twice to close the open dialog boxes.

e. Change the time to one hour later using the Date and Time icon in the Control Panel.

f. Return the settings to the original time and format, then close all open windows.

▼ INDEPENDENT CHALLENGE 3

Calculator is a Windows accessory that you can use to perform calculations.

a. Start the Calculator, click Help on the menu bar, then click Help Topics.

b. Click the Calculator book in the left pane, click Perform a simple calculation to view that help topic, then print it if you have a printer connected.

c. Open the Perform a scientific calculation topic, then view the definition of a number system.

d. Determine how many months you have to work to earn an additional week of vacation if you work for a company that provides one additional day of paid vacation for every 560 hours you work. (*Hint:* Divide 560 by the number of hours you work per month.)

e. Close all open windows.

▼ INDEPENDENT CHALLENGE 4

You can customize many Windows features, including the appearance of the taskbar on the desktop.

a. Right-click the taskbar, then click Lock the Taskbar to uncheck the command, if necessary.

b. Position the pointer over the top border of the taskbar. When the pointer changes shape, drag up an inch.

c. Resize the taskbar back to its original size.

d. Right-click the Start button, then click Properties. Click the Taskbar tab.

e. Click the Help button (a question mark), then click each check box to view the pop-up window describing it.

f. Click the Start Menu tab, then click the Classic Start menu option button and view the change in the preview. (*Note:* Do not click OK.) Click Cancel.

▼ VISUAL WORKSHOP

Use the skills you have learned in this unit to customize your desktop so it looks like the one in Figure A-18. Make sure you include the following:

- Calculator program minimized
- Vertical scroll bar in Control Panel window
- Large icons view in Control Panel window
- Rearranged icons on desktop; your icons may be different. (*Hint*: If the icons snap back to where they were, they are set to be automatically arranged. Right-click a blank area of the desktop, point to Arrange Icons By, then click Auto Arrange to deselect this option.)

Use the Print Screen key to make a copy of the screen, then print it from the Paint program. (To print from the Paint program, click the Start button on the taskbar, point to All Programs, point to Accessories, then click Paint; in the Paint program window, click Edit on the menu bar, then click Paste; click Yes to fit the image on the bitmap, click the Print button on the toolbar, then click Print in the Print dialog box. See your instructor or technical support person for assistance.)

When you have completed this exercise, be sure to return your settings and desktop back to their original arrangement.

FIGURE A-18

Working with Programs, Files, and Folders

OBJECTIVES

Create and save a WordPad document
Open, edit, and save an existing Paint file
Work with multiple programs
Understand file management
View files and create folders with My Computer
Move and copy files with My Computer
Manage files with Windows Explorer
Search for files
Delete and restore files

If you have a SAM user profile, you may have access to hands-on instruction, practice, and assessment of the skills covered in this unit. Log in to your SAM account and go to your assignments page to see what your instructor has assigned.

Most of your work on a computer involves using programs to create files. For example, you might use WordPad to create a resumé or Microsoft Excel to create a budget. The resumé and the budget are examples of **files**, electronic collections of data that you create and save on a disk. In this unit, you learn how to work with files and the programs you use to create them. You create new files, open and edit an existing file, and use the Clipboard to copy and paste data from one file to another. You also explore the file management features of Windows XP, using My Computer and Windows Explorer. Finally, you learn how to work more efficiently by managing files directly on your desktop.

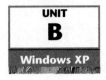

Creating and Saving a WordPad Document

As with most programs, when you start WordPad, a new, blank document opens. To create a new file, such as a memo, you simply begin typing. Your work is automatically stored in your computer's random access memory (RAM) until you turn off your computer, at which point anything stored in the computer's RAM is erased. To store your work permanently, you must save your work as a file on a disk. You can save files either on an internal **hard disk**, which is built into your computer, usually the C: drive, or on a removable 3½" **floppy disk**, which you insert into a drive on your computer, usually the A: or B: drive, or on a **CD-ROM** or **Zip disk**, two other kinds of removable storage devices. (Before you can save a file on a floppy disk, the disk must be formatted; see the Appendix, "Formatting a Floppy Disk.") When you name a file, you can use up to 255 characters, including spaces and punctuation, using either upper- or lowercase letters. In this lesson, you start WordPad and create a file that contains the text shown in Figure B-1 and save the file to the drive and folder where your Project Files are stored.

STEPS

QUICK TIP

If you make a mistake, press [Backspace] to delete the character to the left of the insertion point.

1. **Click the** Start button **on the taskbar, point to** All Programs, **point to** Accessories, **click** WordPad, **then click the** Maximize **button** ▣ **if the window does not fill your screen**
The WordPad program window opens. The blinking insertion point indicates where the text you type will appear.

2. **CType** Memo, **then press** [Enter] **to move the insertion point to the next line**

3. **Press** [Enter] **again, then type the remaining text shown in Figure B-1, pressing** [Enter] **at the end of each line**

4. **Click** File **on the menu bar, then click** Save As
The Save As dialog box opens, as shown in Figure B-2. In this dialog box, you specify where you want your file saved and give your document a name.

TROUBLE

This unit assumes that you are using the A: drive for your Project Files. If not, substitute the correct drive when you are instructed to use the 3 1/2 Floppy (A:) drive. See your instructor or technical support person for help.

5. **Click the** Save in list arrow, **then click** 3½ Floppy (A:), **or whichever drive contains your Project Files**
The drive containing your Project Files is now active, meaning that the contents of the drive appear in the Save in dialog box and that the file will now be saved in this drive.

6. **Click in the** File name text box, **type** Memo, **then click the** Save button
Your memo is now saved as a WordPad file with the name "Memo" on your Project Disk. The WordPad title bar contains the name of the file. Now you can **format** the text, which changes its appearance to make it more readable or attractive.

QUICK TIP

You can double-click to select a word or triple-click to select a paragraph.

7. **Click to the left of the word** Memo, **drag the mouse to the right to highlight the word, then release the mouse button**
Now the text is highlighted, indicating that it is **selected**. This means that any action you make will be performed on the highlighted text.

8. **Click the** Center button ▤ **on the Formatting toolbar, then click the** Bold button Ⓑ **on the Formatting toolbar**
The text is centered and bold.

9. **Click the** Font Size list arrow 10 ▾, **click** 16 **in the list, then click the** Save button 🖫
A **font** is a set of letters and numbers sharing a particular shape of type. The **font size** is measured in points; one **point** is 1/72 of an inch in height.

FIGURE B-1: Text to enter in WordPad

Press [Enter] three and four times (respectively) to insert blank lines

Bold button

Center button

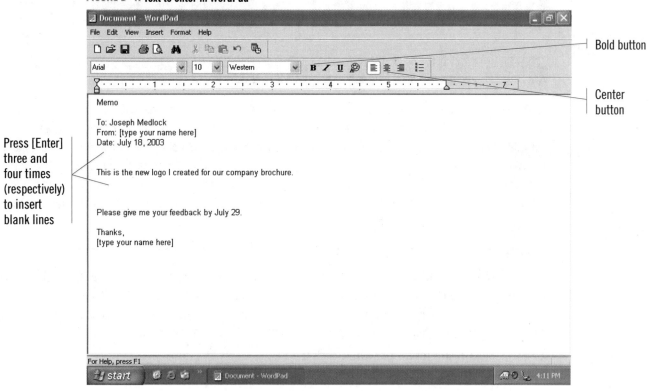

FIGURE B-2: Save As dialog box

Type new filename here

Click to select the location in which to save the file

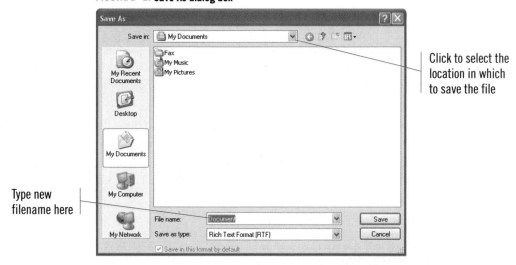

Opening, Editing, and Saving an Existing Paint File

Sometimes you create files from scratch, as you did in the previous lesson, but often you may want to work with a file you or someone else has already created. To do so, you need to open the file. Once you open a file, you can **edit** it, or make changes to it, such as adding or deleting text or changing the formatting. After editing a file, you can save it with the same filename, which means that you no longer will have the file in its original form, or you can save it with a different filename, so that the original file remains unchanged. 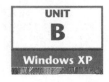 In this lesson, you use Paint (a graphics program that comes with Windows XP) to open a file, edit it by changing a color, and then save the file with a new filename to leave the original file unchanged.

STEPS

1. **Click the** Start button **on the taskbar, point to** All Programs, **point to** Accessories, **click** Paint, **then click the** Maximize button ▣ **if the window doesn't fill the screen**

   The Paint program opens with a blank work area. If you wanted to create a file from scratch, you would begin working now. However, you want to open an existing file, located on your Project Disk.

2. **Click** File **on the menu bar, then click** Open

   The Open dialog box works similarly to the Save As dialog box that you used in the previous lesson.

3. **Click the** Look in list arrow, **then click** 3½ Floppy (A:)

   The Paint files on your Project Disk are listed in the Open dialog box, as shown in Figure B-3.

   > **QUICK TIP**
   > You can also open a file by double-clicking it in the Open dialog box.

4. **Click** Win B-1 **in the list of files, and then click the** Open button

   The Open dialog box closes and the file named Win B-1 opens. Before you change this file, you should save it with a new filename, so that the original file is unchanged.

5. **Click** File **on the menu bar, then click** Save As

6. **Make sure** 3½ Floppy (A:) **appears in the Save in text box, select the text** Win B-1 **in the File name text box, type** Logo, **click the** Save as type list arrow, **click** 256 Color Bitmap, **then click the** Save button

   The Logo file appears in the Paint window, as shown in Figure B-4. Because you saved the file with a new name, you can edit it without changing the original file. You saved the file as a 256 Color Bitmap to conserve space on your floppy disk. You will now modify the logo by using buttons in the **Tool Box**, a toolbar of drawing tools, and the **Color Box**, a palette of colors from which you can choose.

7. **Click the** Fill With Color button 🖍 **in the Tool Box, then click the** Light blue color box, **which is the fourth from the right in the bottom row**

   Notice how clicking a button in the Tool Box changes the mouse pointer. Now when you click an area in the image, it will be filled with the color you selected in the Color Box. See Table B-1 for a description of the tools in the Tool Box.

8. **Move the pointer into the white area that represents the sky until the pointer changes to** 🖍, **then click**

   The sky is now blue.

9. **Click** File **on the menu bar, then click** Save

   The change you made is saved to disk, using the same Logo filename.

FIGURE B-3: Open dialog box

List of files ⊢

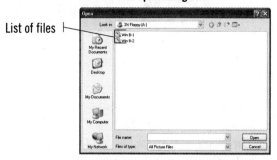

FIGURE B-4: Paint file saved with new filename

Name of file
appears in
title bar

Tool Box ⊢

Sky area to
fill with
light blue

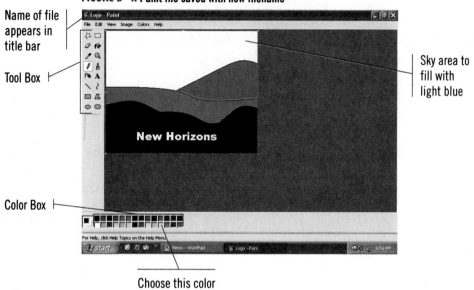

Color Box ⊢

Choose this color

TABLE B-1: Paint Tool Box buttons

tool	description
Free-Form Select button	Selects a free-form section of the picture to move, copy, or edit
Select button	Selects a rectangular section of the picture to move, copy, or edit
Eraser button	Erases a portion of the picture using the selected eraser size and foreground color
Fill With Color button	Fills a closed shape or area with the current drawing color
Pick Color button	Picks up a color from the picture to use for drawing
Magnifier button	Changes the magnification; lists magnifications under the toolbar
Pencil button	Draws a free-form line one pixel wide
Ellipse button	Draws an ellipse with the selected fill style; hold down [Shift] to draw a circle
Brush button	Draws using a brush with the selected shape and size
Airbrush button	Produces a circular spray of dots
Text button	Inserts text into the picture
Line button	Draws a straight line with the selected width and foreground color
Curve button	Draws a wavy line with the selected width and foreground color
Rectangle button	Draws a rectangle with the selected fill style; hold down [Shift] to draw a square
Polygon button	Draws polygons from connected straight-line segments
Rounded Rectangle button	Draws rectangles with rounded corners using the selected fill style; hold down [Shift] to draw a rounded square

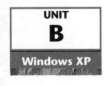

Working with Multiple Programs

A powerful feature of Windows is its capability to run more than one program at a time. For example, you might be working with a document in WordPad and want to search the Internet to find the answer to a question. You can start your **browser**, a program designed to access information on the Internet, without closing WordPad. When you find the information, you can leave your browser open and switch back to WordPad. Each open program is represented by a program button on the taskbar that you click to switch between programs. You can also copy data from one file to another (whether or not the files were created with the same Windows program) using the Clipboard, an area of memory on your computer's hard drive, and the Cut, Copy, and Paste commands. See Table B-2 for a description of these commands. ▰▰▱▱ In this lesson, you copy the logo graphic you worked with in the previous lesson into the memo you created in WordPad.

STEPS

1. **Click Edit on the menu bar, then click Select All to select the entire picture**
   A dotted rectangle surrounds the picture, indicating it is selected, as shown in Figure B-5.

2. **Click Edit on the menu bar, then click Copy**
   The logo is copied to the Clipboard. When you **copy** an object onto the Clipboard, the object remains in its original location and is also available to be pasted into another location.

> **QUICK TIP**
> To switch between programs using the keyboard, press and hold down [Alt], press [Tab] until you select the program you want, then release [Alt].

3. **Click the WordPad program button on the taskbar**
   WordPad becomes the active program.

4. **Click in the first line below the line that ends "for our company brochure."**
   The insertion point indicates where the logo will be pasted.

5. **Click the Paste button 📋 on the WordPad toolbar**
   The contents of the Clipboard, in this case the logo, are pasted into the WordPad file, as shown in Figure B-6.

6. **Click the WordPad Close button; click Yes to save changes**
   Your WordPad document and the WordPad program close. Paint is now the active program.

7. **Click the Paint Close button; if you are prompted to save changes, click Yes**
   Your Paint document and the Paint program close. You return to the desktop.

Clues to Use

Other Programs that Come with Windows XP

WordPad and Paint are just two of many programs that come with Windows XP. From the All Programs menu on the Start menu, you can access everything from games and entertainment programs to powerful communications software and disk maintenance programs without installing anything other than Windows XP. For example, from the Accessories menu, you can open a simple calculator; start Windows Movie Maker to create, edit, and share movie files; and use the Address Book to keep track of your contacts. From the Communications submenu, you can use NetMeeting to set up a voice and/or video conference over the Internet, or use the Remote Desktop Connection to allow another person to access your computer for diagnosing and solving computer problems. Several other menus and submenus display programs and tools that come with Windows XP. You can get a brief description of each by holding your mouse pointer over the name of the program in the menu. You might have to install some of these programs from the Windows CD if they don't appear on the menus.

FIGURE B-5: Selecting the logo to copy and paste into the Memo file

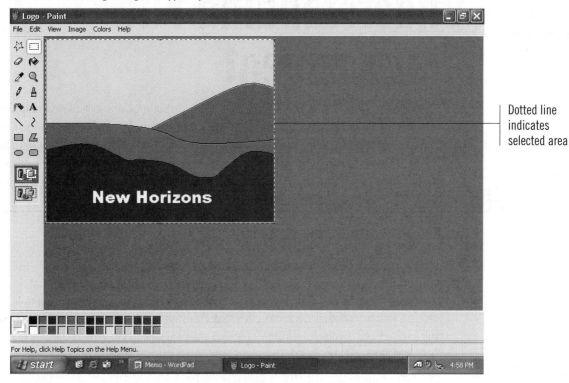

Dotted line indicates selected area

FIGURE B-6: Memo with pasted logo

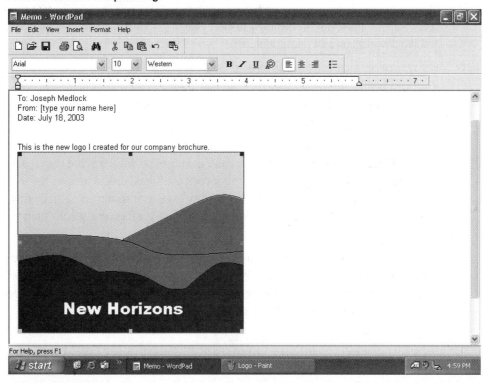

TABLE B-2: Overview of cutting, copying, and pasting

toolbar button	function	keyboard shortcut
✂ Cut	Removes selected information from a file and places it on the Clipboard	[Ctrl][X]
📋 Copy	Places a copy of the selected information on the Clipboard, leaving the file intact	[Ctrl][C]
📋 Paste	Inserts whatever is currently on the Clipboard into another location within the same file or into another file (depending on where you place the insertion point)	[Ctrl][V]

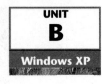

Understanding File Management

After you have created and saved numerous files, the process of organizing and keeping track of all of your files (referred to as **file management**) can be a challenge. Fortunately, Windows provides tools to keep everything organized so you can easily locate the files you need, move files to new locations, and delete files you no longer need. There are two main tools for managing your files: My Computer and Windows Explorer. ▓▓▓▓ In this lesson, you preview the ways you can use My Computer and Windows Explorer to manage your files.

Windows XP gives you the ability to:

- **Create folders in which you can save and organize your files**

    Folders are areas on a floppy disk (or other removable storage medium) or hard disk that help you organize your files, just as folders in a filing cabinet help you store and organize your papers. For example, you might create a folder for your work documents and another folder for your personal files. Folders can also contain other folders, which creates a more complex structure of folders and files, called a **file hierarchy**. See Figure B-7 for an example of how files can be organized.

- **Examine and organize the hierarchy of files and folders**

    You can use either My Computer or Windows Explorer to see and manipulate the overall structure of your files and folders. By examining your file hierarchy with these tools, you can better organize the contents of your computer and adjust the hierarchy to meet your needs. Figures B-8 and B-9 illustrate how My Computer and Windows Explorer list folders and files.

- **Copy, move, and rename files and folders**

    If you decide that a file belongs in a different folder, you can move it to another folder. You can also rename a file if you decide a different name is more descriptive. If you want to keep a copy of a file in more than one folder, you can copy it to new folders.

- **Delete files and folders you no longer need and restore files you delete accidentally**

    Deleting files and folders you are sure you don't need frees up disk space and keeps your file hierarchy more organized. The **Recycle Bin**, a space on your computer's hard disk that stores deleted files, allows you to restore files you deleted by accident. To free up disk space, you should occasionally check to make sure you don't need the contents of the Recycle Bin and then delete the files permanently from your hard drive.

- **Locate files quickly with the Windows XP Search feature**

    As you create more files and folders, you may forget where you placed a certain file or you may forget what name you used when you saved a file. With Search, you can locate files by providing only partial names or other facts you know about the file, such as the file type (for example, a WordPad document or a Paint graphic) or the date the file was created or modified.

- **Use shortcuts**

    If a file or folder you use often is located several levels down in your file hierarchy (in a folder within a folder, within a folder), it might take you several steps to access it. To save time accessing the files and programs you use frequently, you can create shortcuts to them. A **shortcut** is a link that gives you quick access to a particular file, folder, or program.

> **QUICK TIP**
>
> To browse My Computer using multiple windows, click Tools on the menu bar, and then click Folder Options. In the Folder Options dialog box, click the General tab, and then under Browse Folders, click the Open each folder in its own window option button. Each time you open a new folder, a new window opens, leaving the previous folder's window open so that you can view both at the same time.

FIGURE B-7: Sample file hierarchy

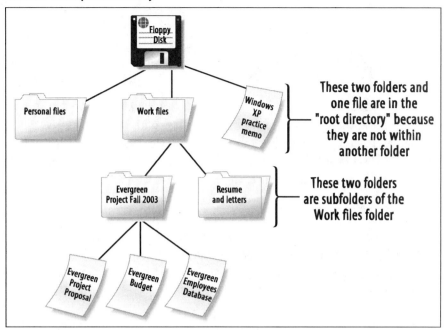

These two folders and one file are in the "root directory" because they are not within another folder

These two folders are subfolders of the Work files folder

FIGURE B-8: Evergreen Project folder shown in My Computer

Tasks related to selected object appear here

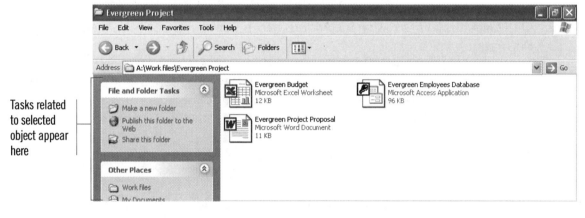

FIGURE B-9: Evergreen Project folder shown in Windows Explorer

File hierarchy is visible; the selected folder's contents appear in the right pane

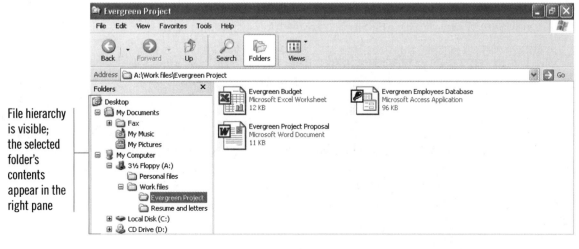

Viewing Files and Creating Folders with My Computer

My Computer shows the contents of your computer, including files, folders, programs, disk drives, and printers. You can click the icons to view that object's contents or properties. You use the My Computer Explorer Bar, menu bar, and toolbar to manage your files. See Table B-3 for a description of the toolbar buttons. ▉▉▉ In this lesson, you use My Computer to look at your computer's file hierachy, then you create two new folders on your Project Disk.

STEPS

1. Double-click the My Computer icon 💻 **on your desktop, then click the** Maximize button ▣ **if the My Computer window does not fill the screen**

My Computer displays the contents of your computer, as shown in Figure B-10. The left pane, called the **Explorer Bar**, displays tasks related to whatever is selected in the right pane.

2. Make sure your Project Disk is in the floppy disk drive, then double-click the 3½ Floppy (A:) icon

The contents of your Project Disk appear in the window. Each file is represented by an icon, which varies in appearance depending on the program that was used to create the file. If Microsoft Word is installed on your computer, the Word icon appears for the WordPad files; if not, the WordPad icon appears.

3. Click the Address list arrow **on the Address bar, as shown in Figure B-10, then click** My Documents

The window changes to show the contents of the My Documents folder on your computer's hard drive. The Address bar allows you to open and view a drive, folder, or even a Web page. You can also type in the Address bar to go to a different drive, folder, or Web page. For example, typing "C:\" will display the contents of your C: drive, and typing "http://www.microsoft.com" opens Microsoft's Web site if your computer is connected to the Internet.

4. Click the Back button ◉ **on the Standard Buttons toolbar**

The Back button displays the previous location, in this case, your Project Disk.

5. Click the Views button list arrow ▦▾ **on the Standard Buttons toolbar, then click** Details

Details view shows not only the files and folders, but also the sizes of the files, the types of files, folders, or drives and the date the files were last modified.

6. In the File and Folder Tasks pane, click Make a new folder

A new folder called "New Folder" is created on your Project Disk, as shown in Figure B-11. You can also create a new folder by right-clicking in the blank area of the My Computer window, clicking New, then clicking Folder.

7. If necessary, click to select the folder, then click Rename this folder **in the File and Folder Tasks pane; type** Windows XP Practice, **then press** [Enter]

Choosing descriptive names for your folders helps you remember their contents.

8. Double-click the Windows XP Practice folder, **repeat Steps 6 and 7 to create a new folder in the Windows XP Practice folder, name the folder** Brochure, **then press** [Enter]

9. Click the Up button ▧ **to return to the root directory of your Project Disk**

FIGURE B-10: My Computer window

Menu bar

Address bar

Standard Buttons toolbar

Address list arrow

Your icons may differ

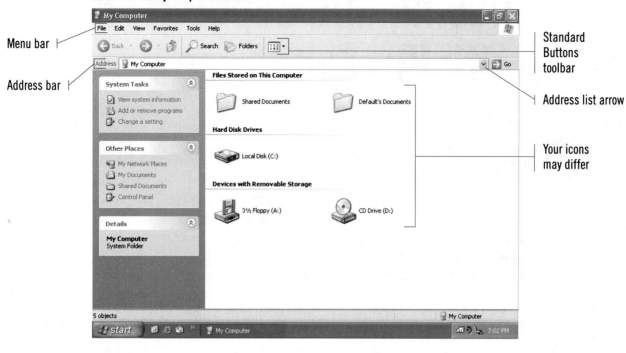

FIGURE B-11: Creating a new folder

Back button

Folder is located on the A: drive

You'll rename the new folder; yours might appear selected

TABLE B-3: Buttons on the Standard Buttons toolbar in My Computer

button	function
Back button	Moves back one location in the list of locations you have recently viewed
Forward button	Moves forward one location in the list of locations you have recently viewed
Up button	Moves up one level in the file hierarchy
Search button	Opens the Search Companion task pane, where you can choose from various options to search for files, computers, Web pages, or people on the Internet
Folders button	Opens the Folders task pane, where you can easily view and manage your computer's file hierarchy
▾ Views button	Lists the contents of My Computer using different views

Moving and Copying Files with My Computer

You can move a file or folder from one location to another using a variety of methods in My Computer. If the file or folder and the location to which you want to move it are both visible, you can simply drag the item from one location to another. You can also use the Cut, Copy, and Paste commands on the Edit menu, or right-click a file or folder and click the appropriate option on the menu that appears. Perhaps the most powerful file management tool in My Computer is the Common Tasks pane. When you select any item in My Computer, the Common Tasks pane changes to the File and Folder Tasks pane, listing tasks you can typically perform with the selected item. For example, if you select a file, the options in the Files and Folders task pane include "Rename this file," "Move this file," and "Delete this file," among many others. If you select a folder, file management tasks for folders appear. If you select more than one object, tasks appear that relate to manipulating multiple objects. You can also right-click any file or folder and choose the Send To command to "send" it to another location – most often a floppy disk or other removable storage medium. This **backs up** the files, making copies of them in case you have computer trouble (which can cause you to lose files from your hard disk). ▓▓▓ In this lesson, you move your files into the folder you created in the last lesson.

STEPS

1. **Click the** Win B-1 file, **hold down the mouse button and drag the file onto the** Windows XP Practice folder, **as shown in Figure B-12, then release the mouse button**
   Win B-1 is moved into the Windows XP Practice folder.

2. **Double-click the** Windows XP Practice folder **and confirm that the folder contains the Win B-1 file as well as the Brochure folder**

> **QUICK TIP**
> It is easy to confuse the Back button with the Up button. The Back button returns you to the last location you viewed, no matter where it is in your folder hierarchy. The Up button displays the next level up in the folder hierarchy, no matter what you last viewed.

3. **Click the** Up button 🗁 **on the Standard Buttons toolbar, as shown in Figure B-12**
   You return to the root directory of your Project Disk. The Up button shows the next level up in the folder hierarchy.

4. **Click the** Logo file, **press and hold down** [Shift], **then click the** Memo file
   Both files are selected. Table B-4 describes methods for selecting multiple objects.

5. **Click** Move the selected items **in the File and Folder Tasks pane**
   The filenames turn gray, and the Move Items dialog box opens, as shown in Figure B-13.

6. **Click the plus sign next to My Computer if you do not see 3½ Floppy (A:) listed, click the** 3½ Floppy (A:) **drive, click the** Windows XP Practice folder, **click the** Brochure folder, **then click** Move
   The two files are moved to the Brochure folder. Only the Windows XP Practice folder and the Win B-2 file remain in the root directory.

7. **Click the** Close button **in the 3½ Floppy (A:) (My Computer) window**

FIGURE B-12: Dragging a file from one folder to another

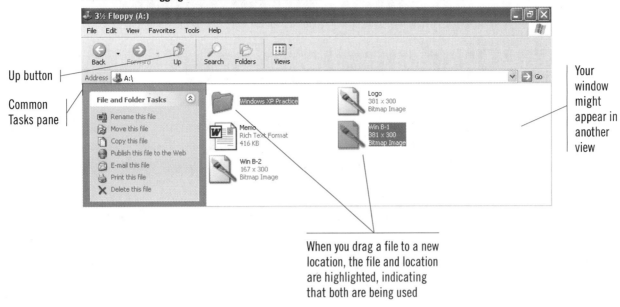

Up button

Common Tasks pane

Your window might appear in another view

When you drag a file to a new location, the file and location are highlighted, indicating that both are being used

FIGURE B-13: Moving files

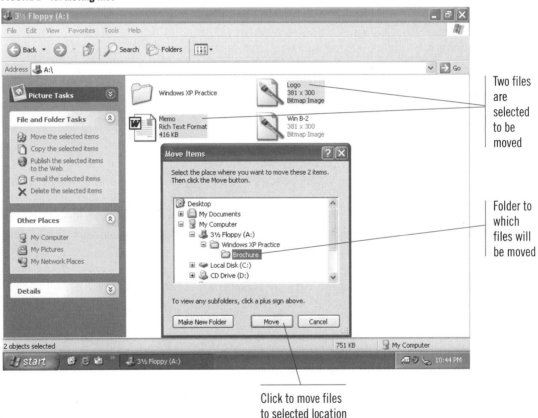

Two files are selected to be moved

Folder to which files will be moved

Click to move files to selected location

TABLE B-4: Techniques for selecting multiple files and folders

to select	do this
Individual objects not grouped together	Click the first object you want to select, then press and hold down [Ctrl] as you click each additional object you want to add to the selection
Objects grouped together	Click the first object you want to select, then press and hold down [Shift] as you click the last object in the list of objects you want to select; all the objects listed between the first and last objects are selected

Managing Files with Windows Explorer

As with My Computer, you can use Windows Explorer to copy, move, delete, and rename files and folders. However, in their default settings, My Computer and Windows Explorer look a little different and work in slightly different ways. In My Computer, the Explorer Bar displays the File and Folder Tasks pane when you select files or folders. In Windows Explorer, the Explorer Bar displays the Folders pane, which allows you to see and manipulate the overall structure of the contents of your computer or network while you work with individual files and folders within that structure. This allows you to work with more than one computer, folder, or file at once. Note that you can change the view in My Computer to show the Folders pane, and in Windows Explorer to view the File and Folder Tasks pane. ▰▰▰▰ In this lesson, you copy a folder from your Project Disk into the My Documents folder on your hard disk and then rename the folder.

STEPS

TROUBLE

If you do not see the toolbar, click View on the menu bar, point to Toolbars, then click Standard Buttons. If you do not see the Address bar, click View, point to Toolbars, then click Address Bar.

1. **Click the** Start button, **point to** All Programs, **point to** Accessories, **click** Windows Explorer, **then maximize the window if necessary**

Windows Explorer opens, as shown in Figure B-14. The Folders pane on the left displays the drives and folders on your computer in a hierarchy. The right pane displays the contents of whatever drive or folder is currently selected in the Folders pane. Each pane has its own set of scroll bars, so that scrolling in one pane won't affect the other.

2. **Click** View **on the menu bar, then click** Details **if it is not already selected**

Remember that a bullet point or check mark next to a command on the menu indicates that it's selected.

TROUBLE

If you cannot see the A: drive, you may have to click the plus sign (+) next to My Computer to view the available drives on your computer.

3. **In the Folders pane, scroll to and click** 3½ Floppy (A:)

The contents of your Project Disk appear in the right pane.

4. **In the Folders pane, click the** plus sign (+) **next to** 3½ Floppy (A:), **if necessary**

You click the plus sign (+) or minus sign (-) next to any item in the left pane to show or hide the different levels of the file hierarchy, so that you don't always have to look at the entire structure of your computer or network. A plus sign (+) next to an item indicates there are additional folders within that object. A minus sign (-) indicates the next level of the hierarchy is shown. Clicking the + displays (or "expands") the next level; clicking the − hides (or "collapses") it. When neither a + nor a − appears next to an icon, it means that the object does not have any folders in it, although it may have files.

5. **In the Folders pane, click the** Windows XP Practice folder

The contents of the Windows XP Practice folder appear in the right pane, as shown in Figure B-15. Double-clicking an item in the Folders pane that has a + next to it displays its contents in the right pane and also expands the next level in the Folders pane.

TROUBLE

If you are working in a lab setting, you may not be able to add items to your My Documents folder. Skip, but read carefully, Steps 6, 7, and 8 if you are unable to complete them.

6. **In the Folders pane, drag the** Windows XP Practice folder **on top of the** My Documents folder, **then release the mouse button**

When you drag files or folders from one drive to a different drive, they are copied rather than moved.

7. **In the Folders pane, click the** My Documents folder

The Windows XP Practice folder should now appear in the list of folders in the right pane. You may have to scroll to see it. Now you should rename the folder so you can distinguish the original folder from the copy.

8. **Right-click the** Windows XP Practice folder **in the right pane, click** Rename **in the shortcut menu, type** Windows XP Copy, **then press** [Enter]

FIGURE B-14: Windows Explorer window

Left pane, known as the Folders list or the Explorer Bar

Your list of devices, folders, and files will differ

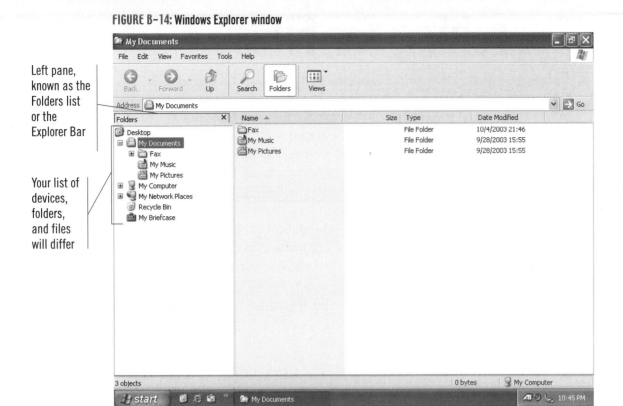

FIGURE B-15: Contents of Windows XP Practice folder

Windows XP Practice folder selected in left pane

Contents of Windows XP Practice folder appear in right pane

Your window might appear in a different view

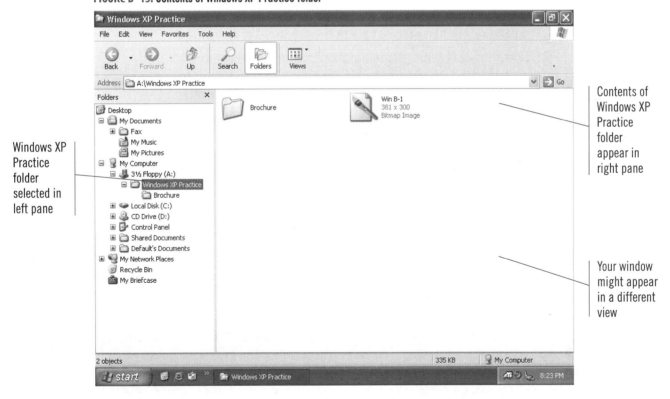

Searching for Files

After you've worked a while on your computer, saving, deleting, and modifying files and folders, you may forget where you've saved an item or what you named it. Or, you may want to send an e-mail to someone, but you can't remember how the name is spelled. You can use the **Windows XP Search** feature to quickly find any kind of object, from a Word document or a movie file to a computer on your network or a person in your address book. If you're connected to the Internet, you can use Search to locate Web pages and people on the Internet. ▧▨▩ In this lesson, you search for a file on your Project Disk.

STEPS

QUICK TIP

You can also start the Search Companion by clicking the Start button and then clicking Search. To change the way the Search tool works (such as whether the animated dog appears), click Change preferences at the bottom of the Search Companion pane.

1. **Click the** Search button 🔎 **on the Standard Buttons toolbar**

   The Explorer Bar changes to display the Search Companion pane, as shown in Figure B-16. Let's assume you can't remember where you placed the Logo file you created earlier. You know that it is a picture file and that it is somewhere on your floppy disk.

2. **In the Search Companion pane, click** Pictures, music, or video; **in the list that appears, click the** Pictures and Photos check box, **then type** Logo **in the All or part of the file name text box, as shown in Figure B-17**

3. **Click** Use advanced search options **to open a larger pane, click the** Look in list arrow, **click** 3½ Floppy (A:), **then click the** Search button **at the bottom of the Search Companion pane**

   The search results are displayed in the right pane and options for further searching are displayed in the Search Companion pane.

4. **Click the** Logo icon **in the right pane, click** File **on the menu bar, point to** Open With, **and then click** Paint

TROUBLE

If you don't like the way your clouds look, click Edit on the menu bar, click Undo, then repeat Step 5.

5. **Click the** Airbrush tool 🖌, **click the** white color box **in the Color box (the first one in the second row), then drag or click in the sky to make clouds**

6. **Save the file without changing the name and close Paint**

Clues to Use

Accessing files, folders, programs, and drives you use often

As you continue to use your computer, you will probably find that you use certain files, folders, programs, and disk drives almost every day. You can create a **shortcut**, an icon that represents an object stored somewhere else, and place it on the desktop. From the desktop, you double-click the shortcut to open the item, whether it's a file, folder, program, or disk drive. To create a shortcut on the desktop, view the object in My Computer or Windows Explorer, size the window so you can see both the object and part of the desktop at the same time, use the *right* mouse button to drag the object to the desktop, and then click Create Shortcuts Here. To delete the shortcut, select it and press [Delete]. The original file, folder, or program will not be affected. To **pin** a program to the Start menu, which places it conveniently at the top of the left side of the menu, open the Start menu as far as needed to view the program you want to pin, right-click the program name, and then click Pin to Start menu. To remove it, right-click it in its new position and then click Unpin from Start menu.

FIGURE B-16: Getting ready to search

Search button

Search Companion pane

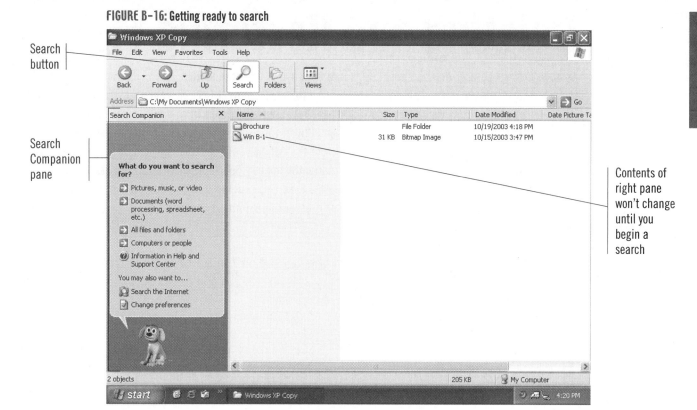

Contents of right pane won't change until you begin a search

FIGURE B-17: Specifying search options

Select this check box

Enter search text here

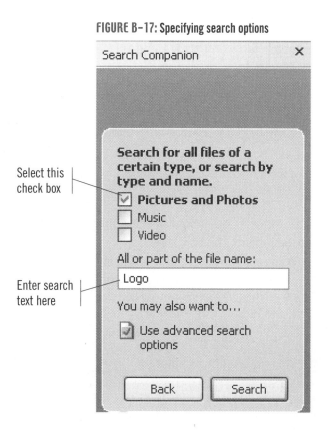

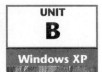

Deleting and Restoring Files

To save disk space and manage your files more effectively, you should **delete** (or remove) files you no longer need. There are many ways to delete files and folders from the My Computer and Windows Explorer windows, as well as from the Windows XP desktop. Because files deleted from your hard disk are stored in the Recycle Bin until you remove them permanently by emptying the Recycle Bin, you can restore any files you might have deleted accidentally. However, note that when you delete files from your floppy disk, they are not stored in the Recycle Bin – they are permanently deleted. See Table B-5 for an overview of deleting and restoring files. █████ In this lesson, you delete a file by dragging it to the Recycle Bin, you restore it, and then you delete a folder by using the Delete command in Windows Explorer.

STEPS

1. **Click the** Folders button 📁, **then click the** Restore button 🗗 **on the Search Results (Windows Explorer) title bar**
   You should be able to see the Recycle Bin icon on your desktop, as shown in Figure B-18. If you can't see the Recycle Bin, resize or move the Windows Explorer window until it is visible.

2. **If necessary, select the** Windows XP Copy folder **in the left pane of Windows Explorer**

QUICK TIP
If you are unable to delete the file, it might be because your Recycle Bin is full or the properties have been changed so that files are deleted right away. See your instructor or technical support person for assistance.

3. **Drag the** Windows XP Copy folder **from the left pane to the** Recycle Bin **on the desktop, as shown in Figure B-18, then click** Yes **to confirm the deletion, if necessary**
   The folder no longer appears in Windows Explorer because you have moved it to the Recycle Bin.

4. **Double-click the** Recycle Bin icon **on the desktop, then scroll if necessary until you can see the** Windows XP Copy folder
   The Recycle Bin window opens, as shown in Figure B-19. Depending on the number of files already deleted on your computer, your window might look different.

TROUBLE
If the Recycle Bin window blocks your view of Windows Explorer, minimize the Recycle Bin window. You might need to scroll the right pane to find the restored folder in Windows Explorer.

5. **Click the** Windows XP Copy folder, **then click** Restore this item **in the Recycle Bin Tasks pane**
   The Windows XP Copy folder is restored and should now appear in the Windows Explorer window.

6. **Right-click the** Windows XP Copy folder **in the right pane of Windows Explorer, click** Delete **on the shortcut menu, then click** Yes
   When you are sure you no longer need files you've moved into the Recycle Bin, you can empty the Recycle Bin. You won't do this now, in case you are working on a computer that you share with other people. But when you're working on your own machine, open the Recycle Bin window, verify that you don't need any of the files or folders in it, then click Empty the Recycle Bin in the Recycle Bin Tasks pane.

7. **Close the Recycle Bin and Windows Explorer**
   If you minimized the Recycle Bin in Step 5, click its program button to open the Recycle Bin window, and then click the Close button.

FIGURE B-18: Dragging a folder to delete it

Your desktop background and icons might differ

Drag the folder here

Folder located in the My Documents folder

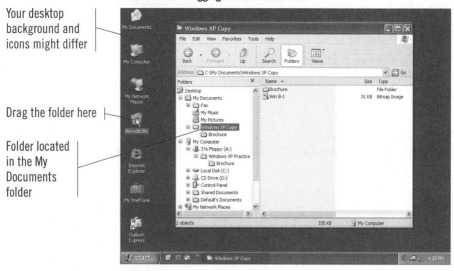

FIGURE B-19: Recycle Bin window

Deleted folder

The buttons on your toolbar might differ

You may see more files and folders, and they may be displayed in a different view

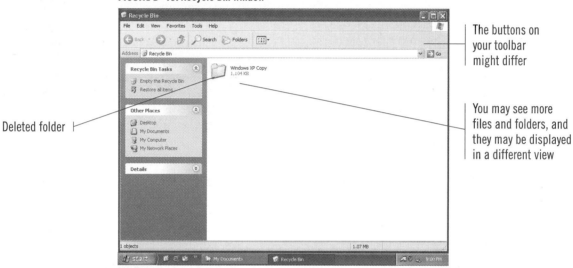

TABLE B-5: Methods for deleting and restoring files

ways to delete a file	ways to restore a file from the Recycle Bin
If File and Folder Tasks pane is open, click the file, then click Delete this file	Click Edit, then click Undo Delete
Select the file, then press [Delete]	Select the file in the Recycle Bin window, then click Restore this file
Right-click the file, then click Delete on the shortcut menu	Right-click the file in the Recycle Bin window, then click Restore
Drag the file to the Recycle Bin	Drag the file from the Recycle Bin to any other location

Clues to Use

Customizing your Recycle Bin

You can set your Recycle Bin according to how you like to delete and restore files. For example, if you do not want files to go to the Recycle Bin but rather want them to be immediately and permanently deleted, right-click the Recycle Bin, click Properties, then click the Do Not Move Files to the Recycle Bin check box. If you find that the Recycle Bin fills up too fast and you are not ready to delete the files permanently, you can increase the amount of disk space devoted to the Recycle Bin by moving the Maximum Size of Recycle Bin slider to the right. This, of course, reduces the amount of disk space you have available for other things. Also, you can choose not to have the Confirm File Delete dialog box open when you send files to the Recycle Bin. See your instructor or technical support person before changing any of the Recycle Bin settings.

Practice

▼ CONCEPTS REVIEW

Label each of the elements of the Windows Explorer window shown in Figure B-20.

FIGURE B-20

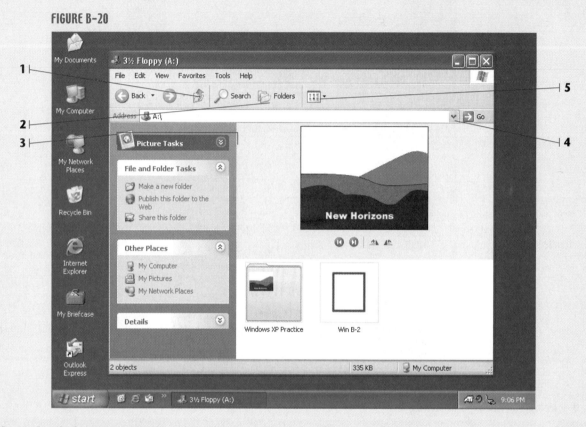

Match each of the statements with the term it describes.

6. Electronic collections of data

7. Your computer's temporary storage area

8. Temporary location of information you wish to paste into another location

9. Storage areas on your hard drive for files, folders, and programs

10. Structure of files and folders

a. RAM
b. Folders
c. Files
d. File hierarchy
e. Clipboard

Select the best answer from the list of choices.

11. To prepare a floppy disk to save your files, you must first make sure
   a. files are copied to the disk.
   b. the disk is formatted.
   c. all the files that might be on the disk are erased.
   d. the files are on the Clipboard.

12. You can use My Computer to
   a. create a drawing of your computer.
   b. view the contents of a folder.
   c. change the appearance of your desktop.
   d. add text to a WordPad file.

13. Which of the following best describes WordPad?
   a. A program for organizing files
   b. A program for performing financial analysis
   c. A program for creating basic text documents
   d. A program for creating graphics

14. **Which of the following is NOT a way to move a file from one folder to another?**
    a. Open the file and drag its program window to the new folder.
    b. In My Computer or Windows Explorer, drag the selected file to the new folder.
    c. Use the Move this file command in the File and Folder Tasks pane.
    d. Use the [Ctrl][X] and [Ctrl][V] keyboard shortcuts while in the My Computer or the Windows Explorer window.

15. **In which of the following can you, by default, view the hierarchy of drives, folders, and files in a split pane window?**
    a. Windows Explorer
    b. All Programs
    c. My Computer
    d. WordPad

16. **To restore files that you have sent to the Recycle Bin,**
    a. click File, then click Empty Recycle Bin.
    b. click Edit, then click Undo Delete.
    c. click File, then click Undo.
    d. You cannot retrieve files sent to the Recycle Bin.

17. **To select files that are not grouped together, select the first file, then**
    a. press [Shift] while selecting the second file.
    b. press [Alt] while selecting the second file.
    c. press [Ctrl] while selecting the second file.
    d. click the second file.

18. **Pressing [Backspace]**
    a. deletes the character to the right of the cursor.
    b. deletes the character to the left of the cursor.
    c. moves the insertion point one character to the right.
    d. deletes all text to the left of the cursor.

19. **The size of a font is measured in**
    a. centimeters.
    b. points.
    c. places.
    d. millimeters.

20. **The Back button on the My Computer toolbar**
    a. starts the last program you used.
    b. displays the next level of the file hierarchy.
    c. backs up the currently selected file.
    d. displays the last location you visited.

▼ SKILLS REVIEW

1. **Create and save a WordPad file.**
    a. Start Windows, then start WordPad.
    b. Type **My Drawing Ability**, then press [Enter] three times.
    c. Save the document as **Drawing Ability** to your Project Disk, but do not close it.

2. **Open, edit, and save an existing Paint file.**
    a. Start Paint and open the file Win B-2 on your Project Disk.
    b. Save the picture with the filename **First Unique Art** as a 256-color bitmap file to your Project Disk.
    c. Inside the picture frame, use [Shift] with the Ellipse tool to create a circle, fill it with purple, switch to yellow, then use [Shift] with the Rectangle tool to place a square inside the circle. Fill the square with yellow.
    d. Save the file, but do not close it. (Click Yes, if necessary to replace the file.)

3. **Work with multiple programs.**
    a. Select the entire graphic and copy it to the Clipboard, then switch to WordPad.
    b. Place the insertion point in the last blank line, paste the graphic into your document, then deselect the graphic.
    c. Save the changes to your WordPad document. Switch to Paint.
    d. Using the Fill With Color tool, change the color of a filled area of your graphic.
    e. Save the revised graphic with the new name **Second Unique Art** as a 256-color bitmap on your Project Disk.
    f. Select the entire graphic and copy it to the Clipboard.
    g. Switch to WordPad, move the insertion point to the line below the graphic by clicking below the graphic and pressing [Enter], type **This is another version of my graphic:** below the first picture, then press [Enter].
    h. Paste the second graphic under the text you just typed.
    i. Save the changed WordPad document as **Two Drawing Examples** to your Project Disk. Close Paint and WordPad.

4. **View files and create folders with My Computer.**
   a. Open My Computer. Double-click the drive that contains your Project Disk.
   b. Create a new folder on your Project Disk by clicking File, pointing to New, then clicking Folder, and name the new folder **Review**.
   c. Open the folder to display its contents (it is empty).
   d. Use the Address bar to view the My Documents folder.
   e. Create a folder in the My Documents folder called **Temporary**, then use the Back button to view the Review folder.
   f. Create two new folders in the Review folder, one named **Documents** and the other named **Artwork**.
   g. Click the Forward button as many times as necessary to view the contents of the My Documents folder.
   h. Change the view to Details if necessary.

5. **Move and copy files with My Computer.**
   a. Use the Address bar to view your Project Disk. Switch to Details view, if necessary.
   b. Press the [Shift] key while selecting First Unique Art and Second Unique Art, then cut and paste them into the Artwork folder.
   c. Use the Back button to view the contents of Project Disk.
   d. Select the two WordPad files, Drawing Ability and Two Drawing Examples, then move them into the Review folder.
   e. Open the Review folder, select the two WordPad files again, move them into the Documents folder, then close My Computer.

6. **Manage files with Windows Explorer.**
   a. Open Windows Explorer and view the contents of the Artwork folder in the right pane.
   b. Select the two Paint files.
   c. Drag the two Paint files from the Artwork folder to the Temporary folder in the My Documents folder to copy – not move – them.
   d. View the contents of the Documents folder in the right pane, then select the two WordPad files.
   e. Repeat Step c to copy the files to the Temporary folder in the My Documents folder.
   f. View the contents of the Temporary folder in the right pane to verify that the four files are there.

7. **Search for files.**
   a. Open the Search companion from Windows Explorer.
   b. Search for the First Unique Art file on your Project Disk.
   c. Close the Search Results window.

8. **Delete and restore files and folders.**
   a. If necessary, open and resize the Windows Explorer window so you can see the Recycle Bin icon on the desktop, then scroll in Windows Explorer so you can see the Temporary folder in the left pane.
   b. Delete the Temporary folder from the My Documents folder by dragging it to the Recycle Bin.
   c. Click Yes to confirm the deletion, if necessary.
   d. **Open the Recycle Bin, restore the Temporary folder and its files to your hard disk, and then close the Recycle Bin.** (*Note*: If your Recycle Bin is empty, your computer is set to automatically delete items in the Recycle Bin.)
   e. Delete the Temporary folder again by clicking to select it and then pressing [Delete]. Click Yes to confirm the deletion.

▼ INDEPENDENT CHALLENGE 1

You have decided to start a bakery business and you want to use Windows XP to create and organize the files for the business.

   a. Create two new folders on your Project Disk, one named **Advertising** and one named **Customers**.
   b. Use WordPad to create a letter inviting new customers to the open house for the new bakery, then save it as **Open House Letter** in the Customers folder.
   c. Use WordPad to create a new document that lists five tasks that need to get done before the business opens (such as purchasing equipment, decorating the interior, and ordering supplies), then save it as **Business Plan** to your Project Disk, but don't place it in a folder.

▼ INDEPENDENT CHALLENGE 1 (CONTINUED)

d. Use Paint to create a simple logo for the bakery, save it as a 256-color bitmap named **Bakery Logo**, then place it in the Advertising folder.

e. Print the three files.

▼ INDEPENDENT CHALLENGE 2

To complete this Independent Challenge, you will need a second formatted, blank floppy disk. Write **IC2** on the disk label, then complete the steps below. Follow the guidelines listed here to create the file hierarchy shown in Figure B-21.

a. In the My Documents folder on your hard drive, create one folder named IC2 and a second named Project Disk 1.

b. Copy the contents of your first Project Disk into the new Project Disk 1 folder. This will give you access to your files as you complete these steps.

c. Place your blank IC2 disk into the floppy drive.

d. Start WordPad, then create a new file that contains a list of things to get done. Save the file as **To Do List** to your IC2 Disk.

e. Start My Computer and copy the To Do List from your IC2 Disk to the IC2 folder and rename the file in the IC2 folder **Important List**.

f. Copy the Open House Letter file from your Project Disk 1 folder to the IC2 folder. Rename the file **Article**.

g. Copy the Memo file from your Project Disk 1 folder to the IC2 folder in the My Documents folder and rename it **Article Two**.

h. Copy the Logo file from your Project Disk 1 folder to the IC2 folder and rename the file **Sample Logo**.

i. Move the files into the folders shown in Figure B-21.

j. Copy the IC2 folder to your IC2 Disk, then delete the Project Disk 1 and IC2 folders from the My Documents folder.

FIGURE B-21

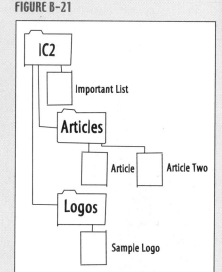

▼ INDEPENDENT CHALLENGE 3

With Windows XP, you can access the Web from My Computer and Windows Explorer, allowing you to search for information located not only on your computer or network but also on any computer on the Internet.

a. Start Windows Explorer, then click in the Address bar so the current location is selected, type **www.microsoft.com**, then press [Enter].

b. Connect to the Internet if necessary. The Microsoft Web page appears in the right pane of Windows Explorer.

c. Click in the Address bar, then type **www.course.com**, press [Enter], and then wait a moment while the Course Technology Web page opens.

d. Make sure your Project Disk is in the floppy disk drive, then click 3½ Floppy (A:) in the left pane.

e. Click the Back button list arrow, then click Microsoft's home page.

f. Capture a picture of your desktop by pressing [Print Screen] (usually located on the upper-right side of your keyboard). This stores the picture on the Clipboard. Open the Paint program, paste the contents of the Clipboard into the drawing window, clicking No if asked to enlarge the Bitmap, then print the picture.

g. Close Paint without saving your changes.

h. Close Windows Explorer, then disconnect from the Internet if necessary.

▼ INDEPENDENT CHALLENGE 4

Open Windows Explorer, make sure you can see the drive that contains your Project Disk listed in the left pane, use the right mouse button to drag the drive to a blank area on the desktop, then click Create Shortcuts Here. Then capture a picture of your desktop showing the new shortcut: press [Print Screen], located on the upper-right side of your keyboard. Then open the Paint program and paste the contents of the Clipboard into the drawing window. Print the screen, close Paint without saving your changes, then delete the shortcut when you are finished.

▼ VISUAL WORKSHOP

Recreate the screen shown in Figure B-22, which shows the Search Results window with the Memo file listed, one shortcut on the desktop, and one open (but minimized) file. Press [Print Screen] to make a copy of the screen, (a copy of the screen is placed on the Clipboard), open Paint, click Paste to paste the screen picture into Paint, then print the Paint file. Close Paint without saving your changes, and then return your desktop to its original state. Your desktop might have different icons and a different background.

FIGURE B-22

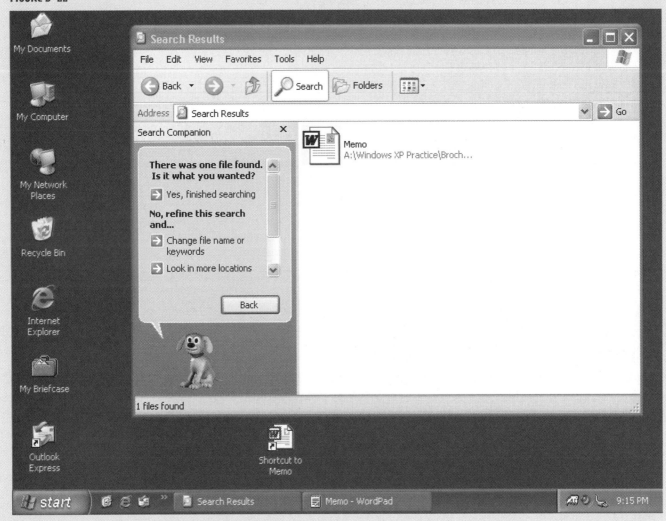

Formatting a Floppy Disk

A **disk** is a device on which you can store electronic data. Disks come in a variety of sizes and have varying storage capacities. Your computer's **hard disk**, one of its internal devices, can store large amounts of data. **Floppy disks**, on the other hand, are smaller, inexpensive, and portable. Most floppy disks that you buy today are 3 ½-inch disks (the diameter of the inside, circular part of the disk) and are already formatted. Check the package that your disk came in for the word "formatted" or "pre-formatted;" such disks do not require further formatting.  If your package says "unformatted," then you should follow the steps in this appendix. In this appendix, you will prepare a floppy disk for use.

Formatting a Floppy Disk

In order for an operating system to be able to store data on a disk, the disk must be formatted. **Formatting** prepares a disk so it can store information. Usually, floppy disks are formatted when you buy them, but if not, you can format them yourself using Windows XP. To complete the following steps, you need a blank floppy disk or a disk containing data you no longer need. Do not use your Project Disk for this lesson, as all information on the disk will be erased.

STEPS

TROUBLE

This appendix assumes that the drive that will contain your floppy disks is drive A. If not, substitute the correct drive when you are instructed to use the 3 ½ Floppy (A:) drive.

1. **Start your computer and** Windows XP **if necessary, then place a 3 ½-inch floppy disk in drive A**

2. **Double-click the** My Computer icon 🖳 **on the desktop**

   My Computer opens, as shown in Figure AP-1. This window lists all the drives and printers that you can use on your computer. Because computers have different drives, printers, programs, and other devices installed, your window will probably look different.

3. **Right-click the** 3 ½ Floppy (A:) icon

   When you click with the right mouse button, a shortcut menu of commands that apply to the item you right-clicked appears. Because you right-clicked a drive, the Format command is available.

TROUBLE

Windows cannot format a disk if it is write-protected; therefore, you may need to slide the write-protect tab over until it clicks to continue. See Figure AP-3 to locate the write-protect tab on your disk.

4. **Click** Format **on the shortcut menu**

   The Format dialog box opens, as shown in Figure AP-2. In this dialog box, you specify the capacity of the disk you are formatting, the File system, the Allocation unit size, the kind of formatting you want to do, and if you want, a volume label. You are doing a standard format, so you will accept the default settings.

5. **Click** Start, **then, when you are warned that formatting will erase all data on the disk, click** OK **to continue**

   Windows formats your disk. After the formatting is complete, you might see a summary about the size of the disk.

6. **Click** OK **when the message telling you that the format is complete appears, then click** Close **in the Format dialog box**

QUICK TIP

Once a disk is formatted, you do not need to format it again. However, some people use the Quick Format option to erase the contents of a disk quickly, rather than having to select the files and then delete them.

7. **Click the** Close button ☒ **in the My Computer window**

   My Computer closes and you return to the desktop.

FIGURE AP-1: My Computer window

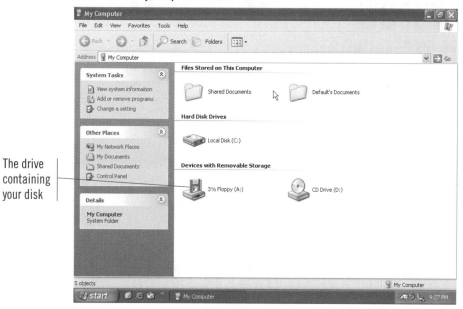

The drive containing your disk

FIGURE AP-2: Format dialog box

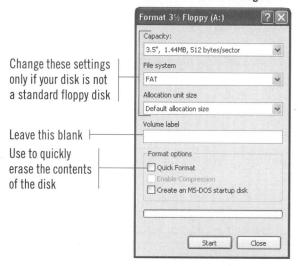

Change these settings only if your disk is not a standard floppy disk

Leave this blank

Use to quickly erase the contents of the disk

FIGURE AP-3: Write-protect tab

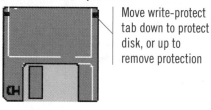

Move write-protect tab down to protect disk, or up to remove protection

3.5" disk

Clues to Use

More about disks

Disks are sometimes called **drives**, but this term really refers to the name by which the operating system recognizes the disk (or a portion of the disk). The operating system typically assigns a drive letter to a drive (which you can reassign if you want). For example, on most computers the hard disk is identified by the letter "C" and the floppy drive by the letter "A." The amount of information a disk can hold is called its capacity, usually measured in megabytes (MB). The most common floppy disk **capacity** is 1.44 MB. Computers also come with other disk drives, such as a **CD drives** and **Zip drives**. Such drives handle CDs and Zip disks, respectively. Both are portable like floppy disks, but they can contain far more data than floppy disks.

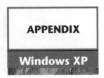

Data Files

Read the following information carefully!

It is very important to organize and keep track of the files you need for this book.

1. **Find out from your instructor the location of the Data Files you need and the location where you will store your files.**

   - To complete many of the units in this book, you need to use Data Files. Your instructor will either provide you with a copy of the Data Files or ask you to make your own copy.
   - If you need to make a copy of the Data Files, you will need to copy a set of files from a file server, stand-alone computer, or the Web to the drive and folder where you will be storing your Data Files.
   - Your instructor will tell you which computer, drive letter, and folders contain the files you need, and where you will store your files.
   - You can also download the files by going to www.course.com. A copy of a Data Files list is provided on the Review Pack for this book or may be provided by your instructor.

2. **Copy and organize your Data Files.**

   Floppy disk users

   - If you are using floppy disks to store your Data Files, the Data Files List shows which files you'll need to copy onto your disk(s).
   - Unless noted in the Data Files List, you will need one formatted, high-density disk for each unit. For each unit you are assigned, copy the files listed in the **Data File Supplied column** onto one disk.
   - Make sure you label each disk clearly with the unit name (e.g., Word Unit A).
   - When working through the unit, save all your files to this disk.

   Users storing files in other locations

   - If you are using a zip drive, network folder, hard drive, or other storage device, use the Data Files List to organize your files.
   - Create a subfolder for each unit in the location where you are storing your files, and name it according to the unit title (e.g., Word Unit A).
   - For each unit you are assigned, copy the files listed in the **Data File Supplied column** into that unit's folder.
   - Store the files you modify or create for each unit in the unit folder.

3. **Find and keep track of your Data Files and completed files.**

   - Use the **Data File Supplied column** to make sure you have the files you need before starting the unit or exercise indicated in the **Unit and Location column**.
   - Use the **Student Saves File As column** to find out the filename you use when saving your changes to a Data File that was provided.
   - Use the **Student Creates File column** to find out the filename you use when saving a file you create new for the exercise.

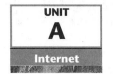

Getting Started with Internet Explorer

OBJECTIVES

Understand Web browsers
Start Internet Explorer
Explore the browser window
View and navigate Web pages
Save a favorite Web page
Print a Web page
Search for information
Get Help
Exit Internet Explorer

 If you have a SAM user profile, you may have access to hands-on instruction, practice, and assessment of the skills covered in this unit. Log in to your SAM account and go to your assignments page to see what your instructor has assigned.

In this unit, you learn how to use the Internet Explorer browser to find information on the World Wide Web (WWW or the Web). You learn how to navigate to sites on the Web, how to navigate from one Web page to another, and how to search for information on the Web. You also learn how to print Web pages and how to get helpful information about using Internet Explorer. You need to connect to the Internet to complete this unit. MediaLoft is a chain of bookstore cafés founded in 1988. MediaLoft stores offer customers the opportunity to purchase books, music, and movies while enjoying a variety of coffees, teas, and freshly baked desserts. Martin Smith is a community relations manager at MediaLoft. Martin wants to continue to encourage MediaLoft employees to participate in community service and contribute to charitable organizations. As his assistant, you research nonprofit organizations to add to the list of organizations that MediaLoft supports financially and through volunteer services.

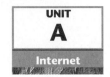
Understanding Web Browsers

The **World Wide Web** (the **Web** or **WWW**) is the part of the Internet that contains linked Web pages. **Web pages** are documents that contain text, graphics, and/or sound. **Web browsers (browsers)** are software programs used to access and display Web pages. You must use a browser to view Web pages that are on the Web. Browsers, such as Microsoft Internet Explorer, Opera, and Netscape Navigator, make navigating the Web easy by providing a graphical, point-and-click environment. When you view Web pages with a browser you click words, phrases, or graphics called **hyperlinks**, or simply **links**, to connect to and view other Web pages. Figure A-1 shows a sample Web page. Links on a Web page also can open graphics files or play sound or video files. This unit features **Internet Explorer**, a popular browser that is part of the Microsoft Windows operating system. ▰▰▰ Martin asks you to use Internet Explorer and the Web to research nonprofit charitable organizations that can be supported by MediaLoft employees. You discuss the features and benefits of using Internet Explorer.

DETAILS

Using Internet Explorer, you can:

- **Display Web pages**

  You can access Web sites from all over the world. A **Web site** is a group of Web pages focused on a particular subject. Web sites exist for individuals, businesses, museums, governments, charitable organizations, and educational institutions. There are Web sites for the arts, music, politics, education, sports, and commerce—for any topic, interest, or endeavor in the world. As you research nonprofit charitable organizations that MediaLoft may be interested in supporting, you can find in-depth information about each organization by visiting its Web site.

- **Use links to move from one Web page to another**

  You can click the hyperlinks on a charitable organization's Web page to get more specific information about its work and affiliations.

- **Play audio and video clips**

  A Web browser can play audio and video clips if it has been configured to do so and your computer has the appropriate hardware, such as speakers. In your research, you might find some Web pages that include video clips of group projects, success stories, or additional information about the organization.

- **Search the Web for information**

  A **search engine** is a special Web site that searches the Internet for Web sites based on words or phrases that you enter. You can take advantage of search engines to look for organizations that focus on projects and issues that MediaLoft employees might find interesting, such as literacy, health care, or environmental protection.

- **Save a list of favorite Web pages**

  You can save a list of links to Web pages that you might need to visit again, such as a page for a specific organization or information about local volunteer services. Internet Explorer makes it easy to compile a list of your favorite Web sites that is quickly accessible when you want to view those Web sites later.

- **Print or save the text and graphics on Web pages**

  If you want to keep a hard copy of the information or images you find on the Web, you can easily print the Web page, including any graphics. You also can save the text or graphics on a Web page, or copy this information temporarily to the Clipboard, where it is available for pasting into other programs.

- **E-mail Web pages**

  If you want to share a Web page with a colleague, you can easily e-mail the link or the page directly from the browser window to another person who is set up for e-mail. The person receives the page or link to the page as part of an e-mail message.

FIGURE A-1: A sample Web page

Clues to Use

The Internet, computer networks, and intranets

A **computer network** is the hardware and software that makes it possible for two or more computers to share information and resources. An **intranet** is a computer network that connects computers in a local area only, such as computers in a company's office. Users can dial into intranets from remote locations to share company information and resources. The **Internet** is a network of connected computers and computer networks located around the world. The Internet is an international community; Web pages exist from nearly every country in the world. There are over 200 million users worldwide currently connected to the Internet through telephone lines, cables, satellites, and other telecommunications media. Through the Internet, these computers can share many types of information, including text, graphics, sound, video, and computer programs. Anyone who has access to a computer and a connection to the Internet through a computer network or modem can use this rich information source.

Internet

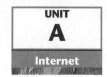

Starting Internet Explorer

Internet Explorer is a Web browser that connects your computer to the Web through an Internet connection. You can start Internet Explorer by clicking the Start button on the taskbar, pointing to All Programs, then clicking Internet Explorer. After Internet Explorer is installed, its icon appears on your Windows desktop, and you can double-click the icon to start Internet Explorer. You can also start Internet Explorer by clicking the Internet Explorer button on the Quick Launch toolbar. ▦▦▦ Before you can take advantage of the Web's many features to start your search for nonprofit organizations, you must start Internet Explorer.

STEPS

TROUBLE

If an Internet Connection Wizard dialog box opens at any point, you either need to connect to the Internet or enter your Internet settings. Ask your technical support person for assistance.

1. **If you connect to the Internet using a modem and a telephone, follow your normal procedure to establish your connection; if you connect through an always-on broadband connection, you can begin with Step 2**

2. **Locate the Internet Explorer icon on your Windows desktop**
   The icon appears on the left side of your screen, as shown in Figure A-2. The exact location of the Internet Explorer icon might vary on different computers. Ask your instructor or technical support person for assistance if you are unable to locate the Internet Explorer icon.

QUICK TIP

You can also start Internet Explorer by clicking the Start button on the taskbar, pointing to All Programs on the Start menu, then clicking Internet Explorer.

3. **Double-click the Internet Explorer icon on the Windows desktop**
   Internet Explorer opens and displays your home page. The home page for the National Science Foundation is shown in Figure A-3. A **home page** is the first page that opens every time you start Internet Explorer. Your home page might be one for your school, one for your employer, or one that you specify. The term "home page" also applies to the main page that opens when you first go to a Web site. Because the Internet is an active environment, many of the Web pages shown in the figures will have changed since this book was written.

4. **If necessary, click the Maximize button on the Internet Explorer title bar to maximize the program window**

Internet Explorer icon

Text

Graphic

Links

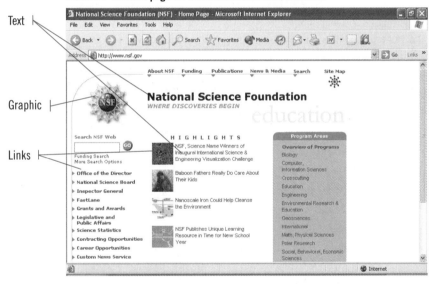

Clues to Use

History of the Internet and the World Wide Web

The Internet has its roots in the U.S. Department of Defense Advanced Research Projects Agency Network (ARPANET), which began in 1969. In 1986 the National Science Foundation formed NSFNET, which replaced ARPANET. NSFNET expanded the foundation of the U.S. portion of the Internet with high-speed, long-distance lines. By the end of the 1980s, corporations begin to use the Internet to communicate with each other and with their customers. In 1991, the U.S. Congress further expanded the Internet's capacity and speed and opened it to commercial use.

The World Wide Web was created in Switzerland in 1991 to allow links between documents on the Internet. The first graphical Web browser, Mosaic, was introduced at the University of Illinois in 1993, leading to the development of browsers such as Netscape Navigator and Internet Explorer. With the boom in the personal computer industry and the expanding availability of inexpensive desktop machines and powerful, network-ready servers, many companies were able to join the Internet for the first time in the early 1990s. The Web is now an integral component of corporate culture, educational institutions, and individuals' personal lives. The Web is used daily for commerce, education, and entertainment by millions of people around the world.

Internet

Exploring the Browser Window

The elements of the Internet Explorer browser window let you view, print, and search for information on the Web. You can customize elements of the window, such as the toolbar and Address bar. For example, you can choose to view the buttons on the toolbar with or without their corresponding text labels, or with text labels on the right. 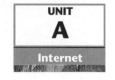 Before viewing Web pages and navigating from one page to another, you need to become more familiar with the components of the Internet Explorer browser window. Look at the home page on your screen and find and compare the elements below using Figure A-4 as a guide.

DETAILS

The elements of the Internet Explorer browser window are:

- The **title bar** at the top of the page usually contains the name of the Web page currently displayed in the Web browser window.

- The **menu bar** provides access to most of the browser's features through a series of menus.

- The **Standard Buttons toolbar** provides buttons for many options, such as stopping the loading of a Web page, moving from one Web page to another, printing Web pages, and searching for information on the Internet. Table A-1 explains buttons that are available on the Standard Buttons toolbar. You can add and remove the buttons to customize the toolbar to your preferences. The toolbar can show large or small icons and have different text settings. The default setting for the toolbar is "Selective text on right." Many commonly used commands available on menus are more readily accessed using the toolbar buttons. Depending on the programs installed on your computer, you may have additional buttons.

- The **Address bar** displays the address of the Web page currently opened. The **Uniform Resource Locator (URL)**, or the Web page's address, appears in the Address bar after you open (or load) the page. If you click the Address bar list arrow, you see a list of addresses you have recently entered in the Address bar.

QUICK TIP
You can resize the Links bar to view more links by placing your mouse pointer to the left of the word Links on the Links bar and dragging to the left.

- The **Links bar** is a convenient place to store links to Web pages that you use often. You can add a link to the Links bar by dragging the Internet Explorer icon 🔲 that precedes the URL in the Address bar to the Links bar. Links placed in the Links bar are also found in the Links folder under the Favorites menu.

- The **Go button** is used along with the Address bar to help you search for Web sites about a particular topic. You can enter a keyword or words in the Address bar, then click the Go button to activate the search. When the search is complete, a list of related Web sites opens in a search results Web page.

- The **status indicator** is animated while a new Web page loads.

- The **browser window** is the specific area where the current Web page appears. You might need to scroll down the page to view its entire contents.

- The **vertical scroll bar** allows you to move the current Web page up or down in the browser window. The **scroll box** indicates your relative position within the Web page.

QUICK TIP
You can hide or display the status bar by clicking View on the menu bar and then clicking Status Bar.

- The **status bar** performs three main functions: 1) it displays information about your connection progress whenever you open a new Web page; 2) it notifies you when you connect to another Web site; and 3) it identifies the percentage of information transferred from the Web server to your browser. The status bar also displays the Web addresses of any links on the Web page when you move your mouse pointer over them.

FIGURE A-4: Elements of the Internet Explorer window

Title bar
Menu bar
Address bar
Status bar
Status indicator
Standard Buttons toolbar
Links bar
Go button
Scroll box
Vertical scroll bar

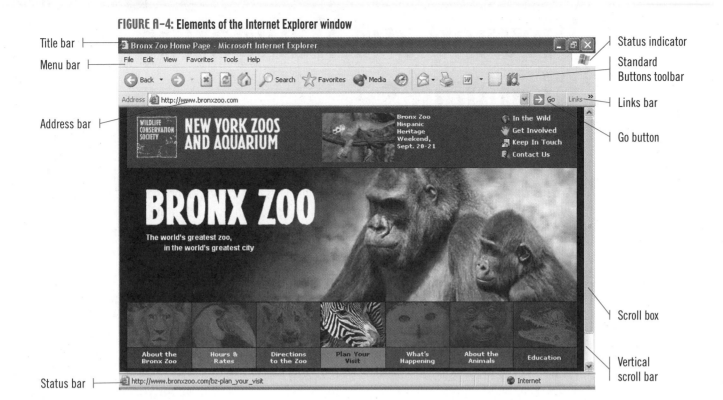

TABLE A-1: Standard Buttons toolbar buttons

button name	button	description
Back	Back	Opens the previous page
Forward		Opens the next page
Stop		Stops loading the page
Refresh		Refreshes the contents of the current page
Home		Opens the home page
Search	Search	Opens the Search Companion in the Search bar
Favorites	Favorites	Opens the Favorites bar
Media	Media	Opens the Media bar
History		Opens the History bar
Mail		Displays options for working with mail and news
Print		Prints the current Web page
Edit		Transfers the currently displayed Web page to Microsoft FrontPage or Microsoft Word for editing; the Edit icon in your browser window depends on which text editing software programs you have installed on your computer
Full Screen		Expands the browser window and removes the menu bar and title bar, leaving only the toolbar
Discuss		Lets you add or edit discussion servers and open the Discussion bar
Research		Opens the Research task pane to find information on the Web

Internet

Viewing and Navigating Web pages

Every Web page has a unique address on the Web, also known as the **URL** for the page. Browser software locates a Web page based on its address. All Web page addresses begin with "http," which stands for Hypertext Transfer Protocol, the set of rules for exchanging files on the Web. This is followed by a colon and two forward slashes. Most pages begin with "www" (which identifies that the page is on the World Wide Web), followed by a dot, or period, and then the Web site's name, known as the **domain name**. Following the domain name is another dot and the top-level domain, such as com, edu, or org. The **top-level domain** tells you the type of site you are visiting. After the top-level domain, another slash and one or more folder names and a filename might appear.

Moving between Web pages located at different addresses is simple with hyperlinks. **Hyperlinks** enable you to navigate to, or open, another location on the same Web page or to jump to an entirely different Web page. You can follow these links to obtain more information about a topic by clicking a linked word or phrase. In addition to links on Web pages themselves, you can use the navigation tools in Internet Explorer to move around the Web. You can navigate from page to page using the Forward and Back buttons, as well as the Home button. If you click the list arrow on the Back or Forward button, you see the recently viewed Web pages, and you can click the name of the page you want to view at that time. You want to investigate how MediaLoft can participate in a national library program. You look at the Library of Congress Web site for information about the National Digital Preservation program.

STEPS

1. **Click anywhere in the Address bar**

   The current address is highlighted; any text you type replaces it.

QUICK TIP

If you change your mind or if a page takes too long to load, you can click the Stop button 🗙 on the toolbar to stop a new Web page from loading.

2. **Type www.loc.gov, then press [Enter]**

   Internet Explorer automatically adds the http:// protocol to the beginning of the address you type, after you press [Enter]. If you have typed a specific address in the Address bar previously, the AutoComplete feature recognizes the first few characters you type, then completes the name of the address for you. As the page is loading, the status bar displays the connection process. After a few seconds, the home page for the Library of Congress opens in the browser window, as shown in Figure A-5, and the status bar displays "Done". The page contains pictures and text, some of which are hyperlinks.

3. **Place your mouse pointer on the National Digital Preservation Program**

   When you place the pointer on a hyperlink, the pointer changes to 🖑. A ScreenTip may also appear giving you more information about the linked page.

TROUBLE

Web pages change frequently. The hyperlink may be in a new location on the page.

4. **Click the National Digital Preservation Program link**

   The status indicator is animated while the new linked Web page loads. The **Digital Preservation Program** page opens in your Web browser window, as shown in Figure A-6.

5. **Click the Back button ⊙ Back on the Standard Buttons toolbar**

   The Web page that you just viewed, the Library of Congress home page, opens in the browser window.

QUICK TIP

Place the pointer on the Back or Forward button to display the ScreenTip for which page will appear when the button is clicked.

6. **Click the Forward button ⊙ on the Standard Buttons toolbar**

   The Forward button opens the Digital Preservation Program page in the browser window again.

7. **Click the Home button 🏠 on the Standard Buttons toolbar**

   Clicking the Home button opens the home page designated for your installation of Internet Explorer.

8. **Click the Back button list arrow ⊙ Back ▾ on the Standard Buttons toolbar, then click The Library of Congress**

FIGURE A-5: Home page for the Library of Congress

Web page address

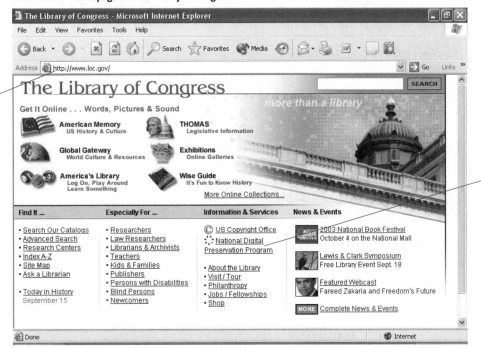

National Digital Preservation Program link

FIGURE A-6: Digital Preservation Program home page

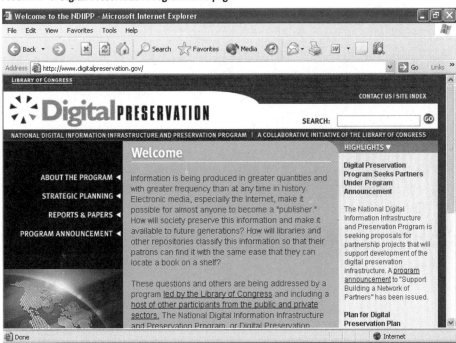

Clues to Use

Selecting a home page

When you click the Home button on the toolbar, the page that is specified as the home page opens in your Web browser window. Each time you start Internet Explorer, the first page that appears is your home page. When you install Internet Explorer, the default home page is the Welcome to MSN.com home page at the MSN Web site. You can easily select a different home page to open each time you start Internet Explorer. Simply go to the page that you want to be your home page in your Web browser window, click Tools on the menu bar, click Internet Options, click the General tab if necessary, click Use Current in the Home page area, then click OK to specify the current page as your home page.

Internet

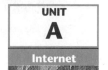

Saving a Favorite Web Page

The **Favorites list** and the **Favorites toolbar button** allow you to create your own list of frequently visited Web pages. When you find a Web page you know you will want to revisit, add the site address to the Favorites list. You can then access the site by clicking a link rather than having to type the URL. After you add a Web page to your Favorites list, you can automatically access that page by clicking the Favorites button on the toolbar or by clicking Favorites on the menu bar and then clicking the link name. ⬛⬛⬛ You know you will want to be able to revisit the pages for some of the charitable organizations you have found. Rather than writing the URLs on a sheet of paper and having to type the URLs in the Address bar each time, you save the sites in the Favorites list. You can return to these saved sites often as you do your research.

STEPS

1. **Click the Address bar, type** www.habitat.org**, then press** [Enter]

    The home page for Habitat for Humanity International opens as shown in Figure A-7. You want to see what volunteer opportunities are available.

> **TROUBLE**
> Web pages change frequently. The hyperlink may be in a new location on the page.

2. **Click the** Get Involved link**, read the information, then click the** Back button ⬅ Back **on the Standard Buttons toolbar**

    This site offers great volunteer opportunities you are certain are of interest to MediaLoft employees, so you decide to save the home page link in the Favorites list.

3. **Click** Favorites **on the menu bar, then click** Add to Favorites

    The Add Favorite dialog box opens as shown in Figure A-8. Favorites can be placed in folders or listed as menu items under the Favorites menu.

4. **Click** Create in **to open the Create in list (if necessary)**

    The Add Favorite dialog box expands to show the folders in which you can place the URL for the Habitat for Humanity International Web page. The name of the Web page appears in the Name text box and the Favorites folder is selected by default. If the default name of the Web page is unclear, you can change the default page name by typing a new name in the Name text box.

5. **Click** OK

    The name and URL for the Habitat for Humanity International Web page are added to your Favorites list. It is now a link on the Favorites list.

6. **Click the** Home button 🏠 **on the Standard Buttons toolbar to return to your home page**

> **QUICK TIP**
> You can click the Favorites button
> ⭐ Favorites on the Standard Buttons toolbar to open the Favorites task pane, which enables you to keep your list of favorites open on the screen.

7. **Click** Favorites **on the menu bar, then click the** Habitat for Humanity International link **on the Favorites list**

    The Habitat for Humanity International home page opens in your Web browser window.

FIGURE A-7: Habitat for Humanity International home page

Get Involved link

FIGURE A-8: Add Favorite dialog box

Name of Web page

Click to display folders

Clues to Use

Creating and organizing favorites

Once you add a Web page to your Favorites list, returning to that page is much easier. To keep your Favorites list manageable, only add pages that you expect to visit again. You can organize your list of favorites by placing them into folders by category. For example, you may want to create folders according to your interests, such as Sports, Cooking, and Travel. You may want to create folders in which each member of the household can place their favorites. To add a folder to your Favorites list, click Favorites on the menu bar, then click Organize Favorites. The Organize Favorites dialog box opens, as shown in Figure A-9. Click the Create Folder button to add a new folder to the list of folders and favorites. You can add a favorite to a specific folder by clicking the favorite, then clicking the Move to Folder button. You can also drag and drop a favorite into a folder. To see the contents of a folder, simply click the folder to open it, then click it again to close it.

FIGURE A-9: Organize Favorites dialog box

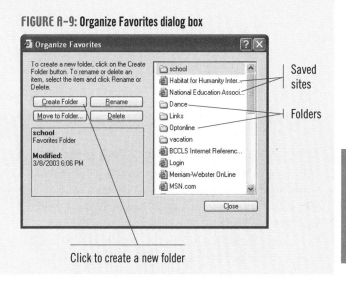

Saved sites

Folders

Click to create a new folder

Printing a Web Page

You can quickly print the Web page that appears in the browser window by clicking the Print button on the Standard Buttons toolbar. When you click File on the menu bar, then click Print, the options in the Print dialog box allow you to specify print options such as the number of copies and the page range. When you print a Web page, its text and any graphics appear on the printed page. With Internet Explorer, you can preview a Web page prior to printing by using Print Preview, which is helpful because some Web pages are lengthy and you may only want to print the pages that have the information relevant to your task. Table A-3 explains printing options in more detail. ▰▰▰▰ You decide to print a copy of a Web page to post on a bulletin board to publicize an organization of interest to MediaLoft employees.

STEPS

1. **Click the Address bar, type www.americorps.org, then press [Enter]**
   The home page for AmeriCorps opens.

2. **Click File on the menu bar, then click Print Preview**
   The Print Preview window opens. You want to print this page to post on the bulletin board, so you want to make sure all the relevant information from the Web page fits on one sheet of paper.

3. **Click the Zoom list arrow, then click Whole Page**
   You screen looks similar to Figure A-10. You confirm that the Web page only fills one printed page.

QUICK TIP

To print a Web page without previewing the page or changing any settings, click the Print button 🖨 on the Standard Buttons toolbar.

4. **Click the Print button to open the Print dialog box**

5. **Make sure 1 appears in the Number of copies text box, and that the All option button is selected in the Page Range area, as shown in Figure A-11**
   These settings indicate that once printing starts, one copy of all the pages for that Web page will print using the default printer. The printers listed in your Print dialog box will differ.

6. **Make sure your computer is connected to a printer, that it is turned on, and that it contains paper**

TROUBLE

If your computer is not connected to a printer or if an error message appears, ask your technical support person for assistance.

7. **Click Print**
   The Print dialog box closes, and one copy of the current Web page prints.

Clues to Use

Copying information from a Web page

You can select text on a Web page and use the Copy and Paste commands to use the same information in another program, such as Microsoft Word or other Office programs. You can also save a graphic image from a Web page by right-clicking the image, clicking Save Picture As on the shortcut menu, and then specifying where to save the image. If you just need to copy an image, click the Copy command on the shortcut menu. Using the Copy command saves the text or image to the Clipboard.

Keep in mind that the same laws that protect printed works generally protect information and graphics published on a Web page. Do not use material on a Web page without citing its source and checking the site carefully for any usage restrictions.

FIGURE A-10: Print Preview window

Print button ⊢

Number of
possible
printed pages

Zoom list arrow ⊢

FIGURE A-11: Print dialog box

Selected printer ⊢

All option button ⊢

Number of copies

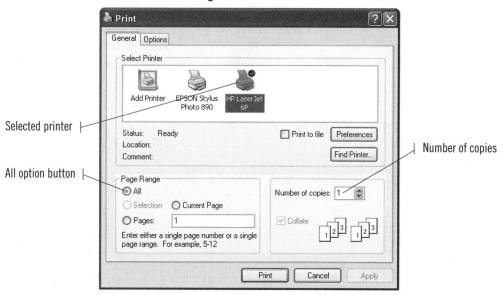

TABLE A-2: Printing options

option	tab	description
Select Printer	General	Displays information about the name, status, type, and location of the active printer
Page range	General	Allows you to choose to print all pages, a range of pages, or a selection on a page
Number of copies	General	Indicates the number of copies of each page to print and their sequence
Print all linked documents	Options	Opens and prints each document referenced by a link on the current page
Print frames	Options	Allows you to print only the current frame or all frames, separately or together
Print table of links	Options	Prints links in a table at the end of the document
Orientation	(Depends on printer)	Allows you to specify landscape or portrait page orientation

Internet

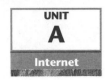

Searching for Information

A vast and ever-increasing number of Web pages and other information sources are available through the Internet. Searching using Internet Explorer's **Address bar** is based on criteria or **keywords**, which are words related to the topic for which you are searching. To search using the Address bar, you can enter a keyword or words in the Address bar, then click the Go button to start the search. The **Search Companion** enables you to search in two ways: it can provide a list of links similar in content or topic to the Web page you are currently viewing; or you can use the Search Companion text box to search for information based on keywords. If you use Web **search engines** such as Google or Yahoo! to locate information, the result is a list of links to Web sites related to your search topic. You can click one of the links to go quickly to a site. You decide to look for volunteer opportunities in a new area, environmental conservation. You start the search at a familiar site and then plan to search the Internet for similar Web sites using the Search Companion and a popular search engine.

STEPS

1. **Click the Address bar, type www.nature.org, then press [Enter]**

   The site for The Nature Conservancy opens in the browser window.

QUICK TIP

You can also click View on the menu bar, point to the Explorer Bar, then click Search to open the Search Companion.

2. **Click the Tools on the menu bar, then click Show Related Links**

   As shown in Figure A-12, the browser window splits into two panes. The right pane shows the Web page you were viewing before beginning your search. The Search Companion opens in the left pane. Your search results appear as a list of links to related Web sites called **Related Links**.

3. **Click any link to view a related Web page, click the Back button Back on the Standard Buttons toolbar to return to The Nature Conservancy Web site, then click the Close button in the Search Companion task pane to close the Search Companion**

   You want to include directions for some of the volunteer opportunities when you communicate them to the MediaLoft employees. You decide to investigate online map services.

4. **Click the Search button Search on the Standard Buttons toolbar, type maps in the Search Companion Please type your query here text box, then click Search**

   As shown in Figure A-13, your search results appear as a list of related Web sites in the right pane of the browser window. Other categories and additional options are available in the Search Companion task pane. Some search engines list results by category or topic, whereas others list Web page names. You can click any hyperlink to open a Web page or a list of Web pages relating to a specific category.

5. **Examine the results list by scrolling up or down, then click a hyperlink of your choice**

   The related page containing information about maps opens in the browser window.

6. **Click Search on the Standard Buttons toolbar to close the Search Companion task pane, click the Address bar, type www.google.com, then press [Enter]**

   Google is a commercial company that runs a search engine. Search engines such as Yahoo!, Google, Lycos, WebCrawler, and Excite routinely use software programs to methodically catalog, or crawl, through the entire Internet and create huge databases with links to Web pages and their URLs. When you enter a keyword or phrase, the search engine examines its database index for relevant information and displays a list of Web sites. Each search engine differs slightly in the way it formats information, the way it records the number of Internet sites in the database, and how often it updates the database.

7. **Type Volunteer opportunities for corporations in the text box, as shown in Figure A-14, then click Google Search**

8. **Review the list of results by scrolling up or down, then click a hyperlink of your choice**

   Based on your search you see that there are many opportunities available to give back to the community.

9. **Click the Home button on the Standard Buttons toolbar**

   Your home page appears in the browser window.

FIGURE A-12: Related Links

Search button

Search companion

Close button

Related links

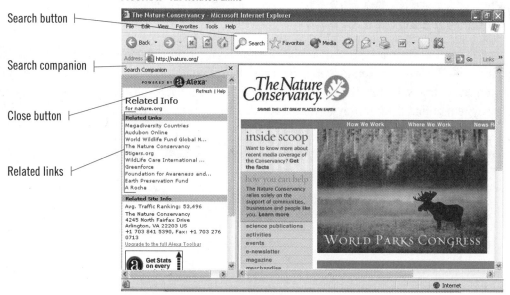

FIGURE A-13: Search Companion

Additional search options

Keyword used in search

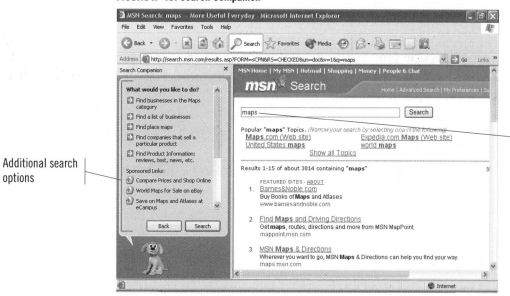

FIGURE A-14: Search engine

Keywords

Google Search button

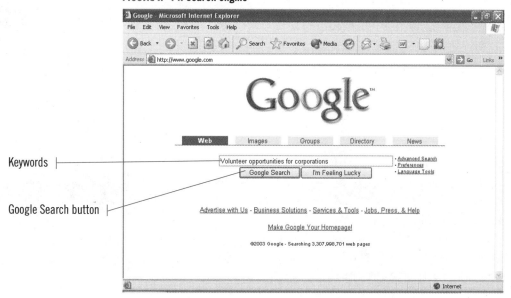

Internet

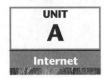

Getting Help

Internet Explorer provides a Help system with information and instructions on various features and commands. While exploring Web pages from the search results, Martin viewed a page that had a video on one of the Web sites. That video contains information that he needs, so he asks you to access the Help system to find the best way to view that video through the browser.

STEPS

1. **Click Help on the menu bar**
   The Help menu opens.

2. **Click Contents and Index**
   The Microsoft Internet Explorer Help window opens, with the Contents tab in view. The Contents tab works like a table of contents in a book. Table A-4 explains how each of the four tabs in the Help window provides a different way to access Help information.

3. **Click the Index tab**
   Your screen should look like Figure A-15.

4. **Click the Search tab**
   The Search tab allows you to search for a specific word or phrase in the Help contents.

5. **Type video in the Type in the keyword to find text box, click List Topics to display a list of relevant topics in the Select Topic to display list box, click Play an audio or video file using the Media bar, then click Display**
   As shown in Figure A-16, the text in the right pane of the Microsoft Internet Explorer Help window provides information on how to view an audio or video file. The word "video" is highlighted in the right pane because it was your keyword in the search.

6. **Double-click Using the Media bar in Internet Explorer in the left pane**
   The Help Window shown in Figure A-17 explains the buttons on the Media bar.

7. **Click the Close button in the upper-right corner of the Mocrosoft Internet Explorer Help window**
   The Help window closes.

TABLE A–3: Help options

tab	function
Contents	Lists the categories available in Help
Index	Lists available Help topics in alphabetical order, and lets you locate specific topics
Search	Locates the desired Help topic based on the keyword or phrase you enter
Favorites	Lists links to user-defined Help topics for easy reference

Clues to Use

Viewing sites in other languages

The Web is an international forum; as you surf the Web, you may find sites that display text in the native language of the country where the site originates. If you are a native English-speaking person, most Web sites have an English link somewhere on the site's home page that you can click to display the site in English.

FIGURE A-15: Help window Index tab

Index tab

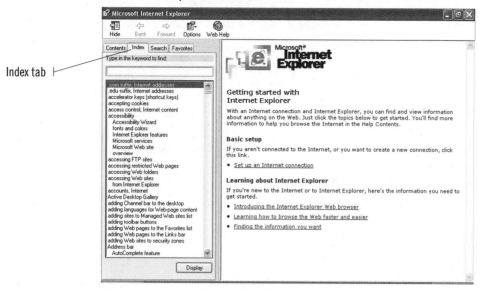

FIGURE A-16: Help on viewing video

Search keyword highlighted

List topics button

Selected topic

Display button

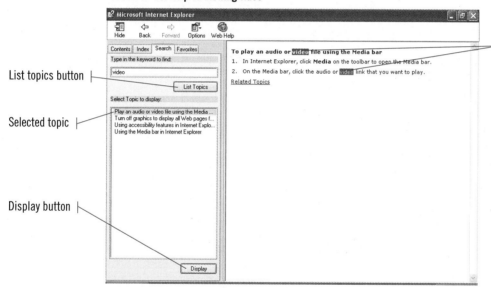

FIGURE A-17: Help on using the Media bar in Internet Explorer

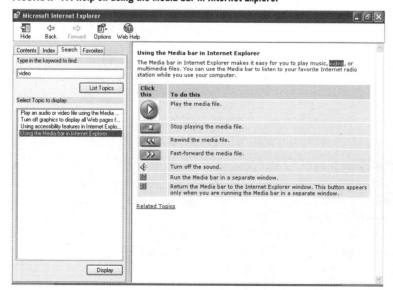

UNIT A

Internet

Exiting Internet Explorer

When you are ready to exit Internet Explorer, you can click the Close button in the upper-right corner of the browser window or click Close on the File menu. You do not need to save files before you exit. However, you may want to clear out your Favorites folder. ◢◣◤◥ You have completed your research on the Web and you are ready to exit Internet Explorer.

STEPS

1. **Click Favorites on the menu bar, click Organize Favorites, select the Favorites that you created in this unit, click Delete, click Yes in the Confirm File Delete dialog box, then click Close to close the Organize Favorites dialog box**

2. **Click File on the menu bar**
   The File menu opens, as shown in Figure A-18.

> **QUICK TIP**
> You can also exit from Internet Explorer by clicking the Close button in the upper-right corner of the browser window.

3. **Click Close**
   The Internet Explorer browser window closes.

4. **If you connected to the Internet by telephone, follow your normal procedure to close your connection**

Clues to Use

Saving or sending a Web page

Before exiting Internet Explorer, you may want to save a copy of the current page or send someone a copy of the page. By selecting Save As on the File menu, you can save the complete Web page, including any graphics—or just the text from the page—in a file on your computer. If you want to send the complete page to someone, click File on the menu bar, point to Send, click Page By Email, and then use your e-mail program to address and send the message to the intended recipient. If you want to send the Link only, not the whole page, click File on the menu bar, point to Send, then click Link by Email. You can also click Tools on the menu bar, point to Mail and News, and then click either Send a Link or Send Page.

FIGURE A-18: File menu

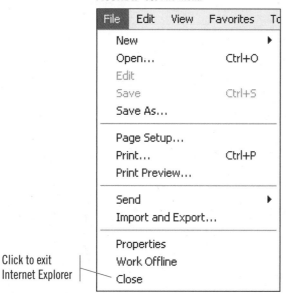

Click to exit
Internet Explorer

Clues to Use

Using media players

As you surf the Web, you may encounter a Web site with links to video or audio clips. Without the proper "player" software, your computer is unable to play the clips. You can download a free copy of RealOne (formerly called RealPlayer) from www.real.com. RealOne allows you to play audio and video clips and listen to your favorite radio stations. You can also view video or listen to music through Windows Media Player, as shown in Figure A-19. Windows Media Player comes with "skins", which display graphics that you can customize as the music plays. Windows Media Player is included with Windows, or you can download it or get updates from www.windowsmedia.com. Most Web sites direct you to either the RealOne Web site or the Windows Media Web site if you try to play a video clip unsuccessfully. You can also watch partner channels, such as CNN, Comedy Central, MSN Music, and others using MediaPlayer or RealOne. Before you download any new software to any computer, be sure you have permission to do so for the computer on which you are working.

FIGURE A-19: Windows Media Player

Practice

▼ CONCEPTS REVIEW

Label each element of the Internet Explorer browser window shown in Figure A-20.

FIGURE A-20

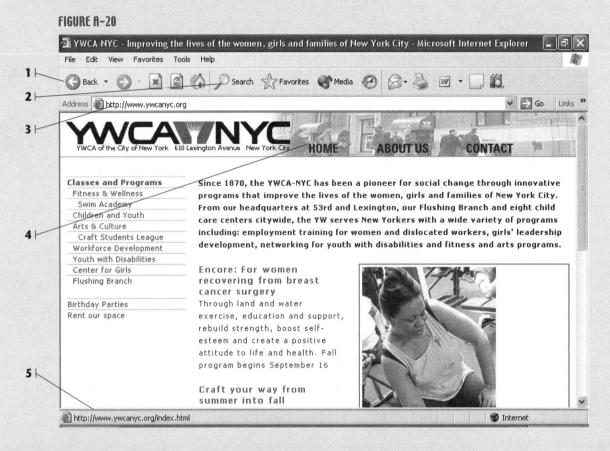

Match each term with the statement that best describes it.

6. **Address bar**
7. **Search Companion**
8. **Favorites button**
9. **Hyperlink**
10. **Back button**

a. Click to view a new Web page
b. Displays the URL for the currently displayed page
c. Use to find related Web sites
d. Displays a list of saved Web pages
e. Displays the previously viewed page

Select the best answer from the list of choices.

11. **Software programs used to access and display Web pages are called:**
    a. Web companions.
    b. Web browsers.
    c. Web documents.
    d. Web windows.

12. **If you want to save the name and URL of a Web page and return to it later, you can add it to:**
    a. Book links.
    b. Preferences.
    c. Home links.
    d. The Favorites list.

13. **An international network that consists of hyperlinked documents is called:**
    a. Internet Explorer.
    c. Netscape Navigator.
    b. The Internet.
    d. The World Wide Web.

14. **The _____ has buttons used to perform many common functions, such as printing Web pages and returning to the home page.**
    a. Address bar
    c. Status bar
    b. Link bar
    d. Standard Buttons toolbar

15. **You can search for Web sites by category by entering a keyword in the Address bar, then clicking the:**
    a. Go button.
    c. Home button.
    b. Search button.
    d. Link button.

16. **Which of the following URLs is valid?**
    a. htp://www.usf.edu
    c. http:/www.usf.edu
    b. http://www.usf.edu
    d. http//www.usf.edu

17. **Which button on the Standard Buttons toolbar should you click if you want to view the previous Web page on your computer?**
    a. Home
    c. Back
    b. Last
    d. Link

18. **Words on a Web page that, when clicked, enable you to navigate to another Web page location are called:**
    a. Favorites.
    c. Web browsers.
    b. Hyperlinks.
    d. Buttons.

19. **To locate information on a specific topic on the Internet, you can use a:**
    a. Search engine.
    c. Favorites list.
    b. Web browser.
    d. URL engine.

20. **When viewing a Web page, which of the following type of file requires that you use a media player?**
    a. Graphic image
    c. Audio clip
    b. Video clip
    d. E-mail message

▼ SKILLS REVIEW

1. **Start Internet Explorer.**
   a. Make sure your computer is connected to the Internet.
   b. Start Internet Explorer.

2. **Explore the browser window.**
   a. Identify the toolbar, menu bar, Address bar, Go button, Links bar, status bar, status indicator, URL, browser window, and scroll bars.
   b. Identify the toolbar buttons for printing, searching, viewing favorites, and returning to the home page.
   c. Identify the complete URL of the current Web page.

3. **View and navigate Web pages.**
   a. Open the Web page **www.usps.com** using the Address bar.
   b. Click a link on the Web page to view a new Web page.
   c. Return to the default home page for your browser.
   d. Click the Back button.
   e. Follow another link to investigate the content.
   f. Return to the default home page for your browser.

4. **Save favorite Web pages.**
   a. Open the Web page **www.nps.gov** using the Address bar.
   b. Add the Web page to your Favorites list.
   c. Return to the default home page for your browser.
   d. Using the Favorites list, return to the National Park Service home page.

▼ SKILLS REVIEW (CONTINUED)

5. **Print a Web page.**
   a. Open the Web page **www.microsoft.com** using the Address bar.
   b. Use Print Preview to preview the Web page in printed form.
   c. Print one copy of the first page only.

6. **Search for information on the Web.**
   a. Open the Search Companion.
   b. Type any keyword or phrase for which you would like to find information, then execute the search and review the results.
   c. Open the Web page **www.nationalgeographic.com** using the Address Bar.
   d. Use the Show Related Links command to find Web sites similar to the National Geographic Web site.
   e. Click any link in the Search Companion Related Links list and read the Web page.
   f. When you finish reviewing the results of your search, close the Search Companion.
   g. Enter the URL for a search engine in the Address Bar (you can use www.google.com, www.dogpile.com, or www.yahoo.com).
   h. Type any keyword or phrase for which you would like to find information, then start the search using the search engine.
   i. View the resulting list of links, then click a link and review the Web page.
   j. Return to the search results page, then explore some of the other hyperlinks you found.

7. **Get Help.**
   a. Open Microsoft Internet Explorer Help, then click the Contents tab if necessary.
   b. Click Understanding Security and Privacy on the Internet.
   c. Click Understanding security and privacy features.
   d. Read about working safely on the Internet.
   e. Close the Microsoft Internet Explorer Help window.

8. **Exit Internet Explorer.**
   a. Delete any Favorites you created using the Organize Favorites dialog box.
   b. Exit Internet Explorer.

▼ INDEPENDENT CHALLENGE 1

You are an aspiring journalist interested in understanding how different journalists approach the same story. You decide to use the Web to find some articles for comparison.

a. Start Internet Explorer.
b. Read and compare the coverage of a current international news story using two of the following sites:

   • CNN   www.cnn.com
   • MSNBC News   www.msnbc.com
   • Fox News Channel   www.foxnews.com
   • ABCNews   www.abcnews.com
   • CBSNews   www.cbsnews.com

c. Print one page of the same story from both sites that you chose.

Advanced Challenge Exercise

■ Use your favorite search engine to locate an online news media source from a country other than the United States. You can search on keywords such as "Asian newspapers" or "European news." You should be able to find many English-language versions of non-U.S. papers.
■ See if you can find the news story you researched in Step b. Read the article.
■ Print one page of the article from the site that you chose.

d. Exit Internet Explorer.

▼ INDEPENDENT CHALLENGE 2

You have been asked by your local library to create an exhibit in the lobby that parallels in content a current exhibit at the National Gallery of Art in Washington, DC. You decide to use the Web to research the exhibit.

    a. Start Internet Explorer.

    b. Go to **www.nga.gov**, then search the site to find out what exhibits are currently at the museum.

    c. Click several links on the site and review the online resources.

    d. Add a page from the site that you want to visit again to the Favorites list.

    e. Print one page from the site on the topic of interest.

Advanced Challenge Exercise

    ■ Find one page that includes a link for media such as audio or video.

    ■ Click the link and listen to the audio or play the video, noticing the player in which the media plays by default.

    ■ After listening to or viewing the media file, close the media player.

    f. Exit Internet Explorer.

▼ INDEPENDENT CHALLENGE 3

As a student of American political history, you want to learn about the structure of the U.S. government. You decide to use the Web to get information about this topic.

    a. Start Internet Explorer, then access the following government Web site: **www.senate.gov**.

    b. Explore the site to find a page containing information on the history of the U.S. Senate, then print one page from that site.

    c. Return to the U.S. Senate home page, navigate through the site to find the Web site for a senator who represents the state that you would most like to visit, then print one page from that site.

    d. Find sites related to the senator's Web site. Click several links to learn more about those related links.

    e. Print one page from one of the related sites.

    f. Exit Internet Explorer.

▼ INDEPENDENT CHALLENGE 4

You would like to decide on a search engine to use consistently when you search the Web. You decide to compare several search engines to determine which one you like the most.

    a. Start Internet Explorer. Using two of the search engines listed below, type **space travel nasa** in the Search text box.

      • Yahoo!   www.yahoo.com

      • MSN   www.msn.com

      • Google   www.google.com

    b. Print the first page of the results from each search. Circle the name of the search engine and the number of hits it produced.

    c. On a piece of paper, write down which search engine you think is better and why. Write down a few reasons for your preference.

Advanced Challenge Exercise

    ■ Create a folder on the Favorites list called **Search**.

    ■ Add the home page for your favorite search engine to the Favorites list, in the Search folder.

    ■ Return to your home page, then use the Favorites list to go to the search engine home page.

    ■ Delete the Search folder and search engine home page from the Favorites list.

    d. Exit Internet Explorer.

Internet

▼ VISUAL WORKSHOP

Graphics you find as you view pages on the Web can be static images, video, or animated graphics. Use the Search Companion to find and print a Web page that includes an animated graphic, such as the one shown in Figure A-21. Often a Web site's home page includes animation to "invite" a visitor to browse the site. The graphic can come from any one of several Web pages identified in your search results. Be sure to identify the Web site on which the graphic was located.

FIGURE A-21

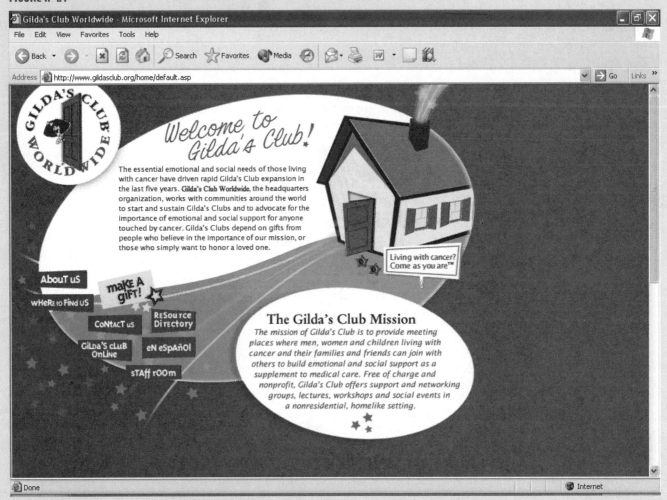

Introducing Microsoft Office 2003

OBJECTIVES

Define the Office 2003 Suite
Create a document with Word 2003
Build a worksheet with Excel 2003
Manage data with Access 2003
Create a presentation with PowerPoint 2003
Browse the World Wide Web with Internet Explorer
Integrate Office information
Manage office tasks with Outlook 2003

If you have a SAM user profile, you may have access to hands-on instruction, practice, and assessment of the skills covered in this unit. Log in to your SAM account and go to your assignments page to see what your instructor has assigned.

Microsoft Office 2003 is a collection of software programs designed to help you accomplish tasks quickly and efficiently. Each Office program is designed to complete specific tasks and has similar buttons and commands that make switching among the programs easy and seamless. The Microsoft Office programs are supplied together in a group called a **suite** (although you can also purchase them separately). Suite programs are designed so that you can easily transfer information among them. This unit introduces you to the Microsoft Office suite programs, as well as to MediaLoft, a chain of bookstore cafés founded in 1988. MediaLoft stores offer customers the opportunity to purchase books, music, and movies while enjoying a variety of coffees, teas, and freshly baked desserts. By exploring how MediaLoft uses Microsoft Office components, you will learn how each program can be used in a business environment.

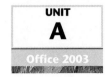

UNIT
A
Office 2003

Defining the Office 2003 Suite

Microsoft Office 2003, or Office, is a collection of software programs known as **business productivity software** because it helps business people work efficiently. Office is available in several configurations, and the most commonly used programs are Word, Excel, Access, PowerPoint, and Outlook. Internet Explorer is a Web browser that comes with Windows and can be downloaded from the Web. The Office programs have a similar "look and feel," and are designed to exchange information seamlessly. ▓▓▓▓ All MediaLoft employees use Office programs to create business documents, communicate with associates, and access the Internet. See Figure A-1 for an overview of MediaLoft's stores and Figure A-2 for sample Office documents.

DETAILS

- **The basic tools: Microsoft Office 2003 Suite components**

  The Office suite components work individually and with each other to help people accomplish tasks and work together. **Microsoft Office Word** [W] lets you create powerful text documents. Isaac Robinson, MediaLoft's marketing director, uses Word to create letters, reports, faxes, and flyers. You can automatically calculate and analyze data with **Microsoft Office Excel** [X]. Jim Fernandez, MediaLoft's office manager, uses Excel to create budgets, financial statements, and payroll summaries. **Microsoft Office Access** [A] lets you organize, track, and update complex data. Kelsey Lang, a MediaLoft marketing manager, uses Access to create and maintain a customer information database. You can create powerful visual presentations using **Microsoft Office PowerPoint** [P]. Maria Abbott, MediaLoft's general sales manager, uses PowerPoint to create a slide show summarizing the company's performance; she will show it at an annual meeting of store managers. You can easily track contacts, appointments, and e-mail with **Microsoft Office Outlook** [O]. Marketing manager Alice Wegman uses Outlook to stay in touch with MediaLoft employees around the world.

  Internet Explorer [e] enables you to find information on the Internet and World Wide Web. Alice Wegman uses Internet Explorer to find out about competitors in geographic areas the company is considering as sites for expansion.

- **Working together: Program compatibility and integration**

  Because the Office suite programs have a similar "look and feel," you can use your knowledge of one program's tools in other suite programs. For example, you can use the same commands and icons for common tasks such as printing and saving. Some tasks that are universally available in the suite, such as the Office Clipboard and Help, are organized in an area called the **task pane**, which is located on the right side of the screen in each program. Office documents are **compatible** with one another, meaning that you can easily place, or **integrate**, an Excel chart into a PowerPoint slide, or you can insert an Access table into a Word document. You can specify that information in one file be automatically updated whenever information in another file changes. The Office programs also share a common dictionary, so that special words you use often can be used consistently across all of your Office documents. And you can use the Office Clipboard to easily transfer up to 24 entries between any Office programs.

- **Supporting collaboration and teamwork: The new business model**

  Office recognizes the way people do business today, and supports the emphasis on communication and knowledge sharing within companies and across the globe via company intranets and the Internet. All Office programs include the ability to share information over the Internet—called **online collaboration**. Employees can share documents, schedule online meetings, and have discussions over the World Wide Web. Office supports teamwork by allowing people to share documents and incorporate team members' feedback into one central place.

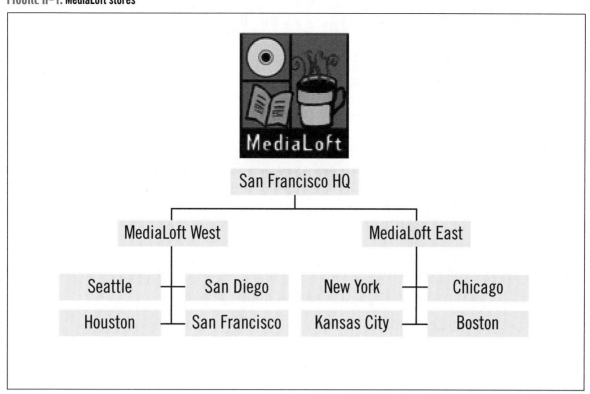

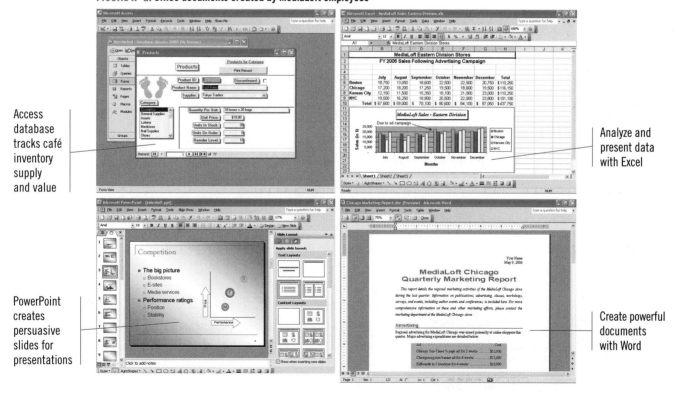

Access database tracks café inventory supply and value

Analyze and present data with Excel

PowerPoint creates persuasive slides for presentations

Create powerful documents with Word

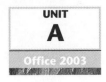

Creating a Document with Word 2003

Microsoft Word 2003 is a **word processing** program that allows you to create and edit text documents. You can also format text with characteristics such as bold and italics to make text information easier to understand and to make important information stand out. You can use a word processor to create reports, memos, or letters that contain text, tables, and graphics. Sophisticated text-handling tools, such as an electronic thesaurus, indexes, and footnotes make Word ideal for long and complex text documents such as books. ▰▰▰ MediaLoft employees use Word to create a variety of documents necessary for putting together the company's Annual Report. A document can contain many elements that make it readable and professional looking.

DETAILS

The following are some of the benefits of using Word:

* **Enter text quickly and easily**

  Word makes it easy to enter and edit text. Rather than having to retype a document if you make a mistake or want the information to be presented differently, you can rearrange and revise the text on-screen. Bullets or numbers can make lists more attractive and easier to understand. When you move items in a numbered list, Word automatically corrects the numbers to reflect the new order.

* **Organize information in a table to make it easier to read**

  Some information is easier to read in rows and columns, and it's easy to create and modify a table in Word. Once you create a table, you can edit its contents and modify its appearance using your own formatting or using predesigned formats. You can also sort table data without any additional typing.

* **Create error-free copy**

  You can use the Word Spelling and Grammar checker after you finish typing to help you create error-free documents. It compares each word in a document to a built-in dictionary and notifies you if it does not recognize a word. The Word AutoCorrect feature can automatically correct misspelled words as you type them. Word provides entries for commonly misspelled words, and you can also add your own.

* **Combine text and graphics**

  Using Word, you can combine text and graphics easily in the same document.

* **Communicate with others**

  You can use special Word features to communicate with teammates. For example, you can insert **comments** within a document that coworkers can see. You can use the **tracking** feature to keep a record of edits and view edits others make in a document. Figure A-3 shows a Word document containing tracked changes, text, a graphic, and a table as they look on the screen; Figure A-4 shows the printed memo. In addition to collaborating using Word features, you can also control who can view, edit, or distribute the content of a document using rights management tools.

* **See different document views**

  Depending on your need, you can view a document in a variety of ways. For example, you can use the Print Layout view to see how the document will look when it is printed as you create it. If you want to read a document before printing, you can use the Reading Layout view. This view makes minor alterations to the layout and improves the font display, making it easier to read a document on-screen.

* **Add special effects**

  Word lets you create columns of text, drop caps (capital letters that take up two or three lines), and WordArt (customized text with a three-dimensional or shadowed appearance), adding a polished quality to your documents.

FIGURE A-3: Memo created in Word

Tracked changes

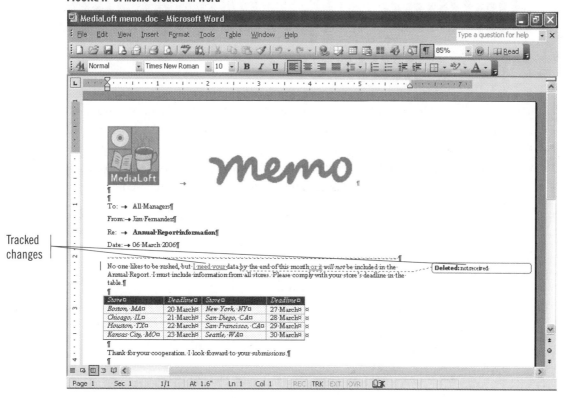

FIGURE A-4: Printout of completed memo

Graphic containing company logo

Table makes data easier to read

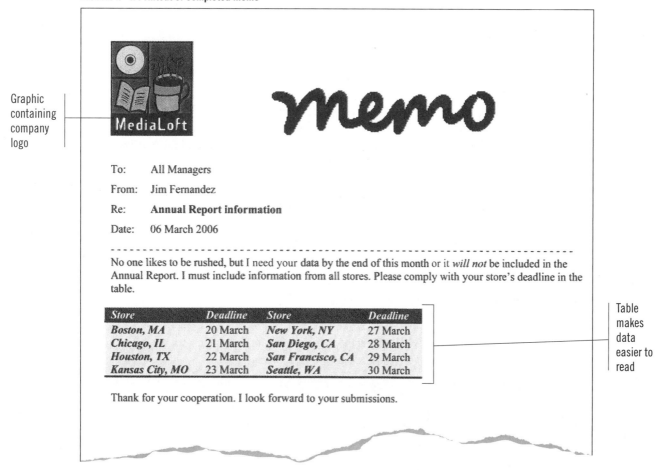

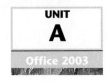
Building a Worksheet with Excel 2003

Microsoft Excel 2003 is a **spreadsheet** program you can use to analyze data, perform calculations, and create charts. Excel performs numeric calculations rapidly and accurately. Like traditional paper-based spreadsheets, this electronic spreadsheet contains a **worksheet** area that is divided into columns and rows that form individual cells. **Cells** can contain text, numbers, formulas, or a combination of all three. 🖉🖉🖉 MediaLoft employees use Excel to store and analyze sales data as well as other numeric information they have collected. They can then format the data for insertion into the Annual Report.

DETAILS

The following are some of the benefits of using Excel:

- **Calculate results quickly and accurately**

  With Excel, you can enter data quickly and accurately using formulas. Excel then calculates the results.

- **Recalculate easily**

  Excel makes updating data easy by automatically recalculating when you change or correct an entry.

- **Perform what-if analysis**

  Because Excel automatically recalculates formulas when data changes, you can ask "what-if?" and create a variety of business scenarios, such as, "What if the interest rate on a corporate credit card changes?" Anticipating possible outcomes helps you make better business decisions.

- **Complete complex mathematical formulas**

  Using Excel, you can easily complete complicated mathematical computations by using built-in formulas. The program tells you what data to enter, then you fill in the blanks, saving valuable time.

- **Communicate with others**

  In today's offices it is common for a group of people to review the same document. Readers can use the Comments feature to attach explanatory comments to worksheet cells. You can also keep track of changes others make to your worksheets by using powerful change-tracking tools. In addition, the Excel rights-management tools enable you to control who can view, edit, or distribute a workbook.

- **Create charts**

  Excel makes it easy to create charts based on worksheet information. With Excel, charts are automatically updated as worksheet data changes. The worksheet in Figure A-5 contains a bar chart that illustrates sales revenue for the eight MediaLoft stores over a three-year period.

- **Analyze worksheet data**

  Worksheet data in a long list is easy to summarize and analyze quickly using the PivotTable feature. Once you create a PivotTable, you can chart its output. Without the PivotTable feature, it would be time-consuming and very difficult to analyze lengthy Excel data.

- **Create attractive output**

  You can enhance the overall appearance of numeric data by using charts, graphics, and text formatting, as shown in Figure A-5. Figure A-6 shows the printed worksheet.

FIGURE A-5: Worksheet created in Excel

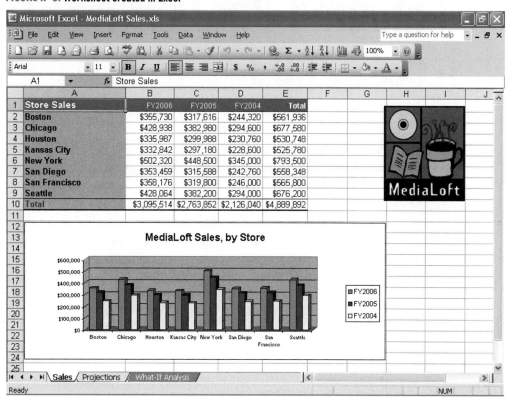

FIGURE A-6: Printout of annual revenue data with corresponding chart

Formatting makes data easier to read

Company logo graphic inserted

Legend identifies colors used in chart

Corresponds to FY 2006 sales for Boston

Sales Summary

Store Sales	FY2006	FY2005	FY2004	Total
Boston	$355,730	$317,616	$244,320	$561,936
Chicago	$428,938	$382,980	$294,600	$677,580
Houston	$335,987	$299,988	$230,760	$530,748
Kansas City	$332,842	$297,180	$228,600	$525,780
New York	$502,320	$448,500	$345,000	$793,500
San Diego	$353,459	$315,588	$242,760	$558,348
San Francisco	$358,176	$319,800	$246,000	$565,800
Seattle	$428,064	$382,200	$294,000	$676,200
Total	$3,095,514	$2,763,852	$2,126,040	$4,889,892

MediaLoft Sales, by Store

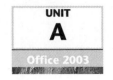

Managing Data with Access 2003

Microsoft Access 2003 is a database management system. A **database** is a collection of related information such as a list of employees, their Social Security numbers, salaries, and accumulated vacation time. A **database management system** organizes databases and allows you to link multiple groups of information. With Access, you can arrange and analyze large amounts of data in grids called **tables**, such as an inventory of products, or the members of a sales department. The tables in a database are related to one another by a common piece of information, such as a product number, which makes the database a powerful information retrieval tool. You can rearrange and combine the information in the tables in a variety of ways. For example, an inventory database might be listed alphabetically, by stocking location, or by the number of units on order. You might use a salesperson's name from a Sales Rep table and a product description from a Products table to create a sales report. A powerful database program like Access lets you use your data in a wide variety of ways. MediaLoft stores use Access databases to keep track of inventory. Information from these databases is used to generate inventory lists and data for the Annual Report.

DETAILS

The following are some of the benefits of using Access:

- **Enter data easily**

  Employees can enter data in an existing table as the database grows or changes. Because Access organizes the data for you, the order in which you enter items is not a concern.

- **Retrieve data easily**

  Access makes it easy for you to specify **criteria**, or conditions, and then produce a list of all data that conforms to those criteria. You might want to see a list of products by supplier or a list of discontinued products. Figure A-7 shows an inventory table containing music sold at MediaLoft's stores.

- **Create professional forms**

  You can enter data into an on-screen form that you create in Access. Using a form makes entering data more efficient, and you'll be less prone to making errors. Figure A-8 shows a screen form that the MediaLoft music department uses for data entry.

- **Create flexible, professional reports**

  You can create a report that summarizes any or all of the information in an Access table. You can create your own layout, and add summaries of data within the report. For example, a MediaLoft inventory report could include all the information in the Music Inventory table and contain subtotals of the number of items in each music category.

- **Eliminate common errors automatically**

  The AutoCorrect feature makes it possible to eliminate common errors in forms and reports automatically. This feature helps you identify errors (such as a report that exceeds the printable page width) and quickly fix them. This saves you valuable time, improves your productivity, and increases the professional quality of your work.

- **Add graphics to printed screen forms and reports**

  Forms and reports can contain graphic images, text formatting, and special effects, such as WordArt, to make them look more professional.

FIGURE A-7: List of inventory items in Access

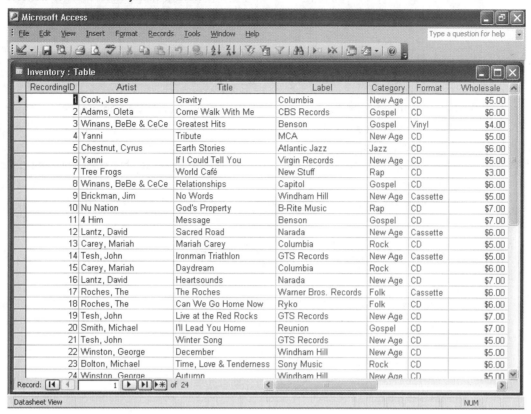

FIGURE A-8: On-screen Access data entry form

Inserted
graphic
image

Formatted
text

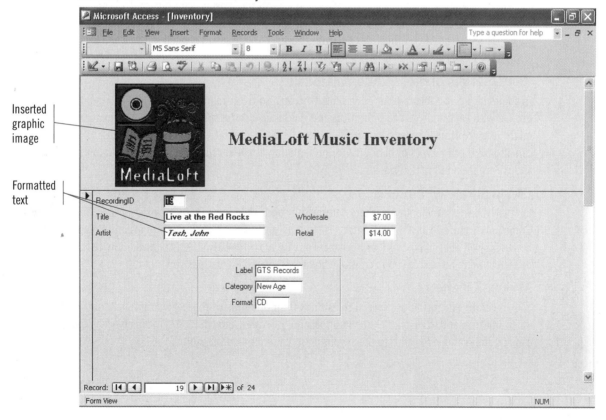

Creating a Presentation with PowerPoint 2003

Microsoft PowerPoint 2003 is a **presentation graphics** program you can use to develop slides and hand-outs for visual presentations. In PowerPoint, a **slide** is a "page" in an on-screen display called a **slide show**, in which consecutive images appear on a computer screen. The computer can be connected to a projector so a roomful of people can see the presentation. You can then use your on-screen slide content to create handouts, outlines, notes, and 35-mm slides. ▓▓▓▓ Store managers present highlights of the Annual Report to MediaLoft executives using a slide show and notes created in PowerPoint.

DETAILS

The following are some of the benefits of using PowerPoint:

- **Create and edit slides easily**

  You can enter text directly on a PowerPoint slide, enabling you to see how your slide will look. After you have learned how to edit text in Word, you can use the same techniques in PowerPoint. You can cut, copy, paste, and move slide text quickly and easily.

- **Combine information from Office programs**

  You can use data you create in Word, Excel, Access, and other Office programs in your PowerPoint slides. This means that you can easily insert a worksheet you created in Excel, for example, without having to retype the information.

- **Add graphics**

  Predesigned images called **clip art**, an Excel chart, or a corporate logo can further enhance any presentation. PowerPoint comes with many clip art images and accepts the most commonly available graphic file formats. PowerPoint also allows you to create your own shapes and enhance text with special effects using WordArt. Figure A-9 shows a PowerPoint slide containing both a chart that was created in Excel and a graphic image of a corporate logo.

- **Print a variety of presentation materials**

  In addition to being able to print out a slide, you can also create many other types of printed materials. Notes printed with each slide can contain hints and reminders for the speaker or for the audience members, who might receive printed copies of the presentation slides. Figure A-10 shows notes created in PowerPoint. You can also print other types of handouts for presentation attendees that contain a reduced image of each slide and a place for handwritten notes.

- **Communicate with others**

  In many businesses, employees share information and often contribute to others' work. You can use the Comments feature to insert explanatory comments on a slide. This makes communication more efficient, because co-workers can point out areas that are unclear or particularly effective. In addition, rights-management tools in PowerPoint enable you to control who has access to presentations you create.

- **Add special effects**

  You can create slides that use special transitions from one slide to the next. Animation effects allow you to determine how and when slide elements appear on the screen and which sound effects accompany them. You can add audio and video clips to make your presentation look professional.

FIGURE A-9: Slide created in PowerPoint

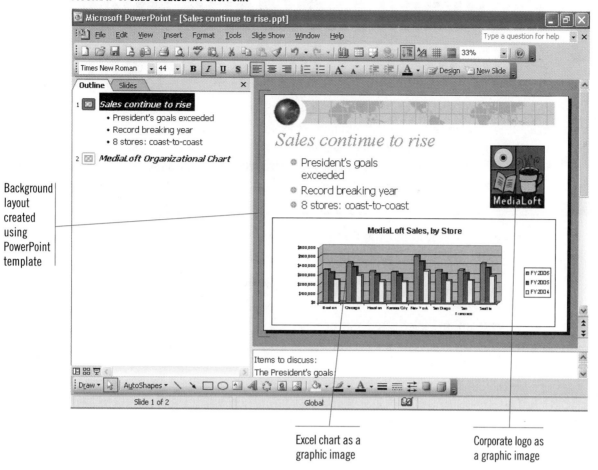

Background layout created using PowerPoint template

Excel chart as a graphic image

Corporate logo as a graphic image

FIGURE A-10: Notes created in PowerPoint

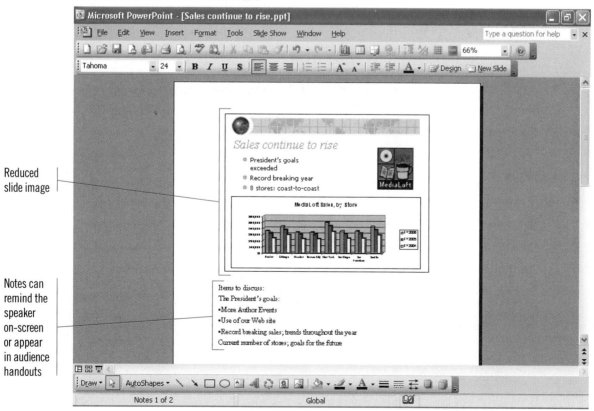

Reduced slide image

Notes can remind the speaker on-screen or appear in audience handouts

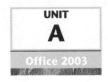

Browsing the World Wide Web with Internet Explorer

The **World Wide Web**—also known as the **Web**—is the part of the Internet that brings text, graphics, and multimedia information to your desktop. Internet Explorer is a **browser**, a program designed to help you view the text, graphic images, and multimedia on the Web. Many Web sites let you move to other sites with the click of your mouse using **links**, special areas that take you to different Web site addresses. MediaLoft employees keep informed on the latest trends and research competitors by using Internet Explorer.

DETAILS

The following are some of the benefits of using Internet Explorer:

- **Display Web sites**

  Once you're connected to the Internet, you can view interesting and informative Web sites from all around the globe. The MediaLoft Web site is shown in Figure A-11.

- **Move from one Web site to another**

  Web page links let you effortlessly move from site to site. You can easily find information related to the topic in which you're interested.

- **Save your favorite Web site locations**

  Once you've located interesting Web sites, you can save their Web site addresses so you can return to them later without performing another search or remembering a long address. Internet Explorer makes it easy to compile a list of your favorite locations.

- **Use multimedia**

  Web pages frequently contain video and audio clips. Internet Explorer allows you to experience the multimedia capabilities of the Web.

- **Communicate with others**

  You can use your browser to participate in online discussions with other users.

- **Incorporate Web information**

  Internet Explorer makes it easy to combine the immediacy of the Web with the power of Office suite programs: you can import data—whether it is text, graphics, or numbers—from the Web and edit it in the Office program you select, such as Word or Excel.

- **Print Web pages**

  As you travel the Web, you may want to print the information you find. You can easily print an active Web page—including its text and graphics.

FIGURE A-11: Browsing with Internet Explorer

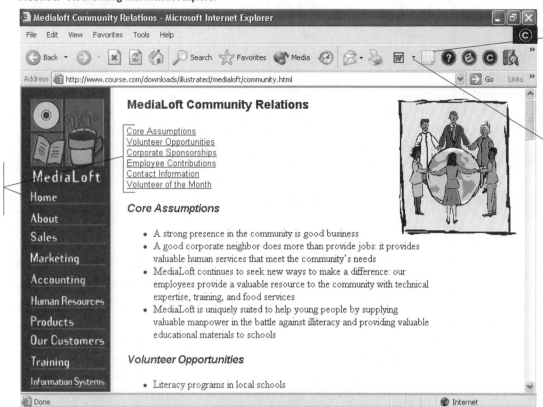

Click to participate in a discussion

Click to import and edit Web data in an Office program

Click links to display other Web pages

Office 2003

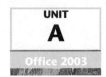
Integrating Office Information

Information created in one Office program can be used in another. This means that a chart created in Excel can be used in Word without having to be retyped or reentered. Information in an Access table can be exported to Excel and analyzed, or pasted into a Word document. An outline created in Word can be imported into PowerPoint, saving you time and allowing you to work more efficiently. Using Office, integrating information is easy and can be accomplished in many ways. ▓▓▓▓ MediaLoft employees use integration as a means of working efficiently.

DETAILS

The following are some of the benefits of using integration:

- **Create information once**

  It is not necessary to retype information each time you want to use it in another document or program. For example, the same Excel chart can be pasted into a Word document and a PowerPoint slide, as shown in Figure A-12. Because you can copy information into the Office Clipboard, it is easy to paste it into any other Office program. Data can also be linked, so that when the original document is changed, the pasted data is changed too.

- **Merge data**

  In addition to simple copy-and-paste techniques, Office programs offer more sophisticated processes, such as merging Access data with Word. This feature makes it possible to combine information in a database with text in a letter. The result is that you can easily create form letters with the click of a few buttons.

- **Export data**

  Data in an Access table can be exported to Excel. Once in Excel, the data can be further analyzed and charted. Or, a PowerPoint presentation can be exported to Word, where you can save and edit the document to create special handouts to accompany the presentation. See Figure A-13.

- **Create hyperlinks**

  With so many interrelated documents being used in business, it's helpful to know that Office lets you link on-screen documents. You can click on specially formatted text or graphics called **hyperlinks** and automatically be transferred to another area of your current document, or to another document entirely.

FIGURE A-12: Excel chart used in a Word document and a PowerPoint slide

Chart in Word
document

Chart in Excel
worksheet

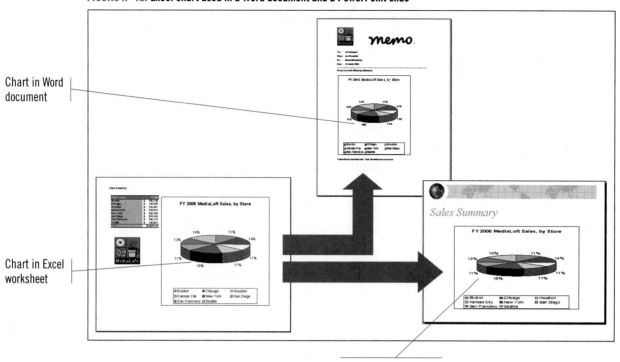

Chart in PowerPoint slide

FIGURE A-13: PowerPoint presentation in a Word document

Slides in
PowerPoint
presentation

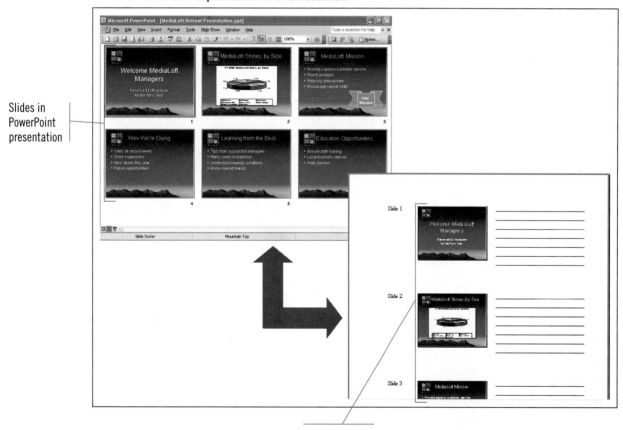

PowerPoint slides
after sending to
Word document

Managing Office Tasks with Outlook 2003

There's more to office work than creating documents, worksheets, databases, and presentations. Microsoft Outlook 2003 is an electronic **personal information manager** that helps you manage a typical business day. You can use it to schedule appointments, keep track of contacts, and send e-mail and files to people on your local network or intranet, as well as across the Internet to anyone with an Internet address. For example, using the Inbox, you can send electronic mail messages—or **e-mail**—to anyone with an e-mail address. Table A-1 describes tasks you can perform with Outlook. 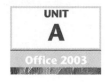 MediaLoft employees work more efficiently by using Outlook to send messages between stores, schedule appointments, and keep track of deadlines.

DETAILS

The following are some of the benefits of using Outlook:

- **Process mail**

  Use the Inbox to read, forward, reply to, and create e-mail. The Inbox displays unread messages in bold text, so you can tell which messages still need to be read.

- **Create an address book**

  Keep track of e-mail addresses in an address book so that you don't have to type an e-mail address each time you create a new message. You can also create distribution lists so that you can easily send messages to a group of people with whom you communicate frequently, without having to enter each e-mail address over and over.

- **Send attachments**

  In addition to the actual content of a message, you can attach individual files to an e-mail message. This means you can send a colleague a spreadsheet created in Excel, for example, along with an explanatory message.

- **Organize mail**

  Organizational tools in Outlook make it easy to keep track of large volumes of mail. Outlook enables users to sort mail in a variety of ways and automatically categorizes mail in groups, such as mail received "today", "yesterday", and "last week". In addition, folders called Search Folders cut down on the need to file e-mail messages because each Search Folder provides a current view of e-mail that fits specific criteria (such as flagged e-mail or e-mail relating to a specific person). Outlook also provides a variety of ways to filter unwanted junk e-mail.

TABLE A-1: Additional Outlook tasks

task	description
Manage appointments	Use Calendar to make appointments, plan meetings, and keep track of events
Manage tasks	Use Tasks to keep track of pending jobs, set priorities, assign due dates, and express completion expectations for tasks
Track contacts	Use Contacts to record information such as names, addresses, phone numbers, and e-mail addresses for business and personal associates
Maintain a journal of your activities	Use Journal to track project phases, record activities, and manage your time
Create reminders	Use Notes—an electronic equivalent of yellow sticky notes—to leave reminders for yourself

Getting Started with Word 2003

OBJECTIVES

Understand word processing software
Start Word 2003
Explore the Word program window
Start a document
Save a document
Print a document
Use the Help system
Close a document and exit Word

If you have a SAM user profile, you may have access to hands-on instruction, practice, and assessment of the skills covered in this unit. Log in to your SAM account and go to your assignments page to see what your instructor has assigned.

Microsoft Office Word 2003 is a word processing program that makes it easy to create a variety of professional-looking documents, from simple letters and memos to newsletters, research papers, Web pages, business cards, resumes, financial reports, and other documents that include multiple pages of text and sophisticated formatting. In this unit, you will explore the editing and formatting features available in Word, learn how to start Word, and create a document. You have just been hired to work in the Marketing Department at MediaLoft, a chain of bookstore cafés that sells books, music, and videos. Shortly after reporting to your new office, Alice Wegman, the marketing manager, asks you to familiarize yourself with Word and use it to create a memo to the marketing staff.

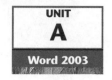

Understanding Word Processing Software

A **word processing program** is a software program that includes tools for entering, editing, and formatting text and graphics. Microsoft Word is a powerful word processing program that allows you to create and enhance a wide range of documents quickly and easily. Figure A-1 shows the first page of a report created using Word and illustrates some of the Word features you can use to enhance your documents. The electronic files you create using Word are called **documents**. One of the benefits of using Word is that document files can be stored on a disk, making them easy to transport, exchange, and revise. ▓▓▓ You need to write a memo to the marketing staff to inform them of an upcoming meeting. Before beginning your memo, you explore the editing and formatting capabilities available in Word.

DETAILS

You can use Word to accomplish the following tasks:

- **Type and edit text**

  The Word editing tools make it simple to insert and delete text in a document. You can add text to the middle of an existing paragraph, replace text with other text, undo an editing change, and correct typing, spelling, and grammatical errors with ease.

- **Copy and move text from one location to another**

  Using the more advanced editing features of Word, you can copy or move text from one location and insert it in a different location in a document. You also can copy and move text between documents. Being able to copy and move text means you don't have to retype text that is already entered in a document.

- **Format text and paragraphs with fonts, colors, and other elements**

  The sophisticated formatting tools available in Word allow you to make the text in your documents come alive. You can change the size, style, and color of text, add lines and shading to paragraphs, and enhance lists with bullets and numbers. Formatting text creatively helps you highlight important ideas in your documents.

- **Format and design pages**

  The Word page-formatting features give you power to design attractive newsletters, create powerful resumes, and produce documents such as business cards, CD labels, and books. You can change the paper size and orientation of your documents, add headers and footers to pages, organize text in columns, and control the layout of text and graphics on each page of a document.

- **Enhance documents with tables, charts, diagrams, and graphics**

  Using the powerful graphic tools available in Word, you can spice up your documents with pictures, photographs, lines, shapes, and diagrams. You also can illustrate your documents with tables and charts to help convey your message in a visually interesting way.

- **Create Web pages**

  The Word Web page design tools allow you to create documents that others can read over the Internet or an intranet. You can enhance Web pages with themes and graphics, add hyperlinks, create online forms, and preview Web pages in your Web browser.

- **Use Mail Merge to create form letters and mailing labels**

  The Word Mail Merge feature allows you to easily send personalized form letters to many different people. You can also use Mail Merge to create mailing labels, directories, e-mail messages, and many other types of documents.

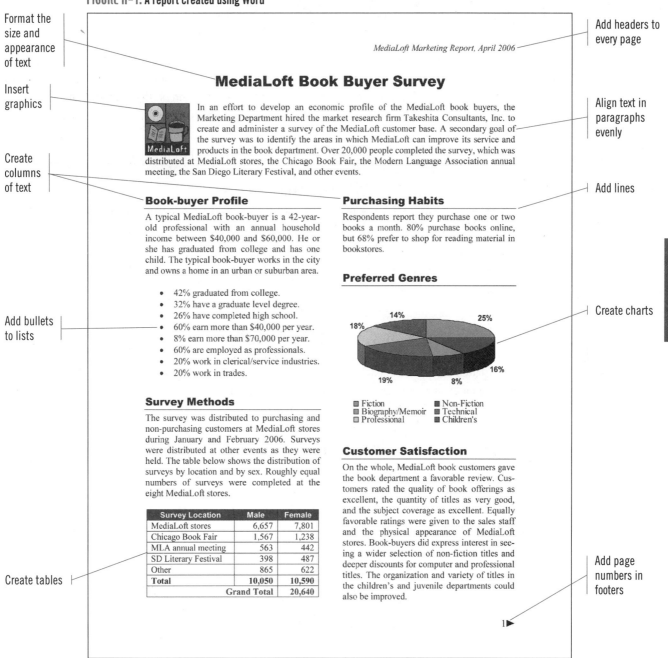

Format the size and appearance of text

Insert graphics

Create columns of text

Add bullets to lists

Create tables

Add headers to every page

Align text in paragraphs evenly

Add lines

Create charts

Add page numbers in footers

MediaLoft Marketing Report, April 2006

MediaLoft Book Buyer Survey

In an effort to develop an economic profile of the MediaLoft book buyers, the Marketing Department hired the market research firm Takeshita Consultants, Inc. to create and administer a survey of the MediaLoft customer base. A secondary goal of the survey was to identify the areas in which MediaLoft can improve its service and products in the book department. Over 20,000 people completed the survey, which was distributed at MediaLoft stores, the Chicago Book Fair, the Modern Language Association annual meeting, the San Diego Literary Festival, and other events.

Book-buyer Profile

A typical MediaLoft book-buyer is a 42-year-old professional with an annual household income between $40,000 and $60,000. He or she has graduated from college and has one child. The typical book-buyer works in the city and owns a home in an urban or suburban area.

- 42% graduated from college.
- 32% have a graduate level degree.
- 26% have completed high school.
- 60% earn more than $40,000 per year.
- 8% earn more than $70,000 per year.
- 60% are employed as professionals.
- 20% work in clerical/service industries.
- 20% work in trades.

Survey Methods

The survey was distributed to purchasing and non-purchasing customers at MediaLoft stores during January and February 2006. Surveys were distributed at other events as they were held. The table below shows the distribution of surveys by location and by sex. Roughly equal numbers of surveys were completed at the eight MediaLoft stores.

Survey Location	Male	Female
MediaLoft stores	6,657	7,801
Chicago Book Fair	1,567	1,238
MLA annual meeting	563	442
SD Literary Festival	398	487
Other	865	622
Total	**10,050**	**10,590**
	Grand Total	**20,640**

Purchasing Habits

Respondents report they purchase one or two books a month. 80% purchase books online, but 68% prefer to shop for reading material in bookstores.

Preferred Genres

14% 18% 25% 19% 8% 16%

- Fiction
- Biography/Memoir
- Professional
- Non-Fiction
- Technical
- Children's

Customer Satisfaction

On the whole, MediaLoft book customers gave the book department a favorable review. Customers rated the quality of book offerings as excellent, the quantity of titles as very good, and the subject coverage as excellent. Equally favorable ratings were given to the sales staff and the physical appearance of MediaLoft stores. Book-buyers did express interest in seeing a wider selection of non-fiction titles and deeper discounts for computer and professional titles. The organization and variety of titles in the children's and juvenile departments could also be improved.

1▶

Word 2003

Clues to Use

Planning a document

Before you create a new document, it's a good idea to spend time planning it. Identify the message you want to convey, the audience for your document, and the elements, such as tables or charts, you want to include. You should also think about the tone and look of your document—is it a business letter, which should be written in a pleasant, but serious tone and have a formal appearance, or are you creating a flyer that must be colorful, eye-catching, and fun to read?

The purpose and audience for your document determines the appropriate design. Planning the layout and design of a document involves deciding how to organize the text, selecting the fonts to use, identifying the graphics to include, and selecting the formatting elements that will enhance the document's message and appeal. For longer documents, such as newsletters, it can be useful to sketch the layout and design of each page before you begin.

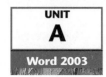

Starting Word 2003

Before starting Word, you must start Windows by turning on your computer. Once Windows is running, you can start Word or any other application by using the Start button on the Windows taskbar. You can also start Word by clicking the Word icon on the Windows desktop or the Word icon on the Microsoft Office Shortcut bar, if those items are available on your computer. You use the Start button to start Word so you can familiarize yourself with its features.

STEPS

1. **Click the** Start button **on the Windows taskbar**
   The Start menu opens on the desktop. The left pane of the Start menu includes shortcuts to the most frequently used programs on the computer.

2. **Point to** All Programs **on the Start menu**
   The All Programs menu opens. The All Programs menu displays the list of programs installed on your computer.

> **TROUBLE**
> If Microsoft Office is not on your All Programs menu, ask your technical support person for assistance.

3. **Point to** Microsoft Office
   A menu listing the Office programs installed on your computer opens, as shown in Figure A-2.

4. **Click** Microsoft Office Word 2003 **on the Microsoft Office menu**
   The **Word program window** opens and displays a blank document in the document window and the Getting Started task pane, as shown in Figure A-3. The blank document opens in the most recently used view. **Views** are different ways of displaying a document in the document window. Figure A-3 shows a blank document in Print Layout view. The lessons in this unit will use Print Layout view.

5. **Click the** Print Layout View button ▣ **as shown in Figure A-3**
   If your blank document opened in a different view, the view changes to Print Layout view.

> **TROUBLE**
> If your toolbars are on one row, click the Toolbar Options button at the end of the Formatting toolbar, then click Show Buttons on Two Rows.

6. **Click the** Zoom list arrow **on the Standard toolbar as shown in Figure A-3, then click** Page Width
   The blank document fills the document window. Your screen should now match Figure A-3. The blinking vertical line in the upper-left corner of the document window is the **insertion point**. It indicates where text appears as you type.

7. **Move the mouse pointer around in the Word program window**
   The mouse pointer changes shape depending on where it is in the Word program window. In the document window in Print Layout view, the mouse pointer changes to an **I-beam pointer** I or a **click and type pointer** $I^{\equiv}$. You use these pointers to move the insertion point in the document or to select text to edit. Table A-1 describes common Word pointers.

8. **Place the mouse pointer over a toolbar button**
   When you place the pointer over a button or some other element of the Word program window, a ScreenTip appears. A **ScreenTip** is a label that identifies the name of the button or feature.

TABLE A-1: Common Word pointers

pointer	use to
I	Move the insertion point in a document or to select text
$I^{\equiv}$ or $\underset{\equiv}{I}$	Move the insertion point in a blank area of a document in Print Layout or Web Layout view; automatically applies the paragraph formatting required to position text at that location in the document
�	Click a button, menu command, or other element of the Word program window; appears when you point to elements of the Word program window
⍒	Select a line or lines of text; appears when you point to the left edge of a line of text in the document window
�	Open a hyperlink; appears when you point to a hyperlink in the task pane or a document

FIGURE A-2: Starting Word from the All Programs menu

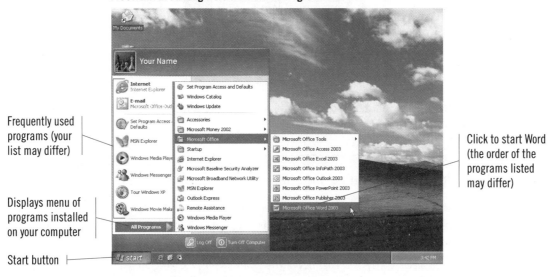

Frequently used programs (your list may differ)

Displays menu of programs installed on your computer

Start button

Click to start Word (the order of the programs listed may differ)

FIGURE A-3: Word program window in Print Layout view

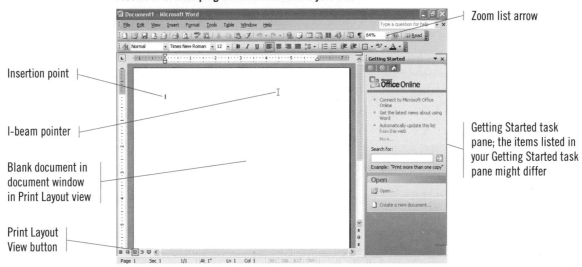

Insertion point

I-beam pointer

Blank document in document window in Print Layout view

Print Layout View button

Zoom list arrow

Getting Started task pane; the items listed in your Getting Started task pane might differ

Clues to Use

Using Word document views

Each Word view provides features that are useful for working on different types of documents. The default view, **Print Layout view**, displays a document as it will look on a printed page. Print Layout view is helpful for formatting text and pages, including adjusting document margins, creating columns of text, inserting graphics, and formatting headers and footers. Also useful is **Normal view**, which shows a simplified layout of a document, without margins, headers and footers, or graphics. When you want to quickly type, edit, and format text, it's often easiest to work in Normal view. **Web Layout view** allows you to accurately format Web pages or documents that will be viewed on a computer screen. In Web Layout view, a document appears just as it will when viewed with a Web browser. **Outline view** is useful for editing and formatting longer documents that include multiple headings. Outline view allows you to reorganize text by moving the headings. You switch between these views by clicking the view buttons to the left of the horizontal scroll bar or by using the commands on the View menu.

Two additional views make it easier to read documents on the screen. **Reading Layout view** displays document text so that it is easy to read and annotate. When you are working with highlighting or comments in a document, it's useful to use Reading Layout view. You switch to Reading Layout view by clicking the Read button on the Standard toolbar or the Reading Layout button to the left of the horizontal scroll bar. You return to the previous view by clicking the Close button on the Reading Layout toolbar. **Full Screen view** displays only the document window on screen. You switch to Full Screen view by using the Full Screen command on the View menu; you return to the previous view by pressing [Esc].

Changing views does not affect how the printed document will appear. It simply changes the way you view the document in the document window.

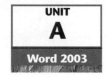

Exploring the Word Program Window

When you start Word, a blank document appears in the document window and the Getting Started task pane appears. You examine the elements of the Word program window.

DETAILS

Using Figure A-4 as a guide, find the elements described below in your program window.

*   The **title bar** displays the name of the document and the name of the program. Until you give a new document a different name, its temporary name is Document1. The title bar also contains resizing buttons and the program Close button, buttons that are common to all Windows programs.

*   The **menu bar** contains the names of the Word menus. Clicking a menu name opens a list of commands. The menu bar also contains the **Type a question for help box** and the Close Window button. You use the Type a question for help box to access the Word Help system.

*   The **toolbars** contain buttons for the most commonly used commands. The **Standard toolbar** contains buttons for frequently used operating and editing commands, such as saving a document, printing a document, and cutting, copying, and pasting text. The **Formatting toolbar** contains buttons for commonly used formatting commands, such as changing font type and size, applying bold to text, and changing paragraph alignment. The Clues to Use in this lesson provides more information about working with toolbars and menus in Word.

*   The **Getting Started task pane** contains shortcuts for opening a document, for creating new documents, and for accessing information on the Microsoft Web site. The blue words in the Open section of the task pane are **hyperlinks** that provide quick access to existing documents and the New Document task pane. If your computer is connected to the Internet, you can use the Microsoft Office Online section of the task pane to search the Microsoft Web site for information related to Office programs. As you learn more about Word, you will work with other task panes that provide shortcuts to Word formatting, editing, and research features. Clicking a hyperlink in a task pane can be quicker than using menu commands and toolbar buttons to accomplish a task.

*   The **document window** displays the current document. You enter text and format your document in the document window.

*   The horizontal and vertical rulers appear in the document window in Print Layout view. The **horizontal ruler** displays left and right document margins as well as the tab settings and paragraph indents, if any, for the paragraph in which the insertion point is located. The **vertical ruler** displays the top and bottom document margins.

*   The **vertical and horizontal scroll bars** are used to display different parts of the document in the document window. The scroll bars include **scroll boxes** and **scroll arrows**, which you can use to easily move through a document.

*   The **view buttons** to the left of the horizontal scroll bar allow you to display the document in Normal, Web Layout, Print Layout, Outline, or Reading Layout view.

*   The **status bar** displays the page number and section number of the current page, the total number of pages in the document, and the position of the insertion point in inches, lines, and characters. The status bar also indicates the on/off status of several Word features, including tracking changes, overtype mode, and spelling and grammar checking.

FIGURE A-4: Elements of the Word program window

Title bar

Menu bar

Standard toolbar

Formatting toolbar

Horizontal ruler

Document window

Vertical ruler

View buttons

Status bar

Type a question for help box

Getting Started task pane

Task pane Close button

Hyperlink

Scroll box

Vertical scroll bar

Scroll arrow

Horizontal scroll bar

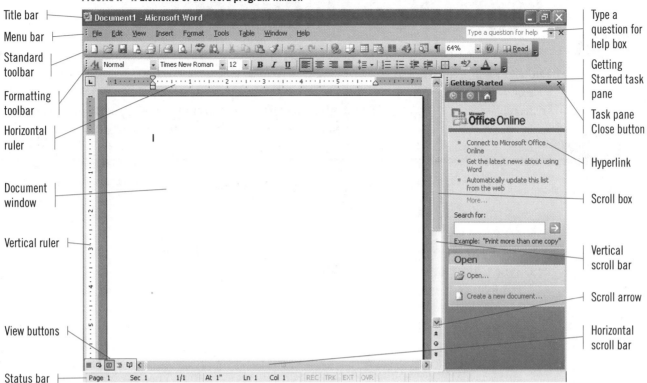

Clues to Use

Working with toolbars and menus in Word 2003

The lessons in this book assume you are working with full menus and toolbars visible, which means the Standard and Formatting toolbars appear on two rows and display all the buttons, and the menus display the complete list of menu commands.

You can also set Word to use personalized toolbars and menus that modify themselves to your working style. When you use personalized toolbars, the Standard and Formatting toolbars appear on the same row and display only the most frequently used buttons. To use a button that is not visible on a toolbar, click the Toolbar Options button ⬚ at the end of the toolbar, and then click the button you want on the Toolbar Options list. As you work, Word adds the buttons you use to the visible toolbars, and moves the buttons

you haven't used recently to the Toolbar Options list. Similarly, Word menus adjust to your work habits, so that the commands you use most often appear on shortened menus. You double-click the menu name or click the double arrow at the bottom of a menu to view additional menu commands.

To work with full toolbars and menus visible, you must turn off the personalized toolbars and menus features. To turn off personalized toolbars and menus, double-click Tools on the menu bar, click Customize, click the Options tab, select the Show Standard and Formatting toolbars on two rows and Always show full menus check boxes, and then click Close.

Starting a Document

You begin a new document by simply typing text in a blank document in the document window. Word includes a **word-wrap** feature, so that as you type Word automatically moves the insertion point to the next line of the document when you reach the right margin. You only press [Enter] when you want to start a new paragraph or insert a blank line. You can easily edit text in a document by inserting new text or by deleting existing text. You type a quick memo to the marketing staff to inform them of an upcoming meeting.

STEPS

1. **Click the Close button in the Getting Started task pane**

   The task pane closes and the blank document fills the screen.

2. **Type Memorandum, then press [Enter] four times**

   Each time you press [Enter] the insertion point moves to the start of the next line.

3. **Type DATE:, then press [Tab] twice**

   Pressing [Tab] moves the insertion point several spaces to the right. You can use the [Tab] key to align the text in a memo header or to indent the first line of a paragraph.

4. **Type April 21, 2006, then press [Enter]**

   When you press [Enter], a purple dotted line appears under the date. This dotted underline is a **smart tag**. It indicates that Word recognizes the text as a date. If you move the mouse pointer over the smart tag, a **Smart Tag Actions button** ⓢ appears above the date. Smart tags are one of the many automatic features you will encounter as you type. Table A-2 describes other automatic features available in Word. You can ignore the smart tags in your memo.

5. **Type:**   TO: [Tab] [Tab] Marketing Staff [Enter]
                  FROM: [Tab] Your Name [Enter]
                  RE: [Tab] [Tab] Marketing Meeting [Enter] [Enter]

   Red or green wavy lines may appear under the words you typed. A red wavy line means the word is not in the Word dictionary and might be misspelled. A green wavy line indicates a possible grammar error. You can correct any typing errors you make later.

6. **Type The next marketing meeting will be held May 6th at 10 a.m. in the Bloomsbury room on the ground floor., then press [Spacebar]**

   As you type, notice that the insertion point moves automatically to the next line of the document. You also might notice that Word corrects typing errors or makes typographical adjustments as you type. This feature is called **AutoCorrect**. AutoCorrect automatically detects and adjusts typos, certain misspelled words (such as "taht" for "that"), and incorrect capitalization as you type. For example, Word automatically changed "6th" to "6th" in the memo.

7. **Type Heading the agenda will be a discussion of our new cafe music series, scheduled for August. Please bring ideas for promoting this exciting new series to the meeting.**

   When you type the first few characters of "August," the Word AutoComplete feature displays the complete word in a ScreenTip. **AutoComplete** suggests text to insert quickly into your documents. You can ignore AutoComplete for now. Your memo should resemble Figure A-5.

8. **Position the I pointer after for (but before the space) in the second sentence, then click**

   Clicking moves the insertion point after "for."

9. **Press [Backspace] three times, then type to debut in**

   Pressing [Backspace] removes the character before the insertion point.

10. **Move the insertion point before marketing in the first sentence, then press [Delete] ten times to remove the word marketing and the space after it**

    Pressing [Delete] removes the character after the insertion point. Figure A-6 shows the revised memo.

FIGURE A-5: Memo text in the document window

Blank lines between paragraphs

Purple dotted underline indicates a smart tag

Green wavy underline indicates a possible grammar error (your memo will show your name)

Text wraps to the next line (yours might wrap differently)

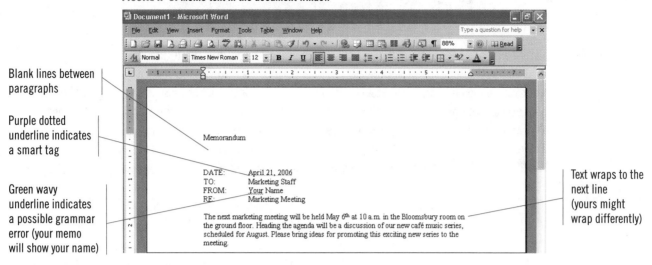

FIGURE A-6: Edited memo text

Text inserted in the memo

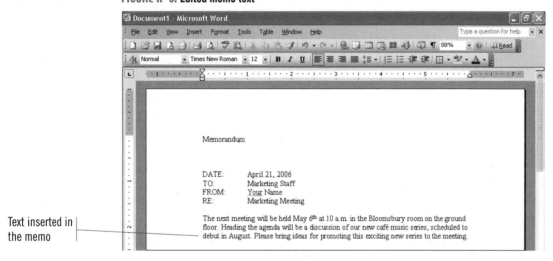

TABLE A-2: Automatic features in Word

feature	what appears	to use
AutoComplete	A ScreenTip suggesting text to insert appears	Press [Enter] to insert the text suggested by the ScreenTip; continue typing to reject the suggestion
Spelling and Grammar	A red wavy line under a word indicates a possible misspelling; a green wavy line under text indicates a possible grammar error	Right-click red- or green-underlined text to display a shortcut menu of correction options; click a correction to accept it and remove the wavy underline
AutoCorrect	A small blue box appears when you place the pointer under text corrected by AutoCorrect; an AutoCorrect Options button appears when you point to the corrected text	Word automatically corrects typos, minor spelling errors, and capitalization, and adds typographical symbols (such as © and ™) as you type; to reverse an AutoCorrect adjustment, click the AutoCorrect Options button, then click Undo or the option that will undo the action
Smart tag	A purple dotted line appears under text Word recognizes as a date, name, address, or place; a Smart Tag Actions button appears when you point to a smart tag	Click the Smart Tag Actions button to display a shortcut menu of options (such as adding a name to your address book in Outlook or opening your Outlook calendar); to remove a smart tag, click Remove this Smart Tag on the shortcut menu

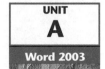

Saving a Document

To store a document permanently so you can open it and edit it in the future, you must save it as a **file**. When you **save** a document you give it a name, called a **filename**, and indicate the location where you want to store the file. Files can be saved to your computer's internal hard disk, to a floppy disk, or to a variety of other locations. You can save a document using the Save button on the Standard toolbar or the Save command on the File menu. Once you have saved a document for the first time, you should save it again every few minutes and always before printing so that the saved file is updated to reflect your latest changes. You save your memo with the filename Marketing Memo.

STEPS

TROUBLE
If you don't see the extension .doc on the filename in the Save As dialog box, don't worry. Windows can be set to display or not to display the file extensions.

1. Click the Save button on the Standard toolbar

   The first time you save a document, the Save As dialog box opens, as shown in Figure A-7. The default filename, Memorandum, appears in the File name text box. The default filename is based on the first few words of the document. The .doc extension is assigned automatically to all Word documents to distinguish them from files created in other software programs. To save the document with a different filename, type a new filename in the File name text box, and use the Save in list arrow to select where you want to store the document file. You do not need to type .doc when you type a new filename. Table A-3 describes the functions of the buttons in the Save As dialog box.

2. Type Marketing Memo in the File name text box

   The new filename replaces the default filename. It's a good idea to give your documents brief filenames that describe the contents.

TROUBLE
This book assumes your Data Files for Unit A are stored in a folder titled UnitA. Substitute the correct drive or folder if this is not the case.

3. Click the Save in list arrow, then navigate to the drive or folder where your Data Files are located

   The drive or folder where your Data Files are located appears in the Save in list box. Your Save As dialog box should resemble Figure A-8.

4. Click Save

   The document is saved to the location you specified in the Save As dialog box, and the title bar displays the new filename, "Marketing Memo.doc."

5. Place the insertion point before August in the second sentence, type early, then press [Spacebar]

   You can continue to work on a document after you have saved it with a new filename.

6. Click

   Your change to the memo is saved. Saving a document after you give it a filename saves the changes you make to the document. You also can click File on the menu bar, and then click Save to save a document.

Clues to Use

Recovering lost document files

Sometimes while you are working on a document, Word might freeze, making it impossible to continue working, or you might experience a power failure that shuts down your computer. Should this occur, Word has a built-in recovery feature that allows you to open and save the files that were open at the time of the interruption. When you restart Word after an interruption, the Document Recovery task pane opens on the left side of your screen and lists both the original and the recovered versions of the Word files. If

you're not sure which file to open (original or recovered), it's usually better to open the recovered file because it includes your latest changes to the document. You can, however, open and review all the versions of the file that were recovered and select the best one to save. Each file listed in the Document Recovery task pane has a list arrow with options that allow you to open the file, save the file, delete the file, or show repairs made to the file.

FIGURE A-7: Save As dialog box

Active folder or drive

Folders and files in the active folder or drive (yours will differ)

Default filename and file extension are selected

Click to create a new folder in the active folder or drive

Click the Save in list arrow to change the active folder or drive

Click to change the file type

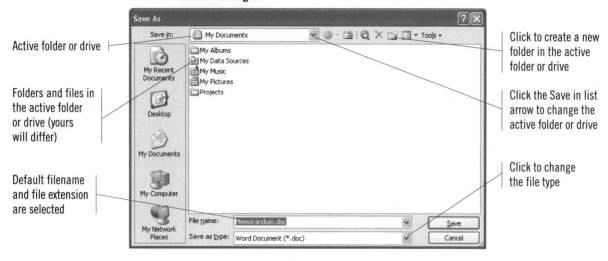

FIGURE A-8: File to be saved to the UnitA folder

Location of Data Files (yours might differ)

New filename

Your dialog box might list the files and folders in the active folder or drive here

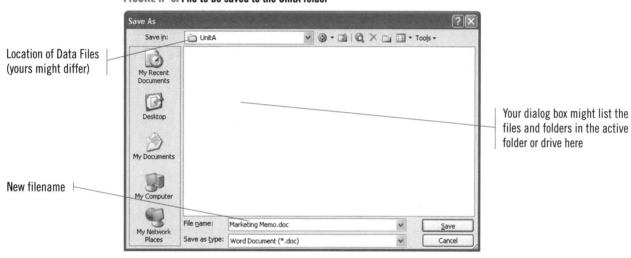

TABLE A-3: Save As dialog box buttons

button	use to
⊕ Back	Navigate to the drive or folder previously shown in the Save in list box; click the Back list arrow to navigate to a recently displayed drive or folder
🗁 Up One Level	Navigate to the next highest level in the folder hierarchy (to the drive or folder that contains the current folder)
🔍 Search the Web	Connect to the World Wide Web to locate a folder or file
✕ Delete	Delete the selected folder or file
🗀 Create New Folder	Create a new folder in the current folder or drive
▦ ▾ Views	Change the way folder and file information is shown in the Save As dialog box; click the Views list arrow to open a menu of options
Tools ▾ Tools	Open a menu of commands related to the selected drive, folder, or file

Printing a Document

Before you print a document, it's a good habit to examine it in **Print Preview** to see what it will look like when printed. When a document is ready to print, you can print it using the Print button on the Standard toolbar or the Print command on the File menu. When you use the Print button, the document prints using the default print settings. If you want to print more than one copy of a document or select other printing options, you must use the Print command. You display your memo in Print Preview and then print a copy.

STEPS

1. **Click the** Print Preview button 🔍 **on the Standard toolbar**

   The document appears in Print Preview. It is useful to examine a document carefully in Print Preview so that you can correct any problems before printing it.

2. **Move the pointer over the memo text until it changes to** 🔍 **, then click**

   Clicking with the 🔍 pointer magnifies the document in the Print Preview window and changes the pointer to 🔍. The memo appears in the Print Preview window exactly as it will look when printed, as shown in Figure A-9. Clicking with the 🔍 pointer reduces the size of the document in the Print Preview window.

   > **QUICK TIP**
   > You can also use the Zoom list arrow on the Print Preview toolbar to change the magnification in the Print Preview window.

3. **Click the** Magnifier button 🔍 **on the Print Preview toolbar**

   Clicking the Magnifier button turns off the magnification feature and allows you to edit the document in Print Preview. In edit mode, the pointer changes to I. The Magnifier button is a **toggle button**, which means you can use it to switch back and forth between magnification mode and edit mode.

4. **Compare the text on your screen with the text in Figure A-9, examine your memo carefully for typing or spelling errors, correct any mistakes, then click the** Close Preview button Close **on the Print Preview toolbar**

   Print Preview closes and the memo appears in the document window.

5. **Click the** Save button 💾 **on the Standard toolbar**

   If you made any changes to the document since you last saved it, the changes are saved.

6. **Click** File **on the menu bar, then click** Print

   The Print dialog box opens, as shown in Figure A-10. Depending on the printer installed on your computer, your print settings might differ slightly from those in the figure. You can use the Print dialog box to change the current printer, change the number of copies to print, select what pages of a document to print, and modify other printing options.

7. **Click** OK

   The dialog box closes and a copy of the memo prints using the default print settings. You can also click the Print button 🖨 on the Standard toolbar or the Print Preview toolbar to print a document using the default print settings.

FIGURE A-9: **Memo in the Print Preview window**

Print Preview
toolbar

Magnifier
button

Close Preview
button

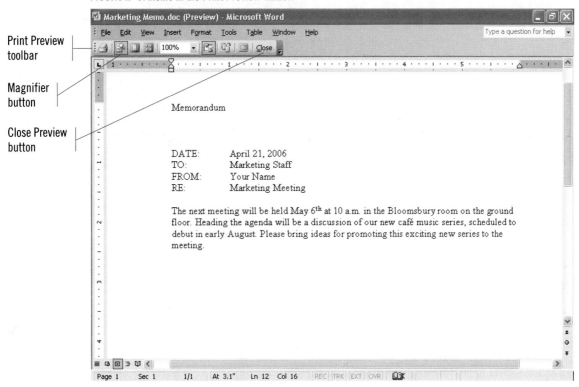

FIGURE A-10: **Print dialog box**

Change document
properties for printing,
such as orientation,
page order, and paper
source

Default
printer (yours
might differ)

Select the range of
pages to print

Select the special
aspects of the
document to print

Change the number of
copies to print

Change the number of
pages to print on a sheet
of paper

Print using the
current settings

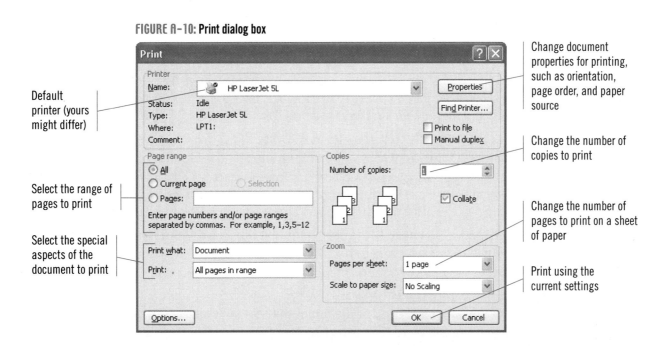

Using the Help System

Word includes an extensive Help system that provides immediate access to definitions, instructions, and useful tips for working with Word. You can quickly access the Help system by typing a question in the Type a question for help box on the menu bar, by clicking the Microsoft Office Word Help button on the Standard toolbar, or by selecting an option from the Help menu. If you are working with an active Internet connection, your queries to the Help system will also return information from the Microsoft Office Online Web site. Table A-4 describes the many ways to get help while using Word. You are curious to learn more about typing with AutoCorrect and viewing and printing documents. You search the Word Help system to discover more about these features.

STEPS

TROUBLE
The figures in this lesson reflect an active Internet connection. If you are not connected to the Internet, then connect if possible.

1. **Type** AutoCorrect **in the Type a question for help box on the menu bar, then press** [Enter]

   The Search Results task pane opens. Help topics related to AutoCorrect are listed in blue in the task pane. Notice that the pointer changes to 🖑 when you move it over the blue hyperlink text. If you are working online, it may take a few seconds for information to appear in the task pane.

2. **Click** About automatic corrections **in the Search Results task pane**

   The Microsoft Office Word Help window opens, as shown in Figure A-11. The Help window displays the "About automatic corrections" Help topic you selected. The colored text in the Help window indicates a link to a definition or to more information about the topic. Like all windows, you can maximize the Help window by clicking the Maximize button on its title bar, or you can resize the window by dragging a top, bottom, or side edge.

TROUBLE
If the hyperlink is not visible in your Help window, click the down scroll arrow until it appears.

3. **Read the information in the Help window, then click the colored text** hyperlinks

   Clicking the link expands the Help topic to display more detailed information. A definition of the word "hyperlink" appears in colored text in the Help window.

4. **Read the definition, then click** hyperlinks **again to close the definition**

5. **Click** Using AutoCorrect to correct errors as you type **in the Help window, then read the expanded information, clicking the** down scroll arrow **as necessary to read the entire Help topic**

   Clicking the up or down scroll arrow allows you to navigate through the Help topic when all the text does not fit in the Help window. You can also **scroll** by clicking the scroll bar above and below the scroll box, or by dragging the scroll box up or down in the scroll bar.

6. **Click the** Close button **in the Microsoft Office Word Help window title bar, then click the** Microsoft Office Word Help button 🔘 **on the Standard toolbar**

   The Word Help task pane opens, as shown in Figure A-12. You use this task pane to search for Help topics related to a keyword or phrase, to browse the Table of Contents for the Help system, or to connect to the Microsoft Office Online Web site, where you can search for more information on a topic.

7. **Type** print a document **in the Search for text box in the Word Help task pane, then click the green** Start searching button ➡

   When you click the green Start searching button, a list of Help topics related to your query appears in the Search Results task pane. You can also press [Enter] to return a list of Help topics.

8. **Click the** Back button 🔵 **at the top of the Search Results task pane, then click** Table of Contents **in the Word Help task pane**

   The table of contents for the Help system appears in the Word Help task pane. To peruse the table of contents, you simply click a category in the list to expand it and see a list of subcategories and Help topics. Categories are listed in black text in the task pane and are preceded by a book icon. Help topics are listed in blue text and are preceded by a question mark icon.

QUICK TIP
Click the Back and Forward buttons on the Word Help window toolbar to navigate between the Help topics you have viewed.

9. **Click** Viewing and Navigating Documents, **click a blue** Help topic, **read the information in the Microsoft Office Word Help window, then click the** Close button **in the Help window**

FIGURE A-11: Microsoft Office Word Help window

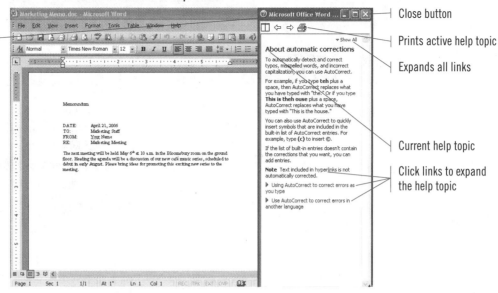

Microsoft Office Word Help window

Close button

Prints active help topic

Expands all links

Current help topic

Click links to expand the help topic

FIGURE A-12: Word Help task pane

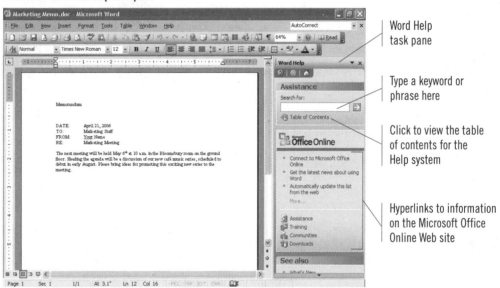

Word Help task pane

Type a keyword or phrase here

Click to view the table of contents for the Help system

Hyperlinks to information on the Microsoft Office Online Web site

Word 2003

TABLE A-4: Word resources for getting Help

resource	function	to use
Type a question for help box	Provides quick access to the Help system	Type a word or question in the Type a question for help box, then press [Enter]
Word Help task pane	Displays the table of contents for the Help system, provides access to a search function, and includes hyperlinks to Help information on the Microsoft Office Online Web site	Press [F1] or click the Microsoft Office Word Help button ⓘ on the Standard toolbar; in the Word Help task pane, type a word or phrase in the Search for text box to return a list of possible Help topics, click Table of Contents to browse the complete list of Help topics, or click a link to access information on the Microsoft Office Online Web site
Microsoft Office Online Web site	Connects to the Microsoft Office Online Web site, where you can search for information on a topic	Click the Microsoft Office Online command on the Help menu, or click a link in the Word Help task pane
Office Assistant	Displays tips related to your current task and provides access to the Help system	Click Show the Office Assistant on the Help menu to display the Office Assistant; click Hide the Office Assistant on the Help menu to hide the Office Assistant

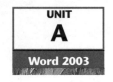

Closing a Document and Exiting Word

When you have finished working on a document and have saved your changes, you can close the document using the Close Window button on the menu bar or the Close command on the File menu. Closing a document closes the document only, it does not close the Word program window. To close the Word program window and exit Word, you can use the Close button on the title bar or the Exit command on the File menu. Using the Exit command closes all open documents. It's good practice to save and close your documents before exiting Word. Figure A-13 shows the Close buttons on the title bar and menu bar. ◄ You close the memo and exit Word.

STEPS

1. **Click the Close button on the Word Help task pane**

   The task pane closes. It is not necessary to close the task pane before closing a file or the program, but it can be helpful to reduce the amount of information displayed on the screen. Table A-5 describes the functions of the Word task panes.

2. **Click File on the menu bar, then click Close**

   If you saved your changes to the document before closing it, the document closes. If you did not save your changes, an alert box opens asking if you want to save the changes.

3. **Click Yes if the alert box opens**

   The document closes, but the Word program window remains open, as shown in Figure A-14. You can create or open another document, access Help, or close the Word program window.

4. **Click File on the menu bar, then click Exit**

   The Word program window closes. If any Word documents were still open when you exited Word, Word closes all open documents, prompting you to save changes to those documents if necessary.

> **QUICK TIP**
>
> To create a new blank document, click the New Blank Document button ☐ on the Standard toolbar.

TABLE A-5: Word task panes

task pane	use to
Getting Started	Open a document, create a new blank document, or search for information on the Microsoft Office Online Web site
Word Help	Access Help topics and connect to Help on the Microsoft Office Online Web site
Search Results	View the results of a search for Help topics and perform a new search
Clip Art	Search for clip art and insert clip art in a document
Research	Search reference books and other sources for information related to a word, such as for synonyms
Clipboard	Cut, copy, and paste items within and between documents
New Document	Create a new blank document, XML document, Web page, or e-mail message, or create a new document using a template
Shared Workspace	Create a Web site (called a document workspace) that allows a group of people to share files, participate in discussions, and work together on a document
Document Updates	View information on a document that is available in a document workspace
Protect Document	Apply formatting and editing restrictions to a shared document
Styles and Formatting	Apply styles to text
Reveal Formatting	Display the formatting applied to text
Mail Merge	Perform a mail merge
XML Structure	Apply XML elements to a Word XML document

FIGURE A-13: Close and Close Window buttons

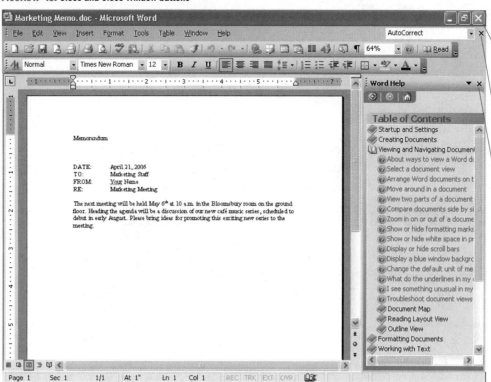

Close button on title bar closes all open documents and exits Word

Close Window button closes the current document

Close button closes the task pane

FIGURE A-14: Word program window with no documents open

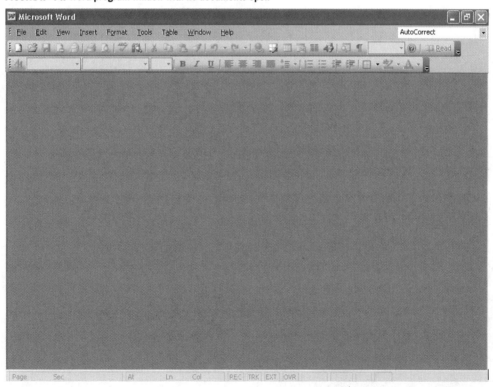

Practice

▼ CONCEPTS REVIEW

Label the elements of the Word program window shown in Figure A-15.

FIGURE A-15

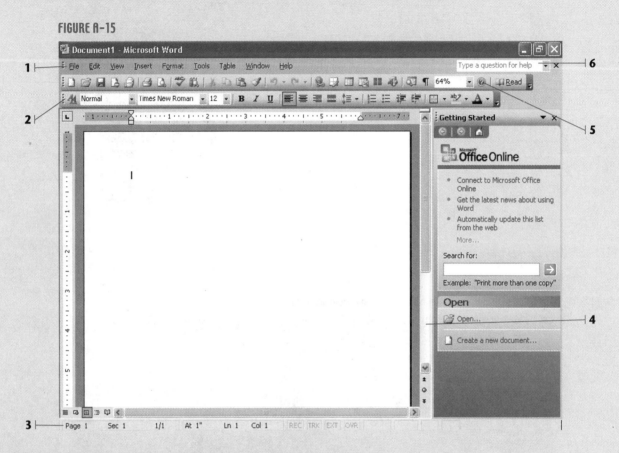

Match each term with the statement that best describes it.

7. **Print Preview**   a. Displays a simple layout view of a document

8. **Office Assistant**   b. Displays tips on using Word

9. **Status bar**   c. Displays the document exactly as it will look when printed

10. **Menu bar**   d. Suggests text to insert into a document

11. **AutoComplete**   e. Fixes certain errors as you type

12. **Horizontal ruler**   f. Displays the number of pages in the current document

13. **AutoCorrect**   g. Displays tab settings and document margins

14. **Normal view**   h. Provides access to Word commands

Select the best answer from the list of choices.

15. **Which task pane opens automatically when you start Word?**
    a. Document Updates
    b. Getting Started
    c. Word Help
    d. New Document

16. **Which element of the Word program window shows the settings for the left and right document margins?**
    a. Formatting toolbar
    b. Status bar
    c. Horizontal ruler
    d. Getting Started task pane

17. **What is the function of the Exit command on the File menu?**
    a. To close the current document without saving changes
    b. To close all open documents and the Word program window
    c. To save changes to and close the current document
    d. To close all open programs

18. **Which view do you use when you want to adjust the margins in a document?**
    a. Outline view
    b. Web Layout view
    c. Normal view
    d. Print Layout view

19. **Which of the following does not appear on the status bar?**
    a. The current page number
    b. The current tab settings
    c. The Overtype mode status
    d. The current line number

20. **Which of the following is not used to access the Help system?**
    a. Type a question for help box
    b. The Office Assistant
    c. Microsoft Office Online
    d. The Research task pane

▼ SKILLS REVIEW

1. **Start Word 2003.**
   a. Start Word.
   b. Switch to Print Layout view if your blank document opened in a different view.
   c. Change the zoom level to Page Width.

2. **Explore the Word program window.**
   a. Identify as many elements of the Word program window as you can without referring to the unit material.
   b. Click each menu name on the menu bar and drag the pointer through the menu commands.
   c. Point to each button on the Standard and Formatting toolbars and read the ScreenTips.
   d. Point to each hyperlink in the Getting Started task pane.

  e. Click the view buttons to view the blank document in Normal, Web Layout, Print Layout, Outline, and Reading Layout view.

  f. Click the Close button in Reading Layout view, then return to Print Layout view.

3. **Start a document.**

  a. Close the Getting Started task pane.

  b. In a new blank document, type FAX at the top of the page, then press [Enter] four times.

  c. Type the following, pressing [Tab] as indicated and pressing [Enter] at the end of each line:
  To: [Tab] Dr. Beatrice Turcotte
  From: [Tab] Your Name
  Date: [Tab] Today's date
  Re: [Tab] Travel arrangements
  Pages: [Tab] 1
  Fax: [Tab] (514) 555-3948

  d. Press [Enter], then type I have reserved a space for you on the March 4-18 Costa Rica Explorer tour. You are scheduled to depart Montreal's Dorval Airport on Plateau Tours and Travel charter flight 234 at 7:45 a.m. on March 4th, arriving in San Jose at 4:30 p.m. local time.

  e. Press [Enter] twice, then type Please call me at (514) 555-4983 or stop by our offices on rue St-Denis.

  f. Insert this sentence at the beginning of the second paragraph: I must receive full payment within 48 hours to hold your reservation.

  g. Using the [Backspace] key, delete Travel in the Re: line, then type Costa Rica tour.

  h. Using the [Delete] key, delete 48 in the last paragraph, then type 72.

4. **Save a document.**

  a. Click File on the menu bar, then click Save.

  b. Save the document as Turcotte Fax to the drive and folder where your Data Files are located.

  c. After your name, type a comma, press [Spacebar], then type Plateau Tours and Travel.

  d. Click the Save button to save your changes to the document.

5. **Print a document.**

  a. Click the Print Preview button to view the document in Print Preview.

  b. Click the word FAX to zoom in on the document, then proofread the fax.

  c. Click the Magnifier button to switch to edit mode, then correct any typing errors in your document.

  d. Close Print Preview, then save your changes to the document.

  e. Print the fax using the default print settings.

6. **Use the Help system.**

  a. Click the Microsoft Office Word Help button to open the Word Help task pane.

  b. Type open a document in the Search text box, then press [Enter].

  c. Click the topic Open a file.

  d. Read about saving documents in Word by clicking the links to expand the Help topic.

  e. Close the Help window, type viewing documents in the Type a question for help box, then press [Enter].

  f. Click the link Zoom in on or out of a document in the Search Results task pane, then read the Help topic.

  g. Close the Help window, then close the Search Results task pane.

7. **Close a document and exit Word.**

  a. Close the Turcotte Fax document, saving your changes if necessary.

  b. Exit Word.

▼ INDEPENDENT CHALLENGE 1

You are a performance artist, well known for your innovative work with computers. The Missoula Arts Council president, Sam McCrum, has asked you to be the keynote speaker at an upcoming conference in Missoula, Montana, on the role of technology in the arts. You are pleased at the invitation, and write a letter to Mr. McCrum accepting the invitation and confirming the details. Your letter to Mr. McCrum should reference the following information:

- The conference will be held October 10–12, 2006, at the civic center in Missoula.
- You have been asked to speak for one hour on Saturday, October 11, followed by a half hour for questions.
- Mr. McCrum suggested the lecture topic "Technology's Effect on Art and Culture."
- Your talk will include a 20-minute slide presentation.
- The Missoula Arts Council will make your travel arrangements.
- Your preference is to arrive in Missoula on Friday, October 10, and depart on Sunday, October 12.
- You want to fly in and out of the airport closest to your home.

a. Start Word.

b. Save a new blank document as **McCrum Letter** to the drive and folder where your Data Files are located.

c. Model your letter to Mr. McCrum after the sample business letter shown in Figure A-16. Use the following formatting guidelines: 3 blank lines after the date, 1 blank line after the inside address, 1 blank line after the salutation, 1 blank line after each body paragraph, and 3 blank lines between the closing and your typed name.

d. Begin the letter by typing today's date.

e. Type the inside address. Be sure to include Mr. McCrum's title and the name of the organization. Make up a street address and zip code.

f. Type a salutation.

g. Using the information listed above, type the body of the letter:

- In the first paragraph, accept the invitation to speak and confirm the important conference details.
- In the second paragraph, confirm your lecture topic and provide any relevant details.
- In the third paragraph, state your travel preferences.
- Type a short final paragraph.

h. Type a closing, then include your name in the signature block.

Advanced Challenge Exercise

- View the letter in Normal view, then correct your spelling and grammar errors, if any, by right-clicking any red- or green-underlined text and then choosing from the options on the shortcut menu.
- View the letter in Print Layout view, then remove any smart tags.
- View the letter in Reading Layout view, then click the Close button on the Reading Layout toolbar to close Reading Layout view.

FIGURE A-16

June 12, 2006

Dr. Leslie Morris
Professor of American Literature
Department of Literature
Manchester State College
Manchester, NH 03258

Dear Dr. Morris:

Thank you very much for your kind invitation to speak at your upcoming conference on the literature of place. I will be happy to oblige. I understand the conference will be held September 16 and 17 in the Sanders Auditorium.

I will address my remarks to the topic you suggested, "Writers of the Monadnock region." I understand you would like me to speak at 2:30 p.m. on September 16 for forty minutes, with twenty minutes of questions to follow. My talk will include a slide show. I presume you will have the necessary equipment—a slide projector and viewing screen—on hand.

My preference is to arrive in Manchester on the morning of September 16, and to depart that evening. It is easiest for me to use New York's LaGuardia Airport. I am grateful that your office will be taking care of my travel arrangements.

I look forward to meeting you in September.

Sincerely,

Jessica Grange

---

i. Proofread your letter, make corrections as needed, then save your changes.

j. Preview the letter, print the letter, close the document, then exit Word.

▼ INDEPENDENT CHALLENGE 2

Your company has recently installed Word 2003 on its company network. As the training manager, it's your responsibility to teach employees how to use the new software productively. Now that they have begun working with Word 2003, several employees have asked you about smart tags. In response to their queries, you decide to write a memo to all employees explaining how to use the smart tag feature. You know that smart tags are designed to help users perform tasks in Word that normally would require opening a different program, such as Microsoft Outlook (a desktop information-management program that includes e-mail, calendar, and address book features). Before writing your memo, you'll learn more about smart tags by searching the Word Help system.

a. Start Word and save a new blank document as **Smart Tags Memo** to the drive and folder where your Data Files are located.

b. Type **WORD TRAINING MEMORANDUM** at the top of the document, press [Enter] four times, then type the memo heading information shown in Figure A-17. Make sure to include your name in the From line and the current date in the Date line.

c. Press [Enter] twice to place the insertion point where you will begin typing the body of your memo.

d. Search the Word Help system for information on working with smart tags.

e. Type your memo after completing your research. In your memo, define smart tags, then explain what they look like, how to use smart tags, and how to remove smart tags from a document.

FIGURE A-17

> WORD TRAINING MEMORANDUM
>
>
> To: All employees
> From: Your Name, Training Manager
> Date: Today's date
> Re: Smart tags in Microsoft Word

Advanced Challenge Exercise

■ Search the Help system for information on how to check for new smart tags developed by Microsoft and third-party vendors.

■ Print the information you find.

■ Add a short paragraph to your memo explaining how to find new smart tags.

f. Save your changes, preview and print the memo, then close the document and exit Word.

▼ INDEPENDENT CHALLENGE 3

Yesterday you interviewed for a job as marketing director at Komata Web Designs. You spoke with several people at Komata, including Shige Murata, Director of Operations, whose business card is shown in Figure A-18. You need to write a follow-up letter to Mr. Murata, thanking him for the interview and expressing your interest in the company and the position. He also asked you to send him some samples of your marketing work, which you will enclose with the letter.

FIGURE A-18

a. Start Word and save a new blank document as **Komata Letter** to the drive and folder where your Data Files are located.

b. Begin the letter by typing today's date.

c. Four lines below the date, type the inside address, referring to Figure A-18 for the address information. Be sure to include the recipient's title, company name, and full mailing address in the inside address. (*Hint*: When typing a foreign address, type the name of the country in capital letters by itself on the last line.)

d. Two lines below the inside address, type the salutation.

> **Komata Web Designs**
>
> 5-8, Edobori 4-chome
> Minato-ku
> Tokyo 108-0034
> Japan
>
> **Shige Murata**   Phone: (03) 5555-3299
> *Director of Operations*   Fax: (03) 5555-7028
>   Email: smurata@komata.co.jp

e. Two lines below the salutation, type the body of the letter according to the following guidelines:

- In the first paragraph, thank him for the interview. Then restate your interest in the position and express your desire to work for the company. Add any specific details you think will enhance the power of your letter.

- In the second paragraph, note that you are enclosing three samples of your work and explain something about the samples you are enclosing.

- Type a short final paragraph.

f. Two lines below the last body paragraph, type a closing, then four lines below the closing, type the signature block. Be sure to include your name in the signature block.

g. Two lines below the signature block, type an enclosure notation. (*Hint*: An enclosure notation usually includes the word "Enclosures" or the abbreviation "Enc." followed by the number of enclosures in parentheses.)

h. Save your changes.

i. Preview and print the letter, then close the document and exit Word.

▼ **INDEPENDENT CHALLENGE 4**

Unlike personal letters or many e-mail messages, business letters are formal in tone and format. The World Wide Web is one source for information on writing styles, proper document formatting, and other business etiquette issues. In this independent challenge, you will research guidelines and tips for writing effective and professional business letters. Your online research should seek answers to the following questions: What is important to keep in mind when writing a business letter? What are the parts of a business letter? What are some examples of business letter types? What are some useful tips for writing business letters?

a. Use your favorite search engine to search the Web for information on writing and formatting business letters. Use the keywords **business letters** to conduct your search.

b. Review the Web sites you find. Print at least two Web pages that offer useful guidelines for writing business letters.

c. Start Word and save a new blank document as **Business Letters** to the drive and folder where your Data Files are located.

d. Type your name at the top of the document, then press [Enter] twice.

e. Type a brief report on the results of your research. Your report should answer the following questions:

- What are the URLs of the Web sites you visited to research guidelines for writing a business letter? (*Hint*: A URL is a Web page's address. An example of a URL is www.eHow.com.)

- What is important to keep in mind when writing a business letter?

- What are the parts of a business letter?

- In what situations do people write business letters? Provide at least five examples.

f. Save your changes to the document, preview and print it, then close the document and exit Word.

Create the cover letter shown in Figure A-19. Save the document with the name Publishing Cover Letter to the drive and folder where your Data Files are stored, print a copy of the letter, then close the document and exit Word.

FIGURE A-19

July 17, 2006

Ms. Charlotte Janoch
Managing Editor
Sunrise Press
6354 Baker Street
Townsend, MA 02181

Dear Ms. Janoch:

I read of the opening for an editorial assistant on the July 15 edition of Boston.com, and I would like to be considered for the position. A recent graduate of Merrimack College, I am interested in pursuing a career in publishing.

My desire for a publishing career springs from my interest in writing and editing. At Merrimack College, I was a frequent contributor to the student newspaper and was involved in creating a Web site for student poetry and short fiction.

I have a wealth of experience using Microsoft Word in professional settings. For the past several summers I worked as an office assistant for Packer Investment Consultants, where I used Word to create newsletters and financial reports for clients. During the school year, I also worked part-time in the Merrimack College admissions office. Here I used Word's mail merge feature to create form letters and mailing labels.

My enclosed resume details my talents and experience. I would welcome the opportunity to discuss the position and my qualifications with you. I can be reached at 617-555-3849.

Sincerely,

Your Name

Enc.

Editing Documents

OBJECTIVES

Open a document
Select text
Cut and paste text
Copy and paste text
Use the Office Clipboard
Find and replace text
Check spelling and grammar
Use the Thesaurus
Use wizards and templates

If you have a SAM user profile, you may have access to hands-on instruction, practice, and assessment of the skills covered in this unit. Log in to your SAM account and go to your assignments page to see what your instructor has assigned.

The sophisticated editing features in Word make it easy to revise and polish your documents. In this unit, you learn how to open an existing file, revise it by replacing, copying, and moving text, and then save the document as a new file. You also learn how to perfect your documents using proofing tools and how to quickly create attractive, professionally designed documents using wizards and templates. ████ You have been asked to create a press release about a new MediaLoft lecture series in New York. The press release should provide information about the series so that newspapers, radio stations, and other media outlets can announce it to the public. MediaLoft press releases are disseminated by fax, so you also need to create a fax coversheet to use when you fax the press release to your list of press contacts.

Opening a Document

Sometimes the easiest way to create a document is to edit an existing document and save it with a new file-name. To modify a document, you must first **open** it so that it displays in the document window. Word offers several methods for opening documents, described in Table B-1. Once you have opened a file, you can use the Save As command to create a new file that is a copy of the original. You can then edit the new file without making changes to the original. ▂▂▂ Rather than write your press release from scratch, you decide to modify a press release written for a similar event. You begin by opening the press release document and saving it with a new filename.

TROUBLE

If the task pane is not open, click View on the menu bar, then click Task Pane.

1. **Start Word**

   Word opens and a blank document and the Getting Started task pane appear in the program window, as shown in Figure B-1. The Getting Started task pane contains links for opening existing documents and for creating new documents.

2. **Click the Open or More hyperlink at the bottom of the Getting Started task pane**

   The Open dialog box opens. You use the Open dialog box to locate and select the file you want to open. The Look in list box displays the current drive or folder. You also can use the Open button 📂 on the Standard toolbar or the Open command on the File menu to open the Open dialog box.

3. **Click the Look in list arrow, click the drive containing your Data Files, then double-click the folder containing your Data Files**

   A list of the Data Files for this unit appears in the Open dialog box, as shown in Figure B-2.

QUICK TIP

You also can double-click a filename in the Open dialog box to open the file.

4. **Click the filename WD B-1.doc in the Open dialog box to select it, then click Open**

   The document opens. Notice that the filename WD B-1.doc appears in the title bar. Once you have opened a file, you can edit it and use the Save or the Save As command to save your changes. You use the **Save** command when you want to save the changes you make to a file, overwriting the file that is stored on a disk. You use the **Save As** command when you want to create a new file with a different filename, leaving the original file intact.

5. **Click File on the menu bar, then click Save As**

   The Save As dialog box opens. By saving a file with a new filename, you create a document that is identical to the original document. The original filename is selected (highlighted) in the File name text box. Any text you type replaces the selected text.

6. **Type NY Press Release in the File name text box, then click Save**

   The original file closes and the NY Press Release file is displayed in the document window. Notice the new filename in the title bar. You can now make changes to the press release file without affecting the original file.

Clues to Use

Managing files and folders

The Open and Save As dialog boxes include powerful tools for navigating, creating, deleting, and renaming files and folders on your computer, a network, or the Web. By selecting a file or folder and clicking the Delete button ✕, you can delete the item and send it to the Recycle Bin. You can also create a new folder for storing files by clicking the Create New Folder button 📁 and typing a name for the folder. The new folder is created in the current folder. To rename a file or folder, simply right-click it in the dialog box, click Rename, type a new name, and then press [Enter].

Using the Save As dialog box, you can create new files that are based on existing files. To create a new file, you can save an existing file with a different filename or save it in a different location on your system. You also can save a file in a different file format so that it can be opened in a different software program. To save a file in a different format, click the Save as type list arrow, then click the type of file you want to create. For example, you can save a Word document (which has a .doc file extension) as a plain text file (.txt), as a Web page file (.htm), or in a variety of other file formats.

FIGURE B-1: **Getting Started task pane**

Open button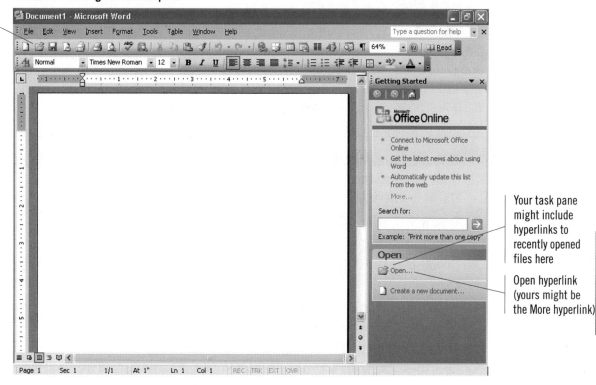

Your task pane might include hyperlinks to recently opened files here

Open hyperlink (yours might be the More hyperlink)

FIGURE B-2: **Open dialog box**

Current drive or folder

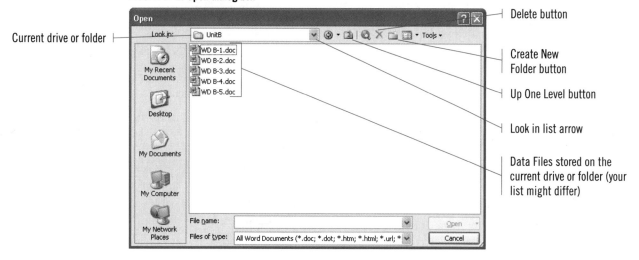

Delete button

Create New Folder button

Up One Level button

Look in list arrow

Data Files stored on the current drive or folder (your list might differ)

TABLE B-1: **Methods for opening documents**

use	to	if you want to
The Open button 📂 on the Standard toolbar, the Open command on the File menu, the Open or More hyperlink in the Getting Started task pane, or [Ctrl][O]	Open the Open dialog box	Open an existing file
A filename hyperlink in the Getting Started task pane	Open the file in the document window	Open the file; a fast way to open a file that was recently opened on your computer
The From existing document hyperlink in the New Document task pane	Open the New from Existing Document dialog box	Create a copy of an existing file; a fast way to open a document you intend to save with a new filename

Selecting Text

Before deleting, editing, or formatting text, you must **select** the text. Selecting text involves clicking and dragging the I-beam pointer across text to highlight it. You also can click with the ⏳ pointer in the blank area to the left of text to select lines or paragraphs. Table B-2 describes the many ways to select text. You revise the press release by selecting text and replacing it with new text.

STEPS

1. **Click the** Zoom list arrow **on the Standard toolbar, click** Page Width, **click before** April 14, 2006, **then drag the** I **pointer over the text to select it**
   The date is selected, as shown in Figure B-3.

2. **Type** May 1, 2006
   The text you type replaces the selected text.

3. **Double-click** James, **type your first name, double-click** Callaghan, **then type your last name**
   Double-clicking a word selects the entire word.

4. **Place the pointer in the margin to the left of the phone number so that the pointer changes to** ⏳, **click to select the phone number, then type** (415) 555-8293
   Clicking to the left of a line of text with the ⏳ pointer selects the entire line.

5. **Click the** down scroll arrow **at the bottom of the vertical scroll bar until the headline Alex Fogg to Speak... is at the top of your document window**
   The scroll arrows or scroll bars allow you to scroll through a document. You scroll through a document when you want to display different parts of the document in the document window.

6. **Select** SAN FRANCISCO, **then type** NEW YORK

7. **In the fourth body paragraph, select the sentence** All events will be held at the St. James Hotel., **then press** [Delete]
   Selecting text and pressing [Delete] removes the text from the document.

8. **Select and replace text in the second and last paragraphs using the following table:**

select	type
May 12	June 14
St. James Hotel in downtown San Francisco	Waldorf-Astoria Hotel
National Public Radio's Helen DeSaint	New York Times literary editor Janet Richard

   The edited press release is shown in Figure B-4.

9. **Click the** Save button 🖫 **on the Standard toolbar**
   Your changes to the press release are saved. Always save before and after editing text.

TABLE B-2: Methods for selecting text

to select	use the mouse pointer to
Any amount of text	Drag over the text
A word	Double-click the word
A line of text	Click with the ⏳ pointer to the left of the line
A sentence	Press and hold [Ctrl], then click the sentence
A paragraph	Triple-click the paragraph or double-click with the ⏳ pointer to the left of the paragraph
A large block of text	Click at the beginning of the selection, press and hold [Shift], then click at the end of the selection
Multiple nonconsecutive selections	Select the first selection, then press and hold [Ctrl] as you select each additional selection
An entire document	Triple-click with the ⏳ pointer to the left of any text, click Select All on the Edit menu, or press [Ctrl][A]

FIGURE B-3: Date selected in the press release

Selected text

Left document margin

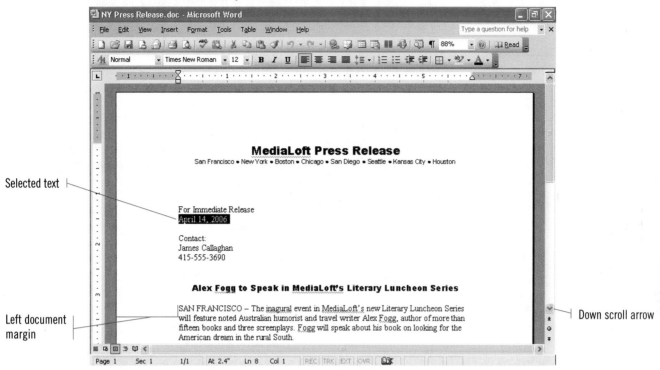

FIGURE B-4: Edited press release

Replacement text

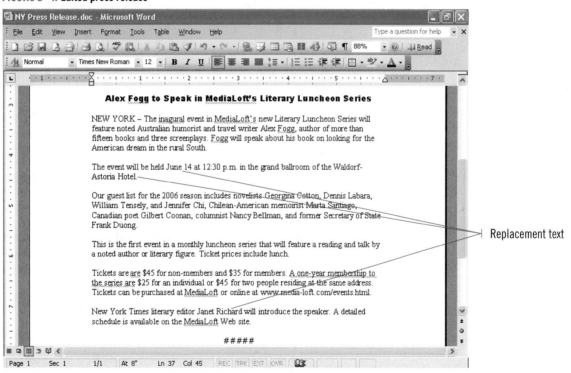

Clues to Use

Replacing text in Overtype mode

Normally you must select text before typing to replace the existing characters, but by turning on **Overtype mode** you can type over existing characters without selecting them first. To turn Overtype mode on and off on your computer, double-click OVR in the status bar. On some computers you also can turn Overtype mode on and off by pressing [Insert]. When Overtype mode is on, OVR appears in black in the status bar. When Overtype mode is off, OVR is dimmed.

Cutting and Pasting Text

The editing features in Word allow you to move text from one location to another in a document. The operation of moving text is often called **cut and paste**. When you cut text from a document, you remove it from the document and add it to the **Clipboard**, a temporary storage area for text and graphics that you cut or copy from a document. You cut text by selecting it and using the Cut command on the Edit menu or the Cut button. To insert the text from the Clipboard into the document, you place the insertion point where you want to insert the text, and then use the Paste command on the Edit menu or the Paste button to paste the text at that location. You also can move text by dragging it to a new location using the mouse. This operation is called **drag and drop**. ▰▰▰ You reorganize the information in the press release using the cut-and-paste and drag-and-drop methods.

STEPS

1. **Click the** Show/Hide ¶ button ¶ **on the Standard toolbar**

   Formatting marks appear in the document window. **Formatting marks** are special characters that appear on your screen and do not print. Common formatting marks include the paragraph symbol (¶), which shows the end of a paragraph—wherever you press [Enter]; the dot symbol (•), which represents a space—wherever you press [Spacebar]; and the arrow symbol (➜), which shows the location of a tab stop—wherever you press [Tab]. Working with formatting marks turned on can help you to select, edit, and format text with precision.

   TROUBLE
   If the Clipboard task pane opens, close it.

2. **In the third paragraph, select** Canadian poet Gilbert Coonan, **(including the comma and the space after it), then click the** Cut button ✂ **on the Standard toolbar**

   The text is removed from the document and placed on the Clipboard. Word uses two different clipboards: the **system Clipboard** (the Clipboard), which holds just one item, and the **Office Clipboard**, which holds up to 24 items. The last item you cut or copy is always added to both clipboards. You'll learn more about the Office Clipboard in a later lesson.

3. **Place the insertion point before** novelists **(but after the space) in the first line of the third paragraph, then click the** Paste button 📋 **on the Standard toolbar**

   The text is pasted at the location of the insertion point, as shown in Figure B-5. The Paste Options button 📋 appears below text when you first paste it in a document. You'll learn more about the Paste Options button in the next lesson. For now, you can ignore it.

4. **Press and hold** [Ctrl]**, click the sentence** Ticket prices include lunch. **in the fourth paragraph, then release** [Ctrl]

   The entire sentence is selected.

   TROUBLE
   If you make a mistake, click the Undo button ↺ on the Standard toolbar, then try again.

5. **Press and hold the mouse button over the selected text until the pointer changes to** ▷**, then drag the pointer's vertical line to the end of the fifth paragraph (between the period and the paragraph mark) as shown in Figure B-6**

   The pointer's vertical line indicates the location the text will be inserted when you release the mouse button.

6. **Release the mouse button**

   The selected text is moved to the location of the insertion point. It's convenient to move text using the drag-and-drop method when the locations of origin and destination are both visible on the screen. Text is not removed to the Clipboard when you move it using drag-and-drop.

7. **Deselect the text, then click the** Save button 💾 **on the Standard toolbar**

   Your changes to the press release are saved.

FIGURE B-5: Moved text with Paste Options button

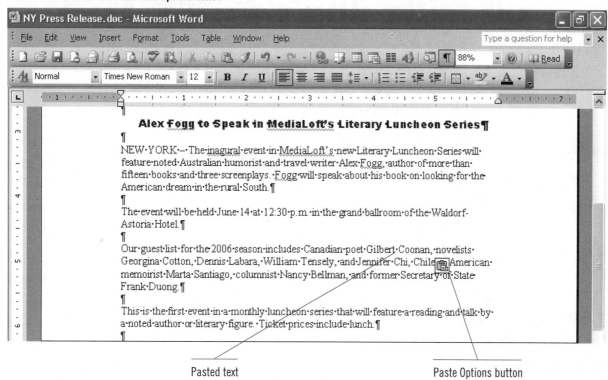

Pasted text   Paste Options button

FIGURE B-6: Text being dragged to a new location

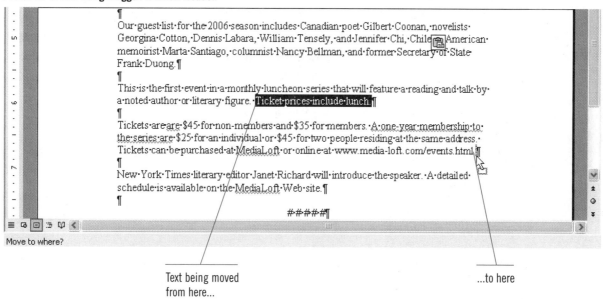

Text being moved   ...to here
from here...

Clues to Use

Using keyboard shortcuts

Instead of using the Cut, Copy, and Paste commands to edit text in Word, you can use the **keyboard shortcuts** [Ctrl][X] to cut text, [Ctrl][C] to copy text, and [Ctrl][V] to paste text. A **shortcut key** is a function key, such as [F1], or a combination of keys, such as [Ctrl][S], that you press to perform a command. For example, pressing [Ctrl][S] saves changes to a document just as clicking the Save button or using the Save command on the File menu saves a document. Becoming skilled at using keyboard shortcuts can help you to quickly accomplish many of the tasks you perform frequently in Word. If a keyboard shortcut is available for a menu command, then it is listed next to the command on the menu.

Copying and Pasting Text

Copying and pasting text is similar to cutting and pasting text, except that the text you copy is not removed from the document. Rather, a copy of the text is placed on the Clipboard, leaving the original text in place. You can copy text to the Clipboard using the Copy command on the Edit menu or the Copy button, or you can copy text by pressing [Ctrl] as you drag the selected text from one location to another. You continue to edit the press release by copying text from one location to another.

STEPS

TROUBLE
If the Clipboard task pane opens, close it.

1. **In the headline, select** Literary Luncheon, **then click the** Copy button 📋 **on the Standard toolbar**

   A copy of the text is placed on the Clipboard, leaving the text you copied in place.

2. **Place the insertion point before** season **in the third body paragraph, then click the** Paste button 📋 **on the Standard toolbar**

   "Literary Luncheon" is inserted before "season," as shown in Figure B-7. Notice that the pasted text is formatted differently than the paragraph in which it was inserted.

QUICK TIP
If you don't like the result of a paste option, try another option or click the Undo button ↺ and then paste the text again.

3. **Click the** Paste Options button 📋, **then click** Match Destination Formatting

   The Paste Options button allows you to change the formatting of pasted text. The formatting of "Literary Luncheon" is changed to match the rest of the paragraph. The options available on the Paste Options menu depend on the format of the text you are pasting and the format of the surrounding text.

4. **Scroll down if necessary so that the last two paragraphs are visible on your screen**

5. **In the fifth paragraph, select** www.media-loft.com, **press and hold** [Ctrl], **then press the mouse button until the pointer changes to** ▹

6. **Drag the pointer's vertical line to the end of the last paragraph, placing it between** site **and the period, release the mouse button, then release** [Ctrl]

   The text is copied to the last paragraph. Since the formatting of the text you copied is the same as the formatting of the paragraph in which you inserted it, you can ignore the Paste Options button. Text is not copied to the Clipboard when you copy it using the drag-and-drop method.

7. **Place the insertion point before** www.media-loft.com **in the last paragraph, type** at **followed by a space, then click the** Save button 💾 **on the Standard toolbar**

   Compare your document with Figure B-8.

Clues to Use

Copying and moving items in a long document

If you want to copy or move items between parts of a long document, it can be useful to split the document window into two panes so that the item you want to copy or move is displayed in one pane and the destination for the item is displayed in the other pane. To split a window, click the Split command on the Window menu, drag the horizontal split bar that appears to the location you want to split the window, and then click. Once the document window is split into two panes, you can drag the split bar to resize the panes and use the scroll bars in each pane to display different parts of the document. To copy or move an item from one pane to another, you can use the Cut, Copy, and Paste commands, or you can drag the item between the panes. When you are finished editing the document, double-click the split bar to restore the window to a single pane.

FIGURE B-7: Text pasted in document

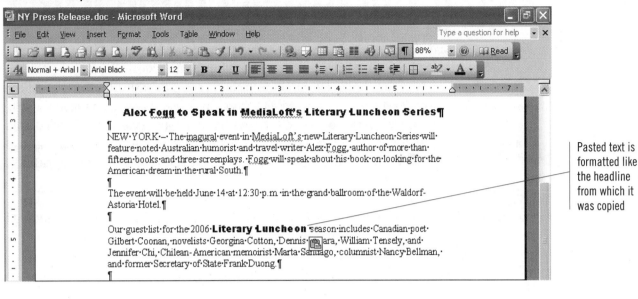

Pasted text is formatted like the headline from which it was copied

FIGURE B-8: Copied text in press release

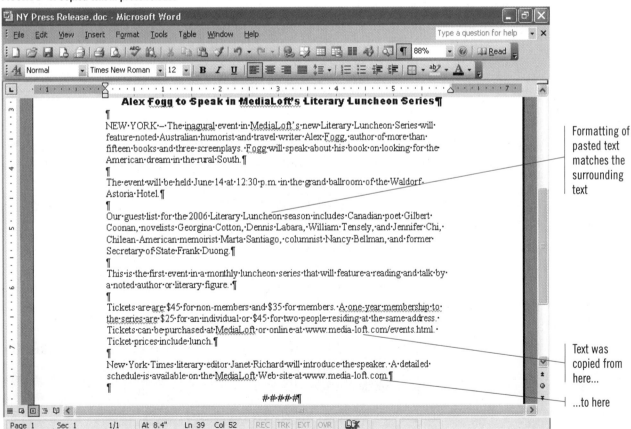

Formatting of pasted text matches the surrounding text

Text was copied from here...

...to here

Using the Office Clipboard

The Office Clipboard allows you to collect text and graphics from files created in any Office program and insert them into your Word documents. It holds up to 24 items and, unlike the system Clipboard, the items on the Office Clipboard can be viewed. By default, the Office Clipboard opens automatically when you cut or copy two items consecutively. You can also use the Office Clipboard command on the Edit menu to manually display the Office Clipboard if you prefer to work with it open. You add items to the Office Clipboard using the Cut and Copy commands. The last item you collect is always added to both the system Clipboard and the Office Clipboard. ▰▰▰ You use the Office Clipboard to move several sentences in your press release.

STEPS

TROUBLE

If the Office Clipboard does not open, click Office Clipboard on the Edit menu, click the Undo button on the Standard toolbar two times, click Clear All on the Clipboard task pane, then repeat Steps 1 and 2. To restore the default, click Options on the Clipboard task pane, click Show Office Clipboard Automatically to select it, then click outside the menu.

1. **In the last paragraph, select the sentence** New York Times literary editor... **(including the space after the period), then click the** Cut button 🗷 **on the Standard toolbar**

   The sentence is cut to the Clipboard.

2. **Select the sentence** A detailed schedule is... **(including the ¶ mark), then click** 🗷

   The Office Clipboard opens in the Clipboard task pane, as shown in Figure B-9. It displays the items you cut from the press release. The icon next to each item indicates the items are from a Word document.

3. **Place the insertion point at the end of the second paragraph (after Hotel. but before the ¶ mark), then click the** New York Times literary editor... **item on the Office Clipboard**

   Clicking an item on the Office Clipboard pastes the item in the document at the location of the insertion point. Notice that the item remains on the Office Clipboard even after you pasted it. Items remain on the Office Clipboard until you delete them or close all open Office programs. Also, if you add a 25th item to the Office Clipboard, the first item is deleted.

4. **Place the insertion point at the end of the third paragraph (after Duong.), then click the** A detailed schedule is... **item on the Office Clipboard**

   The sentence is pasted in the document.

QUICK TIP

To delete an individual item from the Office Clipboard, click the list arrow next to the item, then click Delete.

5. **Select the fourth paragraph, which contains the sentence** This is the first event... **(including the ¶ mark), then click** 🗷

   The sentence is cut to the Office Clipboard. Notice that the last item collected displays at the top of the Clipboard task pane. The last item collected is also stored on the system Clipboard.

6. **Place the insertion point at the beginning of the third paragraph (before Our...), click the** Paste button 🗎 **on the Standard toolbar, then press** [Backspace]

   The "This is the first..." sentence is pasted at the beginning of the "Our guest list..." paragraph. You can paste the last item collected using either the Paste command or the Office Clipboard.

7. **Place the insertion point at the end of the third paragraph (after www.media-loft.com and before the ¶ mark), then press** [Delete] **twice**

   The ¶ symbols and the blank line between the third and fourth paragraphs are deleted.

QUICK TIP

Many Word users prefer to work with formatting marks turned on at all times. Experiment for yourself and see which method you prefer.

8. **Click the** Show/Hide ¶ button 🔳 **on the Standard toolbar**

   Compare your press release with Figure B-10.

9. **Click the** Clear All button **on the Office Clipboard to remove the items from it, close the Clipboard task pane, press** [Ctrl][Home], **then click the** Save button 🖫

   Pressing [Ctrl][Home] moves the insertion point to the top of the document.

FIGURE B-9: Office Clipboard in Clipboard task pane

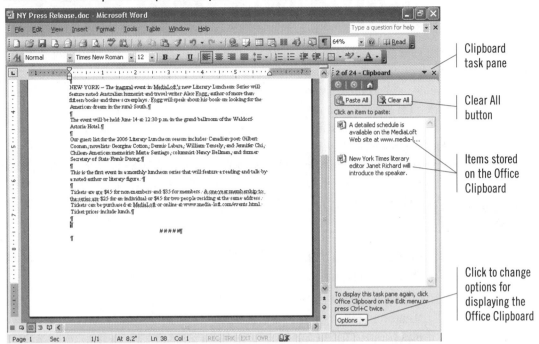

Clipboard task pane

Clear All button

Items stored on the Office Clipboard

Click to change options for displaying the Office Clipboard

Word 2003

FIGURE B-10: Revised press release

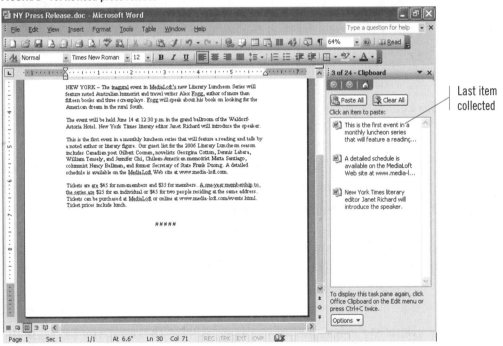

Last item collected

Clues to Use

Copying and moving items between documents

The system and Office Clipboards also can be used to copy and move items between Word documents. To copy or cut items from one Word document and paste them into another, first open both documents and the Clipboard task pane in the program window. With multiple documents open, you can copy and move items between documents by copying or cutting the item(s) from one document and then switching to another document and pasting the item(s). To switch between open documents, click the button on the taskbar for the document you want to appear in the document window. You can also display both documents at the same time by clicking the Arrange All command on the Window menu. The Office Clipboard stores all the items collected from all documents, regardless of which document is displayed in the document window. The system Clipboard stores the last item collected from any document.

Finding and Replacing Text

The Find and Replace feature in Word allows you to automatically search for and replace all instances of a word or phrase in a document. For example, you might need to substitute "bookstore" for "store," and it would be very time-consuming to manually locate and replace each instance of "store" in a long document. Using the Replace command you can automatically find and replace all occurrences of specific text at once, or you can choose to find and review each occurrence individually. You also can use the Find command to locate and highlight every occurrence of a specific word or phrase in a document. ▰▰▰▰ MediaLoft has decided to change the name of the New York series from "Literary Luncheon Series" to "Literary Limelight Series." You use the Replace command to search the document for all instances of "Luncheon" and replace them with "Limelight."

1. **Click** Edit **on the menu bar, click** Replace, **then click** More **in the Find and Replace dialog box**
    The Find and Replace dialog box opens, as shown in Figure B-11.

2. **Click the** Find what text box, **then type** Luncheon
    "Luncheon" is the text that will be replaced.

3. **Press** [Tab], **then type** Limelight **in the Replace with text box**
    "Limelight" is the text that will replace "Luncheon."

4. **Click the** Match case check box **in the Search Options section to select it**
    Selecting the Match case check box tells Word to find only exact matches for the uppercase and lowercase characters you entered in the Find what text box. You want to replace all instances of "Luncheon" in the proper name "Literary Luncheon Series." You do not want to replace "luncheon" when it refers to a lunchtime event.

5. **Click** Replace All
    Clicking Replace All changes all occurrences of "Luncheon" to "Limelight" in the press release. A message box reports three replacements were made.

6. **Click** OK **to close the message box, then click** Close **to close the Find and Replace dialog box**
    Word replaced "Luncheon" with "Limelight" in three locations, but did not replace "luncheon."

7. **Click** Edit **on the menu bar, then click** Find
    The Find and Replace dialog box opens with the Find tab displayed. The Find command allows you to quickly locate all instances of text in a document. You can use it to verify that Word did not replace "luncheon."

8. **Type** luncheon **in the Find what text box, click the** Highlight all items found in check box **to select it, click** Find All, **then click** Close
    The Find and Replace dialog box closes and "luncheon" is selected in the document, as shown in Figure B-12.

9. **Deselect the text, press** [Ctrl][Home], **then click the** Save button 🖬 **on the Standard toolbar**

Clues to Use

Inserting text with AutoCorrect

As you type, AutoCorrect automatically corrects many commonly misspelled words. By creating your own AutoCorrect entries, you also can set Word to quickly insert text that you type often, such as your name or contact information, or to correct words you frequently misspell. For example, you could create an AutoCorrect entry so that the name "Alice Wegman" is automatically inserted whenever you type "aw" followed by a space. To create an AutoCorrect entry, click AutoCorrect Options on the Tools menu. On the AutoCorrect tab in the AutoCorrect dialog box, type the text you want to be automatically corrected in the Replace text box (such as "aw"), type the text you want to be automatically inserted in its place in the With text box (such as "Alice Wegman"), then click Add. The AutoCorrect entry is added to the list. Note that Word inserts an AutoCorrect entry in a document only when you press [Spacebar] after typing the text you want Word to correct. For example, Word will insert "Alice Wegman" when you type "aw" followed by a space, but not when you type "awful."

FIGURE B-11: Find and Replace dialog box

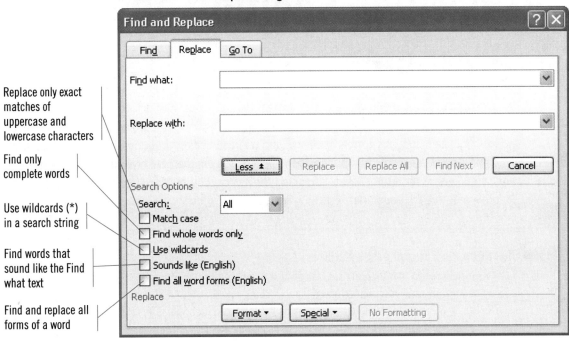

Replace only exact matches of uppercase and lowercase characters

Find only complete words

Use wildcards (*) in a search string

Find words that sound like the Find what text

Find and replace all forms of a word

FIGURE B-12: Found text highlighted in document

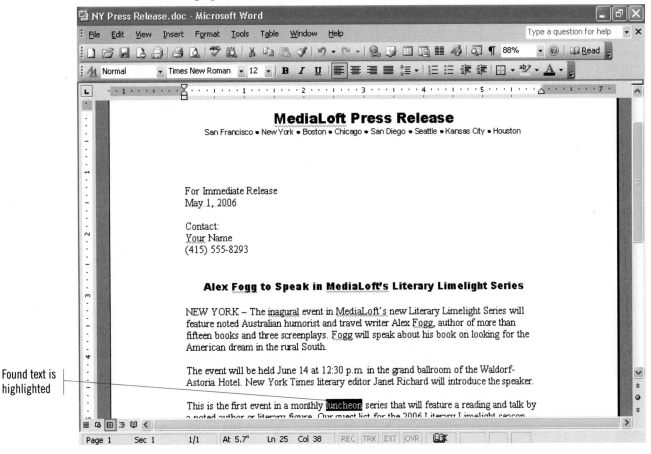

Found text is highlighted

Checking Spelling and Grammar

When you finish typing and revising a document, you can use the Spelling and Grammar command to search the document for misspelled words and grammar errors. The Spelling and Grammar checker flags possible mistakes, suggests correct spellings, and offers remedies for grammar errors such as subject-verb agreement, repeated words, and punctuation. ▓▓▐▐▐▐ You use the Spelling and Grammar checker to search your press release for errors. Before beginning the search, you set the Spelling and Grammar checker to ignore words, such as Fogg, that you know are spelled correctly.

STEPS

1. **Right-click Fogg in the headline**

   A shortcut menu that includes suggestions for correcting the spelling of "Fogg" opens. You can correct individual spelling and grammar errors by right-clicking text that is underlined with a red or green wavy line and selecting a correction. Although "Fogg" is not in the Word dictionary, it is spelled correctly in the document.

2. **Click Ignore All**

   Clicking Ignore All tells Word not to flag "Fogg" as misspelled.

3. **Right-click MediaLoft at the top of the document, click Ignore All, right-click MediaLoft's in the headline, then click Ignore All**

   The red wavy underline is removed from all instances of "MediaLoft" and "MediaLoft's."

4. **Press [Ctrl][Home], then click the Spelling and Grammar button ▧ on the Standard toolbar**

   The Spelling and Grammar: English (U.S.) dialog box opens, as shown in Figure B-13. The dialog box identifies "inagural" as misspelled and suggests possible corrections for the error. The word selected in the Suggestions box is the correct spelling.

5. **Click Change**

   Word replaces the misspelled word with the correctly spelled word. Next, the dialog box indicates "are" is repeated in a sentence.

6. **Click Delete**

   Word deletes the second occurrence of the repeated word. Next, the dialog box flags a subject-verb agreement error and suggests using "is" instead of "are," as shown in Figure B-14. The phrase selected in the Suggestions box is correct.

7. **Click Change**

   The word "is" replaces the word "are" in the sentence and the Spelling and Grammar dialog box closes. Keep in mind that the Spelling and Grammar checker identifies many common errors, but you cannot rely on it to find and correct all spelling and grammar errors in your documents. Always proofread your documents carefully.

8. **Click OK to complete the spelling and grammar check, press [Ctrl][Home], then click the Save button ▧ on the Standard toolbar**

FIGURE B-13: Spelling and Grammar: English (U.S.) dialog box

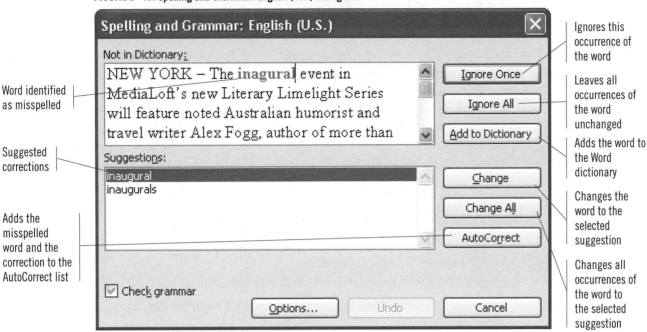

Word identified as misspelled

Suggested corrections

Adds the misspelled word and the correction to the AutoCorrect list

Ignores this occurrence of the word

Leaves all occurrences of the word unchanged

Adds the word to the Word dictionary

Changes the word to the selected suggestion

Changes all occurrences of the word to the selected suggestion

FIGURE B-14: Grammar error identified in Spelling and Grammar dialog box

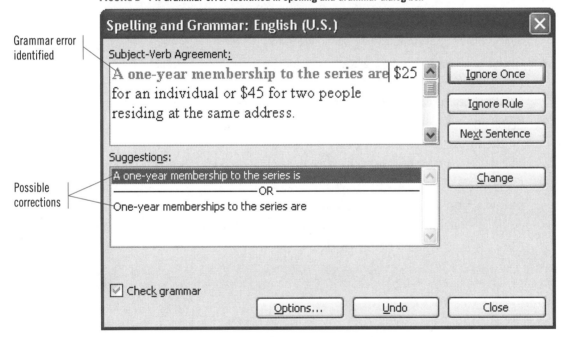

Grammar error identified

Possible corrections

Clues to Use

Using the Undo, Redo, and Repeat commands

Word remembers the editing and formatting changes you make so that you can easily reverse or repeat them. You can reverse the last action you took by clicking the Undo button on the Standard toolbar, or you can undo a series of actions by clicking the Undo list arrow and selecting the action you want to reverse. When you undo an action using the Undo list arrow, you also undo all the actions above it in the list; that is, all actions that were performed after the action you selected. Similarly, you can keep the changes you just reversed by using the Redo button and the Redo list arrow.

If you want to repeat a change you just made, use the Repeat command on the Edit menu. The name of the Repeat command changes depending on the last action you took. For example, if you just typed "thank you," the name of the command is Repeat Typing. Clicking the Repeat Typing command inserts "thank you" at the location of the insertion point. You also can repeat the last action you took by pressing [F4].

Using the Thesaurus

Word also includes a Thesaurus, which you can use to look up synonyms for awkward or repetitive words. The Thesaurus is one of the reference sources available in the Research task pane. This task pane allows you to quickly search reference sources for information related to a word or phrase. When you are working with an active Internet connection, the Research task pane provides access to dictionary, encyclopedia, translation, and other reference sources and research services. ▰▰▰ After proofreading your document for errors, you decide the press release would read better if several adjectives were more descriptive. You use the Thesaurus to find synonyms for "noted" and "new".

STEPS

1. **Scroll down until the headline is displayed at the top of your screen**

2. **In the first sentence of the third paragraph, select noted, then click the Research button 🔍 on the Standard toolbar**

   The Research task pane opens. "Noted" appears in the Search for text box.

QUICK TIP
You can also select a word, click Tools on the menu bar, point to Language, and then click Thesaurus to open the Research task pane and display a list of synonyms for the word.

3. **Click the All Reference Books list arrow under the Search for text box, then click Thesaurus: English (U.S.)**

   Possible synonyms for "noted" are listed under the Thesaurus: English (U.S.) heading in the task pane, as shown in Figure B-15.

4. **Point to distinguished in the list of synonyms**

   A box containing an arrow appears around the word.

QUICK TIP
Right-click a word, then click Look up to open the Research task pane.

5. **Click the arrow in the box, click Insert on the menu that appears, then close the Research task pane**

   "Distinguished" replaces "noted" in the press release.

6. **Scroll up, right-click new in the first sentence of the first paragraph, point to Synonyms on the shortcut menu, then click innovative**

   "Innovative" replaces "new" in the press release.

7. **Press [Ctrl][Home], click the Save button 🖫 on the Standard toolbar, then click the Print button 🖨 on the Standard toolbar**

   A copy of the finished press release prints. Compare your document to Figure B-16.

8. **Click File on the menu bar, then click Close**

Clues to Use

Viewing and modifying the document properties

Document properties are details about a file that can help you to organize and search your files. The author name, the date the file was created, the title, and keywords that describe the contents of the file are examples of document property information. You can view and modify the properties of an open document by clicking Properties on the File menu to open the Properties dialog box. The General, Statistics, and Contents tabs of the Properties dialog box display information about the file that is automatically created and updated by Word. The General tab shows the file type, location, size, and date and time the file was created and last modified; the Statistics tab displays information about revisions to the document along with the number of pages, words, lines, paragraphs, and characters in the file; and the Contents tab shows the title of the document.

You can define other document properties using the Summary and Custom tabs of the Properties dialog box. The Summary tab includes identifying information about the document such as the title, subject, author, and keywords. Some of this information is entered by Word when the document is first saved, but you can modify or add to the summary details by typing new information in the text boxes on the Summary tab. The Custom tab allows you to create new document properties, such as client, project, or date completed. To create a custom property, select a property name in the Name list box on the Custom tab, use the Type list arrow to select the type of data you want for the property, and then type the identifying detail (such as a project name) in the Value text box. When you are finished viewing or modifying the document properties, click OK to close the Properties dialog box.

FIGURE B-15: Research task pane

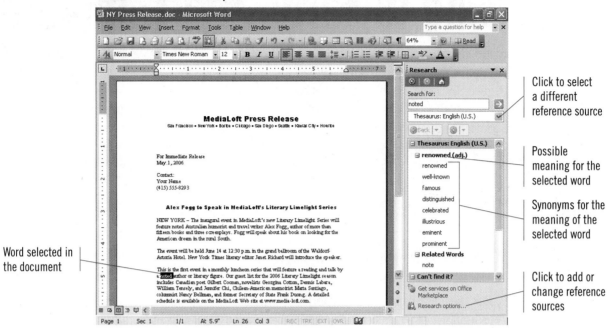

Click to select a different reference source

Possible meaning for the selected word

Synonyms for the meaning of the selected word

Word selected in the document

Click to add or change reference sources

FIGURE B-16: Completed press release

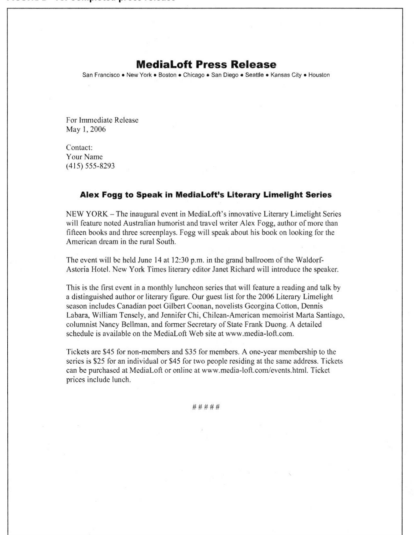

Using Wizards and Templates

Word includes many templates that you can use to quickly create memos, faxes, letters, reports, brochures, and other professionally designed documents. A **template** is a formatted document that contains place-holder text. To create a document that is based on a template, you replace the placeholder text with your own text and then save the document with a new filename. A **wizard** is an interactive set of dialog boxes that guides you through the process of creating a document. A wizard prompts you to provide information and select formatting options, and then it creates the document for you based on your specifications. You can create a document with a wizard or template using the New command on the File menu. ▰▰▰ You will fax the press release to your list of press contacts, beginning with the *New York Times*. You use a template to create a fax coversheet for the press release.

STEPS

1. **Click File on the menu bar, then click New**

   The New Document task pane opens.

2. **Click the On my computer hyperlink in the New Document task pane**

   The Templates dialog box opens. The tabs in the dialog box contain icons for the Word templates and wizards.

3. **Click the Letters & Faxes tab, then click the Professional Fax icon**

   A preview of the Professional Fax template appears in the Templates dialog box, as shown in Figure B-17.

> **QUICK TIP**
>
> Double-clicking an icon in the Templates dialog box also opens a new document based on the template.

4. **Click OK**

   The Professional Fax template opens as a new document in the document window. It contains placeholder text, which you can replace with your own information.

5. **Drag to select Company Name Here, then type MediaLoft**

6. **Click the Click here and type return address and phone and fax numbers placeholder**

   Clicking the placeholder selects it. When a placeholder says Click here... you do not need to drag to select it.

7. **Type MediaLoft San Francisco, press [Enter], then type Tel: (415) 555-8293**

   The text you type replaces the placeholder text.

> **QUICK TIP**
>
> Delete any placeholder text you do not want to replace.

8. **Replace the remaining placeholder text with the text shown in Figure B-18**

   Word automatically inserted the current date in the document. You do not need to replace the current date with the date shown in the figure.

9. **Click File on the menu bar, click Save As, use the Save in list arrow to navigate to the drive or folder where your Data Files are located, type NYT Fax in the File name text box, then click Save**

   The document is saved with the filename NYT Fax.

10. **Click the Print button 🖨 on the Standard toolbar, click File on the menu bar, then click Exit**

    A copy of the fax coversheet prints and the document and Word close.

FIGURE B-17: Letters & Faxes tab in Templates dialog box

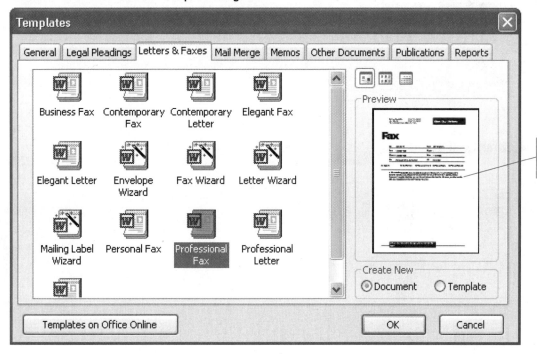

Preview of selected template

FIGURE B-18: Completed fax coversheet

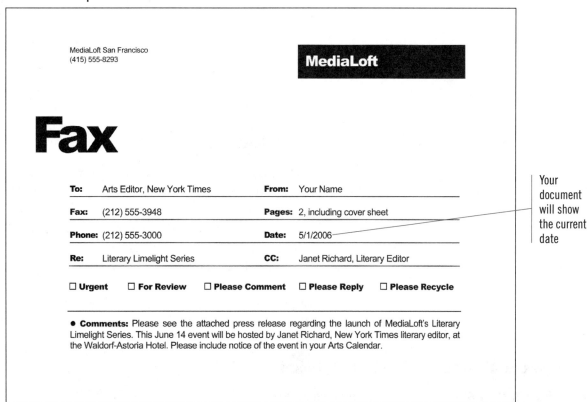

Your document will show the current date

Practice

▼ CONCEPTS REVIEW

Label the elements of the Open dialog box shown in Figure B-19.

FIGURE B-19

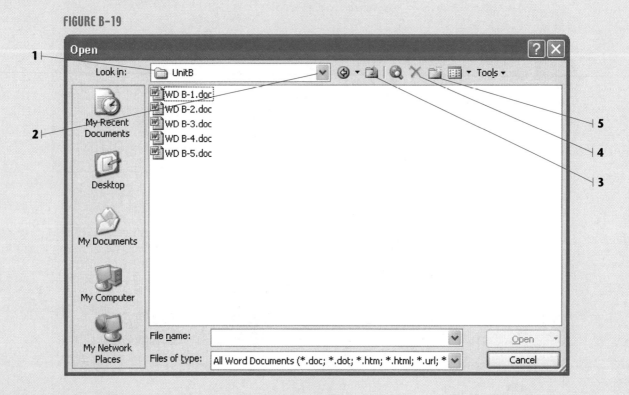

Match each term with the statement that best describes it.

6. **System Clipboard**

7. **Show/Hide**

8. **Select**

9. **Thesaurus**

10. **Undo**

11. **Template**

12. **Office Clipboard**

13. **Paste**

14. **Replace**

a. Command used to insert text stored on the Clipboard into a document

b. Document that contains placeholder text

c. Feature used to suggest synonyms for words

d. Temporary storage area for only the last item cut or copied from a document

e. Command used to display formatting marks in a document

f. Command used to locate and replace occurrences of specific text in a document

g. Command used to reverse the last action you took in a document

h. Temporary storage area for up to 24 items collected from any Office file

i. Action that must be taken before text can be cut, copied, or deleted

Select the best answer from the list of choices.

15. Which of the following is *not* used to open an existing document?

a. Blank document hyperlink in the New Document task pane

b. Open button on the Standard toolbar

c. Open or More hyperlink in the Getting Started task pane

d. Open command on the Edit menu

16. **To locate and change all instances of a word in a document, which menu command do you use?**
    a. Find
    b. Search
    c. Paste
    d. Replace

17. **Which of the following statements is *not* true?**
    a. The last item cut or copied from a document is stored on the system Clipboard.
    b. You can view the contents of the Office Clipboard.
    c. When you move text by dragging it, a copy of the text you move is stored on the system Clipboard.
    d. The Office Clipboard can hold more than one item.

18. **Which Word feature corrects errors as you type?**
    a. Thesaurus
    b. AutoCorrect
    c. Spelling and Grammar
    d. Undo and Redo

19. **Which command is used to display a document in two panes in the document window?**
    a. Split
    b. New Window
    c. Arrange All
    d. Compare Side by Side with...

20. **What does the symbol ¶ represent when it is displayed in the document window?**
    a. Hidden text
    b. A space
    c. A tab stop
    d. The end of a paragraph

▼ SKILLS REVIEW

1. **Open a document.**
   a. Start Word, click the Open button, then open the file WD B-2.doc from the drive and folder where your Data Files are located.
   b. Save the document with the filename CAOS Press Release.

2. **Select text.**
   a. Select Today's Date and replace it with the current date.
   b. Select Your Name and Your Phone Number and replace them with the relevant information.
   c. Scroll down, then select and replace text in the body of the press release using the following table as a guide:

in paragraph	select	replace with
1	13 and 14	**16 and 17**
1	eighth	**eleventh**
4	open his renovated Pearl St studio for the first time this year	**offer a sneak-preview of his Peace sculpture commissioned by the city of Prague**

   d. In the fourth paragraph, delete the sentence Exhibiting with him will be sculptor Francis Pilo.
   e. Save your changes to the press release.

3. **Cut and paste text.**
   a. Display paragraph and other formatting marks in your document if they are not already displayed.
   b. Use the Cut and Paste buttons to switch the order of the two sentences in the fourth paragraph (which begins New group shows...).
   c. Use the drag-and-drop method to switch the order of the second and third paragraphs.
   d. Adjust the spacing if necessary so that there is one blank line between paragraphs, then save your changes.

4. **Copy and paste text.**
   a. Use the Copy and Paste buttons to copy CAOS 2003 from the headline and paste it before the word map in the third paragraph.
   b. Change the formatting of the pasted text to match the formatting of the third paragraph, then insert a space between 2003 and map if necessary.
   c. Use the drag-and-drop method to copy CAOS from the third paragraph and paste it before the word group in the second sentence of the fourth paragraph, then save your changes.

5. Use the Office Clipboard.

   a. Use the Office Clipboard command on the Edit menu to open the Clipboard task pane.

   b. Scroll so that the first body paragraph is displayed at the top of the document window.

   c. Select the fifth paragraph (which begins Studio location maps...) and cut it to the Office Clipboard.

   d. Select the third paragraph (which begins Cambridgeport is easily accessible...) and cut it to the Office Clipboard.

   e. Use the Office Clipboard to paste the Studio location maps... item as the new fourth paragraph.

   f. Use the Office Clipboard to paste the Cambridgeport is easily accessible... item as the new fifth paragraph.

   g. Use any method to switch the order of the two sentences in the fourth paragraph (which begins Studio location maps...).

   h. Adjust the spacing if necessary so that there is one blank line between each of the six body paragraphs.

   i. Turn off the display of formatting marks, clear and close the Office Clipboard, then save your changes.

6. Find and replace text.

   a. Using the Replace command, replace all instances of 2003 with 2006.

   b. Replace all instances of the abbreviation st with street, taking care to replace whole words only when you perform the replace. (*Hint*: Click More to expand the Find and Replace dialog box, and then deselect Match case if it is selected.)

   c. Use the Find command to find all instances of st in the document, and make sure no errors occurred when you replaced st with street. (*Hint*: Deselect the Find whole words only check box.)

   d. Save your changes to the press release.

7. Check Spelling and Grammar and use the Thesaurus.

   a. Set Word to ignore the spelling of Cambridgeport, if it is marked as misspelled. (*Hint*: Right-click Cambridgeport.)

   b. Move the insertion point to the top of the document, then use the Spelling and Grammar command to search for and correct any spelling and grammar errors in the press release.

   c. Use the Thesaurus to replace thriving in the second paragraph with a different suitable word.

   d. Proofread your press release, correct any errors, save your changes, print a copy, then close the document.

8. Use wizards and templates.

   a. Use the New command to open the New Document task pane.

   b. Use the On my computer hyperlink to open the Templates dialog box.

   c. Create a new document using the Business Fax template.

   d. Replace the placeholder text in the document using Figure B-20 as a guide. Delete any placeholders that do not apply to your fax. The date in your fax will be the current date.

   e. Save the document as CAOS Fax, print a copy, close the document, then exit Word.

FIGURE B-20

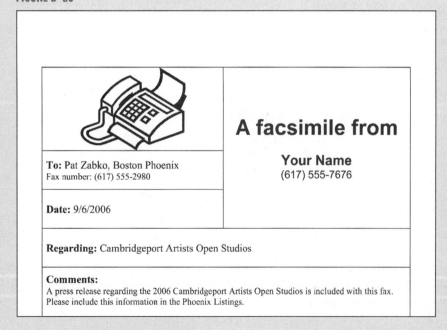

A facsimile from

Your Name
(617) 555-7676

To: Pat Zabko, Boston Phoenix
Fax number: (617) 555-2980

Date: 9/6/2006

Regarding: Cambridgeport Artists Open Studios

Comments:
A press release regarding the 2006 Cambridgeport Artists Open Studios is included with this fax.
Please include this information in the Phoenix Listings.

▼ INDEPENDENT CHALLENGE 1

Because of your success in revitalizing an historic theatre in Hobart, Tasmania, you were hired as the director of The Auckland Lyric Theatre in Auckland, New Zealand, to breathe life into its theatre revitalization efforts. After a year on the job, you are launching your first major fund-raising drive. You'll create a fund-raising letter for the Lyric Theatre by modifying a letter you wrote for the theatre in Hobart.

a. Start Word, open the file WD B-3.doc from the drive and folder where your Data Files are located, then save it as Lyric Theatre Letter.

b. Replace the theatre name and address, the date, the inside address, and the salutation with the text shown in Figure B-21.

c. Use the Replace command to replace all instances of Hobart with Auckland.

d. Use the Replace command to replace all instances of Tasmanians with New Zealanders.

e. Use the Find command to locate the word considerable, then use the Thesaurus to replace the word with a synonym.

f. Create an AutoCorrect entry that inserts Auckland Lyric Theatre whenever you type alt.

g. Select each XXXXX, then type alt followed by a space.

h. Move the fourth body paragraph so that it becomes the second body paragraph.

i. Replace Your Name with your name in the signature block.

j. Use the Spelling and Grammar command to check for and correct spelling and grammar errors.

FIGURE B-21

The Auckland Lyric Theatre
64-70 Queen Street, Auckland, New Zealand

September 24, 2006

Ms. Keri Marshall
718 Elliott Street
Auckland

Dear Ms. Marshall,

Advanced Challenge Exercise

- Open the Properties dialog box, then review the paragraph, line, word, and character count on the Statistics tab.
- On the Summary tab, change the title to Auckland Lyric Theatre and add the keyword fund-raising.
- On the Custom tab, add a property named Project with the value Capital Campaign, then close the dialog box.

k. Proofread the letter, correct any errors, save your changes, print a copy, close the document, then exit Word.

An advertisement for job openings in London caught your eye and you have decided to apply. The ad, shown in Figure B-22, was printed in last weekend's edition of your local newspaper. You'll use the Letter Wizard to create a cover letter to send with your resume.

a. Read the ad shown in Figure B-22 and decide which position to apply for. Choose the position that most closely matches your qualifications.

b. Start Word and open the Templates dialog box.

c. Double-click Letter Wizard on the Letters & Faxes tab, then select Send one letter in the Letter Wizard dialog box.

d. In the Letter Wizard—Step 1 of 4 dialog box, choose to include a date on your letter, select Elegant Letter for the page design, select Modified block for the letter style, include a header and footer with the page design, then click Next.

e. In the Letter Wizard—Step 2 of 4 dialog box, enter the recipient's name (Ms. Katherine Winn) and the delivery address, referring to the ad for the address information. Also enter the salutation **Dear Ms. Winn** using the business style, then click Next.

f. In the Letter Wizard—Step 3 of 4 dialog box, include a reference line in the letter, enter the appropriate position code (see Figure B-22) in the Reference line text box, then click Next.

g. In the Letter Wizard—Step 4 of 4 dialog box, enter your name as the sender, enter your return address (including your country), and select an appropriate complimentary closing. Then, because you will be including your resume with the letter, include one enclosure. Click Finish when you are done.

h. Save the letter with the filename **Global Dynamics Letter** to the drive and folder where your Data Files are located.

i. Replace the placeholder text in the body of the letter with three paragraphs that address your qualifications for the job:

- In the first paragraph, specify the job you are applying for, indicate where you saw the position advertised, and briefly state your qualifications and interest in the position.
- In the second paragraph, describe your work experience and skills. Be sure to relate your experience and qualifications to the position requirements listed in the ad.
- In the third paragraph, politely request an interview for the position and provide your phone number and e-mail address.

j. When you are finished typing the letter, check it for spelling and grammar errors and correct any mistakes.

k. Save your changes to the letter, print a copy, close the document, then exit Word.

FIGURE B-22

GlobalDynamics

Career Opportunities in London

Global Dynamics, an established software development firm with offices in North America, Asia, and Europe, is seeking candidates for the following positions in its London facility:

Instructor

Responsible for delivering software training to our expanding European customer base. Duties include delivering hands-on training, keeping up-to-date with product development, and working with the Director of Training to ensure the high quality of course materials. Successful candidate will have excellent presentation skills and be proficient in Microsoft PowerPoint and Microsoft Word. **Position B12C6**

Administrative Assistant

Proficiency with Microsoft Word a must! Administrative office duties include making travel arrangements, scheduling meetings, taking notes and publishing meeting minutes, handling correspondence, and ordering office supplies. Must have superb multi-tasking abilities, excellent communication, organizational, and interpersonal skills, and be comfortable working with e-mail and the Internet. **Position B16F5**

Copywriter

The ideal candidate will have marketing or advertising writing experience in a high tech environment, including collateral, newsletters, and direct mail. Experience writing for the Web, broadcast, and multimedia is a plus. Fluency with Microsoft Word required. **Position C13D4**

Positions offer salary, excellent benefits, moving expenses, and career growth opportunities.

Send resume and cover letter referencing position code to:

Katherine Winn
Director of Recruiting
Global Dynamics
483 Briar Terrace
London LH3 9JH
United Kingdom

▼ INDEPENDENT CHALLENGE 3

As administrative director of continuing education, you drafted a memo to instructors asking them to help you finalize the course schedule for next semester. Today you'll examine the draft and make revisions before printing it.

a. Start Word and open the file WD B-4.doc from the drive and folder where your Data Files are located.
b. Open the Save As dialog box, navigate to the drive and folder where your Data Files are located, then use the Create New Folder button to create a new folder called **Memos**.
c. Click the Up One Level button in the dialog box, rename the Memos folder **Spring Memos**, then save the document as **Instructor Memo** in the Spring Memos folder.
d. Replace Your Name with your name in the From line, then scroll down until the first body paragraph is at the top of the screen.

Advanced Challenge Exercise

- Use the Split command on the Window menu to split the window under the first body paragraph, then scroll until the last paragraph of the memo is displayed in the bottom pane.
- Use the Cut and Paste buttons to move the sentence **If you are planning to teach...** from the first body paragraph to become the first sentence in the last paragraph of the memo.
- Double-click the split bar to restore the window to a single pane.

e. Use the [Delete] key to merge the first two paragraphs into one paragraph.
f. Use the Office Clipboard to reorganize the list of twelve-week courses so that the courses are listed in alphabetical order. (*Hint*: Use the Zoom list arrow to enlarge the document as needed.)
g. Use the drag-and-drop method to reorganize the list of one-day seminars so that the seminars are listed in alphabetical order.
h. Use the Spelling and Grammar command to check for and correct spelling and grammar errors.
i. Clear and close the Office Clipboard, save your changes, print a copy, close the document, then exit Word.

E-QUEST

▼ INDEPENDENT CHALLENGE 4

Reference sources—dictionaries, thesauri, style and grammar guides, and guides to business etiquette and procedure—are essential for day-to-day use in the workplace. Much of this reference information is available on the World Wide Web. In this independent challenge, you will locate reference sources on the Web and use some of them to look up definitions, synonyms, and antonyms for words. Your goal is to familiarize yourself with online reference sources so you can use them later in your work.

a. Start Word, open the file WD B-5.doc from the drive and folder where your Data Files are located, and save it as **Web References**. This document contains the questions you will answer about the Web reference sources you find. You will type your answers to the questions in the document.
b. Replace the placeholder text at the top of the Web References document with your name and the date.
c. Use your favorite search engine to search the Web for grammar and style guides, dictionaries, and thesauri. Use the keywords **grammar**, **usage**, **dictionary**, **glossary**, and **thesaurus** to conduct your search.
d. Complete the Web References document, then proofread it and correct any mistakes.
e. Save the document, print a copy, close the document, then exit Word.

Using the Elegant Letter template, create the letter shown in Figure B-23. Save the document as Visa Letter. Check the letter for spelling and grammar errors, then print a copy.

FIGURE B-23

YOUR NAME

March 17, 2006

Embassy of Australia
Suite 710
50 O'Connor Street
Ottawa, Ontario K1P 6L2

Dear Sir or Madam:

I am applying for a long-stay (six-month) tourist visa to Australia, valid for four years. I am scheduled to depart for Sydney on July 1, 2006, returning to Vancouver on December 23, 2006.

While in Australia, I plan to conduct research for a book I am writing on coral reefs. I am interested in a multiple entry visa valid for four years so that I can return to Australia after this trip to follow-up on my initial research. I will be based in Cairns, but will be traveling frequently to other parts of Australia to meet with scientists, policy-makers, and environmentalists.

Enclosed please find my completed visa application form, my passport, a passport photo, a copy of my return air ticket, and the visa fee. Please let me know if I can provide further information.

Sincerely,

Your Name

35 HARDY STREET • VANCOUVER, BC • V6C 3K4
PHONE: (604) 555-8989 • FAX: (604) 555-8981

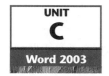

Formatting Text and Paragraphs

OBJECTIVES

Format with fonts
Change font styles and effects
Change line and paragraph spacing
Align paragraphs
Work with tabs
Work with indents
Add bullets and numbering
Add borders and shading

If you have a SAM user profile, you may have access to hands-on instruction, practice, and assessment of the skills covered in this unit. Log in to your SAM account and go to your assignments page to see what your instructor has assigned.

Formatting can enhance the appearance of a document, create visual impact, and help illustrate a document's structure. The formatting of a document can also add personality to it and lend it a degree of professionalism. In this unit you learn how to format text using different fonts and font-formatting options. You also learn how to change the alignment, indentation, and spacing of paragraphs, and how to spruce up documents with borders, shading, bullets, and other paragraph-formatting effects. You have finished drafting the quarterly marketing report for the MediaLoft Chicago store. You now need to format the report so it is attractive and highlights the significant information.

Formatting with Fonts

Formatting text with different fonts is a quick and powerful way to enhance the appearance of a document. A **font** is a complete set of characters with the same typeface or design. Arial, Times New Roman, Comic Sans, Courier, and Tahoma are some of the more common fonts, but there are hundreds of others, each with a specific design and feel. Another way to alter the impact of text is to increase or decrease its **font size**, which is measured in points. A **point** is ¹⁄₇₂ of an inch. When formatting a document with fonts, it's important to pick fonts and font sizes that augment the document's purpose. You apply fonts and font sizes to text using the Font and Font Size list arrows on the Formatting toolbar. You change the font and font size of the title and headings in the report, selecting a font that enhances the business tone of the document. By formatting the title and headings in a font different from the body text, you help to visually structure the report for readers.

STEPS

1. Start Word, open the file WD C-1.doc **from the drive and folder where your Data Files are located, then save it as** Chicago Marketing Report

The file opens in Print Layout view.

2. Click the Normal View button ≡ **on the horizontal scroll bar, click the** Zoom list arrow **on the Standard toolbar, then click** 100% **if necessary**

The document switches to Normal view, a view useful for simple text formatting. The name of the font used in the document, Times New Roman, is displayed in the Font list box on the Formatting toolbar. The font size, 12, appears next to it in the Font Size list box.

3. Select the title MediaLoft Chicago Quarterly Marketing Report, **then click the** Font list arrow **on the Formatting toolbar**

The Font list, which shows the fonts available on your computer, opens as shown in Figure C-1. Fonts you have used recently appear above the double line. All the fonts on your computer are listed in alphabetical order below the double line. You can click the font name in either location on the Font list to apply the font to the selected text.

4. Click Arial

The font of the report title changes to Arial.

5. Click the Font Size list arrow **on the Formatting toolbar, then click** 20

The font size of the title increases to 20 points.

6. Click the Font Color list arrow **on the Formatting toolbar**

A palette of colors opens.

7. Click Plum **on the Font Color palette as shown in Figure C-2, then deselect the text**

The color of the report title text changes to plum. The active color on the Font Color button also changes to plum.

8. Scroll down until the heading Advertising is at the top of your screen, select Advertising, **press and hold** [Ctrl], **select the heading** Events, **then release** [Ctrl]

The Advertising and Events headings are selected. Selecting multiple items allows you to format several items at once.

9. Click the Font list arrow, **click** Arial, **click the** Font Size list arrow, **click** 14, **click the** Font Color button **A, then deselect the text**

The headings are formatted in 14-point Arial with a plum color.

10. Press [Ctrl][Home], **then click the** Save button 🖫 **on the Standard toolbar**

Pressing [Ctrl][Home] moves the insertion point to the beginning of the document. Compare your document to Figure C-3.

FIGURE C-1: Font list

Font list arrow

Font Size list arrow

Font names are formatted in the font (your list of fonts might differ)

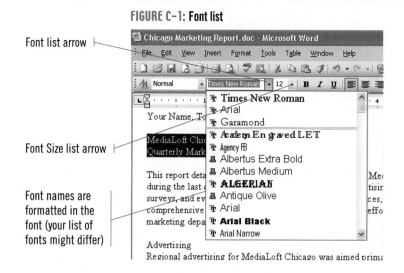

FIGURE C-2: Font Color palette

Font Color list arrow

Name of color appears as a ScreenTip

Click to create a custom color

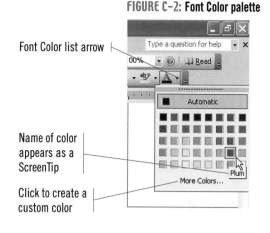

Word 2003

FIGURE C-3: Document formatted with fonts

Title formatted in 20-point Arial, plum

Headings formatted in 14-point Arial, plum

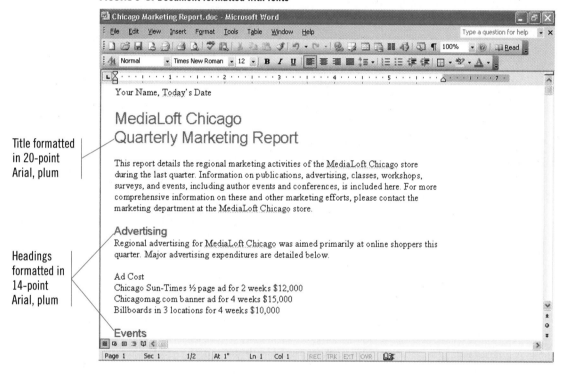

Clues to Use

Adding a drop cap

A fun way to illustrate a document with fonts is to add a drop cap to a paragraph. A **drop cap** is a large initial capital letter, often used to set off the first paragraph of an article. To create a drop cap, place the insertion point in the paragraph you want to format, and then click Drop Cap on the Format menu to open the Drop Cap dialog box. In the Drop Cap dialog box, shown in Figure C-4, select the position, font, number of lines to drop, and the distance you want the drop cap to be from the paragraph text, and then click OK to create the drop cap. The drop cap is added to the paragraph as a graphic object.

    Once a drop cap is inserted in a paragraph, you can modify it by selecting it and then changing the settings in the Drop Cap dialog box. For even more interesting effects, try enhancing a drop cap with font color, font styles, or font effects, or try filling the graphic object with shading or adding a border around it. To enhance a drop cap, first select it, and then experiment with the formatting options available in the Font dialog box and in the Borders and Shading dialog box.

FIGURE C-4: Drop Cap dialog box

Changing Font Styles and Effects

You can dramatically change the appearance of text by applying different font styles, font effects, and character-spacing effects. For example, you can use the buttons on the Formatting toolbar to make text darker by applying **bold**, or to slant text by applying **italic**. You can also use the Font command on the Format menu to apply font effects and character-spacing effects to text. You spice up the appearance of the text in the document by applying different font styles and effects.

STEPS

1. **Select** MediaLoft Chicago Quarterly Marketing Report, **then click the** Bold button **B** **on the Formatting toolbar**

   Applying bold makes the characters in the title darker and thicker.

2. **Select** Advertising, **click** **B**, **select** Events, **then press** [F4]

   Pressing [F4] repeats the last action you took, in this case applying bold. The Advertising and Events headings are both formatted in bold.

3. **Select the** paragraph **under the title, then click the** Italic button **I** **on the Formatting toolbar**

   The paragraph is formatted in italic.

4. **Scroll down until the subheading Author Events is at the top of your screen, select** Author Events, **click** Format **on the menu bar, then click** Font

   The Font dialog box opens, as shown in Figure C-5. You can use options on the Font tab to change the font, font style, size, and color of text, and to add an underline and apply font effects to text.

5. **Scroll up the Font list, click** Arial, **click** Bold Italic **in the Font style list box, select the** Small caps check box, **then click** OK

   The subheading is formatted in Arial, bold, italic, and small caps. When you change text to small caps, the lowercase letters are changed to uppercase letters in a smaller font size.

6. **Select the subheading** Travel Writers & Photographers Conference, **then press** [F4]

   Because you formatted the previous subheading in one action (using the Font dialog box), the Travel Writers subheading is formatted in Arial, bold, italic, and small caps. If you apply formats one by one, then pressing [F4] repeats only the last format you applied.

7. **Under Author Events, select the book title** Just H2O Please: Tales of True Adventure on the Environmental Frontline, **click** **I**, **select** 2 **in the book title, click** Format **on the menu bar, click** Font, **click the** Subscript check box, **click** OK, **then deselect the text**

   The book title is formatted in italic and the character 2 is subscript, as shown in Figure C-6.

8. **Press** [Ctrl][Home], **select the** report title, **click** Format **on the menu bar, click** Font, **then click the** Character Spacing tab **in the Font dialog box**

   You use the Character Spacing tab to change the scale, or width, of the selected characters, to alter the spacing between characters, or to raise or lower the position of the characters.

9. **Click the** Scale list arrow, **click** 150%, **click** OK, **deselect the text, then click the** Save button **on the Standard toolbar**

   Increasing the scale of the characters makes them wider and gives the text a short, squat appearance, as shown in Figure C-7.

FIGURE C-5: Font tab in Font dialog box

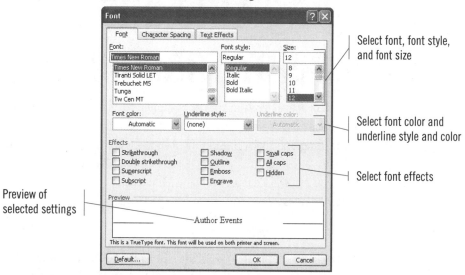

Select font, font style, and font size

Select font color and underline style and color

Select font effects

Preview of selected settings

Author Events

FIGURE C-6: Font effects applied to text

Subhead formatted in 12-point Arial, bold, italic, and small caps

Book title formatted in italic

Subscript text

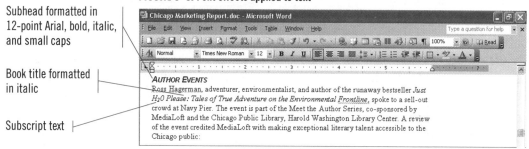

FIGURE C-7: Character spacing effects applied to text

Report title formatted in bold with a character scale of 150%

Paragraph formatted in italic

Headings formatted in bold

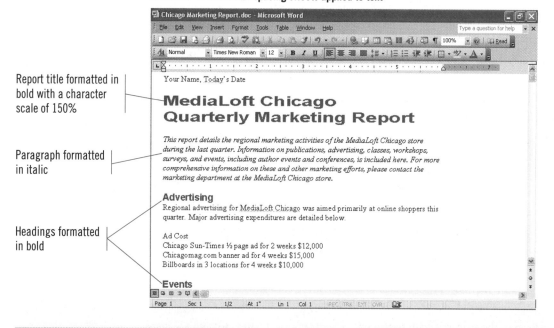

Clues to Use

Changing the case of letters

The Change Case command on the Format menu allows you to quickly change letters from uppercase to lowercase—and vice versa—saving you the time it takes to retype text you want to change. To change the case of selected text, use the Change Case command to open the Change Case dialog box, then select the case style you want to use. Sentence case capitalizes the first letter of a sentence, title case capitalizes the first letter of each word, and toggle case switches all letters to the opposite case.

Changing Line and Paragraph Spacing

Increasing the amount of space between lines adds more white space to a document and can make it easier to read. Adding space between paragraphs can also open up a document and improve its appearance. You can change line and paragraph spacing using the Paragraph command on the Format menu. You can also use the Line Spacing list arrow to quickly change line spacing. You increase the line spacing of several paragraphs and add extra space under each heading to give the report a more open feel. You work with formatting marks turned on, so you can see the paragraph marks (¶).

STEPS

QUICK TIP

The check mark on the Line Spacing list indicates the current line spacing.

1. **Click the** Show/Hide ¶ button **on the Standard toolbar, place the insertion point in the italicized paragraph under the report title, then click the** Line Spacing list arrow **on the Formatting toolbar**

   The Line Spacing list opens. This list includes options for increasing the space between lines.

2. **Click** 1.5

   The space between the lines in the paragraph increases to 1.5 lines. Notice that you do not need to select an entire paragraph to change its paragraph formatting; simply place the insertion point in the paragraph you want to format.

QUICK TIP

Word recognizes any string of text that ends with a paragraph mark as a paragraph, including titles, headings, and single lines in a list.

3. **Scroll down until the heading** Advertising **is at the top of your screen, select the** four-line list **that begins with Ad Cost, click** , **then click** 1.5

   The line spacing between the selected paragraphs changes to 1.5. To change the paragraph-formatting features of more than one paragraph, you must select the paragraphs.

4. **Place the insertion point in the heading** Advertising, **click** Format **on the menu bar, then click** Paragraph

   The Paragraph dialog box opens, as shown in Figure C-8. You can use the Indents and Spacing tab to change line spacing and the spacing above and below paragraphs. Spacing between paragraphs is measured in points.

QUICK TIP

Adjusting the space between paragraphs is a more precise way to add white space to a document than inserting blank lines.

5. **Click the** After up arrow **in the Spacing section so that 6 pt appears, then click** OK

   Six points of space are added below the Advertising heading paragraph.

6. **Select** Advertising, **then click the** Format Painter button **on the Standard toolbar**

   The pointer changes to . The **Format Painter** is a powerful Word feature that allows you to copy all the format settings applied to the selected text to other text that you want to format the same way. The Format Painter is especially useful when you want to copy multiple format settings, but you can also use it to copy individual formats.

QUICK TIP

Using the Format Painter is not the same as using [F4]. Pressing [F4] repeats only the last action you took. You can use the Format Painter at any time to copy multiple format settings.

7. **Select** Events **with the** pointer, **then deselect the text**

   Six points of space are added below the Events heading paragraph and the pointer changes back to the I-beam pointer. Compare your document with Figure C-9.

8. **Select** Events, **then double-click**

   Double-clicking the Format Painter button allows the Format Painter to remain active until you turn it off. By keeping the Format Painter turned on you can apply formatting to multiple items.

9. **Scroll down, select the headings** Classes & Workshops, Publications, **and** Surveys **with the** pointer, **then click** to turn off the Format Painter

   The headings are formatted in 14-point Arial, bold, plum, with six points of space added below each heading paragraph.

10. **Press** [Ctrl][Home], **click** , **then click the** Save button **on the Standard toolbar**

FIGURE C-8: Indents and Spacing tab in Paragraph dialog box

Change the spacing above and below paragraphs

Change line spacing

Spacing After up arrow

Preview of selected settings

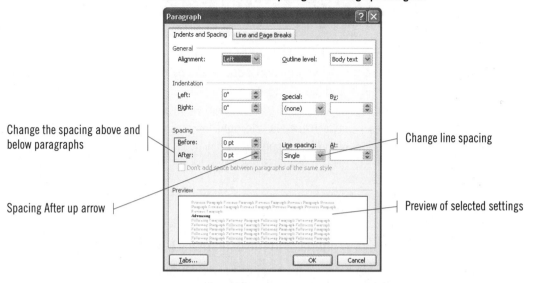

FIGURE C-9: Line and paragraph spacing applied to document

Format Painter button

Style list arrow

6 points of space added below heading paragraphs

Line Spacing list arrow

Line spacing is 1.5

Line spacing is 1

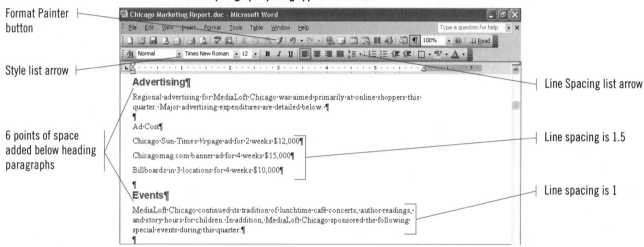

Clues to Use

Formatting with styles

You can also apply multiple format settings to text in one step by applying a style. A **style** is a set of formats, such as font, font size, and paragraph alignment, that are named and stored together. Styles can be applied to text, paragraphs, lists, and tables. To work with styles, click the Styles and Formatting button 🔠 on the Formatting toolbar to open the Styles and Formatting task pane, shown in Figure C-10. The task pane displays the list of available styles and the formats you have created for the current document. To view all the styles available in Word, click the Show list arrow at the bottom of the task pane, then click All Styles.

A **character style**, indicated by **a** in the list of styles, includes character format settings, such as font and font size. A **paragraph style**, indicated by ¶ in the list, is a combination of character and paragraph formats, such as font, font size, paragraph alignment, paragraph spacing, indents, and bullets and numbering. A **table style** indicated by ⊞ in the list, includes format settings for text in tables, as well as for table borders, shading, and alignment. Finally, a **list style**, indicated by ☷ in the list, includes indent and numbering format settings for an outline numbered list.

To apply a style, select the text, paragraph, or table you want to format, then click the style name in the Pick formatting to apply list box. To remove styles from text, select the text, then click Clear Formatting in the Pick formatting to apply list box. You can also apply and remove styles using the Style list arrow on the Formatting toolbar.

FIGURE C-10: Styles and Formatting task pane

Aligning Paragraphs

Changing paragraph alignment is another way to enhance a document's appearance. Paragraphs are aligned relative to the left and right margins in a document. By default, text is **left-aligned**, which means it is flush with the left margin and has a ragged right edge. Using the alignment buttons on the Formatting toolbar, you can **right-align** a paragraph—make it flush with the right margin—or **center** a paragraph so that it is positioned evenly between the left and right margins. You can also **justify** a paragraph so that both the left and right edges of the paragraph are flush with the left and right margins. You change the alignment of several paragraphs at the beginning of the report to make it more visually interesting.

STEPS

1. **Replace** Your Name, Today's Date **with your name, a comma, and the date**

2. **Select your name, the comma, and the date, then click the** Align Right button **on the Formatting toolbar**

   The text is aligned with the right margin. In Normal view, the junction of the white and shaded sections of the horizontal ruler indicates the location of the right margin. The left end of the ruler indicates the left margin.

3. **Place the insertion point between your name and the comma, press** [Delete] **to delete the comma, then press** [Enter]

   The new paragraph containing the date is also right-aligned. Pressing [Enter] in the middle of a paragraph creates a new paragraph with the same text and paragraph formatting as the original paragraph.

4. **Select the** report title, **then click the** Center button **on the Formatting toolbar**

   The two paragraphs that make up the title are centered between the left and right margins.

QUICK TIP

Click the Align Left button on the Formatting toolbar to left-align a paragraph.

5. **Place the insertion point in the** Advertising **heading, then click**

   The Advertising heading is centered.

6. **Place the insertion point in the italicized paragraph under the report title, then click the** Justify button

   The paragraph is aligned with both the left and right margins, as shown in Figure C-11. When you justify a paragraph, Word adjusts the spacing between words so that each line in the paragraph is flush with the left and the right margins.

7. **Place the insertion point in** MediaLoft **in the report title, click** Format **on the menu bar, then click** Reveal Formatting

   The Reveal Formatting task pane opens in the Word program window, as shown in Figure C-12. The Reveal Formatting task pane shows the formatting applied to the text and paragraph where the insertion point is located. You can use the Reveal Formatting task pane to check or change the formatting of any character, word, paragraph, or other aspect of a document.

8. **Select** Advertising, **then click the** Alignment **hyperlink in the Reveal Formatting task pane**

   The Paragraph dialog box opens with the Indents and Spacing tab displayed. It shows the settings for the selected text.

9. **Click the** Alignment list arrow, **click** Left, **click** OK, **then deselect the text**

   The Advertising heading is left-aligned.

10. **Close the Reveal Formatting task pane, then click the** Save button **on the Standard toolbar**

FIGURE C-11: Modified paragraph alignment

Right margin in Normal view

Right-aligned

Center-aligned

Justified

Left-aligned

FIGURE C-12: Reveal Formatting task pane

Insertion point indicates selected text

Click the minus sign to hide information

Click the plus sign to display information

Reveal Formatting task pane

Format settings for selected text

Click hyperlinks to change format settings

Select to show underlying style

Select to show formatting marks in document

Clues to Use

Comparing formatting

When two words or paragraphs in a document do not look exactly the same but you are not sure how they are formatted differently, you can use the Reveal Formatting task pane to compare the two selections to determine the differences. To compare the formatting of two text selections, select the first instance, select the Compare to another selection check box in the Reveal Formatting task pane, and then select the second instance. Differences in formatting between the two selections are listed in the Formatting differences section in the Reveal Formatting task pane. You can then use the hyperlinks in the Formatting differences section to make changes to the formatting of the second selection. If you want to format the second selection so that it matches the first, you can click the list arrow next to the second selection in the Selected text section, and then click Apply Formatting of Original Selection on the menu that appears. On the same menu, you can also click Select All Text with Similar Formatting to select all the text in the document that is formatted the same, or Clear Formatting to return the formatting of the selected text to the default.

Working with Tabs

Tabs allow you to align text vertically at a specific location in a document. A **tab stop** is a point on the horizontal ruler that indicates the location at which to align text. By default, tab stops are located every ½" from the left margin, but you can also set custom tab stops. Using tabs, you can align text to the left, right, or center of a tab stop, or you can align text at a decimal point or bar character. You set tabs using the horizontal ruler or the Tabs command on the Format menu. 🔲🔲🔲 You use tabs to format the information on advertising expenditures so it is easy to read.

STEPS

1. **Scroll down until the heading Advertising is at the top of your screen, then select the four-line list beginning with Ad Cost**

   Before you set tab stops for existing text, you must select the paragraphs for which you want to set tabs.

2. **Point to the tab indicator ⬛ at the left end of the horizontal ruler**

   The icon that appears in the tab indicator indicates the active type of tab; pointing to the tab indicator displays a ScreenTip with the name of the active tab type. By default, left tab is the active tab type. Clicking the tab indicator scrolls through the types of tabs and indents.

3. **Click the tab indicator to see each of the available tab and indent types, make left tab ⬛ the active tab type, then click the 1" mark on the horizontal ruler**

   A left tab stop is inserted at the 1" mark on the horizontal ruler. Clicking the horizontal ruler inserts a tab stop of the active type for the selected paragraph or paragraphs.

4. **Click the tab indicator twice so the Right Tab icon ⬛ is active, then click the 4½" mark on the horizontal ruler**

   A right tab stop is inserted at the 4½" mark on the horizontal ruler, as shown in Figure C-13.

5. **Place the insertion point before Ad in the first line in the list, press [Tab], place the insertion point before Cost, then press [Tab]**

   Inserting a tab before Ad left-aligns the text at the 1" mark. Inserting a tab before Cost right-aligns Cost at the 4½" mark.

6. **Insert a tab at the beginning of each remaining line in the list, then insert a tab before each $ in the list**

   The paragraphs left-align at the 1" mark. The prices right-align at the 4½" mark.

7. **Select the four lines of tabbed text, drag the right tab stop to the 5" mark on the horizontal ruler, then deselect the text**

   Dragging the tab stop moves it to a new location. The prices right-align at the 5" mark.

8. **Select the last three lines of tabbed text, click Format on the menu bar, then click Tabs**

   The Tabs dialog box opens, as shown in Figure C-14. You can use the Tabs dialog box to set tab stops, change the position or alignment of existing tab stops, clear tab stops, and apply tab leaders to tabs. **Tab leaders** are lines that appear in front of tabbed text.

9. **Click 5" in the Tab stop position list box, click the 2 option button in the Leader section, click OK, deselect the text, then click the Save button ⬛ on the Standard toolbar**

   A dotted tab leader is added before each 5" tab stop, as shown in Figure C-15.

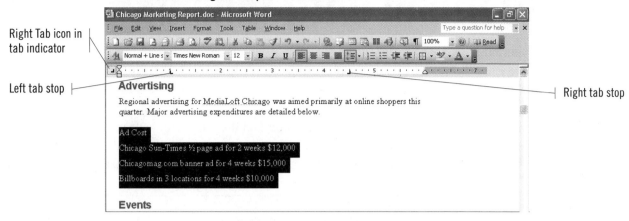

FIGURE C-13: Left and right tab stops on the horizontal ruler

Right Tab icon in tab indicator

Left tab stop

Right tab stop

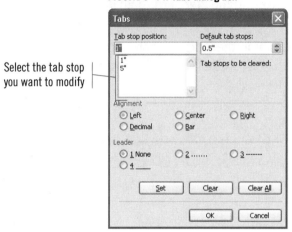

FIGURE C-14: Tabs dialog box

Select the tab stop you want to modify

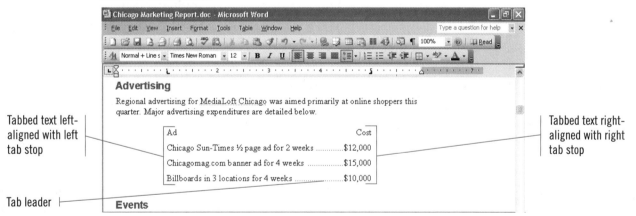

FIGURE C-15: Tab leaders

Tabbed text left-aligned with left tab stop

Tabbed text right-aligned with right tab stop

Tab leader

Clues to Use

Working with Click and Type

The **Click and Type** feature in Word allows you to automatically apply the paragraph formatting (alignment and indentation) necessary to insert text, graphics, or tables in a blank area of a document in Print Layout or Web Layout view. As you move the pointer around in a blank area of a document, the pointer changes depending on its location. Double-clicking with a click and type pointer in a blank area of a document automatically applies the appropriate alignment and indentation for that location, so that when you begin typing, the text

is already formatted. The pointer shape indicates which formatting is applied at each location when you double-click. For example, if you click with the ⊥ pointer, the text you type is center-aligned. Clicking with I⁼ creates a left tab stop at the location of the insertion point so that the text you type is left-aligned at the tab stop. Clicking with ⁼I right-aligns the text you type. The I⁼ pointer creates left-aligned text with a first line indent. The best way to learn how to use Click and Type is to experiment in a blank document.

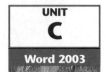
Working with Indents

When you **indent** a paragraph, you move its edge in from the left or right margin. You can indent the entire left or right edge of a paragraph, just the first line, or all lines except the first line. The **indent markers** on the horizontal ruler indicate the indent settings for the paragraph in which the insertion point is located. Dragging the indent markers to a new location on the ruler is one way to change the indentation of a paragraph; using the indent buttons on the Formatting toolbar is another. You can also use the Paragraph command on the Format menu to indent paragraphs. Table C-1 describes different types of indents and the methods for creating each. You indent several paragraphs in the report.

STEPS

1. **Press** [Ctrl][Home], **click the** Print Layout View button 🔲 **on the horizontal scroll bar, click the** Zoom list arrow **on the Standard toolbar, then click** Page Width

   The document is displayed in Print Layout view, making it easier to see the document margins.

> **QUICK TIP**
> Press [Tab] at the beginning of a paragraph to indent the first line ½". You can also set a custom indent using the Indents and Spacing tab in the Paragraph dialog box.

2. **Place the insertion point in the italicized paragraph under the title, then click the** Increase Indent button 🔳 **on the Formatting toolbar**

   The entire paragraph is indented ½" from the left margin, as shown in Figure C-16. The indent marker ⟨ also moves to the ½" mark on the horizontal ruler. Each time you click the Increase Indent button, the left edge of a paragraph moves another ½" to the right.

3. **Click the** Decrease Indent button 🔳 **on the Formatting toolbar**

   The left edge of the paragraph moves ½" to the left, and the indent marker moves back to the left margin.

> **TROUBLE**
> Take care to drag only the First Line Indent marker. If you make a mistake, click the Undo button ↺, then try again.

4. **Drag the** First Line Indent marker ▽ **to the** ¼" **mark on the horizontal ruler as shown in Figure C-17**

   The first line of the paragraph is indented ¼". Dragging the first line indent marker indents only the first line of a paragraph.

5. **Scroll to the bottom of page 1, place the insertion point in the** quotation **(the last paragraph), then drag the** Left Indent marker ☐ **to the** ½" **mark on the horizontal ruler**

   When you drag the Left Indent marker, the First Line and Hanging Indent markers move as well. The left edge of the paragraph is indented ½" from the left margin.

6. **Drag the** Right Indent marker △ **to the** 5½" **mark on the horizontal ruler**

   The right edge of the paragraph is indented ½" from the right margin, as shown in Figure C-18.

7. **Click the** Save button 🔲 **on the Standard toolbar**

TABLE C-1: Types of indents

indent type	description	to create
Left indent	The left edge of a paragraph is moved in from the left margin	Drag the Left Indent marker ☐ right to the position where you want the left edge of the paragraph to align, or click the Increase Indent button 🔳 to indent the paragraph in ½" increments
Right indent	The right edge of a paragraph is moved in from the right margin	Drag the Right Indent marker △ left to the position where you want the right edge of the paragraph to end
First-line indent	The first line of a paragraph is indented more than the subsequent lines	Drag the First Line Indent marker ▽ right to the position where you want the first line of the paragraph to start
Hanging indent	The subsequent lines of a paragraph are indented more than the first line	Drag the Hanging Indent marker ⬠ right to the position where you want the hanging indent to start
Negative indent (or Outdent)	The left edge of a paragraph is moved to the left of the left margin	Drag the Left Indent marker ☐ left to the position where you want the negative indent to start

FIGURE C-16: Indented paragraph

First Line Indent marker

Hanging Indent marker

Left Indent marker

Indented paragraph

Right Indent marker

Increase Indent button

Decrease Indent button

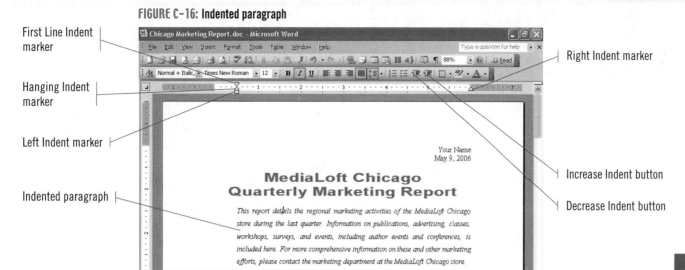

FIGURE C-17: Dragging the First Line Indent marker

First Line Indent marker being dragged to the ¼" mark

Dotted line shows positon of First Line Indent marker

FIGURE C-18: Paragraph indented from the left and right

Paragraph indented ½" from left margin

Paragraph indented ½" from right margin

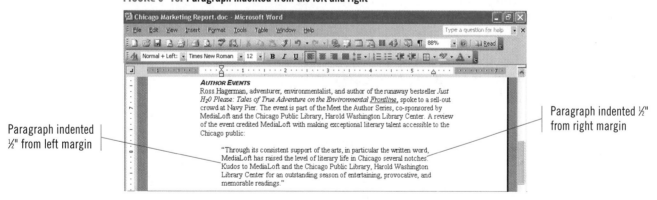

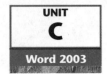

Adding Bullets and Numbering

Formatting a list with bullets or numbering can help to organize the ideas in a document. A **bullet** is a character, often a small circle, that appears before the items in a list to add emphasis. Formatting a list as a numbered list helps illustrate sequences and priorities. You can quickly format a list with bullets or numbering by using the Bullets and Numbering buttons on the Formatting toolbar. You can also use the Bullets and Numbering command on the Format menu to change or customize bullet and numbering styles. You format the lists in your report with numbers and bullets.

STEPS

1. **Scroll down until the first paragraph on the second page (Authors on our...) is at the top of your screen**

2. **Select the** three-line list of names **under the paragraph, then click the** Numbering button ⊞ **on the Formatting toolbar**
   The paragraphs are formatted as a numbered list.

3. **Place the insertion point after** Jack Seneschal, **press** [Enter], **then type** Polly Flanagan
   Pressing [Enter] in the middle of the numbered list creates a new numbered paragraph and automatically renumbers the remainder of the list. Similarly, if you delete a paragraph from a numbered list, Word automatically renumbers the remaining paragraphs.

4. **Click** 1 **in the list**
   Clicking a number in a list selects all the numbers, as shown in Figure C-19.

5. **Click the** Bold button ⊞ **on the Formatting toolbar**
   The numbers are all formatted in bold. Notice that the formatting of the items in the list does not change when you change the formatting of the numbers. You can also use this technique to change the formatting of bullets in a bulleted list.

6. **Select the** list of classes and workshops **under the Classes & Workshops heading, scrolling down if necessary, then click the** Bullets button ⊞ **on the Formatting toolbar**
   The five paragraphs are formatted as a bulleted list.

7. **With the list still selected, click** Format **on the menu bar, then click** Bullets and Numbering
   The Bullets and Numbering dialog box opens with the Bulleted tab displayed, as shown in Figure C-20. You use this dialog box to apply bullets and numbering to paragraphs, or to change the style of bullets or numbers.

8. **Click the** Square bullets box **or select another style if square bullets are not available to you, click** OK, **then deselect the text**
   The bullet character changes to a small square, as shown in Figure C-21.

9. **Click the** Save button ⊞ **on the Standard toolbar**

Clues to Use

Creating outlines

You can create lists with hierarchical structures by applying an outline numbering style to a list. To create an outline, begin by applying an outline numbering style from the Outline Numbered tab in the Bullets and Numbering dialog box, then type your outline, pressing [Enter] after each item. To demote items to a lower level of importance in the outline, place the insertion point in the item, then click the Increase Indent button ⊞ on the Formatting toolbar. Each time you indent a paragraph, the item is demoted to a lower lever in the outline. Similarly, you can use the Decrease Indent button ⊞ to promote an item to a higher level in the outline. You can also create a hierarchical structure in any bulleted or numbered list by using ⊞ and ⊞ to demote and promote items in the list. To change the outline numbering style applied to a list, select a new style from the Outline Numbered tab in the Bullets and Numbering dialog box.

FIGURE C-19: Numbered list

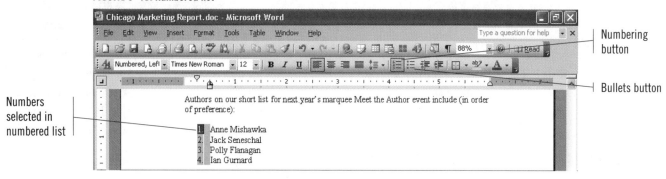

Numbering button

Bullets button

Numbers selected in numbered list

FIGURE C-20: Bulleted tab in the Bullets and Numbering dialog box

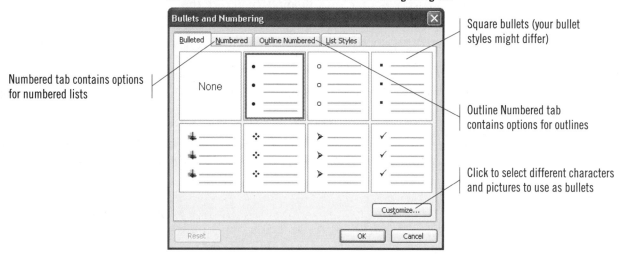

Numbered tab contains options for numbered lists

Square bullets (your bullet styles might differ)

Outline Numbered tab contains options for outlines

Click to select different characters and pictures to use as bullets

FIGURE C-21: Square bullets applied to list

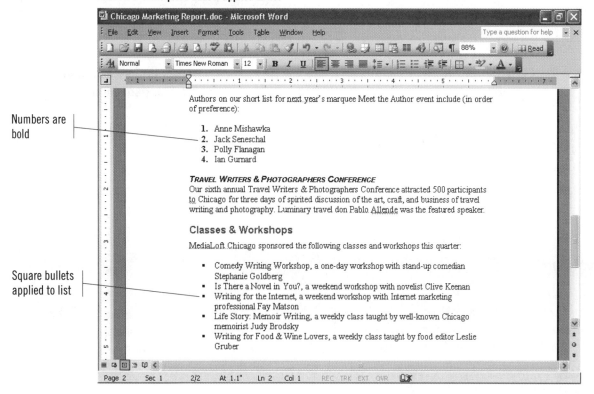

Numbers are bold

Square bullets applied to list

Word 2003

Adding Borders and Shading

Borders and shading can add color and splash to a document. **Borders** are lines you add above, below, to the side, or around words or a paragraph. You can format borders using different line styles, colors, and widths. **Shading** is a color or pattern you apply behind words or paragraphs to make them stand out on a page. You apply borders and shading using the Borders and Shading command on the Format menu. You enhance the advertising expenses table by adding shading to it. You also apply a border under every heading to visually punctuate the sections of the report.

STEPS

1. **Scroll up until the heading Advertising is at the top of your screen**

2. **Select the four paragraphs of tabbed text under the Advertising heading, click Format on the menu bar, click Borders and Shading, then click the Shading tab**
   The Shading tab in the Borders and Shading dialog box is shown in Figure C-22. You use this tab to apply shading to words and paragraphs.

3. **Click the Lavender box in the bottom row of the Fill section, click OK, then deselect the text**
   Lavender shading is applied to the four paragraphs. Notice that the shading is applied to the entire width of the paragraphs, despite the tab settings.

4. **Select the four paragraphs, drag the Left Indent marker ⬚ to the ¾" mark on the horizontal ruler, drag the Right Indent marker △ to the 5¼" mark, then deselect the text**
   The shading for the paragraphs is indented from the left and right, making it look more attractive.

5. **Select Advertising, click Format on the menu bar, click Borders and Shading, then click the Borders tab**
   The Borders tab is shown in Figure C-23. You use this tab to add boxes and lines to words or paragraphs.

> **QUICK TIP**
> When creating custom borders, it's important to select the style, color, and width settings before applying the borders in the Preview section.

6. **Click the Custom box in the Setting section, click the Width list arrow, click ¾ pt, click the Bottom Border button ⊞ in the Preview section, click OK, then deselect the text**
   A ¾-point black border is added below the Advertising paragraph.

7. **Click Events, press [F4], scroll down and use [F4] to add a border under each plum heading, press [Ctrl] [Home], then click the Save button ⊟ on the Standard toolbar**
   The completed document is shown in Figure C-24.

8. **Click the Print button ⊟, close the document, then exit Word**
   A copy of the report prints. Depending on your printer, colors might appear differently when you print. If you are using a black-and-white printer, colors will print in shades of gray.

Clues to Use

Highlighting text in a document

The Highlight tool allows you to mark and find important text in a document. **Highlighting** is transparent color that is applied to text using the Highlight pointer ⬧. To highlight text, click the Highlight list arrow ⬚ on the Formatting toolbar, select a color, then use the I-beam part of the ⬧ pointer to select the text. Click ⬚ to turn off the Highlight pointer. To remove highlighting, select the highlighted text, click ⬚, then click None. Highlighting prints, but it is used most effectively when a document is viewed on screen.

FIGURE C-22: Shading tab in Borders and Shading dialog box

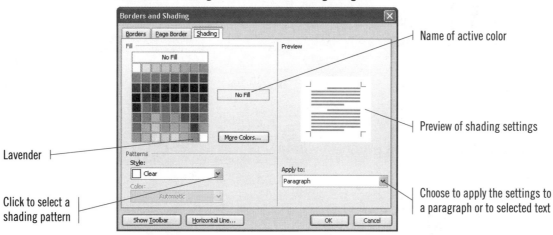

Name of active color

Preview of shading settings

Lavender

Click to select a shading pattern

Choose to apply the settings to a paragraph or to selected text

FIGURE C-23: Borders tab in Borders and Shading dialog box

Select border formats before applying them in the Preview area

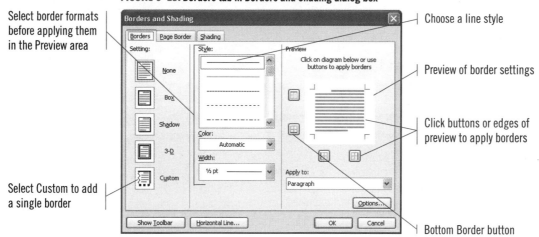

Choose a line style

Preview of border settings

Click buttons or edges of preview to apply borders

Select Custom to add a single border

Bottom Border button

FIGURE C-24: Borders and shading applied to the document

Border under headings

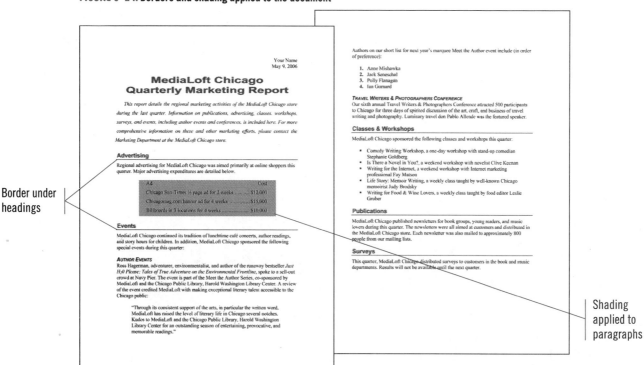

Shading applied to paragraphs

Word 2003

Practice

▼ CONCEPTS REVIEW

Label each element of the Word program window shown in Figure C-25.

FIGURE C-25

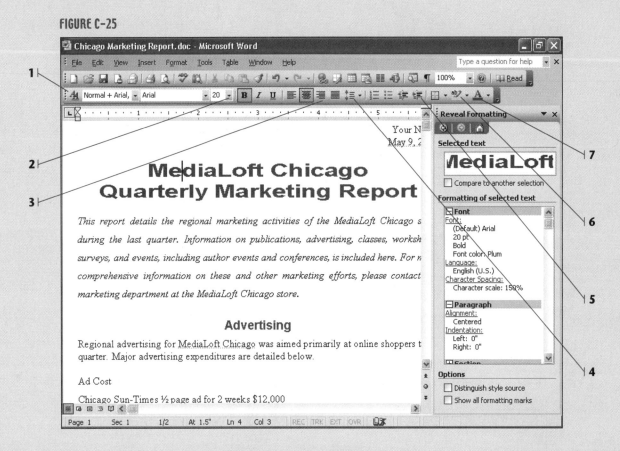

Match each term with the statement that best describes it.

8. **Bold**
9. **Shading**
10. **Point**
11. **Style**
12. **Italic**
13. **Highlight**
14. **Bullet**
15. **Border**

a. A character that appears at the beginning of a paragraph to add emphasis
b. Transparent color that is applied to text to mark it in a document
c. A text style in which characters are slanted
d. Color or a pattern that is applied behind text to make it look attractive
e. A set of format settings
f. A unit of measurement equal to ½ of an inch
g. A line that can be applied above, below, or to the sides of a paragraph
h. A text style in which characters are darker and thicker

Select the best answer from the list of choices.

16. Which button is used to align a paragraph with both the left and right margins?

a. [icon]

b. [icon]

c. [icon]

d. [icon]

17. What is Arial?

a. A style

b. A character format

c. A text effect

d. A font

18. What is the most precise way to increase the amount of white space between two paragraphs?

a. Insert an extra blank line between the paragraphs.

b. Change the line spacing of the paragraphs.

c. Indent the paragraphs.

d. Use the Paragraph command to change the spacing below the first paragraph.

19. What element of the Word program window can be used to check the tab settings applied to text?

a. Formatting toolbar

b. Standard toolbar

c. Reveal Formatting task pane

d. Styles and Formatting task pane

20. Which command would you use to apply color behind a paragraph?

a. Background

b. Styles and Formatting

c. Borders and Shading

d. Paragraph

▼ SKILLS REVIEW

1. Format with fonts.

a. Start Word, open the file WD C-2.doc from the drive and folder where your Data Files are located, save it as **EDA Report**, then scroll through the document to get a feel for its contents.

b. Press [Ctrl][Home], format the report title **Richmond Springs Economic Development Report Executive Summary** in 26-point Tahoma. Choose a different font if Tahoma is not available to you.

c. Change the font color of the report title to Teal, then press [Enter] after Springs in the title.

d. Place the insertion point in the first body paragraph under the title, then add a two-line drop cap to the paragraph using the Dropped position.

e. Format each of the following headings in 14-point Tahoma with the Teal font color: **Mission Statement**, **Guiding Principles**, **Issues**, **Proposed Actions**.

f. Press [Ctrl][Home], then save your changes to the report.

2. Change font styles and effects.

a. Apply bold to the report title and to each heading in the report.

b. Show formatting marks, then format the paragraph under the Mission Statement heading in italic.

c. Format **Years Population Growth**, the first line in the four-line list under the Issues heading, in bold, small caps, with a Teal font color.

d. Change the font color of the next two lines under Years Population Growth to Teal.

e. Format the line **Source: Office of State Planning** in italic.

f. Scroll to the top of the report, change the character scale of **Richmond Springs Economic Development Report** to 80%, then save your changes.

3. Change line and paragraph spacing.

   a. Change the line spacing of the three-line list under the first body paragraph to 1.5 lines.

   b. Add 12 points of space before the Executive Summary line in the title.

   c. Add 12 points of space after each heading in the report (but not the title).

   d. Add 6 points of space after each paragraph in the list under the Guiding Principles heading.

   e. Add 6 points of space after each paragraph under the Proposed Actions heading.

   f. Press [Ctrl][Home], then save your changes to the report.

4. Align paragraphs.

   a. Press [Ctrl][A] to select the entire document, then justify all the paragraphs.

   b. Center the three-line report title.

   c. Press [Ctrl][End], type your name, press [Enter], type the current date, then right-align your name and the date.

   d. Save your changes to the report.

5. Work with tabs.

   a. Scroll up and select the four-line list of population information under the Issues heading.

   b. Set left tab stops at the 1¾" mark and the 3" mark.

   c. Insert a tab at the beginning of each line in the list.

   d. In the first line, insert a tab before Population. In the second line, insert a tab before 4.5%. In the third line, insert a tab before 53%.

   e. Select the first three lines, then drag the second tab stop to the 2¾" mark on the horizontal ruler.

   f. Press [Ctrl][Home], then save your changes to the report.

6. Work with indents.

   a. Indent the paragraph under the Mission Statement heading ½" from the left and ½" from the right.

   b. Indent the first line of the paragraph under the Guiding Principles heading ½".

   c. Indent the first line of the three body paragraphs under the Issues heading ½".

   d. Press [Ctrl][Home], then save your changes to the report.

7. Add bullets and numbering.

   a. Apply bullets to the three-line list under the first body paragraph.

   b. Change the bullet style to small black circles (or choose another bullet style if small black circles are not available to you).

   c. Change the font color of the bullets to Teal.

   d. Scroll down until the Guiding Principles heading is at the top of your screen.

   e. Format the six-paragraph list under Guiding Principles as a numbered list.

   f. Format the numbers in 12-point Tahoma bold, then change the font color to Teal.

   g. Scroll down until the Proposed Actions heading is at the top of your screen, then format the paragraphs under the heading as a bulleted list using check marks as the bullet style. If checkmarks are not available, click Reset or choose another bullet style.

   h. Change the font color of the bullets to Teal, press [Ctrl][Home], then save your changes to the report.

8. Add borders and shading.

   a. Change the font color of the report title to Light Yellow, then apply Teal shading.

   b. Add a 1-point Teal border below the Mission Statement heading.

   c. Use the Format Painter to copy the formatting of the Mission Statement heading to the other headings in the report.

   d. Under the Issues heading, select the first three lines of tabbed text, which are formatted in Teal.

▼ SKILLS REVIEW (CONTINUED)

e. Apply Light Yellow shading to the paragraphs, then add a 1-point Teal box border around the paragraphs.

f. Indent the shading and border around the paragraphs 1½" from the left and 1½" from the right.

g. Press [Ctrl][Home], save your changes to the report, view the report in Print Preview, then print a copy. The formatted report is shown in Figure C-26.

h. Close the file and exit Word.

FIGURE C-26

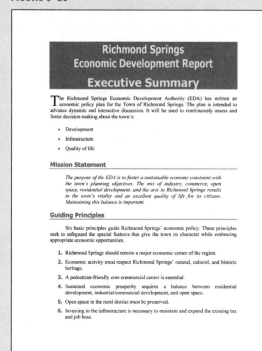

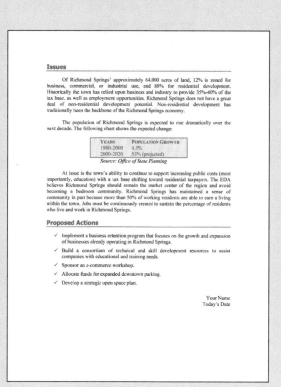

▼ INDEPENDENT CHALLENGE 1

You are an estimator for Zephir Construction in the Australian city of Wollongong. You have drafted an estimate for a home renovation job, and need to format it. It's important that your estimate have a clean, striking design, and reflect your company's professionalism.

a. Start Word, open the file WD C-3.doc from the drive and folder where your Data Files are located, save it as **Zephir Construction**, then read the document to get a feel for its contents. Figure C-27 shows how you will format the letterhead.

FIGURE C-27

ZEPHIRConstruction
73 Corrimal Street, Wollongong, NSW 2500
Tel: 02-4225-3202; www.zephir.com.au

b. In the first paragraph, format **ZEPHIR** in 24-point Arial Black, then apply bold. (*Hint*: Select a similar font if Arial Black is not available to you.)

c. Format **Construction** in 24-point Arial, then change the character scale to 90%.

d. Format the next two lines in 9-point Arial bold, center the three-line letterhead, then add a 1-point black border below the last line.

e. Format the title **Proposal of Renovation** in 16-point Arial Black, then center the title.

f. Format the following headings (including the colons) in 12-point Arial Black: **Date**, **Work to be performed for and at**, **Scope of work**, **Payment schedule**, and **Agreement**.

g. Format the 14-line list under **Scope of work** that begins with **Demo of all ...** as a numbered list, then apply bold to the numbers.

▼ INDEPENDENT CHALLENGE 1 (CONTINUED)

h. Change the paragraph spacing to add 4 points of space after each paragraph in the list. (*Hint*: Select 0 pt in the After text box, then type 4.)

i. With the list selected, set a right tab stop at the 5¾" mark, then insert tabs before every price in the list.

j. Apply bold to the two lines, Total estimated job cost... and Approximate job time... below the list.

k. Replace Your Name with your name in the signature block, select the signature block (Respectfully submitted through your name), set a left tab stop at the 3½" mark, then indent the signature block.

l. Examine the document carefully for formatting errors and make any necessary adjustments.

m. Save and print the document, then close the file and exit Word.

▼ INDEPENDENT CHALLENGE 2

Your employer, The Lange Center for Contemporary Arts in Halifax, Nova Scotia, is launching a membership drive. Your boss has written the text for a flyer advertising Lange membership, and asks you to format it so that it is eye catching and attractive.

a. Open the file WD C-4.doc from the drive and folder where your Data Files are located, save it as Membership Flyer, then read the document. Figure C-28 shows how you will format the first several paragraphs of the flyer.

b. Select the entire document and format it in 10-point Arial Narrow.

FIGURE C-28

c. Center the first line, Membership Drive, and apply indigo shading to the paragraph. Format the text in 26-point Arial Narrow, bold, with a white font color. Expand the character spacing by 7 points.

d. Format the second line, 2006, in 36-point Arial Black. Expand the character spacing by 25 points and change the character scale to 200%. Center the line.

e. Format each What we do for... heading in 12-point Arial, bold, with an indigo font color. Add a single line ½-point border under each heading.

f. Format each subheading (Gallery, Lectures, Library, All members..., and Membership Levels) in 10-point Arial, bold. Add 3 points of spacing before each paragraph.

g. Indent each body paragraph ¼", except for the lines under the What we do for YOU heading.

h. Format the four lines under the All members... subheading as a bulleted list. Use a bullet symbol of your choice and format the bullets in the indigo color.

i. Indent the five lines under the Membership Levels heading ¼". For these five lines, set left tab stops at the 1¼" mark and the 2" mark on the horizontal ruler. Insert tabs before the price and before the word All in each of the five lines.

j. Format the name of each membership level (Artistic, Conceptual, etc.) in 10-point Arial, bold, italic, with an indigo font color.

k. Format the For more information heading in 14-point Arial, bold, with an indigo font color, then center the heading.

l. Format the last two lines in 11-point Arial Narrow, and center the lines. In the contact information, replace Your Name with your name, then apply bold to your name.

Advanced Challenge Exercise

- Change the font color of 2006 to 80% gray and add a shadow effect.
- Add an emboss effect to each subheading.
- Add a 3-point dotted black border above the For more information heading.

m. Examine the document carefully for formatting errors and make any necessary adjustments.

n. Save and print the flyer, then close the file and exit Word.

▼ INDEPENDENT CHALLENGE 3

One of your responsibilities as program coordinator at Solstice Mountain Sports is to develop a program of winter outdoor learning and adventure workshops. You have drafted a memo to your boss to update her on your progress. You need to format the memo so it is professional looking and easy to read.

a. Start Word, open the file WD C-5.doc from the drive and folder where your Data Files are located, then save it as **Solstice Memo**.

b. Select the heading **Solstice Mountain Sports Memorandum**, then apply the paragraph style Heading 1 to it. (*Hint*: Open the Styles and Formatting task pane, click the Show list arrow, click Available Styles if necessary, then click Heading 1.)

c. In the memo header, replace Today's Date and Your Name with the current date and your name.

d. Select the four-line memo header, set a left tab stop at the ¾" mark, then insert tabs before the date, the recipient's name, your name, and the subject of the memo.

e. Double-space the four lines in the memo header, then apply the character style Strong to **Date:**, **To:**, **From:**, and **Re:**.

f. Apply a 1½-point double line border below the blank line under the memo header. (*Hint*: Turn on formatting marks, select the paragraph symbol below the memo header, then apply a border below it.)

g. Apply the paragraph style Heading 3 to the headings **Overview**, **Workshops**, **Accommodation**, **Fees**, and **Proposed winter programming**.

h. Under the Fees heading, format the words **Workshop fees** and **Accommodation fees** in bold italic.

i. Add 6 points of space after the Workshop fees paragraph.

Advanced Challenge Exercise

- Format **Fees** as animated text using the Las Vegas Lights animation style.
- After Fees, type **Verify prices with the Moose Lodge**, then format the text as hidden text.
- In the Fees section, apply yellow highlighting to the prices.

j. On the second page of the document, format the list under the **Proposed winter programming** heading as an outline. Figure C-29 shows the hierarchical structure of the outline. (*Hint*: Format the list as an outline numbered list, then use the Increase Indent and Decrease Indent buttons to change the level of importance of each item.)

k. Change the outline numbering style to the bullet numbering style shown in Figure C-29, if necessary.

l. Save and print the document, then close the file and exit Word.

▼ INDEPENDENT CHALLENGE 4

The fonts you choose for a document can have a major effect on the document's tone. Not all fonts are appropriate for use in a business document, and some fonts, especially those with a definite theme, are appropriate only for specific purposes. The World Wide Web includes hundreds of Web sites devoted to fonts and text design. Some Web sites sell fonts, others allow you to download fonts for free and install them on your computer. In this Independent Challenge, you will research Web sites related to fonts and find examples of fonts you can use in your work.

a. Start Word, open the file WD C-6.doc from the drive and folder where your Data Files are located, and save it as **Fonts**. This document contains the questions you will answer about the fonts you find.

b. Use your favorite search engine to search the Web for Web sites related to fonts. Use the keyword **font** to conduct your search.

c. Explore the fonts available for downloading. As you examine the fonts, notice that fonts fall into two general categories: serif fonts, which have a small stroke, called a serif, at the ends of each character, and sans serif fonts, which do not have a serif. Times New Roman is an example of a serif font and Arial is an example of a sans serif font.

d. Replace Your Name and Today's Date with the current date and your name, type your answers in the Fonts document, save it, print a copy, then close the file and exit Word.

FIGURE C-29

Proposed winter programming

- ❖ Skiing, Snowboarding, and Snowshoeing
  - ➢ Skiing and Snowboarding
    - ▪ Cross-country skiing
      - • Cross-country skiing for beginners
      - • Intermediate cross-country skiing
      - • Inn-to-inn ski touring
      - • Moonlight cross-country skiing
    - ▪ Telemarking
      - • Basic telemark skiing
      - • Introduction to backcountry skiing
      - • Exploring on skis
    - ▪ Snowboarding
      - • Backcountry snowboarding
  - ➢ Snowshoeing
    - ▪ Beginner
      - • Snowshoeing for beginners
      - • Snowshoeing and winter ecology
    - ▪ Intermediate and Advanced
      - • Intermediate snowshoeing
      - • Guided snowshoe trek
      - • Above tree line snowshoeing
- ❖ Winter Hiking, Camping, and Survival
  - ➢ Hiking
    - ▪ Beginner
      - • Long-distance hiking
      - • Winter summits
      - • Hiking for women
  - ➢ Winter camping and survival
    - ▪ Beginner
      - • Introduction to winter camping
      - • Basic winter mountain skills
      - • Building snow shelters
    - ▪ Intermediate
      - • Basic winter mountain skills II
      - • Ice climbing
      - • Avalanche awareness and rescue

Using the file WD C-7.doc found in the drive and folder where your Data Files are located, create the menu shown in Figure C-30. (*Hints*: Use Centaur or a similar font. Change the font size of the heading to 56 points, scale the font to 90%, and expand the spacing by 1 point. For the rest of the text, change the font size of the daily specials to 18 points and the descriptions to 14 points. Format the prices using tabs. Use paragraph spacing to adjust the spacing between paragraphs so that all the text fits on one page.) Save the menu as **Melting Pot Specials**, then print a copy.

FIGURE C-30

The Melting Pot Café

Daily Specials

Monday: Veggie Chili
Hearty veggie chili with melted cheddar in our peasant French bread bowl. Topped with sour cream & scallions..$5.95

Tuesday: Greek Salad
Our large garden salad with kalamata olives, feta cheese, and garlic vinaigrette. Served with an assortment of rolls. $5.95

Wednesday: French Dip
Lean roast beef topped with melted cheddar on our roasted garlic roll. Served with a side of au jus and red bliss mashed potatoes. $6.95

Thursday: Chicken Cajun Bleu
Cajun chicken, chunky blue cheese, cucumbers, leaf lettuce, and tomato on our roasted garlic roll. $6.50

Friday: Clam Chowder
Classic New England thick, rich, clam chowder in our peasant French bread bowl. Served with a garden salad. $5.95

Saturday: Hot Chicken and Gravy
Delicious chicken and savory gravy served on a thick slice of toasted honest white. Served with red bliss mashed potatoes..$6.95

Sunday: Turkey-Bacon Club
Double-decker roasted turkey, crisp bacon, leaf lettuce, tomato, and sun-dried tomato mayo on toasted triple seed...$6.50

Chef: Your Name

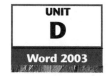

Formatting Documents

OBJECTIVES

Set document margins
Divide a document into sections
Insert page breaks
Insert page numbers
Add headers and footers
Edit headers and footers
Format columns
Insert a table
Insert WordArt
Insert clip art

If you have a SAM user profile, you may have access to hands-on instruction, practice, and assessment of the skills covered in this unit. Log in to your SAM account and go to your assignments page to see what your instructor has assigned.

The page-formatting features of Word allow you to creatively lay out and design the pages of your documents. In this unit, you learn how to change the document margins, determine page orientation, add page numbers, and insert headers and footers. You also learn how to format text in columns and how to illustrate your documents with tables, clip art, and WordArt. You have written and formatted the text for the quarterly newsletter for the marketing staff. You are now ready to lay out and design the newsletter pages. You plan to organize the articles in columns and to illustrate the newsletter with a table, clip art, and WordArt.

Setting Document Margins

Changing a document's margins is one way to change the appearance of a document and control the amount of text that fits on a page. The **margins** of a document are the blank areas between the edge of the text and the edge of the page. When you create a document in Word, the default margins are 1" at the top and bottom of the page, and 1.25" on the left and right sides of the page. You can adjust the size of a document's margins using the Page Setup command on the File menu, or using the rulers. ▓▓▓▓ The newsletter should be a four-page document when finished. You begin formatting the pages by reducing the size of the document margins so that more text fits on each page.

STEPS

1. **Start Word, open the file** WD D-1.doc **from the drive and folder where your Data Files are located, then save it as** MediaLoft Buzz

   The newsletter opens in Print Layout view.

2. **Scroll through the newsletter to get a feel for its contents, then press** [Ctrl][Home]

   The newsletter is currently five pages long. Notice the status bar indicates the page where the insertion point is located and the total number of pages in the document.

3. **Click** File **on the menu bar, click** Page Setup, **then click the** Margins tab **in the Page Setup dialog box if it is not already selected**

   The Margins tab in the Page Setup dialog box is shown in Figure D-1. You can use the Margins tab to change the top, bottom, left, or right document margins, to change the orientation of the pages from portrait to landscape, and to alter other page layout settings. **Portrait orientation** means a page is taller than it is wide; **landscape orientation** means a page is wider than it is tall. This newsletter uses portrait orientation.

4. **Click the** Top down arrow **three times until 0.7" appears, then click the** Bottom down arrow **until 0.7" appears**

   The top and bottom margins of the newsletter will be .7". Notice that the margins in the Preview section of the dialog box change as you adjust the margin settings.

5. **Press** [Tab], **type** .7 **in the Left text box, press** [Tab], **then type** .7 **in the Right text box**

   The left and right margins of the newsletter will also be .7". You can change the margin settings by using the arrows or by typing a value in the appropriate text box.

6. **Click** OK

   The document margins change to .7", as shown in Figure D-2. The bar at the intersection of the white and shaded areas on the horizontal and vertical rulers indicates the location of the margin. You can also change a document's margins by dragging the bar to a new location.

7. **Click the** Zoom list arrow **on the Standard toolbar, then click** Two Pages

   The first two pages of the document appear in the document window.

8. **Scroll down to view all five pages of the newsletter, press** [Ctrl][Home], **click the** Zoom list arrow, **click** Page Width, **then click the** Save button 🔲 **on the Standard toolbar to save the document**

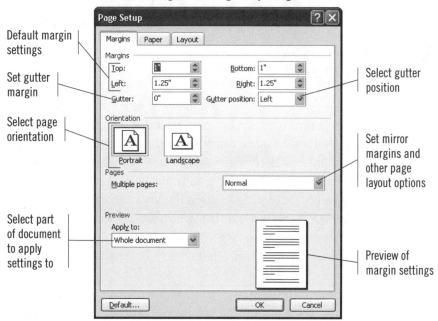

Default margin settings

Set gutter margin

Select page orientation

Select part of document to apply settings to

Select gutter position

Set mirror margins and other page layout options

Preview of margin settings

FIGURE D-2: Newsletter with smaller margins

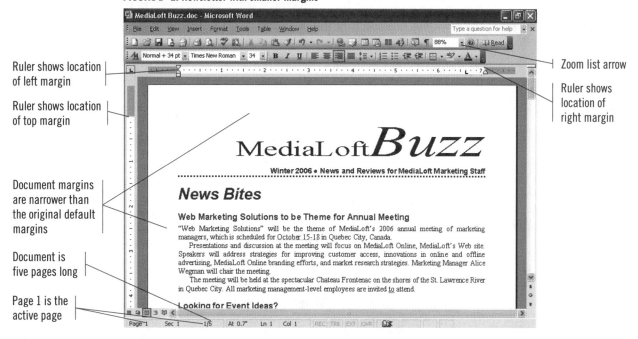

Ruler shows location of left margin

Ruler shows location of top margin

Document margins are narrower than the original default margins

Document is five pages long

Page 1 is the active page

Zoom list arrow

Ruler shows location of right margin

Clues to Use

Changing orientation, margin settings, and paper size

By default, the documents you create in Word use an 8½" × 11" paper size in portrait orientation with the default margin settings. You can adjust these settings in the Page Setup dialog box to create documents that are a different size, shape, or layout. On the Margins tab, change the orientation of the pages by selecting Portrait or Landscape. To change the layout of multiple pages, use the Multiple pages list arrow to create pages that use mirror margins, that include two pages per sheet of paper, or that are formatted like a folded booklet. **Mirror margins** are used in documents with facing pages, such as a magazine, where the margins on the left page of the document are a mirror image of the margins on the right page. Documents with mirror margins have inside and outside margins, rather than right and left margins. Another type of margin is a gutter margin, which is used in documents that are bound, such as books. A **gutter** adds extra space to the left, top, or inside margin to allow for the binding. Add a gutter to a document by adjusting the setting in the Gutter text box on the Margins tab. If you want to change the size of the paper used in a document, use the Paper tab in the Page Setup dialog box. Use the Paper size list arrow to select a standard paper size, or enter custom measurements in the Width and Height text boxes.

Word 2003

Dividing a Document into Sections

Dividing a document into sections allows you to format each section of the document with different page layout settings. A **section** is a portion of a document that is separated from the rest of the document by section breaks. **Section breaks** are formatting marks that you insert in a document to show the end of a section. Once you have divided a document into sections, you can format each section with different column, margin, page orientation, header and footer, and other page layout settings. By default, a document is formatted as a single section, but you can divide a document into as many sections as you like. ▰▰▰▰ You want to format the body of the newsletter in two columns, but leave the masthead and the headline "News Bites" as a single column. You insert a section break before the body of the newsletter to divide the document into two sections, and then change the number of columns in the second section to two.

STEPS

1. **Click the** Show/Hide ¶ button ▣ **on the Standard toolbar to display formatting marks if they are not visible**

   Turning on formatting marks allows you to see the section breaks you insert in a document.

QUICK TIP
When you insert a section break at the beginning of a paragraph, Word inserts the break at the end of the previous paragraph. A section break stores the formatting information for the preceding section.

2. **Place the insertion point before the headline** Web Marketing Solutions to be..., **click** Insert **on the menu bar, then click** Break

   The Break dialog box opens, as shown in Figure D-3. You use this dialog box to insert different types of section breaks. Table D-1 describes the different types of section breaks.

3. **Click the** Continuous option button, **then click** OK

   Word inserts a continuous section break, shown as a dotted double line, above the headline. A continuous section break begins a new section of the document on the same page. The document now has two sections. Notice that the status bar indicates that the insertion point is in section 2.

4. **With the insertion point in section 2, click the** Columns button ▦ **on the Standard toolbar**

   A grid showing four columns opens. You use the grid to select the number of columns you want to create.

5. **Point to the** second column **on the grid, then click**

   Section 2 is formatted in two columns, as shown in Figure D-4. The text in section 1 remains formatted in a single column. Notice the status bar now indicates the document is four pages long. Formatting text in columns is another way to increase the amount of text that fits on a page.

6. **Click the** Zoom list arrow **on the Standard toolbar, click** Two Pages, **then scroll down to examine all four pages of the document**

   The text in section 2—all the text below the continuous section break—is formatted in two columns. Text in columns flows automatically from the bottom of one column to the top of the next column.

7. **Press** [Ctrl][Home], **click the** Zoom list arrow, **click** Page Width, **then save the document**

TABLE D-1: Types of section breaks

section	function
Next page	Begins a new section and moves the text following the break to the top of the next page
Continuous	Begins a new section on the same page
Even page	Begins a new section and moves the text following the break to the top of the next even-numbered page
Odd page	Begins a new section and moves the text following the break to the top of the next odd-numbered page

FIGURE D-3: Break dialog box

FIGURE D-4: Continuous section break and columns

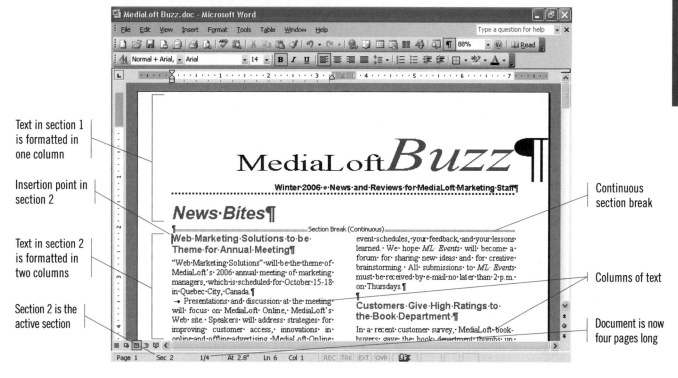

Text in section 1 is formatted in one column

Insertion point in section 2

Text in section 2 is formatted in two columns

Section 2 is the active section

Continuous section break

Columns of text

Document is now four pages long

Clues to Use

Changing page layout settings for a section

Dividing a document into sections allows you to vary the layout of a document. In addition to applying different column settings to sections, you can apply different margins, page orientation, paper size, vertical alignment, header and footer, page numbering, and other page layout settings. For example, if you are formatting a report that includes a table with many columns, you might want to change the table's page orientation to landscape so that it is easier to read. To do this, you would insert a section break before and after the table to create a section that contains only the table. Then you would use the Margins tab in the Page Setup dialog box to change the page orientation of the section that contains the table to landscape.

To change the page layout settings for an individual section, place the insertion point in the section, open the Page Setup (or Columns) dialog box, select the options you want to change, click the Apply to list arrow, click This section, then click OK. When you select This section in the Apply to list box, the settings are applied to the current section only. If you select Whole document in the Apply to list box, the settings are applied to all the sections in the document.

Inserting Page Breaks

As you type text in a document, Word automatically inserts an **automatic page break** (also called a soft page break) when you reach the bottom of a page, allowing you to continue typing on the next page. You can also force text onto the next page of a document by using the Break command to insert a **manual page break** (also called a hard page break). You insert manual page breaks where you know you want to begin each new page of the newsletter.

STEPS

1. **Scroll down to the bottom of page 1, place the insertion point before the headline** Career Corner, **click** Insert **on the menu bar, then click** Break

   The Break dialog box opens. You also use this dialog box to insert page, column, and text-wrapping breaks. Table D-2 describes these types of breaks.

> **QUICK TIP**
> To delete a break, double-click the break to select it, then press [Delete].

2. **Make sure the** Page break option button **is selected, then click** OK

   Word inserts a manual page break before "Career Corner" and moves all the text following the page break to the beginning of the next page, as shown in Figure D-5. The page break appears as a dotted line in Print Layout view when formatting marks are displayed. Page break marks are visible on the screen but do not print. Manual and automatic page breaks are always visible in Normal view.

3. **Scroll down to the bottom of page 2, place the insertion point before the headline** Webcasts Slated for Spring, **press and hold** [Ctrl], **then press** [Enter]

   Pressing [Ctrl][Enter] is a fast way to insert a manual page break. The headline is forced to the top of the third page.

> **QUICK TIP**
> To fit more text on the screen in Print Layout view, you can hide the white space on the top and bottom of each page and the gray space between pages. To toggle between hiding and showing white space, move the pointer to the top of a page until the pointer changes to ⊥⊤, then click.

4. **Scroll down page 3, place the insertion point before the headline** Staff News, **then press** [Ctrl][Enter]

   The headline is forced to the top of the fourth page.

5. **Press** [Ctrl][Home], **click the** Zoom list arrow **on the Standard toolbar, then click** Two Pages

   The first two pages of the document are displayed, as shown in Figure D-6.

6. **Scroll down to view pages 3 and 4, click the** Zoom list arrow, **click** Page Width, **then save the document**

Clues to Use

Vertically aligning text on a page

By default, text is vertically aligned with the top margin of a page, but you can change the vertical alignment of text so that it is centered between the top and bottom margins, justified between the top and bottom margins, or aligned with the bottom margin of the page. You vertically align text on a page only when the text does not fill the page; for example, if you are creating a flyer or a title page for a report. To change the vertical alignment of text in a section (or a document), place the insertion point in the section you want to align, open the Page Setup dialog box, use the Vertical alignment list arrow on the Layout tab to select the alignment you want—top, center, justified, or bottom—use the Apply to list arrow to select the part of the document you want to align, and then click OK.

FIGURE D-5: Manual page break in document

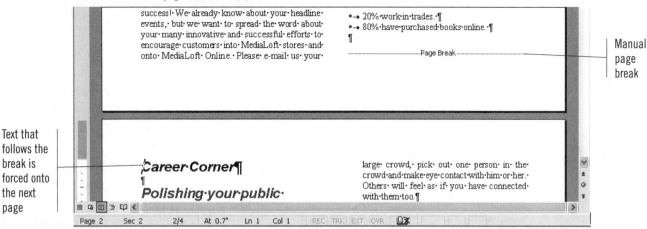

Text that follows the break is forced onto the next page

Manual page break

FIGURE D-6: Pages 1 and 2

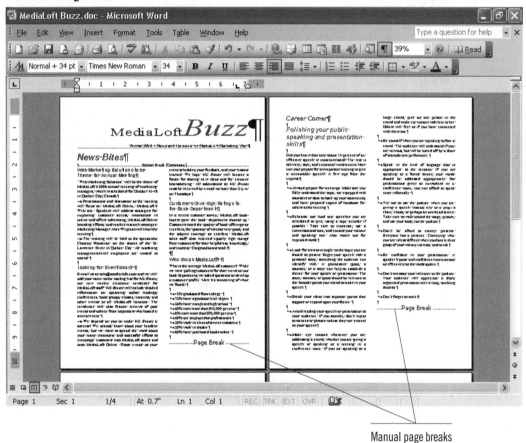

Manual page breaks

TABLE D-2: Types of breaks

break	function
Page break	Forces the text following the break to begin at the top of the next page
Column break	Forces the text following the break to begin at the top of the next column
Text wrapping break	Forces the text following the break to begin at the beginning of the next line

Inserting Page Numbers

If you want to number the pages of a multiple-page document, you can insert a page number field at the top or bottom of each page. A **field** is a code that serves as a placeholder for data that changes in a document, such as a page number or the current date. When you use the Page Numbers command on the Insert menu to add page numbers to a document, Word automatically numbers the pages for you. You insert a page number field so that page numbers will appear at the bottom of each page in the document.

STEPS

1. **Click** Insert **on the menu bar, then click** Page Numbers

   The Page Numbers dialog box opens, as shown in Figure D-7. You use this dialog box to specify the position—top or bottom of the page—and the alignment for the page numbers. Bottom of page (Footer) is the default position.

> **QUICK TIP**
> You can also align page numbers with the left, right, inside, or outside margins of a document.

2. **Click the** Alignment list arrow, **then click** Center

   The page numbers will be centered between the left and right margins at the bottom of each page.

3. **Click** OK, **then scroll to the bottom of the first page**

   The page number 1 appears in gray at the bottom of the first page, as shown in Figure D-8. The number is gray, or dimmed, because it is located in the Footer area. When the document is printed, the page numbers appear as normal text. You will learn more about headers and footers in the next lesson.

4. **Click the** Print Preview button ⬚ **on the Standard toolbar, then click the** One Page button ⬚ **on the Print Preview toolbar if necessary**

   The first page of the newsletter appears in Print Preview. Notice the page number.

5. **Click the** page number **with the** ⊕ **pointer to zoom in on the page**

   The page number is centered at the bottom of the page, as shown in Figure D-9.

6. **Scroll down the document to see the page number at the bottom of each page**

   Word automatically numbered each page of the newsletter.

> **QUICK TIP**
> To display more than six pages of a document in Print Preview, drag to expand the Multiple Pages grid.

7. **Click the** Multiple Pages button ⬚ **on the Print Preview toolbar, point to the** second box **in the bottom row on the grid to select** 2 × 2 pages, **then click**

   All four pages of the newsletter appear in the Print Preview window.

8. **Click** Close **on the Print Preview toolbar, press** [Ctrl][Home], **then save the document**

Clues to Use

Inserting the date and time

Using the Date and Time command on the Insert menu, you can insert the current date or the current time into a document, either as a field or as static text. Word uses the clock on your computer to compute the current date and time. To insert the current date or time at the location of the insertion point, click Date and Time on the Insert menu, then select the date or time format you want to use from the list of available formats in the Date and Time dialog box. If you want to insert the date or time as a field that is updated automatically each time you open or print the document, select the Update automatically check box, and then click OK. If you want the current date or time to remain in the document as static text, deselect the Update automatically check box, and then click OK.

FIGURE D-7: Page Numbers dialog box

Set location for page number (header or footer)

Set alignment of page number

Clear to hide the page number on the first page

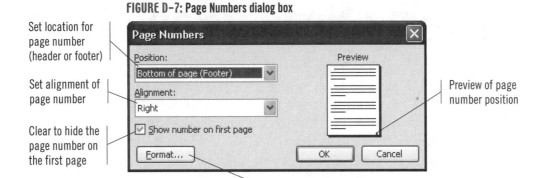

Preview of page number position

Click to change numbering format

FIGURE D-8: Page number in document

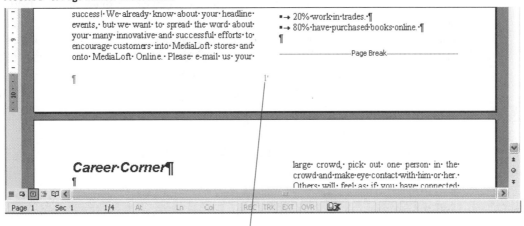

Page number is dimmed

FIGURE D-9: Page number in Print Preview

One Page button

Multiple Pages button

Page number in Print Preview

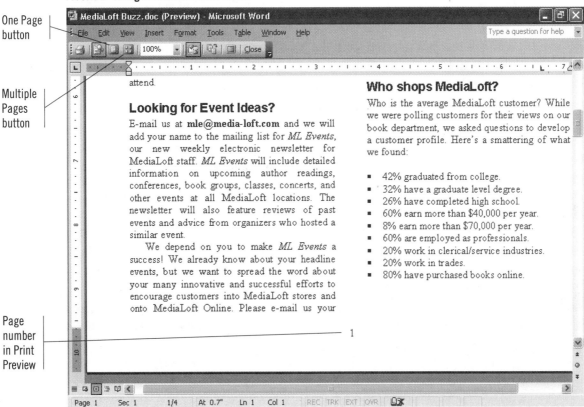

Adding Headers and Footers

A **header** is text or graphics that appears at the top of every page of a document. A **footer** is text or graphics that appears at the bottom of every page. In longer documents, headers and footers often contain information such as the title of the publication, the title of the chapter, the name of the author, the date, or a page number. You can add headers and footers to a document by using the Header and Footer command on the View menu to open the Header and Footer areas, and then inserting text and graphics in them. You create a header that includes the name of the newsletter and the current date.

STEPS

1. **Click View on the menu bar, then click Header and Footer**

   The Header and Footer areas open and the document text is dimmed, as shown in Figure D-10. When the document text is dimmed, it cannot be edited. The Header and Footer toolbar also opens. It includes buttons for inserting standard text into headers and footers and for navigating between headers and footers. See Table D-3. The Header and Footer areas of a document are independent of the document itself and must be formatted separately. For example, if you select all the text in a document and then change the font, the header and footer font does not change.

2. **Type Buzz in the Header area, press [Spacebar] twice, then click the Insert Date button** 🔲 **on the Header and Footer toolbar**

   Clicking the Insert Date button inserts a date field into the header. The date is inserted using the default date format (usually month/date/year, although your default date format might be different). The word "Buzz" and the current date will appear at the top of every page in the document.

3. **Select Buzz and the date, then click the Center button** 🔳 **on the Formatting toolbar**

   The text is centered in the Header area. In addition to the alignment buttons on the Formatting toolbar, you can use tabs to align text in the Header and Footer areas. Notice the tab stops shown on the ruler. The tab stops are the default tab stops for the Header and Footer areas and are based on the default margin settings. If you change the margins in a document, you can adjust the tab stops in the Header or Footer area to align with the new margin settings.

4. **With the text still selected, click the Font list arrow on the Formatting toolbar, click Arial, click the Bold button** 🔲 **, then click in the Header area to deselect the text**

   The header text is formatted in 12-point Arial bold.

5. **Click the Switch Between Header and Footer button** 🔲 **on the Header and Footer toolbar**

   The insertion point moves to the Footer area, where a page number field is centered in the Footer area.

6. **Double-click the page number to select the field, click the Font list arrow, click Arial, click** 🔲 **, then click in the Footer area to deselect the field**

   The page number is formatted in 12-point Arial bold.

7. **Click Close on the Header and Footer toolbar, save the document, then scroll down until the bottom of page 1 and the top of page 2 appear in the document window**

   The Header and Footer areas close and the header and footer text is dimmed, as shown in Figure D-11. The header text—"Buzz" and the current date—appear at the top of every page in the document, and a page number appears at the bottom of every page.

FIGURE D-10: Header area

Header area is open

Header and Footer toolbar (yours may open in a different location)

Tab stops for the header are set for the default document margins

Document text is dimmed

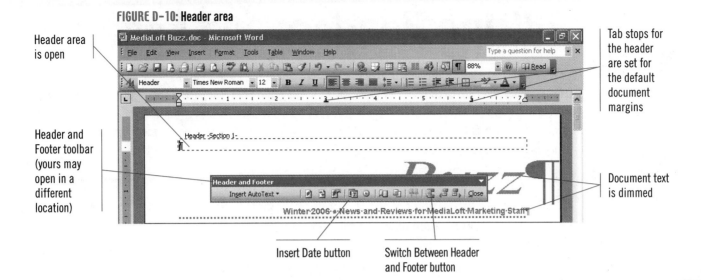

Insert Date button

Switch Between Header and Footer button

Word 2003

FIGURE D-11: Header and footer in document

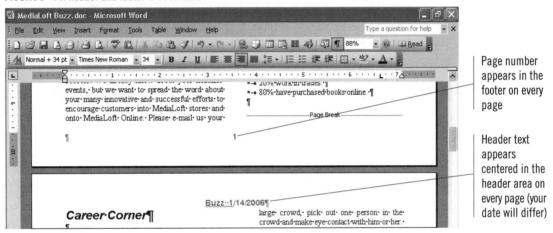

Page number appears in the footer on every page

Header text appears centered in the header area on every page (your date will differ)

TABLE D-3: Buttons on the Header and Footer toolbar

button	function
Insert AutoText ▾	Inserts an AutoText entry, such as a field for the filename, or the author's name
Insert Page Number	Inserts a field for the page number so that the pages are numbered automatically
Insert Number of Pages	Inserts a field for the total number of pages in the document
Format Page Number	Opens the Page Number Format dialog box; use to change the numbering format or to begin automatic page numbering with a specific number
Insert Date	Inserts a field for the current date
Insert Time	Inserts a field for the current time
Page Setup	Opens the Page Setup dialog box
Show/Hide Document Text	Hides and displays the document text
Link to Previous	Switches the link between headers and footers in adjoining sections on and off; use to make headers and footers in adjoining sections the same or different
Switch Between Header and Footer	Moves the insertion point between the Header and Footer areas
Show Previous	Moves the insertion point to the header or footer in the next section
Show Next	Moves the insertion point to the header or footer in the previous section

Editing Headers and Footers

To change header and footer text or to alter the formatting of headers and footers, you must first open the Header and Footer areas. You open headers and footers by using the Header and Footer command on the View menu or by double-clicking a header or footer in Print Layout view. ▓▓▓ You modify the header by adding a small circle symbol between "Buzz" and the date. You also add a border under the header text to set it off from the rest of the page. Finally, you remove the header and footer text from the first page of the document.

STEPS

1. **Place the insertion point at the top of page 2, position the pointer over the header text at the top of page 2, then double-click**

   The Header and Footer areas open.

2. **Place the insertion point between the two spaces after Buzz, click Insert on the menu bar, then click Symbol**

   The Symbol dialog box opens and is similar to Figure D-12. **Symbols** are special characters, such as graphics, shapes, and foreign language characters, that you can insert into a document. The symbols shown in Figure D-12 are the symbols included with the (normal text) font. You can use the Font list arrow on the Symbols tab to view the symbols included with each font on your computer.

3. **Scroll the list of symbols if necessary to locate the black circle symbol shown in Figure D-12, select the black circle symbol, click Insert, then click Close**

   A circle symbol is added at the location of the insertion point.

4. **With the insertion point in the header text, click Format on the menu bar, then click Borders and Shading**

   The Borders and Shading dialog box opens.

5. **Click the Borders tab if it is not already selected, click Custom in the Setting section, click the dotted line in the Style scroll box (the second line style), click the Width list arrow, click 2¼ pt, click the Bottom border button in the Preview section, make sure Paragraph is selected in the Apply to list box, click OK, click Close on the Header and Footer toolbar, then scroll as needed to see the top of page 2**

   A dotted line border is added below the header text, as shown in Figure D-13.

6. **Press [Ctrl][Home] to move the insertion point to the beginning of the document**

   The newsletter already includes the name of the document at the top of the first page, making the header information redundant. You can modify headers and footers so that the header and footer text does not appear on the first page of a document or a section.

7. **Click File on the menu bar, click Page Setup, then click the Layout tab**

   The Layout tab of the Page Setup dialog box includes options for creating a different header and footer for the first page of a document or a section, and for creating different headers and footers for odd- and even-numbered pages. For example, in a document with facing pages, such as a magazine, you might want the publication title to appear in the left-page header and the publication date to appear in the right-page header.

8. **Click the Different first page check box to select it, click the Apply to list arrow, click Whole document, then click OK**

   The header and footer text is removed from the Header and Footer areas on the first page.

9. **Scroll to see the header and footer on pages 2, 3, and 4, then save the document**

FIGURE D-12: Symbol dialog box

Special Characters tab

The subset changes as you scroll the list of symbols

Black circle symbol (yours might be located in a different position)

Available symbols (yours might differ)

Name of selected symbol

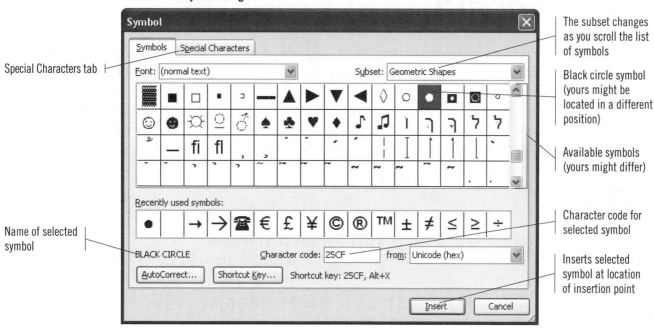

Character code for selected symbol

Inserts selected symbol at location of insertion point

FIGURE D-13: Symbol and border added to header

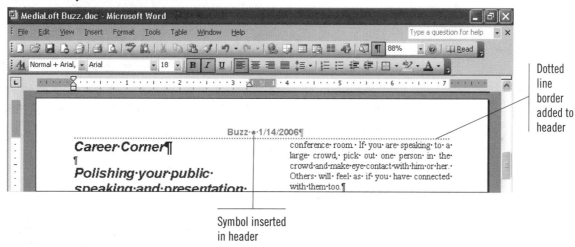

Dotted line border added to header

Symbol inserted in header

Clues to Use

Inserting and creating AutoText entries

Word includes a number of built-in AutoText entries, including salutations and closings for letters, as well as information for headers and footers. To insert a built-in AutoText entry at the location of the insertion point, point to AutoText on the Insert menu, point to a category on the AutoText menu, then click the AutoText entry you want to insert. You can also use the Insert AutoText button on the Header and Footer toolbar to insert an AutoText entry from the Header/Footer category into a header or footer.

The Word AutoText feature also allows you to store text and graphics that you use frequently so that you can easily insert them in a document. To create a custom AutoText entry, enter the text or graphic you want to store—such as a company name or logo—in a document, select it, point to AutoText on the Insert menu, and then click New. In the Create AutoText dialog box, type a name for your AutoText entry, then click OK. The text or graphic is saved as a custom AutoText entry. To insert a custom AutoText entry in a document, point to AutoText on the Insert menu, click AutoText, select the entry name on the AutoText tab in the AutoCorrect dialog box, click Insert, then click OK.

Formatting Columns

Formatting text in columns often makes the text easier to read. You can apply column formatting to a whole document, to a section, or to selected text. The Columns button on the Standard toolbar allows you to quickly create columns of equal width. In addition, you can use the Columns command on the Format menu to create columns and to customize the width and spacing of columns. To control the way text flows between columns, you can insert a **column break**, which forces the text following the break to move to the top of the next column. You can also balance columns of unequal length on a page by inserting a continuous section break at the end of the last column on the page. ███████ You format the Staff News page in three columns, and then adjust the flow of text.

STEPS

1. **Scroll to the top of page 4, place the insertion point before** Boston, **click** Insert **on the menu bar, click** Break, **click the** Continuous option button, **then click** OK

   A continuous section break is inserted before Boston. The newsletter now contains three sections.

> **QUICK TIP**
> To change the width and spacing of existing columns, you can use the Columns dialog box or drag the column markers on the horizontal ruler.

2. **Refer to the status bar to confirm that the insertion point is in section 3, click** Format **on the menu bar, then click** Columns

   The Columns dialog box opens, as shown in Figure D-14.

3. **Select** Three **in the Presets section, click the** Spacing down arrow **twice until 0.3" appears, select the** Line between check box, **then click** OK

   All the text in section 3 is formatted in three columns of equal width with a line between the columns, as shown in Figure D-15.

> **QUICK TIP**
> To create a banner headline that spans the width of a page, select the headline text, click the Columns button, then click 1 Column.

4. **Click the** Zoom list arrow **on the Standard toolbar, then click** Whole Page

   Notice that the third column of text is much shorter than the first two columns. Page 4 would look better if the three columns were balanced—each the same length.

5. **Place the insertion point at the end of the third column, click** Insert **on the menu bar, click** Break, **click the** Continuous option button, **then click** OK

   The columns in section 3 adjust to become roughly the same length.

6. **Scroll up to page 3**

   The two columns on page 3 are also uneven. You want the information about Jack Niven to appear at the top of the second column.

> **QUICK TIP**
> If a section contains a column break, you cannot balance the columns by inserting a continuous section break.

7. **Click the** Zoom list arrow, **click** Page Width, **scroll down page 3, place the insertion point before the heading** Jack Niven, **click** Insert **on the menu bar, click** Break, **click the** Column break option button, **then click** OK

   The text following the column break is forced to the top of the next column.

8. **Click the** Zoom list arrow, **click** Two Pages, **then save the document**

   The columns on pages 3 and 4 are formatted as shown in Figure D-16.

Clues to Use

Hyphenating text in a document

Hyphenating a document is another way to control the flow of text in columns. Hyphens are small dashes that break words that fall at the end of a line. Hyphenation diminishes the gaps between words in justified text and reduces ragged right edges in left-aligned text. If a document includes narrow columns, hyphenating the text can help give the pages a cleaner look. To hyphenate a document automatically, point to Language on the Tools menu, click Hyphenation, select the Automatically hyphenate document check box in the Hyphenation dialog box, and then click OK. You can also use the Hyphenation dialog box to change the hyphenation zone—the distance between the margin and the end of the last word in the line. A smaller hyphenation zone results in a greater number of hyphenated words and a cleaner look to columns of text.

FIGURE D-14: Columns dialog box

Select a preset format for columns

Change the number of columns

Select to add a line between columns

Set custom width and spacing for columns

Preview of current settings

Select to create columns of equal width

Select part of document to apply format to

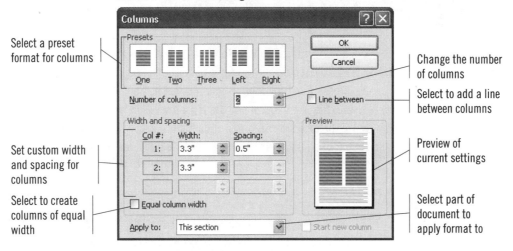

FIGURE D-15: Text formatted in three columns

Text in section 3 is formatted in three columns

Column markers show the width and spacing of columns

Section break is at end of section 2

Line added between columns

FIGURE D-16: Columns on pages 3 and 4 of the newsletter

Text following column break is forced to top of next column

Column break

Continuous section break

Columns in section are balanced

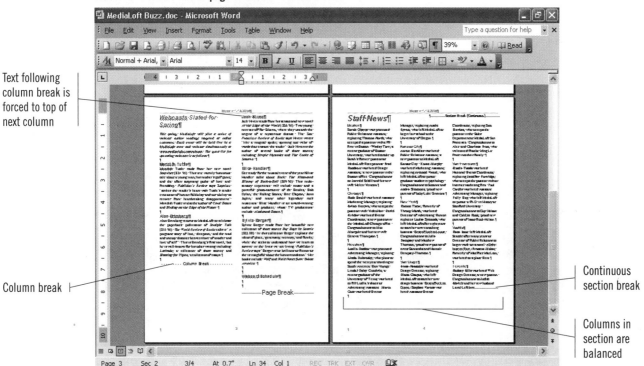

Inserting a Table

Adding a table to a document is a useful way to illustrate information that is intended for quick reference and analysis. A **table** is a grid of columns and rows of cells that you can fill with text and graphics. A **cell** is the box formed by the intersection of a column and a row. The lines that divide the columns and rows of a table and help you see the grid-like structure of the table are called **borders**. A simple way to insert a table into a document is to use the Insert command on the Table menu. This command allows you to determine the dimensions and format of a table before it is inserted. ▰▰▰▰▰ You add a table showing the schedule for Webcasts to the bottom of page 3.

STEPS

1. **Click the Zoom list arrow on the Standard toolbar, click Page Width, then scroll down page 3 until the heading Webcast Schedule is at the top of your screen**

   The bottom of page three is displayed.

2. **Place the insertion point before the heading Webcast Schedule, click Insert on the menu bar, click Break, click the Continuous option button, then click OK**

   A continuous section break is inserted before the heading Webcast Schedule. The document now includes four sections, with the heading Webcast Schedule in the third section.

3. **Click the Columns button ▦ on the Standard toolbar, point to the first column on the grid, then click**

   Section 3 is formatted as a single column.

4. **Place the insertion point before the second paragraph mark below the heading Webcast Schedule, click Table on the menu bar, point to Insert, then click Table**

   The Insert Table dialog box opens, as shown in Figure D-17. You use this dialog box to create a blank table with a set number of columns and rows, and to choose an option for sizing the width of the columns in the table.

QUICK TIP

To apply a different table style to a table once it is created, place the insertion point in the table, click Table Auto-Format on the Table menu, and then modify the selections in the Table Auto-Format dialog box.

5. **Type 4 in the Number of columns text box, press [Tab], type 6 in the Number of rows text box, make sure the Fixed column width option button is selected, then click AutoFormat**

   The Table AutoFormat dialog box opens. You use this dialog box to apply a table style to the table. Table styles include format settings for the text, borders, and shading in a table. A preview of the selected style appears in the Preview section of the dialog box.

6. **Scroll down the list of table styles, click Table Grid 8, clear the First column, Last row, and Last column check boxes in the Apply special formats to section, then click OK twice**

   A blank table with four columns and six rows is inserted in the document at the location of the insertion point. The table is formatted in the Table Grid 8 style, with blue shading in the header row and blue borders that define the table cells. The insertion point is in the upper-left cell of the table, the first cell in the header row.

7. **Type Date in the first cell in the first row, press [Tab], type Time, press [Tab], type Guest, press [Tab], type Store, then press [Tab]**

   Pressing [Tab] moves the insertion point to the next cell in the row. At the end of a row, pressing [Tab] moves the insertion point to the first cell in the next row. You can also click in a cell to move the insertion point to it.

TROUBLE

If you pressed [Tab] after the last row, click the Undo button ↩ on the Standard toolbar to remove the blank row.

8. **Type the text shown in Figure D-18 in the table cells, pressing [Tab] to move from cell to cell**

   You can edit the text in a table by placing the insertion point in a cell and then typing. You can also select the text in a table and then format it using the buttons on the Formatting toolbar. If you want to modify the structure of a table, you can use the Insert and Delete commands on the Table menu to add and remove rows and columns. You can also use the AutoFit command on the Table menu to change the width of table columns and the height of table rows. To select a column, row, or table before performing an action, place the insertion point in the row, column, or table you want to select, and then use the Select command on the Table menu.

9. **Save the document**

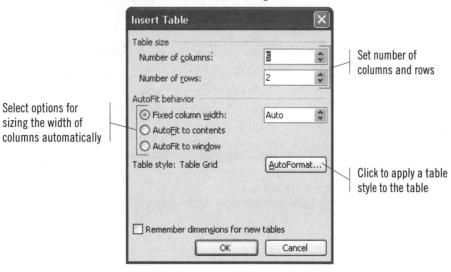

FIGURE D-17: Insert Table dialog box

Set number of columns and rows

Select options for sizing the width of columns automatically

Click to apply a table style to the table

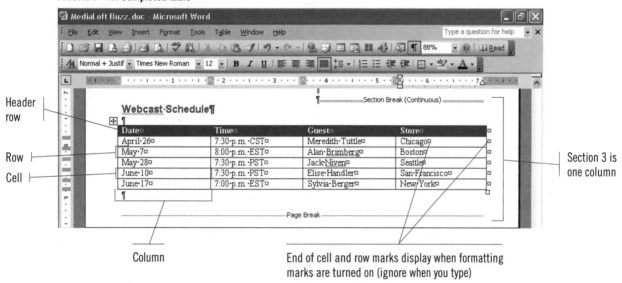

FIGURE D-18: Completed table

Header row

Row

Cell

Section 3 is one column

Column

End of cell and row marks display when formatting marks are turned on (ignore when you type)

Clues to Use

Moving around in a long document

Rather than scrolling to move to a different place in a long document, you can use the Browse by Object feature, the Go To command, or the Document Map to quickly move the insertion point to a specific location. Browse by Object allows you to browse to the next or previous page, section, line, table, graphic, or other item of the same type in a document. To do this, first click the Select Browse Object button ⊙ below the vertical scroll bar to open a palette of object types. On this palette, click the button for the type of item by which you want to browse, and then click the Next ⬇ or Previous ⬆ buttons to scroll through the items of that type in the document.

To move a specific page, section, or other item in a document,

you can click the Go To command on the Edit menu. On the Go To tab in the Find and Replace dialog box, select the type of item in the Go to what list box, type the item number in the text box, and then click Go To to move the insertion point to the item.

If your document is formatted with heading styles, you can also use the Document Map to navigate a document. The Document Map is a separate pane in the document window that displays a list of headings in the document. You click a heading in the Document Map to move the insertion point to that heading in the document. To open and close the Document Map, click Document Map on the View menu or click the Document Map button 🔲 on the Standard toolbar.

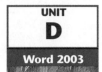

Inserting WordArt

Illustrating a document with WordArt is a fun way to spice up the layout of a page. **WordArt** is an object that contains specially formatted, decorative text. The text in a WordArt object can be skewed, rotated, stretched, shadowed, patterned, or fit into shapes to create interesting effects. To insert a WordArt object into a document, you use the WordArt command on the Insert menu. ░▓▓ You decide to format the Staff News headline as WordArt to add some zest to the final page of the newsletter.

STEPS

1. **Scroll down until the heading** Staff News **is at the top of your screen, select** Staff News **(not including the paragraph mark), then press** [Delete]
   The insertion point is at the top of page 4 in the third section of the document. The third section is formatted as a single column.

2. **Click** Insert **on the menu bar, point to** Picture, **then click** WordArt
   The WordArt Gallery dialog box opens, as shown in Figure D-19. You use the WordArt Gallery to select a style for the WordArt object.

3. **Click the** fourth style in the third row, **then click** OK
   The Edit WordArt Text dialog box opens. You type the text you want to format as WordArt in this dialog box. You can also use the Edit WordArt Text dialog box to change the font and font size of the WordArt text.

> **QUICK TIP**
> Use the Text Wrapping button on the WordArt toolbar to convert the object to a floating graphic.

4. **Type** Staff News, **then click** OK
   The WordArt object appears at the location of the insertion point. The object is an **inline graphic**, or part of the line of text in which it was inserted.

5. **Click the** WordArt object **to select it**
   The black squares that appear on the corners and sides of the object are the **sizing handles**. Sizing handles appear when a graphic object is selected. You can drag a sizing handle to change the size of the object. The WordArt toolbar also appears when a WordArt object is selected. You use the buttons on the WordArt toolbar to edit and modify the format of WordArt objects.

6. **Position the pointer over the** lower-right sizing handle, **when the pointer changes to** ⬉⬊ **drag down and to the right to make the object about** 1½" **tall and** 5½" **wide**
   Refer to the vertical and horizontal rulers for guidance as you drag the sizing handle to resize the object. When you release the mouse button, the WordArt object is enlarged, as shown in Figure D-20.

7. **Click the** Center button ▤ **on the Formatting toolbar**
   The WordArt object is centered between the margins.

8. **Click the** WordArt Shape button ▤ **on the WordArt toolbar, then click the** Wave 1 **shape (the fifth shape in the third row)**
   The shape of the WordArt text changes.

> **TROUBLE**
> If the newsletter is five pages instead of four, reduce the height of the WordArt object.

9. **Click outside the WordArt object to deselect it, click the** Zoom list arrow **on the Standard toolbar, click** Two Pages, **then save the document**
   The completed pages 3 and 4 are displayed, as shown in Figure D-21.

FIGURE D-19: WordArt Gallery dialog box

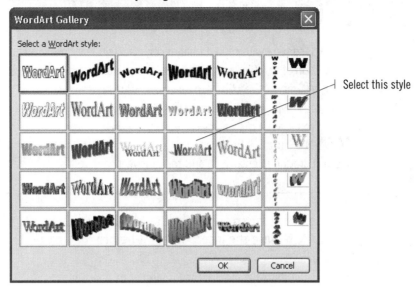

Select this style

FIGURE D-20: Resized WordArt object

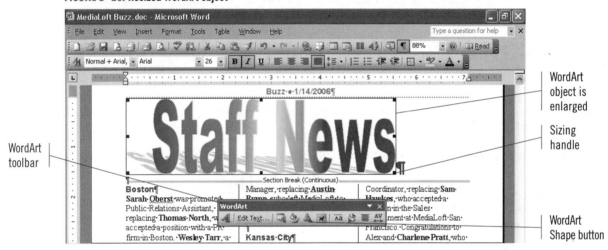

WordArt object is enlarged

Sizing handle

WordArt toolbar

WordArt Shape button

FIGURE D-21: Completed pages 3 and 4

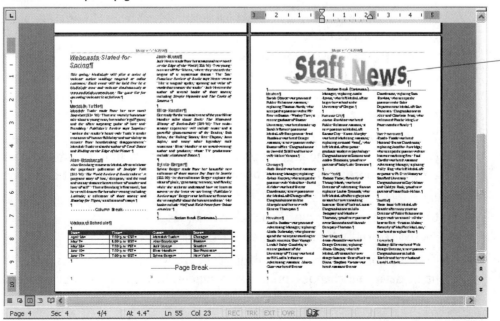

WordArt centered with the Wave 1 shape applied

Inserting Clip Art

Illustrating a document with clip art images can give it visual appeal and help to communicate your ideas. **Clip art** is a collection of graphic images that you can insert into a document. Clip art images are stored in the **Clip Organizer**, a library of the **clips**—media files, including graphics, photographs, sounds, movies, and animations—that come with Word. You can add a clip to a document using the Clip Art command on the Insert menu. Once you insert a clip art image, you can wrap text around it, resize it, and move it to a different location. 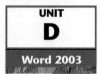 You illustrate the second page of the newsletter with a clip art image. After you insert the image, you wrap text around it, enlarge it, and then move it so that it is centered between the two columns of text.

STEPS

1. **Click the** Zoom list arrow **on the Standard toolbar, click** Page Width, **scroll to the top of page 2, then place the insertion point before the first body paragraph, which begins** Did you know...

   You insert the clip art graphic at the location of the insertion point.

2. **Click** Insert **on the menu bar, point to** Picture, **then click** Clip Art

   The Clip Art task pane opens. You can use this task pane to search for clips related to a keyword. If you are working with an active Internet connection, your search results will include clip art from the Microsoft Office Online Web site.

TROUBLE

Make sure the All media types check box in the Results should be in list box has a check mark. Select a different clip if the clip shown in Figure D-22 is not available to you.

3. **Select the text in the Search for text box if necessary, type** communication, **then click** Go

   Clips that include the keyword "communication" appear in the Clip Art task pane, as shown in Figure D-22. When you point to a clip, a ScreenTip showing the first few keywords applied to the clip (listed alphabetically), the width and height of the clip in pixels, and the file size and file type for the clip appears.

4. **Point to the** clip **called out in Figure D-22, click the** list arrow **that appears next to the clip, click** Insert **on the menu, then close the Clip Art task pane**

   The clip is inserted at the location of the insertion point. You want to center the graphic on the page. Until you apply text wrapping to a graphic, it is part of the line of text in which it was inserted (an **inline graphic**). To move a graphic independently of text, you must wrap the text around it to make it a **floating graphic**, which can be moved anywhere on a page.

5. **Double-click the** clip art image, **click the** Layout tab **in the Format Picture dialog box, click** Tight, **then click** OK

   The text in the first body paragraph wraps around the irregular shape of the clip art image. The white circles that appear on the square edges of the graphic are the sizing handles. The white sizing handles indicate the graphic is a floating graphic.

QUICK TIP

To verify the size of a graphic or to set precise measurements, double-click the graphic to open the Format Picture dialog box, then adjust the Height and Width settings on the Size tab.

6. **Position the pointer over the** lower-right sizing handle, **when the pointer changes to** ↖ **drag down and to the right until the graphic is about 2½" wide and 2½" tall**

   As you drag a sizing handle, the dotted lines show the outline of the graphic. Refer to the dotted lines and the rulers as you resize the graphic. When you release the mouse button, the image is enlarged.

7. **With the graphic still selected, position the pointer over the graphic, when the pointer changes to** ⊹ **drag the graphic down and to the right so it is centered on the page as shown in Figure D-23, release the mouse button, then deselect the graphic**

   The graphic is now centered between the two columns of text.

TROUBLE

If page 3 is a blank page or contains text continued from page 2, reduce the size of the graphic on page 2.

8. **Click the** Zoom list arrow, **then click** Two Pages

   The completed pages 1 and 2 are displayed, as shown in Figure D-24.

9. **Click the** Zoom list arrow, **click** Page Width, **press** [Ctrl][End], **press** [Enter] **twice, type your name, save your changes, print the document, then close the document and exit Word**

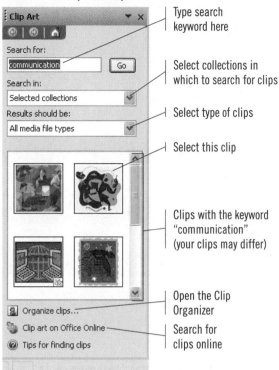

Type search keyword here

Select collections in which to search for clips

Select type of clips

Select this clip

Clips with the keyword "communication" (your clips may differ)

Open the Clip Organizer

Search for clips online

Sizing handle

Text is wrapped around graphic

Dotted line shows square outline of graphic as it is being dragged; position top of square between the last two lines of the first paragraph in column 2

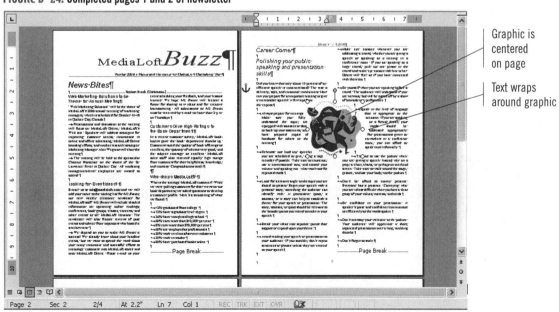

Graphic is centered on page

Text wraps around graphic

Word 2003

Practice

▼ CONCEPTS REVIEW

Label each element shown in Figure D-25.

FIGURE D-25

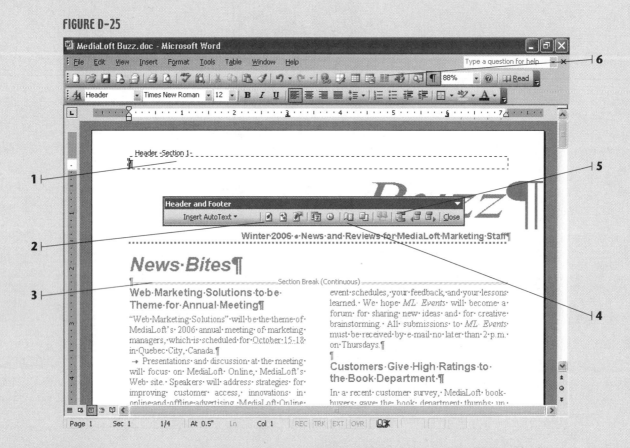

Match each term with the statement that best describes it.

7. **Section break**
8. **Header**
9. **Footer**
10. **Field**
11. **Manual page break**
12. **Margin**
13. **Inline graphic**
14. **Floating graphic**

a. A placeholder for information that changes
b. A formatting mark that divides a document into parts that can be formatted differently
c. The blank area between the edge of the text and the edge of the page
d. A formatting mark that forces the text following the mark to begin at the top of the next page
e. An image that is inserted as part of a line of text
f. An image to which text wrapping has been applied
g. Text or graphics that appear at the bottom of every page in a document
h. Text or graphics that appear at the top of every page in a document

Select the best answer from the list of choices.

15. Which of the following do documents with mirror margins always have?

 a. Inside and outside margins

 b. Different first page headers and footers

 c. Gutters

 d. Landscape orientation

16. Which button is used to insert a field into a header or footer?

 a. 🔲   **c.** 🔲

 b. 🔲   **d.** 🔲

17. Which type of break do you insert if you want to force text to begin on the next page?

 a. Text wrapping break   **c.** Automatic page break

 b. Manual page break   **d.** Continuous section break

18. Which type of break do you insert if you want to balance the columns in a section?

 a. Text wrapping break   **c.** Continuous section break

 b. Column break   **d.** Automatic page break

19. What must you do to change an inline graphic to a floating graphic?

 a. Move the graphic   **c.** Anchor the graphic

 b. Resize the graphic   **d.** Apply text wrapping to the graphic

20. Pressing [Ctrl][Enter] does which of the following?

 a. Inserts a manual page break

 b. Moves the insertion point to the beginning of the document

 c. Inserts a continuous section break

 d. Inserts an automatic page break

▼ SKILLS REVIEW

1. Set document margins.

 a. Start Word, open the file WD D-2.doc from the drive and folder where your Data Files are located, then save it as **Happy Valley Fitness**.

 b. Change the top and bottom margins to 1.2" and the left and right margins to 1".

 c. Save your changes to the document.

2. Divide a document into sections.

 a. Hide the white space in the document by moving the pointer to the top of a page, then clicking the Hide White Space pointer that appears.

 b. Scroll down, then insert a continuous section break before the **Facilities** heading.

 c. Format the text in section 2 in two columns, then save your changes to the document.

3. Insert page breaks.

 a. Insert a manual page break before the heading **Welcome to the Happy Valley Fitness Center!**.

 b. Scroll down and insert a manual page break before the heading **Services**.

 c. Scroll down and insert a manual page break before the heading **Membership**.

 d. Show the white space in the document by moving the pointer over the thick black line that separates the pages, then clicking the Show White Space pointer that appears.

 e. Press [Ctrl][Home], then save your changes to the document.

4. Insert page numbers.

 a. Insert page numbers in the document. Center the page numbers at the bottom of the page.

 b. View the page numbers on each page in Print Preview, close Print Preview, then save your changes to the document.

5. Add headers and footers.

  a. Change the view to Page Width, then open the Header and Footer areas.

  b. Type your name in the Header area, press [Tab] twice, then use the Insert Date button on the Header and Footer toolbar to insert the current date.

  c. On the horizontal ruler, drag the right tab stop from the 6" mark to the 6½" mark so that the date aligns with the right margin of the document.

  d. Move the insertion point to the Footer area.

  e. Double-click the page number to select it, then format the page number in bold italic.

  f. Close headers and footers, preview the header and footer on each page in Print Preview, close Print Preview, then save your changes to the document.

6. Edit headers and footers.

  a. Open headers and footers, then apply italic to the text in the header.

  b. Move the insertion point to the Footer area, double-click the page number to select it, then press [Delete].

  c. Click the Align Right button on the Formatting toolbar.

  d. Use the Symbol command on the Insert menu to open the Symbol dialog box.

  e. Insert a black right-pointing triangle symbol (character code: 25BA), then close the Symbol dialog box.

  f. Use the Insert Page Number button on the Header and Footer toolbar to insert a page number.

  g. Use the Page Setup button on the Header and Footer toolbar to open the Page Setup dialog box.

  h. Use the Layout tab to create a different header and footer for the first page of the document.

  i. Scroll to the beginning of the document, type your name in the First Page Header area, then apply italic to your name.

  j. Close headers and footers, preview the header and footer on each page in Print Preview, close Print Preview, then save your changes to the document.

7. Format columns.

  a. On page 2, select Facilities and the paragraph mark below it, use the Columns button to format the selected text as one column, then center Facilities on the page.

  b. Balance the columns on page 2 by inserting a continuous section break at the bottom of the second column.

  c. On page 3, select Services and the paragraph mark below it, format the selected text as one column, then center the text.

  d. Balance the columns on page 3.

  e. On page 4, select Membership and the paragraph mark below it, format the selected text as one column, then center the text.

  f. Insert a column break before the Membership Cards heading, press [Ctrl][Home], then save your changes to the document.

8. Insert a table.

  a. Click the Document Map button on the Standard toolbar to open the Document Map.

  b. In the Document Map, click the heading Membership Rates, then close the Document Map. (*Hint*: The Document Map button is a toggle button.)

  c. Select the word Table at the end of the Membership Rates section, press [Delete], then open the Insert Table dialog box.

  d. Create a table with two columns and five rows, open the AutoFormat dialog box, and then apply the Table Classic 3 style to the table, clearing the Last row check box. Close the dialog box.

  e. Press [Tab] to leave the first cell in the header row blank, then type Rate.

  f. Press [Tab], then type the following text in the table, pressing [Tab] to move from cell to cell.

Enrollment/Individual	$100
Enrollment/Couple	$150
Monthly membership/Individual	$35
Monthly membership/Couple	$60

g. With the insertion point in the table, right-click the table, point to AutoFit on the shortcut menu, then click AutoFit to Contents.

h. With the insertion point in the table, right-click again, point to AutoFit, then click AutoFit to Window.

i. Save your changes to the document.

9. Insert WordArt.

a. Scroll to page 3, place the insertion point before the Personal Training heading, then insert a WordArt object.

b. Select any horizontal WordArt style, type Get Fit!, then click OK.

c. Click the WordArt object to select it, click the Text Wrapping button on the WordArt toolbar, then apply the Tight text-wrapping style to the object so that it is a floating object.

d. Move the object so that it is centered below the text at the bottom of the page (below the page break mark).

e. Adjust the size and position of the object so that the page looks attractive. (*Hint*: The sizing handles on floating objects are white circles.)

f. Apply a different WordArt shape to the object, preview the page, adjust the size and position if necessary, then save your changes to the document.

10. Insert clip art.

a. On page 1, place the insertion point in the second blank paragraph below A Rehabilitation and Exercise Facility. (*Hint*: Place the insertion point to the left of the paragraph mark.)

b. Open the Clip Art task pane. Search for clips related to the keyword fitness.

c. Insert the clip shown in Figure D-26. (*Note*: An active Internet connection is needed to select the clip shown in the figure. Select a different clip if this one is not available to you. If you are working offline, you might need to search using a keyword such as sports.)

d. Select the graphic, then drag the lower-right sizing handle down and to the right so that the graphic is about 2.5" wide and 3" tall. Size the graphic so that all the text and the manual page break fit on page 1. (*Hint*: The sizing handles on inline graphics are black squares.)

e. Save your changes to the document. Preview the document, print a copy, then close the document and exit Word.

FIGURE D-26

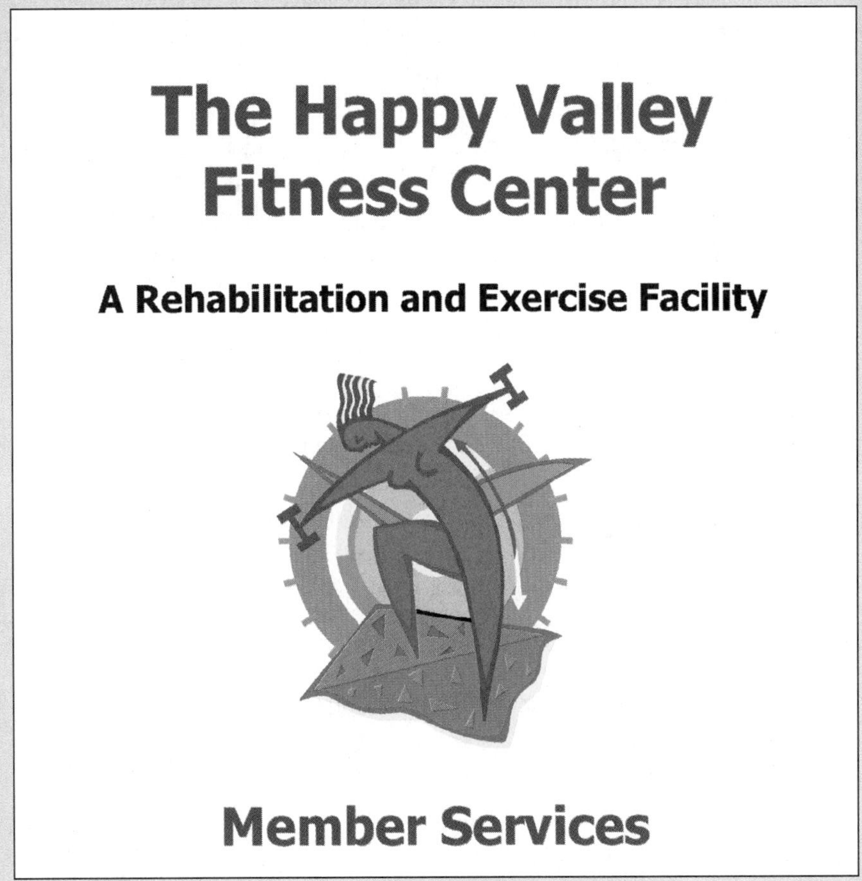

The Happy Valley Fitness Center

A Rehabilitation and Exercise Facility

Member Services

▼ INDEPENDENT CHALLENGE 1

You are the owner of a small business in Latona, Ontario, called Small World Catering. You have begun work on the text for a brochure advertising your business and are now ready to lay out the pages and prepare the final copy. The brochure will be printed on both sides of an 8½" × 11" sheet of paper, and folded in thirds.

a. Start Word, open the file WD D-3.doc from the drive and folder where your Data Files are located, then save it as Small World. Read the document to get a feel for its contents.

b. Change the page orientation to landscape, and change all four margins to .6".

c. Format the document in three columns of equal width.

d. Insert a manual page break before the heading Catering Services.

e. On page 1, insert column breaks before the headings Sample Indian Banquet Menu and Sample Tuscan Banquet Menu.

f. On page 1, insert a continuous section break at the end of the third column to create separate sections on pages one and two.

g. Add lines between the columns on the first page, then center the text in the columns.

h. Create a different header and footer for the first page. Type Call for custom menus designed to your taste and budget in the First Page Footer area.

i. Center the text in the footer area, format it in 20-point Comic Sans MS, all caps, with a violet font color, then close headers and footers.

j. On page 2, insert a column break before Your Name. Press [Enter] as many times as necessary to move the contact information to the bottom of the second column. Be sure all five lines of the contact information are in column 2 and do not flow to the next column.

k. Replace Your Name with your name, then center the contact information in the column.

l. Insert a column break at the bottom of the second column. Then, type the text shown in Figure D-27 in the third column. Refer to the figure as you follow the instructions for formatting the text in the third column.

m. Use the Font dialog box to format Small World Catering in 32-point Comic Sans MS, bold, with a violet font color.

n. Format the remaining text in 12-point Comic Sans MS, with a violet font color. Center the text in the third column.

o. Insert the clip art graphic shown in Figure D-27 or another appropriate clip art graphic. Do not wrap text around the graphic.

p. Resize the graphic and add and remove blank paragraphs in the third column of your brochure so that the spacing between elements roughly matches the spacing shown in Figure D-27.

Advanced Challenge Exercise

- Format Small World as a WordArt object using a WordArt style and shape of your choice.
- Format Catering as a WordArt object using a WordArt style and shape of your choice.
- Adjust the size, position, and spacing of the WordArt objects, clip art graphic, and text in the third column so that the brochure is attractive and eye-catching.

q. Save your changes, preview the brochure in Print Preview, then print a copy. If possible, print the two pages of the brochure back to back so that the brochure can be folded in thirds.

r. Close the document and exit Word.

FIGURE D-27

Small World

Catering

Complete catering services available for all types of events. Menus and estimates provided upon request.

▼ INDEPENDENT CHALLENGE 2

You work in the Campus Safety Department at Hudson State College. You have written the text for an informational flyer about parking regulations on campus and now you need to format the flyer so it is attractive and readable.

a. Start Word, open the file WD D-4.doc from the drive and folder where your Data Files are located, then save it as **Hudson Parking FAQ**. Read the document to get a feel for its contents.

b. Change all four margins to .7".

c. Insert a continuous section break before **1. May I bring a car to school?** (*Hint*: Place the insertion point before May.)

d. Scroll down and insert a next page section break before **Sample Parking Permit**.

e. Format the section 2 text in three columns of equal width with .3" of space between the columns.

f. Hyphenate the document using the automatic hyphenation feature. (*Hint*: If the Hyphenation feature is not installed on your computer, skip this step.)

g. Add a 3-point dotted-line bottom border to the blank paragraph under Hudson State College. (*Hint*: Place the insertion point before the paragraph mark under Hudson State College, then apply a bottom border to the paragraph.)

h. Add your name to the header. Right-align your name and format it in 10-point Arial.

i. Add the following text to the footer, inserting symbols between words as indicated: **Parking and Shuttle Service Office • 54 Buckley Street • Hudson State College • 942-555-2227**.

j. Format the footer text in 9-point Arial Black and center it in the footer. Use a different font if Arial Black is not available to you. If necessary, adjust the font and font size so that the entire address fits on one line.

k. Apply a 3-point dotted-line border above the footer text. Make sure to apply the border to the paragraph.

l. Balance the columns in section 2.

m. Add the clip art graphic shown in Figure D-28 or another appropriate clip art graphic to the upper-right corner of the document, above the border. Make sure the graphic does not obscure the border. (*Hint*: Apply text wrapping to the graphic before positioning it.)

FIGURE D-28

Frequently Asked Questions (FAQ)
of the Department of Campus Safety

Parking & Shuttle Service Office
Hudson State College

n. Place the insertion point on page 2 (which is section 4). Change the left and right margins in section 4 to 1". Also change the page orientation of section 4 to landscape.

o. Change the vertical alignment of section 4 to Center.

p. Save your changes, preview the flyer in Print Preview, then print a copy. If possible, print the two pages of the flyer back to back.

q. Close the document and exit Word.

▼ INDEPENDENT CHALLENGE 3

A book publisher would like to publish an article you wrote on stormwater pollution in Australia as a chapter in a forthcoming book called *Environmental Issues for the New Millennium*. The publisher has requested that you format your article like a book chapter before submitting it for publication, and has provided you with a style sheet.

a. Start Word, open the file WD D-5.doc from the drive and folder where your Data Files are located, then save it as **Stormwater**.

b. Change the font of the entire document to 11-point Book Antiqua. If this font is not available to you, select a different font suitable for the pages of a book. Change the alignment to justified.

c. Change the paper size to 6" × 9".

d. Create mirror margins. (*Hint*: Use the Multiple Pages list arrow.) Change the top and bottom margins to .8", change the inside margin to .4", change the outside margin to .6", and create a .3" gutter to allow room for the book's binding.

e. Change the Zoom level to Two Pages, then apply the setting to create different headers and footers for odd- and even-numbered pages.

f. Change the Zoom level to Page Width. In the odd-page header, type **Chapter 5**, insert a symbol of your choice, then type **Stormwater Pollution in the Fairy Creek Catchment**.

g. Format the header text in 9-point Book Antiqua italic, then right-align the text.

h. In the even-page header, type your name, insert a symbol of your choice, then insert the current date. (*Hint*: Scroll down or use the Show Next button to move the insertion point to the even-page header.)

i. Change the format of the date to include just the month and the year. (*Hint*: Right-click the date field, then click Edit Field.)

j. Format the header text in 9-point Book Antiqua italic. The even-page header should be left-aligned.

k. Insert page numbers that are centered in the footer. Format the page number in 10-point Book Antiqua. Make sure to insert a page number field in both the odd- and even-page footer areas.

l. Format the page numbers so that the first page of your chapter, which is Chapter 5 in the book, begins on page 53. (*Hint*: Select a page number field, then use the Format Page Number button.)

m. Go to the beginning of the document, press [Enter] 10 times, type **Chapter 5: Stormwater Pollution in the Fairy Creek Catchment**, press [Enter] twice, type your name, then press [Enter] twice.

n. Format the chapter title in 16-point Book Antiqua bold, format your name in 14-point Book Antiqua using small caps, then left-align the title text and your name.

Advanced Challenge Exercise

■ Use the Browse by Object feature to move the insertion point to page 4 in the document, scroll down, place the insertion point at the end of the paragraph above the Potential health effects... heading, press [Enter] twice, type **Table 1: Total annual pollutant loads per year in the Fairy Creek Catchment**, format the text as bold, then press [Enter] twice.

■ Insert a table with four columns and four rows that is formatted in the Table Professional style.

■ Type the text shown in Figure D-29 in the table. Do not be concerned when the text wraps to the next line in a cell.

■ Format the text as bold in the header row, then remove the bold formatting from the text in the remaining rows.

■ Place the insertion point in the table, point to AutoFit on the Table menu, click Distribute Rows Evenly, point to AutoFit on the Table menu a second time, then click AutoFit to Contents.

o. Save your changes, preview the chapter in Print Preview, print the first four pages of the chapter, then close the document and exit Word.

FIGURE D-29

Area	Nitrogen	Phosphorus	Suspended solids
Fairy Creek	9.3 tonnes	1.2 tonnes	756.4 tonnes
Durras Arm	6.2 tonnes	.9 tonnes	348.2 tonnes
Cabbage Tree Creek	9.8 tonnes	2.3 tonnes	485.7 tonnes

▼ INDEPENDENT CHALLENGE 4

One of the most common opportunities to use the page layout features of Word is when formatting a research paper. The format recommended by the *MLA Handbook for Writers of Research Papers*, a style guide that includes information on preparing, writing, and formatting research papers, is the standard format used by many schools, colleges, and universities. In this independent challenge, you will research the MLA (Modern Language Association) guidelines for formatting a research paper and use the guidelines you find to prepare a sample first page of a research report.

a. Start Word, open the file WD D-6.doc from the drive and folder where your Data Files are located, then save it as **MLA Style**. This document contains the questions you will answer about MLA style guidelines.

b. Use your favorite search engine to search the Web for information on the MLA guidelines for formatting a research report. Use the keywords **MLA Style** and **research paper format** to conduct your search.

c. Look for information on the proper formatting for the following aspects of a research paper: paper size, margins, title page or first page of the report, line spacing, paragraph indentation, page numbers, and works cited.

d. Type your answers to the questions in the MLA Style document, save it, print a copy, then close the document.

e. Using the information you learned, start a new document and create a sample first page of a research report. Use **MLA Format for Research Papers** as the title for your sample report, and make up information about the course and instructor, if necessary. For the body of the report, type several sentences about MLA style. Make sure to format the page exactly as the MLA style dictates.

f. Save the document as **MLA Sample Format** to the drive and folder where your Data Files are located, print a copy, close the document, then exit Word.

Use the file WD D-7.doc, found on the drive and folder where your Data Files are located, to create the article shown in Figure D-30. (*Hint*: Change all four margins to .6". To locate the flower clip art image, search using the keyword **flower**, and be sure only the Photographs check box in the Results should be in list box in the Clip Art task pane has a check mark. Select a different clip if the clip shown in the figure is not available to you.) Save the document with the filename **Gardener's Corner**, then print a copy.

FIGURE D-30

GARDENER'S CORNER

Putting a Perennial Garden to Bed

By Your Name

A certain sense of peace descends when a perennial garden is put to bed for the season. The plants are safely tucked in against the elements, and the garden is ready to welcome the first signs of life. When the work is done, you can sit back and anticipate the bright blooms of spring. Many gardeners are uncertain of how to close a perennial garden. This week's column demystifies the process.

Clean up

Garden clean up can be a gradual process—plants will deteriorate at different rates, allowing you to do a little bit each week.

1. Edge beds and borders and remove stakes and other plant supports.
2. Dig and divide irises, daylilies, and other early bloomers.
3. Cut back plants when foliage starts to deteriorate.
4. Rake all debris out of the garden and pull any weeds that remain.

Plant perennials

Fall is the perfect time to plant perennials! The warm, sunny days and cool nights provide optimal conditions for new root growth.

1. Dig deeply and enhance soil with organic matter.
2. Use a good starter fertilizer to speed up new root growth.
3. Untangle the roots of new plants before planting them.
4. Water deeply after planting as the weather dictates.

Add compost

Organic matter is the key ingredient to healthy soil. If you take care of the soil, your plants will become strong and disease resistant.

1. Use an iron rake to loosen the top few inches of soil.
2. Spread a one to two inch layer of compost over the entire garden.
3. Refrain from stepping on the area and compacting the soil.

To mulch or not to mulch?

Winter protection for perennial beds can only help plants survive the winter. Here's what works and what doesn't:

1. Always apply mulch after the ground is frozen.
2. Never apply generic hay because is contains billions of weed seeds. Also, whole leaves and bark mulch hold too much moisture.
3. Straw and salt marsh hay are excellent choices for mulch.

For copies of earlier Gardener's Corner columns, call 1-800-555-3827.

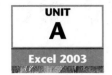
Getting Started with Excel 2003

OBJECTIVES

Define spreadsheet software
Start Excel 2003
View the Excel window
Open and save a workbook
Enter labels and values
Name and move a sheet
Preview and print a worksheet
Get Help
Close a workbook and exit Excel

If you have a SAM user profile, you may have access to hands-on instruction, practice, and assessment of the skills covered in this unit. Log in to your SAM account and go to your assignments page to see what your instructor has assigned.

In this unit, you will learn how to start Microsoft Office Excel 2003 and identify elements in the Excel window. You will also learn how to open and save existing files, enter data in a worksheet, manipulate worksheets, and use the extensive Help system. ▆▆▆ Jim Fernandez is the office manager at MediaLoft, a chain of bookstore cafés founded in 1988. MediaLoft stores offer customers the opportunity to purchase books, music, and movies while enjoying a variety of coffees, teas, and freshly baked desserts. Jim wants you, his assistant, to learn how to use Excel and help him analyze a worksheet summarizing budget information for the MediaLoft café in the New York City location.

Defining Spreadsheet Software

Microsoft Excel is an electronic spreadsheet program that runs on Windows computers. You use an **electronic spreadsheet** to produce professional-looking documents that perform numeric calculations rapidly and accurately. These calculations are updated automatically so that accurate information is always available. See Table A-1 for common ways spreadsheets are used in business. The electronic spreadsheet that you produce when using Excel is also referred to as a **worksheet**. Individual worksheets are stored within a **workbook**, which is a file with the .xls file extension. Each new workbook automatically contains three worksheets, although you can have up to 255 sheets. 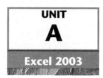 Jim uses Excel extensively to track MediaLoft finances, and as you work with Jim, you will also use Excel to complete many tasks. Figure A-1 shows a budget worksheet that Jim created using pencil and paper, while Figure A-2 shows the same worksheet Jim created using Excel.

DETAILS

When you use Excel you have the ability to:

- **Enter data quickly and accurately**

  With Excel, you can enter information faster and more accurately than with pencil and paper. For example, in the MediaLoft NYC Café Budget, certain expenses, such as rent, cleaning supplies, and products supplied on a yearly contract (coffee, creamers, and sweeteners), remain constant for the year. You can copy the expenses that don't change from quarter to quarter, then use Excel to calculate Total Expenses and Net Income for each quarter by supplying the data and formulas.

- **Recalculate data easily**

  Fixing typing errors or updating data using Excel is easy, and the results of a changed entry are recalculated automatically. For example, if you receive updated expense figures for Quarter 4, you enter the new numbers, and Excel recalculates the worksheet.

- **Perform a what-if analysis**

  The ability in Excel to change data and quickly view the recalculated results makes it a powerful decision-making tool. For instance, if the salary budget per quarter is increased to $17,200, you can enter the new figure into the worksheet and immediately see the impact on the overall budget. Any time you use a worksheet to ask the question "what if?" you are performing a **what-if analysis**.

- **Change the appearance of information**

  Excel provides powerful features for making information visually appealing and easy to understand. For example, you can use boldface type and colored or shaded text headings or numbers to emphasize important worksheet data and trends.

- **Create charts**

  Excel makes it easy to create charts based on worksheet information. Charts are updated automatically as data changes. The worksheet in Figure A-2 includes a 3-D pie chart that shows the distribution of the budget expenses for the MediaLoft NYC Café.

- **Share information with other users**

  Because everyone at MediaLoft is now using Microsoft Office, it's easy for them to share worksheet data. For example, you can complete the MediaLoft budget that Jim started creating in Excel. Simply access the files you need or want to share through the network or from a disk, or through the use of online collaboration tools (such as intranets and the Internet), and make any changes or additions.

- **Create new worksheets from existing ones quickly**

  It's easy to take an existing Excel worksheet and quickly modify it to create a new one. When you are ready to create next year's budget, you can open the file for this year's budget, save it with a new filename, and use the existing data as a starting point. An Excel file can also be created using a special format called a **template**, which lets you open a new file based on an existing workbook's design or content. Excel comes with many prepared templates you can use.

FIGURE A-1: Traditional paper worksheet

MediaLoft NYC Café Budget

	Qtr 1	Qtr 2	Qtr 3	Qtr 4	Total
Net Sales	56,000	84,000	72,000	79,000	291,000
Expenses					
Salary	17,200	17,200	17,200	17,200	68,800
Rent	4,000	4,000	4,000	4,000	16,000
Advertising	3,750	8,000	3,750	3,750	19,250
Cleansers	2,200	2,200	2,200	2,200	8,800
Pastries	2,500	2,500	2,500	2,500	10,000
Milk/Cream	1,000	1,000	1,000	1,000	4,000
Coffee/Tea	4,700	4,750	4,750	4,750	18,950
Sweeteners	650	650	650	650	2,600
Total Expenses	36,000	40,300	36,050	36,050	148,400
Net Income	20,000	43,700	35,950	42,950	142,600

FIGURE A-2: Excel worksheet

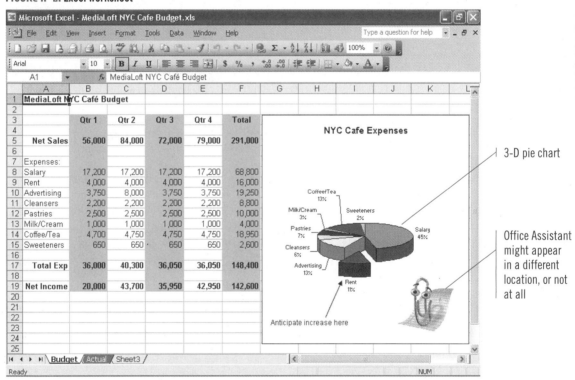

3-D pie chart

Office Assistant might appear in a different location, or not at all

TABLE A-1: Common business uses for electronic spreadsheets

spreadsheets are used to	by
Maintain values	Calculating numbers
Represent values graphically	Creating charts based on worksheet figures
Create reports to summarize data	Creating workbooks containing multiple worksheets of related data, and numbering and printing the worksheets as consecutively numbered pages
Organize data	Sorting data in ascending or descending order
Analyze data	Creating data summaries and short lists using PivotTables or AutoFilters
Create what-if data scenarios	Using variable values to investigate and sample different outcomes

Starting Excel 2003

To start any Windows program, you use the Start button on the taskbar. A slightly different procedure might be required for computers on a network and those that use Windows-enhancing utilities. If you need assistance, ask your instructor or technical support person. ▄▄▄▄▄ Jim has asked you to work on the budget for the MediaLoft café in New York City, which he created using Excel. You begin by starting Excel.

1. **Point to the Start button 🏁 start on the taskbar**

   The Start button is on the left side of the taskbar. You use it to start programs on your computer.

   > **QUICK TIP**
   > You might also see Microsoft Office Excel 2003 listed on the left side of the Start menu, which you can also click to start Excel.

2. **Click 🏁 start**

   Microsoft Office Excel is located on the All Programs menu, which is located at the bottom of the Start menu, as shown in Figure A-3.

3. **Point to All Programs**

   The All Programs menu opens. All the programs on your computer, including Microsoft Excel, are listed on this menu. Your All Programs menu might look different, depending on the programs installed on your computer.

4. **Point to Microsoft Office**

   A submenu displays listing all the Microsoft Office programs installed on your computer. See Figure A-4.

   > **TROUBLE**
   > If you don't see the Microsoft Office Excel 2003 icon, see your instructor or technical support person.

5. **Click the Microsoft Office Excel 2003 program icon on the Microsoft Office submenu**

   Excel opens and a blank worksheet is displayed. In the next lesson, you will learn about the elements of the Excel worksheet window.

6. **If necessary, click the Maximize button ▣ on the title bar**

   In the next lesson, you will learn about the elements of the Excel worksheet window.

FIGURE A-3: Start menu

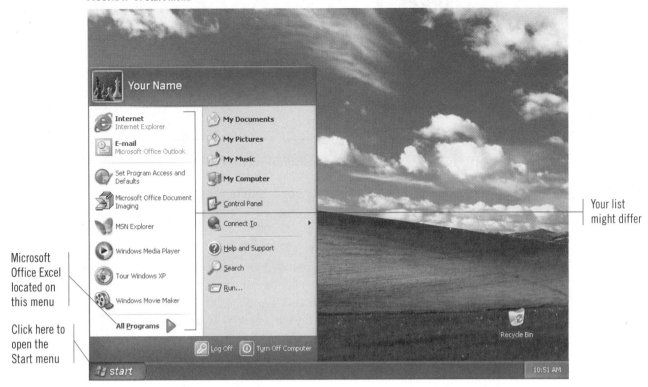

Microsoft Office Excel located on this menu

Click here to open the Start menu

Your list might differ

FIGURE A-4: All Programs menu

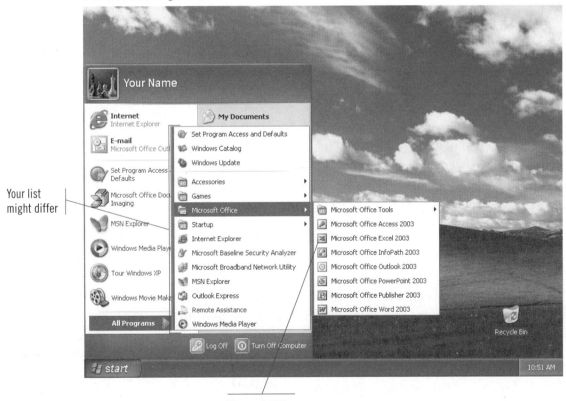

Your list might differ

Microsoft Office Excel 2003 program icon

Viewing the Excel Window

When you start Excel, the worksheet window appears on your screen. The **worksheet window** includes the tools that enable you to create and work with worksheets. You need to familiarize yourself with the Excel worksheet window and its elements before you start working on the budget worksheet. Compare the descriptions below to the elements shown in Figure A-5.

DETAILS

The elements of the Excel worksheet window include:

QUICK TIP

There are two sets of resizing buttons: one for the program and another for the active workbook. The program's resizing buttons are located on the title bar, while the workbook's resizing buttons appear below the program resizing buttons, on the menu bar (when the workbook is maximized).

- The **title bar** displays the program name (Microsoft Excel) and the filename of the open worksheet (in this case the default filename, Book1). As shown in Figure A-5, the title bar also contains a control menu box, a Close button, and resizing buttons, which are common to all Windows programs. The **control menu box** provides a menu of commands that allow you to move, size, open, or close the program window.

- The **menu bar** contains menus from which you select Excel commands. As with all Windows programs, you can select a menu command by clicking it with the mouse pointer or by pressing [Alt] plus the underlined letter in the menu command name. When you click a menu, only a short list of commonly used commands might appear at first; you can wait or click the double arrows at the bottom of the menu to see expanded menus with a complete list of commands.

- The **Name box** displays the active cell address. In Figure A-5, "A1" appears in the Name box, indicating that A1 is the active cell.

- The **formula bar** allows you to enter or edit data in the worksheet.

- The **toolbars** contain buttons for frequently used Excel commands. The **Standard toolbar** is located just below the menu bar and contains buttons that perform actions within the worksheet. The **Formatting toolbar**—beneath the Standard toolbar—contains buttons that change the worksheet's appearance. Each button contains an image representing its function. For instance, the Print button contains an image of a printer. To select any button, click it with the left mouse button.

QUICK TIP

You can always return to the Getting Started task pane by clicking the Home button 🏠 at the top of any task pane.

- The worksheet window contains a grid of columns and rows. Columns are labeled alphabetically (A, B, C, etc.) and rows are labeled numerically (1, 2, 3, etc.). The worksheet window displays only a small fraction of the whole worksheet, which has a total of 256 columns and 65,536 rows. The intersection of a column and a row is called a **cell**. Cells can contain text, numbers, formulas, or a combination of all three. Every cell has its own unique location or **cell address**, which is identified by the coordinates of the intersecting column and row. For example, the cell address of the cell in the upper-left corner of a worksheet is A1.

- A **task pane** is an organizational tool that allows you to perform routine tasks quickly and easily. The **Getting Started task pane** appears to the right of the worksheet window and lets you quickly open new or existing workbooks. The **Task pane list arrow** lets you choose from 12 different panes.

TROUBLE

If your screen does not display cells in orange and gray as shown in the figure, ask your technical support person to check your Windows color settings.

- The **cell pointer** is a dark rectangle that outlines the cell in which you are working. This cell is called the **active cell**. In Figure A-5, the cell pointer is located at A1, so A1 is the active cell. The column and row headings for the active cell are orange; inactive column and row headings are gray. To activate a different cell, just click any other cell or press the arrow keys on your keyboard to move the cell pointer elsewhere.

- **Sheet tabs** below the worksheet grid let you keep your work in a collection called a workbook. Each workbook contains three worksheets by default and can contain a maximum of 255 sheets. Sheet tabs allow you to name your worksheets with meaningful names. **Sheet tab scrolling buttons** help you display hidden worksheets.

- The **status bar** is located at the bottom of the Excel window. The left side of the status bar provides a brief description of the active command or task in progress. The right side of the status bar shows the status of important keys such as [Caps Lock] and [Num Lock].

FIGURE A-5: Excel worksheet window elements

Title bar
Control menu box
Menu bar
Standard toolbar
Formatting toolbar
Name box
Cell pointer highlights active cell
Formula bar
Sheet tab scrolling buttons

Close button
Resizing buttons
Task pane list arrow
Getting Started task pane lets you open or create a workbook
Worksheet window

Status bar   Sheet tabs

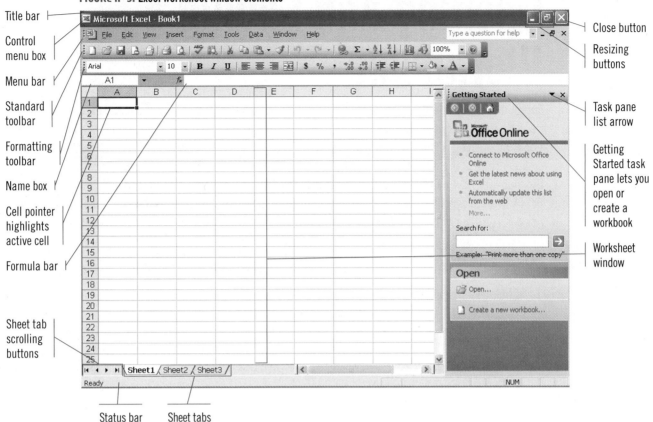

Clues to Use

Working with toolbars and menus in Excel 2003

Although you can configure Excel so that your toolbars and menus modify themselves to conform to your working style, the lessons in this book assume you have turned off personalized menus and toolbars and are working with all menu commands and toolbar buttons displayed. When you use personalized toolbars, the Standard and Formatting toolbars appear on the same row and display only the most frequently used buttons, as shown in Figure A-6. To use a button that is not visible on a toolbar, you click the Toolbar Options button ⬚ at the end of the toolbar, then click the button on the Toolbar Options list. As you work, Excel adds the buttons you use to the visible toolbars and drops the buttons you don't often use to the Toolbar Options list. Similarly, Excel menus adjust to your work habits, so that

the commands you use most often appear on shortened menus. You can see all the menu commands by clicking the Expand button (double arrows) at the bottom of a menu. It is often easier to work with full toolbars and menus displayed. To turn off personalized toolbars and menus, click Tools on the menu bar, click Customize, then click the Options tab in the Customize dialog box. Select the Show Standard and Formatting toolbars on two rows and Always show full menus check boxes, then click Close. The Standard and Formatting toolbars appear on separate rows and display most of the buttons, and the menus display the complete list of menu commands. (You can also quickly display the toolbars on two rows by clicking a Toolbar Options button, then clicking Show Buttons on Two Rows.)

FIGURE A-6: Toolbars on one row

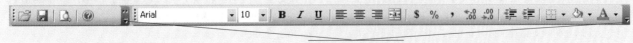

Toolbar Options buttons

Excel 2003

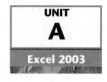

Opening and Saving a Workbook

Sometimes it's more efficient to create a new workbook by modifying one that already exists. This saves you from having to retype information from previous work. Throughout this book, you will create new workbooks by opening a file from the location where your Data Files are stored, using the Save As command to create a copy of the file with a new name, then modifying the new file by following the lesson steps. Saving the files with new names keeps your original Data Files intact, in case you have to start the unit over again or you wish to repeat an exercise. Use the Save command to store changes made to an existing file. It is a good idea to save your work every 10 or 15 minutes and before printing. ▰▰▰ You want to complete the MediaLoft budget on which Jim has been working.

STEPS

> **QUICK TIP**
>
> If the task pane is not open, click View on the menu bar, then click Task Pane to display the Getting Started task pane.

1. **Click the Open button 🗁 in the Getting Started task pane**

   The Open dialog box opens. See Figure A-7. You can also click the Open button 🗁 on the Standard toolbar.

2. **Click the Look in list arrow, then click the drive and folder where your Data Files are located**

   The Look in list arrow lets you navigate to folders and disk drives on your computer. A list of your Data Files appears in the Open dialog box.

> **QUICK TIP**
>
> If you don't see the three-letter extension .xls on the filenames in the Open dialog box, don't worry. Windows can be set up to display or not to display the file extensions.

3. **Click the file EX A-1.xls, then click Open**

   The file EX A-1.xls opens. The Getting Started task pane no longer appears on the screen.

4. **Click File on the menu bar, then click Save As**

   The Save As dialog box opens, displaying the drive where your Data Files are stored. You can create a new folder from within the Save As dialog box by clicking 🖆 on the dialog box toolbar, typing a name in the Name text box, then clicking OK. To open a file from a folder you create, double-click folders, or use the Look in list arrow in the Open dialog box to open the folder, click the filename, then click Open.

5. **In the File name text box, select the current filename if necessary, type MediaLoft Cafe Budget, as shown in Figure A-8, then click Save**

   Both the Save As dialog box and the file EX A-1.xls close, and a duplicate file named MediaLoft Cafe Budget opens, as shown in Figure A-9.

Clues to Use

Creating a new workbook

You can create your own worksheets from scratch by opening a new workbook. To create a new workbook, click the New button 🗋 on the Standard toolbar. You can also use the Getting Started or New Workbook task panes to open a new workbook. Click the Go to New Workbook task pane button 🗋 in the Getting Started task pane to open the New Workbook task pane, then click the Blank Workbook button 🗋 to open a new workbook.

FIGURE A-7: Open dialog box

My Documents folder opens by default

Your files and folders appear here; your contents might differ

Selected filename will appear here

Look in list arrow

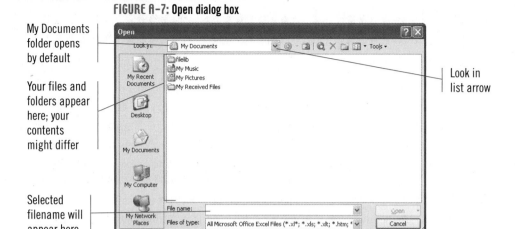

FIGURE A-8: Save As dialog box

Current drive or folder (yours might differ)

Your list of files might differ

Type new filename here

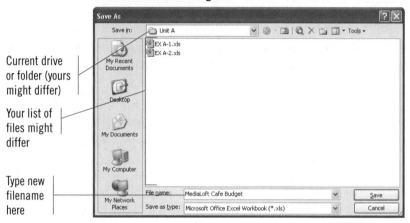

FIGURE A-9: MediaLoft Café Budget workbook

Orange column and row headers define the active cell

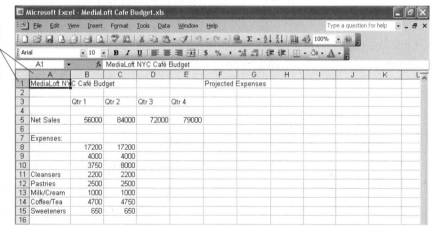

Clues to Use

Opening a workbook using a template

You can create a workbook by entering data and formats into a blank workbook, or you can use predesigned workbooks called templates that are included with Excel. Templates let you automatically create workbooks such as balance sheets, expense statements, loan amortizations, sales invoices, or timecards. Templates save you time because they contain labels, values, formulas, and formatting. To open a new workbook based on a template, click the Other Task Panes list arrow

from the Getting Started task pane, then click New Workbook. Click the On my computer link under the Templates section, then click the Spreadsheet Solutions tab in the Templates dialog box. Click one of the samples, save it under a new name, then add your own information. You may need to have the Office CD available to install the templates. You can also find more templates by clicking the Templates home page link.

Entering Labels and Values

Labels help you identify the data in worksheet rows and columns, making your worksheet more readable and understandable. You should try to enter all labels in your worksheet before entering the data. Labels can contain text and numerical information not used in calculations, such as dates, times, or addresses. Labels are left-aligned by default. **Values**, which include numbers, formulas, and functions, are used in calculations. Excel recognizes an entry as a value when it is a number, or begins with one of these special symbols: +, -, =, @, #, or $. All values are right-aligned by default. When you ask Excel to total data in a column, it ignores those cells that have numbers within labels (such as 2006 Sales), and only totals those cells that contain values. When a cell contains both text and numbers, Excel recognizes the entry as a label. You notice that Jim's budget worksheet is missing some data. You want to enter labels identifying the rest of the expense categories, and the values for Qtr 3 and Qtr 4 into the MediaLoft Café Budget worksheet.

STEPS

1. **Click cell A8 to make it the active cell**

    Notice that the cell address A8 appears in the Name box. As you work, the mouse pointer takes on a variety of appearances, depending on where it is and what the program is doing. Table A-2 lists and identifies some mouse pointers. The labels in cells A8:A15 identify the expenses.

2. **Type Salary, as shown in Figure A-10, then click the Enter button ✓ on the formula bar**

    As you type, the word "Enter" appears in the status bar. Clicking the Enter button indicates that you are finished typing or changing your entry, and the word "Ready" appears in the status bar. Because the cell is still selected, its contents still appear in the formula bar. You can also confirm a cell entry by pressing [Enter], [Tab], or one of the keyboard arrow keys. These three methods also select an adjacent cell. To confirm an entry and leave the same cell selected, you can press [Ctrl][Enter]. If a label does not fit in a cell, Excel displays the remaining characters in the next cell to the right, as long as it is empty. Otherwise, the label is **truncated**, or cut off.

3. **Click cell A9, type Rent, press [Enter] to confirm the entry and move the cell pointer to cell A10, type Advertising in cell A10, then press [Enter]**

    The remaining expense values have to be added to the worksheet for Quarters 3 and 4.

4. **Click cell D8, press and hold down the left mouse button, drag ✛ to cell E8 then down to cell E15, then release the mouse button**

    You have selected a **range**, which consists of two or more adjacent cells. The active cell is still cell D8, and the cells in the range are shaded in blue.

5. **Type 17200, press [Enter], type 4000 in cell D9, press [Enter], type 3750 in cell D10, press [Enter], type 2200 in cell D11, press [Enter], type 2500 in cell D12, press [Enter], type 1000 in cell D13, press [Enter], type 4750 in cell D14, press [Enter], type 650 in cell D15, then press [Enter]**

    You often enter data in multiple columns and rows; selecting a range makes working with data entry easier because pressing [Enter] makes the next cell in the range active. You have entered all the values in the Qtr 3 column. The cell pointer is now in cell E8.

6. **Type the remaining values for cells E8 through E15 as shown in Figure A-11**

    Before confirming a cell entry, you can click the Cancel button on the formula bar or press [Esc] to cancel or delete the entry.

7. **Click cell D8, type 17250, then press [Enter]**

8. **Press [Ctrl][Home] to return to cell A1**

9. **Click the Save button 🖫 on the Standard toolbar**

    You can also press [Ctrl][S] to save a worksheet.

FIGURE A-10: Worksheet with first label entered

Name box

Cancel button

Enter button

Formula bar

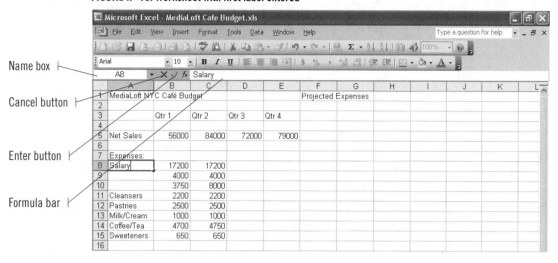

FIGURE A-11: Worksheet with new labels and values

Type these values

Labels entered

Values entered

AutoCalculate value

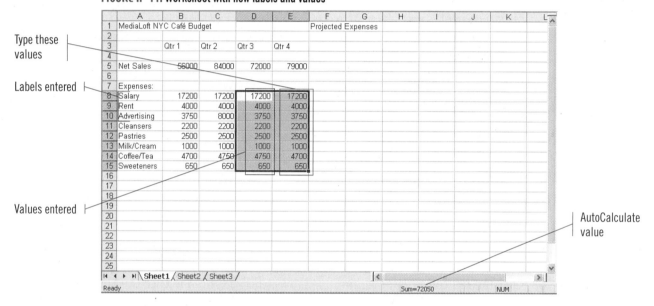

TABLE A-2: Commonly used pointers

name	pointer	use to
Normal	✛	Select a cell or range; indicates Ready mode
Copy	▹ +	Create a duplicate of the selected cell(s)
Fill handle	✚	Create an alphanumeric series in a range
I-beam	I	Edit contents of formula bar
Move	✛	Change the location of the selected cell(s)

Clues to Use

Navigating a worksheet

With over a million cells available to you, it is important to know how to move around, or navigate, a worksheet. You can use the arrow keys on the keyboard (↑, ↓, ←, or →) to move a cell at a time, or use [Page Up] or [Page Down] to move a screen at a time. To move a screen to the left press [Alt][Page Up]; to move a screen to the right press [Alt][Page Down]. You can also use the mouse pointer to click the desired cell. If the desired cell is not visible in the worksheet window, use the scroll bars or the Go To command on the Edit menu to move the location into view. To return to the first cell in a worksheet, click cell A1, or press [Ctrl][Home].

Naming and Moving a Sheet

Each workbook initially contains three worksheets, named Sheet1, Sheet2, and Sheet3. The sheet name appears on the sheet tab. When you open a workbook, the first worksheet is the active sheet. To move from sheet to sheet, you can click any sheet tab at the bottom of the worksheet window. The sheet tab scrolling buttons, located to the left of the sheet tabs, allow you to display hidden sheet tabs. To make it easier to identify the sheets in a workbook, you can rename each sheet and add color to the tabs. You can also organize them in a logical way. For instance, to better track performance goals, you could name each workbook sheet for an individual salesperson; then you could move the sheets so they appeared in alphabetical order. 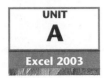 You have added data to Sheet1 of the budget workbook, which contains information on projected expenses. Jim tells you that Sheet2 contains data for the actual expenses. You want to be able to easily identify the actual expenses and the projected expenses, so you want to name the two sheets in the workbook, add color to distinguish them, then change their order.

STEPS

1. **Click the Sheet2 tab**

   Sheet2 becomes active; this is the worksheet that contains the actual quarterly expenses. Its tab moves to the front, and Sheet1 moves to the background.

2. **Click the Sheet1 tab**

   Sheet1, which contains the projected expenses, becomes active again. Once you have confirmed which sheet is which, you can assign them each a name that identifies their contents.

> **QUICK TIP**
>
> You can also rename a sheet by right-clicking the tab, clicking Rename on the shortcut menu, typing the new name, then pressing [Enter].

3. **Double-click the Sheet2 tab**

   Sheet 2 becomes the active sheet with the default sheet name of Sheet2 selected on the sheet tab.

4. **Type Actual, then press [Enter]**

   The new name automatically replaces the default name on the tab. Worksheet names can have up to 31 characters, including spaces and punctuation.

5. **Right-click the Actual tab, then click Tab Color on the shortcut menu**

   The Format Tab Color dialog box opens, as shown in Figure A-12.

> **QUICK TIP**
>
> To delete a worksheet, select the worksheet you want to delete, click Edit on the menu bar, then click Delete sheet. To insert a worksheet, click Insert on the menu bar, then click Worksheet.

6. **Click the red color (first column, third row), click OK, double-click the Sheet1 tab, type Projected, then press [Enter]**

   Notice that when you renamed Sheet1, the color of the entire Actual tab changed to red. You decide to rearrange the order of the sheets, so that Actual comes before Projected.

7. **Click the Actual sheet tab and hold down the mouse button, then drag it to the left of the Projected sheet tab**

   As you drag, the pointer changes to 🔖, the sheet relocation pointer, and a small, black triangle shows its position. See Figure A-13. The first sheet in the workbook is now the Actual sheet. To see hidden sheets, click the far left tab scrolling button to display the first sheet tab; click the far right navigation button to display the last sheet tab. The left and right buttons move one sheet in their respective directions.

8. **Click the Projected sheet tab, enter your name in cell A20, then press [Ctrl][Home]**

   Your name identifies your worksheet as yours, which is helpful if you are sharing a printer.

9. **Click the Save button 🖫 on the Standard toolbar**

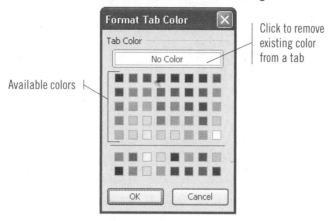

FIGURE A-12: Format Tab Color dialog box

Click to remove existing color from a tab

Available colors

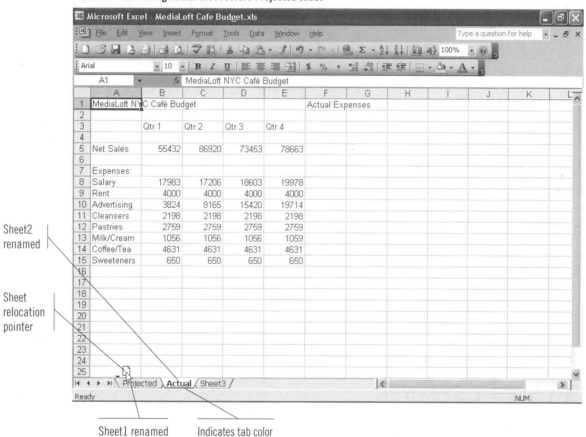

FIGURE A-13: Moving Actual sheet before Projected sheet

Sheet2 renamed

Sheet relocation pointer

Sheet1 renamed

Indicates tab color

Clues to Use

Copying worksheets

There are times when you may want to copy a worksheet. To copy it, press [Ctrl] as you drag the sheet tab, then release the mouse button before you release [Ctrl]. You can also move and copy worksheets between workbooks. You must have the workbook that you are copying to, as well as the workbook that you are copying from, open.

Select the sheet to copy or move, click Edit on the menu bar, then click Move or Copy sheet. Complete the information in the Move or Copy dialog box. Be sure to click the Create a copy check box if you are copying rather than moving the worksheet. Carefully check your calculation results whenever you move or copy a worksheet.

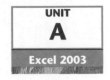

UNIT A
Excel 2003

Previewing and Printing a Worksheet

After you complete a worksheet, you may want to print it to have a paper copy for reference or to give to others. You can also print a worksheet that is not complete to review your work when you are not at a computer. Before you print a worksheet, you should save any changes. That way, if anything happens to the file as it is being sent to the printer, you have your latest work saved. Then you should preview it to make sure it fits on the page the way you want. When you **preview** a worksheet, you see a copy of the worksheet exactly as it will appear on paper. See Table A-3 for a summary of printing tips. ▦▦▦ You are finished entering the labels and values into the MediaLoft budget. You have already saved your changes, so you preview the worksheet, then print a copy which you can review later.

STEPS

QUICK TIP

To print the worksheet using existing settings without previewing it, click the Print button 🖨 on the Standard toolbar.

1. **Make sure the printer is on and contains paper**

   If a file is sent to print and the printer is off, an error message appears on your screen.

2. **Click the Print Preview button 🔍 on the Standard toolbar**

   A miniature version of the worksheet appears in the Print Preview window, as shown in Figure A-14. If your worksheet requires more than one page, you can click the Next button or the Previous button to move between pages. Because your worksheet is only one page, the Next and Previous buttons are dimmed to signify they are inactive.

3. **Click Print**

   The Print dialog box opens, as shown in Figure A-15.

4. **Make sure that the Active sheet(s) option button is selected in the Print what section and that 1 appears in the Number of copies text box in the Copies section**

   Adjusting the value in the Number of copies text box enables you to print multiple copies. You can also print a selected range by clicking the Selection option button.

QUICK TIP

After previewing or printing a worksheet, dotted lines appear on the screen indicating individual page breaks in the printout. Page break positions vary with each printer.

5. **Click OK**

   A Printing dialog box appears briefly while the file is sent to the printer. Note that the dialog box contains a Cancel button. You can use it to cancel the print job while it is waiting in the print queue.

TABLE A-3: Worksheet printing tips

before you print	recommendation
Save the workbook	Make sure your work is saved before executing the command to print
Check the printer	Make sure that the printer is turned on and is online, that it has paper, and that there are no error messages or warning signals
Preview the worksheet	Check the formatted image for page breaks, page setup (vertical or horizontal), and overall appearance of the worksheet
Check the printer selection	Look in the Print dialog box to verify that the correct printer is selected
Check the Print what options	Look in the Print dialog box to verify that you are printing the active sheet, the entire workbook, or a range

FIGURE A-14: Print Preview window

Move to another page

Enlarge the screen image

Print the worksheet

Change print options

Zoom pointer

Return to worksheet

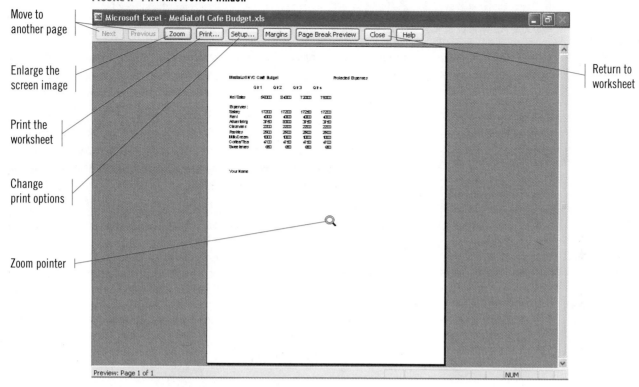

FIGURE A-15: Print dialog box

Your printer might differ

Prints the current worksheet

Indicates the number of copies to be printed

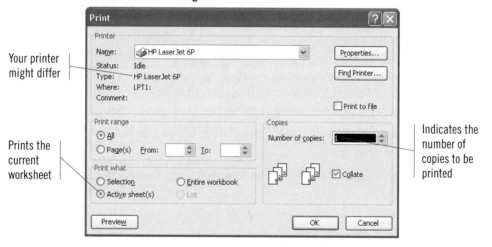

Clues to Use

Using Zoom in Print Preview

When you are in the Print Preview window, you can enlarge the image by clicking the Zoom button. You can also position the Zoom pointer ⊙ over a specific part of the worksheet page, then click it to view that section of the page. Figure A-16 shows a magnified section of a document. While the image is zoomed in, use the scroll bars to view different sections of the page.

FIGURE A-16: Enlarging the preview using Zoom

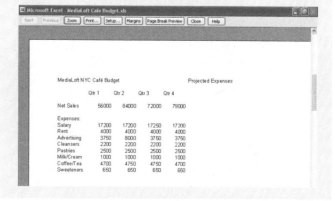

UNIT
A
Excel 2003

Getting Help

Excel features an extensive **Help system** that gives you immediate access to definitions, how to complete tasks, explanations, and useful tips. The Help task pane lets you search the Microsoft online Help database stored on the Web or the Excel Help database stored on your computer. You can type a **keyword**, a representative word on which Excel can search your area of interest, or you can access a question-and-answer format to research your Help topic. In addition, you can press [F1] at any time to display the Help task pane and get immediate assistance. Alternately, the **Type a question for help box** on the menu bar is always available for asking questions. You can click in the text box and type a question at any time to display related Help topics. Questions from your current Excel session are stored, and you can access them at any time by clicking the Type a question for help list arrow, then clicking the question of interest. Jim wants you to find out more about formulas so you can work more efficiently with them. He suggests you find out more information by using the Microsoft Excel Help task pane.

STEPS

QUICK TIP

You can also display the Microsoft Excel Help task pane from any open task pane. To do this, click the Other Task Panes list arrow, then click Help.

1. **Click the** Microsoft Excel Help button ⊚ **on the Standard toolbar**

   The Excel Help task pane opens. You can get information by typing a keyword or question in the Search text box.

2. **Type** Create a formula **in the Search for text box**

   See Figure A-18.

3. **Click the** Start searching button →

   Excel searches for relevant topics from the Help files and displays a list of topics from which you can choose.

4. **Click** Create a formula

   A Help window containing information about creating formulas opens, as shown in Figure A-19. Microsoft Excel Help is an online feature that by default assumes you are connected to the Internet. If you are not connected to the Internet, then your search results might differ from Figure A-19. You may have fewer search results, reflecting those topics stored locally in the Excel Help database on your computer.

QUICK TIP

Clicking the Print button in the Help window prints the information.

5. **Read the text, then click the** Close button ☒ **on the Help window title bar**

   The Help window closes.

6. **Click the** Close button ☒ **on the Search Results task pane to close it.**

   The task pane is no longer displayed in the worksheet window.

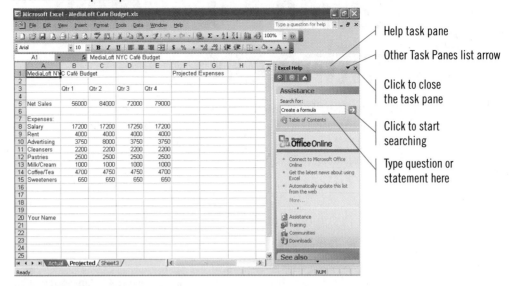

Help task pane

Other Task Panes list arrow

Click to close
the task pane

Click to start
searching

Type question or
statement here

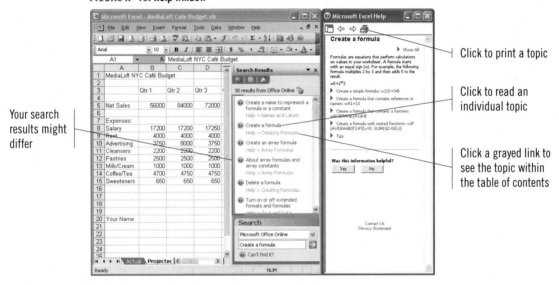

Your search
results might
differ

Click to print a topic

Click to read an
individual topic

Click a grayed link to
see the topic within
the table of contents

Excel 2003

Clues to Use

Using the Office Assistant

If the Office Assistant is displayed, click it to access Help. If it is not displayed, click Help on the menu bar, then click Show the Office Assistant. (You may need to install additional components from your Microsoft Office CD in order to see the Office Assistant.) This feature provides help based on the text you type in the query box. To ask a question, click the Office Assistant. Type a question, statement, or word, as shown in Figure A-17, then click Search. The Search Results task pane searches the database and displays any matching topics. The animated Office Assistant provides Office Assistant Tips (indicated by a light bulb) on the current action you are performing. You can click the light bulb to display a dialog box containing relevant choices to which you can refer as you work. The default Office Assistant character is Clippit, but there are others from which you can choose. To change the appearance of the Office Assistant, right-click the Office Assistant, then click Options on the shortcut menu. Click the Gallery tab in the Options dialog box, click the Back and Next buttons until

you find an Assistant you want to use, then click OK. (You may need to insert your Microsoft Office CD to perform this task.)

FIGURE A-17: Office Assistant dialog box

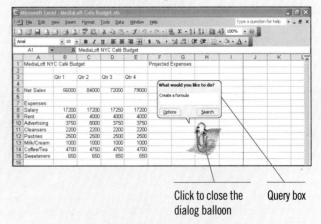

Click to close the
dialog balloon

Query box

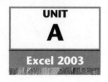

Closing a Workbook and Exiting Excel

When you have finished working, you need to save the workbook file and close it. When you have completed all your work in Excel you need to exit the program. You can exit Excel by clicking Exit on the File menu. ▰▰▰▰▰ You have completed your work on the MediaLoft budget. You want to close the workbook, then exit Excel.

1. **Click File on the menu bar**

   The File menu opens. See Figure A-20.

2. **Click Close**

   Excel closes the workbook, asking if you want to save your changes; if you have made any changes be sure to save them. You can also click the workbook Close button instead of clicking Close on the File menu.

3. **Click File on the menu bar, then click Exit**

   You can also click the program Close button to exit the program. Excel closes, and you return to the desktop.

FIGURE A-20: Closing a workbook using the File menu

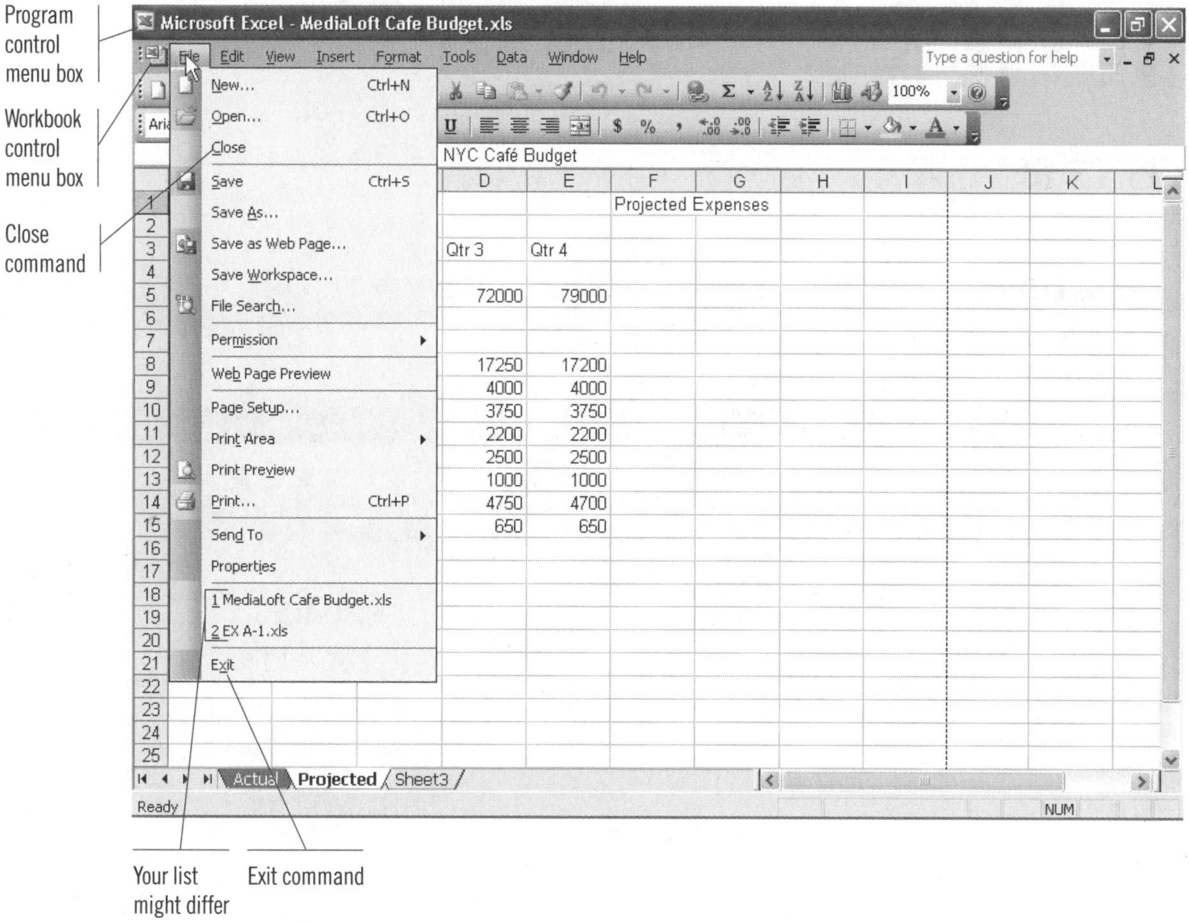

Program control menu box

Workbook control menu box

Close command

Your list might differ   Exit command

Practice

▼ CONCEPTS REVIEW

Label the elements of the Excel worksheet window shown in Figure A-21.

FIGURE A-21

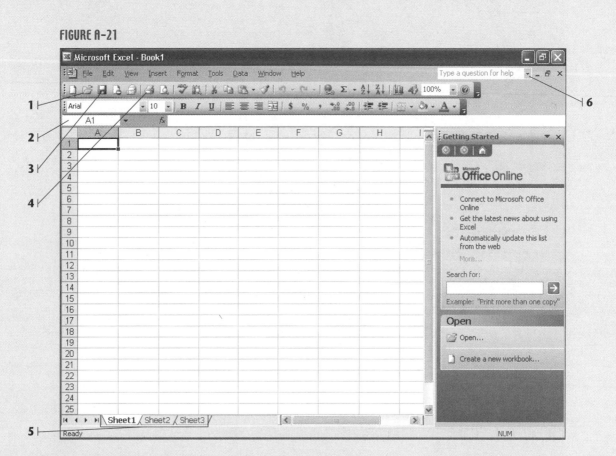

Match each term with the statement that best describes it.

7. Cell
8. Worksheet window
9. Workbook
10. Name Box
11. Cell pointer
12. Formula bar

a. Area that contains a grid of columns and rows
b. The intersection of a column and row
c. Allows you to enter or edit worksheet data
d. Collection of worksheets
e. Rectangle indicating the active cell
f. Displays the active cell address

Select the best answer from the list of choices.

13. The following key(s) can be used to confirm cell entries, except:

   a. [Enter].

   b. [Tab].

   c. [Esc].

   d. [Ctrl][Enter].

14. Each of the following is true about labels, except:

   a. They are left-aligned by default.

   b. They are not used in calculations.

   c. They are right-aligned by default.

   d. They can include numerical information.

15. An electronic spreadsheet can perform all of the following tasks, except:

   a. Display information visually.

   b. Calculate data accurately.

   c. Plan worksheet objectives.

   d. Recalculate updated information.

16. What symbol is typed before a number to make the number a label?

   a. '

   b. !

   c. "

   d. ;

17. You can get Excel Help in any of the following ways, except:

   a. Clicking Help on the menu bar, then clicking Microsoft Excel Help.

   b. Minimizing the program window.

   c. Clicking 🔘.

   d. Pressing [F1].

18. Each of the following is true about values, except:

   a. They can include labels.

   b. They are right-aligned by default.

   c. They are used in calculations.

   d. They can include formulas.

19. Which button is used to preview a worksheet?

   a. 🗋

   b. 💾

   c. 🔍

   d. 🖨

20. Each of the following is true about the Help feature, except:

   a. You can use the Type a question for help text box.

   b. You can search your computer and Microsoft.com.

   c. You can change the appearance of the Office Assistant.

   d. It can complete certain tasks for you.

21. Which feature is used to enlarge a Print Preview view?

   a. Magnify

   b. Enlarge

   c. Amplify

   d. Zoom

▼ SKILLS REVIEW

1. Define spreadsheet software.

   a. Identify five disadvantages of using a nonelectronic spreadsheet.

   b. Identify five common business uses for electronic spreadsheets.

2. Start Excel 2003.

   a. Point to **All Programs** on the Start menu.

   b. Point to Microsoft Office, then click the **Microsoft Office Excel 2003** program icon.

   c. What appears when Excel opens?

▼ SKILLS REVIEW (CONTINUED)

3. **View the Excel window.**
   a. Identify as many elements in the Excel window without looking back in the unit.
   b. If the program and workbook are both maximized, which set of resizing buttons is used to minimize the workbook? (*Hint*: Would you use the upper or lower set?)

4. **Open and save a workbook.**
   a. Open the workbook EX A-2.xls from the drive and folder where your Data Files are located.
   b. Use the Create New Folder button in the Save As dialog box to create a folder called **Toronto** in the drive and folder where your Data Files are located.
   c. Save the workbook as **MediaLoft Toronto Café** in the **Toronto** folder where your Data Files are located.
   d. Close the file.
   e. Open it again from the new folder you created.
   f. Open a new workbook based on the Balance Sheet template: open the New Workbook task pane, click the On my computer link under the Templates section, display the Spreadsheet Solutions tab, then double-click Balance Sheet.
   g. Save the workbook as **MediaLoft Balance Sheet** in the drive and folder where your Data Files are stored, then close the workbook.

5. **Enter labels and values.**
   a. Enter the necessary labels shown in Table A-4. (The entry for "Water" should be in cell A4.)
   b. Enter the values shown in Table A-4.
   c. Clear the contents of cell A9 using the Edit menu, then type **Tea** in cell A9.
   d. Save the workbook using the Save button.

6. **Name and move a sheet.**
   a. Name the Sheet1 tab **Inventory**, then name the Sheet2 tab **Sales**.
   b. Move the Inventory sheet so it comes after the Sales sheet.
   c. Change the tab color of the Inventory sheet to yellow (third column, fourth row in the pallette).
   d. Change the tab color of the Sales sheet to aqua (fifth column, fourth row in the pallette).

7. **Preview and print a worksheet.**
   a. Make the Inventory sheet active.
   b. View it in Print Preview.
   c. Use the Zoom button to get a better look at your worksheet.
   d. Add your name to cell A11, then print one copy of the worksheet.
   e. Save the workbook.

8. **Get Help.**
   a. Display the Help task pane.
   b. Ask for information about defining a range.
   c. Print the information offered by the Help task pane using the Print button in the Help window.
   d. Close the Help window and task pane.

9. **Close a workbook and exit Excel.**
   a. Close the file using the Close command.
   b. Exit Excel.

TABLE A-4

	On-Hand	Cost Each	Sale Price
Water	32	10.03	
Coffee	52	13.71	
Bread	39	15.22	
Muffins	25	16.99	
Sweets	43	11.72	
Sodas	52	9.91	

▼ INDEPENDENT CHALLENGE 1

The Excel Help feature provides definitions, explanations, procedures, and other helpful information. It also provides examples and demonstrations to show you how Excel features work. Topics include elements such as the active cell, status bar, buttons, and dialog boxes, as well as detailed information about Excel commands and options.

  a. Start Excel and open a blank workbook using the Getting Started task pane.

  b. Display the Help task pane.

  c. Find information about displaying toolbar buttons.

Advanced Challenge Exercise

  ■ Display the Office Assistant, if necessary, using the Show Office Assistant command on the Help menu.

  ■ Click the Office Assistant, then type a question about saving a workbook in another file format. (*Hint*: You may have to ask the Office Assistant more than one question.)

  d. Print the information, close the Help window, then exit Excel.

▼ INDEPENDENT CHALLENGE 2

Spreadsheet software has many uses that can affect the way people work. The beginning of this unit discusses some examples of people using Excel. Use your own personal or business experiences to come up with five examples of how Excel can be used in a business setting.

  a. Start Excel.

  b. Write down five business tasks that you can complete more efficiently by using an Excel worksheet.

  c. Sketch a sample of each worksheet. See Table A-5, a sample payroll worksheet, as a guide.

  d. Open a new workbook and save it as **Sample Payroll** in the drive and folder where your Data Files are stored.

  e. Give your worksheet a title in cell A1, then type your name in cell D1.

  f. Enter the labels shown in Table A-5. Enter Hours Worked in column C and Hourly Wage in column E.

  g. Create and enter your own sample data for Hours Worked and Hourly Wage in the worksheet. (The entry for "Dale Havorford" should be in cell A4.)

  h. Save your work, then preview and print the worksheet.

  i. Close the worksheet and exit Excel.

TABLE A-5

Employee Name	Hours Worked	Hourly Wage
Dale Havorford		
Chris Wong		
Sharon Martinez		
Belinda Swanson		
Total		

▼ INDEPENDENT CHALLENGE 3

You are the office manager for Christine's Car Parts, a small auto parts supplier. Although the company is just three years old, it is expanding rapidly, and you are continually looking for ways to make your job easier. Last year, you began using Excel to manage and maintain data on inventory and sales, which has greatly helped you to track information accurately and efficiently. The owner of the company has just approved your request to hire an assistant, who will be starting work in a week. You want to create a short training document that acquaints your new assistant with basic Excel skills.

   a. Start Excel.

   b. Create a new workbook and save it as **Training Workbook** in the drive and folder where your Data Files are located.

   c. Model your worksheet after the sample shown in Figure A-22. Enter a title for the worksheet in cell A1.

   d. Enter your name in cell D1.

   e. Create and enter values and labels for a sample spreadsheet. Make sure you have labels in column A.

   f. Change the name of Sheet1 to Sample Data, then change the tab color of the Sample Data worksheet to another color.

   g. Preview the worksheet, then print it.

Advanced Challenge Exercise

- Open a workbook based on a template from the Spreadsheet Solutions tab in the Templates dialog box. (You may need to insert your Office CD in order to do this.)
- Preview the worksheet, then print it.
- Save the workbook as **Template Sample**.

   h. Close the file(s) and exit Excel.

FIGURE A-22

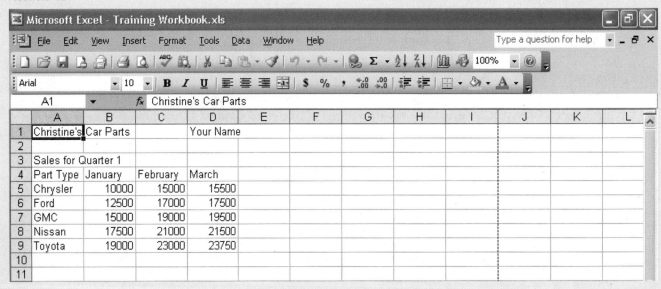

▼ INDEPENDENT CHALLENGE 4

You can use the World Wide Web to help make informed purchasing decisions. Your supervisor has just given you approval for buying a new computer. While cost is not a limiting factor, you do need to provide a list of hardware and software requirements. You can use data found on the World Wide Web, and use Excel to create a worksheet that details your purchase decision.

a. Connect to the Internet, then use your favorite search engine to find your own information sources on computer hardware and software you can purchase.

b. Locate data for the type of system you want by using at least two different vendor's Web sites. When you find systems that meet your needs, print out the information. Be sure to identify each system's key features, such as the processor chip, hard drive capacity, RAM, and monitor size.

c. When you are finished gathering data, disconnect from the Internet.

d. Start Excel, open a new workbook, then save it in the drive and folder where your Data Files are stored as **New Computer Data**.

e. Enter the manufacturers' names in columns and computer features (RAM, etc.) in rows. List the systems you found through your research, including the features you want (e.g., CD-ROM drive, etc.) and the cost for each system.

f. Indicate on the worksheet your final purchase decision by including descriptive text in a prominent cell. Enter your name in one of the cells.

g. Save, preview, then print your worksheet.

h. Close the file and exit Excel.

▼ VISUAL WORKSHOP

Create a worksheet similar to Figure A-23 using the skills you learned in this unit. Save the workbook as **Carrie's Camera and Darkroom** in the drive and folder where your Data Files are stored. Type your name in cell A11, then preview and print the worksheet.

FIGURE A-23

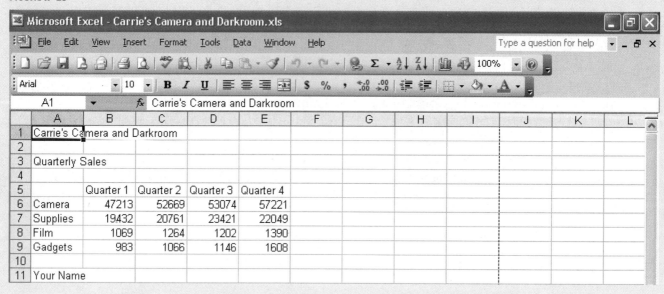

Building and Editing Worksheets

OBJECTIVES

Plan and design a worksheet
Edit cell entries
Enter formulas
Create complex formulas
Introduce Excel functions
Use Excel functions
Copy and move cell entries
Understand relative and absolute cell references
Copy formulas with relative cell references
Copy formulas with absolute cell references

If you have a SAM user profile, you may have access to hands-on instruction, practice, and assessment of the skills covered in this unit. Log in to your SAM accont and go to your assignments page to see what your instructor has assigned.

Using your understanding of Excel basics, you can now plan and build your own worksheets. When you build a worksheet, you enter labels, values, and formulas into worksheet cells. Once you create a worksheet, you can save it in a workbook file and then print it. ▰▰▰ The MediaLoft Marketing Department has asked Jim Fernandez for an estimate of the average number of author appearances this summer. Marketing hopes that the number of appearances will increase 20% over last year's figures. Jim asks you to create a worksheet that summarizes appearances for last year and forecasts the summer appearances for this year.

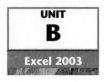

Planning and Designing a Worksheet

Before you start entering data into a worksheet, you need to know the purpose and approximate layout of the worksheet. To increase store traffic and sales, MediaLoft encourages authors to come to stores and sign their books. Jim wants to forecast MediaLoft's 2006 summer author appearances. The goal, already identified by the Marketing Department, is to increase the year 2005 signings by 20%. Using the planning guidelines below, Jim works with you to plan this worksheet and create it in Excel.

DETAILS

In planning and designing a worksheet it is important to:

- **Determine the purpose of the worksheet and give it a meaningful title**

  You need to forecast summer appearances for 2006. Jim suggests you title the worksheet "Summer 2006 MediaLoft Author Events Forecast."

- **Determine your worksheet's desired results, or output**

  Jim needs to begin scheduling author events and will use these forecasts to determine staffing and budget needs if the number of author events increases by 20%. He also wants to calculate the average number of author events because the Marketing Department uses this information for corporate promotions.

- **Collect all the information, or input, that will produce the results you want**

  Jim helps you by gathering together the number of author events that occurred at four stores during the 2005 summer season, which runs from June through August.

- **Determine the calculations, or formulas, necessary to achieve the desired results**

  Jim states you will first need to total the number of events at each of the selected stores during each month of the summer of 2005. Then you will need to add these totals together to determine the grand total of summer appearances. Because you need to determine the goal for the 2006 season, the 2005 monthly totals and grand total are multiplied by 1.2 to calculate the projected 20% increase for the 2006 summer season. Jim suggests you use the Average function to determine the average number of author appearances for the Marketing Department.

- **Sketch on paper how you want the worksheet to look; identify where to place the labels and values**

  Jim suggests you put the store locations in rows and the months in columns. Jim creates a sketch, in which he enters the data and notes the location of the monthly totals and the grand total. Below the totals, he writes out the formula for determining a 20% increase in 2005 appearances. He also includes a label for the calculations of the average number of events. Jim's sketch of this worksheet is shown in Figure B-1.

- **Create the worksheet**

  Jim begins creating the worksheet for you, by entering the labels first, to establish the structure of the worksheet. He then enters the values—the data summarizing the events—into the worksheet. Finally, he enters the formulas necessary to calculate totals, averages, and forecasts. These values and formulas will be used to calculate the necessary output. The worksheet Jim creates is shown in Figure B-2.

FIGURE B-1: Worksheet sketch showing labels, values, and calculations

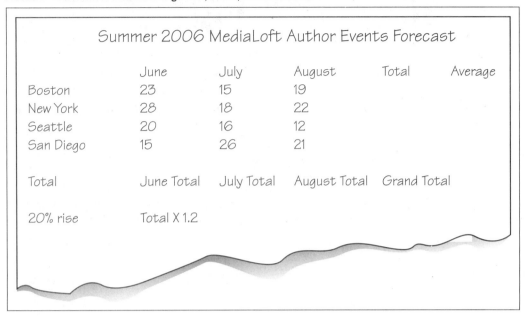

FIGURE B-2: Forecasting worksheet

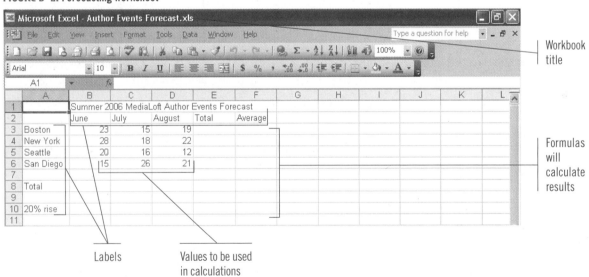

Editing Cell Entries

You can change the contents of a cell at any time. To edit the contents of a cell, you first select the cell you want to edit. Then you have two options: you can click the formula bar or press [F2]. This puts Excel into Edit mode. Alternately, you can double-click any cell and start editing. To make sure you are in Edit mode, look at the **mode indicator** on the far left of the status bar. ▨▨▨▨▨ After planning and creating the worksheet with Jim, you notice that he entered the wrong value for the August Seattle events, and that Houston should replace San Diego. You can edit these entries to correct them.

STEPS

QUICK TIP

In the Open dialog box, you can double-click the filename to open the workbook in one step.

1. **Start Excel, open the file** EX B-1.xls **from the drive and folder where your Data Files are stored, then save it as** Author Events Forecast

2. **Click cell** D5, **then click to the right of** 12 **in the formula bar**

   This cell contains August events for the Seattle store, which you want to change to reflect the correct numbers. Excel goes into Edit mode, and the mode indicator on the status bar displays "Edit." A blinking vertical line called the **insertion point** appears in the formula bar, and if you move the mouse pointer to the formula bar, the pointer changes to I, which is used for editing. See Figure B-3.

QUICK TIP

The Undo button ↺ allows you to reverse up to 16 previous actions, one at a time.

3. **Press** [Backspace], **type** 8, **then click the** Enter button ✓ **on the formula bar**

   The value in cell D5 is changed from 12 to 18, and cell D5 remains selected.

4. **Click cell** A6, **then press** [F2]

   Excel returns to Edit mode, and the insertion point appears in the cell.

5. **Press and hold** [Shift], **press** [Home], **then release** [Shift]

   The contents of the cell is selected, and the next typed character will replace the selection.

6. **Type** Houston, **then press** [Enter]

   The label changes to Houston, and cell A7 becomes the active cell. If you make a mistake, you can click the Cancel button ✕ on the formula bar *before* confirming the cell entry. If you notice the mistake *after* you have confirmed the cell entry, click the Undo button ↺ on the Standard toolbar.

QUICK TIP

Double-clicking when the pointer is to the left of the cell's contents positions the insertion point to the left of the data.

7. **Position the** ⊕ **pointer to the left of** 26 **in cell** C6, **then double-click cell** C6

   Double-clicking a cell also puts Excel into Edit mode with the insertion. point in the cell.

8. **Press** [Delete] **twice, then type** 19

   The number of book signings for July in Houston has been corrected. See Figure B-4.

9. **Click** ✓ **to confirm the entry, then click the** Save button 🖫 **on the Standard toolbar**

FIGURE B-3: Worksheet in Edit mode

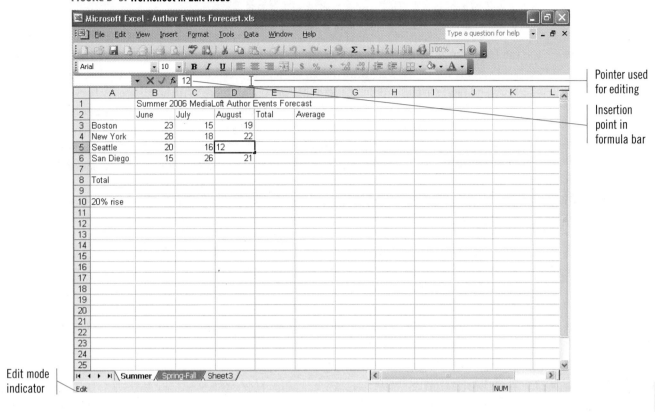

Pointer used for editing

Insertion point in formula bar

Edit mode indicator

FIGURE B-4: Edited worksheet

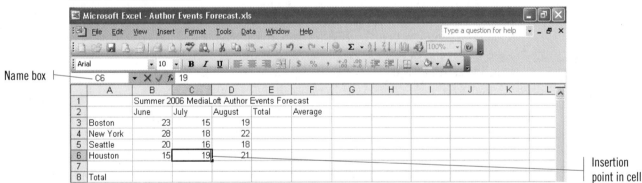

Name box

Insertion point in cell

Clues to Use

Recovering a lost workbook file

Sometimes while you are using Excel, you may experience a power failure or your computer may "freeze," making it impossible to continue working. If this type of interruption occurs, Excel has a built-in recovery feature that allows you to open and save files that were open at the time of the interruption. When you restart Excel after an interruption, the Document Recovery task pane opens on the left side of your screen displaying both original and recovered versions of the files that were open. If you're not sure which file to open (original or recovered), it's usually better to open the recovered file because it will have retained the latest information. You can, however, open and review all the versions of the file that were recovered and save the best one. Each file listed in the Document Recovery task pane has a list arrow with options that allow you to open the file, save the file, delete the file, or show repairs made to the file.

Entering Formulas

You use **formulas** to perform numeric calculations such as adding, multiplying, and averaging. Formulas in an Excel worksheet usually start with the equal sign (=), called the **formula prefix**, followed by cell addresses and range names. Arithmetic formulas use one or more **arithmetic operators** to perform calculations; see Table B-1 for a list of common arithmetic operators. Using a cell address or range name in a formula is called **cell referencing**. If you change a value in a cell, any formula containing that cell reference will be automatically recalculated using the new value. You need to total the values for the monthly author events for June, July, and August. You create formulas to perform these calculations.

STEPS

1. **Click cell B8**

   This is the cell where you want to enter the calculation that totals the number of June events.

2. **Type = (the equal sign)**

   Placing an equal sign at the beginning of an entry tells Excel that a formula is about to be entered, rather than a label or a value. "Enter" appears in the status bar. The total number of June events is equal to the sum of the values in cells B3, B4, B5, and B6.

3. **Type b3+b4+b5+b6**

   Compare your worksheet to Figure B-5. Each cell address in the equation is shown in a matching color in the worksheet. For example, the cell address B3 is written in blue in the equation and is outlined in blue in the worksheet. This makes it easy to identify each cell in a formula.

4. **Click the Enter button ✓ on the formula bar**

   The result, 86, appears in cell B8. Cell B8 remains selected, and the formula appears in the formula bar. Excel is not case sensitive: it doesn't matter if you type uppercase or lowercase characters when you enter cell addresses. Typing cell addresses is only one way of creating a formula. A more accurate method involves **pointing** at cells using the mouse, then using the keyboard to supply arithmetic operators.

5. **Click cell C8, type =, click cell C3, type +, click cell C4, type +, click cell C5, type +, click cell C6, then click ✓**

   When you clicked cell C3, a moving border surrounded the cell. This **moving border** indicates the cell used in the calculation. Moving borders can appear around a single cell or a range of cells. The total number of author appearances for July is 68 and appears in cell C8. The pointing method of creating a formula is more accurate than typing, because it is easy to type a cell address incorrectly. You also need to enter a total for the August events in cell D8.

6. **Click cell D8, type =, click cell D3, type +, click cell D4, type +, click cell D5, type +, click cell D6, then click ✓**

   The total number of appearances for August is 80 and appears in cell D8. Compare your worksheet to Figure B-6.

7. **Click the Save button 🖫 on the Standard toolbar**

FIGURE B-5: Worksheet showing cells in a formula

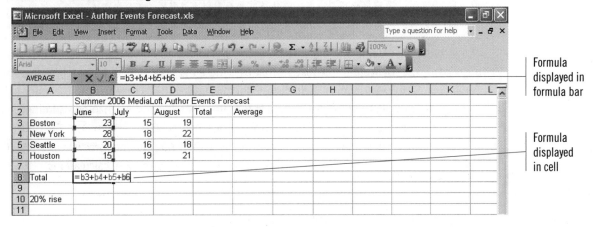

Formula displayed in formula bar

Formula displayed in cell

FIGURE B-6: Completed formulas

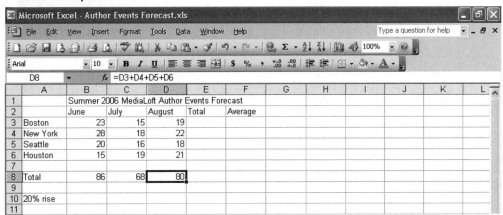

TABLE B-1: Excel arithmetic operators

operator	purpose	example
+	Addition	=A5+A7
–	Subtraction or negation	=A5–10
*	Multiplication	=A5*A7
/	Division	=A5/A7
%	Percent	=35%
^ (caret)	Exponent	=6^2 (same as 6^2)

Excel 2003

Creating Complex Formulas

The formula you entered is a simple formula containing one arithmetic operator, the plus sign. You can create a **complex formula**—an equation that uses more than one type of arithmetic operator. For example, you may need to create a formula that uses addition and multiplication. You can use arithmetic operators to separate tasks within a complex equation. In formulas containing more than one arithmetic operator, Excel uses the order of precedence rules to determine which operation to perform first. ▰▰▰▰ You want to total the values for the monthly author events for June, July, and August, and forecast what the 20% increase in appearances will be. You can create a complex formula to perform these calculations.

STEPS

1. **Click cell B10, type =, click cell B8, then type *.2**

   This part of the formula calculates 20% of the cell contents by multiplying the June total by .2 (or 20%). Because this part of the formula uses multiplication, it is calculated first according to the rules of precedence.

QUICK TIP
Press [Esc] to turn off a moving border and deselect the range.

2. **Type +, then click cell B8**

   The second part of the formula adds the 20% increase to the original value of the cell. The mode indicator says Point, indicating you can add more cell references. Compare your worksheet to Figure B-7.

3. **Click the Enter button ☑ on the formula bar**

   The result, 103.2, appears in cell B10.

4. **Click cell C10, type =, click cell C8, type *.2, type +, click cell C8, then click ☑**

   The result, 81.6, appears in cell C10.

5. **Click cell D10, type =, click cell D8, type *.2, type +, click D8, then click ☑**

   The result, 96, appears in cell D10. Compare your completed worksheet to Figure B-8.

6. **Click the Save button ☐ on the Standard toolbar**

Clues to Use

Order of precedence in Excel formulas

A formula can include several mathematical operations. When you work with formulas that have more than one operator, the order of precedence is very important. If a formula contains two or more operators, such as 4+.55/4000*25, the computer performs the calculations in a particular sequence based on these rules: Operations inside parentheses are calculated before any other operations. Exponents are calculated next, then any multiplication and division—from left to right. Finally, addition and subtraction are calculated from left to right. In the example 4+.55/4000*25, Excel performs the arithmetic operations by first dividing 4000 into .55, then multiplying the result by 25, then adding 4. You can change the order of calculations by using parentheses. For example, in the formula (4+.55)/4000*25, Excel would first add 4 and .55, then divide that amount by 4000, then finally multiply by 25.

FIGURE B-7: Elements of a complex formula

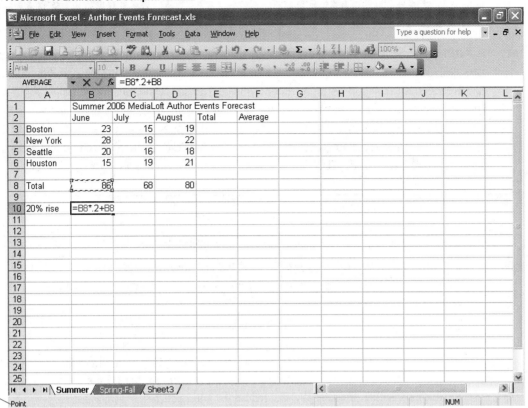

Mode
indicator

FIGURE B-8: Multiple complex formulas

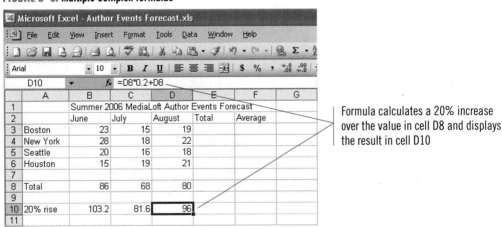

Formula calculates a 20% increase over the value in cell D8 and displays the result in cell D10

Clues to Use

Editing formulas

You edit formulas the same way you edit cell entries: you click the cell containing the formula then edit it in the formula bar; you can also double-click a cell or press [F2] to enter Edit mode, and then edit the formula in the cell. After you are in Edit mode, use the arrow keys to move the insertion point left or right in the formula. Use [Backspace] or [Delete] to delete characters to the left or right of the insertion point, then type or point to new cell references or operators.

Introducing Excel Functions

Functions are predefined worksheet formulas that enable you to perform complex calculations easily. Like formulas, functions always begin with the formula prefix = (the equal sign). You can type functions, or you can use the Insert Function button on the formula bar to select the function you need from a dialog box. The **AutoSum button** on the Standard toolbar enters the most frequently used function, SUM. A function can be used by itself within a cell, or as part of a formula. For example, to calculate monthly sales tax, you could create a formula that adds a range of cells (using the SUM function) and then multiplies the total by a decimal. ▓▓▓ You use the SUM function to calculate the grand totals in the worksheet.

STEPS

1. **Click cell E3**

   This is where you want the total of all Boston author events for June, July, and August to appear.

QUICK TIP

The AutoSum list arrow displays commonly used functions, as well as the More Functions command that opens the Insert Function dialog box.

2. **Click the AutoSum button Σ on the Standard toolbar**

   The formula =SUM(B3:D3) appears in the formula bar and a moving border surrounds cells in the worksheet, as shown in Figure B-9.

3. **Click the Enter button ✓ on the formula bar**

   The result, 57, appears in cell E3. By default, AutoSum adds the values in the cells above the cell pointer. If there are one or fewer values there, AutoSum adds the values to its left—in this case, the values in cells B3, C3, and D3. The information inside the parentheses is the **argument**, or the information Excel uses to calculate the function result. In this case, the argument is the range B3:D3.

4. **Click cell E4, click Σ, then click ✓**

   The total for the New York events, 68, appears in cell E4.

5. **Click cell E5, then click Σ**

   AutoSum sets up a function to add the two values in the cells above the active cell, but this time the default argument is not correct.

QUICK TIP

The ScreenTip 1R × 3C tells you the size of the range is 1 row and 3 columns.

6. **Click cell B5 and hold down the mouse button, drag to cell D5 to select the range B5:D5, then click ✓**

   As you drag, the argument in the SUM function changes to reflect the selected range, and a yellow **Argument ScreenTip** shows the function syntax. You can click any part of the Argument ScreenTip to display Help on the function.

QUICK TIP

Excel automatically enters the final ")".

7. **Click cell E6, type =SUM(, click cell B6 and drag to cell D6, then click ✓**

8. **Click cell E8, type =SUM(, click cell B8 and drag to cell D8, then click ✓**

9. **Click cell E10, type =SUM(, click cell B10 and drag to cell D10, click ✓, then click the Save button 💾 on the Standard toolbar**

   Compare your screen to Figure B-10.

FIGURE B-9: Formula and moving border

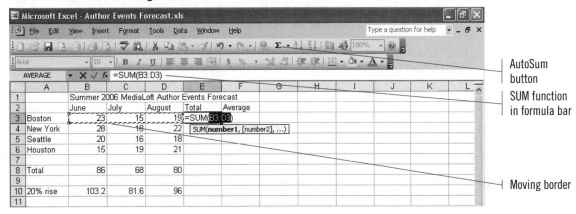

AutoSum button

SUM function in formula bar

Moving border

FIGURE B-10: Worksheet with SUM functions entered

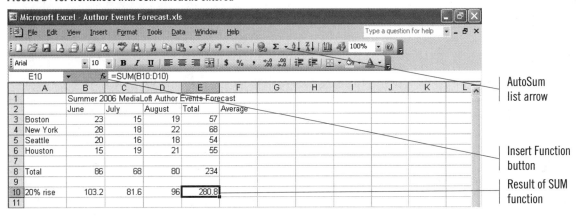

AutoSum list arrow

Insert Function button

Result of SUM function

Clues to Use

Using the MIN and MAX functions

Other commonly used functions include MIN and MAX. You use the MIN function to calculate the minimum, or smallest, value in a selected range; the MAX function calculates the maximum, or largest, value in a selected range. The MAX function is included in the Most Recently Used function category in the Insert Function dialog box, while both the MIN and MAX function can be found in the Statistical category. These functions are particularly useful in larger worksheets and can be selected using the Insert Function button on the formula bar or the AutoSum list arrow on the Standard toolbar.

Using Excel Functions

Functions can be typed directly from the keyboard, or by using the Insert Function button on the formula bar. Clicking this button opens the Insert Function dialog box, which provides a guided method of choosing a function, describes what each function does, and helps you choose which cells to select to complete each equation. ▨▨▨ You need to use the AVERAGE function to calculate the average number of author events per store.

STEPS

1. **Click cell F3, then click the Insert Function button 𝑓ₓ on the formula bar**
    The Insert Function dialog box opens, as shown in Figure B-11. Here you can select a function from a list. See Table B-2 for frequently used functions. The function you need to calculate averages—named AVERAGE—appears in the Most Recently Used function category.

2. **Click AVERAGE in the Select a function list box, then click OK**
    The Function Arguments dialog box opens.

3. **Type B3:D3 in the Number 1 text box, as shown in Figure B-12, then click OK**
    The value 19 appears in cell F3.

4. **Click cell F4, click 𝑓ₓ to open the Insert Function dialog box, verify that AVERAGE is selected in the Select a function list, click OK, type B4:D4, then click OK**

5. **Click cell F5, click 𝑓ₓ, click AVERAGE if necessary, click OK, type B5:D5, then click OK**

6. **Click cell F6, click 𝑓ₓ, click AVERAGE if necessary, click OK, type B6:D6, then click OK**
    The result for Boston (cell F3) is 19; the result for New York (cell F4) is 22.66667; the result for Seattle (cell F5) is 18; and the result for Houston (cell F6) is 18.33333, giving you the averages for all four stores. See Figure B-13.

7. **Enter your name in cell A25, then click the Save button 🖫 on the Standard toolbar**

8. **Click the Print button 🖨 on the Standard toolbar**

TABLE B-2: Frequently used functions

function	description
SUM (argument)	Calculates the sum of the arguments
AVERAGE (argument)	Calculates the average of the arguments
MAX (argument)	Displays the largest value among the arguments
MIN (argument)	Displays the smallest value among the arguments
COUNT (argument)	Calculates the number of values in the arguments
PMT (rate, number of payments, loan amount)	Calculates loan payment amounts
IF (condition, if true, if false)	Determines a value if a condition is true or false
TODAY ()	Returns the current date using a date format

FIGURE B-11: Insert Function dialog box

Your list might be ordered differently

Description of selected function is displayed here

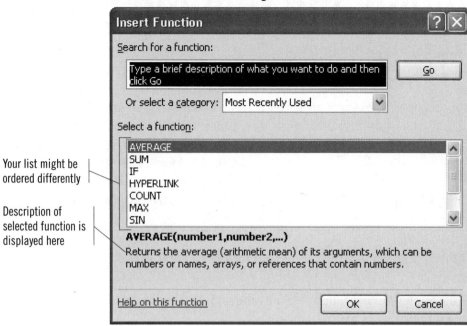

FIGURE B-12: Function Arguments dialog box

Argument is displayed here

Click the Collapse Dialog Box button to define an argument using the mouse

Formula result is displayed here

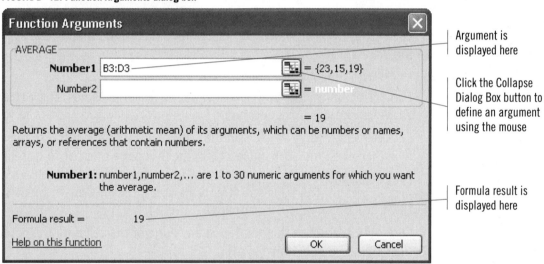

FIGURE B-13: Completed functions

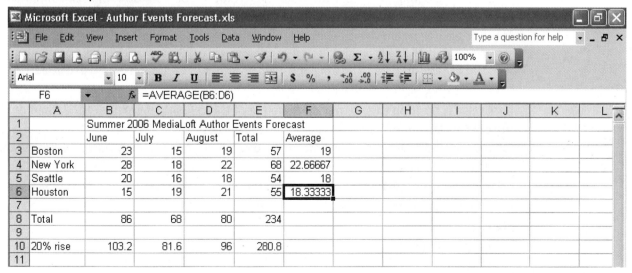

Copying and Moving Cell Entries

You can copy or move information from one cell or range in your worksheet to another using either the Cut, Copy, and Paste buttons, or the Excel drag-and-drop feature. When you cut or move information, the original data does not remain in the original location. You can also cut, copy, and paste labels and values from one worksheet to another. ░░░░░ You need to include the 2006 forecast for spring and fall author events. Jim has already entered the spring data in the second worksheet in the workbook, and asks you to finish entering the labels and data for the fall. You copy information from the spring report to the fall report.

STEPS

1. **Click the** Spring-Fall sheet tab **of the Author Events Forecast workbook**

   The store names in cells A6:A7 are incorrect.

2. **Click the** Summer sheet tab, **select the range** A5:A6, **then click the** Copy button 📋 **on the Standard toolbar**

   The selected range (A5:A6) is copied to the **Office Clipboard**, a temporary storage area that holds the selected information you copy or cut. A moving border surrounds the selected range until you press [Esc] or copy additional information to the Clipboard. The information you copied remains in the selected range.

3. **Click the** Spring-Fall sheet tab, **select the range** A6:A7, **then click the** Paste button 📋 **on the Standard toolbar**

4. **Select the range** A4:A9, **then click** 📋

   The Clipboard task pane opens when you copy a selection to the already occupied Clipboard. You can use the Clipboard task pane to copy, cut, store, and paste up to 24 items. Each item in the pane displays its contents.

5. **Click cell** A13, **click** [Boston New York Seattle Houston Total] **in the Clipboard task pane to paste the contents in cell A13, then click the** Close button ✖ **in the task pane title bar to close it**

   The item is copied into the range A13:A18. When pasting an item from the Clipboard into the worksheet, you only need to specify the upper-left cell of the range where you want to paste the selection. The Total label in column E is missing from the fall forecast.

6. **Click cell** E3, **position the pointer on any edge of the cell until the pointer changes to** ⛶, **then press and hold down** [Ctrl]

   The pointer changes to the Copy pointer ⛶.

7. **While still pressing** [Ctrl], **press and hold the left mouse button, drag the cell contents to cell** E12, **release the mouse button, then release** [Ctrl]

   As you dragged, an outline of the cell moved with the pointer, as shown in Figure B-14, and a ScreenTip appeared tracking the current position of the item as you moved it. When you released the mouse button, the Total label appeared in cell E12. This **drag-and-drop technique** is useful for copying cell contents. You can also use drag and drop to move data to a new cell.

8. **Click cell** C1, **position the pointer on the edge of the cell until it changes to** ⛶, **then drag the cell contents to** A1

   You don't use [Ctrl] when moving information with drag and drop. You can easily enter the fall events data into the range B13:D16.

9. **Select the range** B13:D16, **then using the information shown in Figure B-15, enter the author events data for the fall into this range, then click the** Save button 💾 **on the Standard toolbar**

   The **AutoCalculate** area in the status bar displays "Sum=245," which is the sum of the values in the selected range.

FIGURE B-14: Using drag and drop to copy information

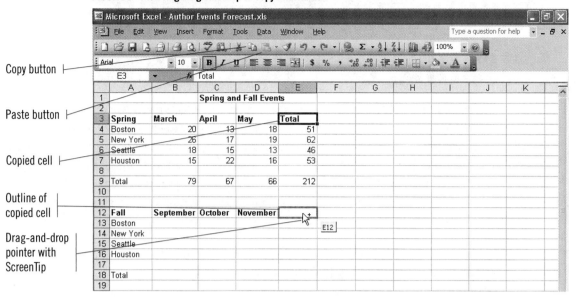

Copy button

Paste button

Copied cell

Outline of copied cell

Drag-and-drop pointer with ScreenTip

FIGURE B-15: Worksheet with fall author event data entered

	Fall	September	October	November	Total
12	Fall	September	October	November	Total
13	Boston	22	17	20	
14	New York	28	16	24	
15	Seattle	20	19	19	
16	Houston	15	25	20	
18	Total				

Summer \ Spring-Fall / Sheet3

Ready   Sum=245   NUM

AutoCalculate displays sum of selected range

Excel 2003

Clues to Use

Using the Office Clipboard

The Office Clipboard, shown in the task pane in Figure B-16, lets you copy and paste multiple items such as text, images, tables, or Excel ranges within or between Microsoft Office applications. The Office Clipboard can hold up to 24 items copied or cut from any Office or Windows-compatible program. The Clipboard task pane displays the items stored on the Office Clipboard. You choose whether to delete the first item from the Clipboard when you copy the 25th item. The collected items remain on the Office Clipboard and are available to you until you close all open Office programs. You can specify when and where to show the Office Clipboard task pane by clicking the Options list arrow at the bottom of the Clipboard task pane.

FIGURE B-16: Office Clipboard task pane

3 of 24 - Clipboard

Paste All   Clear All

Click an item to paste:

Clipboard entry from another program

MediaLoft Author Events Forecast Workbook

Boston New York Seattle Houston Total

Seattle Houston

To display this task pane again, click Office Clipboard on the Edit menu or press Ctrl+C twice.

Options

NUM

Understanding Relative and Absolute Cell References

As you work in Excel, you will often want to reuse formulas in different parts of the worksheet. This will save you time because you won't have to retype them. For example, you may want to perform a what-if analysis showing one set of sales figures using a lower forecast in one part of the worksheet and another set using a higher forecast in another area. But when you copy formulas, it is important to make sure that they refer to the correct cells. To do this, you need to understand relative and absolute cell references. 🖊️ Jim often reuses formulas in different parts of his worksheets to examine different possible outcomes, so he wants you to understand relative and absolute cell references.

- **Use relative references when cell relationships remain unchanged**

  When you create a formula that references other cells, Excel normally does not "record" the exact cell references, but instead the relationship to the cell containing the formula. For example, in Figure B-17, cell E5 contains the formula: =SUM(B5:D5). When Excel retrieves values to calculate the formula in cell E5, it actually looks for "the cell three columns to the left of the formula, which in this case is cell B5," "the cell two columns to the left of the formula," and so on. This way, if you copy the cell to a new location such as cell E6, the results will reflect the new formula location, and will automatically retrieve the values in cells B6, C6, and D6. This is called **relative cell referencing**, because Excel is recording the input cells *in relation to* the formula cell.

  In most cases, you will use relative cell references, which is the Excel default. In Figure B-17, the formulas in E5:E9 and in B9:E9 contain relative cell references. They total the "three cells to the left of" or the "four cells above" the formulas.

- **Use absolute cell references when one relationship changes**

  There are times when you want Excel to retrieve formula information from a specific cell, and you don't want that cell to change when you copy the formula to a new location. For example, you might have a price in a specific cell that you want to use in all formulas, regardless of their location. If you used relative cell referencing, the formula results would be incorrect, because Excel would use a different cell every time you copied the formula. Therefore you need to use an **absolute cell reference**, a reference that does not change when you copy the formula.

  You create an absolute cell reference by placing a $ (dollar sign) before both the column letter and the row number for the cell's address, using the [F4] function key on the keyboard. Figure B-18 displays the formulas used in Figure B-17. The formulas in cells B15 to D18 use absolute cell references to refer to a potential sales increase of 50%, shown in cell B12.

Clues to Use

Using a mixed reference

Sometimes when you copy a formula, you'll want to change the row reference, but keep the column reference the same. This type of cell referencing combines elements of both absolute and relative referencing and is called a **mixed reference**. When copied, the mixed reference C$14 changes the column relative to its new location, but prevents the row from changing. In the mixed reference $C14, the column would not change, but the row would be updated relative to its location. Like the absolute reference, a mixed reference can be created using the [F4] function key. With each press of the [F4] key, you cycle through all the possible combinations of relative, absolute, and mixed references ($C$14, C$14, $C14, C14).

FIGURE B-17: Location of relative references

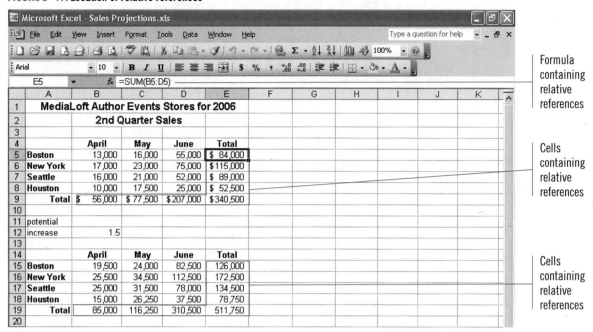

Formula containing relative references

Cells containing relative references

Cells containing relative references

FIGURE B-18: Absolute and relative reference formulas

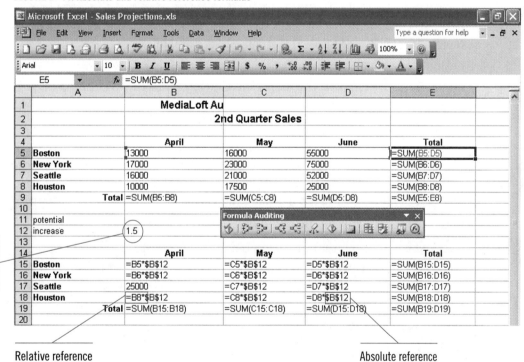

Cell referenced in absolute formulas

Relative reference

Absolute reference

Clues to Use

Printing worksheet formulas

As you create a worksheet, you may find it valuable to print the sheet showing the formulas rather than the cell contents. You can do this by clicking Tools on the menu bar, clicking Options, then clicking the View tab in the Options dialog box. Make sure a check is displayed in the Formulas check box, then click OK. When the Options dialog box closes, the cells are expanded to display the formulas, as shown in Figure B-18, and you can print the worksheet. To return the worksheet to its normal appearance, reopen the Options dialog box and deselect the Formulas check box.

Copying Formulas with Relative Cell References

Copying and moving formulas allows you to reuse formulas you've already created. Copying formulas, rather than retyping them, is faster and helps to prevent typing errors. You can use the Copy and Paste commands or the Fill Right method to copy formulas. ▆▆▆▆ You want to copy the formulas that total the author appearances by region and by month from the spring to the fall.

1. **Click cell E4, then click the Copy button 📋 on the Standard toolbar**
   The formula for calculating the total number of spring Boston author events is copied to the Clipboard. Notice that the formula =SUM(B4:D4) appears in the formula bar.

2. **Click cell E13, then click the Paste button 📋 on the Standard toolbar**
   The formula from cell E4 is copied into cell E13, where the new result of 59 appears. Notice in the formula bar that the cell references have changed, so that the range B13:D13 appears in the formula. This formula contains relative cell references, which tell Excel to copy the formula to a new cell, but to substitute new cell references so that the relationship of the cells to the formula in its new location remains unchanged. In this case, Excel adjusted the formula so that cells D13, C13, and B13—the three cell references immediately to the left of E13—replaced cells D4, C4, and B4, the three cell references to the left of E4. Notice that the lower-right corner of the active cell contains a small square, called the **fill handle**. You can use the fill handle to copy labels, formulas, and values. This option is called **AutoFill**.

3. **Position the pointer over the fill handle until it changes to ✛, press and hold the left mouse button, then drag the fill handle to select the range E13:E16**
   See Figure B-19.

4. **Release the mouse button**
   A formula similar to the one in cell E13 now appears in the range E14:E16. Again, because the formula uses relative cell references, cells E14 through E16 correctly display the totals for the fall author events. After you release the mouse button, the **AutoFill Options button** appears. If you move the pointer over it and click its list arrow, you can specify what you want to fill and whether or not you want to include formatting.

5. **Click cell B9, click Edit on the menu bar, then click Copy**

6. **Click cell B18, click Edit on the menu bar, then click Paste**
   See Figure B-20. The formula for calculating the September events appears in the formula bar. You also need totals to appear in cells C18, D18, and E18. You could use the fill handle again, but another option is the Fill command on the Edit menu.

7. **Select the range B18:E18**

8. **Click Edit on the menu bar, point to Fill, then click Right**
   The rest of the totals are filled in correctly. Compare your worksheet to Figure B-21.

9. **Click the Save button 💾 on the Standard toolbar**

FIGURE B-19: Selected range using the fill handle

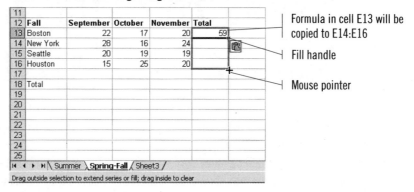

Formula in cell E13 will be copied to E14:E16

Fill handle

Mouse pointer

Drag outside selection to extend series or fill; drag inside to clear

FIGURE B-20: Copied formula

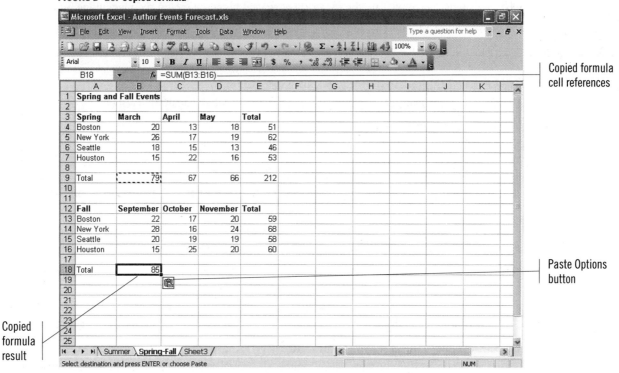

Copied formula cell references

Paste Options button

Copied formula result

FIGURE B-21: Completed worksheet with all formulas copied

12	Fall	September	October	November	Total
13	Boston	22	17	20	59
14	New York	28	16	24	68
15	Seattle	20	19	19	58
16	Houston	15	25	20	60
17					
18	Total	85	77	83	245
19					
20					
21					
22					
23					
24					
25					

⤇ ⤆ ▸ ▸▸ ＼ Summer ＼ Spring-Fall ＼ Sheet3 ／

Ready

Clues to Use

Filling cells with sequential text or values

Often, you'll need to fill cells with sequential text: months of the year, days of the week, years, or text plus a number (Quarter 1, Quarter 2,...). You can easily fill cells using sequences by dragging the fill handle. As you drag the fill handle, Excel automatically extends the existing sequence. (The contents of the last filled cell appear in the ScreenTip.) Use the Fill Series command on the Edit menu to examine all of the available fill series options.

Copying Formulas with Absolute Cell References

When copying formulas, you might want a cell reference to always refer to a particular cell address. In such an instance, you would use an absolute cell reference. An absolute cell reference always refers to a specific cell address when the formula is copied. You create an absolute reference by placing a dollar sign ($) before the row letter and column number of the address (for example $A$1). ▧▧▧▧ The staff in the Marketing Department hopes the number of author events will increase by 20% over last year's figures. Jim asks you to add a column that calculates a possible increase in the number of spring events in 2006. You can then do a what-if analysis and recalculate the spreadsheet several times, changing the percentage by which the number of appearances might increase each time.

STEPS

1. **Click cell G1, type Change, then press [→]**
   You can store the increase factor that will be used in the what-if analysis in cell H1.

2. **Type 1.1, then press [Enter]**
   The value in cell H1 represents a 10% increase in author events.

3. **Click cell G3, type What if?, then press [Enter]**

4. **In cell G4, type =, click E4, type *, click H1, then click the Enter button ☑ on the formula bar**
   The result, 56.1, appears in cell G4. This value represents the total spring events for Boston if there is a 10% increase. Jim wants you to perform a what-if analysis for all the stores.

QUICK TIP
Before you copy or move a formula, check to see if you need to use an absolute cell reference.

5. **Drag the fill handle to extend the selection from G4 to G7**
   The resulting values in the range G5:G7 are all zeros. When you copy the formula it adjusts so that the formula in cell G5 is =E5*H2. Because there is no value in cell H2, the result is 0, an error. You need to use an absolute reference in the formula to keep the formula from adjusting itself. That way, it will always reference cell H1. You can change the relative cell reference to an absolute cell reference by using [F4].

6. **Click cell G4, press [F2] to change to Edit mode, then press [F4]**
   When you press [F2], the range finder outlines the arguments of the equation in blue and green. When you press [F4], dollar signs appear, changing the H1 cell reference to an absolute reference. See Figure B-22.

7. **Click ☑, then drag the fill handle to extend the selection to range G4:G7**
   The formula correctly contains an absolute cell reference, and the value of G4 remains unchanged at 56.1. The correct values for a 10% increase appear in cells G4:G7. You complete the what-if analysis by changing the value in cell H1 to indicate a 20% increase in events.

8. **Click cell H1, type 1.2, then click ☑**
   The values in the range G4:G7 change to reflect the 20% increase. Compare your completed worksheets to Figure B-23. Because events only occur in whole numbers, the appearance of the numbers can be changed later.

9. **Enter your name in cell A25, click the Save button ▤ on the Standard toolbar, click the Print button ▤ on the Standard toolbar, close the workbook, then exit Excel**

FIGURE B-22: Absolute cell reference in cell G4

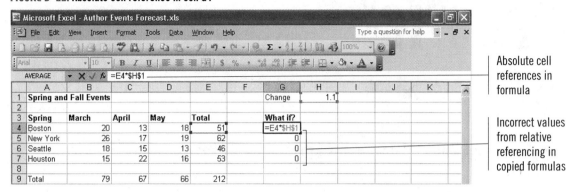

Absolute cell references in formula

Incorrect values from relative referencing in copied formulas

FIGURE B-23: Completed worksheets

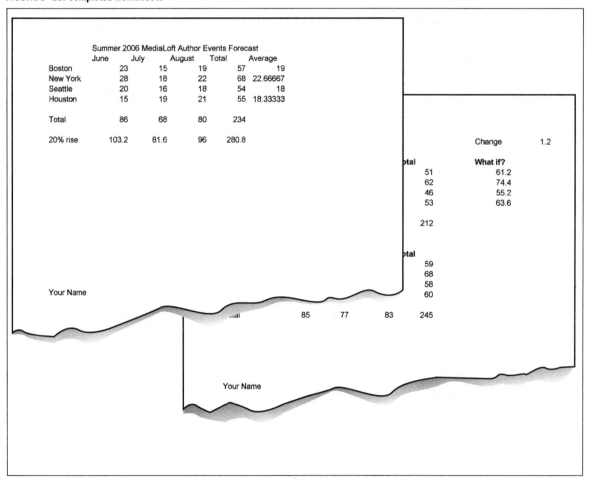

Clues to Use

Inserting and deleting selected cells

As you add formulas to your workbook, you may need to insert or delete cells, not entire rows or columns. When you do this, Excel automatically adjusts cell references to reflect their new locations. To insert cells, click Insert on the menu bar, then click Cells. The Insert dialog box opens, asking if you want to insert a cell and move the selected cell down or to the right of the new one. To delete one or more selected cells, click Edit on the menu bar, click Delete, and in the Delete dialog box, indicate which way you want to move the adjacent cells. When using this option, be careful not to disturb row or column alignment that may be necessary to make sense of the worksheet.

Practice

▼ CONCEPTS REVIEW

Label each element of the Excel worksheet window shown in Figure B-24.

FIGURE B-24

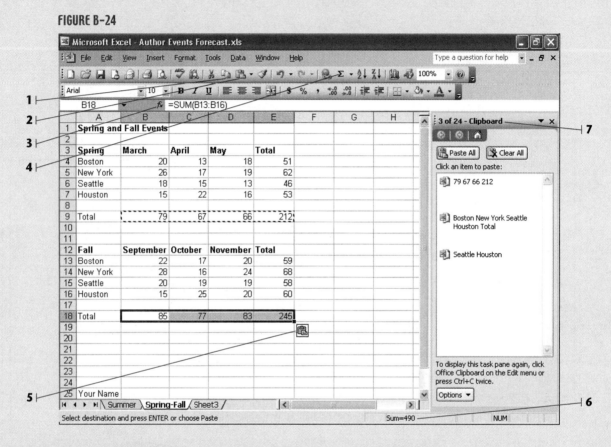

Match each term or button with the statement that best describes it.

8. ☐

9. **Function**

10. **Formula**

11. **Fill handle**

12. ☐

a. A predefined formula that provides a shortcut for commonly used calculations

b. A cell entry that performs a calculation in an Excel worksheet

c. Used to copy labels, formulas, and values

d. Adds the selected range to the Office Clipboard

e. Used to paste cells

Select the best answer from the list of choices.

13. Which button is used to enter data in a cell?

    a.   **c.**

    b.   **d**

14. What type of cell reference changes when it is copied?

    a. Circular   **c.** Looping

    b. Absolute   **d.** Relative

15. What character is used to make a reference absolute?

    a. $ **c.** @

    b. ^   **d.** &

▼ SKILLS REVIEW

1. Plan and design a worksheet.

    a. Using the scenario of tracking quarterly sales at a formal-wear rental shop, determine what sort of output would be required.

    b. Determine what kind of input would be required.

    c. What sort of formulas might be needed?

    d. Make a paper sketch of how the worksheet might look.

2. Edit cell entries.

    a. Start Excel, open the workbook EX B-2.xls from the drive and folder where your Data Files are stored, then save it as **Office Furnishings**.

    b. Change the quantity of Tables to **27**.

    c. Change the price of Desks to **285**.

    d. Change the quantity of Easels to **18**.

    e. Enter your name in cell A40, then save the workbook.

3. Enter formulas.

    a. In cell B6, use the pointing method to enter the formula **B2+B3+B4+B5**.

    b. In cell D2, enter the formula **B2*C2**.

    c. Save your work.

4. Create complex formulas.

    a. In cell B8, enter the formula **(B2+B3+B4+B5)/4**.

    b. In cell C8, enter the formula **(C2+C3+C4+C5)/4**.

    c. Save your work.

5. Introduce Excel functions.

    a. Delete the contents of cell B6.

    b. In cell B6, use the AutoSum feature to calculate the sum of B2:B5.

    c. Save your work.

6. Use Excel functions.

    a. Enter the label **Min Price** in cell A9.

    b. In cell C9, enter the function **MIN(C2:C5)**.

    c. Enter the label **Max Price** in cell A10.

    d. Create a formula in cell C10 that determines the maximum price of for the range C2:C5.

    e. Save your work.

7. Copy and move cell entries.

    a. Select the range **A1:C6**, then copy the range to cell A12.

    b. Select the range **D1:E1**, then use drag and drop to copy the range to cell D12.

    c. Move the contents of cell G1 to cell E9, then save your work.

▼ SKILLS REVIEW (CONTINUED)

8. Understand relative and absolute cell references.

   a. Write a brief description of the difference between a relative and absolute reference.

   b. Provide a sketched example of a relative and absolute reference.

9. Copy formulas with relative cell references.

   a. Copy the formula in D2 into cells D3:D5.

   b. Copy the formula in D2 into cells D13:D16.

   c. Save the worksheet.

10. Copy formulas with absolute cell references.

   a. In cell E10, enter the value **1.375**.

   b. In cell E2, create a formula containing an absolute reference that multiplies D2 and E10.

   c. Use the fill handle to copy the formula in E2 into cells **E3:E5**.

   d. Use the Copy and Paste buttons to copy the formula in E2 into cells **E13:E16**.

   e. Use the Delete command on the Edit menu to delete cells A13:E13, shifting the cells up.

   f. Change the amount in cell E10 to **3.45**.

   g. Select cells A1:E1 and insert cells, shifting cells down.

   h. Enter **Inventory Estimate** in cell A1.

   i. Save, preview, print, and close the workbook, then exit Excel.

▼ INDEPENDENT CHALLENGE 1

You are the box office manager for the Young Brazilians Jazz Band, a popular new group. Your responsibilities include tracking seasonal ticket sales for the band's concerts and anticipating ticket sales for the next season. The group sells four types of tickets: reserved, general, senior, and student tickets.

The 2006–2007 season includes five scheduled concerts: Spring, Summer, Fall, Winter, and Thaw. You will plan and build a worksheet that tracks the sales of each of the four ticket types for all five concerts.

   a. Think about the results you want to see, the information you need to build into these worksheets, and what types of calculations must be performed.

   b. Sketch sample worksheets on a piece of paper to indicate how the information should be laid out. What information should go in the columns? What information should go in the rows?

   c. Start Excel, open a new workbook, then save it as **Young Brazilians** in the drive and folder where your Data Files are stored.

   d. Plan and build a worksheet that tracks the sales of each of the four ticket types for all five concerts. Build the worksheets by entering a title, row labels, column headings, and formulas.

   e. Enter your own sales data that shows that no concert sold more than 400 tickets, and the Reserved category was the most popular.

   f. Calculate the total ticket sales for each concert, the total sales for each of the four ticket types, and the total sales for all tickets.

   g. Name the worksheet **Sales Data** and color the worksheet tab red.

   h. Copy the Sales Data worksheet to a blank worksheet, name the copied worksheet **5% Increase**, then color the sheet tab aqua.

   i. Modify the 5% Increase sheet so that a 5% increase in sales of all ticket types is shown in a separate column with an appropriate column label. See Figure B-25 for a sample worksheet.

   j. Enter your name in a cell in each worksheet.

   k. Save your work, preview and print the worksheets, then close the workbook and exit Excel.

FIGURE B-25

	A	B	C	D	E	F	G	H	I	J	K	L
1			2006-2007 Season									
2			Young Brazilians Jazz Band					Increase				
3								1.05				
4		Reserved	General	Senior	Student							
5	Concerts	Seating	Admission	Citizens	Tickets	Totals		What if?				
6	Spring	285	50	40	20	395		414.75				
7	Summer	135	25	35	20	215		225.75				
8	Fall	130	50	25	20	225		236.25				
9	Winter	160	100	30	20	310		325.5				
10	Thaw	250	75	35	20	380		399				
11	Total	960	300	165	100	1525		1601.25				
12												

▼ INDEPENDENT CHALLENGE 2

The Beautiful You Salon is a small but growing beauty salon that has hired you to organize its accounting records using Excel. The owners want you to track the salon's expenses using Excel. Before you were hired, one of the bookkeepers entered last year's expenses in a workbook, but the analysis was never completed.

a. Start Excel, open the workbook EX B-3.xls, then save it as **Beautiful You Finances** in the drive and folder where your Data Files are stored. The worksheet includes labels for functions such as the Average, Maximum, and Minimum amounts of each of the expenses in the worksheet.

b. Think about what information would be important for the bookkeeping staff to know.

c. Create your sketch using the existing worksheet as a foundation.

d. Create formulas in the Total column and row using the AutoSum function.

e. Rename Sheet1 **Expenses** and add a color to the sheet tab.

Advanced Challenge Exercise

- Create formulas in the Average, Maximum, and Minimum columns and rows using the appropriate functions, dragging to select the range.
- Create a formula using the COUNT function that determines the total number of expense categories listed per quarter.

f. Enter your name in a worksheet cell, then compare your screen to the sample worksheet shown in Figure B-26.

g. Preview the worksheet, then print it.

h. Save the workbook, then close the workbook and exit Excel.

FIGURE B-26

	A	B	C	D	E	F	G	H	I	J	K	L
1	Beautiful You Salon											
2												
3	Operating Expenses for 2006											
4												
5	Expense	Quarter 1	Quarter 2	Quarter 3	Quarter 4	Total	Average	Maximum	Minimum			
6	Rent	4750	4750	4750	4750	19000	4750	4750	4750			
7	Utilities	8624	7982	7229	8096	31931	7982.75	8624	7229			
8	Payroll	23456	26922	25876	29415	105669	26417.25	29415	23456			
9	Insurance	8355	8194	8225	8327	33101	8275.25	8355	8194			
10	Education	4749	3081	6552	4006	18388	4597	6552	3081			
11	Inventory	29986	27115	25641	32465	115207	28801.75	32465	25641			
12	Total	79920	78044	78273	87059	323296						
13												
14	Average	13320	13007.33	13045.5	14509.83							
15	Maximum	29986	27115	25876	32465							
16	Minimum	4749	3081	4750	4006							
17	Count	6										

▼ INDEPENDENT CHALLENGE 3

You have been promoted to computer lab manager at Learn-It-All, a local computer training center. It is your responsibility to make sure there are enough computers for students during scheduled classes. Currently, you have five classrooms: four with IBM PCs and one with Macintoshes. Classes are scheduled Monday, Wednesday, and Friday in two-hour increments from 9 a.m. to 5 p.m. (the lab closes at 7 p.m.), and each room can currently accommodate 32 computers.

You plan and build a worksheet that tracks the number of students who can currently use the available computers per room. You create your enrollment data. Using an additional worksheet, you show the impact of an enrollment increase of 25%.

   a. Think about how to construct these worksheets to create the desired output.
   b. Sketch sample paper worksheets to indicate how the information should be laid out.
   c. Start Excel, open a new workbook, then save it as **Learn-it-All** in the drive and folder where your Data Files are stored.
   d. Create a worksheet by entering a title, row labels, column headings, data, and formulas. Name the sheet to easily identify its contents.
   e. Create a second sheet by copying the information from the initial sheet.
   f. Name the second sheet to easily identify its contents.
   g. Add color to each sheet tab, then compare your screen to the sample shown in Figure B-27.
   h. Enter your name in a cell in each sheet.
   i. Save your work, preview and print each worksheet, then close the workbook and exit Excel.

FIGURE B-27

	A	B	C	D	E	F	G	H	I	J
1	Computer Lab Schedule - Increased enrollment									
2										
3	Monday	PC room #1	PC room #2	PC room #3	PC room #4	Mac room #1				
4	9:00	40	40	40	40	40				
5	11:00	40	40	40	40	40				
6	1:00	40	40	40	40	40				
7	3:00	40	40	40	40	40				
8	5:00	40	40	40	40	40				
9		200	200	200	200	200				
10										
11	Wednesday	PC room #1	PC room #2	PC room #3	PC room #4	Mac room #1				
12	9:00	40	40	40	40	40				
13	11:00	40	40	40	40	40				
14	1:00	40	40	40	40	40				
15	3:00	40	40	40	40	40				
16	5:00	40	40	40	40	40				
17		200	200	200	200	200				
18										
19	Friday	PC room #1	PC room #2	PC room #3	PC room #4	Mac room #1				
20	9:00	40	40	40	40	40				
21	11:00	40	40	40	40	40				
22	1:00	40	40	40	40	40				
23	3:00	40	40	40	40	40				
24	5:00	40	40	40	40	40				
25		200	200	200	200	200				

Actual \ **Increased** / Sheet3 /

Ready   NUM

▼ INDEPENDENT CHALLENGE 4

Your company is opening a branch office in Great Britain and your boss is a fanatic about keeping the thermostats at a constant temperature during each season of the year. Because she grew up in the United States, she is only familiar with Fahrenheit temperatures and doesn't know how to convert them to Celsius. She has asked you to find out the Celsius equivalents for the thermostatic settings she wants to use. She prefers the temperature to be 65 degrees F in the winter, 62 degrees F in the spring, 75 degrees F in the summer, and 70 degrees F in the fall. You can use the Web and Excel to determine the new settings.

a. Start Excel, open a new workbook, then save it as **Temperature Conversions** in the drive and folder where your Data Files are stored.

b. Use your favorite search engine to find your own information sources on calculating temperature conversions.

c. Think about how to create an Excel equation that can perform the conversion.

d. Create column and row titles using Table B-3 to get started.

e. In the appropriate cell, create an equation that calculates the conversion of a Fahrenheit temperature to a Celsius temperature.

f. Copy the equation, then paste it in the remaining Celsius cells.

Advanced Challenge Exercise

- Copy the contents of Sheet1 to Sheet2.
- In Sheet2, change the display so the formulas are visible, then print it.

g. Enter your name in one of the cells in each sheet, preview Sheet1, then print it.

h. Save the workbook, then close the files and exit Excel.

TABLE B-3

Temperature Conversions		
Season	Fahrenheit	Celsius
Spring	62	
Winter	65	
Summer	75	
Fall	70	

Excel 2003

▼ VISUAL WORKSHOP

Create a worksheet similar to Figure B-28 using the skills you learned in this unit. Save the workbook as **Annual Budget** in the drive and folder where your Data Files are stored. Enter your name in cell A13, then preview and print the worksheet.

FIGURE B-28

	A	B	C	D	E	F	G	H	I	J	K	L
1	Computer Consultants, Inc.											
2												
3		Hardware	Software	Training	Contracts	Total						
4	Quarter 1	86600	14200	6100	21000	127900						
5	Quarter 2	96000	16800	5000	24600	142400						
6	Quarter 3	79200	14600	9000	21000	123800						
7	Quarter 4	100600	24900	6750	30600	162850						
8	Total	362400	70500	26850	97200							
9												
10	1.7											
11	Increase	616080	119850	45645	165240							
12												
13	Your Name											
14												
15												
16												
17												
18												
19												
20												
21												
22												
23												
24												
25												

Budget / Sheet2 / Sheet3 /

Ready — NUM

UNIT C
Excel 2003

Formatting a Worksheet

OBJECTIVES

| Format values |
| Use fonts and font sizes |
| Change attributes and alignment |
| Adjust column widths |
| Insert and delete rows and columns |
| Apply colors, patterns, and borders |
| Use conditional formatting |
| Check spelling |

If you have a SAM user profile, you may have access to hands-on instruction, practice, and assessment of the skills covered in this unit. Log in to your SAM accont and go to your assignments page to see what your instructor has assigned.

You can use Excel formatting features to make a worksheet more attractive, to make it easier to read, or to emphasize key data. You do this by using different colors and fonts for the cell contents, adjusting column and row widths, and inserting and deleting columns and rows. The marketing managers at MediaLoft have asked Jim Fernandez to create a workbook that lists advertising expenses for all MediaLoft stores. Jim has prepared a worksheet for the New York City store containing this information, which he can adapt later for use in other stores. He asks you to use formatting to make the worksheet easier to read and to call attention to important data.

Formatting Values

If you enter a value in a cell and you don't like the way the data appears, you can adjust the cell's format. A cell's **format** determines how labels and values appear in it, such as boldface, italic, with or without dollar signs or commas, and the like. Formatting changes only the way a value or label appears; it does not alter cell data in any way. To format a cell, first select it, then apply the formatting. You can format cells and ranges before or after you enter data. The Marketing Department has requested that Jim begin by listing the New York City store's advertising expenses. Jim developed a worksheet that lists advertising invoices, entered all the information, and now he wants you to format some of the labels and values. Because some of the changes might also affect column widths, you make all formatting changes before widening the columns.

STEPS

QUICK TIP

To save a workbook in a different location, you click File on the menu bar, click Save As, click the Save in list arrow in the Save As dialog box, navigate to a new drive or folder, type a new filename if necessary, then click Save.

1. **Start Excel, open the file** EX C-1.xls **from the drive and folder where your Data Files are stored, then save it as** Ad Expenses.

   The NYC advertising worksheet appears in Figure C-1. You can display numeric data in a variety of ways, such as with decimals or leading dollar signs. Excel provides a special format for currency, which adds two decimal places and a dollar sign.

2. **Select the range E4:E32, then click the** Currency Style button $ **on the Formatting toolbar**

   Excel adds dollar signs and two decimal places to the Cost data. Excel automatically resizes the column to display the new formatting. Another way to format dollar values is to use the comma format, which does not include the dollar sign ($).

QUICK TIP

Select any range of contiguous cells by clicking the top-left cell, pressing and holding [Shift], then clicking the bottom-right cell. Add a row to the selected range by continuing to hold down [Shift] and pressing ↓; add a column by pressing →.

3. **Select the range G4:I32, then click the** Comma Style button , **on the Formatting toolbar**

   The values in columns G, H, and I display the comma format. You can also format percentages by using the Formatting toolbar.

4. **Select the range J4:J32, click the** Percent Style button % **on the Formatting toolbar, then click the** Increase Decimal button **on the Formatting toolbar to show one decimal place**

   The data in the % of Total column is now formatted with a percent sign (%) and one decimal place. You decide that you prefer the percentages rounded to the nearest whole number.

5. **Click the** Decrease Decimal button **on the Formatting toolbar**

   You can also apply a variety of formats to dates in a worksheet.

6. **Select the range B4:B31, click** Format **on the menu bar, click** Cells, **then if necessary click the** Number tab **in the Format Cells dialog box**

   The Format Cells dialog box opens with the Date category already selected on the Number tab. See Figure C-2.

7. **Select the format** 14-Mar-01 **in the Type list box, then click** OK

   The dates in column B appear in the format you selected. You decide you don't need the year to appear in the Inv. Due column. You can quickly open the Format Cells dialog box by right-clicking a selected range.

QUICK TIP

The 3-14-01 date format displays a single-digit date (such as 5/9/06) as does 9-May-06. The date format below it displays the same date as 5/09/06.

8. **Select the range** C4:C31, **right-click the range, click** Format Cells **on the shortcut menu, click** 14-Mar **in the Type list box in the Format Cells dialog box, then click** OK

   Compare your worksheet to Figure C-3.

9. **Click the** Save button **on the Standard toolbar**

FIGURE C-1: Advertising expense worksheet

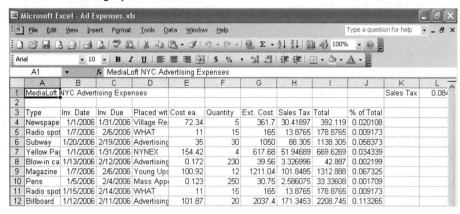

FIGURE C-2: Format Cells dialog box

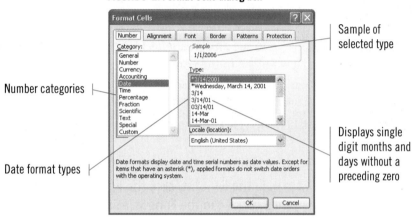

Sample of selected type

Number categories

Date format types

Displays single digit months and days without a preceding zero

FIGURE C-3: Worksheet with formatted values

Dates formatted to appear without year

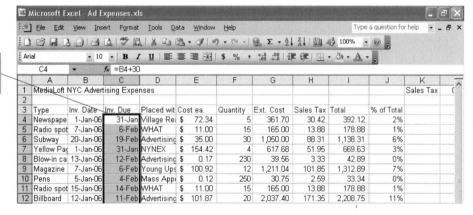

Clues to Use

Using the Format Painter

You can "paint" a cell's format into other cells by using the Format Painter button [image] on the Standard toolbar. This is similar to using copy and paste to copy information, but instead of copying cell contents, you copy only the cell format. Select the cell containing the desired format, then click [image]. The pointer changes to ✚🖌. Use this pointer to select the cell or range you want to contain the new format. You can paint a cell's format into multiple cells by double-clicking [image], then clicking each cell that you want to paint with ✚🖌. When you are finished painting formats, you can turn off the Format Painter by pressing [Esc] or by clicking [image] again.

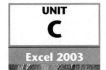

Using Fonts and Font Sizes

A **font** is the name for a collection of characters (letters, numerals, symbols, and punctuation marks) with a similar, specific design. The **font size** is the physical size of the text, measured in units called points. A **point** is equal to 1/72 of an inch. The default font in Excel is 10-point Arial. You can change the font, the size, or both of any worksheet entry or section by using the Format command on the menu bar or by using the Formatting toolbar. Table C-1 shows several fonts in different sizes. Now that the data is formatted, Jim wants you to change the font and size of the labels and the worksheet title so that they stand out more from the data.

STEPS

1. **Press [Ctrl][Home] to select cell A1**

2. **Right-click cell A1, click Format Cells on the shortcut menu, then click the Font tab in the Format Cells dialog box**
   See Figure C-4.

3. **Scroll down the Font list to see an alphabetical listing of the fonts available on your computer, click Times New Roman in the Font list box, click 24 in the Size list box, then click OK**
   The title font appears in 24-point Times New Roman, and the Formatting toolbar displays the new font and size information. The column headings should stand out more from the data.

4. **Select the range A3:J3, then click the Font list arrow** `Arial ▾` **on the Formatting toolbar**
   Notice that the font names on this font list are displayed in the font they represent.

5. **Click Times New Roman in the Font list, click the Font Size list arrow** `10 ▾` **on the Formatting toolbar, then click 14 in the Font Size list**
   Compare your worksheet to Figure C-5. Notice that some of the column headings are now too wide to appear fully in the column. Excel does not automatically adjust column widths to accommodate cell formatting; you have to adjust column widths manually. You'll learn to do this in a later lesson.

6. **Click the Save button 🖫 on the Standard toolbar**

> **QUICK TIP**
> Once you've clicked the Font list arrow, you can quickly locate a font in the list by typing the first few characters in its name.

TABLE C-1: Types of fonts

font	12 point	24 point
Arial	Excel	Excel
Playbill	Excel	Excel
Comic Sans MS	Excel	Excel
Times New Roman	Excel	Excel

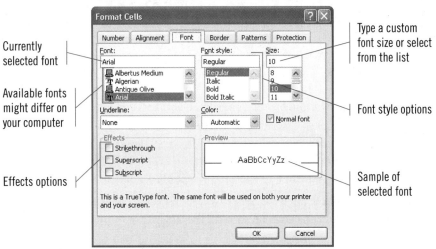

FIGURE C-4: Font tab in the Format Cells dialog box

Currently selected font

Available fonts might differ on your computer

Effects options

Type a custom font size or select from the list

Font style options

Sample of selected font

FIGURE C-5: Worksheet with formatted title and labels

Font and size of active cell or range

Title appears in 24-point Times New Roman

Column headings now 14-point Times New Roman

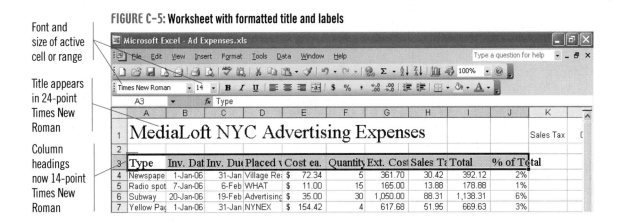

Excel 2003

Clues to Use

Inserting and adjusting clip art

You can add clips to your worksheets to make them look more professional. A **clip** is an individual media file, such as art, sound, animation, or a movie. **Clip art** refers to images such as a corporate logo, a picture, or a photo; Excel comes with many clips that you can use. To add clip art to your worksheet, click Insert on the menu bar, point to Picture, then click Clip Art. The Insert Clip Art task pane appears. Here you can search for clips by typing one or more keywords (words related to your subject) in the Search text box, then clicking Search. Clips that relate to your keywords appear in the Clip Art task pane, as shown in Figure C-6. Click the image you want. (If you have a standard Office installation and have an active Internet connection, you will have more images available.) You can also add your own images to a worksheet by clicking Insert on the menu bar, pointing to Picture, then clicking From File. Navigate to the file you want, then click Insert. To resize an image, drag its lower-right corner. To move an image, drag it to a new location.

FIGURE C-6: Results of Clip Art search

Changing Attributes and Alignment

Attributes are styling formats such as bold, italics, and underlining that you can apply to affect the way text and numbers look in a worksheet. You can also change the **alignment** of labels and values in cells to be left, right, or center. You can apply attributes and alignment options using the Formatting toolbar or using the Alignment tab of the Format Cells dialog box. See Table C-2 for a list and description of the available attribute and alignment toolbar buttons. 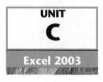 Now that you have applied new fonts and font sizes to the worksheet labels, Jim wants you to further enhance the worksheet's appearance by adding bold and underline formatting and centering some of the labels.

STEPS

1. **Press [Ctrl][Home] to select cell A1, then click the Bold button B on the Formatting toolbar**

   The title appears in bold.

> **QUICK TIP**
> Use formatting shortcuts on any selected range: [Ctrl][B] to bold, [Ctrl][I] to italicize, and [Ctrl][U] to underline.

2. **Click cell A3, then click the Underline button U on the Formatting toolbar**

   Excel underlines the text in the column heading in the selected cell.

3. **Click the Italics button I on the Formatting toolbar, then click B**

   The word "Type" appears in boldface, underlined, italic type. Notice that the Bold, Italics, and Underline buttons are all selected.

> **QUICK TIP**
> Overuse of any attribute can be distracting and make a workbook less readable. Be consistent, adding emphasis the same way throughout.

4. **Click I**

   Excel removes italics from cell A3, but the bold and underline formatting attributes remain.

5. **Click the Format Painter button on the Formatting toolbar, then select the range B3:J3**

   Bold formatting is added to the rest of the labels in the column headings. The title would look better if it were centered over the data columns.

6. **Select the range A1:J1, then click the Merge and Center button on the Formatting toolbar**

   The Merge and Center button creates one cell out of the 10 cells across the row, then centers the text in that newly created large cell. The title "MediaLoft NYC Advertising Expenses" is centered across the 10 columns you selected. You can change the alignment within individual cells using toolbar buttons; you can split merged cells into their original components by selecting the merged cells, then clicking.

> **QUICK TIP**
> To clear all formatting for a selected range, click Edit on the menu bar, point to Clear, then click Formats.

7. **Select the range A3:J3, then click the Center button on the Formatting toolbar**

   Compare your screen to Figure C-7. Although they may be difficult to read, notice that all the headings are centered within their cells.

8. **Click the Save button on the Standard toolbar**

Clues to Use

Rotating and indenting cell entries

In addition to applying fonts and formatting attributes, you can rotate or indent cell data within a cell to further change its appearance. You can rotate text within a cell by altering its alignment. To change alignment, select the cells you want to modify, click Format on the menu bar, click Cells, then click the Alignment tab in the Format Cells dialog box. Click a position in the Orientation box, or type a number in the Degrees text box to change from the default horizontal alignment, then click OK. You can indent cell contents using the Increase Indent button on the Formatting toolbar, which moves cell contents to the right one space, or the Decrease Indent button, which moves cell contents to the left one space.

FIGURE C-7: Worksheet with formatting attributes applied

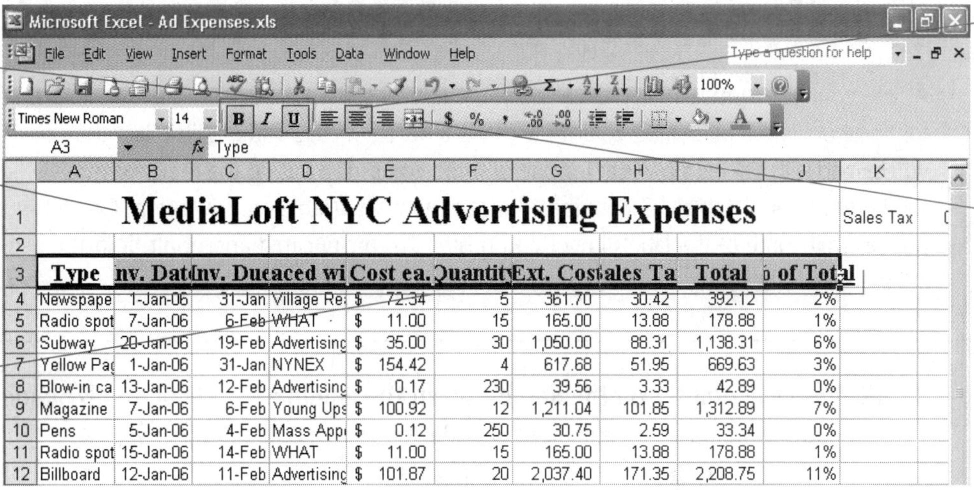

Formatting buttons selected

Title centered across columns

Column headings centered, bold, and underlined

Center button

Merge and Center button

MediaLoft NYC Advertising Expenses

	Type	Inv. Date	Inv. Due	laced wi	Cost ea.	Quantity	Ext. Cost	ales Ta	Total	o of Total
4	Newspape	1-Jan-06	31-Jan	Village Re	$ 72.34	5	361.70	30.42	392.12	2%
5	Radio spot	7-Jan-06	6-Feb	WHAT	$ 11.00	15	165.00	13.88	178.88	1%
6	Subway	20-Jan-06	19-Feb	Advertising	$ 35.00	30	1,050.00	88.31	1,138.31	6%
7	Yellow Pag	1-Jan-06	31-Jan	NYNEX	$ 154.42	4	617.68	51.95	669.63	3%
8	Blow-in ca	13-Jan-06	12-Feb	Advertising	$ 0.17	230	39.56	3.33	42.89	0%
9	Magazine	7-Jan-06	6-Feb	Young Ups	$ 100.92	12	1,211.04	101.85	1,312.89	7%
10	Pens	5-Jan-06	4-Feb	Mass App	$ 0.12	250	30.75	2.59	33.34	0%
11	Radio spot	15-Jan-06	14-Feb	WHAT	$ 11.00	15	165.00	13.88	178.88	1%
12	Billboard	12-Jan-06	11-Feb	Advertising	$ 101.87	20	2,037.40	171.35	2,208.75	11%

Excel 2003

TABLE C-2: Attribute and alignment buttons on the Formatting toolbar

button	description	button	description
B	Bolds text		Aligns text on the left side of the cell
I	Italicizes text		Centers text horizontally within the cell
U	Underlines text		Aligns text on the right side of the cell
	Adds lines or borders		Centers text across columns, and combines two or more selected, adjacent cells into one cell

Clues to Use

Using AutoFormat

Excel has 16 predefined worksheet formats to make formatting your worksheets easier and to give you the option of consistently styling your worksheets. AutoFormats are designed for worksheets with labels in the left column and top rows, and totals in the bottom row or right column. To use AutoFormat, select the data to be formatted—or place your mouse pointer anywhere within the range to be selected (Excel can automatically detect a range of cells)—click Format on the menu bar, click AutoFormat, select a format from the sample boxes in the AutoFormat dialog box, as shown in Figure C-8, then click OK.

FIGURE C-8: AutoFormat dialog box

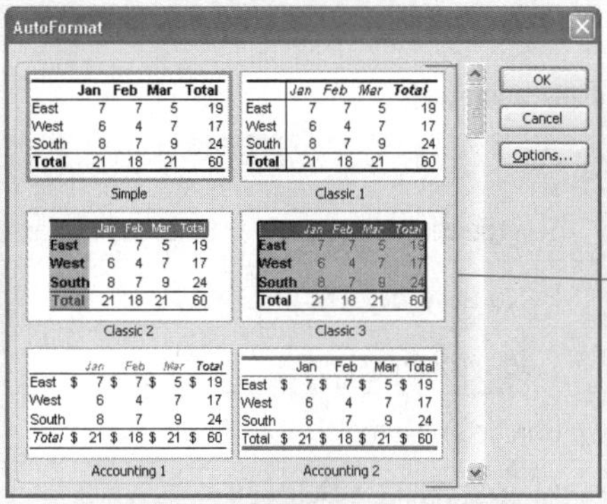

Samples of available formats

Adjusting Column Widths

As you continue formatting a worksheet, you might need to adjust column widths to accommodate a larger font size or style. The default column width is 8.43 characters wide, a little less than one inch. With Excel, you can adjust the column width for one or more columns by using the mouse or the Column command on the Format menu. Table C-3 describes the commands available on the Format Column menu. 🖱️ Jim notices that some of the labels in column A have been truncated and don't fit in the cells. He asks you to adjust the widths of the columns so that the labels appear in their entirety.

STEPS

1. **Position the pointer on the line between the column A and column B headings**

   The **column heading** is the orange box at the top of each column containing a letter. The pointer changes to ↔, as shown in Figure C-9. You position the pointer on the right edge of the column that you are adjusting. The Yellow Pages entries are the widest in the column.

2. **Click and drag the ↔ pointer to the right until the column displays the Yellow Pages entries fully**

   You can use the **AutoFit** feature and your mouse to resize a column so it automatically accommodates the widest entry in a cell.

3. **Position the pointer on the column line between columns B and C headings until it changes to ↔, then double-click**

   Column B automatically widens to fit the widest entry, in this case, the column label.

4. **Use AutoFit to resize columns C, D, and J**

   You can also use the Column Width command on the Format menu to adjust several columns to the same width.

5. **Select the range F5:I5**

   Columns can be adjusted by selecting any cell in the column.

6. **Click Format on the menu bar, point to Column, click Width to open the Column Width dialog box, then move the dialog box, if necessary, by dragging it by its title bar so you can see the selected columns**

   The column width measurement is based on the number of characters in the Normal font (in this case, Arial).

7. **Type 11 in the Column Width text box, then click OK**

   The column widths change to reflect the new setting. See Figure C-10.

8. **Click the Save button 💾 on the Standard toolbar**

TABLE C-3: Format Column commands

command	description
Width	Sets the width to a specific number of characters
AutoFit Selection	Fits to the widest entry
Hide	Hide(s) column(s)
Unhide	Unhide(s) column(s)
Standard Width	Resets width to default widths

FIGURE C-9: Preparing to change the column width

Resize pointer
between
columns
A and B

Row 2 button

Column D
button

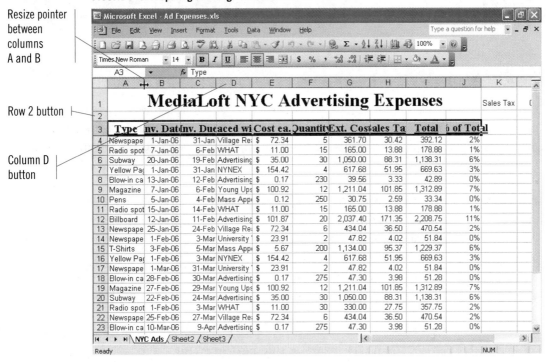

FIGURE C-10: Worksheet with column widths adjusted

Columns
widened
to display
text

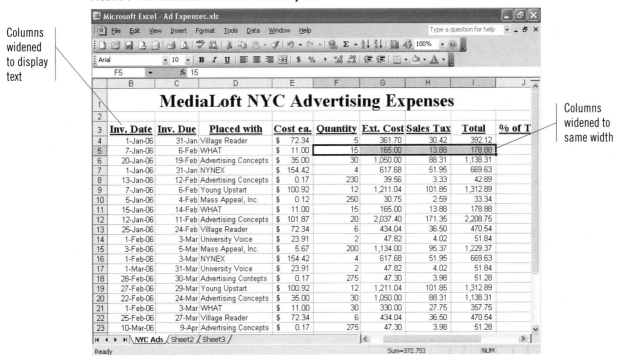

Columns
widened to
same width

Clues to Use

Specifying row height

The Row Height command on the Format menu allows you to customize row height to improve readability. Row height is calculated in points, the same units of measure used for fonts. The row height must exceed the size of the font you are using. Normally, you don't need to adjust row heights manually. If you format something in a row to be a larger point size, Excel adjusts the row to fit the largest point size in the row. You can also adjust row height by placing the ✛ pointer under the row heading and dragging to the desired height.

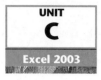

Inserting and Deleting Rows and Columns

As you modify a worksheet, you might find it necessary to insert or delete rows and columns to keep your worksheet current. For example, you might need to insert rows to accommodate new inventory products or remove a column of yearly totals that are no longer necessary. Excel inserts rows above the cell pointer and inserts columns to the left of the cell pointer. When you insert a new row, the contents of the worksheet shift down from the newly inserted row. When you insert a new column, the contents of the worksheet shift to the right from the point of the new column. To insert a single row, you can also right-click the row heading immediately below where you want the new row, then click Insert. To insert multiple rows, drag across row headings to select the same number of rows as you want to insert. ▄▄▄▄▄ You have already improved the appearance of the worksheet by formatting the labels and values. Now Jim asks you to improve the overall appearance of the worksheet by inserting a row between the last row of data and the totals. Also, you have located a row of inaccurate data and an unnecessary column that you need to delete.

STEPS

1. **Right-click cell A32, then click Insert on the shortcut menu**

   The Insert dialog box opens. See Figure C-11. You can choose to insert a column or a row, or you can shift the data in the cells in the active column right or in the active row down. An additional row between the last row of data and the totals will visually separate the totals.

   > **QUICK TIP**
   >
   > Inserting or deleting rows or columns can cause problems in formulas that contain absolute cell references. After adding rows or columns to a worksheet, be sure to proof your formulas.

2. **Click the Entire row option button, then click OK**

   A blank row appears between the totals and the Billboard data, and the formula result in cell E33 has not changed. The Insert Options button 🖍 now appears beside cell A33. When you place ⬚ over 🖍, you can click the Insert Options list arrow and select from the following options: Format Same As Above, Format Same As Below, or Clear Formatting.

3. **Click the row 27 heading**

   Hats from Mass Appeal Inc. are no longer part of the advertising campaign. All of row 27 is selected, as shown in Figure C-12.

   > **QUICK TIP**
   >
   > Use the Edit menu, or right-click the selected row and click Delete to remove a selected row. Pressing [Delete] on the keyboard removes the contents of a selected row; the row itself remains.

4. **Click Edit on the menu bar, then click Delete**

   Excel deletes row 27, and all rows below this shift up one row.

5. **Click the column J heading**

   The percentage information is calculated elsewhere and is no longer necessary in this worksheet.

6. **Click Edit on the menu bar, then click Delete**

   Excel deletes column J. The remaining columns to the right shift left one column.

7. **Click the Save button 🖫 on the Standard toolbar**

Clues to Use

Hiding and unhiding columns and rows

As you work with a worksheet, you may find that you need to make one or more columns or rows invisible. You can hide a selected column by clicking Format on the menu bar, pointing to Column, then clicking Hide. A hidden column is indicated by a black vertical line in its original position. You can display a hidden column by selecting the columns on either side of the black line, clicking Format on the menu bar, pointing to Column, and then clicking Unhide. (To hide/unhide one or more rows, substitute Row for the Column command.)

FIGURE C-11: Insert dialog box

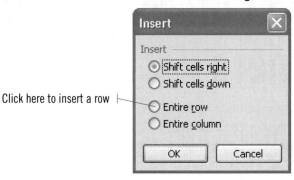

Click here to insert a row

FIGURE C-12: Worksheet with row 27 selected

Row 27 heading

Inserted row

Insert Options button might appear in a different location, or not at all

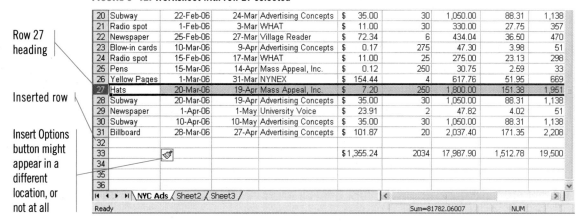

Clues to Use

Adding and editing comments

Much of your Excel work may be in collaboration with teammates with whom you share worksheets. You can share ideas with other worksheet users by adding comments within selected cells. To include a comment in a worksheet, click the cell where you want to place the comment, click Insert on the menu bar, then click Comment. A resizable text box containing the computer user's name opens in which you can type your comments. A small, red triangle appears in the upper-right corner of a cell containing a comment. If the comments are not already displayed, workbook users can point to the triangle to display the comment. To see all worksheet comments, as shown in Figure C-13, click View on the menu bar, then click Comments. To edit a comment, click the cell containing the comment, click Insert on the menu bar, then click Edit Comment. To delete a comment, right-click the cell containing the comment, then click Delete Comment on the shortcut menu.

FIGURE C-13: Comments in worksheet

20	Subway	22-Feb-06	24-Mar	Advertising Concepts	$ 35.00
21	Radio spot	1-Feb-06	3-Mar	WHAT	$ 11.00
22	Newspaper	25-Feb-06	27-Mar	Village Reader	$ 72.34
23	Blow-in cards	10-Mar-06	9-Apr	Advertising Concepts	$ 0.17
24	Radio spot	15-Feb-06	17-Mar		$ 11.00
25	Pens	15-Mar-06	14-Apr		$ 0.12
26	Yellow Pages	1-Mar-06	31-Mar		$ 154.44
27	Subway	20-Mar-06	19-Apr		$ 35.00
28	Newspaper	1-Apr-06	1-May	University Voice	$ 23.91
29	Subway	10-Apr-06	10-May		$ 35.00
30	Billboard	28-Mar-06	27-Apr		$ 101.87
31					
32					$1,348.04
33					
34					

Jim Fernandez: Should we continue with these ads, or expand to other publications?

Jim Fernandez: We need to evaluate whether we should continue these ads.

NYC Ads / Sheet2 / Sheet3 /

Ready

Applying Colors, Patterns, and Borders

You can use colors, patterns, and borders to enhance the overall appearance of a worksheet and to make it easier to read. You can add these enhancements by using the Patterns or Borders tabs in the Format Cells dialog box or by using the Borders and Color buttons on the Formatting toolbar. You can apply color or patterns to the background of a cell, to a range, or to cell contents. You can also apply borders to all the cells in a worksheet or only to selected cells to call attention to individual cells or groups of cells. See Table C-4 for a list of border buttons and their functions. ░░░░ Jim asks you to add a pattern, a border, and color to the title of the worksheet to give the worksheet a more professional appearance.

STEPS

1. **Press [Ctrl][Home] to select cell A1, then click the** Fill Color list arrow ░ ▾ **on the Formatting toolbar**
    The color palette appears.

> **QUICK TIP**
> Use color sparingly. Too much color can divert the reader's attention from the worksheet data.

2. **Click the** Turquoise color **(fourth row, fifth column)**
    Cell A1 has a turquoise background, as shown in Figure C-14. Cell A1 spans columns A through I because of the Merge and Center command used for the title.

3. **Right-click cell A1, then click** Format Cells **on the shortcut menu**
    The Format Cells dialog box opens.

4. **Click the** Patterns tab **if it is not already displayed**
    See Figure C-15. Adding a pattern to cells can add to the visual interest of your worksheet.

5. **Click the** Pattern list arrow, **click the** Thin Diagonal Crosshatch pattern **(third row, last column), then click** OK
    A border also enhances a cell's appearance. Unlike underlining, which is a text-formatting tool, borders extend to the width of the cell.

> **QUICK TIP**
> You can also draw cell borders using the mouse pointer. Click the Borders list arrow on the Formatting toolbar, click Draw Borders, then drag to create borders or boxes.

6. **Click the** Borders list arrow ▦ ▾ **on the Formatting toolbar, then click the** Thick Bottom Border **(second row, second column)** ▦ **on the Borders palette**
    It can be difficult to view a border in a selected cell.

7. **Click cell A3**
    The border is a nice enhancement. Font color can also help distinguish information in a worksheet.

> **QUICK TIP**
> The default color on the Fill Color and Font Color buttons changes to the last color you selected.

8. **Select the range A3:I3, click the** Font Color list arrow **A** ▾ **on the Formatting toolbar, then click the** Blue **color (second row, third column from the right) on the palette**
    The text changes color, as shown in Figure C-16.

9. **Click the** Save button ▦ **on the Standard toolbar**

Clues to Use

Formatting columns or rows

You can save yourself time by formatting an entire column or row using any of the categories that appear in the Format Cells dialog box. You might, for example, want to format all the cells within a column to accept telephone numbers, social security numbers, zip codes, or custom number formats. Click the column or row heading—located at the top of a column or beginning of a row—to select the entire column or row. You can format a selected column or row by clicking Format on the menu bar, clicking Cells, then clicking the appropriate tab in the Format Cells dialog box.

FIGURE C-14: Background color added to cell

Cell A1 with turquoise background

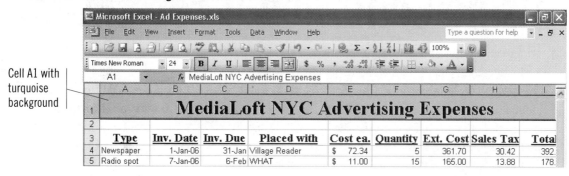

FIGURE C-15: Patterns tab in the Format Cells dialog box

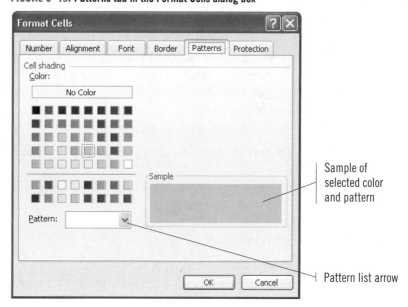

Sample of selected color and pattern

Pattern list arrow

FIGURE C-16: Worksheet with colors, patterns, and border

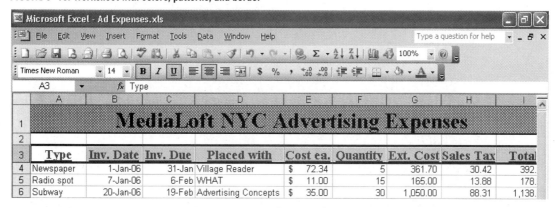

TABLE C-4: Border buttons

button	function	button	function	button	function
	No Border		Bottom Double Border		Top and Thick Bottom Border
	Bottom Border		Thick Bottom Border		All Borders
	Left Border		Top and Bottom Border		Outside Borders
	Right Border		Top and Double Bottom Border		Thick Box Border

Using Conditional Formatting

Formatting makes worksheets look professional and helps distinguish different types of data. You can have Excel automatically apply formatting depending on specific values in cells. You might, for example, want advertising costs above a certain number to appear in red boldface and lower values to appear in blue. Automatically applying formatting attributes based on cell values is called **conditional formatting**. If the data meets your criteria, Excel applies the formats you specify. ▰▰▰▰▰ Jim wants the worksheet to include conditional formatting so that total advertising costs greater than $175 appear in boldface red type. He asks you to create the conditional format in the first cell in the Total cost column.

STEPS

1. **Click cell** G4

   Use the scroll bars if necessary, to make column G visible.

TROUBLE

If the Office Assistant appears, close it by clicking the No, don't provide help now button.

2. **Click** Format **on the menu bar, then click** Conditional Formatting

   The Conditional Formatting dialog box opens. Depending on the logical operator you've selected (such as "greater than" or "not equal to"), the Conditional Formatting dialog box displays different input boxes. You can define up to three different conditions, and then assign formatting attributes to each one. You define the condition first. The default setting for the first condition is "Cell Value Is" "between."

3. **Click the** Operator list arrow **to change the current condition, then click** greater than or equal to

   Because you changed the operator from "between," which required text boxes for two values, only one value text box now appears. The first condition is that the cell value must be greater than or equal to some value. See Table C-5 for a list of options. The value can be a constant, formula, cell reference, or date. That value is set in the third box.

4. **Click the** Value text box, **then type** 175

   Now that you have assigned the value, you need to specify what formatting you want for cells that meet this condition.

5. **Click** Format, **click the** Color list arrow **in the Format Cells dialog box, click the** Red color **(third row, first column), click** Bold **in the Font style list box, then click** OK

6. **Compare your settings to Figure C-17, then click** OK **to close the Conditional Formatting dialog box**

   The value in cell G4, 361.70, is formatted in bold red numbers because it is greater than 175, meeting the condition to apply the format. You can copy conditional formats the same way you would copy other formats.

7. **Verify that** cell G4 **is selected, click the** Format Painter button 🖌 **on the Standard toolbar, then drag** ⬦🖌 **to select the range** G5:G30

8. **Click cell** G4

   Compare your results to Figure C-18. All cells with values greater than or equal to 175 in column G appear in bold red text.

9. **Press** [Ctrl][Home] **to select cell A1, then click the** Save button 🖫 **on the Standard toolbar**

TABLE C-5: Conditional formatting options

option	mathematical equivalent	option	mathematical equivalent
Between	$X > Y < Z$	Greater than	$Z > Y$
Not between	$B \not> C \not< A$	Less than	$Y < Z$
Equal to	$A = B$	Greater than or equal to	$A >= B$
Not equal to	$A \neq B$	Less than or equal to	$Z <= Y$

FIGURE C-17: Completed Conditional Formatting dialog box

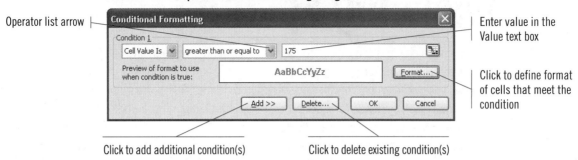

Operator list arrow

Enter value in the Value text box

Click to define format of cells that meet the condition

Click to add additional condition(s)

Click to delete existing condition(s)

FIGURE C-18: Worksheet with conditional formatting

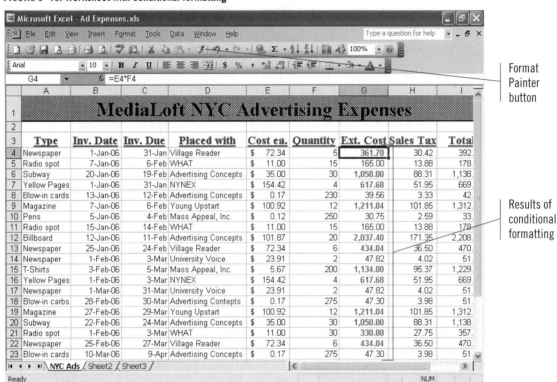

Format Painter button

Results of conditional formatting

Clues to Use

Deleting conditional formatting

Because it's likely that the conditions you define will change, you can delete any conditional format you define. Select the cell(s) containing conditional formatting, click Format on the menu bar, click Conditional Formatting, then click Delete in the Conditional Formatting dialog box. The Delete Conditional Format dialog box opens, as shown in Figure C-19. Select the check boxes for any of the conditions you want to delete, click OK, then click OK again. The previously assigned formatting is deleted—leaving the cell's contents intact.

FIGURE C-19: Delete Conditional Format dialog box

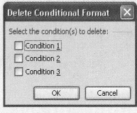

Checking Spelling

A single misspelled word can cast doubt on the validity and professional value of your entire workbook. Excel includes a spelling checker to help you ensure that the words in your worksheet are spelled correctly. The spelling checker scans your worksheet, displays words it doesn't find in its built-in dictionary, and when possible, suggests replacements. To check other sheets in a multiple-sheet workbook, you need to display each sheet and run the spelling checker again. Because the built-in dictionary cannot possibly include all the words that anyone needs, you can add words to the dictionary, such as your company name, an acronym, or an unusual technical term. The spelling checker will no longer consider that word misspelled. Any words you've added to the dictionary using Word, Access, or PowerPoint are also available in Excel. Because he will distribute this workbook to the marketing managers, Jim asks you to check its spelling.

STEPS

TROUBLE
If a language other than English is being used, the Spelling dialog box lists the name of that language in its title bar.

1. **Click the** Spelling button ✓ **on the Standard toolbar**
   The Spelling: English (U.S.) dialog box opens, as shown in Figure C-21, with MediaLoft selected as the first misspelled word in the worksheet. For any word, you have the option to Ignore or to Ignore All cases that the spell checker flags, or to Add the word to the dictionary.

2. **Click** Ignore All **for MediaLoft**
   The spelling checker found the word "cards" misspelled and offers "crabs" as an alternative.

3. **Scroll through the Suggestions list, click** cards, **then click** Change
   The word "Concepts" is also misspelled, and the spelling checker suggests the correct spelling.

4. **Click** Change
   When no more incorrect words are found, Excel displays a message indicating that all the words on the worksheet have been checked.

5. **Click** OK

6. **Enter your name in cell** A34, **then press** [Ctrl][Home]

QUICK TIP
You can set **AutoCorrect** to correct spelling as you type. Click Tools on the menu bar, then click AutoCorrect Options.

7. **Click the** Save button 🖫 **on the Standard toolbar, then preview the worksheet**

8. **In the Preview window, click** Setup **to open the Page Setup dialog box, under Scaling click** Fit to option button **to print the worksheet on one page, click** OK, **click** Print, **then click** OK
   Compare your printout to Figure C-22.

9. **Click** File **on the menu bar, then click** Exit **to close the workbook without saving changes and exit Excel**

Clues to Use

Using e-mail to send a workbook

Once you have checked for spelling errors, you can use e-mail to send an entire workbook from within Excel. To send a workbook as an e-mail message attachment, open the workbook, click File on the menu bar, point to Send To, then click Mail Recipient (as Attachment). You supply the To and optional Cc information, as shown in Figure C-20, then click Send.

FIGURE C-20: E-mailing an Excel workbook

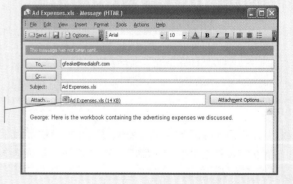

Workbook is automatically attached to message

FIGURE C-21: Spelling English dialog box

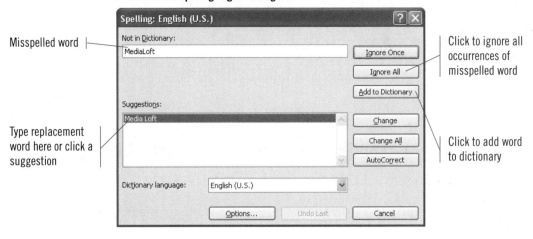

Misspelled word ──| **Not in Dictionary:** MediaLoft | Ignore Once / Ignore All | Click to ignore all occurrences of misspelled word

Add to Dictionary

Type replacement word here or click a suggestion ──| **Suggestions:** Media Loft | Change / Change All / AutoCorrect | Click to add word to dictionary

Dictionary language: English (U.S.)

Options... | Undo Last | Cancel

FIGURE C-22: Completed worksheet

MediaLoft NYC Advertising Expenses

Sales Tax   0.0841

Type	Inv. Date	Inv. Due	Placed with	Cost ea.	Quantity	Ext. Cost	Sales Tax	Total
Newspaper	1-Jan-06	31-Jan	Village Reader	$ 72.34	5	361.70	30.42	392.12
Radio spot	7-Jan-06	6-Feb	WHAT	$ 11.00	15	165.00	13.88	178.88
Subway	20-Jan-06	19-Feb	Advertising Concepts	$ 35.00	30	1,050.00	88.31	1,138.31
Yellow Pages	1-Jan-06	31-Jan	NYNEX	$ 154.42	4	617.68	51.95	669.63
Blow-in cards	13-Jan-06	12-Feb	Advertising Concepts	$ 0.17	230	39.56	3.33	42.89
Magazine	7-Jan-06	6-Feb	Young Upstart	$ 100.92	12	1,211.04	101.85	1,312.89
Pens	5-Jan-06	4-Feb	Mass Appeal, Inc.	$ 0.12	250	30.75	2.59	33.34
Radio spot	15-Jan-06	14-Feb	WHAT	$ 11.00	15	165.00	13.88	178.88
Billboard	12-Jan-06	11-Feb	Advertising Concepts	$ 101.87	20	2,037.40	171.35	2,208.75
Newspaper	25-Jan-06	24-Feb	Village Reader	$ 72.34	6	434.04	36.50	470.54
Newspaper	1-Feb-06	3-Mar	University Voice	$ 23.91	2	47.82	4.02	51.84
T-Shirts	3-Feb-06	5-Mar	Mass Appeal, Inc.	$ 5.67	200	1,134.00	95.37	1,229.37
Yellow Pages	1-Feb-06	3-Mar	NYNEX	$ 154.42	4	617.68	51.95	669.63
Newspaper	1-Mar-06	31-Mar	University Voice	$ 23.91	2	47.82	4.02	51.84
Blow-in cards	28-Feb-06	30-Mar	Advertising Concepts	$ 0.17	275	47.30	3.98	51.28
Magazine	27-Feb-06	29-Mar	Young Upstart	$ 100.92	12	1,211.04	101.85	1,312.89
Subway	22-Feb-06	24-Mar	Advertising Concepts	$ 35.00	30	1,050.00	88.31	1,138.31
Radio spot	1-Feb-06	3-Mar	WHAT	$ 11.00	30	330.00	27.75	357.75
Newspaper	25-Feb-06	27-Mar	Village Reader	$ 72.34	6	434.04	36.50	470.54
Blow-in cards	10-Mar-06	9-Apr	Advertising Concepts	$ 0.17	275	47.30	3.98	51.28
Radio spot	15-Mar-06	17-Apr	WHAT	$ 11.00	25	275.00	23.13	298.13
Pens	15-Mar-06	14-Apr	Mass Appeal, Inc.	$ 0.12	250	30.75	2.59	33.34
Yellow Pages	1-Mar-06	31-Mar	NYNEX	$ 154.44	4	617.76	51.95	669.71
Subway	20-Mar-06	19-Apr	Advertising Concepts	$ 35.00	30	1,050.00	88.31	1,138.31
Newspaper	1-Apr-06	1-May	University Voice	$ 23.91	2	47.82	4.02	51.84
Subway	10-Apr-06	10-May	Advertising Concepts	$ 35.00	30	1,050.00	88.31	1,138.31
Billboard	28-Mar-06	27-Apr	Advertising Concepts	$ 101.87	20	2,037.40	171.35	2,208.75
				$ 1,348.04	1784	16,187.90	1,361.40	17,549.30

Your Name

Practice

▼ CONCEPTS REVIEW

Label each element of the Excel worksheet window shown in Figure C-23.

FIGURE C-23

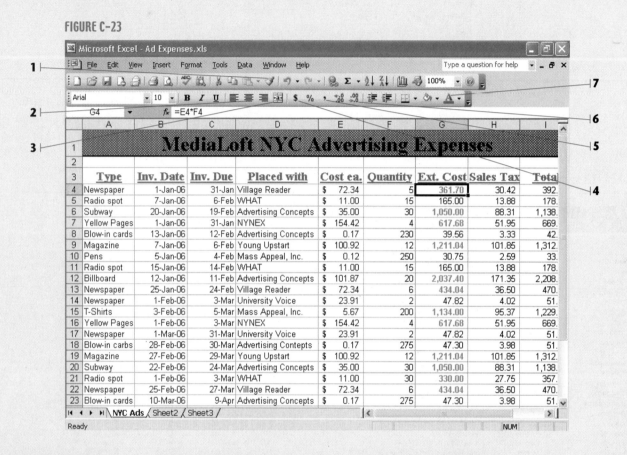

Match each command or button with the statement that best describes it.

8. $
9. [image]
10. [image]
11. Cells command on the Format menu
12. Conditional Formatting
13. Delete command on the Edit menu

a. Changes appearance of a cell depending on result
b. Erases the contents of a cell
c. Used to check the spelling in a worksheet
d. Used to change the appearance of selected cells
e. Pastes the contents of the Clipboard into the current cell
f. Changes the format to Currency

Select the best answer from the list of choices.

14. **What is the name of the feature used to resize a column to its widest entry?**
    a. AutoResize
    b. AutoFormat
    c. AutoFit
    d. AutoAdjust

15. **Which button center-aligns the contents of a single cell?**
    a.
    b.
    c.
    d.

16. **Which button increases the number of decimal places in selected cells?**
    a.
    b.
    c.
    d.

17. **Which of the following is an example of the comma format?**
    a. 5555.55
    b. 55.55%
    c. 5,555.55
    d. $5,555.55

18. **How many conditional formats can be created in any cell?**
    a. 1
    b. 2
    c. 3
    d. 4

19. **Which feature applies formatting attributes according to cell contents?**
    a. AutoFormat
    b. Comments
    c. Conditional Formatting
    d. Merge and Center

20. **Each of the following operators can be used in conditional formatting, *except*:**
    a. Equal to.
    b. Greater than.
    c. Similar to.
    d. Not between.

▼ SKILLS REVIEW

1. Format values.

a. Start Excel and open a new workbook.

b. Enter the information from Table C-6 in your worksheet. Begin in cell A1, and do not leave any blank rows or columns.

c. Save this workbook as **MediaLoft GB Sales** in the drive and folder where your Data Files are stored.

d. Select the range of values in the Average Price column.

e. Format the range using the Currency Style button.

f. Apply the Comma format to the Average Price and Quantity data, and reduce the number of decimals in the Quantity column to 0.

g. Insert formulas in the Totals column (multiply the Average Price by the Quantity).

h. Apply the Currency format to the Totals data.

i. Save your work.

TABLE C-6

MediaLoft Great Britain Quarterly Sales Projections			
Department	Average Price	Quantity	Totals
Sports	30	2250	
Computers	42	3185	
History	37	1325	
Personal Growth	29	2070	

2. Use fonts and font sizes.

a. Select the range of cells containing the column labels.

b. Change the font of the column labels to Times New Roman.

c. Increase the font size of the column labels and the label in cell A1 to 14 point.

d. Resize the columns as necessary.

e. Save your changes.

3. Change attributes and alignment.

a. Select the worksheet title **MediaLoft Great Britain**, then use the Bold button to apply the bold attribute.

b. Use the Merge and Center button to center the title and the Quarterly Sales Projections labels over columns A through D.

c. Select the label **Quarterly Sales Projections**, then apply underlining to the label.

d. Add the bold attribute to the labels in the Department column.

e. Use the Format Painter to paste the format from the data in the Department column to the Department and Totals labels.

f. Add the italics attribute to the Average Price and Quantity labels.

g. Select the range of cells containing the column titles, then center them.

h. Return the underlined, merged and centered Quarterly Sales Projections label to its original alignment.

i. Move the Quarterly Sales Projections label to cell D2 and change the alignment to Align Right.

j. Save your changes.

4. Adjust column widths.

  a. Use the Format menu to change the width of the Average Price column to **25**.

  b. Use the AutoFit feature to resize the Average Price column.

  c. Use the Format menu to resize the Department column to **18** and the Quantity column to **15**.

  d. Change the text in cell C3 to **Sold**, then use AutoFit to resize the column.

  e. Save your changes.

5. Insert and delete rows and columns.

  a. Insert a new row between rows 4 and 5.

  b. Add MediaLoft Great Britain's newest department—**Children's Corner**—in the newly inserted row. Enter **35** for the average price and **1225** for the number sold.

  c. Add the following comment to cell A5: **New department**. Display the comment, if necessary.

  d. Add a formula in cell D5 that multiplies the Average Price column by the Sold column.

  e. Add a new column between the Department and Average Price columns with the title **Location**.

  f. Delete the History row.

  g. Edit the comment in cell A5 so it reads "New department. Needs promotion."

  h. Save your changes.

6. Apply colors, patterns, and borders.

  a. Add an outside border around the Average Price and Sold data.

  b. Apply a light green background color to the labels in the Department column.

  c. Apply a gold background to the column labels in cells **A3:E3**.

  d. Change the color of the font in the column labels in cells A3:E3 to blue.

  e. Add a 12.5% Gray pattern fill to the title in cell A1. (*Hint*: Use the Patterns tab in the Format Cells dialog box to locate the 12.5% Gray pattern.)

  f. Enter your name in cell A20, then save your work.

  g. Preview and print the worksheet, then close the workbook.

7. Use conditional formatting.

  a. Open the file EX C-2.xls from the drive and folder where your Data Files are stored, then save it as **Monthly Operating Expenses**.

  b. Create conditional formatting that changes a monthly data entry to blue if the value is **greater than 2500**, and changes the monthly data entry to red if the value is **less than 700**.

  c. Create a third conditional format that changes the monthly data to green if a value is **between 1000 and 2000**.

  d. Use the Bold button and Center button to format the column headings and row titles.

  e. Make Column A wide enough to accommodate the contents of cells **A4:A9**.

  f. Create formulas in cells F4:F9 and cells B11:F11. Use the Comma Style with no decimals in these cells.

  g. AutoFit the remaining columns.

  h. Use Merge and Center in row 1 to center the title over columns A–F.

  i. Format the title in cell A1 using 14-point text. Fill the cell with a color and pattern of your choice.

  j. Delete the third conditional format.

  k. Enter your name in cell A20, then apply a green background to it and make the text color yellow.

  l. Use the Edit menu to clear the cell formats from the cell with your name, then save your changes.

8. Check spelling.

  a. Check the spelling in the worksheet using the spelling checker, correcting any spelling errors.

  b. Save your changes, then preview and print the workbook.

  c. Close the workbook, then exit Excel.

▼ INDEPENDENT CHALLENGE 1

Beautiful You, a small beauty salon, has been using Excel for several months. Now that the salon's accounting records are in Excel, the manager would like you to work on the inventory. Although more items will be added later, the worksheet has enough items for you to begin your modifications.

a. Start Excel, open the file EX C-3.xls from the drive and folder where your Data Files are stored, then save it as **BY Inventory**.

b. Create a formula that calculates the value of the inventory on hand for each item.

c. Use an absolute reference to calculate the sale price of each item, using the markup percentage shown.

d. Add the bold attribute to the column headings.

e. Make sure all columns are wide enough to display the data and headings.

f. Change the On Hand Value and Sale Price columns so they display the Currency style with two decimal places.

g. Change the Price Paid column so it displays the Comma style with two decimal places.

h. Add a row under #2 Curlers for **Nail Files**, price paid **$0.25**, sold **individually (each)**, with **59** on hand.

i. Verify that all the formulas in the worksheet are correct. Adjust any items as needed, and check the spelling.

j. Use conditional formatting to call attention to items with a quantity of 25 or fewer on hand. Use boldfaced red text.

k. Add an outside border around the data in the Item column.

l. Delete the row with #3 Curlers.

m. Enter your name in an empty cell, then save the file.

n. Preview and print the worksheet, compare your work to the sample shown in Figure C-24, close the workbook, then exit Excel.

FIGURE C-24

	A	B	C	D	E	F	G	H	I	J
1	Beautiful You Salon						markup ->	1.35		
2										
3	**Item**	**Price Paid**	**Sold by**	**On Hand**	**On Hand Value**	**Sale Price**				
4	#2 Curlers	13.80	box	53	$ 731.40	$ 18.63				
5	Nail Files	0.25	each	59	$ 14.75	$ 0.34				
6	Hair dryers	4.25	each	75	$ 318.75	$ 5.74				
7	Nail polish	3.92	each	62	$ 243.04	$ 5.29				
8	Conditioner	2.99	each	35	$ 104.65	$ 4.04				
9	Scrumptious shampoo	8.30	each	25	$ 207.50	$ 11.21				
10	Clips	2.25	box	33	$ 74.25	$ 3.04				
11	Pins	4.75	box	36	$ 171.00	$ 6.41				
12	#1 Curlers	2.10	box	37	$ 77.70	$ 2.84				
13	Jumbo conditioner	10.65	each	22	$ 234.30	$ 14.38				
14	#472 color	16.32	each	13	$ 212.16	$ 22.03				
15										
16										
17										
18										
19										
20	Your Name									
21										
22										
23										
24										
25										

◄ ◄ ► ► \ Sheet1 / Sheet2 / Sheet3 /

Ready   NUM

▼ INDEPENDENT CHALLENGE 2

You volunteer several hours each week with the Community Action Center. You would like to examine the membership list, and decide to use formatting to make the existing data look more professional and easier to read.

a. Start Excel, open the file EX C-4.xls from the drive and folder where your Data Files are stored, then save it as **Community Action**.

b. Remove any blank columns.

c. Format the Annual Revenue figures using the Currency format.

d. Make all columns wide enough to fit their data and headings.

e. Use formatting enhancements, such as fonts, font sizes, and text attributes to make the worksheet more attractive.

f. Center-align the column labels.

g. Use conditional formatting so that entries for Number of Employees that are greater than 50 appear in a contrasting color.

h. Adjust any items as necessary, then check the spelling.

i. Enter your name in an empty cell, then save your work.

j. Before printing, preview the file so you know what the worksheet looks like, then print a copy. Compare your work to the sample shown in Figure C-25.

k. Close the workbook, then exit Excel.

FIGURE C-25

	A	B	C	D	E	F	G
1	Community Action Center Members						
2							
3		Annual	Number of		Type of		
4	Member	Revenue	Employees	Status	Business		
5	Lisa's Photo Studio	$ 56,000.00	5	member	Restaurant		
6	Chip Technology	$ 492,600.00	175	member	Manufacturing, Microchips		
7	Computer Attic	$ 128,000.00	4	member	Computer Consultant		
8	Deluxe Auto Shop	$ 98,420.00	7	member	Automotive		
9	Front Office	$ 162,320.00	25	member	Employment Agency		
10	General Hospital	$ 1,154,000.00	480	member	Health		
11	Grande Table	$ 101,500.00	25	member	Restaurant		
12	Holiday Inn	$ 175,000.00	75	member	Hotel/Motel		
13	Midas Muffler	$ 106,000.00	22	member	Automotive		
14	Mill Shoppe	$ 346,000.00	165	member	Manufacturing, Furniture		
15	Reservation Inn	$ 272,000.00	42	member	Hotel/Motel		
16	State University	$ 975,630.00	422	member	Education		
17	Candy's Candy Shop	$ 100,500.00	3	non-member	Restaurant		
18	Dental Associates	$ 175,000.00	15	non-member	Health		
19	Dr. Rachel	$ 173,000.00	5	non-member	Health		
20	Dunkin' Donuts	$ 66,420.00	7	non-member	Restaurant		
21	Earl's Restaurant	$ 290,000.00	45	non-member	Restaurant		
22	First Federal Bank	$ 1,216,500.00	36	non-member	Bank		
23	Friendly Chevy	$ 289,000.00	17	non-member	Automotive		
24	Ken's Florist Shop	$ 89,900.00	10	non-member	Florist		
25	Mainaka Muffler	$ 107,900.00	24	non-member	Automotive		

Sheet1 / Sheet2 / Sheet3 /

Ready — NUM

▼ INDEPENDENT CHALLENGE 3

Classic Instruments is a Miami-based company that manufactures high-quality pens and markers. As the finance manager, one of your responsibilities is to analyze the monthly reports from your five district sales offices. Your boss, Joanne Bennington, has just asked you to prepare a quarterly sales report for an upcoming meeting. Because several top executives will be attending this meeting, Joanne reminds you that the report must look professional. In particular, she asks you to emphasize the company's surge in profits during the last month and to highlight the fact that the Northeastern district continues to outpace the other districts.

a. Plan a worksheet that shows the company's sales during the first quarter. Assume that all pens are the same price. Make sure you include:

- The number of pens sold (units sold) and the associated revenues (total sales) for each of the five district sales offices. The five sales districts are: Northeastern, Midwestern, Southeastern, Southern, and Western.
- Calculations that show month-by-month totals and a three-month cumulative total
- Calculations that show each district's share of sales (percent of Total Sales)
- Formatting enhancements to emphasize the recent month's sales surge and the Northeastern district's sales leadership

b. Ask yourself the following questions about the organization and formatting of the worksheet: How can you calculate the totals? What formulas can you copy to save time and keystrokes? Do any of these formulas need to use an absolute reference? How do you show dollar amounts? What information should be shown in bold? Do you need to use more than one font? Should you use more than one point size?

c. Start Excel, then build the worksheet with your own price and sales data. Enter the titles and labels first, then enter the numbers and formulas. You can use the information in Table C-7 to get started.

TABLE C-7:

Classic Instruments
1st Quarter Sales Report

Office	Price	January Units Sold	Sales	February Units Sold	Sales	March Units Sold	Sales	Total Units Sold	Sales
Northeastern									
Midwestern									
Southeastern									
Southern									
Western									

d. Save the workbook as **Classic Instruments** in the drive and folder where your Data Files are stored.

e. Adjust the column widths as necessary.

f. Change the height of row 1 to 30 points.

g. Format labels and values, and change the attributes and alignment if necessary.

h. Resize columns and adjust the formatting as necessary.

i. Add a column that calculates a 24% increase in sales dollars. Use an absolute cell reference in this calculation.

j. Create a new column named Increase in Sales that adds the projected increase to the Total Sales. (*Hint*: Make sure the current formatting is applied to the new information.)

Advanced Challenge Exercise

- Use AutoFormat to add color and formatting to the data.
- Insert a clip art image in an appropriate location, adjusting its size and position as necessary.

k. Enter your name in an empty cell.

l. Check the spelling, then save your work.

m. Preview, then print the file in landscape orientation.

n. Close the file, then exit Excel.

▼ INDEPENDENT CHALLENGE 4

After saving for many years, you now have enough funds to take that international trip you have always dreamed about. Your well-traveled friends have told you that you should always have the local equivalent of $100 U.S. dollars in cash with you when you enter a country. You decide to use the Web to determine how much money you will need in each country.

a. Start Excel, open a new workbook, then save it as **Currency Conversions** in the drive and folder where your Data Files are stored.

b. Enter column and row labels using the information in Table C-8 to get started.

c. Use your favorite search engine to find your own information sources on currency conversions.

d. Find out how much cash is equivalent to **$1** in U.S. dollars for the following countries: **Australia**, **Canada**, **France**, **Germany**, **Sweden**, and the **United Kingdom**. Also enter the name of the currency used in each country.

e. Create an equation that calculates the equivalent of **$100** in U.S. dollars for each country in the list, using an absolute value in the formula.

f. Format the entries in columns B and C using the correct currency unit for each country, with two decimal places. (*Hint*: Use the Numbers tab in the Format cells dialog box; choose the appropriate currency format from the Symbol list, using two decimal places.)

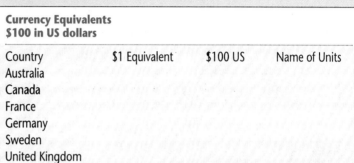

TABLE C-8

Currency Equivalents $100 in US dollars			
Country	$1 Equivalent	$100 US	Name of Units
Australia			
Canada			
France			
Germany			
Sweden			
United Kingdom			

g. Create a conditional format that changes the font attributes of the calculated amount in the "$100 US" column to bold and red if the amount is equals or exceeds **500 units** of the local currency.

h. Merge and center the title over the column headings.

i. Add any formatting attributes to the column headings, and resize the columns as necessary.

j. Add a background color to the title.

Advanced Challenge Exercise

- Apply the AutoFormat of your choice to the conversion table.
- Delete the conditional format in the $100 US column.
- If you have access to an e-mail account, e-mail this workbook to your instructor as an attachment.

k. Enter your name in an empty worksheet cell.

l. Spell check, save, preview, then print the worksheet.

m. Close the workbook and exit Excel.

▼ VISUAL WORKSHOP

Create the worksheet shown in Figure C-26, using skills you learned in this unit. Open the file EX C-5.xls from the drive and folder where your Data Files are stored, then save it as **Projected March Advertising Invoices**. Create a conditional format in the Cost ea. column so that entries greater than 60 appear in red. (*Hint*: The only additional font used in this exercise is Times New Roman. It is 22 point in row 1, and 16 point in row 3.) Enter your name in cell A20, spell check the worksheet, then save and print your work.

FIGURE C-26

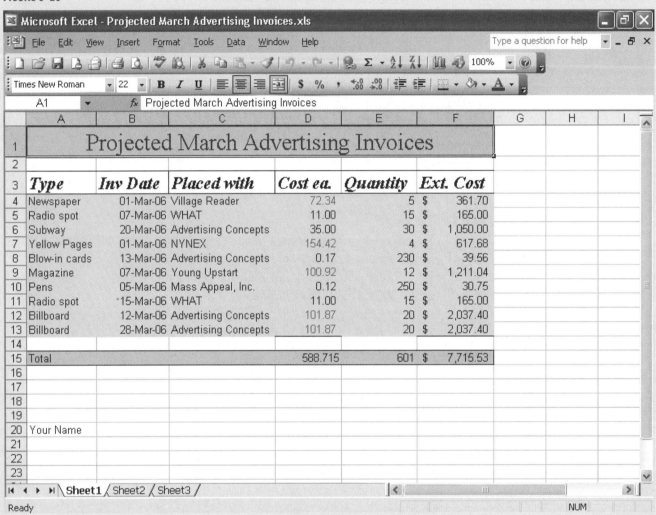

Working with Charts

OBJECTIVES

Plan and design a chart

Create a chart

Move and resize a chart

Edit a chart

Format a chart

Enhance a chart

Annotate and draw on a chart

Preview and print a chart

If you have a SAM user profile, you may have access to hands-on instruction, practice, and assessment of the skills covered in this unit. Log in to your SAM accont and go to your assignments page to see what your instructor has assigned.

Worksheets provide an effective way to organize information, but they are not always the best format for presenting data to others. Information in a selected range or worksheet can easily be displayed as a chart. **Charts**, often called graphs, allow you to communicate the relationships in your worksheet data in readily understandable pictures. In this unit, you will learn how to create a chart, how to edit a chart and change the chart type, how to add text annotations and arrows to a chart, and how to preview and print a chart. For the annual meeting, Jim Fernandez needs you to create a chart showing the six-month sales history for the MediaLoft stores in the Eastern Division. He wants to illustrate the growth trend in this division.

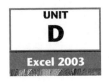

Planning and Designing a Chart

Before creating a chart, you need to plan the information you want your chart to show and how you want it to look. ![diamond] In early June, the Marketing Department launched a regional advertising campaign for the Eastern Division. The results of the campaign were increased sales during the fall months. Jim wants you to create a chart for the annual meeting that illustrates the growth trend for sales in MediaLoft's Eastern Division stores and to highlight this sales increase.

DETAILS

Jim wants you to use the worksheet shown in Figure D-1 and the following guidelines to plan the chart:

- **Determine the purpose of the chart and identify the data relationships you want to communicate graphically**

  You want to create a chart that shows sales throughout MediaLoft's Eastern Division from July through December. In particular, you want to highlight the increase in sales that occurred as a result of the advertising campaign.

- **Determine the results you want to see, and decide which chart type is most appropriate to use**

  Different charts display data in distinctive ways. Some chart types are more appropriate for particular types of data and analyses. How you want your data displayed—and how you want that data interpreted—can help you determine the best chart type to use. Table D-1 describes several different types of charts, the corresponding button on the Chart Type palette located on the Chart toolbar, and indicates when each one is best used. Because you want to compare data (sales in multiple locations) over a time period (the months July through December), you decide to use a column chart.

- **Identify the worksheet data you want the chart to illustrate**

  You are using data from the worksheet titled MediaLoft Eastern Division Stores shown in Figure D-1. This worksheet contains the sales data for the four stores in the Eastern Division from July through December.

- **Sketch the chart, then use your sketch to decide where the chart elements should be placed**

  You sketch your chart as shown in Figure D-2. You put the months on the horizontal axis (the **x-axis**) and the monthly sales figures on the vertical axis (the **y-axis**). The x-axis is often called the **category axis** because it often contains the names of data groups, such as months or years. The y-axis is called the **value axis** because it often contains numerical values that help you interpret the size of chart elements. (In a 3-D chart, the y-axis is referred to as the z-axis.) The area inside the horizontal and vertical axes is called the **plot area**. The **tick marks** on the y-axis create a scale of measure for each value. Each value in a cell you select for your chart is a **data point**. In any chart, a **data marker** visually represents each data point, which in this case is a column. A collection of related data points is a **data series**. In this chart, there are four data series (Boston, Chicago, Kansas City, and New York), so you include a **legend** to make it easy to identify them.

FIGURE D-1: Worksheet containing sales data

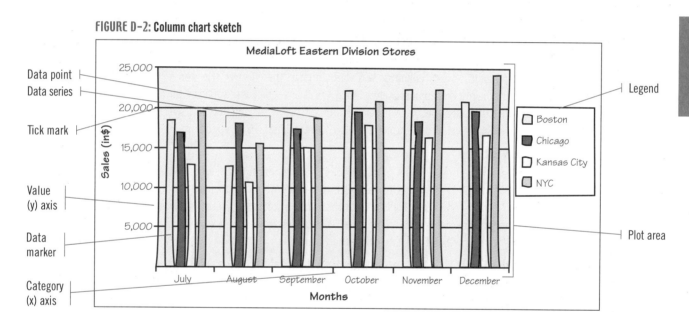

	A	B	C	D	E	F	G	H	I	J	K
1			**MediaLoft Eastern Division Stores**								
2			**FY 2006 Sales Following Advertising Campaign**								
3											
4											
5		**July**	**August**	**September**	**October**	**November**	**December**	**Total**			
6	**Boston**	18,750	13,050	18,600	22,500	22,500	20,750	$116,150			
7	**Chicago**	17,200	18,200	17,250	19,500	18,600	19,500	$110,250			
8	**Kansas City**	12,150	11,500	15,350	18,100	17,050	17,500	$ 91,650			
9	**NYC**	19,500	16,250	18,900	20,500	22,000	23,800	$120,950			
10	**Total**	$ 67,600	$ 59,000	$ 70,100	$ 80,600	$ 80,150	$ 81,550	$439,000			
11											

FIGURE D-2: Column chart sketch

TABLE D-1: Commonly used chart types

type	button	description
Area		Shows how individual volume changes over time in relation to total volume
Bar		Compares distinct object levels over time using a horizontal format; sometimes referred to as a horizontal bar chart in other spreadsheet programs
Column		Compares distinct object levels over time using a vertical format; the Excel default; sometimes referred to as a bar chart in other spreadsheet programs
Line		Compares trends over even time intervals; appears similar to an area chart, but does not emphasize total
Pie		Compares sizes of pieces as part of a whole; used for a single series of numbers
XY (scatter)		Compares trends over uneven time or measurement intervals; used in scientific and engineering disciplines for trend spotting and extrapolation
Combination	none	Combines a column and line chart to compare data requiring different scales of measure

Creating a Chart

To create a chart in Excel, you first select the range containing the data you want to chart. Once you've selected a range, you can use the Excel **Chart Wizard** to lead you through the process of creating the chart. ▰▰▰ Using the worksheet containing the sales data for the Eastern Division, Jim asks you to create a chart that shows the growth trend that occurred.

STEPS

QUICK TIP

When charting any data, make sure all series are for the same time period.

1. **Start Excel, open the File** EX D-1.xls **from the drive and location where your Data Files are stored, then save it as** MediaLoft Sales-Eastern Division

   You want the chart to include the monthly sales figures for each of the Eastern Division stores, as well as month and store labels. You don't include the Total column and row because the monthly figures make up the totals, and these figures would skew the chart.

QUICK TIP

You can create a chart from noncontiguous cells by pressing and holding [Ctrl] while selecting each range.

2. **Select the range** A5:G9, **then click the** Chart Wizard button 📊 **on the Standard toolbar**

   The selected range contains the data you want to chart. The Chart Wizard opens. The Chart Wizard - Step 1 of 4 - Chart Type dialog box lets you choose the type of chart you want to create. The default chart type is a Clustered Column, as shown in Figure D-3. You can see a preview of the chart using your selected data by pressing and holding the Press and Hold to View Sample button.

3. **Click** Next **to accept Clustered Column, the default chart type**

   The Chart Wizard - Step 2 of 4 - Chart Source Data dialog box lets you choose the data to chart and whether the series appear in rows or columns. You want to chart the effect of sales for each store over the time period. Currently, the rows are appropriately selected as the data series, as specified by the Series in option button (located under the Data range). Because you selected the data before clicking the Chart Wizard button, Excel converted the range to absolute values and the correct range, =Sheet1!$A$5:$G$9, appears in the Data range text box.

4. **Click** Next

   The Chart Wizard - Step 3 of 4 - Chart Options dialog box shows a sample chart using the data you selected. The store locations (the rows in the selected range) are plotted against the months (the columns in the selected range), and Excel added the months as labels for each data series. A legend shows each location and its corresponding color on the chart. The Titles tab lets you add titles to the chart and its axes. Other tabs let you modify the axes, legend, and other chart elements.

5. **Click the** Chart title text box, **then type** MediaLoft Sales - Eastern Division

   After a moment, the title appears in the Sample Chart box. See Figure D-4.

6. **Click** Next

   In the Chart Wizard - Step 4 of 4 - Chart Location dialog box, you determine the placement of the chart in the workbook. You can display a chart as an object on the current sheet (called an **embedded chart**), on any other existing sheet, or on a newly created chart sheet. A **chart sheet** in a workbook contains only a chart, which is linked to the workbook data. The default selection—displaying the chart as an object in the sheet containing the data—will help Jim emphasize his point at the annual meeting.

QUICK TIP

If the Chart toolbar does not display, click View on the menu bar, point to Toolbars, and then click Chart.

7. **Click** Finish

   The column chart appears and the Chart toolbar opens, either docked or floating, as shown in Figure D-5. Your chart and the chart toolbar might be in different locations, and the chart may look slightly different. You adjust the chart's location and size in the next lesson. The **sizing handles**, the small squares at the corners and sides of the chart's border, indicate that the chart is selected. Any time a chart is selected, as it is now, a blue border surrounds the worksheet data range, a green border surrounds the row labels, and a purple border surrounds the column labels.

8. **Click the** Save button 💾 **on the Standard toolbar**

FIGURE D-3: First Chart Wizard dialog box

Selected chart

Chart types

Clustered column chart is the default

Chart sub-types for selected chart

Description of selected chart sub-type

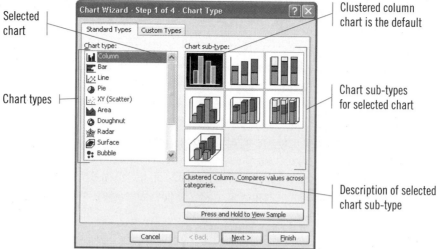

FIGURE D-4: Third Chart Wizard dialog box

Type the chart title here

Sample chart

Title added

Legend

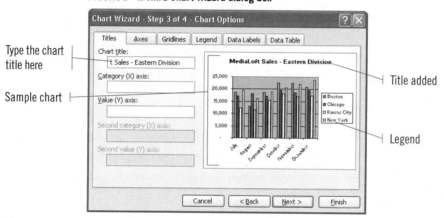

FIGURE D-5: Worksheet with column chart

Column labels

Row labels

Data range

Selected chart object

Chart toolbar

Title

Legend

Sizing handles

Month labels on the x-axis

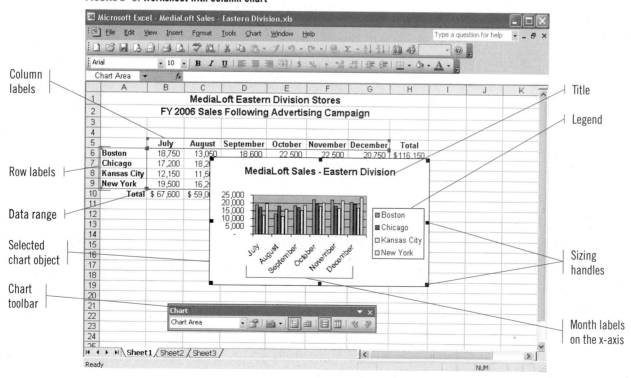

Moving and Resizing a Chart

Charts are graphics, or drawn objects, and are not located in a specific cell or at a specific range address. An **object** is an independent element on a worksheet. You can select an object by clicking within its borders to surround it with sizing handles. You can move a selected chart object anywhere on a worksheet without affecting formulas or data in the worksheet. However, any data changed in the worksheet is automatically updated in the chart. You can resize a chart to improve its appearance by dragging its sizing handles. You can even put a chart on another sheet, and it will still reflect the original data. Chart objects contain other objects, such as a title and legend, which you can move and resize. To move an object, select it, then drag it or cut and copy it to a new location. When you select a chart object, the name of the selected object appears in the Chart Objects list box on the Chart toolbar and in the Name box. ▰▰▰ Jim wants you to increase the size of the chart, position it below the worksheet data, and reposition the legend.

STEPS

QUICK TIP

If you want to delete a chart, select it, then press [Delete].

1. **Make sure the chart is still selected, then position the pointer over the chart**

   The pointer shape ⌖ indicates that you can move the chart or use a sizing handle to resize it. For a table of commonly used chart pointers, refer to Table D-2. On occasion, the Chart toolbar obscures your view. You can dock the toolbar to make it easier to see your work.

2. **If the chart toolbar is floating, click the Chart toolbar's title bar, drag it to the right edge of the status bar until it docks, then release the mouse button**

   The toolbar is docked on the bottom of the screen.

3. **Place ⌖ on a blank area near the edge of the chart, press and hold the left mouse button, using ✛, drag the chart until its upper-left edge is at the top of row 13 and the left edge of the chart is at the left border of column A, then release the mouse button**

   As you drag the chart, you can see a dotted outline representing the chart's perimeter. The chart appears in the new location.

QUICK TIP

Resizing a chart doesn't affect the data in the chart, only the way the chart looks on the sheet.

4. **Position the pointer on the right-middle sizing handle until it changes to ↔, then drag the right edge of the chart to the right edge of column H**

   The chart is widened. See Figure D-6.

5. **Position the pointer over the upper-middle sizing handle until it changes to ↕, then drag it to the top edge of row 12**

6. **Scroll down the screen, position the pointer over the lower-middle sizing handle until it changes to ↕, then drag to position the bottom border of the chart at the bottom border of row 25**

   You can move the legend to improve the chart's appearance. You want to align the top of the legend with the top of the plot area.

QUICK TIP

Placing the mouse pointer over a chart object displays a ScreenTip identifying it, whether the chart is selected or not. If a chart—or any object in it—is selected, the ScreenTips still appear and the name of the selected chart object appears in the Chart Objects list box on the Chart toolbar and in the Name box.

7. **Click the legend to select it, then drag the legend upward using ⌖ so the top of the legend aligns with the top of the plot area**

   Sizing handles appear around the legend when you click it; "Legend" appears in the Chart Objects list box on the Chart toolbar as well as in the Name box, and a dotted outline of the legend border appears as you drag. Changing any label modifies the legend text.

8. **Click cell A9, type NYC, then click the Enter button ✓ on the formula bar**

   See Figure D-7. The legend changes to the text you entered. Because the chart is no longer selected, the chart toolbar no longer appears at the bottom of the screen.

9. **Click the Save button 🖫 on the Standard toolbar**

FIGURE D-6: Worksheet with resized and repositioned chart

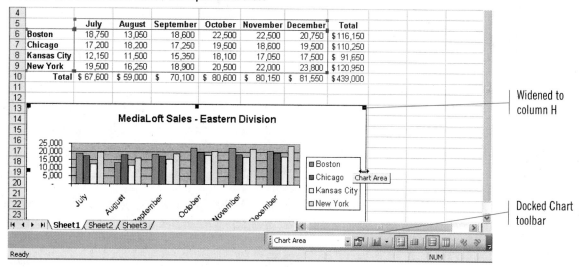

Widened to column H

Docked Chart toolbar

FIGURE D-7: Worksheet with repositioned legend

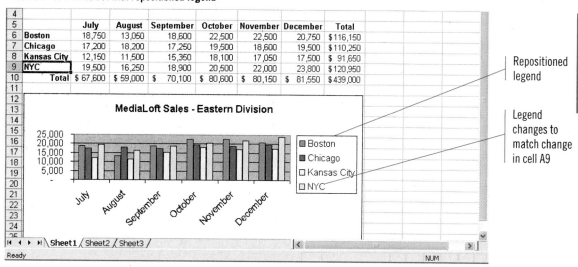

Repositioned legend

Legend changes to match change in cell A9

TABLE D-2: Commonly used pointers

name	pointer	use	name	pointer	use
Diagonal resizing	↙ or ↘	Change chart shape	I-beam	I	Edit chart text from corners
Draw	+	Create shapes	Move chart	↔↕	Change chart location
Horizontal resizing	↔	Change chart shape from left to right	Vertical resizing	↕	Changes chart shape from top to bottom

Clues to Use

Changing the location of a chart

Suppose you have created an embedded chart that you decide would look better on a chart sheet. You can make this change without recreating the entire chart. To change the location of a selected chart, click Chart on the menu bar, then click Location. If the chart is embedded, click the As new sheet option button, then click OK. If the chart is on its own sheet, click the As object in option button, then click OK.

Editing a Chart

Once you've created a chart, it's easy to modify it. You can change data values in the worksheet, and the chart is automatically updated to reflect the new data. You can also change a data point in a chart, and the corresponding data values in the worksheet are automatically updated. You can also easily change the type of chart displayed by using the buttons on the Chart toolbar. ▰▰▰▰ You look over your worksheet and realize the data for the Kansas City store in November and December is incorrect. After you correct this data, Jim asks you to see how the same data looks using different chart types.

STEPS

TROUBLE
If you cannot see the chart and data together on your screen, click View on the menu bar, click Zoom, then click 75%.

1. **If necessary, scroll the worksheet so that you can see both the chart and row 8 containing the Kansas City sales figures, click the November Kansas City data point, then click the data point again**

   Handles surround the data point. You can click and drag these handles to modify the plotted data value.

2. **Drag the upper handle until the ScreenTip displays 21000**

   The value in cell F8 displays 21000.

3. **Click cell G8, type 23000, then click the Enter button ✔ on the formula bar**

   The Kansas City columns for November and December reflect the increased sales figures. See Figure D-8. The totals in column H and row 10 are also updated.

4. **Select the chart by clicking a blank area within the chart border, then click the Chart Type list arrow ▰▾ on the Chart toolbar**

   The Chart Type buttons appear on the Chart Type palette. Table D-3 describes the principal chart types available.

QUICK TIP
As you work with charts, experiment with different formats for your charts until you get just the right look.

5. **Click the Bar Chart button ▰ on the palette**

   The column chart changes to a bar chart. See Figure D-9. You look at the bar chart, take some notes, then decide to see if the large increase in sales would be better presented with a three-dimensional column chart.

6. **Click ▰▾, then click the 3-D Column Chart button ▰ on the palette**

   A three-dimensional column chart appears. You notice that the three-dimensional column format is more crowded than the two-dimensional format, but it gives you a sense of volume.

QUICK TIP
The Chart Type button displays the last chart type selected.

7. **Click ▰▾, then click the Column Chart button ▰ on the palette**

8. **Click the Save button ▰ on the Standard toolbar**

TABLE D-3: Commonly used chart type buttons

click to display a	click to display a	click to display a	click to display a
▰ area chart	▰ pie chart	▰ 3-D area chart	▰ 3-D pie chart
▰ bar chart	▰ (XY) scatter chart	▰ 3-D bar chart	▰ 3-D surface chart
▰ column chart	▰ doughnut chart	▰ 3-D column chart	▰ 3-D cylinder chart
▰ line chart	▰ radar chart	▰ 3-D line chart	▰ 3-D cone chart

FIGURE D-8: Worksheet with new data entered for Kansas City

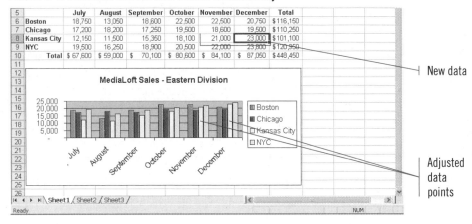

New data

Adjusted
data
points

FIGURE D-9: Bar chart

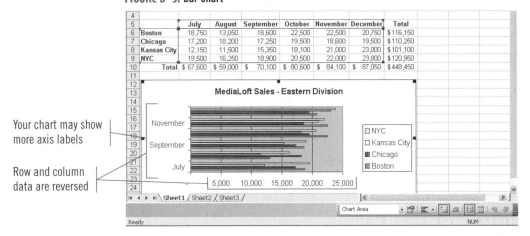

Your chart may show
more axis labels

Row and column
data are reversed

Clues to Use

Rotating a 3-D chart

In a three-dimensional chart, other data series in the same chart can sometimes obscure columns or bars. You can rotate the chart to obtain a better view. Click the chart, click the Corners object located at the tip of one of its axes, then drag the handle until a more pleasing view of the data series appears. See Figure D-10.

FIGURE D-10: 3-D chart rotated with improved view of data series

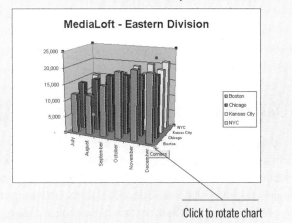

Click to rotate chart

Formatting a Chart

After you've created a chart using the Chart Wizard, you can easily modify its appearance. You can use the Chart toolbar and Chart menu to change the colors of data series and to add or eliminate a legend and gridlines. **Gridlines** are the horizontal and vertical lines in the chart that enable the eye to follow the value on an axis. ◆◆◆◆ Jim wants you to make some changes in the appearance of the chart. He wants to see if the chart looks better without gridlines, and he wants you to change the color of a data series.

STEPS

1. **Make sure the chart is still selected**

   Horizontal gridlines currently extend from the value axis tick marks across the chart's plot area.

QUICK TIP

The Chart menu only appears on the menu bar when a chart or one of its objects is selected.

2. **Click** Chart **on the menu bar, click** Chart Options, **click the** Gridlines tab **in the Chart Options dialog box, then click the** Major Gridlines check box **for the Value (Y) axis to remove the check mark**

   The gridlines disappear from the sample chart in the dialog box, as shown in Figure D-11.

3. **Click the** Major gridlines check box **for the Value (Y) axis to reselect it, then click the** Minor gridlines check box **for the Value (Y) axis**

   Both major and minor gridlines appear in the sample. **Minor gridlines** show the values between the tick marks.

4. **Click the** Minor gridlines check box **for the Value (Y) axis, then click** OK

   The minor gridlines disappear, leaving only the major gridlines on the value axis. You can change the color of the columns to better distinguish the data series.

5. **With the chart selected, double-click any** light blue column **in the NYC data series**

   Handles appear on all the columns in the NYC data series, and the Format Data Series dialog box opens, as shown in Figure D-12.

6. **Click the** fuchsia color **(fourth row, first column) on the Patterns tab, then click** OK

   All the columns for the series become fuchsia, and the legend changes to match the new color. Compare your formatted chart to Figure D-13.

7. **Click the** Save button 🔲 **on the Standard toolbar**

Clues to Use

Adding data labels to a chart

There are times when your audience might benefit by seeing data labels on a chart. These labels can indicate the series name, category name, and/or the value of one or more data points. Once your chart is selected, you can add this information to your chart by clicking

Chart on the menu bar, clicking Chart Options, then clicking the Data Labels tab in the Chart Options dialog box. You can also apply formatting to data labels, or delete individual data labels.

FIGURE D-11: Chart Options dialog box

Sample chart
appears without
gridlines

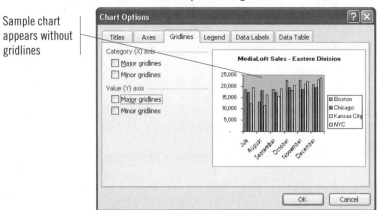

FIGURE D-12: Format Data Series dialog box

Sample of
selected color

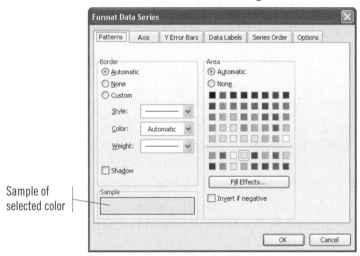

FIGURE D-13: Chart with formatted data series

Gridlines
make it
easy to
follow axis
values

New data
series color

New color
appears in
legend

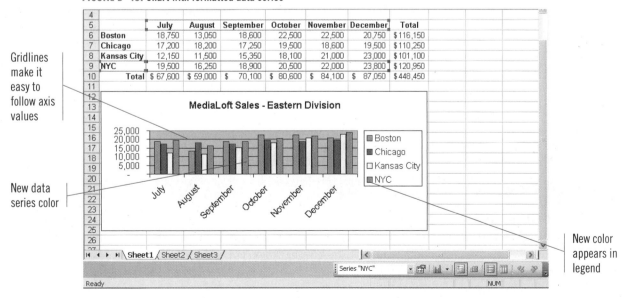

Enhancing a Chart

There are many ways to enhance a chart to make it easier to read and understand. You can create titles for the x-axis and y-axis, add graphics, or add background color. You can even format the text you use in a chart. Many enhancements can be made using the Chart toolbar buttons. These buttons are listed in Table D-4. Jim wants you to improve the appearance of the chart by creating titles for the category axis and value axis and adding a drop shadow to the chart title.

STEPS

1. **Click a blank area of the chart to select the chart, click Chart on the menu bar, click Chart Options, click the Titles tab in the Chart Options dialog box, then type Months in the Category (X) axis text box**

   Descriptive text on the category axis helps readers understand the chart. The word "Months" appears below the month labels in the sample chart, as shown in Figure D-14.

2. **Type Sales (in $) in the Value (Y) axis text box, then click OK**

   A selected text box containing "Sales (in $)" appears rotated 90 degrees to the left of the value axis. Once the Chart Options dialog box is closed, you can move the value or title to a new position by clicking an edge of the object then dragging it.

3. **Press [Esc] on the keyboard to deselect the value axis title**

   Next you decide that a border with a drop shadow will enhance the chart title.

4. **Click the MediaLoft Sales – Eastern Division chart title to select it**

5. **Click the Format Chart Title button on the Chart toolbar to open the Format Chart Title dialog box, make sure the Patterns tab is selected, then click the Shadow check box to select it**

   A border with a drop shadow appears in the sample area.

6. **Click the Font tab in the Format Chart Title dialog box, click Times New Roman in the Font list, click Bold Italic in the Font style list, click OK, then press [Esc] on the keyboard to deselect the chart title**

   A border with a drop shadow appears around the chart title, and the chart title text is reformatted.

7. **Click any one of the months (on the category axis), click , click the Font tab in the Format Axis dialog box if necessary, click 8 in the Size list if necessary, then click OK**

   The size of the category axis text decreases, making more of the plot area visible.

8. **Click any one of the sales values (on the value axis), click , click the Font tab if necessary, click 8 in the Size list, click OK, then press [Esc] on the keyboard to deselect the value axis**

   The text on the value axis becomes smaller. Compare your chart to Figure D-15.

9. **Click the Save button on the Standard toolbar**

Clues to Use

Changing text alignment in charts

You can modify the alignment of axis text to make it fit better within the plot area. With a chart selected, double-click the axis text to be modified. The Format Axis dialog box opens. Click the Alignment tab, then change the alignment by typing the number of degrees in the Degrees text box, or by clicking a marker in the Degrees sample box. When you have made the desired changes, click OK.

FIGURE D-14: Sample chart with Category (X) axis text

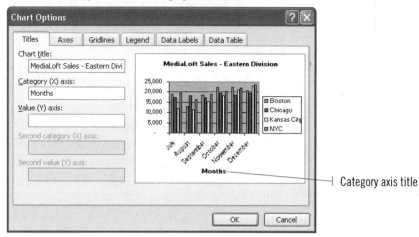

Category axis title

FIGURE D-15: Enhanced chart

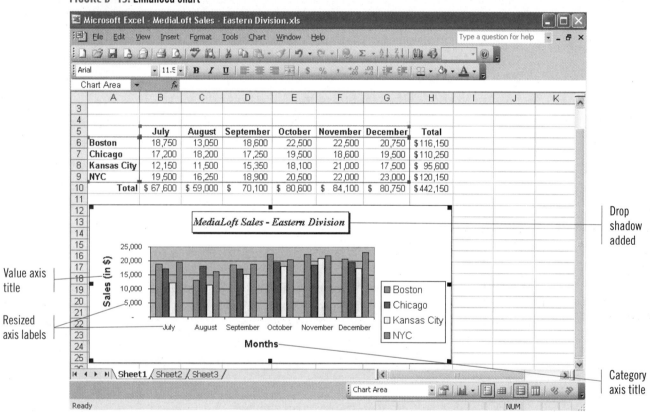

Drop shadow added

Value axis title

Resized axis labels

Category axis title

TABLE D-4: Chart enhancement buttons

button	use
	Displays the Format dialog box for the selected chart object
	Selects chart type (chart type on button changes to last chart type selected)
	Adds/deletes legend
	Creates a data table within the chart
	Charts data by row
	Charts data by column
	Angles selected text downward (clockwise)
	Angles selected text upward (counterclockwise)

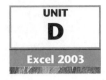

Annotating and Drawing on a Chart

You can add arrows and text annotations to point out critical information in your charts. **Text annotations** are labels that you add to a chart to further describe your data. You can draw lines and arrows that point to the exact locations you want to emphasize. ██████ Jim wants you to add a text annotation and an arrow to highlight the October sales increase.

STEPS

1. **Make sure the chart is selected**

   To call attention to the Boston October sales increase, you can draw an arrow that points to the top of the Boston October data series with the annotation, "Due to ad campaign." With the chart selected, simply typing text in the formula bar creates annotation text.

2. **Type Due to ad campaign, then click the Enter button ✓ on the formula bar**

   As you type, the text appears in the formula bar. After you confirm the entry, the text appears in a selected text box on the chart.

3. **Point to an edge of the text box so that the pointer changes to ⭷**

4. **Drag the text box above the chart, as shown in Figure D-16, then release the mouse button**

   You can add an arrow to point to a specific area or item in a chart by using the Drawing toolbar.

5. **Click the Drawing button ⬙ on the Standard toolbar if necessary to display the Drawing toolbar**

   The Drawing toolbar appears below the worksheet.

6. **Click the Arrow button ⬉ on the Drawing toolbar, then move the pointer over the chart**

   The pointer changes to ✛, and the status bar displays "Click and drag to insert an AutoShape." When you draw an arrow, the point farthest from where you start has the arrowhead.

7. **Position ✛ under the t in the word "to" in the text box, press and hold the left mouse button, drag the line to the Boston column in the October sales series, then release the mouse button**

   An arrow appears, pointing to Boston October sales. The arrow is a selected object in the chart; you can resize, format, or delete it just like any other object. Compare your finished chart to Figure D-17.

8. **Click ⬙ to close the Drawing toolbar**

9. **Click the Save button ⬚ on the Standard toolbar**

TROUBLE

If the pointer changes to ⌶ or ↔, release the mouse button, click outside the text box area to deselect it, select the text box, then repeat Step 3.

QUICK TIP

To annotate charts, you can also use the Callout shapes in the AutoShapes menu on the Drawing toolbar.

QUICK TIP

You can also insert text and an arrow in the data section of a worksheet by clicking the Text Box button ⬚ on the Drawing toolbar, drawing a text box, typing the text, then adding the arrow.

Clues to Use

Adding an organizational chart or other diagram type

In addition to charts, annotations, and drawn objects, you can create a variety of diagrams. Diagram types include an Organization Chart, Cycle, Radial, Pyramid, Venn, or Target diagram. To insert a diagram, click Insert on the menu bar, then click Diagram. In the Diagram Gallery dialog box, click a diagram type, then click OK. The diagram appears on the worksheet as an embedded object with sizing handles, and the Diagram toolbar opens. You can edit placeholder text and use the Diagram toolbar buttons to insert or modify shapes, change the layout or diagram type, or select an AutoFormat. A selected diagram shape can be formatted using the Drawing toolbar buttons.

FIGURE D-16: Repositioning text annotation

Outline of repositioned annotation

Selected text annotation

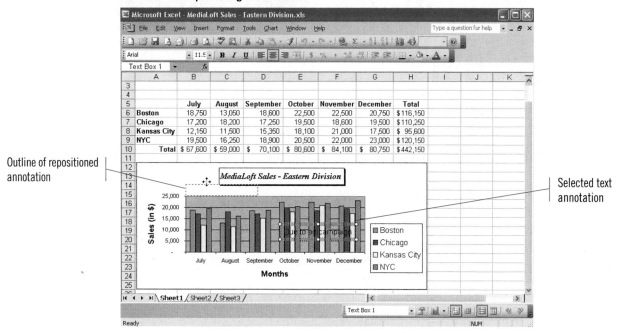

FIGURE D-17: Completed chart with text annotation and arrow

Repositioned text annotation

Arrow

Drawing toolbar

Boston October sales

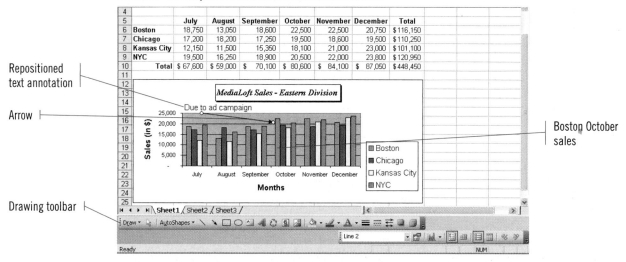

Clues to Use

Exploding a pie slice

Just as an arrow can call attention to a data series, you can emphasize a pie slice by exploding, or pulling it away from, the pie chart. Once the pie chart is selected, click the pie to select it, click the desired slice to select only that slice, then drag the slice away from the pie, as shown in Figure D-18. After you change the chart type, you may need to adjust arrows within the chart.

FIGURE D-18: Exploded pie slice

Eastern Division - 6 Months Sales

$87,050 $67,600 $59,000 $84,100 $80,600 $70,100

☐ July ■ August ☐ September ☐ October ■ November ■ December

Slice pulled from pie

Previewing and Printing a Chart

After you complete a chart, you often need to print it. As with previewing a worksheet, previewing a chart lets you see what your chart looks like before you print it. You can print a chart by itself or as part of the worksheet. ▰▰▰ Jim wants a printed version of the chart for the annual meeting. He wants you to print the worksheet and the chart together, so that the shareholders can see the actual sales numbers for the Eastern Division stores.

STEPS

1. **Press [Esc] on the keyboard to deselect the arrow and the chart, enter your name in cell A35, then press [Ctrl][Home] on the keyboard to select cell A1**

2. **Click the Print Preview button 🔍 on the Standard toolbar**

   The Print Preview window opens. You decide the chart and data would fit better on the page if they were printed in **landscape** orientation—that is, with the text running the long way on the page. You use Page Setup to change the page orientation.

3. **Click Setup on the Print Preview toolbar to open the Page Setup dialog box, then click the Page tab, if necessary**

4. **Click the Landscape option button in the Orientation section, as shown in Figure D-19, then click OK**

   Because each page has a default left margin of 0.75", the chart and data will print too far over to the left of the page. You can change this setting using the Margins tab of the Page Setup dialog box.

5. **Click Setup on the Print Preview toolbar, click the Margins tab, click the Horizontally check box under Center on page, then click OK**

   The data and chart are positioned horizontally on the page. See Figure D-20.

6. **Click Print to display the Print dialog box, then click OK**

   The data and chart print, and you are returned to the worksheet. If you want, you can choose to preview (and print) only the chart.

7. **Select the chart, then click 🔍**

   The chart appears in the Print Preview window. If you wanted to, you could print the chart by clicking the Print button on the Print Preview toolbar.

8. **Click Close on the Print Preview toolbar**

9. **Click the Save button 💾 on the Standard toolbar, close the workbook, then exit Excel**

FIGURE D-19: Page tab of the Page Setup dialog box

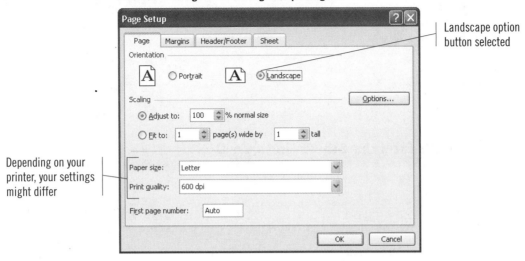

Landscape option
button selected

Depending on your
printer, your settings
might differ

FIGURE D-20: Chart and data ready to print

Centered
on page

Orientation
changed to
landscape

Chart and
data will
print on
one page

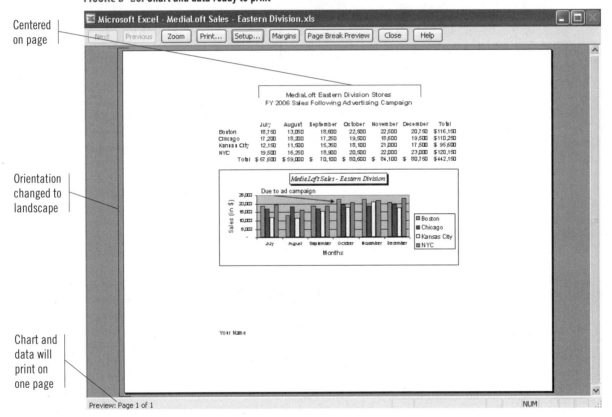

Clues to Use

Using the Page Setup dialog box for a chart

When a chart is selected, a different Page Setup dialog box opens than when neither the chart nor data is selected. The Center on Page options are not always available. To accurately position a chart on the page, you can click the Margins button on the Print Preview toolbar. Margin lines appear on the screen and show you exactly how the margins appear on the page. The exact placement appears in the status bar when you press and hold the mouse button on the margin line. You can drag the lines to the exact settings you want.

Practice

▼ CONCEPTS REVIEW

Label each element of the Excel chart shown in Figure D-21.

FIGURE D-21

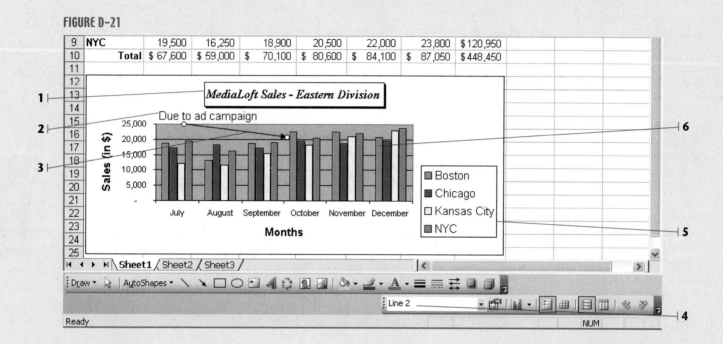

Match each chart type with the statement that best describes it.

7. **Combination**
8. **Column**
9. **Line**
10. **Area**
11. **Pie**

a. Shows how volume changes over time
b. Compares data as parts of a whole
c. Displays a column and line chart using different scales of measurement
d. Compares trends over even time intervals
e. Compares data over time—the Excel default

Select the best answer from the list of choices.

12. **Which pointer is used to resize a chart object?**
    a. I
    b. ↘
    c. ↔
    d. +

13. **The object in a chart that identifies patterns used for each data series is a:**
    a. Data point.
    b. Plot.
    c. Legend.
    d. Range.

14. **The orientation of a page whose dimensions are 11" wide by 8½" tall is:**
    a. Portrait.
    b. Longways.
    c. Landscape.
    d. Sideways.

15. **What is the term for a row or column on a chart?**
    a. Range address
    b. Axis title
    c. Chart orientation
    d. Data series

16. **In a 2-D chart, the category axis is the:**
    a. X-axis.
    b. Z-axis.
    c. D-axis.
    d. Y-axis.

17. **In a 2-D chart, the value axis is the:**
    a. X-axis.
    b. Y-axis.
    c. D-axis.
    d. Z-axis.

▼ SKILLS REVIEW

1. **Plan and design a chart.**
   a. Start Excel, open the Data File EX D-2.xls from the drive and folder where your Data Files are stored, then save it as **MediaLoft Vancouver Software Usage**.
   b. Sketch the type of chart you would use to plot this data.
   c. In what chart type is the y-axis referred to as the z-axis?
   d. What term is used to describe the visual representation of each data point?

2. **Create a chart.**
   a. Select the range containing the data and headings.
   b. Start the Chart Wizard.
   c. In the Chart Wizard, select a clustered column chart, then verify that the series are in rows, add the chart title **Software Usage by Department**, and make the chart an object on the worksheet.
   d. After the chart appears, save your work.

3. Move and resize a chart.

  a. Make sure the chart is still selected.

  b. Move the chart beneath the data.

  c. Resize the chart so it extends to column J.

  d. Use the Legend tab in the Chart Options dialog box to move the legend below the charted data.

  e. Resize the chart so the bottom is at the top of row 25.

  f. Save your work.

4. Edit a chart.

  a. Change the value in cell B3 to **6**. Notice the change in the chart.

  b. Select the chart.

  c. Use the Chart Type list arrow to change the chart to a 3-D Column Chart.

  d. Rotate the chart to move the data.

  e. Change the chart back to a column chart.

  f. Save your work.

5. Format a chart.

  a. Make sure the chart is still selected.

  b. Use the Chart Options dialog box to turn off the displayed gridlines.

  c. Change the font used in the Category and Value labels to Times New Roman.

  d. Turn on the major gridlines for the value axis.

  e. Change the chart title's font to Times New Roman, with a font size of 18.

  f. Save your work.

6. Enhance a chart.

  a. Make sure the chart is selected, then select the Titles tab in the Chart Options dialog box.

  b. Enter **Software** as the x-axis title.

  c. Enter **Users** as the y-axis title.

  d. Change Production in the legend to **Art**. (*Hint*: Change the text entry in the worksheet.)

  e. Add a drop shadow to the chart title.

  f. Save your work.

7. Annotate and draw on a chart.

  a. Make sure the chart is selected, then create the text annotation **Needs More Users**.

  b. Position the text annotation beneath the chart title.

  c. Below the text annotation, use the Drawing toolbar to create an arrow that points to the area containing the Access data.

  d. Compare your work to Figure D-22.

  e. Save your work.

FIGURE D-22

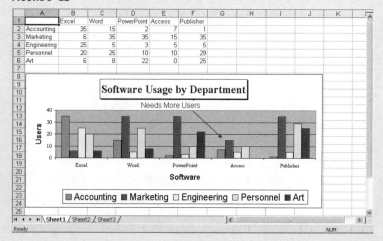

▼ SKILLS REVIEW (CONTINUED)

8. Preview and print a chart.

    a. In the worksheet, enter your name in cell A30.

    b. Preview the chart and data.

    c. Change the page orientation to landscape.

    d. Center the page contents horizontally and vertically on the page.

    e. Print the data and chart from the Print Preview window.

    f. Save your work.

    g. Preview only the chart, then print it.

    h. Close the workbook, then exit Excel.

▼ INDEPENDENT CHALLENGE 1

You are the operations manager for the Springfield Theater Group in Oregon. Each year the group applies to various state and federal agencies for matching funds. For this year's funding proposal, you need to create charts to document the number of productions in previous years.

    a. Sketch a sample worksheet on a piece of paper describing how you will create the charts. Which type of chart is best suited for the information you need to display? What kind of chart enhancements do you want to use? Will a 3-D effect make your chart easier to understand?

    b. Start Excel, open the Data File EX D-3.xls, then save it as **Springfield Theater Group** in the drive and folder where your Data Files are stored.

    c. Create a column chart for the data, accepting all Chart Wizard defaults.

    d. Change at least one of the colors used in a data series.

    e. Create at least two additional charts for the same data to show how different chart types display the same data. Each of these charts should be on its own chart sheet in the workbook.

    f. After creating the charts, make the appropriate enhancements. Include chart titles, legends, and value and category axis titles, using the suggestions in Table D-5.

    g. Add data labels.

    h. Enter your name in a worksheet cell.

    i. Save your work. Before printing, preview the workbook so you know what the charts look like. Adjust any items as necessary.

    j. Print the worksheet (charts and data).

    k. Close the workbook, then exit Excel.

TABLE D-5

suggested chart enhancements	
Title	Types and Number of Plays
Legend	Year 1, Year 2, Year 3, Year 4
Value axis title	Number of Plays
Category axis title	Play Types

▼ INDEPENDENT CHALLENGE 2

Beautiful You, a small beauty salon, has been using Excel for several months. One of your responsibilities at the Beautiful You salon is to re-create the company's records using Excel. Another is to convince the current staff that Excel can help them make daily operating decisions more easily and efficiently. To do this, you've decided to create charts using the previous year's operating expenses, including rent, utilities, and payroll. The manager will use these charts at the next monthly meeting.

    a. Decide which data in the worksheet should be charted. Sketch two sample charts. What type of charts are best suited for the information you need to show? What kind of chart enhancements are necessary?

    b. Start Excel, open the Data File EX D-4.xls from the drive and folder where your Data Files are stored, then save it as **BY Expense Charts**.

    c. Create a column chart on the worksheet, containing the expense data for all four quarters.

    d. Using the same data, create an area chart and one additional chart using any other appropriate chart type. (*Hint*: Move each chart to a new location on the worksheet, then deselect it before using the Wizard to create the next one.)

    e. Add annotated text and arrows to the column chart that highlight any important data or trends.

    f. In one chart, change the color of a data series, then in another chart, use black-and-white patterns only. (*Hint*: Use the Fill Effects button in the Format Data Series dialog box. Then display the Patterns tab. Adjust the Foreground color to black and the Background color to white, then select a pattern.)

    g. Enter your name in a worksheet cell.

    h. Save your work. Before printing, preview each chart so you know what the charts look like. Adjust any items as needed.

    i. Print the charts.

    j. Close the workbook, then exit Excel.

▼ INDEPENDENT CHALLENGE 3

You are working as an account representative at the Bright Light Ad Agency. You have been examining the expenses charged to clients of the firm. The Board of Directors wants to examine certain advertising expenses and has asked you to prepare charts that can be used in this evaluation.

    a. Start Excel, open the Data File EX D-5.xls from the drive and folder where your Data Files are stored, then save it as **Bright Light**.

    b. Decide what types of charts would be best suited for the data in the range A16:B24. Sketch three sample charts. What kind of chart enhancements are necessary?

    c. Use the Chart Wizard to create at least three different types of charts that show the distribution of advertising expenses. (*Hint*: Move each chart to a new location on the worksheet, then deselect it before using the Wizard to create the next one.) One of the charts should be a 3-D pie chart.

    d. Add annotated text and arrows highlighting important data, such as the largest expense.

    e. Change the color of at least one data series.

    f. Add chart titles and category and value axis titles. Format the titles with a font of your choice. Place a drop shadow around the chart title.

Advanced Challenge Exercise

    ■ Explode a slice from the 3-D pie chart.

    ■ Add a data label to the exploded pie slice.

    ■ Change the alignment of labels on an axis.

    ■ Modify the scale of the value axis in one of the charts. (*Hint*: Double-click the gridlines to open the Format Gridlines dialog box, then click the Scale tab.)

    g. Enter your name in a worksheet cell.

    h. Save your work. Before printing, preview the file so you know what the charts look like. Adjust any items as needed. Be sure the chart is placed appropriately on the page.

    i. Print the charts, close the workbook, then exit Excel.

▼ INDEPENDENT CHALLENGE 4

Your company, Film Distribution, is headquartered in Montreal, and is considering opening a new office in the United States. Your supervisor would like you to begin investigating possible locations. You can use the Web to find and compare median pay scales in specific cities to see how relocating will affect the standard of living for those employees who move to the new office.

a. Start Excel, open a new workbook, then save it as **New Location Analysis** in the drive and folder where your Data Files are located.

b. Use your favorite search engine to find your own information sources on salary calculators, or cost-of-living calculators.

c. Determine the median incomes for Seattle, San Francisco, Dallas, Salt Lake City, Memphis, and Boston. Record this data on a sheet named **Median Income** in your workbook. See Table D-6 below for suggested data layout.

d. Format the data so it looks attractive and professional.

e. Create any type of column chart, with the data series in columns, on the same worksheet as the data. Include a descriptive title.

f. Remove the major gridlines in the Median Income chart.

g. On a blank worksheet in the current workbook, determine how much an employee would need to earn in Seattle, San Francisco, Dallas, Memphis, and Boston to maintain the same standard of living as if the company chose to relocate to Salt Lake City and pay $75,000. Name the sheet **Standard of Living**.

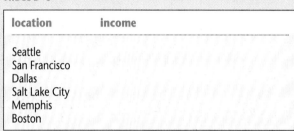

TABLE D-6

location	income
Seattle	
San Francisco	
Dallas	
Salt Lake City	
Memphis	
Boston	

h. Format the data so it looks attractive and professional.

i. Create a 3-D column chart on the same worksheet as the data. Include a descriptive title.

j. Change the color of the data series in the Standard of Living chart to bright green.

Advanced Challenge Exercise

■ Format the value axis in your chart(s) so that the salary income displays a 1000 separator (comma), but no dollar sign or decimal places.

■ Rotate the chart so you get a different view of the data.

■ Change the alignment of the category axis labels.

k. Do not display the legends in your chart(s).

l. Enter your name in a cell in your worksheet(s).

m. Save the workbook. Preview the chart(s) and change margins as necessary.

n. Print your worksheet(s), including the data and chart(s), making setup modifications as necessary.

o. Close the workbook, then exit Excel.

▼ VISUAL WORKSHOP

Modify a worksheet, using the skills you learned in this unit and using Figure D-23 for reference. Open the Data File EX D-6.xls from the drive and folder where your Data Files are stored, then save it as **Quarterly Advertising Budget**. Create the chart, then change the chart to reflect Figure D-23. Enter your name in cell A13, save, preview, then print your results.

FIGURE D-23

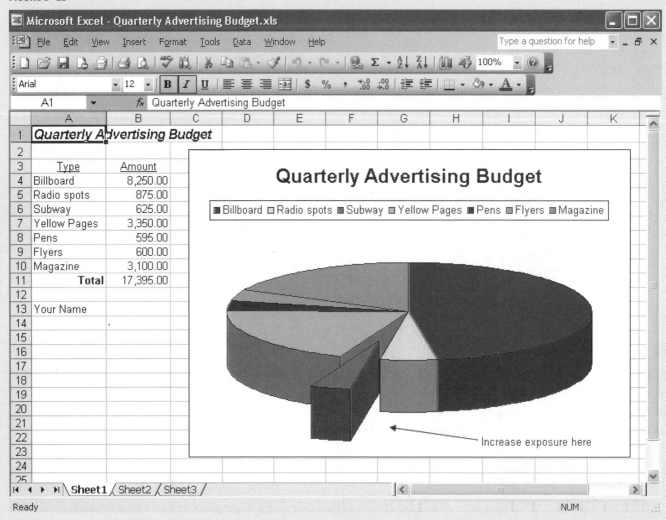

Integrating Word and Excel

OBJECTIVES

Now that you have experienced the power of Word and Excel, you need to learn how to use these two programs together to create sophisticated documents that incorporate data from both applications. For example, suppose that you prepare a report in Word that contains a chart you created in Excel. After preparing the report, you receive new data for the chart. By linking the Excel file with the Word file, you can make sure that any changes you make to the chart in Excel also appear in the chart copied to the Word report. ████ You are working as an assistant to Alice Wegman, the marketing manager for MediaLoft. Alice has asked you to learn about integrating Word and Excel so that you can use the two programs to create a report and a price list.

Understanding Integration

Programs in Microsoft Office are designed to work together. You can share data between documents and among coworkers. The ability to use information across multiple programs is called **integration**. The file from which the information is copied is the **source file**. The file that receives the copied information is the **destination file**. For example, charts created in an Excel worksheet, the source file, can be copied to and edited in a Word document or a PowerPoint presentation, the destination file. Alice asks you to review some of the ways that data can be shared across Office programs.

DETAILS

You can use Microsoft Office integration features to:

- **Copy and paste data**

    You use the Copy and Paste commands to copy text, values, or objects that have been created in one program into another program. You can copy and paste one item at a time using the Windows Clipboard. You can also open the task pane and then use the Office Clipboard to copy and store up to 24 items. Figure A-1 shows the Office Clipboard with three items.

- **Drag and drop data**

    You can also use the drag-and-drop method to move or copy selected text, values, or objects into other programs. First, you open both files and arrange the program windows so that both the source and destination files are visible. To move a selection, you drag it from the source file into the destination file. The object disappears from the source file and appears only in the destination file. To copy a selection, you press and hold [Ctrl], and then drag the selection from the source file into the destination file. The selection then appears in both the source file and destination file.

- **Link objects**

    Sometimes you may want to be able to change data that is included in multiple files. For example, values you originally entered in an Excel spreadsheet may have also been copied to a Word document. If you change the values in Excel, you want the corresponding values to change in Word. You use the Paste Special command to link an object that is copied from the source file to the destination file. A **linked object** maintains a connection to the source file so that the object is updated when the data in the source file changes. Figure A-2 shows the Paste link option in the Paste Special dialog box.

- **Embed objects**

    An **embedded object** maintains a link to the source program, but not to the source file. When you double-click an embedded object, the source program opens and you can edit the object. The source file that the object originally represented does not change.

- **Create hyperlinks**

    You can include **hyperlinks** in a file to other places in the file, other files, or a location on the Web. Figure A-3 shows the Insert Hyperlink dialog box, which is used to create a hyperlink. When you click a hyperlink, the place in the document, the file, or the Web page to which the hyperlink is connected opens. You can also create a hyperlink to an e-mail address. When a user clicks the hyperlink, the mail application (such as Outlook) opens a new blank message with the To field filled in.

- **E-mail files**

    You can share Office files by sending them as attachments to an e-mail message. When you click the E-mail button on the Standard toolbar, your e-mail application opens and attaches the file currently on your screen to the e-mail message.

FIGURE A-1: Entries in Office Clipboard

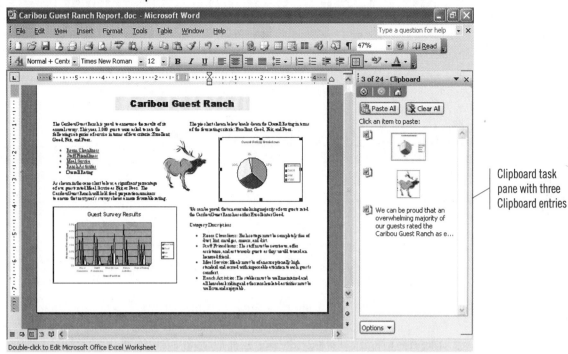

Clipboard task pane with three Clipboard entries

FIGURE A-2: Paste link option in the Paste Special dialog box

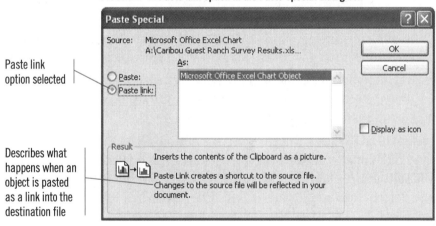

Paste link option selected

Describes what happens when an object is pasted as a link into the destination file

FIGURE A-3: Insert Hyperlink dialog box

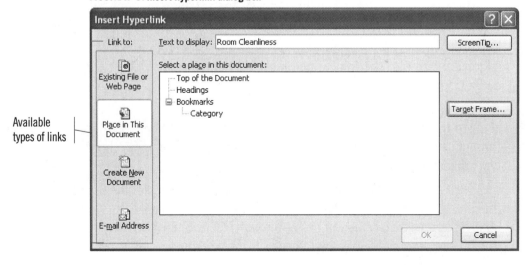

Available types of links

Project 1: Survey Report for Caribou Guest Ranch

MediaLoft's Marketing Department has planned a staff get-together at the Caribou Guest Ranch in the foothills of the Rocky Mountains in British Columbia. The ranch recently surveyed 3,000 guests, and sent you the results so you can evaluate the services offered by the ranch. You decide to include the survey results in a report that you can then give to Alice Wegman in the Marketing Department.

ACTIVITY

Creating the Charts in Excel

STEPS

You start by formatting the survey data in Excel and then creating two charts to visually illustrate the results.

1. **Start Excel, open the file INT A-1.xls from the drive and folder where your Data Files are stored, save it as Caribou Guest Ranch Survey Results, select cells B3 to F3, click the right mouse button, click Format Cells, click the Alignment tab, click the Wrap text check box, then click OK**

2. **Select cells B4 to F8, then click the AutoSum button Σ ▾ on the Standard toolbar**
   Verify that 3000 appears in cells B8 to F8. The values entered in cells B4 to F7 represent the total number of responses to each of the four criteria in each category.

3. **Select cells A3 to F7, click the Copy button 🗐 on the Standard toolbar, click cell A10, click the Paste button 🗐 ▾ on the Standard toolbar, click cell B11, enter the formula =B4/$B$8*100%, then press [Enter]**
   0.36666667 appears in cell B11. The formula divides the value in cell B4 by the value in cell B8 (3000) and then calculates the percentage. The dollar signs indicate that the reference to cell B8 is absolute. When you copy the formula to other cells, the dividend (the value that is divided into) is always the value in cell B8.

4. **Click cell B11, drag the corner fill handle down to cell B14, and with cells B11 to B14 still selected, drag the corner fill handle of cell B14 across to cell F14, then click the Percent Style button % on the Formatting toolbar**

5. **Select cells A10 to F14, click the Chart Wizard button 📊 on the Standard toolbar, scroll down and click Cone, click Next, click Next to accept the selected data range, enter Guest Survey Results as the Chart title, enter Guest Facilities as the Category (X) axis title, enter Response Percentages as the Value (Z) axis title, click Next, then click Finish to create the chart in Sheet1**

6. **Use the mouse to move and resize the chart so it occupies cells A20 through H40, right-click on any x-axis label, such as "Room Cleanliness," click Format Axis, click the Font tab, change the font size to 8 point, click OK, then change the font size of all the labels (the z-axis values, the z-axis title, the Legend text, and the x-axis title) to 8 point**

7. **Right-click the z-axis title (Response Percentages), click Format Axis Title, click the Alignment tab, click the Top diamond in the Orientation diagram to rotate the title 90 degrees, click OK, then click cell A42 below the cone chart**
   The completed cone chart appears, as shown in Figure A-4.

> **QUICK TIP**
> You use [Ctrl] to create a chart from data in non-adjacent columns.

8. **Scroll to the top of the worksheet, click cell A11, press and hold [Ctrl], select cells A11 through A14, select cells F11 through F14, release [Ctrl], click 📊, click Pie under Chart type, then click Next**

9. **Click Next, enter Overall Rating Breakdown as the chart title, click the Data Labels tab, click the Percentage check box, click Next, click Finish, drag and resize the pie chart so that it occupies approximately the range A42 through F60, as shown in Figure A-5, click a worksheet cell to deselect the pie chart, then save the workbook**

FIGURE A-4: Completed cone chart

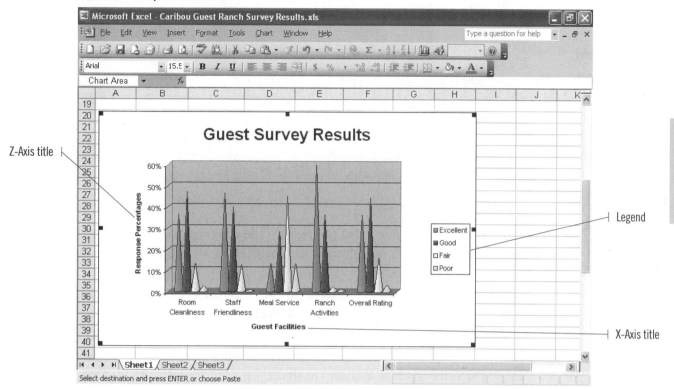

Z-Axis title

Legend

X-Axis title

FIGURE A-5: Completed pie chart

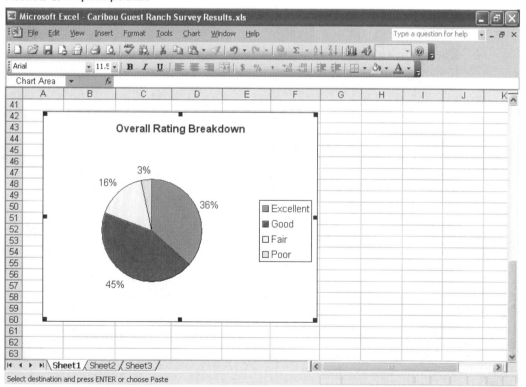

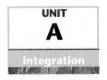

UNIT
A
Integration

Creating the Report in Word

You decide to create a report in Word that communicates information about the survey results. This report will include the charts you created in Excel. To create the report in Word, you first change the margins and select landscape orientation, then you use drag and drop to copy the title in cell A1 in the Excel worksheet to the top of the Word document. Finally, you turn on columns and enter the text.

STEPS

> **TROUBLE**
> If you get an error message about the margins being outside the printable area of the page, click Fix.

1. **Open a blank document in Word, click** File **on the menu bar, click** Page Setup, **change all four margins to** .6", **click** Landscape **under Orientation, click** OK, **then save the document as** Caribou Guest Ranch Report

2. **Click the** Restore Down button ⊟ **if necessary at the upper-right corner of the program window, then resize the window so that it fills half the screen**
   The worksheet in Excel is visible in the other half of the screen.

3. **Click** ⊟ **in the Excel program window if necessary, then resize the Excel window to fit next to the Word window, as shown in Figure A-6**

> **TROUBLE**
> Make sure ⬉ appears before you click and drag cell A1 to the Word document.

4. **Click cell** A1 **in Excel, press and hold** [Ctrl], **move the mouse to the upper-left corner of cell A1 until** ⬉ **appears, click and drag cell** A1 **to the Word document, then release [Ctrl] and the mouse button**

5. **Click the** yellow Caribou Guest Ranch object **in Word, click the** Maximize button ⬜ **at the top right of the document window, then click the** Center button ☰ **on the Formatting toolbar**

6. **Double-click in the left margin below the object, click** Format **on the menu bar, click** Columns, **select the** Two **format in the Presets section, click the** Apply to list arrow, **click** This point forward, **then click** OK

7. **Type the text for the first column, as shown in Figure A-7, then press** [Enter] **twice**
   Make sure you add bullets where indicated in Figure A-7.

8. **Click** Insert **on the menu bar, click** Break, **click the** Column break option button, **click** OK, **then type and format the text for column 2, as shown in Figure A-8**

9. **Save the document**

FIGURE A-6: Word and Excel windows side by side

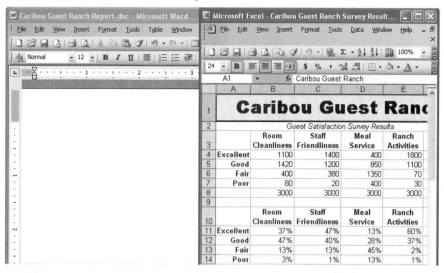

	Room Cleanliness	Staff Friendliness	Meal Service	Ranch Activities
Excellent	1100	1400	400	1800
Good	1420	1200	850	1100
Fair	400	380	1350	70
Poor	80	20	400	30
	3000	3000	3000	3000

	Room Cleanliness	Staff Friendliness	Meal Service	Ranch Activities
Excellent	37%	47%	13%	60%
Good	47%	40%	28%	37%
Fair	13%	13%	45%	2%
Poor	3%	1%	13%	1%

FIGURE A-7: Text for column 1

Caribou Guest Ranch

The Caribou Guest Ranch is proud to announce the results of its annual survey. This year, 3,000 guests were asked to rate the following categories of service in terms of four criteria: Excellent, Good, Fair, and Poor.

- Room Cleanliness
- Staff Friendliness
- Meal Service
- Ranch Activities
- Overall Rating

As shown in the cone chart below, a significant percentage of our guests rated Meal Service as Fair or Poor. The Caribou Guest Ranch will hold food preparation seminars to ensure that next year's survey shows a more favorable rating.

FIGURE A-8: Text for column 2

The pie chart shown below breaks down the Overall Rating in terms of the four rating criteria: Excellent, Good, Fair, and Poor.

We can be proud that an overwhelming majority of our guests rated the Caribou Guest Ranch as either Excellent or Good.

Category Descriptions

- **Room Cleanliness**: Each cottage must be completely free of dust, lint, smudges, smears, and dirt.
- **Staff Friendliness**: The staff must be courteous, offer assistance, and act towards guests as they would toward an honored friend.
- **Meal Service**: Meals must be of an exceptionally high standard and served with impeccable attention to each guest's comfort.
- **Ranch Activities**: The stables must be well maintained and all horseback riding and other ranch-related activities must be well-run and enjoyable.

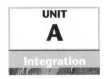

ACTIVITY ## Linking the Charts with the Report

To complete the report, you need to copy the cone chart and the pie chart from Excel and then paste them into Word as links. When you update the chart information in Excel, the charts in Word are also updated. You'll also add hyperlinks to selected text in the Word document. The completed survey report appears in Figure A-9.

STEPS

1. In Word, switch to Whole Page view, click the Excel program button on the taskbar to switch to Excel, click the Cone chart to select it, click the Copy button 📇 on the Standard toolbar, click the Word program button on the taskbar to switch to Word, click after more favorable rating in column 1 (the last line), press [Enter] twice, click Edit on the menu bar, click Paste Special, click the Paste link option button, then click OK

TROUBLE
If you can't see the column 2 text after you size the chart, click in column 2 and press [Delete] to move the text from page 2 to page 1.

2. Click the chart, then drag the lower-left corner handle of the chart up and over about 1" to reduce the size of the chart so that it fits at the bottom of column 1

3. Switch to Excel, click the pie chart to select it, copy and paste it as a link below the first paragraph in column 2 in the Word document, reduce the size of the chart until all the text in the document fits on one page, then click the Center button 📄 on the Formatting toolbar

The charts appear in the Word document, as shown in the completed document in Figure A-9. Now that you've copied the charts into Word, you've discovered that the Overall Rating results are incorrect. Fortunately, you linked the survey data shown in the Excel charts with the report in Word. When you change the values related to the charts in Excel, the charts in Word are also updated.

4. Return to 100% view, look at the pie chart in Word, note the width of the Fair wedge (it's light yellow), switch to Excel, change the value in cell F5 to 910 and the value in cell F6 to 900, save and close the workbook and Excel, switch back to Word, then click away from the chart to deselect it

The Fair slice in the pie chart has increased considerably as a result of the new values you entered in Excel.

TROUBLE
If you can't find a caribou, use another clip.

5. In Word, click Insert on the menu bar, point to Picture, click Clip Art, type caribou in the Search for text box, click Go, then click the picture of the caribou shown in the completed report in Figure A-9

6. Close the Clip Art task pane, double-click the clip art image, click the Layout tab in the Format Picture dialog box, click Square, click OK, then use the mouse to drag the clip art image so that it is positioned on the page, as shown in Figure A-9

7. Select the Category Descriptions heading under the pie chart, click Insert on the menu bar, click Bookmark, type Category, then click Add

8. Select all but the last bullet in the bulleted list in column 1, click Insert on the menu bar, click Hyperlink, click Place in This Document, click Category, then click OK

9. Press [Ctrl], click the Room Cleanliness hyperlink to jump to the Category Descriptions heading, put your name on the document, print it, then save and close the document in Word

The survey report for the Caribou Guest Ranch is complete. When you open the Word file again, you'll see a message asking you to confirm that the file contains links. You need to click Yes to accept the message and open the file.

Caribou Guest Ranch

The Caribou Guest Ranch is proud to announce the results of its annual survey. This year, 3,000 guests were asked to rate the following categories of service in terms of four criteria: Excellent, Good, Fair, and Poor.

- Room Cleanliness
- Staff Friendliness
- Meal Service
- Ranch Activities
- Overall Rating

As shown in the cone chart below, a significant percentage of our guests rated Meal Service as Fair or Poor. The Caribou Guest Ranch will hold food preparation seminars to ensure that next year's survey shows a more favorable rating.

Guest Survey Results

The pie chart shown below breaks down the Overall Rating in terms of the four rating criteria: Excellent, Good, Fair, and Poor.

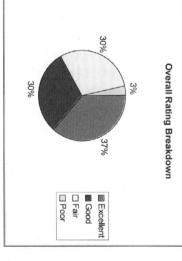

We can be proud that an overwhelming majority of our guests rated the Caribou Guest Ranch as either Excellent or Good.

Category Descriptions

- **Room Cleanliness:** Each cottage must be completely free of dust, lint, smudges, smears, and dirt.
- **Staff Friendliness:** The staff must be courteous, offer assistance, and act towards guests as they would toward an honored friend.
- **Meal Service:** Meals must be of an exceptionally high standard and served with impeccable attention to each guest's comfort.
- **Ranch Activities:** The stables must be well maintained and all horseback riding and other ranch-related activities must be well-run and enjoyable.

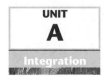

Project 2: Online Price List for Le Bonbon Confections

You recently sampled some of the wonderful candy creations sold at Le Bonbon Confections near the MediaLoft offices and are now thinking that MediaLoft should carry Le Bonbon's products. As one of MediaLoft's product developers, you contact Le Bonbon Company, and they send you information about their prices. You use the information to create a price list in Excel, and then you copy the price list into a Word document where you enter some text.

ACTIVITY

Creating the Price List in Excel

STEPS

As you create the price list, you'll use AutoComplete to save you from typing similar labels more than once.

1. **Open a blank Excel workbook, type Product in cell A1, type Box Size in cell B1, type Price in cell C1, then save your workbook as Le Bonbon Confections Price List**

2. **Click cell A2, type Truffles and Pralines, press [Tab], type 10 pieces, press [Tab], type 15, then widen column A so all the text fits**

3. **Click cell A3, type T, press [Tab] to accept the AutoComplete suggestion, type 25 pieces, press [Tab], type =C2*2, then press [Enter]**

   The formula in cell C3 multiplies the value in cell C2 by 2 to determine the cost of a box containing 25 truffles and pralines.

4. **Click cell C3, then drag the corner handle down to cell C15**

   As you enter the 10-piece box price for each of the products, the values currently entered in cells C4 to C15 change to the correct amounts for the 25-piece boxes.

5. **Click cell A4, type Dark Chocolate Surprises, press [Tab], type 10 p, press [Tab] to accept 10 pieces, type 18, then press [Enter]**

   "10 pieces" appears in cell B4, thanks to AutoComplete. Also note that the price for the 25-piece box (36) appears in cell C5.

6. **As shown in Figure A-10, enter the remaining data for the price list, widen column A so all the labels fit, then bold and center the labels in row 1**

   Note that you still need to enter the prices for the 10-piece boxes in column C. After you enter each 10-piece box price, the prices for the 25-piece boxes appear correctly because of the formula you copied.

7. **Select cells C2 to C15, click Format on the menu bar, click Cells, click the Number tab if necessary, click Currency, click the Symbol list arrow, click the $ sign, click OK, then save and close the workbook**

   You select the Currency number format in the Format Cells dialog box because you want dollar signs to appear immediately to the left of each price, rather than on the left edge of the cell, as they appear when you use the Currency Style button. If you use the Currency Style button, extra spaces appear between the dollar sign and the amount when you copy the Excel worksheet to Word.

8. **Open a new blank document in Word, type Le Bonbon Confections Price List, press [Enter] twice, select the heading, click Format on the menu bar, click Styles and Formatting, click Heading 1 in the Styles and Formatting task pane, then close the task pane**

9. **Type the text as shown in Figure A-11, then save the document as Le Bonbon Confections Price List**

FIGURE A-10: Price list data in Excel

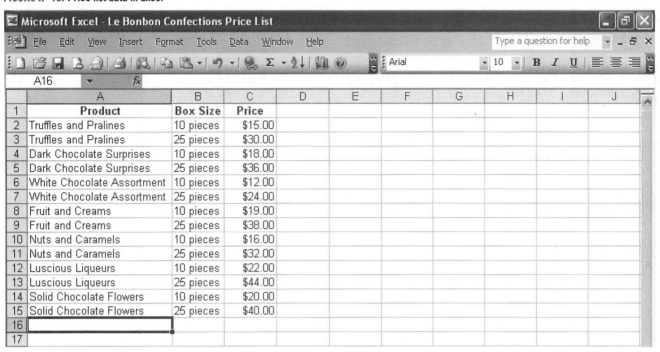

FIGURE A-11: Text for the Word document

Le Bonbon Confections

Make fine chocolate a part of every special occasion. At Le Bonbon Confections, we think about chocolate the way a great artist thinks about paint and canvas. To us, every chocolate we create is a work of art to be savored and enjoyed. Simply put, few things in life can beat the delights of our chocolates made by our team of world-class chocolate chefs. All our luscious confections contain pure cocoa butter and the very finest flavorings with no preservatives.

The price list displayed below lists our full selection of 10-piece and 25-piece boxes. Indulge yourself in a box of solid chocolate flowers or share a box of truffles and pralines with that special someone. To order a box of chocolates from Le Bonbon Confections, call us in Miami, Florida at 1-800-555-1333.

Clues to Use

AutoComplete

When you start to type a label in a cell, Excel checks the surrounding cells for similar data. If Excel finds similar data, it automatically completes the entry for you. You can press [Tab] or [Enter] to accept the AutoComplete suggestion, or you can continue typing to enter different text. For example, if you enter Truffles and Pralines in cell A1, then type T in cell A2, the AutoComplete suggestion of "Truffles and Pralines" appears in cell A2. If you press [Tab] or [Enter], the suggestion is entered into the cell.

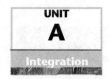

ACTIVITY ## Inserting the Price List into Word

You need to insert the price list into Word as a linked object. A **linked object** is one that you create in a source file and then insert into a destination file. In this project, the source file is an Excel spreadsheet and the destination file is a Word document. When you update data in the source file, the data is also updated in the destination file. You'll then find an appropriate clip art picture from the Microsoft Clip Gallery, and save the document.

STEPS

1. **Double-click about ½" below the last paragraph in the Word document, click Insert on the menu bar, click Object, then click the Create from File tab**
   In the Object dialog box, you select the source file.

2. **Click Browse, navigate to the location where you saved the Excel file Le Bonbon Confections Price List, click Le Bonbon Confections Price List.xls, then click Insert**

3. **Click the Link to file check box, then click OK**
   The price list appears in Word as an object, as shown in Figure A-12.

TROUBLE
You need to be connected to the Internet to access the required clip art picture. If you are not connected to the Internet, substitute a clip art picture of your choice.

4. **Press [Ctrl][Home] to move to the top of the document, show the Drawing toolbar, if necessary, click the Insert Clip Art button 🖼 on the Drawing toolbar, click in the Search text box, type chocolate, then click Go**
   In a few moments, a selection of clip art related to chocolate appears.

5. **Click the picture of the chocolate that appears as shown in the completed price list in Figure A-13, close the Clip Art task pane, right-click the picture, click Format Picture, click the Size tab, enter .8 in the Height text box, then click OK**

QUICK TIP
If the data does not change in Word, right-click the chart, then click Update Link.

6. **Scroll down to view the price list, double-click the price list to open it in Excel, change the price of the 10-piece box of Solid Chocolate Flowers to $17.00, close and save the workbook, then exit Excel**
   When you double-click the price list, it opens in Excel because you originally created the price list in Excel. Changes you make to the price list in Excel appear in the price list in Word because you inserted the Excel file as a linked object.

7. **Save the document in Word, compare your screen to Figure A-13, type your name at the bottom of the price list, print a copy, then close the document and exit Word**

FIGURE A-12: Excel linked object inserted in Word

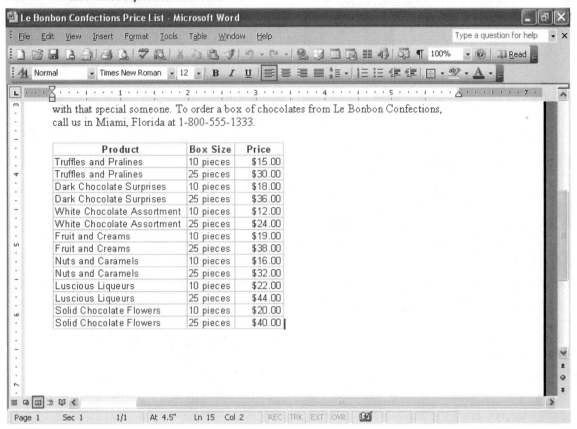

FIGURE A-13: Completed price list

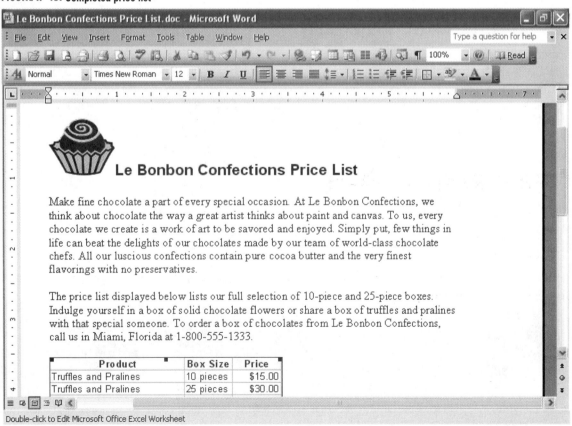

▼ INDEPENDENT CHALLENGE 1

Create a survey report for a company or organization of your choice. For formatting ideas, refer to the report you created in the Caribou Guest Ranch project. Here are some tips for creating your report.

a. Start Excel, then set up a Survey Results worksheet in Excel. Select categories appropriate to your company or organization. For example, if your company is a neighborhood restaurant, you could select such categories as Food Quality, Selection, Service, and Ambiance, or if you choose to analyze a course you're taking at college, you could select such categories as Instructor Presentation, Relevance of Assignments, Course Materials, and Grading System. Make sure you include an Overall Rating column. You can use the rating criteria from the Caribou Guest Ranch project (i.e., Excellent, Good, Fair, and Poor) or select different rating criteria.

b. Enter the number of responses for each category, making sure each category's responses add up to your total number of responses. Use at least 300 total responses.

c. Convert the values that represent the total number of responses to each of the criteria in each category to percentages.

d. Create a pyramid chart or a cylinder chart based on the data in your worksheet.

e. Create a pie chart that shows the breakdown of responses in the Overall Rating column.

f. Switch to Word, save the document as **My Survey Results**, then enter three or four paragraphs of text that describe the survey and its results. Refer to the Caribou Guest Ranch project for ideas. Include text that describes each category evaluated.

g. Copy the charts from Excel to the Word summary. Remember to paste the charts as links into Word.

h. Make some changes to the data in the Excel worksheet. The charts copied into Word should also change. If the data does not change, right-click the chart, then click Update Link.

i. Format the Word summary in Whole Page view, then add an appropriate picture, if you wish.

j. Bookmark the description section, then make the list of categories a hyperlink to their descriptions.

k. Put **Your Name** on both the Word document and the Excel worksheet, and then print both documents.

l. Save both the Excel worksheet and the Word summary as **My Survey Results**, then close Word and Excel.

▼ INDEPENDENT CHALLENGE 2

Create a price list in Excel for a selection of products sold by a company of your choice. As you create the price list, let AutoComplete help minimize your typing. When you complete the price list, set up a Word document as you did in the Le Bonbon Confections project. Make sure to include your name in the Word document. Insert the Excel file into the Word document as a link. Change some of the values in the Excel file, then view the updates in Word. If the values are not updated automatically, right-click the Excel object in Word, then click Update Link. Add an appropriate clip art picture, save both files as **My Price List**, then print the files and close Word and Excel.

▼ INDEPENDENT CHALLENGE 3

Create an Excel worksheet with the projected income and expenses for Gardens Galore, a landscaping business in San Diego, California. Then use the data in the worksheet to create two charts, which you will link to a projected sales summary in Word. Finally, add hyperlinks and a clip art picture.

a. Start Excel, open the file INT A-2.xls from the drive and location where your Data Files are stored, then save it as **Gardens Galore Projected Sales Summary**.

b. Enter and copy the formulas required to calculate the following amounts:
   i. Total monthly income and four-month income (cells B7 to E7 and F5 to F7).
   ii. Cost of Sales: Value of Sales multiplied by 60% (i.e., B6*.6), because the products sold cost the company 60% of the sale price to produce.
   iii. Total monthly and four-month Expenses (cells B16 to E16 and F10 to F16).
   iv. Total Profit (cells B18 to F18): Subtract the total expenses from the total income for each month. When you have completed all the calculations, you should see $21,700.00 in cell F18.

c. Create a pie chart that shows the breakdown of expenses by total amount. You need to select cells A10 to A15 and cells F10 to F15 as the data range, click the Chart Wizard button, and then select the Pie chart type. Use the chart title "Breakdown of Expenses," show percentages in the data labels, and move the chart below the worksheet.

d. Save the workbook, switch to Word, open the file **INT A-3.doc** from the drive and location where your Data Files are stored, then save it as **Gardens Galore Projected Sales Summary**.

e. Select EXPENSES in the paragraph under Projected Expenses, switch to Excel, select the value in cell F16, click the Copy button, switch back to Word, click Edit on the menu bar, click Paste Special, click Paste Link, click Unformatted Text, then click OK. Select Unformatted Text so that the copied text takes on the same formatting used in the Word document. Note that a space is inserted before and after the copied value. You can delete these spaces; however, if you close and reopen the document, the spaces will be reinserted.

f. Use the same procedure to copy the INCOME and PROFIT amounts from Excel to the appropriate locations in the Word document. Make sure you paste the copied values as links in Unformatted Text.

g. Copy the pie chart from Excel and paste it as a link into the Word document below the Projected Expenses paragraph, as shown in the completed sales summary in Figure A-14. Center the chart.

h. Switch to Excel, increase the salaries expense for June to 15,000, increase it to 12,000 for July, then increase the sales income for April and May to 25,000. Note the changes to the pie chart.

i. Switch to Word, enhance the Projected Expenses and Projected Income headings with the Heading 2 style, then enhance the title in the Heading 1 style, as shown in Figure A-14.

j. Insert the clip art picture that appears in Figure A-14 (*Hint*: Search for roses) and reduce the height to 1".

k. Make the Projected Expenses heading a bookmark called **Expenses** and the Projected Income heading a bookmark called **Income**, make a hyperlink from **income** in paragraph 1 to the Income bookmark, then make a hyperlink from **expenses** in paragraph 1 to the Expenses bookmark.

l. Add your name to the document footer, print a copy of the sales summary, compare it to Figure A-14, then save and close the Word and Excel files.

FIGURE A-14: Completed sales summary for Gardens Galore

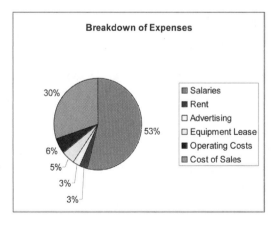

 Gardens Galore Sales Summary

Gerry Watson, our accountant at Gardens Galore, has projected the <u>income</u> and <u>expenses</u> for our landscaping business for the months of April through July.

Projected Expenses

The total projected expenses for April through July are $113,400.00 . The pie chart below displays a breakdown of expenses by total amount.

In order to help decrease our expenses, Marianne Prentiss, one of our own staff members, will create a series of brochures to advertise our products and services, thereby cutting our advertising expenses by 25%.

Projected Income

The total projected income for April through July is $121,900.00 . The projected profit for Gardens Galore from April through July is $8,500.00 . We plan to increase sales by charging a higher rate for our landscaping services in April and May, our busiest months.

▼ VISUAL WORKSHOP

Create the price list shown in Figure A-15 in Excel, use a formula to calculate the prices for 50 items (i.e., C2*5), then format the prices with the Currency style using the Format Cells dialog box. Save the workbook as **Moveable Feast Price List**. Copy the cells containing the price list in Excel, then paste the copied cells into a new Word document as a link (choose Microsoft Excel Worksheet Object in the Paste Special dialog box). In Excel, change the price of 10 King Crab Cakes to $8.00, and verify that the price also changes in Word. Modify the Word document so that it appears as shown in Figure A-16. Save the document as **Moveable Feast Prices**. Enhance the title with the Heading 1 style and Price List with the Heading 2 style. To find the clip art image, search for **picnic**. Change the height of the image to 1" and the Layout to Square, and then use your mouse to position the picture so that it appears as shown in Figure A-16. Add your name to the Word document, print a copy of the price list from Word, then close all files and programs.

FIGURE A-15: Price list worksheet

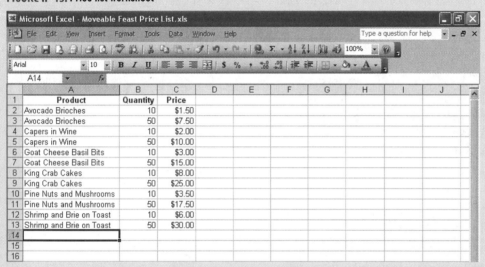

FIGURE A-16: Price List for Moveable Feast

Moveable Feast

Price List

Product	Quantity	Price
Avocado Brioches	10	$1.50
Avocado Brioches	50	$7.50
Capers in Wine	10	$2.00
Capers in Wine	50	$10.00
Goat Cheese Basil Bits	10	$3.00
Goat Cheese Basil Bits	50	$15.00
King Crab Cakes	10	$8.00
King Crab Cakes	50	$40.00
Pine Nuts and Mushrooms	10	$3.50
Pine Nuts and Mushrooms	50	$17.50
Shrimp and Brie on Toast	10	$6.00
Shrimp and Brie on Toast	50	$30.00

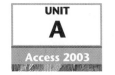

UNIT A
Access 2003

Getting Started with Access 2003

OBJECTIVES

Understand relational databases
Learn database terminology
Start Access and open a database
Work with the database window
Navigate records
Enter records
Edit records
Preview and print a datasheet
Get Help and exit Access

If you have a SAM user profile, you may have access to hands-on instruction, practice, and assessment of the skills covered in this unit. Log in to your SAM accont and go to your assignments page to see what your instructor has assigned.

In this unit, you will learn the purpose, advantages, and terminology of Microsoft Office Access 2003, a relational database software program. You will learn how to use the different elements of the Access window and how to get help. You'll navigate a database, enter and update data, and preview and print data. ▓▓▓ Kelsey Lang is a marketing manager at MediaLoft, a nationwide chain of bookstore cafés that offers customers the opportunity to purchase books, music, and movies while enjoying a variety of coffees, teas, and freshly baked desserts. Recently, MediaLoft switched to Access for storing and maintaining customer information. You use Access to help Kelsey maintain this valuable information for MediaLoft.

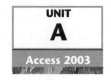

Understanding Relational Databases

Microsoft Access 2003 is a database software program that runs on the Windows operating system. **Relational database software** is used to manage data that can be organized into lists of related information, such as customers, products, vendors, employees, projects, or sales. Many small companies record customer, inventory, and sales information in a spreadsheet program such as Microsoft Excel. While using this electronic format is more productive than using a paper-based system, Excel still lacks many of the database advantages provided by Access. See Table A-1 for a comparison of the two programs. ▟▟▟▟▟ Kelsey asks you to review the advantages of database software over manual and spreadsheet systems.

DETAILS

The advantages of using Access include:

- **Duplicate data is minimized**

  If your database consists of customer, product, and sales data, a paper-based or spreadsheet system would require that you record all of the customer, sales, and product information on index cards as shown in Figure A-1 or in spreadsheet rows as shown in Figure A-2. Both systems duplicate product and customer data each time a sale is made. With Access, however, you enter data about customers or products only once even though it may be related to many sales transactions. Using a relational database eliminates the time-consuming and error-prone process of entering duplicate data.

- **Information is more accurate**

  Because duplicate data is minimized, information in a relational database is more accurate, reliable, and consistent. Data is also easier to maintain because a change in a customer's address, for example, is updated only once rather than each time the customer makes a purchase.

- **Data entry is faster and easier**

  Using a relational database program such as Access, you can create on-screen data entry forms that make data entry easier, faster, and more accurate.

- **Information can be viewed and sorted in multiple ways**

  A manual system or spreadsheet allows you to sort information in only one order at a time. In contrast, Access allows you to view or sort the information in multiple ways in different but simultaneous views. For example, you may want to sort customers in alphabetical order in one window while sorting them according to the value of their total purchases in another. Also, you can save any presentation of data and quickly redisplay it later.

- **Information is more secure**

  You can protect an Access database with a password so only those users with appropriate security clearances can open it. Access databases can be further secured by granting different database capabilities to different users.

- **Information can be shared among several users**

  Access databases are inherently multiuser. More than one person can be entering, updating, and using the database at the same time.

- **Information retrieval is faster and easier**

  With Access you can quickly find, display, and print subsets of information that present or analyze various aspects of the database. Once you create a particular view of the data, you can save and redisplay it.

FIGURE A-1: Using a manual system to record sales data

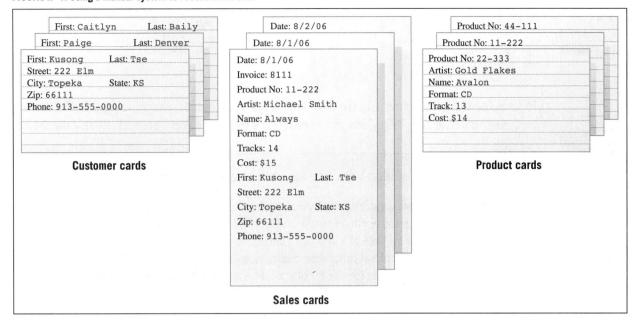

FIGURE A-2: Using a spreadsheet to record sales data

	A	B	C	D	E	F	G	H	I	J	K	L	M	N	O	P
1	Cust No	First	Last	Street	City	State	Zip	Phone	Date	Invoice	Product No	Artist	Name	Format	Tracks	Cost
2	1	Kusong	Tse	222 Elm	Topeka	KS	66111	913-555-0000	8/1/2006	8111	11-222	Michael Smith	Always	CD	14	15
3	2	Paige	Denver	400 Oak	Lenexa	MO	60023	816-555-8877	8/1/2006	8112	11-222	Michael Smith	Always	CD	14	15
4	1	Kusong	Tse	222 Elm	Topeka	KS	66111	913-555-0000	8/2/2006	8113	22-333	Gold Flakes	Avalon	CD	13	14
5	3	Caitlyn	Baily	111 Ash	Ames	IA	50010	515-555-3333	8/3/2006	8114	22-333	Gold Flakes	Avalon	CD	13	14
6	2	Paige	Denver	400 Oak	Lenexa	MO	60023	816-555-8877	8/4/2006	8115	44-1111	Lungwort	Sounds	CD	15	13
7	3	Caitlyn	Baily	111 Ash	Ames	IA	50010	515-555-3333	8/4/2006	8116	44-1111	Lungwort	Sounds	CD	15	13
8	4	Max	Royal	500 Pine	Manilla	NE	55123	827-555-4422	8/5/2006	8117	44-1111	Lungwort	Sounds	CD	15	13
9																

Duplicate customer data is entered each time an existing customer makes an additional purchase

Duplicate product data is entered each time the same product is sold more than once

TABLE A-1: Comparing Excel to Access

feature	Excel	Access
Layout	Provides a natural tabular layout for easy data entry	Provides a natural tabular layout as well as the ability to create customized data entry screens
Storage	Limited to approximately 65,000 records per sheet	Stores any number of records up to 2 GB
Linked tables	Manages single lists of information	Allows links between lists of information to reduce data redundancy
Reporting	Limited to the current spreadsheet arrangement of data	Creates and saves multiple presentations of data
Security	Limited to file security options such as marking the file "read-only" or protecting a range of cells	Allows users to access only the records and fields they need
Multiuser capabilities	Does not easily allow multiple users to simultaneously enter and update data	Allows multiple users to simultaneously enter and update data
Data entry	Provides limited data entry screens	Provides the ability to create extensive data entry screens called forms

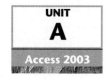

Learning Database Terminology

To be successful with Access, you need to understand basic database terminology. Before you start working with Access, Kelsey asks you to review the terms and concepts that define a database.

You should become familiar with the following database terminology:

- The smallest unit of data organization is called a field. A **field** consists of a specific category of data such as a customer's name, city, state, or phone number. A group of related fields that describe a person, place, or thing is called a **record**. A **key field** is a field that contains unique information for each record, such as a Social Security number for an employee or a customer number for a customer. A collection of records for a single subject, such as all of the customer records, is called a **table**. A collection of tables associated with a general topic (for example, sales of products to customers) is called a **database**.

- An Access database is a **relational database**, in which more than one table, such as the Customers, Sales, and Products tables, may be linked together. The term "relational database" describes a database in which two tables are linked (related) by a common field. For example, in Figure A-3, the Customers and Sales tables are related by the common Cust No field. The Products and Sales tables are related by the common Product No field. Through these relationships a relational database can minimize redundant data and present information from more than one table in a single view. For example, if you want to show the First and Last fields from the Customers table as well as the Product No and Date fields from the Sales table in a single view, the common Cust No field identifies which Sales table records are connected with each record in the Customers table.

- The parts of an Access database that help you enter, view, and manage the data are **tables**, **queries**, **forms**, **reports**, **pages**, **macros**, and **modules**, which are collectively called the database **objects**. They are summarized in Table A-2. Tables are the most important type of **object** in the database because they physically store all of the data within the database. The other objects make it easier to view, modify, or report the data.

- Data can be entered and edited in four objects: tables, queries, forms, and pages. The relationships among tables, queries, forms, and reports are shown in Figure A-4. Regardless of how the data is entered, it is stored in a table object. Furthermore, data can be printed from a table, query, form, page, or report object. The macro and module objects provide additional database productivity and automation features. All of the objects (except for page objects, which create Web pages) are stored in one **Access database file**. In general, however, the phrase "the database" refers only to the data and not the rest of the objects that may be part of an Access database file.

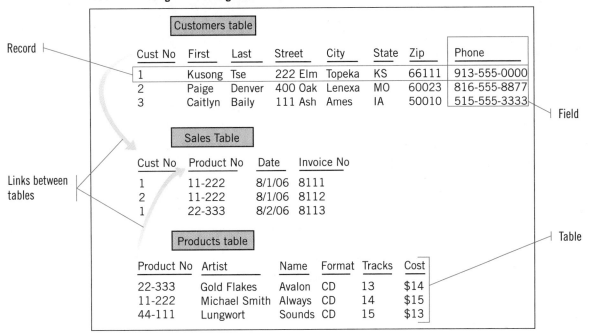

FIGURE A-3: Using Access to organize sales data

FIGURE A-4: Relationships among Access objects

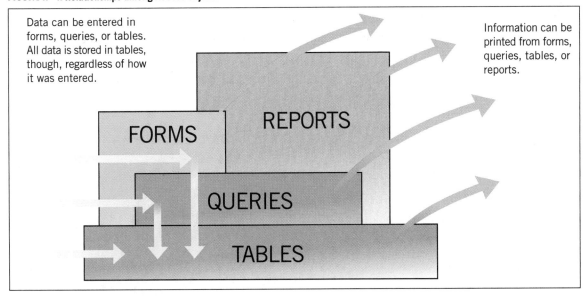

Data can be entered in forms, queries, or tables. All data is stored in tables, though, regardless of how it was entered.

Information can be printed from forms, queries, tables, or reports.

TABLE A-2: Access objects and their purpose

object	purpose
Table	Contains all of the raw data within the database in a spreadsheet-like view; tables are linked with a common field to minimize data redundancy
Query	Provides a spreadsheet-like view of the data similar to tables, but allows the user to select a subset of fields or records from one or more tables; queries are created when a user has a question about the data in the database
Form	Provides an easy-to-use data entry screen which often shows only one record at a time
Report	Provides a professional printout of data that may contain enhancements such as headers, footers, graphics, and calculations on groups of records
Page	Creates dynamic Web pages that interact with an Access database; also called Data Access Page
Macro	Stores a set of keystrokes or commands, such as the commands to display a particular toolbar when a form opens
Module	Stores Visual Basic for Applications programming code that extends the functions and automated processes of Access

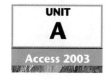

Starting Access and Opening a Database

You can start Access 2003 and open a database in a variety of ways. You can start Access by using the menus found when you click the Start button on the taskbar, or if an Access icon is located on the Windows desktop, you can start Access from that shortcut as well. To open a specific database within Access, click the Open button on the Database toolbar or use the Open portion of the Getting Started task pane. You can also open a specific database within Access by opening the database file from My Computer or Windows Explorer. ▓▓▓▓ You start Access and open the MediaLoft-A.mdb database.

STEPS

1. **Click the** Start button ⟪🏁 start⟫ **on the taskbar**

   The Start button is the first item on the taskbar, and is usually located in the lower-left corner of your screen. You can use the Start menu to start any program on your computer.

   TROUBLE
   If Microsoft Access is not located on the Microsoft Office submenu, look for it on the Start or All Programs menu.

2. **Point to** All Programs, **then point to** Microsoft Office

   Access is generally located on the Microsoft Office submenu of the All Programs menu. All the programs stored on your computer can be found on the All Programs menu or one of its submenus.

3. **Click** Microsoft Office Access 2003

   Access opens and displays a task pane on the right, from which you can open an existing file or create a new database.

   TROUBLE
   If the task pane does not appear on the right side of your screen, click File on the menu bar, then click New.

4. **Click the** More **link in the Open section of the task pane**

   The Open dialog box opens, as shown in Figure A-5. Depending on the databases and folders stored on your computer, your dialog box might look different.

5. **Click the** Look in list arrow, **then navigate to the drive and folder where your Data Files are stored**

   When you navigate to the correct folder, a list of the Microsoft Access database files in that folder appears in the Open dialog box.

6. **Click the** MediaLoft-A.mdb **database file, click** Open, **then click the** Maximize button **on the Microsoft Access title bar if the Access window is not already maximized**

   The MediaLoft-A.mdb database opens as shown in Figure A-6.

FIGURE A-5: Open dialog box

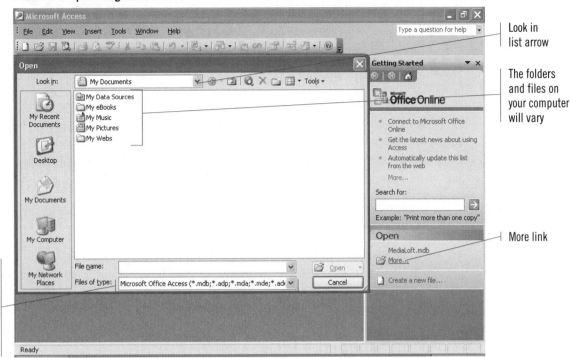

Look in list arrow

The folders and files on your computer will vary

More link

Whether the file extensions are displayed is determined by a Folder Option setting within Windows Explorer

FIGURE A-6: MediaLoft-A database

Microsoft Access title bar

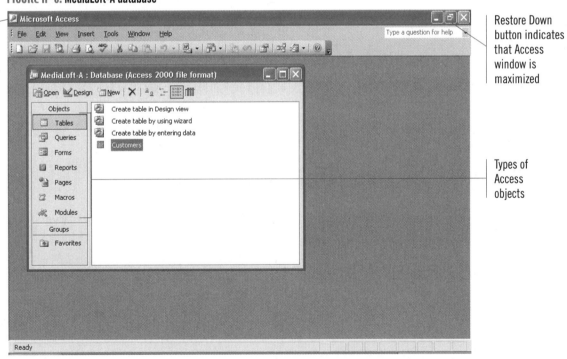

Restore Down button indicates that Access window is maximized

Types of Access objects

Clues to Use

Personalized toolbars and menus in Access 2003

All of the applications within Office 2003 support **personalized toolbars** and **personalized menus** to some extent. "Personalized" means that the toolbars and menus modify themselves to reflect those features that you use most often. To view, modify, or reset the toolbar and menu options, click Tools on the menu bar, and then click Customize. On the Options tab you can reset usage data, eliminate the delay when displaying full menus, and change other toolbar and menu bar characteristics.

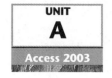
Working with the Database Window

When you start Access and open a database, the **database window** displays familiar Windows elements such as a title bar, menu bar, and toolbar. Specific to Access, however, is the **Objects bar**, which displays the buttons for the seven Access objects. Also, the **Groups bar** below the Objects bar displays folders that contain shortcuts to commonly used objects. Clicking the **Objects button** or **Groups button** alternatively expands and collapses that section of the database window. You are ready to explore the MediaLoft-A database interface.

STEPS

1. **Examine each of the Access window elements shown in Figure A-7**

   The Objects bar on the left side of the database window displays the seven object types. The other elements of the database window are summarized in Table A-3. Because the Tables object button is selected, the single table object, Customers, is displayed within the database window. In addition, the database window displays three "Create table..." shortcuts that help you create new table objects. The database window toolbar also presents buttons that help you work with table objects.

2. **Click File on the menu bar**

   The File menu contains commands for opening a new or existing database, saving data in a variety of formats, and printing. The menu commands vary depending on which window or database object is currently in use.

3. **Point to Edit on the menu bar, point to View, point to Insert, point to Tools, point to Window, point to Help, move the pointer off the menu, then press [Esc] twice**

   All menus close when you press [Esc]. Pressing [Esc] a second time deselects the menu bar.

4. **Point to the New button 🗋 on the Database toolbar**

   When you point to a toolbar button, a descriptive **ScreenTip** automatically appears. The buttons on the toolbars represent the most common Access features. Toolbar buttons change just as menu options change depending on which window and database object are currently in use.

5. **Point to the Open button 🗁 on the Database toolbar, then point to the Save button 🖫 on the Database toolbar**

   Sometimes toolbar buttons or menu options are dimmed, which means they are not currently available. For example, the Save button 🖫 is dimmed because you have not made any changes that need to be saved.

6. **Click Queries on the Objects bar**

   A list of previously created queries is displayed in the database window as shown in Figure A-8. Two shortcuts to create new queries are also displayed.

7. **Click Forms on the Objects bar, then click Reports on the Objects bar**

   The MediaLoft-A database contains the Customers table, three queries, one form, and three reports.

FIGURE A-7: Access window elements

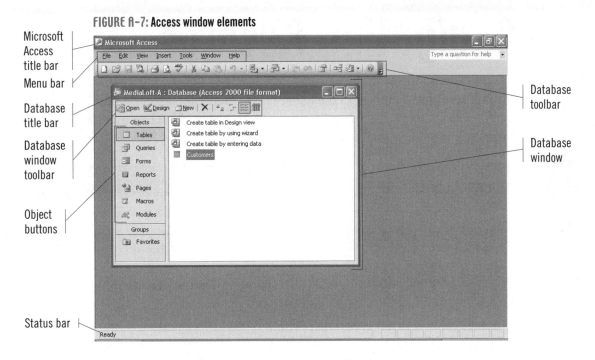

Microsoft Access title bar

Menu bar

Database title bar

Database window toolbar

Object buttons

Status bar

Database toolbar

Database window

FIGURE A-8: Query objects

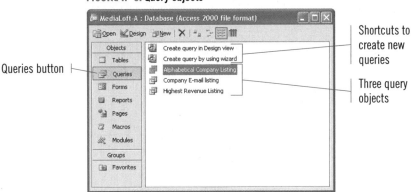

Queries button

Shortcuts to create new queries

Three query objects

TABLE A-3: Elements of the database window

element	description
Title bar	Contains the program name (Microsoft Office Access 2003) or filename (MediaLoft-A)
Menu bar	Contains menu options appropriate for the current view of the database
Database toolbar	Contains buttons for common tasks that affect the entire database (e.g., New, Open, or Relationships) or are common to all database objects (e.g., Print, Copy, or Spelling)
Database window	Presents the objects and shortcuts within the open database
Database window toolbar	Contains buttons used to open, modify, create, delete, or view objects
Object buttons	Provide access to the different types of objects stored within the database
Status bar	Displays messages regarding the current database operation

Clues to Use

Viewing objects

You can change the way you view the objects in the database window by clicking the last four buttons on the database window toolbar. You can view the objects as Large Icons, Small Icons, in a List (default view), and with Details. The Details view shows a description of the object, as well as the date the object was last modified and the date it was originally created.

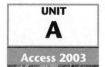

Navigating Records

Your skill in navigating the fields and records of a database helps you productively find, enter, and update data. You use either mouse or keystroke techniques to navigate the data in the table's **datasheet**, a spreadsheet-like grid that displays fields as columns and records as rows. You open the Customers table and practice your record navigation skills.

STEPS

QUICK TIP

You can also select an object and click the Open button on the database window toolbar to open the object.

1. **Click Tables on the Objects bar, then double-click Customers in the database window**

   The datasheet for the Customers table opens, as shown in Figure A-9. The datasheet contains 27 customer records with 13 fields of information for each record. **Field names** are listed at the top of each column. The number of the selected record in the datasheet is displayed in the **Specific Record box** (also called the **record number box**) at the bottom of the datasheet window. Depending on the size of your monitor and your display properties, you may see a different number of fields. To view more fields, scroll to the right.

2. **Press [Tab] to move to Sprint Systems**

   Sprint Systems is selected in the second field, Company, of the first record.

3. **Press [Enter]**

   The focus moves to Aaron in the third column, the field named First. Pressing either [Tab] or [Enter] moves the focus to the next field. The **focus** refers to which field would be edited if you started typing.

4. **Press [↓]**

   The focus moves to Jacob in the second record. The **current record symbol** in the **record selector box** also identifies which record you are navigating. The Next Record and Previous Record **navigation buttons** in the lower-left corner of the datasheet can also be used to navigate the datasheet.

TROUBLE

If [Ctrl][End] doesn't move the focus to the last field of the last record, you are probably working in Edit mode. Press [Tab] to return to Navigation mode, and then press [Ctrl][End].

5. **Press [Ctrl][End]**

   The focus moves to $6,790.33 in the last field, named YTDSales, of the last record. You can also use the Last Record navigation button to move to the last record.

6. **Press [Ctrl][Home]**

   The focus moves to 1 in the field named ID of the first record. You can also use the First Record navigation button to move to the first record. A complete list of navigation keystrokes to move the focus between fields and records is shown in Table A-4.

FIGURE A-9: Customers datasheet

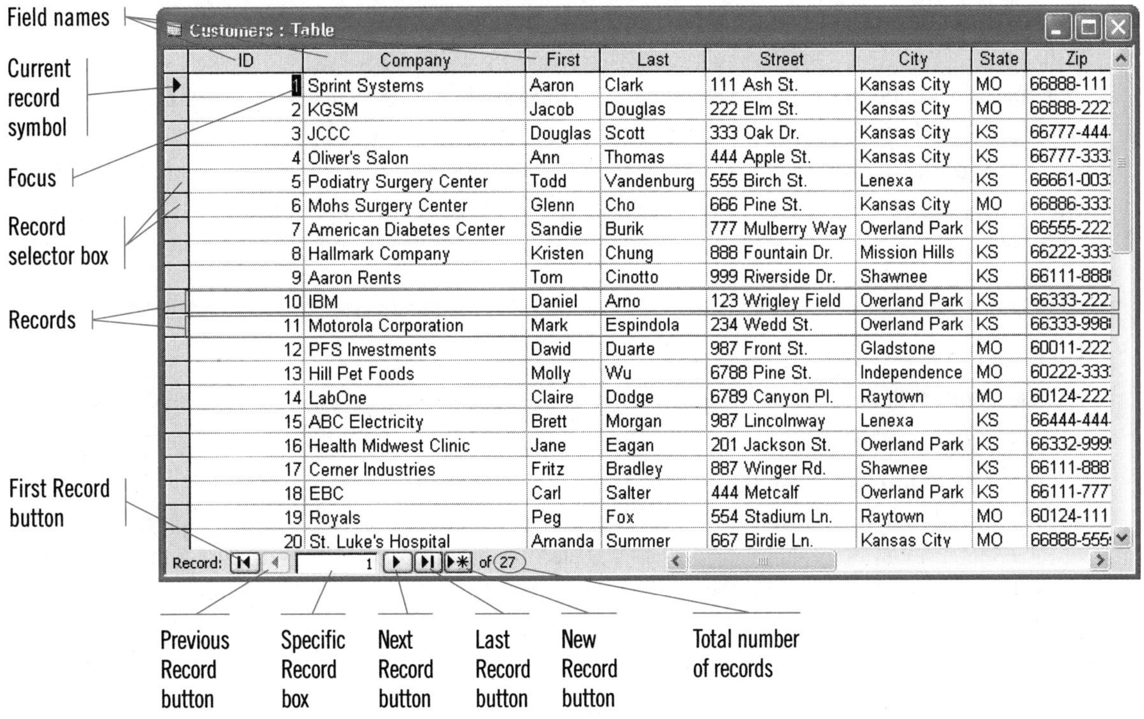

Field names

Current record symbol

Focus

Record selector box

Records

First Record button

ID	Company	First	Last	Street	City	State	Zip
1	Sprint Systems	Aaron	Clark	111 Ash St.	Kansas City	MO	66888-111
2	KGSM	Jacob	Douglas	222 Elm St.	Kansas City	MO	66888-222
3	JCCC	Douglas	Scott	333 Oak Dr.	Kansas City	KS	66777-444
4	Oliver's Salon	Ann	Thomas	444 Apple St.	Kansas City	KS	66777-333
5	Podiatry Surgery Center	Todd	Vandenburg	555 Birch St.	Lenexa	KS	66661-003
6	Mohs Surgery Center	Glenn	Cho	666 Pine St.	Kansas City	MO	66886-333
7	American Diabetes Center	Sandie	Burik	777 Mulberry Way	Overland Park	KS	66555-222
8	Hallmark Company	Kristen	Chung	888 Fountain Dr.	Mission Hills	KS	66222-333
9	Aaron Rents	Tom	Cinotto	999 Riverside Dr.	Shawnee	KS	66111-888
10	IBM	Daniel	Arno	123 Wrigley Field	Overland Park	KS	66333-222
11	Motorola Corporation	Mark	Espindola	234 Wedd St.	Overland Park	KS	66333-998
12	PFS Investments	David	Duarte	987 Front St.	Gladstone	MO	60011-222
13	Hill Pet Foods	Molly	Wu	6788 Pine St.	Independence	MO	60222-333
14	LabOne	Claire	Dodge	6789 Canyon Pl.	Raytown	MO	60124-222
15	ABC Electricity	Brett	Morgan	987 Lincolnway	Lenexa	KS	66444-444
16	Health Midwest Clinic	Jane	Eagan	201 Jackson St.	Overland Park	KS	66332-999
17	Cerner Industries	Fritz	Bradley	887 Winger Rd.	Shawnee	KS	66111-888
18	EBC	Carl	Salter	444 Metcalf	Overland Park	KS	66111-777
19	Royals	Peg	Fox	554 Stadium Ln.	Raytown	MO	60124-111
20	St. Luke's Hospital	Amanda	Summer	667 Birdie Ln.	Kansas City	MO	66888-555

Record: 1 of 27

Previous Record button | Specific Record box | Next Record button | Last Record button | New Record button | Total number of records

TABLE A-4: Navigation mode keyboard shortcuts

shortcut key	moves to the
[Tab], [Enter], or [→]	Next field of the current record
[Shift][Tab] or [←]	Previous field of the current record
[Home]	First field of the current record
[End]	Last field of the current record
[Ctrl][Home]	First field of the first record
[Ctrl][End]	Last field of the last record
[▲]	Current field of the previous record
[▼]	Current field of the next record
[Ctrl] [▲]	Current field of the first record
[Ctrl] [▼]	Current field of the last record
[F5]	Specific record entered in the Specific Record box

Clues to Use

Changing to Edit mode

If you navigate to another area of the datasheet by clicking with the mouse pointer instead of pressing [Tab] or [Enter], you change from **Navigation mode** to Edit mode. In **Edit mode**, Access assumes that you are trying to make changes to the current field value, so keystrokes such as [Ctrl][End], [Ctrl][Home], [←] and [→] move the insertion point *within* the field. To return to Navigation mode, press [Tab] or [Enter] (thus moving the focus to the next field), or press [▼] or [▲] (thus moving the focus to a different record).

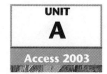

Entering Records

Your ability to add new records into a database is a fundamental skill. You can add a new record by clicking the New Record button ▶* on the Table Datasheet toolbar or by clicking the New Record navigation button. A new record is always added at the end of the datasheet. You can rearrange the order of the records in a datasheet by sorting them, which you will learn later. ◆◆◆◆◆ Kelsey asks you to add two new records to the Customers table. First, you maximize the datasheet window to make the working area as large as possible.

STEPS

1. **Click the** Maximize button **for the Customers table**

   Maximizing both the Access and datasheet windows displays as many fields and records on the screen as possible.

2. **Click the** New Record button ▶* **on the Table Datasheet toolbar, then press** [Tab] **to move through the ID field and into the Company field**

   The ID field is an **AutoNumber** field. Each time you add a record, Access automatically displays the next available integer in an AutoNumber field when you start entering data in that record. You cannot type into an AutoNumber field. The AutoNumber field logs how many records have been added to the datasheet since the creation of the table. It does not tell you how many records are currently in the table because Access does not reuse an AutoNumber value that was assigned to a record that has been deleted.

3. **Type** CIO, **press** [Tab], **type** Taylor, **press** [Tab], **type** McKinsey, **press** [Tab], **type** 420 Locust St., **press** [Tab], **type** Lenexa, **press** [Tab], **type** KS, **press** [Tab], **type** 661118899, **press** [Tab], **type** 9135551189, **press** [Tab], **type** 9135551889, **press** [Tab], **type** 9/6/69, **press** [Tab], **type** taylor@cio.com, **press** [Tab], **type** 5433.22, **then press** [Enter]

   The value of 28 is automatically entered in the ID field for this record. Notice that the navigation buttons indicate that you are now working on record 29 of 29.

4. **Enter the new record for Cooper Michaels shown below**

in field:	type:	in field:	type:
ID	[Tab]	Zip	655554444
Company	Four Winds	Phone	9135551212
First	Cooper	Fax	9135552889
Last	Michaels	Birthdate	8/20/1968
Street	500 Sunset Blvd.	Email	coop@4winds.com
City	Manhattan	YTDSales	5998.33
State	KS		

5. **Press** [Tab], **then compare your updated datasheet with Figure A-10**

   An AutoNumber field displays (AutoNumber) until you start entering data in another field of that record.

> **QUICK TIP**
> You do not need to type the dashes or parentheses in the Zip, Phone, or Fax fields nor the dollar sign or comma in the YTDSales field. These symbols are automatically inserted for these fields. You will learn how to create fields in Unit B.

FIGURE A-10: Customers table with two new records

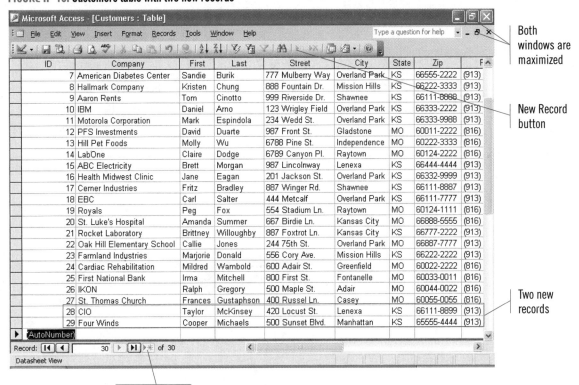

Both windows are maximized

New Record button

Two new records

New Record button

Clues to Use

Moving datasheet columns

You can reorganize the fields in a datasheet by dragging the field name left or right. Figure A-11 shows how the mouse pointer changes to 🗗 as the Email field is moved to the left. The black vertical line between the Fax and Birthdate fields represents the new location for the field you are moving.

FIGURE A-11: Moving a field in a datasheet

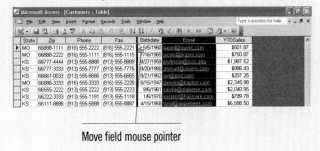

Move field mouse pointer

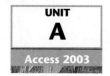

Editing Records

Updating existing information is another critical task. To change the contents of an existing record, click the field you want to change, then type the new information. You can delete unwanted data by clicking the field and using [Backspace] or [Delete] to delete text to the left or right of the insertion point. Other data entry keystrokes are summarized in Table A-5. Kelsey asks you to make some corrections to the datasheet of the Customers table. You start by correcting an error in the Street field of the first record.

STEPS

1. **Press [Ctrl][Home] to move to the first record, click to the right of 111 Ash St. in the Street field, press [Backspace] three times to delete St., then type Dr.**

   When you are editing a record, the **edit record symbol**, which looks like a small pencil, appears in the record selector box to the left of the current record, as shown in Figure A-12.

2. **Click to the right of Hallmark in the Company field in record 8, press [Spacebar], type Cards to change the entry to Hallmark Cards Company, then press [↓] to move to the next record**

   Access automatically saves new records and edits to existing data as soon as you move to another record or close the datasheet.

3. **Click Shawnee in the City field for record 17, then press [Ctrl][']**

   Pressing [Ctrl]['] inserts the data from the same field in the previous record so the entry changes from "Shawnee" to "Overland Park".

4. **Click to the left of EBC in the Company field for record 18, press [Delete] to remove the E, press [Tab] to move to the next field, then type Doug**

   "EBC" becomes "BC" in the Company field, and "Doug" replaces "Carl" in the First field. Notice the edit record symbol in the record selector box to the left of record 18. Because you are still editing this record, you can undo the changes using [Esc].

5. **Press [Esc]**

   The Doug entry changes back to Carl. Pressing [Esc] once removes the current field's editing changes.

6. **Press [Esc] again**

   Pressing [Esc] a second time removes all changes made to the record you are currently editing. The Company entry is restored to EBC. The ability to use [Esc] in Edit mode to remove data entry changes depends on whether you are still editing the record (as evidenced by the edit record symbol to the left of the record). Once you move to another record, the changes are saved, and you return to Navigation mode. In Navigation mode you can no longer use [Esc] to remove editing changes, but you can click the **Undo button** on the Table Datasheet toolbar to undo the last change you made.

7. **Press [↓] to move to Peg in the First field of record 19, type Peggy, press [↓] to move to record 20, then press [Esc]**

   Because you are no longer editing record 19, [Esc] has no effect on the last change.

QUICK TIP
The ScreenTip for the Undo button displays the action you can undo.

8. **Click the Undo button on the Table Datasheet toolbar**

   You undo the last edit and Peggy is changed back to Peg. Some areas of Access allow you to undo multiple actions, but a datasheet allows you to undo only your last action.

9. **Click anywhere in the ABC Electricity (ID 15) record, click the Delete Record button on the Table Datasheet toolbar, then click Yes**

   The message warns that you cannot undo a record deletion operation. Notice that the Undo button is dimmed, indicating that it cannot be used at this time.

FIGURE A-12: Editing a record

Undo button

Edit symbol

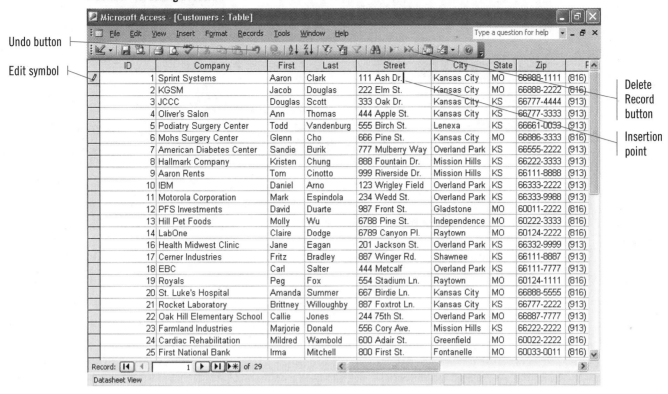

Delete Record button

Insertion point

Record: [◄][◄] 1 [►][►I][►*] of 29

Datasheet View

TABLE A-5: Edit mode keyboard shortcuts

editing keystroke	action
[Backspace]	Deletes one character to the left of the insertion point
[Delete]	Deletes one character to the right of the insertion point
[F2]	Switches between Edit and Navigation mode
[Esc]	Undoes the change to the current field
[Esc][Esc]	Undoes all changes to the current record
[F7]	Starts the spell check feature
[Ctrl][']	Inserts the value from the same field in the previous record into the current field
[Ctrl][;]	Inserts the current date in a Date field

Clues to Use

Resizing datasheet columns

You can resize the width of a field in a datasheet by dragging the thin black line that separates the field names to the left or right. The mouse pointer changes to ↔ as you make the field wider or narrower.

Release the mouse button when you have resized the field. To adjust the column width to accommodate the widest entry in the field, double-click the thin black line that separates the field names.

Access 2003

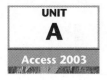

Previewing and Printing a Datasheet

Previewing a datasheet shows you how the data will appear on a physical piece of paper before you send it to the printer. Previewing is important because it allows you to see and make printing adjustments, such as changing the margins or page orientation, before printing it. ![icon] You decide to preview and print the datasheet.

STEPS

QUICK TIP
If you want your name to appear on the printout, enter your name as a new customer in the datasheet before printing.

1. **Click the Print Preview button 🔍 on the Table Datasheet toolbar**

   The datasheet appears as a miniature page in the Print Preview window, as shown in Figure A-14. The Print Preview toolbar provides options for printing, viewing more than one page, and sending the information to Word or Excel.

2. **Click the 🔍 pointer on the field names of the datasheet to zoom in**

   By magnifying the top of the printout, you see that Customers, the name of the table, is positioned in the center of the header. Today's date is positioned in the right section of the header.

3. **Scroll down to view the bottom of the page**

   The word "Page" and the current page number are positioned in the center of the footer.

4. **Click the Two Pages button 🔲 on the Print Preview toolbar**

   The navigation buttons in the lower-left corner are dimmed, indicating that there are no more pages to navigate—the entire printout fits on two pages. To change printing options, use the Page Setup dialog box.

5. **Click the Setup button on the Print Preview toolbar**

   The Page Setup dialog box opens, as shown in Figure A-15. This dialog box provides options for changing margins, removing the print headings (the header and footer), and changing page orientation from portrait (default) to landscape on the Page tab.

6. **Double-click 1 in the Top text box, type 2, then click OK**

   The datasheet now has a two-inch top margin as shown in the Print Preview window.

7. **Click the Print button 🖨 on the Print Preview toolbar, click File on the menu bar, then click Close**

   Closing the Print Preview window takes you back to the database window.

Clues to Use

Hiding fields

Sometimes you may not want all the fields of a datasheet to appear on the printout. To temporarily hide a field, click anywhere in the field, click Format on the datasheet menu bar, and then click Hide Columns. To redisplay the column, click Format, then click Unhide Columns. The Unhide Columns dialog box, shown in Figure A-13, opens. The unchecked boxes indicate which columns are currently hidden.

FIGURE A-13: Unhide Columns dialog box

Unhide Columns	? ✕
Column:	Close
☑ ID	
☑ Company	
☐ First	These fields are
☐ Last	currently hidden
☑ Street	
☑ City	
☑ State	
☑ Zip	
☑ Phone	
☑ Fax	
☑ Birthdate	
☑ Email	

FIGURE A-14: Datasheet in print preview (portrait orientation)

Two pages button

Print Preview toolbar

Print button

Close button

Setup button

Header

Zoom in pointer

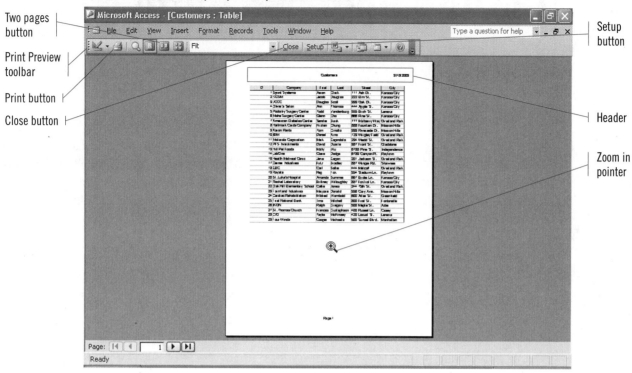

FIGURE A-15: Page Setup dialog box

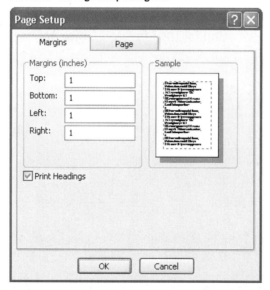

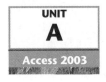
Getting Help and Exiting Access

When you are finished working with a database, you need to close all open objects, close the database, and then exit Access. To close an object, click File on the menu bar and then click Close, or click the object's Close button ☒ located on the right edge of the menu bar. After you close the objects you have been working with, you close the database and exit Access. As with most programs, if you try to exit Access and have not yet saved changes to open objects, Access prompts you to save your changes. You can use the Access Help system to learn more about the program. ▰▰▰ You have finished working with the MediaLoft-A database for now. Before exiting Access, though, you want to learn more about the Help system.

QUICK TIP
If your Data Files are stored on a floppy disk, do not remove your floppy disk from drive A until you have completely exited Access as instructed in Step 6.

1. **Click the** Close button **for the MediaLoft-A database, as shown in Figure A-16**

   The MediaLoft-A database is closed, but Access is still running. At this point you can open another database or explore the Help system to learn more about Access.

2. **Click the** Type a question for help box, **type** naming fields, **then press** [Enter]

   The Search Results task pane opens, listing potential Help topics that relate to your entry. Using the Help text box is similar to initiating keyword searches via the Office Assistant or using the Answer Wizard. Help menu options and terminology are further explained in Table A-6.

3. **Click** About renaming a field in a table (MDB)

   The Help system opens to the specific page that explains how to rename an existing field in a table. **Glossary terms** are shown as blue hyperlinks. Clicking a blue hyperlink displays a definition.

4. **Click the** Show All **link in the upper-right corner of the Microsoft Access Help window, then resize the Help window as desired**

   An expanded view of the Help page with all subcategories and definitions appears, as shown in Figure A-17. The Show All link now becomes the Hide All link.

5. **Click the** Close button **for the Microsoft Office Access Help window**

   You return to the Search Results task pane where you can click another link or initiate another search for information.

6. **Click** File **on the menu bar, then click** Exit

Clues to Use

Compact on Close

The **Compact on Close** option found on the General tab of the Options dialog box compacts and repairs your database each time you close it. To open the Options dialog box, click Tools on the menu bar, and then click Options. *While the Compact on Close feature works well if your database is stored on your hard drive or on another large storage device, it can cause problems if your Data Files are stored on a floppy disk.* The Compact on Close process creates a temporary file that is just as large as the original database file. This temporary file is used during the compaction process, and is deleted after the procedure successfully finishes. Therefore, if your database file grows larger than half of the available storage space on a floppy disk, the Compact on Close process cannot create the necessary temporary file or successfully compact the database. Such an error might result in a harmless error message or, in the worst case, a corrupt database.

FIGURE A-16: Closing a database

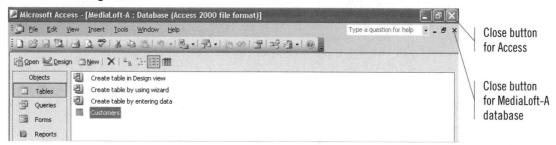

Close button for Access

Close button for MediaLoft-A database

FIGURE A-17: Microsoft Access Help window

Glossary terms are blue

Glossary defintions are green

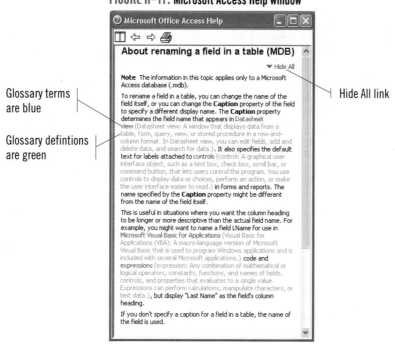

Hide All link

TABLE A-6: Help menu options

Help menu option	description
Microsoft Office Access Help	Opens the Access Help task pane
Show/Hide the Office Assistant	Presents or hides the **Office Assistant**, an automated character that provides tips and interactive prompts while you are working
Microsoft Office Online	If you are connected to the Web, provides additional Microsoft information and support articles stored at the Microsoft Web site
Access Developer Resources	If you are connected to the Web, opens the MSDN Library Web page, which provides information on advanced Access technologies, such as Web development
Contact Us	If you are connected to the Web, opens a Microsoft Office Web page where you can get assistance from Microsoft, such as how-to articles and tips
Sample Databases	Provides easy access to the sample databases installed with Access 2003
Check for Updates	If you are connected to the Web, checks the Microsoft Web site for files you can download to update Office or Access
Detect and Repair	Analyzes a database for possible data corruption and attempts to repair problems
Activate Product	Click to start activation process
Customer Feedback Options	Provides options for working with Microsoft to provide feedback through their Customer Experience Improvement Program
About Microsoft Office Access	Provides the version and product ID of Access

Practice

▼ CONCEPTS REVIEW

Label each element of the Access window shown in Figure A-18.

FIGURE A-18

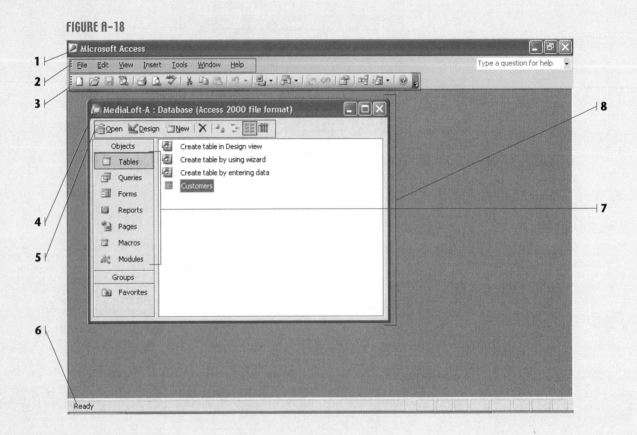

Match each term with the statement that best describes it.

9. **Objects**

10. **Table**

11. **Record**

12. **Field**

13. **Datasheet**

14. **Form**

15. **Compact on Close**

a. A group of related fields, such as all of the demographic information for one customer

b. A collection of records for a single subject, such as all the customer records

c. A category of information in a table, such as a customer's name, city, or state

d. A spreadsheet-like grid that displays fields as columns and records as rows

e. A process that shrinks and repairs a database

f. An Access object that provides an easy-to-use data entry screen

g. Seven types of these are contained in an Access database and are used to enter, enhance, and use the data within the database

Select the best answer from the list of choices.

16. Which of the following is *not* a typical benefit of relational databases?
    a. Easier data entry
    b. Faster information retrieval
    c. Minimized duplicate data entry
    d. Automatic trend analysis

17. Which of the following is *not* an advantage of managing data with a relational database versus a spreadsheet?
    a. Doesn't require planning before data is entered
    b. Allows links between lists of information
    c. Provides greater security
    d. Allows multiple users to enter data simultaneously

18. The object that holds all of the data within an Access database is the:
    a. Query.
    b. Table.
    c. Form.
    d. Report.

19. The object that creates a dynamic Web page is the:
    a. Table.
    b. Form.
    c. Page.
    d. Report.

20. What displays messages regarding the current database operation?
    a. Status bar
    b. Title bar
    c. Database toolbar
    d. Object buttons

▼ SKILLS REVIEW

1. **Understand relational databases.**
    a. Identify five advantages of managing database information in Access versus using a spreadsheet.
    b. Explain how a relational database organizes data to minimize redundant information. Use an example involving a database with two related tables, Customers and Sales, to make your explanation.

2. **Learn database terminology.**
    a. Explain the relationship between a field, a record, a table, and a database.
    b. Identify the seven objects of an Access database, and explain the main purpose of each.
    c. Which object of an Access database is most important? Why?

3. **Start Access and open a database.**
    a. Click the Start button, point to All Programs, point to Microsoft Office, then click Microsoft Office Access 2003.
    b. Open the **Recycle-A.mdb** database from the drive and folder where your Data Files are stored.
    c. Identify the following elements on a printout. (*Hint*: To create a printout of the Recycle-A database window, press [Print Screen] to capture an image of the window to the Windows Clipboard. Start any word processing program, then click the Paste button to paste the image stored on the Clipboard into the document. Print the document that now contains a picture of the opening database window, and identify the elements on the printout.)
    - Microsoft Access title bar
    - Database toolbar
    - Database window
    - Menu bar
    - Database title bar
    - Object buttons
    - Database window toolbar
    - Status bar

4. **Work with the database window.**
    a. Maximize both the Access window and the Recycle-A database window.
    b. Click each of the Object buttons on the Objects bar, then write down the object names of each type that exists in the Recycle-A database.

5. **Navigate records.**
    a. Open the Clubs table datasheet.
    b. Press [Tab] or [Enter] to move through the fields of the first record.
    c. Press [Ctrl][End] to move to the last field of the last record.
    d. Press [Ctrl][Home] to move to the first field of the first record.
    e. Click the Last Record navigation button to quickly move to the Oak Hill Patriots record.

▼ SKILLS REVIEW (CONTINUED)

6. Enter records.

a. In the Clubs table, click the New Record button, then add the following two records:

Club Number	Name	Street	City	State	Zip	Phone	FName	LName
8	EBC Angels	10100 Metcalf	Overland Park	KS	66001	555-333-7711	Steve	Earhart
9	Zoopers	111 Holmes	Kansas City	MO	65001	555-333-8811	Jim	Wheeling

b. Move the Club Number field from the first column of the datasheet to the last column.

7. Edit records.

a. Change the Name field in the first record from Jaycees to JC Club.

b. Change the Name field in the second record from Boy Scouts #11 to Oxford Cub Scouts.

c. Change the FName field in the record for the Lions club from Cory to Clayton.

d. Enter a new record using fictitious but realistic entries for the Name, Street, City, State, Zip, and Phone fields. Enter your name for the FName and LName fields and 99 as the Club Number entry.

e. Resize the datasheet columns so that all field entries are visible.

f. Delete the record for Club Number 3.

8. Preview and print a datasheet.

a. Preview the Clubs table datasheet.

b. Use the Page Setup option on the File menu to change the page orientation from portrait to landscape.

c. Print the Clubs table datasheet.

9. Get Help and exit Access.

a. Close the Clubs table, saving the changes.

b. Close the Recycle-A.mdb database, but leave Access running.

c. Search for Help topics by entering the keyword subdatasheet into the Type a question for help box. Click the link for the About subdatasheets option.

d. Click the Show All link to display all of the glossary terms, then click the Print button on the Help window toolbar to print that page.

e. Close the Microsoft Office Access Help window.

f. Exit Access.

▼ INDEPENDENT CHALLENGE 1

Twelve examples of database tables are given below.

- Telephone directory
- College course offerings
- Restaurant menu
- Cookbook
- Movie listing
- Islands of the Caribbean
- Encyclopedia
- Shopping catalog
- Product inventory
- Party guest list
- Members of the House of Representatives
- Ancient wonders of the world

For each example, write a brief answer for the following.

a. What field names would you expect to find in each table?

b. Provide an example of two possible records for each table.

▼ INDEPENDENT CHALLENGE 2

You are working with several civic groups to coordinate a community-wide cleanup effort. You have started a database called Recycle-A that tracks the clubs, their trash deposits, and the trash collection centers that are participating.

a. Start Access, then open the **Recycle-A.mdb** database from the drive and folder where your Data Files are stored.

b. Open each table's datasheet, and write down the number of records and fields in each of the tables.

c. In the Centers table datasheet, modify the ContactFirst and ContactLast names for Center Number 1 to be your name.

d. Preview the Centers table datasheet, use the Page Setup options to change the left and right margins to 0.5", and also change the page orientation to landscape. The printout should now fit on one page. Print the Centers table datasheet, then close it.

Advanced Challenge Exercise

■ Open the datasheet for the Clubs table. Click the expand button to the left of each record and count the records in each subdatasheet that appears. (*Hint*: To quickly count the records in a subdatasheet, click within the subdatasheet and then view the total number of records displayed to the right of the navigation buttons in the lower-left corner of the datasheet.) How many total records are in the subdatasheets, and what does this tell you about the relationship between the Clubs and Deposits tables? (*Hint*: How many records did you originally find in the Deposits table from Step b?)

■ Close the datasheet for the Clubs table. Open the datasheet for the Centers table. An expand button appears as a small plus sign to the left of the Name field for each record. Click the expand button to the left of each of the records in the Centers datasheet. A subdatasheet for each center appears. Count the records in each subdatasheet. How many total records are in the subdatasheets, and what does this tell you about the relationship between the Centers and Deposits tables?

e. Close the Centers table, close **Recycle-A.mdb**, then exit Access.

▼ INDEPENDENT CHALLENGE 3

You are working with several civic groups to coordinate a community-wide cleanup effort. You have started a database called Recycle-A that tracks the clubs, their trash deposits, and the trash centers that are participating.

a. Start Access and open the **Recycle-A.mdb** database from the drive and folder where your Data Files are stored.

b. Add the following records to the Clubs table:

Name	Street	City	State	Zip	Phone	FName	LName	Club Number
Take Pride	222 Lincoln Way	Olathe	KS	66001	555-888-2211	Franklin	Rivers	10
Cub Scouts #321	333 Ward Pkwy.	Kansas City	MO	65002	555-777-8800	Jacob	Tamar	11

c. Edit the Lions record 4 in the Clubs table. The Street value should be **444 Maple Way**, the City value should be **Shawnee**, and the Zip value should be **68777**.

d. If you haven't entered a record containing your own name in the FName and LName fields, enter this record using **99** as the Club Number.

e. Print the datasheet in landscape orientation.

f. Close the Clubs table.

Advanced Challenge Exercise

■ Click the Queries button, then open the datasheet for the Deposits by Club query by double-clicking it.

■ Click File on the menu bar, click Print, then enter **1** in the From and To boxes to print only the first page. Click OK in the Print dialog box. On the printout, identify which table supplied the three fields in the datasheet. Close the Deposits by Club query.

g. Close the **Recycle-A.mdb** database, then exit Access.

▼ INDEPENDENT CHALLENGE 4

The World Wide Web can be used to research information about almost any topic. In this exercise, you go to Microsoft's Web site for Access, and explore what's new about Access 2003.

a. Connect to the Internet, and use your browser to go to the www.microsoft.com/access Web page.

b. Web sites change often, but you can probably find a link that provides a tour of Access 2003, or an introduction to Access 2003. Click that link and follow the tour or introduction. Based on what you learned, describe two new features or capabilities that you discovered about Access 2003.

c. Go back to the www.microsoft.com/access or www.microsoft.com/office Web page, then click the appropriate hyperlinks to find out how Office 2003 suites are organized. You might find this information within a pricing or ordering link. Find the Web page that describes what is included in the various Office 2003 suites and print it. On the printout, identify which suites include Access.

▼ VISUAL WORKSHOP

Open the Recycle-A.mdb database from the drive and folder where your Data Files are stored, then open the Centers table datasheet. Modify the records in the existing Centers table to reflect the changes shown in Figure A-19. The fields have been reorganized, the Name field for the fourth record has changed, and a new record has been added. If you have not entered your own first and last names in the ContactFirst and ContactLast fields of the first record, do so now. Print the datasheet in landscape orientation, close the Centers table, close the Recycle-A.mdb database, then exit Access.

FIGURE A-19

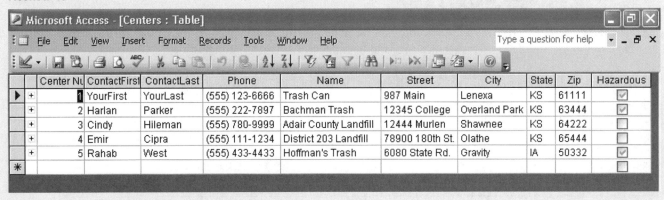

Using Tables and Queries

OBJECTIVES

Organize fields
Plan related tables
Create a table
Modify a table
Format a datasheet
Understand sorting, filtering, and finding
Sort records and find data
Filter records
Create a query
Modify a query

If you have a SAM user profile, you may have access to hands-on instruction, practice, and assessment of the skills covered in this unit. Log in to your SAM account and go to your assignments page to see what your instructor has assigned.

Now that you are familiar with some basic Access terminology and features, you are ready to plan and build your own database. You start by creating tables that store data. Once the tables are created and the data is entered, you use several techniques for finding specific information in the database, including sorting, filtering, and building queries. Kelsey Lang, a marketing manager at MediaLoft, wants you to build a database to track information about MediaLoft's music inventory. You use the database to find, analyze, and report information about MediaLoft's products.

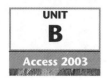

Organizing Fields

Before you build a database in Access, it's wise to carefully plan the fields and tables to avoid rework necessary to later fix a poorly constructed database. To plan a database, start by identifying and organizing the individual fields that the database will store. Each field needs to have a descriptive name and an appropriate data type. The **data type** defines the kind of data that can be stored in each field, such as text, numbers, or dates. Table B-1 lists the data types available within Access. ☞ Before you build the new MediaLoft database, you plan its fields.

DETAILS

To organize the fields of a database:

- **Design the reports that you want the database to produce**

  Designing or sketching the reports that you want the database to produce helps you identify the fields that the database should store. In this case, you want to be able to print inventory reports that list MediaLoft's music products by artist, title, and price.

- **Collect the raw data that is required to produce the reports**

  To produce reports, you need **raw data**, the individual pieces of information entered into each field. The raw data for the reports might be in one or multiple locations, including index cards, paper reports, or computer files, such as word processing documents, spreadsheets, or accounting system files. Or, your reports may require you to start collecting fields of information that have not been recorded in the past.

- **Identify a name and data type for each field**

  Based on the reports you design and the raw data you collect, identify the field name and data type for each field that you want the database to contain, as shown in Figure B-1. Be sure to break down and assign each piece of data to its own field. For example, if you were designing a table to hold information about customers, separate the customer address into several fields such as Street, City, State, Zip, and Country in order to make the data easy to find, sort, and merge. Apply the same rule of thumb to a person's name. In most cases, you will want to break names into several fields such as First, Middle, Last, and Title in order to easily find, sort, and merge any part of a person's name.

  Properly defining the data type for each field helps you maintain data consistency and accuracy. For example, a field with a Currency data type will *not* accept a text entry.

Clues to Use

Choosing between the Text and Number data type

When assigning data types, avoid choosing the Number data type for a Telephone or Zip Code field. Although these fields generally contain only numeric entries, they should still be Text data types. For example, suppose you want to enter 1-800-BUY-BOOK in a telephone number field. This would not be possible if the field were designated as a Number data type. Also, when you sort fields such as Telephone or Zip Code, you want them to sort alphabetically, like Text fields, rather than in numeric order. For example, consider the zip codes of 60011 and 50011-8888. If the Zip Code field is designated as a Number data type, the data is interpreted incorrectly as the values 60,011 and 500,118,888, and sorted in that order. Given a Text data type, the zip codes are sorted based on the value of the first character, so 50011-8888 would come before 60011. Also, a Zip Code entry of 01234 would be stored as 1234 if stored as a number (leading zeros are insignificant when evaluated as numbers and are therefore dropped), making the field value incorrect.

Field Name	Data Type
RecordingID	AutoNumber
Title	Text
ArtistFirst	Text
ArtistLast	Text
Group	Text
Tracks	Number
Wholesale	Currency
Retail	Currency

TABLE B-1: **Data types**

data type	description of data	size
Text	Text information or combinations of text and numbers, such as a street address, name, or phone number	Up to 255 characters
Memo	Lengthy text such as comments or notes	Up to 65,535 characters
Number	Numeric information such as quantities	Several sizes available to store numbers with varying degrees of precision
Date/Time	Dates and times	Size controlled by Access to accommodate dates and times across thousands of years (for example, 1/1/1850 and 1/1/2150 are valid dates)
Currency	Monetary values	Size controlled by Access; accommodates up to 15 digits to the left of the decimal point and 4 digits to the right
AutoNumber	Integers assigned by Access to sequentially order each record added to a table	Size controlled by Access
Yes/No	Only one of two values stored (Yes/No, On/Off, True/False)	Size controlled by Access
OLE Object	Objects and files linked or embedded (OLE) that are created in other programs, such as pictures, sound clips, documents, or spreadsheets	Up to 1 GB
Hyperlink	Web and e-mail addresses	Size controlled by Access
Lookup Wizard	Not a data type, but a wizard that helps link the current table to another table or list	Size controlled through the choices made in the Lookup Wizard

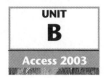

Planning Related Tables

Tables are the most important objects in a database because they store all of the raw data. Each table should contain fields that describe only one subject. A table that repeats data in the same field of several records suggests that the table represents more than one subject. If you see repeated data in the fields of several records, you should consider separating the repeating fields into a second table that has a one-to-many relationship with the original table. A **one-to-many relationship** means that a single record in the "one" table is related to many records in the "many" table. For example, in a database that tracks music products, one artist may have many products for sale, such as different recordings. If you separate the fields that describe the artists and products into two tables—one for artists and another for products—you can create a one-to-many relationship between the tables by establishing a common field used to link the tables together. This organization of data allows you to enter the record that describes the artist only once, yet link it to many records that describe that artist's recordings. Now that you have organized the fields, you plan the tables for the new MediaLoft database.

DETAILS

To plan the tables of a database:

- **Separate the fields into specific subject areas**

  For example, if your database manages the sale of products to customers, you should create separate Customers, Sales, and Inventory tables. For the new MediaLoft database, you need to create at least one table to store the fields that you previously identified. At this point, you may not yet see the need for more than one table.

- **Create sample records and examine the entries to determine if more tables are needed**

  Enter several records into the table and examine each field to see if they repeat data from other records, as shown in Figure B-2. If you see repeated data, the fields that contain the redundant information may need to be separated into another table. The two tables will later be linked in a one-to-many relationship.

- **Identify a primary key field for each table**

  A **primary key field** is a field that contains unique information for each record. For example, you could use the Employee Number field as the primary key field for a table that stores information about employees. Usually it is not a good idea to use a name field for a primary key field because two people could have the same name. The primary key field has two roles—it uniquely identifies each record in that table, and it is also used on the "one" side of a one-to-many relationship between two tables. For the new MediaLoft database, RecordingID will serve as the primary key field for the Inventory table and ArtistID will be the primary key field for the Artists table.

- **Identify a common field to link the tables in a one-to-many relationship**

  Once the tables are designed, a common field must be established to link the tables together. The common field is usually the primary key field in the table on the "one" side of a one-to-many relationship. The common field is called the **foreign key field** in the table on the "many" side of a one-to-many relationship. For the new MediaLoft database, one artist may offer many music products. Therefore, the ArtistID field (the primary key field in the Artists table, the "one" side of this relationship) is added to the Inventory table (the "many" side of this relationship) to serve as the common field to link the two tables together. In this situation, the ArtistID field in the Inventory table is called the foreign key field. Figure B-3 shows the final design for the first two tables of the new MediaLoft database. To see the relationships between tables for any existing database, click the Relationships button.

  Remember, the benefit of separating the fields into two tables is that it minimizes redundant data entries. In this case, you will enter the data that describes each artist in a record in the Artists table. Through the one-to-many relationship to the Inventory table, that artist record in the Artists table will be linked to many records in the Inventory table. Minimizing redundant data helps you increase the accuracy, consistency, efficiency, reliability, and overall value of data. Because the tables are connected in a relational database, you may view and organize the fields of multiple tables in any organization by using queries, forms, reports, and Web pages.

FIGURE B-2: Examining records for repeated data

	RecordingID	Title	ArtistFirst	ArtistLast	Group	Tracks	Wholesale	Retail
	1	Autumn	George	Walters	Justice	7	$5.00	$15.00
	2	Summer	George	Walters	Justice	15	$7.00	$12.00
	3	Spring	George	Walters	Justice	11	$7.00	$15.00
	4	Winter	George	Walters	Justice	10	$6.00	$15.00
	5	KG Live	Kenny	George	KG	11	$5.00	$14.00
	6	Skyline Firedance	Kenny	George	KG	10	$14.00	$18.00
	7	Sacred Road	David	Lantz	Lantz Orchestra	12	$6.00	$17.00
	8	Heartsounds	David	Lantz	Lantz Orchestra	14	$7.00	$17.00
	9	Handel's Messiah	Leonard	Bernard	Leonard Bernard	11	$6.00	$12.00
	10	Favorite Overtures	Leonard	Bernard	Leonard Bernard	5	$10.00	$15.00

Using only one table, some fields contain redundant data in multiple records

FIGURE B-3: Final design for the first two tables

ArtistID is the primary key field in the Artists table

ArtistID is the foreign key field in the Inventory table

Using two tables, fields that describe the artist are separated from the fields that describe the products

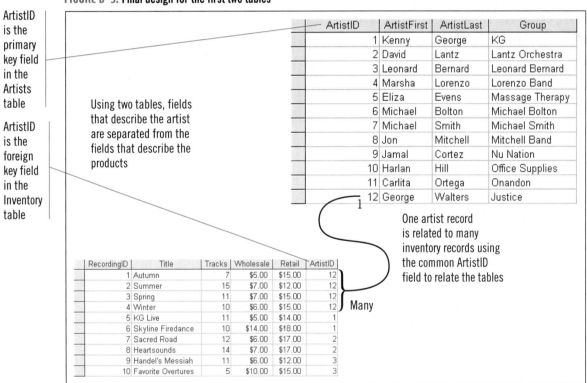

	ArtistID	ArtistFirst	ArtistLast	Group
	1	Kenny	George	KG
	2	David	Lantz	Lantz Orchestra
	3	Leonard	Bernard	Leonard Bernard
	4	Marsha	Lorenzo	Lorenzo Band
	5	Eliza	Evens	Massage Therapy
	6	Michael	Bolton	Michael Bolton
	7	Michael	Smith	Michael Smith
	8	Jon	Mitchell	Mitchell Band
	9	Jamal	Cortez	Nu Nation
	10	Harlan	Hill	Office Supplies
	11	Carlita	Ortega	Onandon
	12	George	Walters	Justice

One artist record is related to many inventory records using the common ArtistID field to relate the tables

	RecordingID	Title	Tracks	Wholesale	Retail	ArtistID
	1	Autumn	7	$5.00	$15.00	12
	2	Summer	15	$7.00	$12.00	12
	3	Spring	11	$7.00	$15.00	12
	4	Winter	10	$6.00	$15.00	12
	5	KG Live	11	$5.00	$14.00	1
	6	Skyline Firedance	10	$14.00	$18.00	1
	7	Sacred Road	12	$6.00	$17.00	2
	8	Heartsounds	14	$7.00	$17.00	2
	9	Handel's Messiah	11	$6.00	$12.00	3
	10	Favorite Overtures	5	$10.00	$15.00	3

Creating a Table

After you plan the structure of the database, your next step is to create the actual database file and the first table object. The database file contains the tables and any other objects that you create to view and work with the data such as queries, forms, and reports. Access offers several methods for creating the database and the first table. For example, you can create a sample database (complete with sample table, query, form, and report objects) using the **Database Wizard**. Or, you could create a blank database and build the objects from scratch. To build your first table, you could import a table from another data source such as a spreadsheet, or use the Access **Table Wizard**. The Table Wizard provides interactive help to create the field names and data types for each field. ▨▨▨▨ You are ready to create the new MediaLoft database and Inventory table. You use the Table Wizard to create the Inventory table.

STEPS

TROUBLE
If the task pane does not appear in the Access window, click File on the menu bar, then click New.

1. **Start Access, click the** Create a new file link **near the bottom of the Getting Started task pane, then click the** Blank database link **in the New File task pane as shown in Figure B-4**
   The File New Database dialog box opens.

2. **Type** MediaLoft **in the File name text box, click the** Save in list arrow, **navigate to the drive and folder where your Data Files are stored, then click** Create
   The MediaLoft.mdb database file is created and saved where your Data Files are stored. There are many ways to create the first table in the database, but the Table Wizard offers an efficient and easy way to get started.

TROUBLE
If the Create table by using wizard option does not appear in the database window, click Tools on the menu bar, then click Options. On the View tab, make sure that the New object shortcuts check box is selected, then click OK.

3. **Double-click** Create table by using wizard **in the MediaLoft database window**
   The Table Wizard dialog box opens. The Table Wizard offers 25 business and 20 personal sample tables from which you can select sample fields. The Recordings table in the Personal database category most closely matches the fields you want to include in the Inventory table.

4. **Click the** Personal option button, **then scroll down and click** Recordings **in the Sample Tables list box**
   The Table Wizard offers several sample fields for the Recordings table from which you can choose for your new table.

5. **Click** RecordingID **in the Sample Fields list, click the** Select Single Field button ⌷ > ⌷, **click** RecordingTitle, **click** ⌷ > ⌷, **click** RecordingArtistID, **click** ⌷ > ⌷, **click** NumberofTracks, **click** ⌷ > ⌷, **click** PurchasePrice, **click** ⌷ > ⌷
   Your Table Wizard dialog box should look like Figure B-5.

6. **Click** Next, **type** Inventory, **click the** No, I'll set the primary key option button, **then click** Next
   The next dialog box asks questions about the primary key field. You want the RecordingID field to be the primary key field with an AutoNumber data type so that Access consecutively numbers each new record automatically. Therefore, you don't need to change the default settings that already specify these options.

TROUBLE
If you are in Table Datasheet View, click the Design View button ⌷ on the Table Datasheet toolbar.

7. **Click** Next, **click the** Modify the table design option button, **then click** Finish
   The table opens in Design View, shown in Figure B-6, which allows you to add, delete, or modify the fields in the table. The **key symbol** indicates that the RecordingID field has been designated as the primary key field.

FIGURE B-4: New File task pane

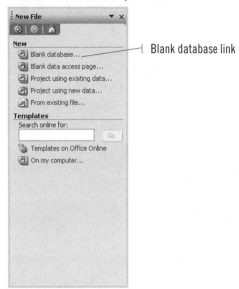

Blank database link

FIGURE B-5: Table Wizard

Sample fields for
Recordings table

Personal category

Recordings table

Select Single
Field button

Fields selected
for the new table

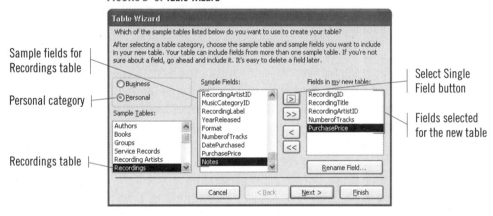

FIGURE B-6: Inventory table in Design View

Inventory table

Key field symbol

Field names

Data types

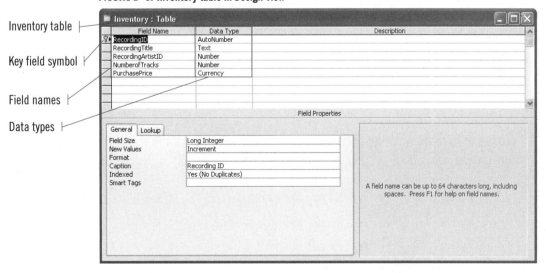

Access 2003

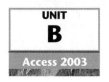

Modifying a Table

Each database object has a **Design View** in which you can modify its structure. The Design View of a table allows you to add or delete fields, add field descriptions, or change other field properties. Field **properties** are additional characteristics of a field such as its size or default value. Using the Table Wizard, you were able to create the Inventory table very quickly. Now in Design View you modify the fields to meet your specific needs.

STEPS

1. **In Design View of the Inventory table, double-click the PurchasePrice field name to select it, then type Wholesale**

   With the Wholesale field clearly named, you need to add another Currency field named Retail to store retail price data.

QUICK TIP
You can also choose a data type by pressing its first letter such as C for Currency.

2. **Click the blank Field Name cell below the Wholesale field, type Retail, press [Tab], click the Data Type list arrow, then click Currency**

   The new field is added to the Inventory table, as shown in Figure B-7. Field names can include any combination of letters, numbers, and spaces, up to 64 characters. The only special characters that are not allowed are the period (.), exclamation point (!), accent grave (`), and square brackets [ ]. Field descriptions are optional, but they help to further identify the field. At this point, you decide to shorten the names of three existing fields.

3. **Double-click RecordingTitle to select it, type Title, double-click RecordingArtistID, type ArtistID, double-click NumberofTracks, then type Tracks**

   You also want to move the ArtistID field to the end of the field list.

4. **Click the row selector button to the left of the ArtistID field to select the entire row, then drag the row selector button to just below the Retail field**

   The black triangle in the row selector button helps you see which field is currently selected. The **Field Properties pane** in the lower half of Table Design View shows you the properties for the currently selected field. The **Caption** property contains the default label for the field when it is displayed in a datasheet or on a form. Without a Caption property, fields are labeled with their field name. The caption that the Table Wizard automatically created for the Wholesale field is "Purchase Price", which is no longer appropriate. Therefore, you decide to delete the Caption property for the Wholesale field.

5. **Click the Wholesale field, then delete Purchase Price in the Caption property**

   Table Design View of the Inventory table should look like Figure B-8. Other field properties, such as **Field Size**, restrict the amount or type of data that can be entered in the field and are helpful in reducing typing errors.

QUICK TIP
The Datasheet View button becomes the Design View button when working in Datasheet View.

6. **Click the Datasheet View button on the Table Design toolbar, click Yes to save the table, then type the following record into the new datasheet:**

in field:	type:
Recording ID	[Tab]
Recording Title	Lift Us Up
Number of Tracks	15
Wholesale	20
Retail	25
Recording Artist ID	12

7. **Close the Inventory table, then close the MediaLoft.mdb database**

   Data is saved automatically, so you are not prompted to save the record when you closed the datasheet.

Wholesale field

Retail field is created with a Currency data type

Field Properties pane

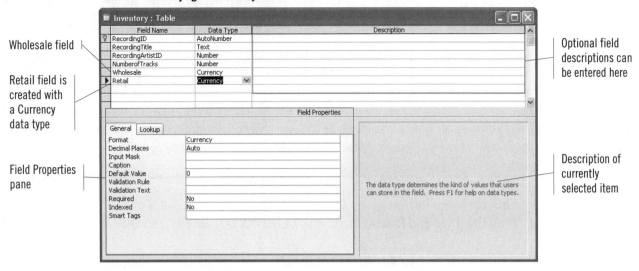

Optional field descriptions can be entered here

Description of currently selected item

Title field has been renamed

Tracks field has been renamed

Wholesale field is selected

Row selector button for ArtistID field

ArtistID field has been renamed and moved

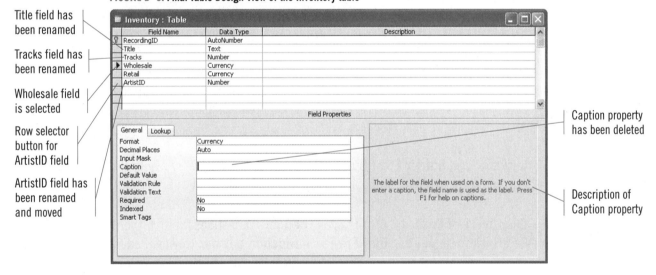

Caption property has been deleted

Description of Caption property

Clues to Use

Learning about field properties

Properties are the characteristics that define the field. Two properties are required for every field: Field Name and Data Type. Many other properties, such as Field Size, Format, Caption, and Default Value, are defined in the Field Properties pane in the lower half of Table Design View. As you add more property entries, you are generally restricting the amount or type of data that can be entered in the field, which in turn increases data entry accuracy. For example, you might change the Field Size property for a State field to 2 in order to eliminate an incorrect entry such as FLL. Field properties change depending on the data type of the selected field. For example, there is no Field Size property for date fields, because Access controls the size of fields with a Date/Time data type.

Access 2003

Formatting a Datasheet

After the database has been designed, the tables have been built, and the data has been entered, you often create printouts. Although the report object is most often used to create professional printouts, you can print data as displayed by a datasheet as well. In a datasheet, you can change the fonts, colors, and gridlines to enhance the appearance of the information. ▰▰▰▰▰ After working with the Table Wizard, you finished building the MediaLoft database to include both the Inventory and Artists tables and entered several records in both tables. Now you want to format and print the Inventory datasheet.

STEPS

1. **Click the** Open button 📂 **on the Database toolbar, select the** MediaLoft-B.mdb **database from the drive and folder where your Data Files are stored, then click** Open

2. **Click the** Inventory **table in the MediaLoft-B database window, then click the** Open button 📇 **on the database window toolbar**

   The Inventory table contains 62 records, as shown in Figure B-9. When you format a datasheet, every record in the datasheet is formatted the same way. You use the options on the Format menu to format a datasheet.

3. **Click** Format **on the menu bar, click** Font, **scroll and click** Comic Sans MS **in the Font list, then click** OK

   Comic Sans MS is an informal font that simulates handwritten text, but is still very readable. Formatting options for a datasheet are also found on the Formatting (Datasheet) toolbar. By default, the Formatting (Datasheet) toolbar does not appear in Datasheet View, but toolbars are easily turned on and off using the View menu.

4. **Click** View **on the menu bar, point to** Toolbars, **then click** Formatting (Datasheet)

   The Formatting (Datasheet) toolbar contains the most common formatting options for changing the font, colors, and gridlines of the datasheet.

5. **Click the** Line/Border Color button list arrow ✏️▾, **click the** red box, **click the** Gridlines button list arrow ▦▾, **then click the** Gridlines: Horizontal box

6. **Click the** Print Preview button 🔍 **on the Table Datasheet toolbar, then click the** Next Page button ▶ **in the Print Preview navigation buttons to view Page 2**

   The First Page ◀◀ and Previous Page ◀ buttons are dimmed if you are viewing the first page of the datasheet. The Next Page ▶ and Last Page ▶▶ buttons are dimmed if you are viewing the last page of the datasheet. By default, the table name and current date print in the datasheet header, and the page number prints in the datasheet footer as shown in Figure B-10.

7. **Click the** Close button `Close` **for the preview window, click the** Close button **on the datasheet, then click** No **when asked to save the changes to the layout of the table**

   All data entries and edits are automatically saved as you move between records or close a datasheet. Therefore, you are never prompted as to whether you want to save data. Access does prompt you as to whether you want to save structural or formatting changes, though.

FIGURE B-9: Inventory table datasheet

	RecordingID	Title	Tracks	Wholesale	Retail	ArtistID
▶	1	Autumn	7	$5.00	$15.00	12
	2	Summer	15	$7.00	$12.00	12
	3	Spring	11	$7.00	$15.00	12
	4	Winter	10	$6.00	$15.00	12
	5	KG Live	11	$5.00	$14.00	1
	6	Skyline Firedance	10	$14.00	$18.00	1
	7	Sacred Road	12	$6.00	$17.00	2
	8	Heartsounds	14	$7.00	$17.00	2
	9	Handel's Messiah	11	$6.00	$12.00	3
	10	Favorite Overtures	5	$10.00	$15.00	3
	11	Mariah Carey	11	$5.00	$12.00	4
	12	Live with Mariah	9	$5.00	$13.00	4
	13	Daydream	12	$6.00	$13.00	4
	14	Watermark	12	$8.00	$13.00	5
	15	Time and Love	10	$6.00	$12.00	6
	16	I'll Lead You Home	14	$7.00	$12.00	7
	17	Blue	10	$10.00	$15.00	8
	18	God's Property	13	$5.00	$14.00	9
	19	Tribute	10	$5.00	$12.00	10
	20	Union	14	$8.00	$12.00	11

Record: 1 of 62 — 62 records

FIGURE B-10: Previewing the formatted datasheet

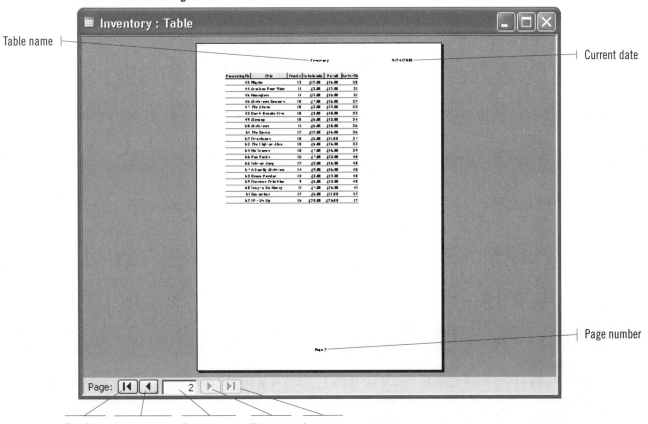

Table name | | Current date

Page number

Page: 2

First Page   Previous page   Current page   Next page   Last page

Access 2003

Understanding Sorting, Filtering, and Finding

The records of a datasheet are automatically sorted according to the data in the primary key field. Often, however, you may want to view or print records in a different sort order, or you may want to display a subset of the records, such as those with the same artist or those less than a certain retail price. Access makes it easy to sort records, find data, and filter a datasheet by using buttons on the Table Datasheet toolbar, summarized in Table B-2. You study the sort, filter, and find features to better learn how to find and retrieve information.

- **Sorting** refers to reorganizing the records in either ascending or descending order based on the contents of a field. In ascending order, Text fields sort from A to Z, Number and Currency fields sort from the lowest to the highest value, and Date/Time fields sort from the oldest date to the date furthest into the future. In Figure B-11 the Inventory table is sorted in descending order based on the values in the Retail field.

- **Filtering** means temporarily isolating a subset of records, as shown in Figure B-12. For example, by using a filter, you can list all records with a value greater than 15 in the Retail field. To redisplay all of the records in the datasheet, click the Remove Filter button. The filtered subset can be formatted and printed just like the entire datasheet.

- **Finding** refers to locating a specific piece of data, such as "Light". The Find and Replace dialog box is shown in Figure B-13. The options in this dialog box are summarized below.

  - **Find What:** Provides a text box for your search criteria. The search criteria might be Amy, Beatles, or Capitol Records.
  - **Look In:** Determines whether Access looks for the search criteria in the current field or in the entire datasheet.
  - **Match:** Determines whether the search criteria must exactly match the contents of the whole field, any part of the field, or the start of the field.
  - **Search:** Allows you to search the entire datasheet (All) or just those records before (Up) or after (Down) the current record.
  - **Match Case:** Determines whether the search criteria are case sensitive (e.g., TX versus Tx or tx).
  - **Search Fields As Formatted:** Determines whether the search criteria are compared to the actual value of the field or the formatted appearance of the value (e.g., 10 versus $10.00).
  - **Replace tab:** Provides a Replace With text box for you to specify replacement text. For example, you can find every occurrence of Corp and replace it with Corporation.

Clues to Use

Using wildcards

Wildcards are symbols you use as substitutes for characters to locate data that matches your criteria. Access uses these wildcards: the **asterisk (*)** represents any group of characters, the **question mark (?)** stands for any single character, and the **pound sign (#)** stands for a single number digit. For example, to find any word beginning with S, type s* in the Find What text box. Wildcards may be used in criteria used to find, filter, or query information. Filters and queries are covered later in this unit.

FIGURE B-11: Descending sort order based on the Retail field

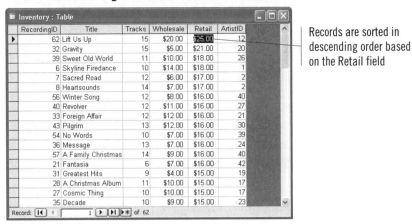

Records are sorted in descending order based on the Retail field

FIGURE B-12: Records filtered for values >15 in the Retail field

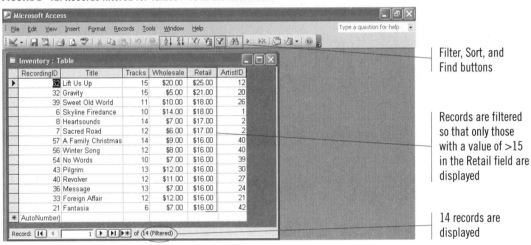

Filter, Sort, and Find buttons

Records are filtered so that only those with a value of >15 in the Retail field are displayed

14 records are displayed

FIGURE B-13: Find and Replace dialog box

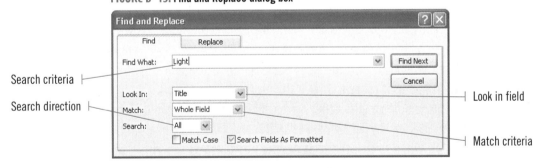

Search criteria

Search direction

Look in field

Match criteria

TABLE B-2: Sort, Filter, and Find buttons

name	button	purpose
Sort Ascending	⅔↓	Sorts records based on the selected field in ascending order (0 to 9, A to Z)
Sort Descending	⅔↓	Sorts records based on the selected field in descending order (Z to A, 9 to 0)
Filter By Selection	⅔	Filters records based on selected data and hides records that do not match
Filter By Form	⅔	Filters records based on more than one selection criteria by using the Filter by Form window
Apply Filter or Remove Filter	⅔	Applies or removes the filter
Find	⅔	Searches for a string of characters in the current field or all fields

Access 2003

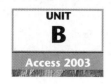
Sorting Records and Finding Data

The sort and find features are powerful tools that help you work more efficiently whether you are working with data in a datasheet or viewing it through a form. ▰▰ You want to create several different printouts of the Inventory datasheet to satisfy various MediaLoft departments. The Marketing Department wants the records sorted by Title. The Accounting Department wants the records sorted from the highest retail price to the lowest.

STEPS

1. **Double-click the** Inventory **table to open its datasheet, click any value in the** Title **field, then click the** Sort Ascending button ↓ **on the Table Datasheet toolbar**

   The records are sorted in ascending order by the values in the Title field, as shown in Figure B-14.

2. **Click any value in the** Retail **field, then click the** Sort Descending button ↓ **on the Table Datasheet toolbar**

   The products that sell for the highest retail price are listed first. If you printed the datasheet now, the records would be listed in the current sort order on the printout. Kelsey also asks you to find the titles that may be hot sellers during the Christmas season. Access lets you find all records based on search criteria.

3. **Click any value in the** Title **field, then click the** Find button ▦ **on the Table Datasheet toolbar**

   The Find and Replace dialog box opens with Title selected as the Look In field.

4. **Type** Christmas **in the Find What text box, click the** Match list arrow, **then click** Any Part of Field, **as shown in Figure B-15**

   "Christmas" is the search criteria. Access finds all occurrences of the word Christmas in the Title field, whether it is the first, middle, or last part of the title.

5. **Click** Find Next, **then drag the** title bar **of the Find and Replace dialog box up and to the right to better view the datasheet**

   The search starts with the record after the current record so if you started the search at the top of the datasheet, A Family Christmas, the thirteenth record in the sorted datasheet, is the first title found.

6. **Click** Find Next **to find the next occurrence of the word Christmas, then click** Find Next **as many times as it takes to move through all the records**

   When no more occurrences of the search criteria Christmas are found, Access provides a dialog box that tells you that no more matching records can be found.

7. **Click** OK **when prompted that Access has finished searching the records, then click** Cancel **to close the Find and Replace dialog box**

   If you close a datasheet without saving the layout changes, the records return to the original sort order based on the values in the primary key field. If you close a datasheet and save layout changes, the last sort order is saved.

FIGURE B-14: Inventory table sorted in ascending order by Title

Records are
sorted
ascending
by title

FIGURE B-15: Christmas is the search criterion for the Title field

Search
criterion

Find the
search
criterion
anywhere
in the field

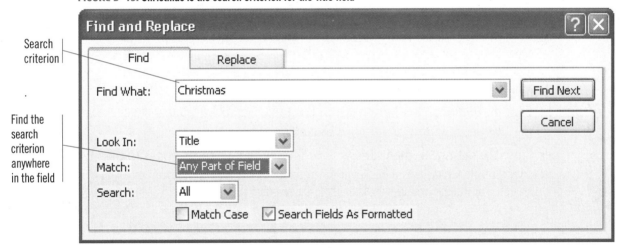

Clues to Use

Using more than one sort field

You may want to apply more than one sort field to a datasheet. For example, the telephone book sorts records by last name (**primary sort field**) and when ties occur on the last name (for example, two or more Johnson entries), the entries are further sorted by the first name (**secondary sort field**). You may sort by more than one field in a datasheet by selecting more than one field name (by dragging through the field name row) before clicking a sort button. Using this method, though, the sort fields must be positioned beside one another. The leftmost field is the primary sort field, the field to its right is the secondary sort field, and so forth. If you want to sort a datasheet by fields that are not positioned next to one another, use a query, which is covered later in this unit.

Filtering Records

Filtering the datasheet temporarily displays only those records that match given criteria. **Criteria** are rules or limiting conditions you set. For example, you may want to show only those records where the Title field contains the word "Christmas" or where the Wholesale field is less than $10. Once you have filtered the records in a datasheet or form, you can sort or find data within the subset of records just as if you were working with all of the records. ▓▓▓▓ The Marketing Department asks you for a listing of titles that contain the word "Christmas" with a retail price of 15 or more. You filter the records to provide this information.

STEPS

1. **Double-click the word** Christmas **in the Title field for RecordingID 28, then click the** Filter By Selection button 🔲 **on the Table Datasheet toolbar**

   Four records are selected, as shown in Figure B-16. Filter By Selection is a fast and easy way to filter the records for an exact match (in this case, where the Title field contains a word that is *equal to* Christmas). To filter for comparative data and to specify more complex criteria including **comparison operators** (for example, where Retail is *equal to or greater than* 15), you must use the Filter By Form feature. See Table B-3 for more information about comparison operators.

   QUICK TIP
   If criteria become lengthy, you can widen a column to display the entire criteria entry by dragging the right edge of the column to the right. If you need to clear previous criteria, click the Clear Grid button 🔲.

2. **Click the** Filter By Form button 🔲 **on the Table Datasheet toolbar, click the** Retail **criteria cell, then type** >=15

   The Filter by Form window is shown in Figure B-17. The previous Filter By Selection criteria that you initiated directly on the datasheet, Like "*Christmas*", in the Title field, is still in the grid. Access distinguishes between text and numeric entries by placing quotation marks around text entries. Access also inserts the operator Like and wildcard asterisks in the "*Christmas*" criteria to help you find Christmas in any location of the Title field. Filter By Form is more powerful than Filter By Selection because it allows you to enter criteria for more than one field so that *both* criteria must be true to show the record in the resulting datasheet.

3. **Click the** Apply Filter button 🔲 **on the Table Datasheet toolbar**

   Only three records are true for both criteria. The record navigation buttons in the lower-left corner of the datasheet display how many records were chosen for the filtered subset. The Apply Filter button becomes the Remove Filter button after a filter is applied.

   QUICK TIP
   Be sure to remove existing filters before applying a new filter or you will apply a filter to the current subset of records instead of applying the filter to the entire datasheet.

4. **Click the** Remove Filter button 🔲 **on the Table Datasheet toolbar**

   The datasheet redisplays all 62 records when the filter is removed.

5. **Close the datasheet, then click** No **if prompted to save the changes to the Inventory table**

   Saving a table layout saves the last sort order, but filters are always removed when you close a datasheet, regardless of whether you save the changes to the layout.

FIGURE B-16: Inventory datasheet filtered for Christmas in the Title field

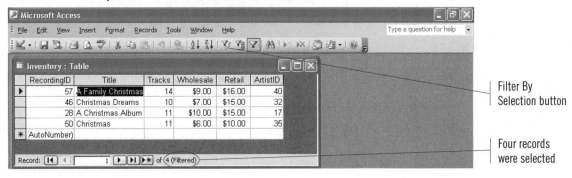

Filter By
Selection button

Four records
were selected

FIGURE B-17: Filter by Form window

Clear Grid
button

* wildcards
used to find
Christmas
anywhere in
Title field

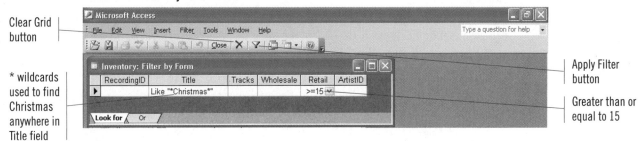

Apply Filter
button

Greater than or
equal to 15

TABLE B-3: Comparison operators

operator	description	expression	meaning
>	Greater than	>500	Numbers greater than 500
>=	Greater than or equal to	>=500	Numbers greater than or equal to 500
<	Less than	<"Braveheart"	Names from A to Braveheart, but not Braveheart
<=	Less than or equal to	<="Bridgewater"	Names from A through, and including, Bridgewater
<>	Not equal to	<>"Fontanelle"	Any name except for Fontanelle

Clues to Use

Searching for blank fields

Is Null and **Is Not Null** are two other types of common criteria. Is Null criteria finds all records where no entry has been made in the field. Is Not Null finds all records where there is any entry in the field, even if the entry is 0. Primary key fields cannot have a null entry.

Creating a Query

A **query** is a database object that creates a datasheet of selected fields and records from one or more tables. You can edit, navigate, sort, find, and filter a query's datasheet just like a table's datasheet. A query is similar to a filter, but much more powerful. For example, a query is a saved object within the database. Filtering creates only a temporary view of the data. Table B-4 compares queries and filters. ▰▰▱▱▱ You use the Simple Query Wizard to build a query to display information from both the Inventory and Artists tables in one datasheet.

STEPS

1. **Click** Queries **on the Objects bar, then double-click** Create query by using wizard
   The Simple Query Wizard dialog box opens asking you to select the fields that you want to view.

2. **Double-click** ArtistFirst, **double-click** ArtistLast, **double-click** Group, **click the** Tables/Queries **list arrow, click** Table:Inventory, **double-click** Title, **then double-click** Retail
   The Simple Query Wizard dialog box should look like Figure B-18.

3. **Click** Next, **click** Next **to accept the** Detail option, **type** Product List **for the query title, then click** Finish
   The Product List query's datasheet opens with 62 records, each with the five fields of information you requested, as shown in Figure B-19. You can use a query datasheet to edit or add information.

4. **Double-click** Kenny **in the ArtistFirst cell for the first record, type** Kenneth, **then press** [↓]
   Editing data through a query datasheet changes the data in the underlying table just as if you were working directly in the table's datasheet. In this case, Kenny changed to Kenneth in the second record as well as the first because this artist's first name is stored only once in the Artists table, but it is selected for this datasheet twice because this artist is related to two records in the Inventory table (via the common ArtistID field). A query is sometimes called a **logical view** of the data because it is not a copy of the data, but rather, a selected view of data from the underlying tables.

5. **Click the** Design View button ▨ **on the Query Datasheet toolbar**
   The Query Design View opens, showing you **field lists** for the Inventory and Artists tables in the upper portion of the window, and the fields you have requested for this query in the **query design grid** (also called the **query grid**) in the lower portion of the window.

   > **QUICK TIP**
   > Query criteria are not case sensitive.

6. **Click the** Criteria cell **for the Group field, then type** Justice **as shown in Figure B-20**
   Query Design View is used to add, delete, or change the order of fields, sort the records, or add criteria to limit the number of records shown in the resulting datasheet. Any change made in Query Design View is saved with the query object.

7. **Click the** Datasheet View button ▦ **on the Query Design toolbar**
   The resulting datasheet has five records that match the Justice criteria in the Group field. To save this query with a more descriptive name than the one currently displayed in the query title bar, use the Save As command on the File menu.

8. **Click** File **on the menu bar, click** Save As, **type** Justice Titles **in the Save Query text box, click** OK, **then close the query datasheet**
   Both the original Product List and the modified Justice Titles queries are saved in this database. You can double-click a query to reopen it in Query Datasheet View.

FIGURE B-18: Simple Query Wizard

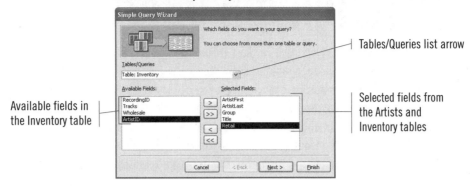

Tables/Queries list arrow

Available fields in the Inventory table

Selected fields from the Artists and Inventory tables

FIGURE B-19: Product List datasheet

Design View button

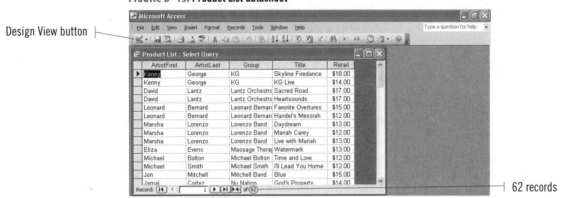

62 records

FIGURE B-20: Query Design View

Datasheet View button

Artists field list

Inventory field list

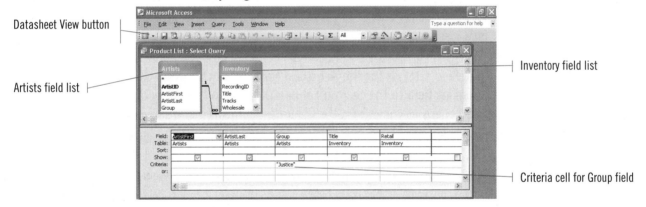

Criteria cell for Group field

TABLE B-4: Queries versus filters

characteristics	filters	queries
Are saved as an object in the database	No	Yes
Can be used to select a subset of records in a datasheet	Yes	Yes
Can be used to select a subset of fields in a datasheet	No	Yes
Its resulting datasheet can be used to enter and edit data	Yes	Yes
Its resulting datasheet can be used to sort, filter, and find records	Yes	Yes
Is commonly used as the source of data for a form or report	No	Yes
Can calculate sums, averages, counts, and other types of summary statistics across records	No	Yes
Can be used to create calculated fields	No	Yes

Access 2003

Modifying a Query

To modify an existing query, you work in **Query Design View**. The upper portion of Query Design View displays the field lists for each table used by the query. The lower portion of Query Design View displays the query grid where you add or change the fields displayed by the query, add criteria to determine which records will be selected, define sort orders, and build calculated fields. To delete or move a field in the query grid, you select it by clicking its field selector. The **field selector** is the thin gray bar above each field in the query grid. ▓▓▓▓ You want to modify the Justice Titles query in a variety of ways. You use Query Design View to make the changes and then print the resulting datasheet.

STEPS

QUICK TIP

Right-click an object and click Design View on the shortcut menu to open it in this view.

1. **Click the** Justice Titles query **in the MediaLoft-B database window, then click the** Design button ▨ **on the database window toolbar**

   Query Design View opens, displaying the fields and criteria for the Justice Titles query. To add fields to the query, drag the fields from their field list to the position in the query design grid where you want them to appear on the datasheet.

TROUBLE

If some information in Query Design View is not visible, use the scroll bars to view other parts of the window.

2. **Drag the** Tracks field **from the Inventory field list to the** Retail Field cell **in the query design grid, double-click the** Wholesale field **in the Inventory field list, then scroll to the right in the query grid**

   The Tracks field is added to the query design grid between the Title and Retail fields. Double-clicking a field adds it to the next available column in the grid, as shown in Figure B-21. You can also delete fields in the existing query grid.

3. **Scroll to the left in the query grid, click the** field selector **for the** ArtistFirst **field, then press** [Delete]

   Deleting a field from Query Design View does not affect the data stored in the underlying table. Deleting a field from a query only means that this field is not displayed on the datasheet for this query. To move fields, drag the field selector.

4. **Click the** field selector **for the ArtistLast field to select it, then drag the** field selector **for the ArtistLast field to the second column position in the query design grid**

   Now that the fields are rearranged in the datasheet as shown in Figure B-22, you're ready to set the sort orders.

TROUBLE

Click the field selector for a field to select it, release the mouse button, then drag the field selector for the chosen field. A thin black vertical bar indicates where the field is positioned as you drag it.

5. **Click the** Sort cell **for the Group field, click the** Sort list arrow, **click** Ascending, **click the** Sort cell **for the Title field, click the** Sort list arrow, **click** Ascending, **then click the** Datasheet View button ▦ **on the Query Design toolbar to view the resulting datasheet**

   Because the only value in the Group field is Justice, the secondary sort field, Title, is used to determine the order of the records. If you add another Group to this datasheet, however, both sort fields are used to determine the order of the records.

6. **Click the** Design View button ▨ **on the Query Datasheet toolbar, click the** or Criteria cell **below "Justice", then type** Clownfish

   The row into which query criteria is entered is extremely important. Criteria entered on the same row must *both* be true for a record to be selected. Criteria entered on different rows are evaluated separately; a record need only be true for *one* row of criteria in order to be selected for the resulting datasheet.

QUICK TIP

If you want your name on the printout, change the ArtistLast field to your own last name before printing the datasheet.

7. **Click** ▦

   The final datasheet is shown in Figure B-23. Seven records matched the criterion entered in the query grid. Also note that the Group field is used as the primary sort order—the Clownfish records sorted before the Justice records. The values in the Title field were used as the secondary sort order. You can specify as many sort orders as you desire in Query Design View, but they are always evaluated from left to right.

8. **Click the** Print button ▤, **close the datasheet without saving changes, close the MediaLoft-B.mdb database, then exit Access**

FIGURE B-21: Tracks field added to query grid

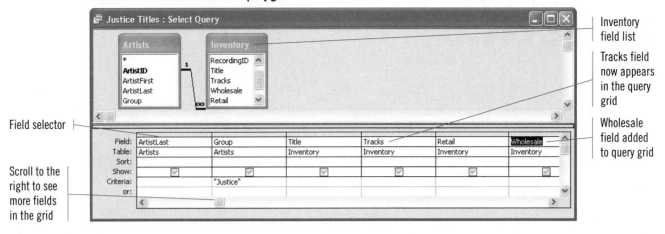

Inventory field list

Tracks field now appears in the query grid

Wholesale field added to query grid

Field selector

Scroll to the right to see more fields in the grid

FIGURE B-22: New field arrangement

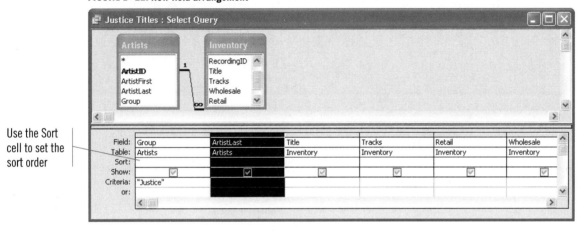

Use the Sort cell to set the sort order

FIGURE B-23: Final datasheet

Primary sort

Secondary sort

Records must match the criteria entered in the query gird

Access 2003

Clues to Use

Understanding And and Or criteria

Criteria placed on different rows of the query design grid are called **Or criteria**. In other words, a record may be true for one row *or* another row in order for it to be displayed on the resulting datasheet. Placing additional criteria in the *same* row, however, creates **And criteria**. In other words, records must meet the criteria for one criterion *and* all other criteria entered on one row in order to be chosen for that datasheet. As you add additional rows of criteria (Or criteria) to the query design grid, you increase the number of records displayed on the resulting datasheet because the record needs to be true for the criteria in only *one* of the rows to be displayed on the datasheet for that query.

Practice

▼ CONCEPTS REVIEW

Label each element of the Access window shown in Figure B-24.

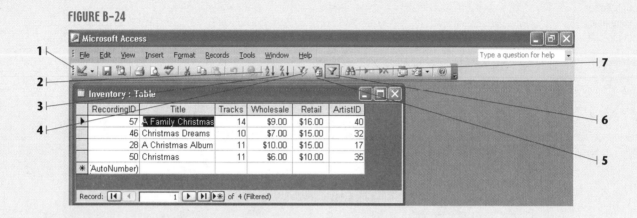

FIGURE B-24

Match each term with the statement that best describes it.

8. **Primary key**

9. **Table Wizard**

10. **Filter**

11. **Data type**

12. **Query**

13. **AutoNumber**

14. **One-to-many relationship**

15. **Foreign key**

a. Determines what type of data can be stored in each field

b. Provides interactive help to create the field names and data types for each field in a new table

c. Creates a datasheet of selected fields and records from one or more tables

d. Contains unique information for each record

e. Creates a temporary subset of records

f. Links two tables together

g. Serves as the common field in the "many" table in a one-to-many relationship

h. Inserts a sequential integer as the field value for each new record

Select the best answer from the list of choices.

16. **Which data type would be best for a field that stores Web addresses?**
   a. Text
   b. Memo
   c. OLE
   d. Hyperlink

17. **Which data type would be best for a field that stores telephone numbers?**
   a. Text
   b. Number
   c. OLE
   d. Hyperlink

18. **Which data type would be best for a field that stores birth dates?**
   a. Text
   b. Number
   c. AutoNumber
   d. Date/Time

19. **Sorting refers to:**
   a. Reorganizing the records in either ascending or descending order.
   b. Selecting a subset of fields and/or records to view as a datasheet from one or more tables.
   c. Displaying only those records that meet certain criteria.
   d. Using Or and And criteria in the query design grid.

20. **Each of the following is true about a filter, *except*:**
   a. It creates a temporary datasheet of records that match criteria.
   b. The resulting datasheet can be sorted.
   c. The resulting datasheet includes all fields.
   d. A filter is automatically saved as an object in the database.

▼ SKILLS REVIEW

1. **Organize fields.**
   a. Organize the fields of a database that contains the names and addresses of physicians and clinics. You might use a telephone book to gather information.
   b. On paper, write down the field names in one column and the data types for each field in the second column.

2. **Plan related tables.**
   a. Organize the fields into two tables: Clinics and Physicians. Identify a primary key field for each table.
   b. Determine how the tables will be related in a one-to-many relationship.
   c. Identify a primary key field for both tables.
   d. Add the foreign key field to the "many" table.

3. **Create a table.**
   a. Start Access and use the Blank database option to create a database. Save the file as **Medical Directory.mdb** in the drive and folder where your Data Files are stored.
   b. Use the Table Wizard to create a new table. Use the Contacts sample table found in the Business database category.
   c. Choose sample fields in the following order: ContactID, FirstName, LastName, Title.
   d. Name the table **Physicians**, and select the No, I'll set the primary key field option button.
   e. Accept the default options for the primary key field.
   f. Click the Modify the table design option button, then click Finish.

4. **Modify a table.**
   a. In the first available blank row, add a new field called **ClinicNo** with a Number data type.
   b. Change the Field Size property of the Title field from 50 to **4**.
   c. Add the field description **M.D. or D.O.** to the Title field.
   d. Save the Physicians table, display its datasheet, and enter one record using your own information in the name fields. Remember that the ContactID field is specified with an AutoNumber data type so Access automatically enters a value in that field as you add the record. Enter **1** for the ClinicNo value.
   e. Preview then print the datasheet.
   f. Close the Physicians table and the Medical Directory.mdb database.

5. **Format a datasheet.**

   a. Open the **Medical Directory-B.mdb** database from the drive and folder where your Data Files are stored. Open the Physicians table datasheet.

   b. Change the font of the datasheet to Arial Narrow, and the font size to **9**.

   c. Change the gridline color to black, and remove the vertical gridlines.

   d. Change the values for the First and Last fields of the first record to your own name, then preview and print the datasheet. Close the Physicians datasheet without saving the formatting changes.

6. **Understand sorting, filtering, and finding.**

   a. On a sheet of paper, identify three ways that you might want to sort a list of addresses. Be sure to specify both the field you would sort on and the sort order (ascending or descending).

   b. On a sheet of paper, identify three ways that you might want to filter a list of addresses. Be sure to specify both the field you would filter on and the criteria that you would use.

7. **Sort records and find data.**

   a. Open the Physicians datasheet, sort the records in ascending order on the Last field, then list the first two last names on paper.

   b. Sort the Physicians records in descending order on the ClinicNo field, then list the first two entries in the Last field on paper.

   c. Find the records in which the Title field contains D.O. Write down how many records you found.

8. **Filter records.**

   a. In the Physicians datasheet, filter the records for all physicians with a last name that starts with the letter "B". (*Hint:* Select only the letter B for an entry that starts with "B" in the Last field, then click the Filter By Selection button).

   b. Filter the records for all physicians with a last name that starts with the letter "B" as well as those with a title of D.O. Change "Baskets" in the Last field to your own last name, then print the datasheet.

   c. Close the Physicians datasheet without saving changes.

9. **Create a query.**

   a. Use the Query Wizard to create a new query with the following fields: First and Last (from the Physicians table), ClinicName, City, State, Zip, and Phone (from the Clinics table).

   b. Name the query **Clinics in Missouri**, then view the datasheet.

   c. In Query Design View, add the criterion **MO** to the State field, then view and print the datasheet.

10. **Modify a query.**

    a. Modify the Clinics in Missouri query to include only those doctors in Kansas City, Missouri. (*Hint:* Both criteria entries must be in the same row of the query grid, but in different columns.)

    b. Save the query with the name **Clinics in Kansas City Missouri**. Print the query results, then close the query datasheet.

    c. Modify the Clinics in Kansas City Missouri query so that the ClinicName field is the First field in the datasheet.

    d. Sort the records in ascending order on the ClinicName field, then in ascending order on the Last field.

    e. Print and save the sorted datasheet, then close the datasheet.

    f. Close the **Medical Directory-B.mdb** database, then exit Access.

▼ INDEPENDENT CHALLENGE 1

You want to start a database to track your personal movie collection.

a. Start Access and create a new database called **Movies.mdb** in the drive and folder where your Data Files are stored.

b. Using the Table Wizard, create a table based on the Video Collection sample table in the Personal category with the following fields: MovieTitle, YearReleased, Rating, Length, DateAcquired, PurchasePrice.

c. Enter the name **Collection** for the table and allow Access to set a primary key field.

d. Modify the Collection table in Design View with the following changes:

- Delete the Rating Field. (*Hint*: Use the Delete Rows button on the Table Design toolbar.)
- Rename the YearReleased field to **Year**, and the DateAcquired field to **PurchaseDate**.
- Give the Length field a Number data type.
- Add a field between Year and Length called **PersonalRating** with a Number data type.
- In the Description of the PersonalRating field, enter: **My personal rating from 1 (bad) to 10 (great)**.
- Add a field between the PersonalRating and Length fields called **Rated** with a Text data type.
- In the Description of the Rated field, enter: **G, PG, PG-13, R**.
- Change the Field Size property of the Rated field to **5**.
- Add a field between the Rated and Length called **Format** with a Text data type.
- In the Description of the Format field, enter: **VCR, DVD**.

e. Save the Collection table, and then open it in Datasheet View.

f. Enter five records with sample data, then preview the datasheet. Use the Setup button to change the page orientation to landscape.

g. If the printout spans two pages, return to Datasheet View, narrow the columns, and then preview the datasheet again. When you have narrowed the columns or formatted the data so that it prints on a single piece of paper, print the datasheet, close the Collection table, close the **Movies.mdb** database, then exit Access.

▼ INDEPENDENT CHALLENGE 2

You work for a marketing company that sells medical supplies to doctors' offices.

a. Start Access and open the **Medical Directory-B.mdb** database from the drive and folder where your Data Files are stored, then open the Clinics table datasheet.

b. Filter the records to find all clinics in the city of **Grandview**, modify column widths so that all data is visible, edit the Grandview entry for Cancer Specialists to the name of your hometown, then preview and print the datasheet in landscape orientation.

c. Remove the filter, sort the records in ascending order by Zip, then change the cell color to silver. (*Hint*: Use the Fill/Back Color button on the Formatting toolbar.) Change the font style to bold, then print the datasheet in landscape orientation.

d. Close the Clinics datasheet without saving the changes.

e. Using the Query Wizard, create a query with the following fields: First and Last from the Physicians table and Phone from the Clinics table.

f. Name the query **Telephone List**. Sort the records in ascending order by last name, then print the datasheet. Close the query without saving the changes.

g. In Query Design View of the Telephone List query, delete the First field, then add the Title field between the existing Last and Phone fields. Add an ascending sort order to the Phone field. Save, view, and print the datasheet.

▼ INDEPENDENT CHALLENGE 2 (CONTINUED)

Advanced Challenge Exercise

- In Query Design View of the Telephone List query, add the Address2 field to the fourth column.
- Add criteria so that only those records where there is no entry in the Address2 field are displayed on the resulting datasheet. (*Hint*: Use **Is Null** criteria for the Address2 field.)
- View the datasheet, then print and close the Telephone List query without saving the changes.

h. Close the **Medical Directory-B.mdb** database, then exit Access.

▼ INDEPENDENT CHALLENGE 3

You want to create a database to keep track of your personal contacts.

a. Start Access and create a new database called **People.mdb** in the drive and folder where your Data Files are stored.

b. Using the Table Wizard, create a table based on the Addresses sample table in the Personal category with the following fields: FirstName, LastName, SpouseName, Address, City, StateOrProvince, PostalCode, EmailAddress, HomePhone, Birthdate.

c. Name the table **Contacts**, allow Access to set the primary key field, and choose the Enter data directly into the table option in the last Table Wizard dialog box.

d. Enter at least five records into the table, making sure that two people have the same last name. Use your name in the First Name and Last Name fields of one of the records. Note that the ContactsID field has an AutoNumber data type.

e. Sort the records in ascending order by last name, then save and close the Contacts datasheet.

f. Using the Query Wizard, create a query with the following fields:
LastName, FirstName, Birthdate. Name the query **Birthday List**.

g. In Query Design View, sort the records in ascending order by LastName and then by FirstName.

h. Save the query as **Sorted Birthday List**, then view the query. Change the Birthdate value to **1/6/71** for your record.

i. Modify the datasheet by making font and color changes, print it, then close it without saving it.

Advanced Challenge Exercise

- Open the datasheet for the Contacts table and observe the Birthdate value for your record. On a piece of paper, explain why the 1/6/71 value appears in the datasheet for the table when you entered this date while working with the datasheet of the Sorted Birthday List query.
- On paper, explain why the 1/6/71 value was saved even though you closed the query without saving the layout changes.

j. Close the Contacts table, close the **People.mdb** database, then exit Access.

▼ INDEPENDENT CHALLENGE 4

You are on the staff of an economic development team whose goal is to encourage tourism in the Baltic Sea region. You have created an Access database called Baltic-B.mdb to track important fields of information on the countries in that region, and use the Internet to find information about the area.

FIGURE B-25

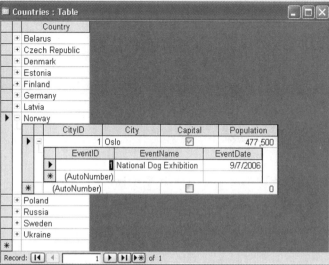

a. Start Access and open the **Baltic-B.mdb** database from the drive and folder where your Data Files are stored.

b. Open the Countries table datasheet, then click the expand button to the left of Norway as well as to the left of Oslo using Figure B-25 as a guide.

c. This arrangement of data shows you how events are tracked by city, and how cities are tracked by country in the Baltic-B database.

d. Create a query that selects the City, Population, Country, and Capital fields from the Cities table. Show details, name the query **City Info**, then display, print, and close the datasheet.

e. Create a query with the City and Country fields from the Cities table, and the EventName and EventDate fields from the Events table. Show details, name the query **List of Events**, then display, print, and close it.

Advanced Challenge Exercise

■ Connect to the Internet, then go your favorite search engine to conduct some research for the database. Your goal is to enter at least one city record (the country's capital city) for each country. Be sure to enter the Population data for that particular city, rather than for the entire country. You can enter the data by expanding the country record sub-datasheets as shown for Norway in Figure B-25, or by entering the records directly into the Cities datasheet.

■ Return to the search engine, and research upcoming tourist events for Oslo, Norway. Enter three more events for Oslo into the database. You can enter the data into the Event subdatasheet shown in Figure B-25, or enter the records directly into the Events datasheet by opening the Events table datasheet. If you enter the records into the Events datasheet, remember that the CityID field value for Oslo is 1.

■ Reopen, then print and close the **City Info** and **List of Event** datasheets.

f. Close the **Baltic-B.mdb** database, then exit Access.

Access 2003

▼ VISUAL WORKSHOP

Open the **MediaLoft-B.mdb** database from the drive and folder where your Data Files are stored. Create a query based on the Inventory and Artists tables that displays the datasheet shown in Figure B-26. Name the query **Most Tracks**. Filter the query for only those records with a value of 15 or greater in the Tracks field, and sort the query by the Group field.

FIGURE B-26

Using Forms

OBJECTIVES

Plan a form
Create a form
Move and resize controls
Modify labels
Use text boxes for calculations
Modify tab order
Enter, edit, and print records
Insert an image

If you have a SAM user profile, you may have access to hands-on instruction, practice, and assessment of the skills covered in this unit. Log in to your SAM account and go to your assignments page to see what your instructor has assigned.

Forms are the primary type of Access object used to enter and edit data. Although the datasheet view of a table or a query object can also be used to navigate, enter, and edit data, some fields for one record are sometimes not visible unless you scroll left or right. A form solves that problem by allowing you to design the layout of fields on the screen in any arrangement. A form also supports graphical elements such as pictures, buttons, and tabs, which make the form's data easy to understand and use. Kelsey Lang, the marketing manager for MediaLoft, asks you to create forms to make information easier to access, enter, and update in the MediaLoft database.

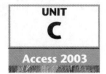

Planning a Form

Properly organized and well-designed forms make a tremendous difference in the productivity of the end user. Forms are often built to match a **source document** (for example, a paper employment application or a medical history form) to facilitate fast and accurate data entry. Now, however, it is becoming more common to type data directly into the database rather than first recording it on paper. Therefore, form design considerations, such as clearly labeled fields and appropriate formatting, are extremely important. Other form design considerations include how the user tabs from field to field, and what type of control is used. A **control** is an element placed on the form to display or describe data. See Table C-1 for more information on form controls. Before you create a form, you plan the form on paper to share your plans with Kelsey.

DETAILS

Consider the following form design tasks to plan a form:

- **Gather the source documents used to design your form**

  Find all existing source documents (if building the form to match an existing process) and sketch the Access form on paper. This helps you make sure that you identify every control, including fields, text, and graphics that you want the form to display.

- **Determine the best type of control to use for each item on the form**

  Figures C-1 and C-2 show examples of several controls. **Bound controls** display data from the underlying record source and are also used to edit and enter data. **Unbound controls** do not change from record to record and exist only to clarify and enhance the appearance of the form.

- **Determine the underlying record source**

  The **record source** supplies the data that is presented by the bound controls on the form. The record source may be either the fields and records of a single table, or those selected by a query. The record source is also called the **recordset**.

- **Name the form**

  Name your form with its specific purpose, such as "Artist Entry Form".

FIGURE C-1: Form controls

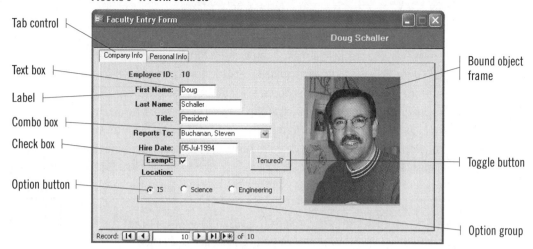

FIGURE C-2: Form controls

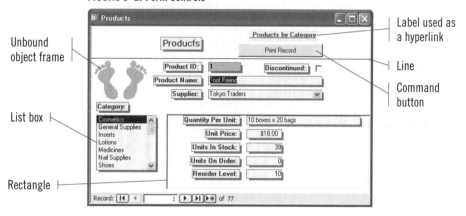

TABLE C-1: Form controls

name	used to	bound	unbound
Label	Provide consistent descriptive text as you navigate from record to record; the label is the most common type of unbound control and can also be used as a hyperlink to another database object, external file, or Web page		x
Text box	Display, edit, or enter data for each record from an underlying record source; the text box is the most common type of bound control	x	
List box	Display a list of possible data entries	x	
Combo box	Display a list of possible data entries for a field, and provide a text box for an entry from the keyboard; combines the list box and text box controls	x	
Tab control	Create a three-dimensional aspect to a form		x
Check box	Display "yes" or "no" answers for a field; if the box is checked, it means "yes"	x	
Toggle button	Display "yes" or "no" answers for a field; if the button is pressed, it means "yes"	x	
Option button	Display a choice for a field	x	
Option group	Display and organize choices (usually presented as option buttons) for a field	x	
Bound object frame	Display data stored by an OLE (Object Linking and Embedding) field, such as a picture	x	
Unbound object frame	Display a picture or clip art image that doesn't change from record to record		x
Line and Rectangle	Draw lines and rectangles on the form		x
Command button	Provide an easy way to initiate a command or run a macro		x

Creating a Form

There are many ways to create a form. You can create a form from scratch using **Form Design View**, or you can use the **Form Wizard** to provide guided steps for developing a form. The Form Wizard prompts you to select the record source for the form, choose a layout, choose a style, and title the form. The Form Wizard is an easy way to create an initial version of a form. Table C-2 summarizes the ways to create a form. No matter what technique is used to create a form, you use Form Design View to modify an existing form object. You decide to use the Form Wizard to build an initial version of your first form in the MediaLoft database, the Artists Entry Form.

1. **Start Access, click the** More **link in the task pane, then open the** MediaLoft-C.mdb **database from the drive and folder where your Data Files are stored**

    QUICK TIP
    To access additional form wizards and AutoForms, click the New button 🔳 on the database window toolbar.

2. **Click** Forms **on the Objects bar in the MediaLoft-C database window, then double-click** Create form by using wizard **in the database window**

    The Form Wizard dialog box opens, prompting you to identify the record source for the form. The Artists table will serve as the record source for this form.

3. **Click the** Select All Fields button >>

    At this point, you could select more fields from other table or query objects if you wanted to add other fields to the form. In this case, you'll base the new form only on the fields of the Artists table.

4. **Click** Next, **click the** Columnar layout option button, **click** Next, **click the** Standard style, **click** Next, **type** Artists Entry Form **as the title for the form, then click** Finish

    The Artists Entry Form opens in **Form View**, as shown in Figure C-3. Descriptive labels appear in the first column, and text boxes that display data from the underlying record source appear in the second column. You can enter, edit, find, sort, and filter records using a form. The sort, filter, and find features work the same way in a form as they do in a datasheet.

    QUICK TIP
    Always click in a text box to identify which field you want to sort or filter before clicking the sort or filter buttons.

5. **Click** KG **in the Group text box, click the** Sort Ascending button ⬆️ **on the Form View toolbar, then click the** Next Record button ▶️ **four times to move to the fifth record**

    Numbers sort before letters in a Text field so the group 4 Him appears before the group Ant Farm. The group Campfire is displayed in the fifth record. Information about the current record number and total number of records appears by the Record navigation buttons.

6. **Click the** Last Record button ▶️❙

    The group Youngsters is the last record when the records are sorted in ascending order by the Group field.

7. **Close the Artists Entry Form**

    The last sort order is automatically saved when you close a form. Filters are automatically removed when you close a form just as they are for a datasheet.

FIGURE C-3: New form open in Form View

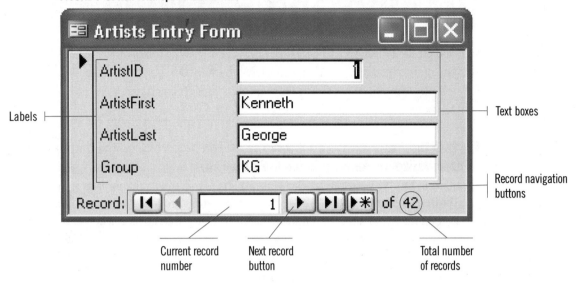

Labels

Text boxes

Record navigation buttons

Current record number

Next record button

Total number of records

TABLE C-2: Form creation techniques

technique	description
Form Design View	Provides a layout screen in which the form developer has complete control over the data, layout, and formatting choices that the form will display. Because Form Design View is the most powerful and flexible technique used to create a form, it is also the most complex. Form Design View is also used to modify existing forms, regardless of how they were created.
Form Wizard	Provides a guided series of steps to create a form. Prompts for record source, layout, style, and title.
AutoForm	Instantly creates a form that displays all the fields in the chosen record source. The five different AutoForm options (Columnar, Tabular, Datasheet, PivotTable, and PivotChart) correspond to five different form layouts in the New Form dialog box.
Chart Wizard	Provides a guided series of steps to create a graphical arrangement of data in the form of a business chart such as a bar, column, line, or pie chart that is placed on a form.
PivotTable Wizard	Provides a guided series of steps to create a summarized arrangement of data in a form called a PivotTable. Fields used for the column and row headings determine how the data is grouped and summarized.

Clues to Use

Using the AutoForm button

You can quickly create a form by clicking a table or query object in the database window, then clicking the New Object: AutoForm button on the Database toolbar. The New Object: AutoForm button offers no prompts or dialog boxes; it instantly creates a new form that contains all the fields in the selected table or query.

Moving and Resizing Controls

After you create a form, you can work in Form Design View to modify the size, location, and appearance of existing controls. Form Design View also allows you to add or delete controls. ▞▞▞▞ You decide to move and resize the controls on the Artists Entry Form to improve the layout.

STEPS

1. **Click the** Artists Entry Form, **click the** Design button ⬛ **on the database window toolbar, then resize the form as shown in Figure C-4**

   In Form Design View, several elements that help you design the form may automatically appear. The **Toolbox toolbar** contains buttons that help you to add controls to the form. The **field list** contains the fields in the record source (in this case, the Artists table). You can drag fields out of the field list to add them to the form. The vertical and horizontal **rulers** help you position controls on the form. If you are not working with the Toolbox or the field list, you can toggle them off to unclutter your screen.

2. **If the Toolbox toolbar is visible, click the** Toolbox button ⬛ **on the Form Design toolbar to toggle it off, and if the field list is visible, click the** Field List button ⬛ **on the Form Design toolbar to toggle it off**

   Before moving, resizing, deleting, or otherwise modifying a control, you must select it.

3. **Click the** ArtistLast label, **then press** [Delete]

   Deleting a control on a form does not delete or modify data; deleting a control only removes it from this form.

4. **Click the** ArtistLast text box **to select it, then drag it to the right of the ArtistFirst text box using the** 🖐 **as shown in Figure C-5**

   The form automatically widens to accommodate the new position for the ArtistLast text box. **Sizing handles**, small black boxes, appear in the corners and edges of a selected control. When you work with controls, the mouse pointer shape is very important. Pointer shapes are summarized in Table C-3. You can move controls using the keyboard as well.

5. **Click the** Group text box **to select it, then press and hold** [Ctrl] **while pressing** [↑] **enough times to position the Group label and text box under the ArtistFirst label and ArtistFirst text box**

   The Group label is associated with the Group text box so it automatically moves as you reposition the Group text box. Use the 🖐 mouse pointer to move a single control.

6. **Click the** 0.5" **mark on the horizontal ruler to select all of the labels, then drag to the right the middle sizing handle on the left edge of any selected control using the** ↔ **pointer**

   Because three labels are selected, all three labels are resized at the same time. Narrowing the width of the labels pulls them closer to the text boxes that they describe.

7. **Click the** Form View button ⬛ **on the Form Design toolbar, then resize the final form as shown in Figure C-6**

   Moving and resizing controls requires great concentration and mouse control. Don't worry if your screen doesn't precisely match the figure, but do make sure that you understand how to use the move and resize mouse pointers in Form Design View. Precision and accuracy naturally develop with practice, but even experienced form designers regularly rely on the Undo button ⬛.

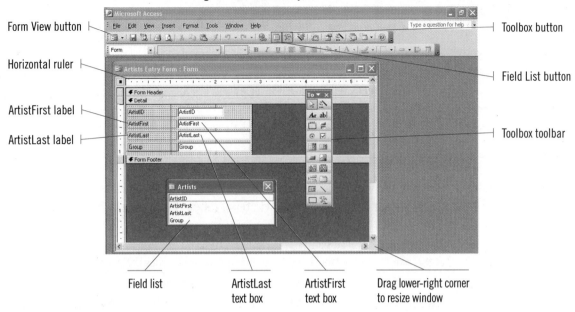

FIGURE C-4: Form Design View of Artists Entry Form

Form View button

Horizontal ruler

ArtistFirst label

ArtistLast label

Toolbox button

Field List button

Toolbox toolbar

Field list

ArtistLast
text box

ArtistFirst
text box

Drag lower-right corner
to resize window

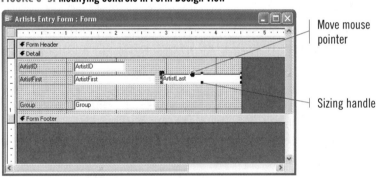

FIGURE C-5: Modifying controls in Form Design View

Move mouse
pointer

Sizing handle

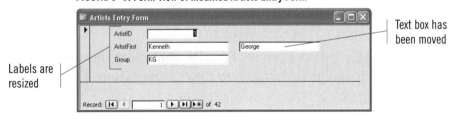

FIGURE C-6: Form View of modified Artists Entry Form

Text box has
been moved

Labels are
resized

TABLE C-3: Form Design View mouse pointer shapes

shape	when does this shape appear?	action
▷	When you point to any unselected control on the form (the default mouse pointer)	Single-clicking with this mouse pointer *selects* a control
✋	When you point to the edge of a selected control (but not when you are pointing to a sizing handle)	Dragging this mouse pointer *moves all selected controls*
☝	When you point to the larger sizing handle in the upper-left corner of a selected control	Dragging this mouse pointer *moves only the single control* where the pointer is currently positioned, not other controls that may also be selected
↔ ↕ ↗ ↖	When you point to any sizing handle (except the larger one in the upper-left corner)	Dragging this mouse pointer *resizes* the control

Modifying Labels

When you create a form with the Form Wizard, it places a label to the left of each text box that displays the name of the field. Often, you'll want to modify those labels to be more descriptive or user friendly. You can modify a label control by directly editing it in Form Design View, or you can use the property sheet to modify a control. The **property sheet** is a comprehensive listing of all **properties** (characteristics) for the selected control. You decide to modify the labels of the Artists Entry Form to be more descriptive.

STEPS

1. **Click the** Design View button ◩ **on the Form View toolbar, click anywhere on the form to deselect the three labels, click the** ArtistFirst label, **double-click the** ArtistFirst **text to select it, type** Artist Name, **then press** [Enter]

   Directly editing labels in Form Design View is tricky because you must single-click the label to select it, then double-click the text within the label to edit the text. If you double-click the edge of the label, you will open its property sheet, which provides another way to modify label text.

2. **Click the** ArtistID label, **click the** Properties button 🖀 **on the Form Design toolbar, then click the** Format tab, **as shown in Figure C-7**

   The title bar of the property sheet indicates what type of control is currently selected (in this case, a label). The **Caption** property on the Format tab controls the text displayed by the label.

3. **Click between the** t **and** I **in the Caption property, press** [Spacebar] **to modify the entry to be Artist ID, then click** 🖀 **to close the property sheet**

   Don't be overwhelmed by the number of properties available for each control on the form. Over time, you may want to learn about most of these properties, but in the beginning you'll be able to make most property changes through menu and toolbar options rather than by accessing the property sheet itself. For example, to right-align the labels you could modify the Text Align property in the property sheet for each label, or use the Align Right button ≣ on the Formatting (Form/Report) toolbar. To right-align all three labels at the same time, you need to select all three controls.

4. **Press and hold** [Shift] **while clicking the** Artist Name **and** Group labels **to add them to the selection, then click the** Align Right button ≣ **on the Formatting (Form/Report) toolbar**

   Now all three labels are positioned closer to the text boxes they describe as shown in Figure C-8. See Table C-4 for a list of techniques to quickly select several controls so that you can apply alignment and formatting changes to more than one control simultaneously.

5. **Click the** Save button 🖫 **on the Form Design toolbar, then click the** Form View button 🖼 **on the Form Design toolbar to view the changes in Form View**

   The labels are more descriptive and positioned closer to the text boxes they describe.

6. **Close the Artists Entry Form**

FIGURE C-7: Modifying a label using its property sheet

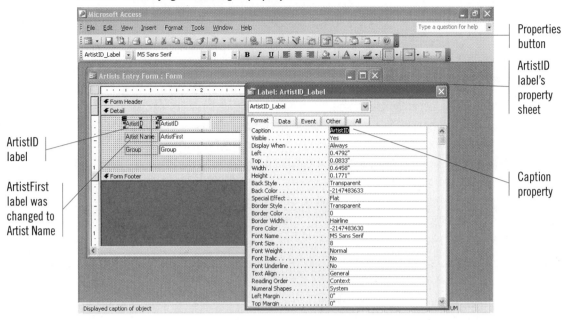

FIGURE C-8: Right-aligning labels

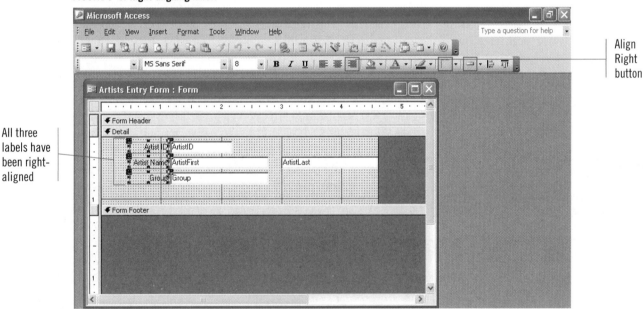

TABLE C-4: Selecting more than one control

technique	description
Click, [Shift]+click	Click a control, then press and hold [Shift] while clicking other controls; each one is selected
Drag a selection box	Drag a selection box (an outline box you create by dragging the pointer in Form Design View); every control that is in or is touched by the edges of the box is selected
Click in the ruler	Click in either the horizontal or vertical ruler to select all controls that intersect the selection line
Drag in the ruler	Drag through either the horizontal or vertical ruler to select all controls that intersect the selection line as it is dragged through the ruler

Using Text Boxes for Calculations

Text boxes are generally used to display data from underlying fields and are therefore *bound* to those fields. The name that appears in a text box control in Form Design View identifies the field to which the text box is bound. A text box control can also display a calculation. To create a calculation in a text box, you enter an **expression**, an equal sign, and a combination of symbols that calculates a result. For example, you could use a text box to store a numeric calculation that determines a commission. Or, you could use a text box to concatenate the values of two Text fields such as FirstName and LastName. You want to add a text box to the Item Entry Form to calculate the difference between the Retail and Wholesale values. You will work in Form Design View to accomplish this.

STEPS

TROUBLE

If the Toolbox is not visible, click ⚒ to toggle it on. Also, the Toolbox might be docked on the edge of your screen. Drag it to a convenient location.

1. **Click the** Item Entry Form **in the database window, then click the** Design button ⬕ **on the database window toolbar**

   The Item Entry Form opens in Form Design View where you can add, delete, or modify controls. To add a new text box control you will use the Toolbox toolbar.

2. **Click the** Text Box button ⓐⓑ **on the Toolbox toolbar, then click just below the** Wholesale text box **on the form**

   Adding a new text box automatically adds a new label to the left of the text box, too. The number in the default caption of the label depends on how many controls you have previously added to the form. First you will create the expression in the **calculated control** and then you will modify the label.

3. **Click** Unbound **in the new text box, type** =[Retail]-[Wholesale], **press [Enter], then widen the text box as necessary to see the entire expression as shown in Figure C-9**

   All expressions entered into a text box start with an equal sign (=). When referencing a field name within an expression, square brackets surround the field name. In an expression, you must type the field name exactly as it was created in Table Design View, but you do not need to worry about capitalization.

TROUBLE

If your calculated control did not work, delete it, then repeat Steps 2 through 4.

4. **Click the** Text18: label **to select the label control, double-click the** Text18: text **to select the text, type** Profit **as the new caption, press [Enter], then click the** Form View button ⊟ **to view the changes**

   The Profit text box for the first record correctly calculates the value of 4 ($18-$14) as shown in Form View in Figure C-10. Because this value represents money, you want to format it like the values in the Retail and Wholesale fields. Text boxes can be formatted in Form View using the Formatting toolbar or the property sheet.

QUICK TIP

If the Formatting (Form/Report) toolbar is not visible, right-click any visible toolbar and click Formatting (Form/Report).

5. **Click** 4 **in the Profit text box, click the** Align Right button ▤ **on the Formatting (Form/Report) toolbar, click** View **on the menu bar, then click** Properties

   Monetary values such as those in the calculated Profit field should be right-aligned and displayed with a currency format. You can give the values a currency format by modifying the Format property in the property sheet.

6. **Click the** Format tab **in the property sheet if it is not already selected, click the** Format list arrow, **then scroll and click** Currency

   A short description of the selected property appears in the status bar. While you can format text boxes in Form View, you can only make some modifications to controls, such as moving, deleting, or adding them, in Form Design View. Also, you can modify labels only in Form Design View.

7. **Click** ⬕, **then click the** Properties button ⚙ **to close the property sheet**

   Your last task is to move and resize the new controls to best match the existing layout of the form.

8. **Use the** ✥ **pointer to move the new label and text box and the** ↔ **pointer to resize the controls directly under the Wholesale label and text box, click the** Save button 🖫, **then click** ⊟

   The final form is shown in Figure C-11.

FIGURE C-9: Adding a text box to calculate a value

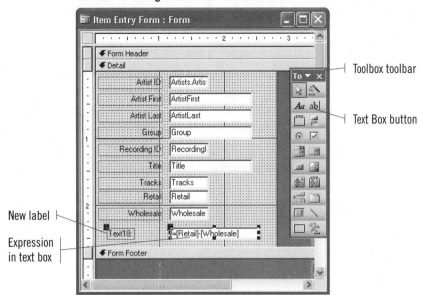

Toolbox toolbar

Text Box button

New label

Expression in text box

FIGURE C-10: Displaying a calculation in Form View

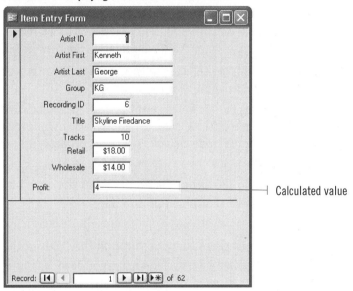

Calculated value

FIGURE C-11: Revised Item Entry Form

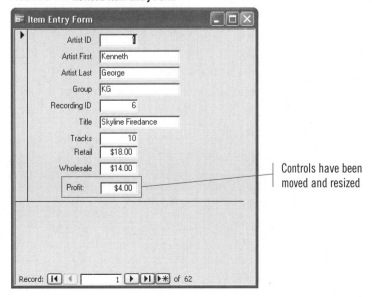

Controls have been moved and resized

Access 2003

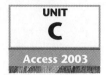

Modifying Tab Order

Once all of the controls have been positioned on the form, you'll want to check the tab order. The **tab order** is the order in which the focus moves as you press [Tab] in Form View. **Focus** refers to which field would be edited if you started typing. Generally, you want the focus to move from the top to the bottom through each consecutive bound control on the form. Unbound controls such as labels and lines cannot have the focus in Form View because they are not used to enter or edit data. ⬛⬛⬛ You check the tab order of the Item Entry Form, then change the tab order as necessary in Form Design View.

TROUBLE

If you press [Tab] 10 times, you will move to the first field of the second record. Press [Shift]+[Tab] to tab backward or click the Previous Record button to return to the first record.

1. **Press [Tab] nine times, watching the focus move through the bound controls of the form**

   Currently, focus moves to the Wholesale field before the Retail field. You want to switch the tab order for those two controls.

2. **Click the Design View button ⬛ on the Form View toolbar, click View on the menu bar, then click Tab Order**

   The Tab Order dialog box allows you to change the tab order of controls in three sections: Form Header, Detail, and Form Footer. You can expand these sections in Form Design View by dragging the bottom edge of a section down to open it. Right now, all of the controls are positioned in the form's Detail section. See Table C-5 for more information on form sections. To change the tab order, drag the **row selector**, positioned to the left of the field name, up or down. A black line shows you the new placement of the field in the list.

QUICK TIP

Click the Auto Order button in the Tab Order dialog box to automatically set a left-to-right, top-to-bottom tab order.

3. **Click the Retail row selector in the Custom Order list, drag it up and position it just above Wholesale as shown in Figure C-12**

   Text18 represents the name of the text box that contains the profit calculation. (The number represents the number of controls you have added to the form). If you wanted to give the text box a more descriptive name, you could change its Name property. The **Name property** for a text box is analogous to the Caption property for a label.

QUICK TIP

In Form Design View, press [Ctrl][.] to switch to Form View. In Form View, press [Ctrl][,] to switch to Form Design View.

4. **Click OK in the Tab Order dialog box, click the Save button ⬛, then click the Form View button ⬛ on the Form Design toolbar**

   Although nothing visibly changes on the form, the tab order is different.

5. **Press [Enter] 10 times to move through the fields of the form with the new tab order**

   Both [Tab] and [Enter] move the focus to the next bound control of a form.

6. **Continue pressing [Enter] until you reach the Retail value of the second record, type 20, then press [Enter]**

   Changing the value in either the Retail or the Wholesale fields automatically recalculates the value in the Profit field as shown in Figure C-13.

7. **Press [Enter] to move the focus to the Profit field, attempt to type any value, and observe the message in the status bar**

   Even though the calculated control can receive the focus, its value cannot be directly edited in Form View. As the message in the status bar indicates, its value is bound to the expression [Retail]-[Wholesale].

8. **Close the Item Entry Form**

FIGURE C-12: Changing tab order

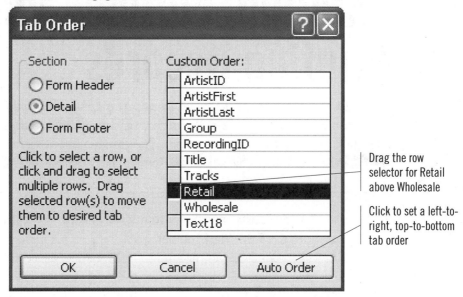

Drag the row selector for Retail above Wholesale

Click to set a left-to-right, top-to-bottom tab order

FIGURE C-13: Profit field automatically recalculates

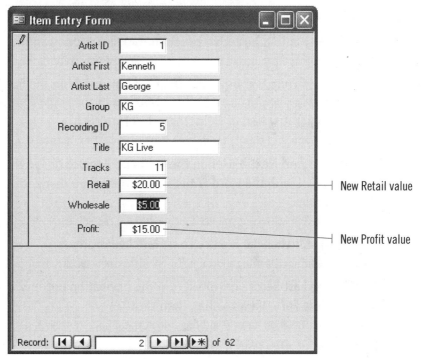

New Retail value

New Profit value

TABLE C-5: Form sections

section	description
Form Header	Controls placed in the Form Header section print only once at the top of the printout; by default, this section is closed in Form Design View
Detail	Controls placed in the Detail section appear in Form View and print once for every record in the underlying table or query object; all controls created by the Form Wizard are placed in this section
Form Footer	Controls placed in the Form Footer section print only once at the end of the printout; by default, this section is closed in Form Design View

Entering, Editing, and Printing Records

You use a form to quickly find, enter, or edit records in the underlying record source. You can also print a form, but printing all records in a form layout produces a very long printout because of the vertical orientation of the fields. To print only a single record in a form, you use the Selected Record option in the Print dialog box. You are ready to use the Artists Entry Form to add new information to the MediaLoft database.

STEPS

QUICK TIP

The New Record button is also located in the navigation buttons at the bottom of the form.

1. **Double-click the** Artists Entry Form **to open it in Form View, then click the** New Record **button** ▶* **on the Form View toolbar**

   A new, blank record is displayed. The Artist ID field is an AutoNumber field that automatically increments when you begin to enter data. The Specific Record box indicates the current record number.

2. **Press [Tab] to move the focus to the Artist Name text box, type your first name, press [Tab], type your last name, press [Tab] to move the focus to the Group text box, then type** Snowboards

   Data is automatically saved as you work in a form so you do not need to worry about saving data.

TROUBLE

The Print button 🖨 on the Form View toolbar prints *all* records.

3. **Click** File **on the menu bar, click** Print **to open the Print dialog box, click the** Selected Record(s) option button **in the Print Range section as shown in Figure C-14, then click** OK

   Forms are also often used to find, edit, or delete existing records in the database.

QUICK TIP

Drag the title bar of the Find and Replace dialog box if it covers the Artists Entry Form.

4. **Click the** Group text box, **click the** Find button 🔍 **on the Form View toolbar to open the Find and Replace dialog box, type** Mitchell **in the Find What text box, click the** Match list arrow, **click** Any Part of Field, **then click** Find Next

   Record 16 appears behind the Find and Replace dialog box, as shown in Figure C-15.

5. **Click the** Find Next button **in the Find and Replace dialog box to find the next occurrence of an artist with the word "Mitchell" in the group name, click the** Find Next button, **then click** Cancel

   Once you find the record you need to change, you can edit data using a form.

6. **Edit the Mitchell Band entry to be** Mitchell Brothers

   Besides editing data using a form, it's also easy to delete records using a form.

7. **Click the** Last Record button ▶▮ **in the navigation buttons, click the** Delete Record button ▶✗ **on the Form View toolbar, then click** Yes

   As the confirmation message indicates, you cannot undo the deletion of a record.

8. **Close the Artists Entry Form**

FIGURE C-14: Printing a selected record of a form

Click to print only the selected record

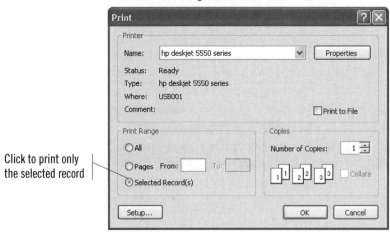

FIGURE C-15: Finding data in a form

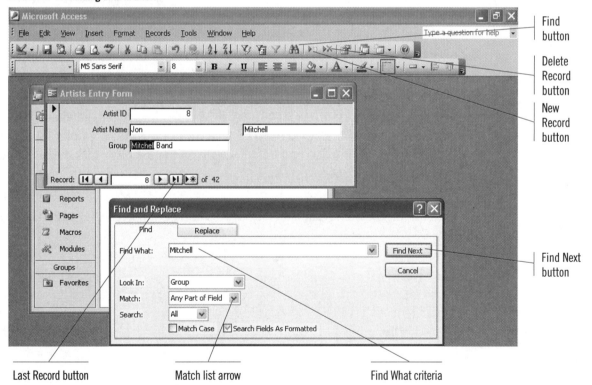

Find button

Delete Record button

New Record button

Find Next button

Last Record button

Match list arrow

Find What criteria

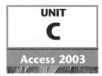
Inserting an Image

Graphic images, such as pictures, logos, or clip art, can add style and professionalism to a form. The form section in which they are placed is significant. For example, if you add a company logo to the Form Header section, the image appears at the top of the form in Form View as well as at the top of a printout. If you add the same image to the Detail section, it would print beside each record in a printout because the Detail section is printed for every record. ▰▰▰▰▰ Kelsey suggests that you add the MediaLoft logo and a descriptive title to the top of the form. You add the logo by inserting an unbound image control in the Form Header section.

STEPS

1. **Right-click the Item Entry Form, then click Design View on the shortcut menu**

   The Item Entry Form opens in Design View.

2. **Maximize the form, then drag the top edge of the Detail section down about 1" to open the Form Header section**

   The Form Header section opens so that you can add controls to that section.

3. **Click the Image button ⊞ on the Toolbox toolbar, click in the Form Header section, click the Look in list arrow, navigate to the drive and folder where your Data Files are stored, click Smallmedia.bmp, then click OK**

   The MediaLoft logo is inserted into the Form Header in an image control, as shown in Figure C-16. Table C-6 summarizes other types of multimedia controls that may be added to a form using the Toolbox toolbar. Placing a title in the Form Header section adds a finishing touch to the form.

4. **Click the Label button Aa on the Toolbox toolbar, click to the right of the MediaLoft logo in the Form Header section, type MediaLoft Music, then press [Enter]**

   Labels can be formatted to enhance their appearance on the form.

5. **Click the Font Size list arrow 8 , click 24, double-click a sizing handle so that the MediaLoft Music label is completely displayed, click the Font/Fore Color list arrow A ·, click the dark blue box (second from the right on the top row), click the Save button 🖫, then click the Form View button 🖼**

   The final form is shown in Figure C-17.

6. **Click File on the menu bar, click Print, click the Selected Record(s) option button, then click OK**

   The first record as displayed by the Item Entry Form is sent to the printer.

7. **Close the Item Entry Form, close the MediaLoft-C database, then exit Access**

FIGURE C-16: Adding an image to the Form Header section

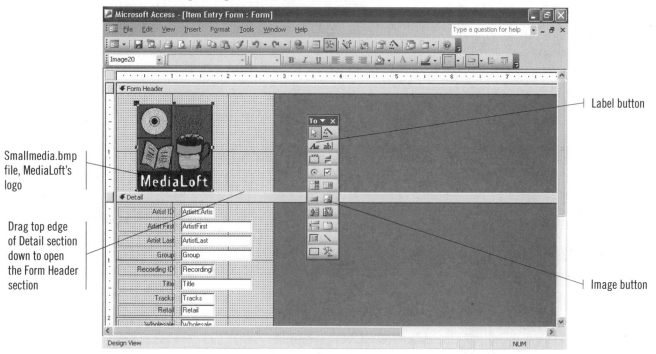

Smallmedia.bmp file, MediaLoft's logo

Label button

Drag top edge of Detail section down to open the Form Header section

Image button

FIGURE C-17: Final Item Entry Form

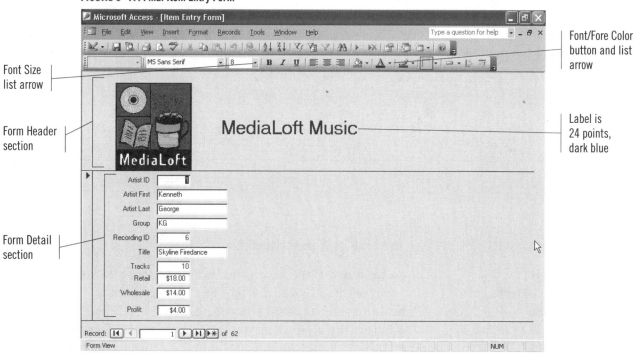

Font Size list arrow

Form Header section

Form Detail section

Font/Fore Color button and list arrow

Label is 24 points, dark blue

TABLE C-6: Multimedia controls

control	button	description
Image		Adds a single piece of clip art, a photo, or a logo to a form
Unbound object frame		Adds a sound clip, a movie clip, a document, or other type of unbound data (data that isn't stored in a table of the database) to a form
Bound object frame		Displays the contents of a field with an **OLE Object** (object linking and embedding) data type; an OLE Object field might contain pictures, sound clips, documents, or other data created by other software applications

Practice

▼ CONCEPTS REVIEW

Label each element of the Form View shown in Figure C-18.

FIGURE C-18

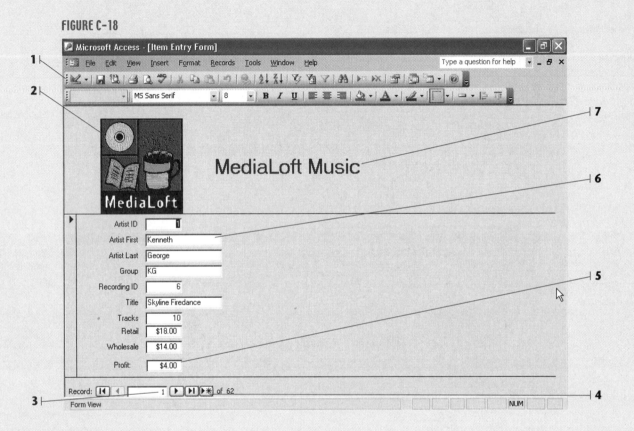

Match each term with the statement that best describes it.

8. **Bound control**
9. **Calculated control**
10. **Detail section**
11. **Form**
12. **Sizing handles**
13. **Tab order**

a. An Access database object that allows you to arrange the fields of a record in any layout and is used to enter, edit, and delete records
b. Used on a form to display data from a field
c. Squares that appear in the corners and edges of the selected control
d. The way in which the focus moves from one bound control to the next in Form View
e. Created by entering an expression in a text box
f. Controls placed here print once for every record in the underlying record source

Select the best answer from the list of choices.

14. Every element on a form is called a(n):

a. Property.

b. Attribute.

c. Tool.

d. Control.

15. The mouse pointer that could be used to resize a control is:

a. ⬍

b. ↔

c. 👆

d. ✋

16. The most common bound control is the:

a. List box.

b. Check box.

c. Combo box.

d. Text box.

17. The most common unbound control is the:

a. Label.

b. Command Button.

c. Line.

d. Image.

18. Form _____ View is used to move or resize form controls.

a. Control

b. Design

c. Preview

d. Datasheet

19. The _____ control is commonly used to display data on a form from a field with a Yes/No data type.

a. Check box

b. Boolean

c. Text box

d. Combo box

20. The _____ Object Frame control is used to display data from a field with an OLE Object data type.

a. Bound

b. Caption

c. Unbound

d. Target

▼ SKILLS REVIEW

1. Plan a form.
a. Plan a form to use for entering business contacts by looking at several business cards.
b. Sketch the form.
c. Determine what type of control you will use for each bound field.
d. Identify the labels you would like to display on the form.

2. Create a form.
a. Start Access and open the **Membership-C.mdb** database from the drive and folder where your Data Files are stored.
b. Click the Forms button in the Membership-C database window, then double-click the Create form by using wizard option.
c. Base the form on the Contacts table, and include all of the fields.
d. Use a Columnar layout, a Standard style, title the form **Contact Entry Form**, and display the form in Form View.

3. Move and resize controls.
a. Open and maximize Form Design View for the Contact Entry Form.
b. Delete the LNAME label, then move the LNAME text box to the right of the FNAME text box.
c. Move the DUESOWED and DUESPAID text boxes and corresponding labels to the right of the COMPANY and STREET text boxes.
d. Resize the CITY text box to be the same width as the COMPANY and STREET text boxes.
e. Move the PHONE text box and corresponding label between the FNAME and COMPANY controls. The resulting form should look similar to Figure C-19.

FIGURE C-19

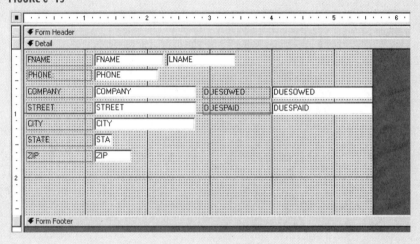

4. Modify labels.
a. Right-align all of the labels. Be careful to right-align only the labels, and not the text boxes.
b. Edit the caption of the FNAME label to **NAME**, the DUESOWED label to **DUES OWED**, and the DUESPAID label to **DUES PAID**. Be careful to modify the labels and not the text boxes.

5. Use text boxes for calculations.
a. Add a new text box below the DUESPAID text box.
b. Type the expression **=[DUESOWED]-[DUESPAID]** in the new unbound text box. (*Hint*: Remember that you must use the *exact field names* surrounded by square brackets in a calculated expression.)
c. In the property sheet for the new calculated control, change the Format property to Currency.
d. Right-align the new calculated control.
e. Change the accompanying label for the new calculated control to **BALANCE**.
f. Move and resize the new calculated control and label so that they are aligned beneath the DUESOWED and DUESPAID controls.

6. **Modify tab order.**
   a. Change the tab order so that pressing [Tab] moves the focus through the text boxes in the following order: FNAME, LNAME, PHONE, COMPANY, STREET, CITY, STATE, ZIP, DUESOWED, DUESPAID, Text20 (Text20 represents the text box with the calculated control).
   b. Save your changes, open the form in Form View, then test the new tab order.

7. **Enter, edit, and print records.**
   a. Use the Contact Entry Form to enter the following new records:

	FIRST NAME	LAST NAME	PHONE	COMPANY	STREET
Record 1	Your first name	Your last name	555-223-1166	Cummins Construction	1515 Maple St.
Record 2	Sena	Tsao	555-777-2277	Magpie Industries	1010 Green St.

	CITY	STATE	ZIP	DUES OWED	DUES PAID
1 continued	Greely	CO	77888-1111	$50.00	$25.00
2 continued	Alva	CO	77889-3333	$50.00	$50.00

   b. Find the record with your name, and print only that record.
   c. Find the Lois Grayson record, enter IBM in the COMPANY text box, then change Barnes in the STREET field to Washington.
   d. Filter for all records with a ZIP that starts with 64145. (*Hint*: Use Filter By Form with a filter criteria entry of 64145*.)
   e. Sort the filtered 64145 zip code records in ascending order by LAST NAME, change the COMPANY name for this record to Your Last Name Industries, then print only this record.

8. **Insert an image.**
   a. In Form Design View, expand the Form Header section by about 1".
   b. Use the Image control to insert the Hand.bmp file in the left side of the Form Header. (*Hint*: The Hand.bmp file is on the drive and folder where your Data Files are stored.)
   c. Centered and below the image, add the label MEMBERSHIP INFORMATION in a 24-point font. Be sure to resize the label so that all of the text is visible.
   d. Below the MEMBERSHIP INFORMATION label, add your name as a label.
   e. View the form in Form View, then sort the records in descending order based on the COMPANY values.
   f. Print only the first record.
   g. Save and close the form, close the database, then exit Access.

▼ INDEPENDENT CHALLENGE 1

As the office manager of a cardiology clinic, you need to create a data entry form for new patients.

a. Start Access, then open the **Clinic-C.mdb** database from the drive and folder where your Data Files are stored.

b. Using the Form Wizard, create a form that includes all the fields in the Outcomes Data table, using the Columnar layout and Standard style. Title the form **Medical Chart Information**.

c. Move the four text boxes in the second column down to make room to move the three text boxes at the bottom of the first column (Dietary Cholesterol, Chol, and HDL) to the top of the second column.

d. Drag the top of the Form Footer up to close up the empty space at the bottom of the form.

e. Right-align all labels so that they are closer to the text boxes they describe.

f. Resize the MR# text box to be the same size as the Date text box. Resize all other text boxes to be the same size as the Height text box. (*Hint*: Select several text boxes to resize at the same time, then use the Format, Size, To Narrowest menu option to automatically size the selected text boxes to the narrowest text box.)

g. Add a label with your name to the Form Header, then save the form and display it in Form View.

h. In Form View, check the tab order to make sure it works in a top-to-bottom order for both columns. Modify the tab order as needed.

i. Sort the records in ascending order based on the Height field, then print the first record.

Advanced Challenge Exercise

- In Form Design View, add an Image control to the Form Header. Use the Insert Picture dialog box to search for and find an appropriate piece of clip art to insert on the form. One folder to explore for available clip art images is C:\Program Files\Microsoft Office\media. (*Hint*: If you are having trouble finding an appropriate piece of medical clip art on your computer, use either the Medical.bmp or Medstaff.bmp images provided in your Data Files.)
- To resize the image to fit within the form, open its property sheet. Click the Format tab, click the Size Mode property, and press F1 to read the Microsoft Access Help page about this property. After reading about the property in Help, close Help and change the Size Mode property of the image to Zoom.

j. Save and display the Medical Chart Information in Form View as shown in Figure C-20, sort the records in ascending order on the Weight field, then print the first record.

k. Close the form, close the database, then exit Access.

FIGURE C-20

Medical Chart Information

Your Name

Graphic appears if you perform the Advanced Steps

MR# 027675	Dietary Cholesterol 206
Date 6/11/2006	Chol 0
Height 69	HDL 0
Weight 124	LDL 0
Functional Capacity 0	TRG 0
Energy Expenditure 0	Fasting BG 0
Dietary Fat 36	HbA1c 0
Dietry Sat Fat #Nam	

Record: 1 of 59

▼ INDEPENDENT CHALLENGE 2

As office manager of a cardiology clinic, you want to build a form that quickly calculates a height-to-weight ratio value based on information in the Outcomes Data table.

   a. Start Access, then open the **Clinic-C.mdb** database from the drive and folder where your Data Files are stored.

   b. Using the Form Wizard, create a form based on the Outcomes Data table with only the following fields: MR#, Date, Height, and Weight.

   c. Use the Columnar layout and Standard style, and name the form **Height to Weight Ratio Form**.

   d. In Design View, use the Text Box button to add a text box and accompanying label below the Weight text box.

   e. Enter the expression **=[Height]/[Weight]** in the unbound text box.

   f. Modify the new label from Text6: to **Ratio**.

   g. Resize the Ratio label so that it is closer to the calculated expression control, then right-align all of the labels. Resize the Weight and calculated text boxes to be the same width as the Height text box.

   h. Change the Format property of the calculated control to **Fixed**, and the Decimal Places property to **2**.

   i. Open the Form Header section about **0.5"**, then add a label to that section that displays your name. Modify the MR# label to be **Medical Record #**.

   j. Save and view the form in Form View, then print only the record with the Medical Record # of 017771.

   k. Sort the records in descending order by Height, change the value in the Weight field to **200**, press [Tab], then print only this record.

Advanced Challenge Exercise

   ■ Open the Height to Weight Ratio Form in Form Design View, then open the field list.

   ■ Drag the Chol, HDL, and LDL fields from the field list to the right of the Height, Weight, and Ratio text boxes.

   ■ Move the new labels and text boxes as necessary so that all of the controls on the form are clearly presented. (*Hint*: Once the controls are moved so that they are not touching, you can align the top edges of controls in a row by selecting the controls, then choosing the Format, Align, Top menu option.)

   l. Save and display the form in Form View. Find the record for Medical Record # 058231, then print only that record.

   m. Close the Height to Weight Ratio Form, close the Clinic-C database, then exit Access.

▼ INDEPENDENT CHALLENGE 3

As office manager of a cardiology clinic, you want to build a form to enter new insurance information.

    a. Open the Clinic-C.mdb database from the drive and folder where your Data Files are stored.

    b. Using the Form Wizard, create a form based on all of the fields in the Insurance Company Information table. Use the Columnar layout, Standard style, and accept Insurance Company Information as the title.

    c. In Form Design View, change the Insurance Company Name label to Insurance Company. Be sure to modify the Insurance Company Name label, and not the text box.

    d. Resize the State text box so that it is the same size as the City text box.

    e. Expand the Form Header section, then add the graphic image Medical.bmp to the left side of the Form Header section. The Medical.bmp file is in the drive and folder where your Data Files are stored.

    f. Add a label Insurance Entry Form and another for your name to the right of the medical clip art in the Form Header section.

    g. Increase the size of the Insurance Entry Form label to 18 points. Resize the label to display the entire caption.

    h. Switch to Form View, then find the record for the Cigna Insurance Company. Change Sherman in the City field to Bridgewater, then print this record.

Advanced Challenge Exercise

- Filter for all records with a State entry of KS. Preview the filtered records, then use the Setup button to modify the top and bottom margins of the printout so that it fits on one page.
- In Form Design View, drag the medical clip art image to the Detail section, then redisplay the form in Form View and preview it again. Notice how the printout differs when you place the image in the Detail section versus the Form Header section.
- If the printout fits on one page (the records should still be filtered for KS), print it. If not, continue modifying the margins or work in Form Design View to make the form small enough so that this filtered printout fits on one page, then print the page.

    i. Save and close the Insurance Company Information Form, close the Clinic-C database, then exit Access.

▼ INDEPENDENT CHALLENGE 4

You are on the staff of an economic development team whose goal is to encourage tourism in the Baltic Sea region. You have created an Access database called Baltic-C.mdb to track important fields of information for the countries in that region, and will use the Internet to find information about the area and enter it into existing forms.

a. Start Access and open the **Baltic-C.mdb** database from the drive and folder where your Data Files are stored.

b. Connect to the Internet, then go to any general search engine to conduct research for your database. Your goal is to find information for at least one new city record for each country.

c. Open the Countries form. You can enter the data you found on the Internet for each city by using the City fields shown in Figure C-21. This arrangement of data organizes cities within countries using a main form/subform arrangement. The main form contains a single text box bound to the Country field. The subform presents a datasheet of four City fields. Be sure to enter the Population data for that particular city, rather than for the entire country. CityID is an AutoNumber field, so it automatically increments as you enter the City, Capital, and Population data.

FIGURE C-21

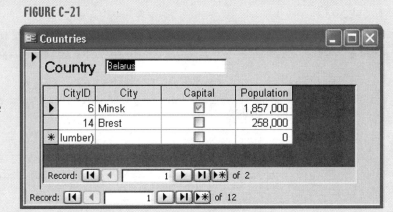

d. After you have entered one new city for each country, print the record for Sweden.

e. Close the Countries form, then open the Countries table datasheet. Click all of the expand buttons to the left of each Country record to show the city records that you just entered through the Countries form. Close the Countries table.

f. Open the Cities form and find the Oslo, Norway, record shown in Figure C-22. This form shows another main form/subform arrangement. The main form contains fields that describe the city, and the subform contains a datasheet with fields that describe the events for that city.

FIGURE C-22

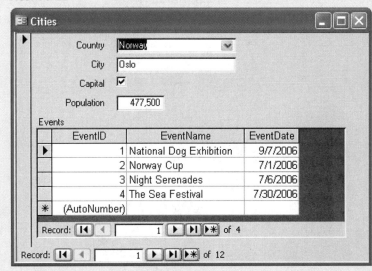

g. Return to the search engine, and research upcoming tourist events for Copenhagen, Denmark.

h. In the Cities form, find the Copenhagen record, then enter three events for Copenhagen. EventID is an AutoNumber field, so it automatically increments as you enter the EventName and EventDate information.

i. Print the Copenhagen record, close the Cities form, close the Baltic-C database, then exit Access.

Access 2003

▼ VISUAL WORKSHOP

Open the **Clinic-C.mdb** database, then use the Form Wizard to create the form based on the Demographics table, as shown in Figure C-23. Notice that the label **Patient Form** is 24 points and has been placed in the Form Header section. The clip art, **Medstaff.bmp**, can be found in the drive and folder where your Data Files are stored. The image has been placed on the right side of the Detail section, and many controls were moved and resized. Also notice that the labels are right-aligned. To change the background color of the Detail section to white, double-click the Detail section bar in Form Design View, then modify the Back Color property on the Format tab of the property sheet to **16777215**, the value that corresponds to white. Enter your own name and gender for the first record, then print it.

FIGURE C-23

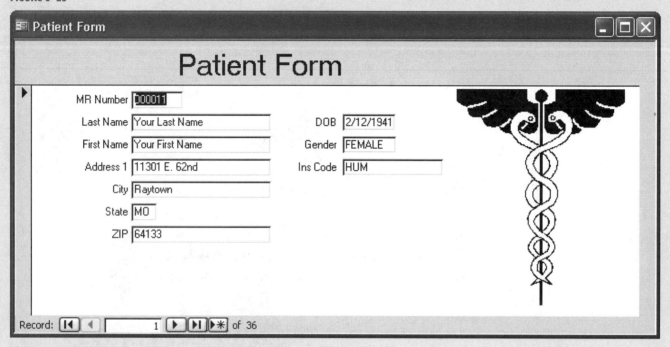

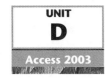

UNIT
D
Access 2003

Using Reports

OBJECTIVES

Plan a report
Create a report
Use group sections
Change the sort order
Add a calculation
Align controls
Format controls
Change page layout

If you have a SAM user profile, you may have access to hands-on instruction, practice, and assessment of the skills covered in this unit. Log in to your SAM account and go to your assignments page to see what your instructor has assigned.

A **report** is an Access object used to create professional printouts. Although you can print a datasheet or form, reports are the primary object used to create professional printouts because reports provide many more printing options. For example, a report may include formatting embellishments such as multiple fonts and colors, extra graphical elements such as clip art and lines, and multiple headers and footers. Reports are also very powerful analysis tools. A report can calculate subtotals, averages, counts, or other statistics for groups of records. You cannot enter or edit data through a report. Kelsey Lang, a marketing manager at MediaLoft, wants you to produce some reports to distribute to MediaLoft employees.

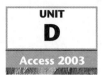

Planning a Report

Hard copy reports are often the primary tool used to communicate database information at internal meetings or with customers. Time spent planning your report not only increases your productivity but also ensures that the report meets its intended objectives. Creating a report is similar to creating a form, in that you work with bound, unbound, and calculated controls in Report Design View just as you do in Form Design View. Reports, however, have more sections than forms. A **section** determines how often and where controls placed within that section print in the final report. See Table D-1 for more information on report sections. Kelsey asks you to create a report that summarizes inventory items within each music category.

DETAILS

Use the following guidelines to plan a new report:

- **Determine the information (the fields and records) that the report will show**

  You can base a report on a table, but usually you create a query to gather the specific fields from one or more tables upon which the report is based. If you base the report on a query, you can also set criteria within the query to limit the number of records displayed by the report.

- **Determine how the fields should be organized on the report**

  Most reports display fields in a horizontal layout across the page, but you can arrange them any way you want. Just as in forms, bound text box controls are used on a report to display the data stored in the underlying fields. These text boxes are generally placed in the report **Detail section**. The Detail section of a report is always visible in Report Design View.

- **Determine how the records should be grouped and sorted within the report**

  In an Access report, **grouping** means to sort records in a particular order *plus* provide a section before each group of records called the Group Header section and a section after the group of records called the Group Footer section. The **Group Header** section usually introduces the upcoming group of records. The **Group Footer** section is most often used to calculate statistics such as subtotals for the group of records it follows. Group Header and Footer sections are created by choices made when initially creating the report using the Report Wizard, or by specifying a Yes value to these field properties in the Sorting and Grouping dialog box in Report Design View. To view or edit the grouping and sorting orders for any report, click the Sorting and Grouping button 🔳 on the Report Design toolbar. In Figure D-1, the field used to group the records is the Category field. Therefore, the Group Header section for this report is called the Category Header section and the Group Footer section is called the Category Footer section.

- **Identify any other descriptive information that should be placed at the beginning or end of the report, or at the top or bottom of each page**

  You use the **Report Header**, **Report Footer**, **Page Header**, and **Page Footer** sections to add information that you want to print on every page, or at the beginning or end of the report. For example, you might add a text box that contains an expression to display the current date in the Page Header section, or you might add a text box that contains an expression to display the current page number in the Page Footer section. The Report Header and Report Footer sections of a report can be opened using the Report Header/Footer option on the View menu in Report Design View.

- **Identify a meaningful title for the report**

  The title should clearly identify the purpose of the report. The title is created with a label control placed in the Report Header section.

  The sketch of your first report is shown in Figure D-1.

FIGURE D-1: Sketch of the Inventory Report

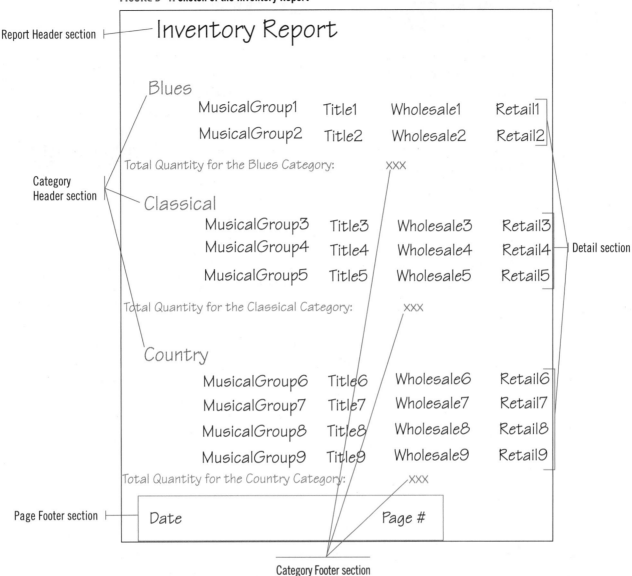

TABLE D-1: Report sections

section	where does this section print?	which controls are most commonly placed in this section?
Report Header	At the top of the first page of the report	Label controls containing the report title; can also include clip art, a logo image, or a line separating the title from the rest of the report
Page Header	At the top of every page (but below the Report Header on page one)	Text box controls containing a page number or date expression
Group Header	Before every group of records	Text box controls for the field by which the records are grouped
Detail	Once for every record	Text box controls for the rest of the fields in the recordset (the table or query upon which the report is built)
Group Footer	After every group of records	Text box controls containing calculated expressions, such as subtotals or counts, for the records in that group
Page Footer	At the bottom of every page	Text box controls containing a page number or date expression
Report Footer	At the end of the entire report	Text box controls containing expressions such as grand totals or counts that calculate a value for all of the records in the report

Creating a Report

You can create reports in Access in Report Design View, or you can use the Report Wizard to help you get started. The **Report Wizard** asks questions that guide you through the initial development of the report, similar to the Form Wizard. Your responses to the Report Wizard determine the record source, style, and layout of the report. The Report Wizard also helps you determine how the records will be sorted, grouped, and analyzed. Another way to quickly create a report is by selecting a table or query, clicking the New Object list arrow ⊞ ▾ on the Database toolbar, and then clicking AutoReport. ▰▰▰▰▰ You use the Report Wizard to create the Inventory Report that you previously sketched.

STEPS

1. **Start Access, click the** More link **in the Open section of the Getting Started task pane, then open the** MediaLoft-D.mdb database **from the drive and folder where your Data Files are stored**

    This database contains the Inventory and Artists tables.

2. **Click** Reports **on the Objects bar in the MediaLoft-D database window, then double-click** Create report by using wizard

    The Report Wizard dialog box opens and prompts you to select the fields you want on the report. You can select fields from one or more tables or queries. You need the MusicalGroup field from the Artists table and the Category, Title, Wholesale, and Retail fields from the Inventory table. These fields have been previously selected in the Inventory Items query.

3. **Click the** Tables/Queries list arrow, **click** Query: Inventory Items, **then click the** Select All Fields button ⟩⟩

    The five fields are selected and the first dialog box of the Report Wizard should look like Figure D-2.

4. **Click** Next

    The next question asks how you want to view your data. Your response determines how the records will be grouped. Viewing the data "by Artists" makes the MusicalGroup field the grouping field as shown in the sample. Because you want to use Category as the grouping field, you select the "by Inventory" option.

> **TROUBLE**
> Click Back to review previous dialog boxes within a wizard.

5. **Click** by Inventory, **click** Next, **click** Category, **click the** Select Single field button ⟩ **to select Category as the grouping field, then click** Next

    You can use the Report Wizard to specify up to four sort fields in either an ascending or descending sort order for each field. For now, you decide not to choose any sort fields and to finish the steps of the Report Wizard.

6. **Click** Next, **accept the** Stepped **layout and** Portrait **orientation, click** Next, **click** Corporate **for the style, click** Next, **then type** Inventory Report **for the report title**

7. **Verify that the** Preview the report option button **is selected, click** Finish, **then maximize the Inventory Report**

    The Inventory Report opens in Print Preview, as shown in Figure D-3. Notice that the records are grouped by Category.

FIGURE D-2: Report Wizard dialog box

Base the report on the Inventory Items query

Select All Fields button

Fields selected for the report

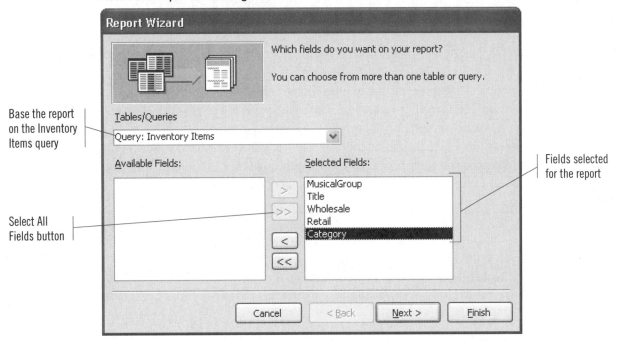

FIGURE D-3: Inventory Report in Print Preview

Report Header section

Page Header section

Category Header section

Detail section

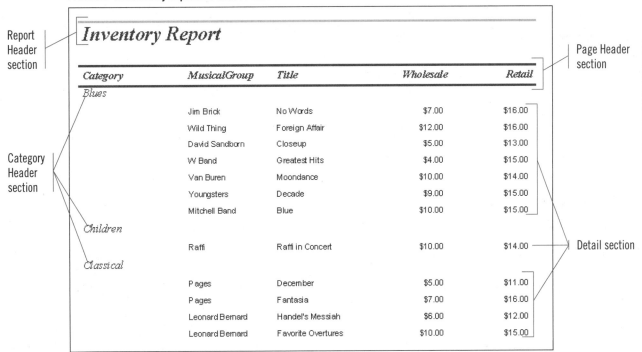

Clues to Use

Why reports should be based on queries

The first dialog box of the Report Wizard asks you to select the fields you want to see on the report. Your choices determine the value of the report's **Record Source** property, which identifies the **recordset** (fields and records) passed to the report. You can modify the Record Source property of any report, thus changing the recordset that is passed to the report. If you choose the fields from a single query (versus selecting fields from different tables), however, the recordset is already defined as a query object, which makes it very easy to modify. For example, you may want to add more fields to the report at a later time. If your report is based on a query, simply open the query used as the report's recordset in Query Design View and add the field to the query grid. The new field will automatically be made available to the report as well.

Access 2003

Using Group Sections

Grouping means to sort records in a particular order *plus* provide a section before and after each group, the Group Header and Group Footer. The Group Header and Group Footer sections take the name of the field by which you are grouping the records. If grouping records by the State field, for example, the sections would be called the State Header and State Footer sections. You can create groups on a report through the Report Wizard, or you can change an existing report's grouping fields in Report Design View. The Inventory Report is grouped by the Category field. The name of each category appears in the Category Header section before each group of records within that category. You will open the Category Footer section and add the controls needed to count the number of items within each category.

STEPS

TROUBLE
If the Field List button 📄 or Properties button 📑 on the Report Design toolbar are selected, click them to toggle these windows off for now.

1. **Click the Design View button 🗹 on the Print Preview toolbar to switch to Report Design View**

   Report Design View shows you the sections of the report as well as the controls within each section. Report Design View is where you make all structural changes to a report object including making changes to grouping fields.

2. **Click the Sorting and Grouping button 🗐 on the Report Design toolbar, click the Group Footer text box, click the Group Footer list arrow, then click Yes**

   Specifying Yes for the Group Footer property as shown in Figure D-4 opens that section of the report in Report Design View.

TROUBLE
To resize a floating toolbar, drag its edge. To move a floating toolbar, drag its title bar. If your Toolbox toolbar is docked to a side of the screen, you can move it by dragging its topmost or leftmost edge.

3. **Click 🗐 to close the Sorting and Grouping dialog box, then click the Toolbox button 🛠 on the Report Design toolbar to toggle it on if it is not already visible**

   You can add a calculated control to count the number of records in each group by placing a text box in the Category Footer section and entering an expression that counts the records into the text box.

4. **Click the Text Box button 🔳 on the Toolbox toolbar, then click in the Category Footer section directly below the Title text box**

   Your screen should look like Figure D-5. When adding a new text box to the report, a new label is also automatically added to the left of the text box. You want to modify the Text16 label to be more descriptive of the information it identifies.

TROUBLE
If you double-click the edge of the label, you open the control's property sheet. Close the property sheet, then double-click Text16 to select it.

5. **Click the Text16: label in the Category Footer section to select the label, double-click Text16 to select the text within the label, type Count, then press [Enter]**

   With the label modified, your next task is to enter the expression that counts the number of items in each category.

6. **Click the Unbound text box control in the Category Footer section to select the text box, click Unbound within the text box, type =Count([Title]), then press [Enter]**

   Expressions start with an equal sign and each character including the parentheses must be entered exactly as shown. Field names used in expressions are not case sensitive but must be surrounded by [square brackets] and match the exact name of the field as defined in Table Design View. This expression counts the number of items in the Title field. Additional information on expressions is covered later in this unit.

TROUBLE
If you see #Error on the report, return to Report Design View, edit the expression in the new text box as shown in Step 6, then preview the report again.

7. **Click the Print Preview button 🔍 on the Report Design toolbar**

   Each group of records is followed by a Group Footer that identifies how many titles are in each category as shown in Figure D-6.

8. **Click the Close button on the Print Preview toolbar, click the Save button, then close the Inventory Report**

FIGURE D-4: Sorting and Grouping dialog box

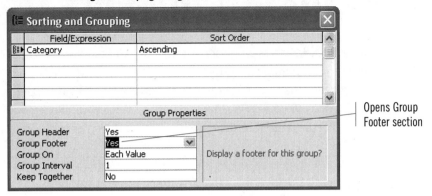

Opens Group
Footer section

FIGURE D-5: Inventory Report in Report Design View

Toolbox
toolbar
button

Field list
button

New label

New
text box

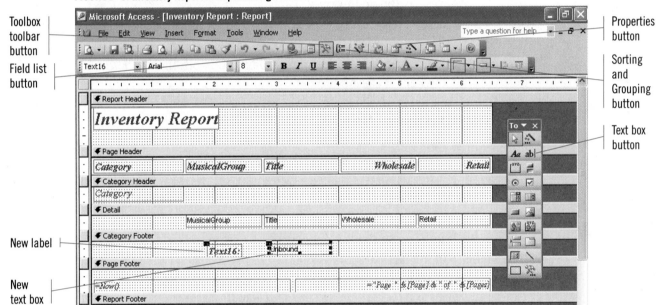

Properties
button

Sorting
and
Grouping
button

Text box
button

FIGURE D-6: Adding a calculation in the Category Footer section

Category Footer
section

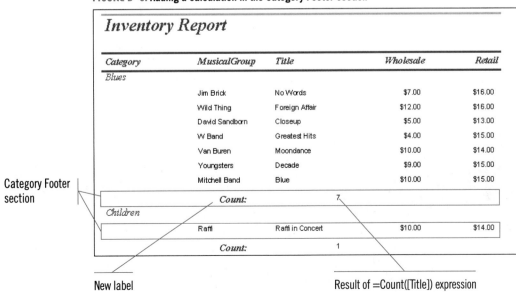

New label

Result of =Count([Title]) expression

Changing the Sort Order

The grouping field acts as a primary sort field, but you can define additional sort fields within each group. The Report Wizard prompts you for group and sort information at the time you create the report, but you can change the group and sort orders on an existing report by using the Sorting and Grouping dialog box in Report Design View. After reviewing the report with Kelsey, you decide to modify the Inventory Report so that the Detail records are sorted in ascending order by the value in the MusicalGroup field.

STEPS

1. **Right-click the** Inventory Report, **then click** Design View

   The Inventory Report opens in Report Design View.

2. **Click the** Sorting and Grouping button 🔳 **on the Report Design toolbar, click the** Field/Expression text box **in the second row, click the** Field/Expression list arrow, **then click** MusicalGroup **as shown in Figure D-7**

   Both the Group Header and Group Footer property values for the MusicalGroup field are set to No, which indicates that the MusicalGroup field is providing a sort order only.

3. **Click** 🔳 **to toggle the Sorting and Grouping dialog box off, then click the** Print Preview button 🔳 **on the Report Design toolbar**

   Part of the report is shown in Print Preview, as shown in Figure D-8. You can use the buttons on the Print Preview toolbar to view more of the report.

   > **QUICK TIP**
   > The grid expands to a maximum of 4 x 5 pages if you keep dragging to expand it.

4. **Click the** One Page button 🔳 **on the Print Preview toolbar to view one miniature page, click the** Two Pages button 🔳 **to view two pages, click the** Multiple Pages button 🔳, **point to** 1 x 3 Pages **as shown in Figure D-9, then click the** 1 x 3 Pages **option**

   The Print Preview window displays the three pages of the report. You can click the **Zoom pointers** 🔍 and 🔍 to change the zoom magnification.

   > **QUICK TIP**
   > You can also type a number into the Fit text box to zoom at a specific percent.

5. **Point to the** last count **on the last page of the report with the** 🔍 **pointer, click to read the number** 5 **in the last Category Footer of the report, then click again to view all three pages of the report in the Preview window**

   To zoom the preview to a specific percentage, click the **Zoom list arrow** `100%` on the Print Preview toolbar, then click a percentage. The **Fit** option automatically adjusts the preview to display all pages in the report.

6. **Close the Inventory Report, then click** Yes **when prompted to save it**

FIGURE D-7: Specifying a sort order

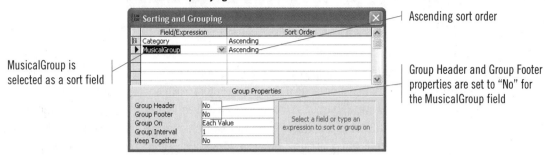

Ascending sort order

MusicalGroup is selected as a sort field

Group Header and Group Footer properties are set to "No" for the MusicalGroup field

FIGURE D-8: Inventory Report sorted by MusicalGroup

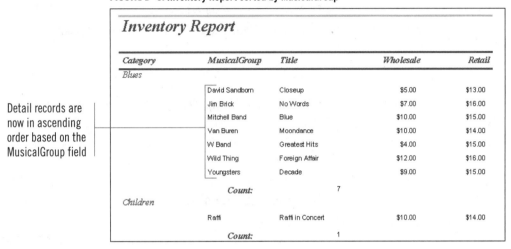

Detail records are now in ascending order based on the MusicalGroup field

Inventory Report

Category	MusicalGroup	Title	Wholesale	Retail
Blues				
	David Sandborn	Closeup	$5.00	$13.00
	Jim Brick	No Words	$7.00	$16.00
	Mitchell Band	Blue	$10.00	$15.00
	Van Buren	Moondance	$10.00	$14.00
	W Band	Greatest Hits	$4.00	$15.00
	Wild Thing	Foreign Affair	$12.00	$16.00
	Youngsters	Decade	$9.00	$15.00
	Count:		7	
Children				
	Raffi	Raffi in Concert	$10.00	$14.00
	Count:		1	

FIGURE D-9: Two Page Print Preview

One Page button

Two Pages button

Multiple Pages button

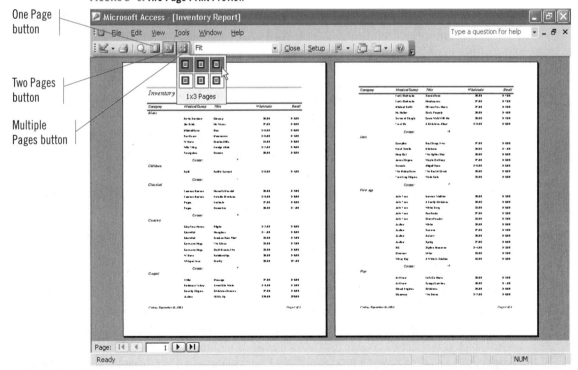

Clues to Use

Adding a field to a report

To add a new field to a report, click the Field List button 🗒 on the Report Design toolbar, then drag the field from the field list to the appropriate position on the report in Report Design View. This action creates both a label that displays the field name and a text box that displays the value of the field on the resulting report.

Adding a Calculation

In a report, you create a **calculation** by entering an expression into an unbound text box. When a report is previewed or printed, the expression is evaluated and the resulting calculation is placed on the report. An **expression** is a combination of field names, operators (such as +, –, /, and *), and functions that result in a single value. A **function** is a built-in formula such as Sum or Count that helps you quickly create a calculation. See Table D-2 for examples of common expressions that use Access functions. Notice that every expression starts with an equal sign, and when it uses a function, the arguments for the function are placed in parentheses. **Arguments** are the pieces of information that the function needs to create the final answer. When an argument is a field name, the field name must be surrounded by square brackets. Kelsey asks you to add another calculation to the Inventory Report to show the average Retail value for each category of items.

STEPS

1. **Right-click the** Inventory Report, **click** Design View, **click the** Text Box button ab **on the Toolbox toolbar, then click in the** Category Footer section **just below the Retail text box**

   Adding a new text box automatically adds a new label as well. You will modify the label to better describe the value that will be calculated by the text box. (*Note*: If you wanted to add only a descriptive label to the report, you would use the Label button Aa on the Toolbox toolbar.)

2. **Click the new** Text18: label **to select the label, double-click** Text18 **to select the text within the label, type** Average, **then press** [Enter]

   Now that the label displays descriptive text, you will enter the appropriate expression in the text box to calculate the average Retail value for each group of records.

3. **Click the new** Unbound text box control **in the Category Footer section to select the text box, click** Unbound **within the text box, type** =Avg([Retail]), **then press** [Enter]

   You used the Avg function to create the expression to average the values in the Retail field as shown in Figure D-10.

4. **Click the** Print Preview button 🔍 **on the Report Design toolbar, then click** 🔍 **to zoom in on the report as shown in Figure D-11**

   The average Retail value calculation is correct, but is not formatted to look like a monetary value.

5. **Click the** Design View button 📐 **on the Print Preview toolbar, click the** =Avg([Retail]) text box **to select it, click the** Properties button 📰 **on the Report Design toolbar to open the property sheet for the text box, click the** Format tab, **click the** Format list arrow, **then scroll and click** Currency

   The **property sheet** is a list of all of the characteristics of the selected control that you can modify. In this case, you modified the Format property, which changes the way the resulting calculation will appear on the report.

6. **Click** 📰 **to toggle off the property sheet, click the** Save button 💾 **on the Report Design toolbar, then click** 🔍 **to preview the report again**

   When you save a report object, you are saving the report definition, not the data displayed by the report. The data that the report displays was automatically saved when it was previously entered into the database. Once a report object is saved, it always shows the most up-to-date data when you preview or print the report. The average Retail calculation is now formatted with the Currency format, so it matches the values shown in the Retail field, which has a Currency data type.

FIGURE D-10: Adding a new calculation

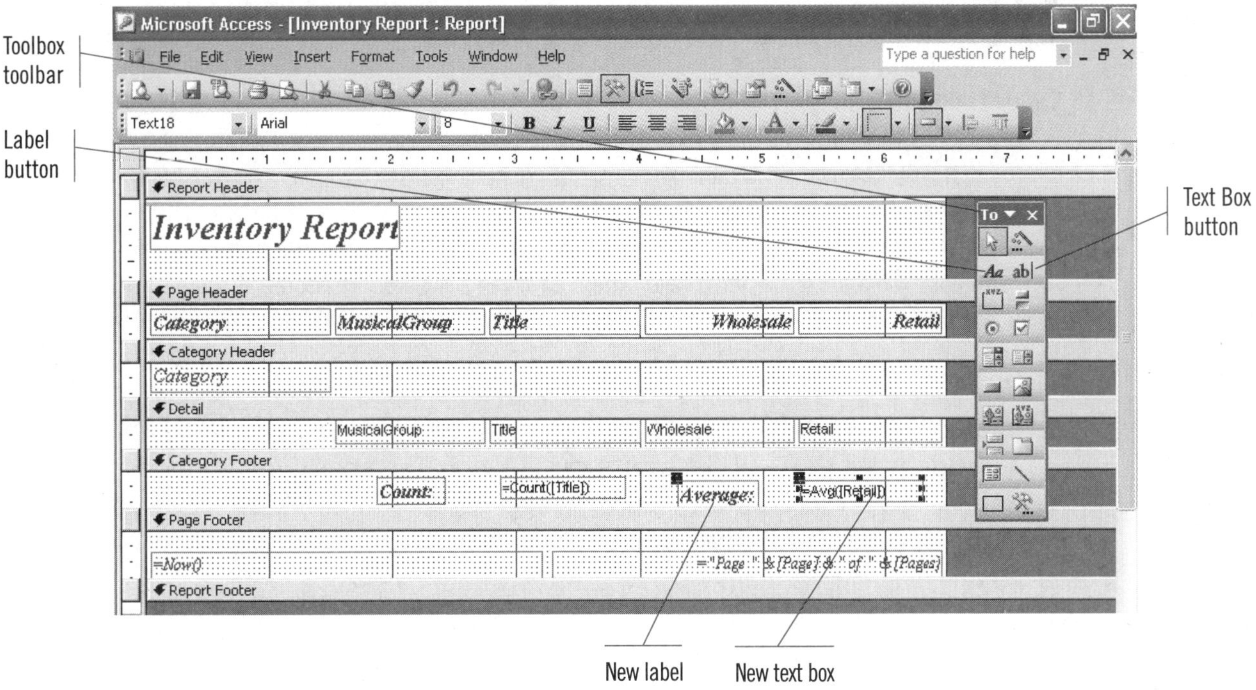
Toolbox toolbar
Label button
Text Box button
New label
New text box
Microsoft Access - [Inventory Report : Report]
Report Header
Inventory Report
Page Header
Category
MusicalGroup
Title
Wholesale
Retail
Category Header
Category
Detail
MusicalGroup
Title
Wholesale
Retail
Category Footer
Count:
=Count([Title])
Average:
=Avg([Retail])
Page Footer
=Now()
="Page " & [Page] & " of " & [Pages]
Report Footer

FIGURE D-11: Previewing the new calculation

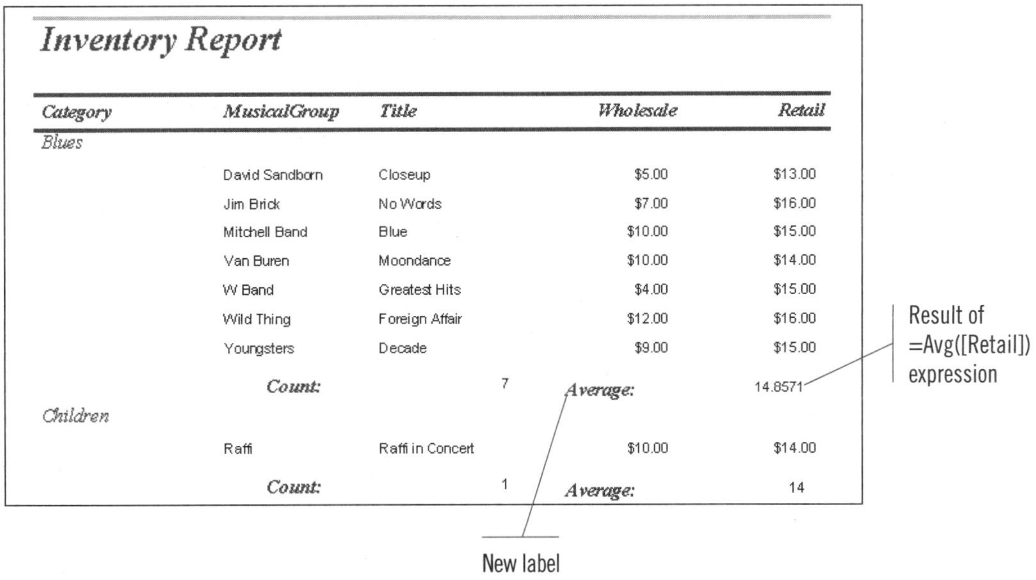
Inventory Report
Category
MusicalGroup
Title
Wholesale
Retail
Blues
David Sandborn
Closeup
$5.00
$13.00
Jim Brick
No Words
$7.00
$16.00
Mitchell Band
Blue
$10.00
$15.00
Van Buren
Moondance
$10.00
$14.00
W Band
Greatest Hits
$4.00
$15.00
Wild Thing
Foreign Affair
$12.00
$16.00
Youngsters
Decade
$9.00
$15.00
Count:
7
Average:
14.8571
Children
Raffi
Raffi in Concert
$10.00
$14.00
Count:
1
Average:
14
Result of =Avg([Retail]) expression
New label

TABLE D-2: Sample Access expressions

sample expression	description
=[Price]*1.05	Multiplies the Price field by 1.05 (adds 5% to the Price field)
=[Subtotal]+[Shipping]	Adds the value of the Subtotal field to the value of the Shipping field
=Avg([Freight])	Uses the **Avg** function to display an average of the values in the Freight field
=Date()	Uses the **Date** function to display the current date in the form of mm-dd-yy
="Page "&[Page]	Displays the word Page, a space, and the result of the **[Page]** field, an Access field that contains the current page number
=[FirstName]& " "&[LastName]	Displays the value of the FirstName and LastName fields in one control separated by a space
=Left([ProductNumber],2)	Uses the **Left** function to display the first two characters in the ProductNumber field

Aligning Controls

Once the information that you want to present has been added to the appropriate section of a report, you may also want to align the data on the report. Aligning controls in precise columns and rows makes the information easier to read. There are two different types of **alignment** commands: you can left-, right-, or center-align a control *within its own border* using the Alignment buttons on the Formatting (Form/Report) toolbar, or you can align the edges of controls *with respect to one another* using the Align command on the Format menu. ▓▓▓▓ You decide to align the controls in the Category Footer section to improve the readability of the report.

QUICK TIP

You can drag through the horizontal ruler to select all controls that intersect with the selection line.

1. **Click the** Design View button 🖾 **on the Print Preview toolbar, then click in the** vertical ruler **to the left of the Count label in the Category Footer section**

   When you click a ruler, a selection line crosses the report at that point. In this case, the selection line touched all four controls in the Category Footer section as shown in Figure D-12. All four controls are now selected.

2. **Click the** Align Right button ▤ **on the Formatting (Form/Report) toolbar**

   Now the information displayed by these controls is right-aligned within the border of each control. In addition to aligning the information *within* the controls, you want to align the controls *with respect to each other*.

QUICK TIP

If you make a mistake, click the Undo button ↺.

3. **With the four controls still selected, click** Format **on the menu bar, point to** Align, **then click** Bottom

   Now the bottom edges of the four controls are aligned with respect to one another. You can also align controls in different sections with respect to one another to form perfect columns.

4. **Click the** Retail text box **in the Detail section, press and hold** [Shift], **click the** =Avg([Retail]) text box **in the Category Footer section, click** Format **on the menu bar, point to** Align, **then click** Right

   The right edges of the Retail text box and =Avg([Retail]) text box are now aligned with respect to each other so they will form a perfect column on the report.

5. **Click the** Save button 🖫, **click the** Print Preview button 🔍, **then scroll and zoom so that your report looks similar to Figure D-13**

FIGURE D-12: Selecting multiple controls

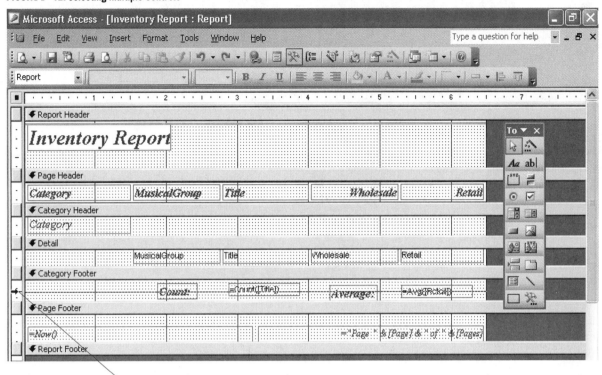

Click in the vertical ruler to select all controls in that section

FIGURE D-13: Controls are aligned

Inventory Report

Category	MusicalGroup	Title	Wholesale	Retail
Blues				
	David Sandborn	Closeup	$5.00	$13.00
	Jim Brick	No Words	$7.00	$16.00
	Mitchell Band	Blue	$10.00	$15.00
	Van Buren	Moondance	$10.00	$14.00
	W Band	Greatest Hits	$4.00	$15.00
	Wild Thing	Foreign Affair	$12.00	$16.00
	Youngsters	Decade	$9.00	$15.00
	Count:	7	Average:	$14.86
Children				
	Raffi	Raffi in Concert	$10.00	$14.00
	Count:	1	Average:	$14.00

Right edges of controls are aligned

Bottom edges of controls are aligned

Clues to Use

Precisely moving and resizing controls

You can move and resize controls using the mouse, but precise movements are often easier to accomplish using the keyboard. Pressing the arrow keys while holding [Ctrl] moves selected controls one **pixel** (picture element) at a time in the direction of the arrow. Pressing the arrow keys while holding [Shift] resizes selected controls one pixel at a time.

Formatting Controls

Formatting refers to enhancing the appearance of the information. Table D-3 lists several of the most popular formatting commands found on the Formatting (Form/Report) toolbar. Although the Report Wizard automatically applies many formatting embellishments to a report, you often want to improve the appearance of the report to fit your particular needs. ░░░░ In reviewing the Inventory Report with Kelsey, you decide to format the category names on the report to make it more prominent.

STEPS

1. **Click the** Design View button ▨ **on the Print Preview toolbar, then click the** Category text box **in the Category Header section**

   Before you can format any control, it must be selected.

2. **Click the** Font Size list arrow `11 ▾` **on the Formatting (Form/Report) toolbar, click** 12, **then click the** Bold button **B** **on the Formatting (Form/Report) toolbar**

   Increasing the font size and applying bold are common ways to make information more visible on a report. You can also change the colors of the control.

   QUICK TIP
   When the color on the Fill/Back Color ░, Font/Fore Color **A**, or Line/Border Color ▨ button displays the color you want, you simply click the button to apply that color.

3. **With the Category text box still selected, click the** Font/Fore Color button **A** **to select red as the font color**

   Many buttons on the Formatting (Form/Report) toolbar include a list arrow that you can click to reveal a list of formatting choices. When you click the color list arrow, a palette of available colors is displayed.

4. **With the Category text box still selected, click the** Fill/Back Color list arrow ░ ▾, **then click the** light gray color **(fourth row, last column on the right) as shown in Figure D-14**

   Be careful about relying too heavily on color formatting. Background shades often become solid black boxes when printed on a black-and-white printer or fax machine. Fortunately, Access allows you to undo up to your 20 most recent actions in Report Design View.

   QUICK TIP
   The quick keystroke for Undo is [Ctrl][Z]. The quick keystroke for Redo is [Ctrl][Y].

5. **With the Category text box still selected, click the** Undo button ▨ **on the Report Design toolbar to remove the background color, click** ▨ **to remove the font color, then click the** Redo button ▨ **to redo the font color**

   If you undo more actions than desired, use the Redo command on the Edit menu to redo the last undone action. The Redo menu command changes depending on the last undone action, and it can be used to redo up to 20 undone actions.

6. **Click the** Line/Border Color list arrow ▨ ▾, **click the** dark blue color **(first row, second to last column), then click the** Print Preview button ▨

   The screen should look like Figure D-15.

   QUICK TIP
   If you want your name on the printout, switch to Report Design View and add your name as a label to the Page Header section.

7. **Click** File **on the menu bar, click** Print, **type** 1 **in the From text box, type** 1 **in the To text box, then click** OK

8. **Close the Inventory Report, then click** Yes **when prompted to save it**

FIGURE D-14: Formatting a report

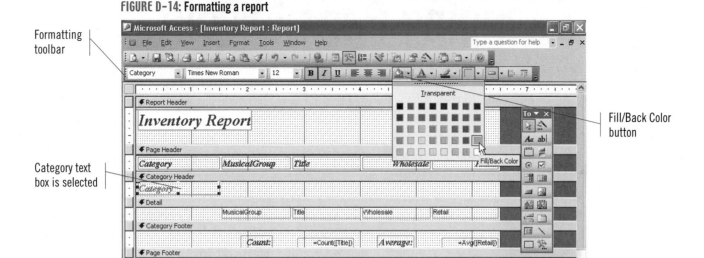

Formatting toolbar

Fill/Back Color button

Category text box is selected

FIGURE D-15: Formatted Inventory Report

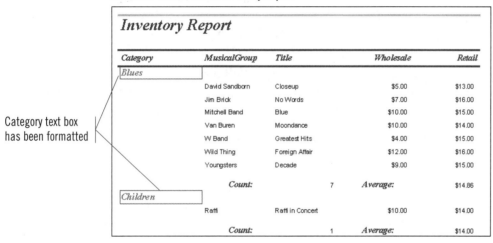

Category text box has been formatted

TABLE D-3: Useful formatting commands

button	button name	description
B	Bold	Toggles bold on or off for the selected control(s)
I	Italic	Toggles italics on or off for the selected control(s)
<u>U</u>	Underline	Toggles underline on or off for the selected control(s)
≣	Align Left	Left-aligns the selected control(s) within its own border
≣	Center	Center-aligns the selected control(s) within its own border
≣	Align Right	Right-aligns the selected control(s) within its own border
⬥ ▾	Fill/Back Color	Changes the background color of the selected control(s)
A ▾	Font/Fore Color	Changes the text color of the selected control(s)
✎ ▾	Line/Border Color	Changes the border color of the selected control(s)
▾	Line/Border Width	Changes the style of the border of the selected control(s)
▭ ▾	Special Effect	Changes the special visual effect of the selected control(s)

Changing Page Layout

In order to fit all of the information on a report on a physical sheet of paper, you may need to change the page layout options such as margins or page orientation. If a report contains a large number of columns, for example, you may want to expand the print area by narrowing the margins. Or, you might want to switch from a portrait (8.5" wide by 11" tall) to a landscape (11" wide by 8.5" tall) paper orientation. ▰▰▰▰ Kelsey has created a report called Inventory by Artist Report that doesn't display all of the information properly. You modify the page layout options to provide more room on the paper to help solve this problem.

STEPS

1. **Double-click the** Inventory by Artist Report **to open it in Print Preview, then click with the** 🔍 **pointer to zoom in on the report as shown in Figure D-16**

   In examining the report, you see that you need more horizontal space on the paper to display all of the labels and field values properly. One way to provide more horizontal space on the report is to switch from portrait to landscape orientation.

2. **Click the** Setup button **on the Print Preview toolbar, click the** Page tab, **click the** Landscape option button, **then click** OK

   In landscape orientation the paper is wider (11") than tall (8.5"). While this orientation works well for reports with many columns of data, you decide that this report doesn't really need to be printed in landscape orientation, but rather, could fit in portrait orientation with an extra inch of horizontal space. You add the extra inch by narrowing the left and right margins from 1" to 0.5".

3. **Click the** Setup button, **click the** Page tab, **click the** Portrait option button, **click the** Margins tab, **select** 1 **in the Left box, type** 0.5, **select** 1 **in the Right box, type** 0.5, **then click** OK

   By narrowing the margins, you have an extra inch of horizontal space to work with Report Design View.

TROUBLE

Do not drag the right edge of the paper beyond the 7.5" mark or your printout will not fit on a single sheet of paper.

4. **Click the** Design View button 📐 **on the Print Preview toolbar, then drag the right edge of the report from the** 6.5" **mark on the horizontal ruler to the** 7.5" **mark on the horizontal ruler**

   The horizontal ruler tells you the width of the print area. Because a piece of paper is 8.5" wide in portrait orientation and you have specified 0.5" left and right margins, you can expand the width of the print area to 7.5" to give the existing controls more horizontal space.

5. **Use your moving, resizing, and aligning skills to make Report Design View look like Figure D-17**

   Don't worry if your report doesn't look exactly like Figure D-17, but make sure that all of the labels are wide enough to display the text within them, and be sure to widen the MusicalGroup and Title text boxes so that the field values are not cut off when you preview the report. To increase your productivity, use the [Shift] key to click and select more than one control at a time before you move, resize, or align them.

TROUBLE

To select the lines in the Page Header section, you may need to expand that section slightly in order to clearly see and select the lines.

6. **Click the** Save button 💾, **then click the** Print Preview button 🔍

   Your new report should look like Figure D-18. You may need to move back and forth between Report Design View and Print Preview making several adjustments before you are satisfied with your report.

7. **When finished improving the report, click** File **on the menu bar, click** Print, **click the** Pages option button, **type** 1 **in the From box, type** 1 **in the To box, and then click** OK

8. **Close the Inventory by Artist Report, close the MediaLoft-D.mdb database, then exit Access**

QUICK TIP

If you want your name on the printout, switch to Report Design View and add your name as a label to the Page Header section.

FIGURE D-16: Initial Inventory by Artist List Report

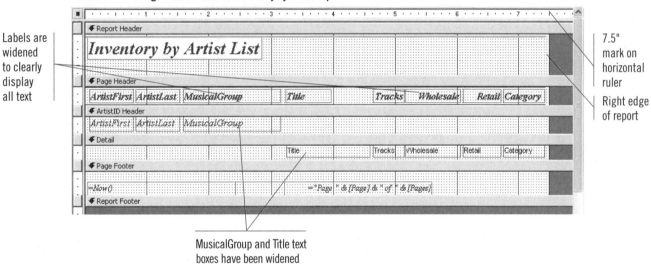

Inventory by Artist List

ArtistFirst	ArtistLast	MusicalG━	Title	Tracks	Wholesale	Retail	Category
Kenneth	George	KG					
			KG Live	11	$5.00	$20.00	Rock
			Skyline Fire	10	$14.00	$18.00	NewAge
David	Lantz	Lantz Orc					
			Sacred Roa	12	$6.00	$17.00	Gospel
			Heartsound	14	$7.00	$17.00	Gospel
Leonard	Bernard	Leonard B					
			Favorite Ov	5	$10.00	$15.00	Classical
			Handel's M	11	$6.00	$12.00	Classical

These labels are not displaying properly

Information in MusicalGroup and Title text boxes doesn't display properly

FIGURE D-17: Design View of widened Inventory by Artist Report

Labels are widened to clearly display all text

7.5" mark on horizontal ruler

Right edge of report

MusicalGroup and Title text boxes have been widened

Report Header
Inventory by Artist List
Page Header
ArtistFirst ArtistLast MusicalGroup Title Tracks Wholesale Retail Category
ArtistID Header
ArtistFirst ArtistLast MusicalGroup
Detail
Title Tracks Wholesale Retail Category
Page Footer
=Now() ="Page " & [Page] & " of " & [Pages]
Report Footer

FIGURE D-18: Final Inventory by Artist Report

Inventory by Artist List

ArtistFirst	ArtistLast	MusicalGroup	Title	Tracks	Wholesale	Retail	Category
Kenneth	George	KG					
			KG Live	11	$5.00	$20.00	Rock
			Skyline Firedance	10	$14.00	$18.00	NewAge
David	Lantz	Lantz Orchestra					
			Sacred Road	12	$6.00	$17.00	Gospel
			Heartsounds	14	$7.00	$17.00	Gospel
Leonard	Bernard	Leonard Bernard					
			Favorite Overtures	5	$10.00	$15.00	Classical
			Handel's Messiah	11	$6.00	$12.00	Classical

Report now clearly displays all labels

All text boxes are wide enough to display field values

Practice

▼ CONCEPTS REVIEW

Label each element of the Report Design View window shown in Figure D-19.

FIGURE D-19

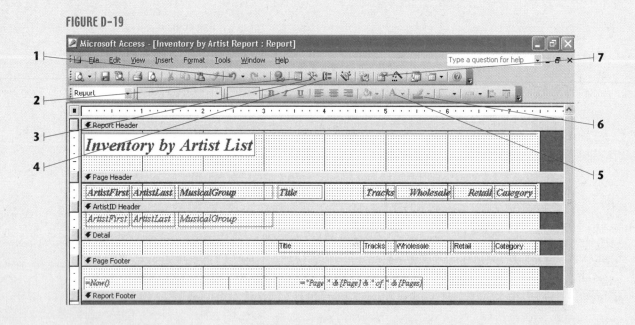

Match each term with the statement that best describes it.

8. **Expression**

9. **Section**

10. **Detail section**

11. **Record Source property**

12. **Formatting**

13. **Grouping**

a. Prints once for every record

b. Determines where a control will display on the report and how often it will print

c. Used to identify which fields and records are passed to the report

d. Enhancing the appearance of information displayed in the report

e. Sorting records *plus* providing a section before and after the group of records

f. A combination of field names, operators, and functions that result in a single value

Select the best answer from the list of choices.

14. Press and hold which key to select more than one control in Report Design View?
    a. [Alt]
    b. [Ctrl]
    c. [Shift]
    d. [Tab]

15. Which type of control is most commonly placed in the Detail section?
    a. Combo box
    b. Label
    c. List box
    d. Text box

16. Which type of control is most commonly placed in the Page Header section?
    a. Bound image
    b. Combo box
    c. Command button
    d. Label

17. A calculated expression is most often placed in which report section?
    a. Detail
    b. Formulas
    c. Group Footer
    d. Report Header

18. Which of the following would be the appropriate expression to count the number of records using the FirstName field?
    a. =Count(FirstName)
    b. =Count[FirstName]
    c. =Count{FirstName}
    d. =Count([FirstName])

19. To align the edges of several controls with respect to one another, you use the alignment commands on the:
    a. Format menu.
    b. Formatting toolbar.
    c. Print Preview toolbar.
    d. Standard toolbar.

20. Which of the following may *not* be changed in the Page Setup dialog box?
    a. Font size
    b. Margins
    c. Paper orientation
    d. Paper size

▼ SKILLS REVIEW

1. Plan a report.

a. Plan a report to use for tracking members of a ski club. You want to list the member names, their employer, address, dues owed, dues paid, and membership status (Active or Inactive).

b. Sketch the Report Header, Group Header, and Detail sections of the report by using sample data based on the following information:

- The title of the report should be **Membership Report**.
- The records should be grouped by the Status field so that Active members are listed before Inactive members.
- The Detail section should include information on the person, their employer, address, dues owed, and dues paid.

2. Create a report.

a. Start Access and open the **Club-D.mdb database** from the drive and folder where your Data Files are stored.

b. Use the Report Wizard to create a report based on the MEMBERS table.

c. Include the following fields in the following order for the report: STATUS, FNAME, LNAME, DUESOWED, DUESPAID.

d. Use STATUS as the grouping field, but do not specify any sort orders.

e. Use the Stepped layout and Portrait orientation.

f. Use a Casual style and title the report **Membership Status Report**.

g. Preview the first page of the new report.

3. Use Group sections.

a. In Report Design View, open the Sorting and Grouping dialog box, then open the STATUS Footer section using the Sorting and Grouping dialog box.

b. Close the Sorting and Grouping dialog box.

c. Preview the first page of the new report.

4. Change the sort order.

a. In Report Design View, open the Sorting and Grouping dialog box, then add LNAME as a sort field in ascending order immediately below the STATUS field.

b. Close the Sorting and Grouping dialog box, then preview the first page of the new report.

5. Add a calculation.

a. In Report Design View, add a text box control to the STATUS Footer section just below the DUESOWED field. Change the label to **Subtotal:** and enter the expression **=Sum([DUESOWED])** in the text box.

b. Add a text box control to the STATUS Footer section just below the DUESPAID field. Delete the accompanying label, and enter the expression **=SUM([DUESPAID])** in the text box.

c. Use the property sheet to change the Format property for both of the new calculations to Currency, then close the property sheet.

d. Click the Label button on the Toolbox toolbar, then click in the Report Header section to add a label control. Modify the label to display your name.

e. Preview both pages of the report.

6. Align controls.

  a. In Report Design View, right-align the new calculated controls in the STATUS Footer section.

  b. Select the three controls in the STATUS Footer section, then align the bottoms of the controls with respect to one another.

  c. Select the DUESOWED text box in the Detail section, and the =Sum([DUESOWED]) calculated expression in the STATUS Footer section, then right-align the controls with respect to one another.

  d. Select the DUESPAID text box in the Detail section, and the =Sum([DUESPAID]) calculated expression in the STATUS Footer section, then right-align the controls with respect to one another.

7. Format controls.

  a. Select the STATUS text box in the STATUS Header section, change the font size to 12 points, bold and italicize the control, then change the Fill/Back color to bright yellow. The Report Design View should look like Figure D-20.

  b. Save, then preview the report.

8. Change page layout.

  a. Use the Page Setup dialog box to change the top margin of the report to 1.5".

  b. Preview, then print the report.

  c. Close and save the Membership Status Report.

  d. Close the Club-D.mdb database, then exit Access.

FIGURE D-20

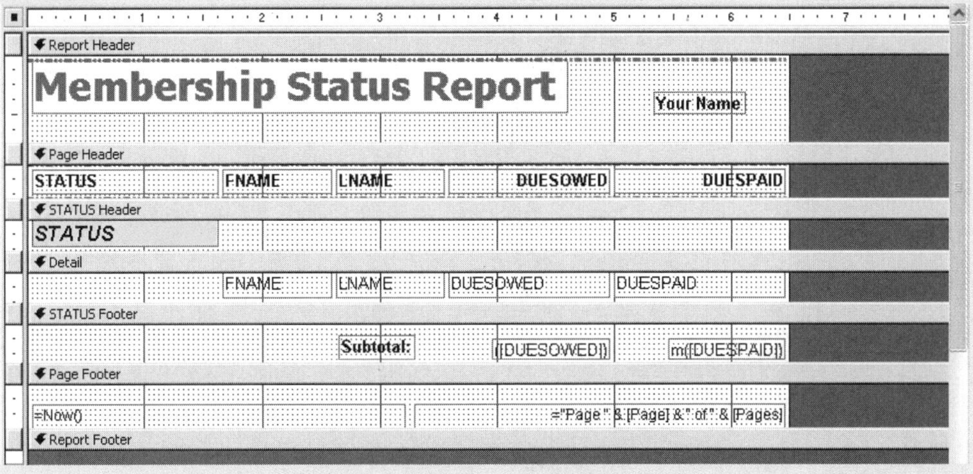

▼ INDEPENDENT CHALLENGE 1

You have been hired to create a report for a physical therapy clinic.

   a. Start Access then open the Therapy-D.mdb database from the drive and folder where your Data Files are stored.

   b. Use the Report Wizard to create a report using all of the fields from the Location Financial Query.

   c. View your data by Surveys, group by Street, and sort by PatientLast.

   d. Use the Stepped layout, Portrait orientation, and Soft Gray style.

   e. Name the report Location Financial Report.

   f. In Report Design View, open the Street Footer section, then add a text box to the Street Footer section just below the Charges text box in the Detail section.

   g. Modify the label to the left of the new text box to display Subtotal:

   h. Enter an expression in the new text box to sum the Charges field.

   i. Right-align the new text box in the Street Footer section and then align the right edges of the new text box in the Street Footer section and the Charges text box in the Detail section with respect to each other.

   j. Choose Currency for the Format property of the new text box in the Street Footer section.

   k. Click the Label button in the Toolbox toolbar, then click in the Report Header section to add a label control. Modify the label to display your name.

   l. Save, then print the first page of the report.

   m. Close Location Financial Report, close the Therapy-D.mdb database, then exit Access.

▼ INDEPENDENT CHALLENGE 2

You have been hired to create a report for a physical therapy clinic.

a. Start Access and open the **Therapy-D.mdb database** from the drive and folder where your Data Files are stored.

b. Use the Report Wizard to create a report using all of the fields from the Therapist Satisfaction Query except for the Initials and First fields.

c. View the data by Therapists. Do not add any additional grouping or sorting fields.

d. Use the Block layout, Portrait orientation, and Bold style.

e. Title the report **Physical Therapist Satisfaction Report**, then view the report.

f. In Report Design View, click the Label button in the Toolbox toolbar, then click in the Report Header section to add a label control. Modify the label to display your name.

g. Use the Sorting and Grouping dialog box to group the records by Last. Open the Group Footer section for the Last field.

h. Use the Sorting and Grouping dialog box to further sort the records by PatientLast, then close the Sorting and Grouping dialog box.

i. Add a text box to the Last Footer section below the Courtesy text box in the Detail section. Change the accompanying label to display **Averages:** and enter an expression into the new text box to calculate the average value in the Courtesy field.

j. Add another text box to the Last Footer section below the Knowledge text box in the Detail section. Delete the accompanying label and enter an expression into the new text box to calculate the average in the Knowledge field.

k. Modify the Format property of the two new text boxes in the Last Footer section to be Fixed. Modify the Decimal Places property of the two new text boxes in the Last Footer section to be 1.

l. Resize the new calculated controls so that they are the same size as the Courtesy and Knowledge text boxes in the Detail section.

m. Right-align the two new calculated controls within their own borders.

n. Align the right edge of the text box that calculates the average for the Courtesy field with respect to the Courtesy text box above it. Align the right edge of the text box that calculates the average for the Knowledge field with respect to the Knowledge text box above it.

o. Align the top edges of the new controls in the Last Footer section with respect to each other.

p. Modify the Last label in the Page Header section to read **Therapist**. Be careful to modify the Last label in the Page Header section and not the Last text box in the Detail section.

q. If the report is wider than 6.5" wide, drag the right edge of the report to the left so that the final report is no wider than 6.5".

r. Save, then preview the report. The report should look like Figure D-21.

s. Print then close the Physical Therapist Satisfaction Report.

t. Close the Therapy-D.mdb database, then exit Access.

Access 2003

FIGURE D-21

Physical Therapist Satisfaction Report

Your Name

Therapist	PatientFirst	PatientLast	Courtesy	Knowledge
Breckenridge	Kelsey	Beuchant	5	4
	Oliva	Copper	4	4
	Elizabeth	Custone	4	4
	Lily	Moon	2	3
	Raymond	Parker	5	4
		Averages:	4.0	3.8
Lopez	Aparna	Chaffee	5	4
	Thomas	Green	5	4
	Lance	Lyon	5	5
	Lisa	Modic	5	4
	Sumei	Ouyang	5	5
	Sonnie	Rich	5	5
		Averages:	5.0	4.5

▼ INDEPENDENT CHALLENGE 3

You have been hired to modify a report for a physical therapy clinic.

a. Start Access and open the **Therapy-D.mdb database** from the drive and folder where your Data Files are stored.

b. Open the Overall Statistics Report in Print Preview, then print the first page so you can examine the problems this report presents because the controls do not have enough horizontal space to display all of the information.

c. Change the page orientation to landscape, then open Report Design View.

d. Drag the right edge of the report to the 8" mark on the horizontal ruler.

e. Click the Label button in the Toolbox toolbar, then click in the Report Header section to add a label control. Modify the label to display your name.

Advanced Challenge Exercise

- Delete the PatientLast label in the Page Header section. Be careful not to delete the PatientLast text box in the Detail section.
- Change the PatientFirst label in the Page Header section to display only the text **Patient**. Be careful to modify the PatientFirst label in the Page Header section and not the PatientFirst text box in the Detail section.
- Change the Font face from Arial to Arial Narrow for the Scheduling, Location, Hours, Courtesy, and Knowledge labels in the Page Header section.
- Use your moving, resizing, and alignment skills so that all of the labels in the Page Header section clearly display all of the text and so that the right edges of these labels are aligned with the right edges of their respective text boxes in the Detail section.

f. Save, preview, and then print the first page of the report. It should look similar to Figure D-22.

g. Close the Overall Statistics report, close the Therapy-D.mdb database, then exit Access.

FIGURE D-22

Overall Statistics

Your Name

First	Last	Date	Street	Patient		Scheduling	Location	Hours	Courtesy	Knowledge
Cesar	Lopez									
		10/4/2005	985 North 18th Street	Lance	Lyon	5	4	5	5	5
		12/5/2005	2626 West 74th Street	Sumei	Ouyang	4	4	4	5	5
		2/15/2005	105 South 18th Street	Lisa	Modic	2	4	2	5	4
		7/31/2006	105 South 18th Street	Aparna	Chaffee	5	5	5	5	4
		8/1/2006	985 North 18th Street	Thomas	Green	5	4	4	5	4
		8/2/2006	2626 West 74th Street	Sonnie	Rich	5	5	4	5	5
Douglas	North									
		10/5/2005	985 North 18th Street	Terrance	George	4	4	4	4	4
		2/22/2005	2626 West 74th Street	Lomu	Confetti	1	4	4	4	4
		7/31/2006	105 South 18th Street	Hagrid	Tann	4	3	4	4	4
		8/1/2006	985 North 18th Street	Brook	Black	5	5	5	5	5
		8/1/2006	985 North 18th Street	Karter	Brownline	5	5	4	4	5
		8/1/2006	2626 West 74th Street	Robert	Choe	4	4	5	5	4

▼ **INDEPENDENT CHALLENGE 4**

You are on the staff of an economic development team whose goal is to encourage tourism in the Baltic Sea region. You have created an Access database called Baltic-D.mdb to track important fields of information for the countries in that region. You have been using the Internet to find information about events and demographics in the area and are entering that information into the database using existing forms. You need to create and then print reports to present to the team.

a. Start Access and open the **Baltic-D.mdb database** from the drive and folder where your Data Files are stored.

b. Connect to the Internet, then go to www.google.com, www.yahoo.com, or another search engine to conduct research for your database. Your goal is to find three upcoming events for Helsinki and Finland and to print the Web pages.

c. Open the Cities form, find the Helsinki record, and enter three events for Helsinki into the Events fields. EventID is an AutoNumber field, so it will automatically increment as you enter the EventName and EventDate information.

Advanced Challenge Exercise

- Use the Simple Query Wizard to create a query with these fields: City and Country from the Cities table and EventName and EventDate from the Events table. Make the query a Detail query that shows every field of every record and name the query **Baltic Area Festivals**.
- Use the Report Wizard to create a report based on the Baltic Area Festivals query. Use all of the fields. View the data by Cities, do not add any more grouping levels, and sort the records in ascending order by EventDate.
- Use an Outline 1 layout, a Portrait orientation, and a Corporate style.
- Title the report **Baltic Festivals Report**.
- In Report Design View, click the Label button in the Toolbox toolbar, then click in the Report Header section to add a label control. Modify the label to display your name.
- Format the report as desired.
- Save, preview, and print the Baltic Festivals Report, then close it.

d. Close the Baltic-D.mdb database, then exit Access.

▼ VISUAL WORKSHOP

Open the **Club-D.mdb database** from the drive and folder where your Data Files are stored to create the report based on the MEMBERS table. The report is shown in Figure D-23. The Report Wizard, Stepped layout, Portrait orientation, and the Corporate style were used to create this report. Note that the records are grouped by the CITY field and sorted within each group by the LNAME field. A calculated control that counts the number of records is displayed in the City Footer. Add a label with your name to the Report Header section, then save and print the report.

FIGURE D-23

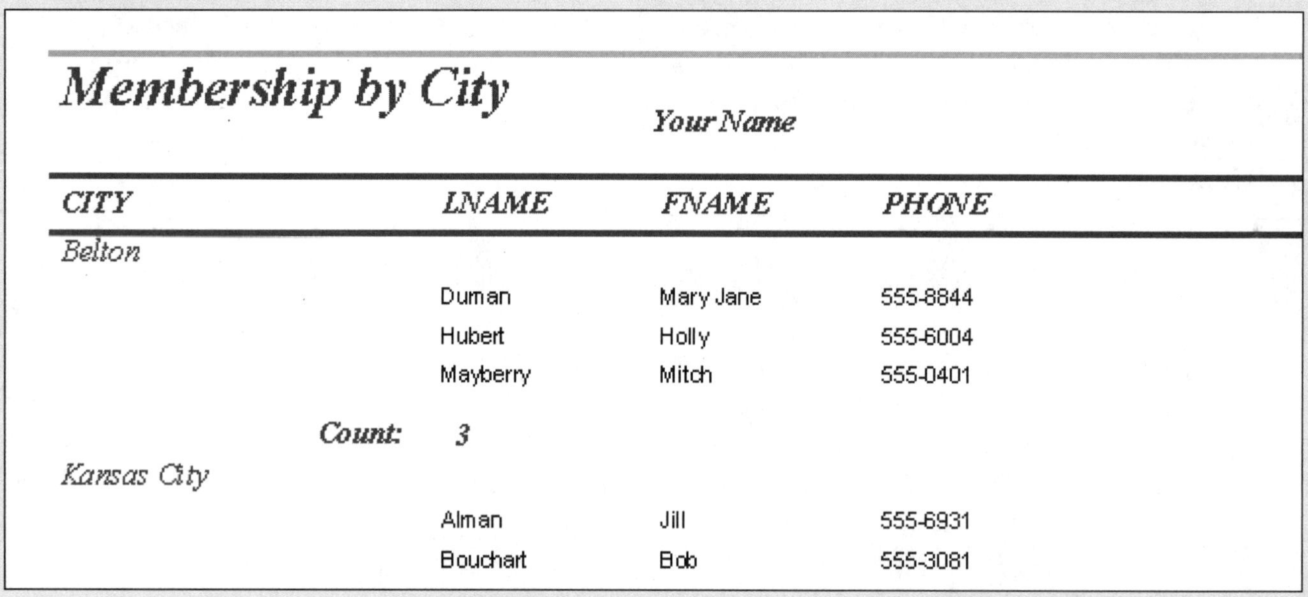

Membership by City

Your Name

CITY	LNAME	FNAME	PHONE
Belton			
	Duman	Mary Jane	555-8844
	Hubert	Holly	555-6004
	Mayberry	Mitch	555-0401
Count: 3			
Kansas City			
	Alman	Jill	555-6931
	Bouchart	Bob	555-3081

Integrating Word, Excel, and Access

OBJECTIVES

As the administrator of a business, your typical to-do list might include creating sales charts, identifying new inventory items to order, completing purchase orders, and producing a proposal to secure a new contract. To accomplish such diverse tasks quickly and easily, you need to use each program in the Office suite to its maximum efficiency. A good strategy is to build an Access database that contains the names and addresses of customers and suppliers, information about inventory, and sales records. You can then include selected tables from the database in reports and other documents that you create in Word. You can also analyze data from the Access database in Excel and then produce charts and spreadsheets. ▓▓▓ Karen Rosen, the director of human resources at MediaLoft, maintains an extensive database of employees. She asks you to identify the kinds of documents you can create and tasks you can accomplish by combining data from an Access database with Word and Excel. She then asks you to use the three programs to create a company profile and a memo report.

Identifying Integration Opportunities

You can integrate information created in different Office 2003 programs in a variety of ways. For example, you can enter data into an Access database, create a chart from that data in Excel, and then create a report in Word that includes a copy of the Excel chart and copies of tables created in Access. 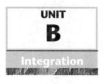 Karen asks you to review the various ways in which information can be shared between Access, Word, and Excel.

Access, Word, and Excel can be used together to:

- **Publish an Access table in Word**

  You use the Publish It with Microsoft Office Word feature to export a table created in Access to Word as shown in Figure B-1. The table is exported to a new Word document that is automatically saved in rich text format (.rtf) with the same name as the Access table. You can then format the table in Word just as you would any table. You can also copy the table into an existing Word document.

- **Analyze Access data in Excel**

  You use the Analyze It with Microsoft Office Excel feature to export an Access table to Excel. You can then use Excel features to manipulate and analyze the data. For example, you can calculate totals, create charts, and sort the data in a variety of ways. Figure B-2 shows how the data contained in an Access table can be analyzed and illustrated in chart form in Excel.

- **Merge data between Access and Word**

  An Access database can contain names, addresses, and other information about a company's customers, contacts, and suppliers. You can **merge** data from the database with a letter you've created in Word to create a series of individually addressed form letters. You can initiate the merge process from either Access or Word. In Access, you use the Merge It with Microsoft Office Word feature to merge an active table with a main document you've created in Word. In Word, you open the Mail Merge task pane and select an Access database as the data source. The document containing the standard text (the text that remains the same for each recipient) is called the **main document**. The file containing unique data for each individual recipient is called the **data source**.

Clues to Use

Understanding objects

An object is self-contained information in the form of text, spreadsheet data, graphics, a chart, table, or even a sound or video clip. Objects provide a means of sharing information between programs. You can use an object from one file or application in another file or application by selecting Object on the Insert menu or by selecting Paste Special on the Edit menu. You can create an embedded object within the destination file or you can copy it from the source file and then edit it within the destination program using the editing features of the source program. Any changes you make to an embedded object appear only in the destination file; the changes are not made to the information in the source file. A linked object is created in a source file, then inserted into a destination file and linked to the source file. When you link an object to its source, changes made to the data in the source file are reflected in the destination file. You create linked objects when you want to include information that is maintained independently, such as data collected by a different department, or when you need to keep that information up to date in the document that links to it. In a linked object, the connection between the source file and the destination file is called a **Dynamic Data Exchange (DDE) link**.

FIGURE B-1: Access table published in Word

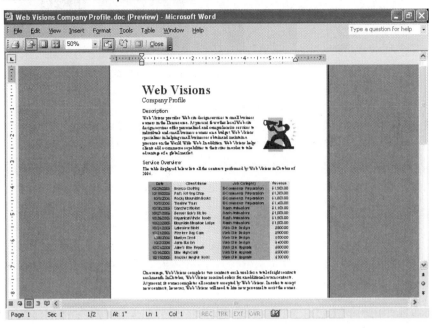

FIGURE B-2: Access table analyzed in Excel

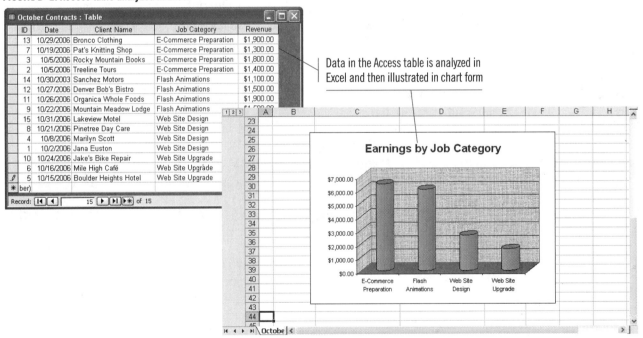

Data in the Access table is analyzed in Excel and then illustrated in chart form

Project 1: Company Profile for Web Visions

MediaLoft's Human Resources Department wants to hire Web Visions, a Web site design company in Denver, Colorado, to maintain the MediaLoft Web site. You are asked to work with the owner of Web Visions to put together a company profile that includes information about recent contracts and a chart that illustrates the most popular—and profitable—Web site design services offered.

ACTIVITY Creating the Web Visions Database

You need to create a database that contains information about the contracts completed by Web Visions in October 2006, and then create a query table that lists all contracts that paid more than $1200.

STEPS

1. Start Access, create a new database called Web Visions Database in the drive and folder where your Data Files are stored, double-click Create table in Design view, then enter the field names for the table, as shown in Figure B-3

2. Click Text in the Data Type column for Date, click the list arrow, click Date/Time, then change the data type for the Revenue field to Currency

3. Click the View button, click Yes to save the table, type October Contracts, click OK, then click Yes to create a primary key

> **QUICK TIP**
> You can enter dates as October 2, October 5, etc., and Access converts them to the correct date format when you press [Tab].

4. Enter the records for the October Contracts table and format the column widths as shown in Figure B-4

5. Close and save the October Contracts table, click Queries on the Objects bar, double-click Create query by using wizard, click the Select All Fields button >> to select all the fields for the query, click Next, click Next again, type High Revenue Contracts as the query title, click the Modify the query design option button, then click Finish

> **TROUBLE**
> The Revenue criteria cell is the blank cell directly under the check mark in the Revenue column. Seven of the 15 contracts the company completed in October generated revenues of more than $1200.

6. Click the Revenue criteria cell, type >1200, then click the Run button on the Query Design toolbar

7. Close and save the High Revenue Contracts query, click the OfficeLinks list arrow on the Database toolbar, then click Analyze It with Microsoft Office Excel
   In a few seconds, the Access table appears in Excel in a workbook called High Revenue Contracts.xls.

8. In Excel, click cell E9, click the AutoSum button Σ on the Standard toolbar twice, click cell D9, type Total Revenue, then press [Enter]

9. Format the worksheet so that it appears as shown in Figure B-5, then save and close the workbook

FIGURE B-3: Fields for the October Contracts table

Field Name	Data Type	Description
Date	Text	
Client Name	Text	
Job Category	Text	
▸ Revenue	Text ⌄	

`▦ Table1 : Table`

FIGURE B-4: Records for the October Contracts table

`▦ October Contracts : Table`

The year you create the database is entered here →

ID	Date	Client Name	Job Category	Revenue
1	10/2/2006	Jana Euston	Web Site Design	$400.00
2	10/5/2006	Treeline Tours	E-Commerce Preparation	$1,400.00
3	10/5/2006	Rocky Mountain Books	E-Commerce Preparation	$1,800.00
4	10/8/2006	Marilyn Scott	Web Site Design	$500.00
5	10/15/2006	Boulder Heights Hotel	Web Site Upgrade	$300.00
6	10/16/2006	Mile High Café	Web Site Upgrade	$500.00
7	10/19/2006	Pat's Knitting Shop	E-Commerce Preparation	$1,300.00
8	10/21/2006	Pinetree Day Care	Web Site Design	$900.00
9	10/22/2006	Mountain Meadow Lodge	Flash Animations	$1,500.00
10	10/24/2006	Jake's Bike Repair	Web Site Upgrade	$800.00
11	10/26/2006	Organica Whole Foods	Flash Animations	$1,900.00
12	10/27/2006	Denver Bob's Bistro	Flash Animations	$1,500.00
13	10/29/2006	Bronco Clothing	E-Commerce Preparation	$1,900.00
14	10/30/2006	Sanchez Motors	Flash Animations	$1,100.00
15	10/31/2006	Lakeview Motel	Web Site Design	$800.00
▸ At				$0.00

Record: ◄◄ ◄ 16 ► ►◄ ►* of 16

FIGURE B-5: Completed High Revenue Contracts worksheet in Excel

	A	B	C	D	E	F	G	H	I
1	ID	Date	Client Name	Job Category	Revenue				
2	2	05-Oct-06	Treeline Tours	E-Commerce Preparation	$1,400.00				
3	3	05-Oct-06	Rocky Mountain Books	E-Commerce Preparation	$1,800.00				
4	7	19-Oct-06	Pat's Knitting Shop	E-Commerce Preparation	$1,300.00				
5	9	22-Oct-06	Mountain Meadow Lodge	Flash Animations	$1,500.00				
6	11	26-Oct-06	Organica Whole Foods	Flash Animations	$1,900.00				
7	12	27-Oct-06	Denver Bob's Bistro	Flash Animations	$1,500.00				
8	13	29-Oct-06	Bronco Clothing	E-Commerce Preparation	$1,900.00				
9				Total Revenue	$11,300.00				
10									
11									
12									
13									
14									

Bold and right-align cell D9

Add the Top and Double Bottom Border

Bold labels

Integration

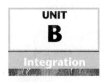

ACTIVITY **Creating a Cylinder Chart in Excel**

In the company profile that you create in Word, you want to include a cylinder chart that shows which job category generates the highest earnings. You create this chart in Excel from the data entered in the October Contracts table. To simplify the task of creating the cylinder chart, you first display the October Contracts table, and then you sort the Job Category records in alphabetical order. You then use the Excel Subtotal function to create the cylinder chart in Excel that shows the total earnings for each job category.

STEPS

1. **In Access, click** Tables **on the Objects bar, double-click** October Contracts **to open it, click** Job Category, **then click the** Sort Ascending button ⬇️ **on the Table Datasheet toolbar**

2. **Close and save the October Contracts table, make sure it is selected, then click the** OfficeLinks button ▦ ▾

   A second Excel workbook, automatically saved as October Contracts.xls, opens with the October Contracts table entered.

3. **Select the range of cells** A1:E16, **click** Data **on the menu bar, then click** Subtotals

   The Subtotal dialog box appears. You need to specify that you want the subtotals to appear after each series of jobs.

4. **Click the** At each change in list arrow, **click** Job Category, **verify that** Revenue **is selected in the Add subtotal to box, as shown in Figure B-6, then click** OK

   The total revenue from each of the four job categories now appears in your worksheet. For example, the company made a total of $6,000.00 on developing Flash animations for Web sites in October.

5. **Click away from the selected cells to deselect them, click the** Chart Wizard button 📊 **on the Standard toolbar, scroll down the list of chart types, click** Cylinder, **click** Next, **then click the** Collapse dialog box button 📑 **at the far right of the Data range text box**

6. **Click cell** E6, **press and hold** [Ctrl], **click cells** E11, E16, **and** E20, **click the** Restore dialog box button 📑, **click the** Series tab, **click the** Category (X) axis labels text box, **click** 📑, **use** [Ctrl] **to select cells** D5, D10, D15, **and** D19, **then click** 📑

7. **Click** Next, **click the** Titles tab **if necessary, click the** Chart title text box, **type** Earnings by Job Category **as the chart title, click** Finish, **move the chart down so that it begins in approximately cell** A25, **then drag the lower-right corner handle to approximately cell** E43

8. **Click** Series1 **(the legend) to select it, press** [Delete], **right-click anywhere on the gray walls of the chart, click** Format Walls, **click** Fill Effects, **click the** Texture tab, **select the** Canvas **texture as shown in Figure B-7, click** OK, **then click** OK

9. **Right-click the** x-axis labels, **click** Format Axis, **click the** Font tab, **select the** 8 point **font size, click** OK, **change the font size of the** y-axis labels **to** 8 point, **then save the workbook**

   Your chart appears as shown in Figure B-8.

FIGURE B-6: Subtotal dialog box

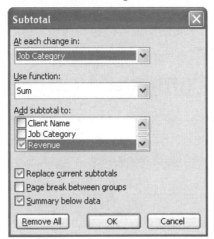

FIGURE B-7: Canvas texture selected

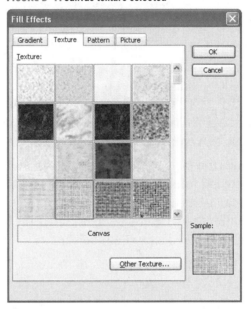

FIGURE B-8: Completed cylinder chart in Excel

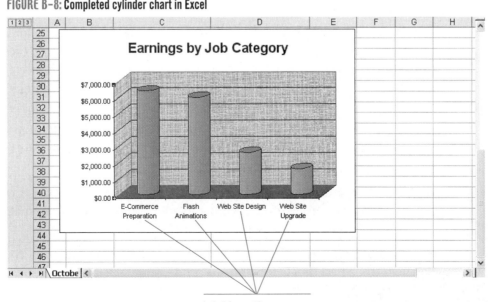

Label formatting may vary

UNIT
B

Integration

ACTIVITY | **Creating a Company Profile in Word**

The company profile will consist of the two pages shown in Figure B-9. You first create the heading and type the text, and then you insert the October Contracts table from Access, the cylinder chart from Excel, and the High Revenue Contracts worksheet from Excel.

STEPS

1. **Open a new Word document, type and enhance just the text (not the tables) shown in Figure B-9, then save the document as Web Visions Company Profile**
   Make sure you press [Enter] three times between the paragraphs where the data from Access and Excel is inserted.

2. **In Access, verify that the October Contracts table is selected, click the OfficeLinks button list arrow ⬛ ▾ on the Database toolbar, then click Publish It with Microsoft Office Word**
   The table is pasted into a new Word document that has been automatically named October Contracts.rtf. You need to copy the table into your company profile.

TROUBLE

To view the paragraph marks, click the Show/Hide ¶ button ¶ on the Standard toolbar.

3. **Move the insertion point over the upper-left corner of the table to show the table select icon ⊞, click ⊞, click the Copy button 🔲 on the Standard toolbar, click Window on the menu bar, click Web Visions Company Profile.doc, click the second paragraph mark below the Service Overview paragraph, then click the Paste button 🔳**

4. **Click ⊞ to select the table, click Table on the menu bar, click Table AutoFormat, select the Table Columns 2 format, click Apply, double-click the column division between ID and Date to automatically resize all the columns, select just the ID column, click the right mouse button, click Delete Columns, select the table again, then click the Center button ≡ on the Formatting toolbar**

5. **Apply bold to the labels in the first row of the table, then select the remaining rows in the table and remove the bold**

6. **Click the cylinder chart in Excel in the October Contracts.xls file, click 🔲, click after the first Service Breakdown paragraph in the Web Visions Company Profile document, click 🔳, click the copied chart, then click ≡**

7. **Click after the second to last paragraph (ending with "Flash Animation for Web sites"), click Insert on the menu bar, click Object, click the Create from File tab, click Browse, navigate to the drive and folder where you saved the High Revenue Contracts file, select High Revenue Contracts.xls, click Insert, click OK, then center the worksheet object in Word**

QUICK TIP

To show the document in Two Pages view, click the Zoom list arrow 114% ▾ on the Standard Toolbar, then click Two Pages.

8. **Switch to Two Pages view, click in the first paragraph, show the Drawing toolbar, click the Insert Clip Art button 🖼 on the Drawing toolbar, click in the Search for text box, type Vision, press [Enter], then insert the picture of your choice and close the Clip Art task pane**
   The picture does not appear in the correct location.

9. **Right-click the image, click Format Picture, click the Layout tab, click Square, click Right, click OK, then drag the lower-right corner handle of the picture up to reduce its size so it appears similar to the picture shown in Figure B-9**

10. **Return to 100% view, click Insert on the menu bar, click Page Numbers, change the Alignment to Center, click OK, enter your name below the last paragraph, print a copy of the document, then save and close all files and all programs**

FIGURE B-9: Completed company profile for Web Visions

Web Visions

Company Profile

Description

Web Visions provides Web site design services to small business owners in the Denver area. At present, few other local Web site design services offer personalized and comprehensive services to individuals and small business owners on a budget. Web Visions specializes in helping small businesses obtain and maintain a presence on the World Wide Web. In addition, Web Visions helps clients add e-commerce capabilities to their sites in order to take advantage of a global market.

Service Overview

The table displayed below lists all the contracts performed by Web Visions in October of 2006.

Date	Client Name	Job Category	Revenue
10/29/2006	Bronco Clothing	E-Commerce Preparation	$1,900.00
10/19/2006	Pat's Knitting Shop	E-Commerce Preparation	$1,300.00
10/5/2006	Rocky Mountain Books	E-Commerce Preparation	$1,800.00
10/5/2006	Treeline Tours	E-Commerce Preparation	$1,400.00
10/30/2006	Sanchez Motors	Flash Animations	$1,100.00
10/27/2006	Denver Bob's Bistro	Flash Animations	$1,500.00
10/26/2006	Organica Whole Foods	Flash Animations	$1,900.00
10/22/2006	Mountain Meadow Lodge	Flash Animations	$1,500.00
10/31/2006	Lakeview Motel	Web Site Design	$800.00
10/21/2006	Pinetree Day Care	Web Site Design	$900.00
10/8/2006	Marilyn Scott	Web Site Design	$500.00
10/2/2006	Jana Euston	Web Site Design	$400.00
10/24/2006	Jake's Bike Repair	Web Site Upgrade	$800.00
10/16/2006	Mile High Café	Web Site Upgrade	$500.00
10/15/2006	Boulder Heights Hotel	Web Site Upgrade	$300.00

On average, Web Visions completes two contracts each week for a total of eight contracts each month. In October, Web Visions received orders for an additional seven contracts. At present, its owner completes all contracts accepted by Web Visions. In order to accept new contracts, however, Web Visions will need to hire new personnel to assist the owner.

1

Service Breakdown

The cylinder chart below shows the breakdown of contracts in terms of the revenue generated in October of 2006. The highest revenue is generated from contracts related to E-Commerce and Flash Animation.

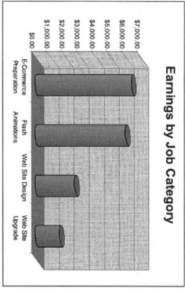

Since January of 2006, E-Commerce and Flash Animation contracts have become the number one priority of Web Visions. The table below lists all contracts in October 2006 that generated more than $1,200. The total revenue of $11,300.00 comes exclusively from contracts involving either E-Commerce preparation of Web sites or the designing of Flash Animation for Web sites.

ID	Date	Client Name	Job Category	Revenue
2	05-Oct-06	Treeline Tours	E-Commerce Preparation	$1,400.00
3	05-Oct-06	Rocky Mountain Books	E-Commerce Preparation	$1,800.00
7	19-Oct-06	Pat's Knitting Shop	E-Commerce Preparation	$1,300.00
9	22-Oct-06	Mountain Meadow Lodge	Flash Animations	$1,500.00
11	26-Oct-06	Organica Whole Foods	Flash Animations	$1,900.00
12	27-Oct-06	Denver Bob's Bistro	Flash Animations	$1,500.00
13	29-Oct-06	Bronco Clothing	E-Commerce Preparation	$1,900.00
			Total Revenue	$11,300.00

Web Visions has outgrown its home-based operation. In November 2006 Web Visions will move to a commercial office space and hire two Web site designers.

2

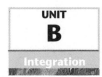
Project 2: Memo Report for LifeWorks Software

MediaLoft Online recently started selling educational software manufactured by LifeWorks Software from the MediaLoft Web site, and business is booming. Karen Rosen, your supervisor in the Human Resources Department, has asked you to analyze data sent from the Ordering Department and then write a memo that describes the orders filled over the past week. The memo needs to include an Access table that lists the products sold from the Web site from May 7 through May 13, 2006, a line chart that shows the daily sales, and a pie chart that shows the breakdown of sales by buyer location.

ACTIVITY Creating the Database and Analyzing the Data

You first create a database in Access that contains information about all the sales for the week of May 7 to May 13, 2006. Then, you analyze the data in Excel and use the Subtotals function to sort the data.

STEPS

1. **Create a database called** LifeWorks Software **in the drive and folder where your Data Files are stored, double-click** Create table by entering data, **then enter the labels and data shown in Figure B-10 and save the table as** Web Sales

   Note that you need to switch to Design View to change the data type for the Sale Date column to Date/Time and the data type for the Sale column to Currency. You also need to answer Yes to set a primary key.

2. **Close and save the table, click** Web Sales, **click the** OfficeLinks button list arrow 📑 ▾, **then click** Analyze It with Microsoft Office Excel

> **TROUBLE**
> Widen columns in Excel as necessary.

3. **In Excel, select the range of cells** A1:G14, **click** Data **on the menu bar, click** Subtotals, **click the** At each change in list arrow, **select** Sale Day, **make sure that** Sale **is selected in the Add the subtotal to list, then click** OK

4. **Click away from the table, click the** Chart Wizard button 📊, **select** Line, **click** Next, **click the** Collapse dialog box button 📑 **to the right of the Data range text box, click cell** G3, **press and hold [Ctrl], click cells** G7, G9, G12, G14, G19, **and** G21 **as the data range and cells** C2, C6, C8, C11, C13, C18, **and** C20 **as the x-axis labels**

5. **Enter** May 7 to 13 Sales **as the Chart title and remove the chart legend**

6. **Size and position the chart so that it extends from cell** A24 **to** G45, **then change the font sizes of the x-axis and y-axis labels to** 10 point

7. **Right-click the gray plot area, click** Format Plot Area, **click** Fill Effects, **click the** Gradient tab **if necessary, click the** Preset option button, **click the** Preset colors list arrow, **click** Wheat, **click** OK, **then click** OK

8. **Right-click the line representing the data series, click** Format Data Series, **click the** Weight list arrow **in the Line section, select the bottom weight, then click** OK

9. **Click away from the chart and compare it to Figure B-11, then save the workbook**

FIGURE B-10: Data for the Web Sales table

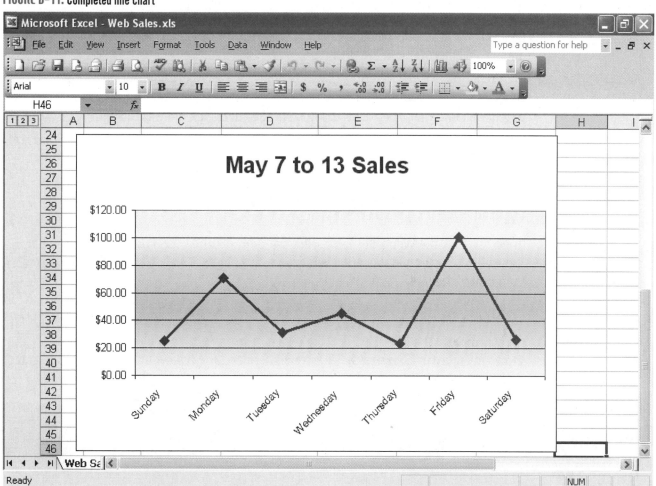

ID	Sale Date	Sale Day	Product	Category	Buyer Location	Sale
1	5/7/2006	Sunday	Eat Right	Lifestyle	England	$24.95
2	5/8/2006	Monday	Resume Writing	Business	Canada	$19.95
3	5/8/2006	Monday	Astrology Kit	Lifestyle	United States	$24.95
4	5/8/2006	Monday	Eat Right	Lifestyle	England	$25.95
5	5/9/2006	Tuesday	Card Games Plus	Entertainment	United States	$30.95
6	5/10/2006	Wednesday	Astrology Kit	Lifestyle	United States	$24.95
7	5/10/2006	Wednesday	Word Games	Entertainment	Canada	$19.95
8	5/11/2006	Thursday	Typing Tutor	Business	France	$22.95
9	5/12/2006	Friday	Wills & Estates	Business	United States	$24.95
10	5/12/2006	Friday	Cartoon Clips	Entertainment	Australia	$25.95
11	5/12/2006	Friday	Astrology Kit	Lifestyle	Japan	$24.95
12	5/12/2006	Friday	Astrology Kit	Lifestyle	Australia	$24.95
13	5/13/2006	Saturday	Eat Right	Lifestyle	Canada	$25.95
A|						$0.00

Record: 14 of 14

FIGURE B-11: Completed line chart

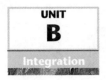

| ACTIVITY | # Creating the Memo in Word |

First, you create a pie chart in Excel and then you open the text for the memo in Word. You then format the memo in Word and copy the Web Sales table from Access and the two charts from Excel. The completed memo is shown in Figure B-12.

| STEPS |

1. **Return to Access, right-click Web Sales in the Database window, click Copy, click the right mouse button, click Paste, name the copied table Buyer Location, then click OK**

2. **Double-click the Buyer Location table to open it, click the Buyer Location field, click the Sort Ascending button ⬇, close and save the table, then analyze it in Excel**

3. **In Excel, create a Subtotals list that calculates total sales at each change in the Buyer Location**

4. **Click away from the Subtotals list, click the Chart Wizard button 📊, click Pie, click Next, collapse the dialog box, use [Ctrl] to select cells G4, G8, G11, G13, G15, and G20 as the data range, expand the dialog box, click the Series tab, click in the Category Labels text box, collapse the dialog box, use [Ctrl] to select cells F3, F7, F10, F12, F14, and F19 as the data labels, then expand the dialog box**

5. **Click Next, name the chart Breakdown of Sales by Buyer Location, click the Legend tab, click the Show legend check box to deselect it, click the Data Labels tab, click the Category name check box, click the Percentage check box, then click Finish**

6. **Size and position the pie chart so that it extends from cell A22 to G44, reduce the font size of the data labels to 10 point, click the chart title, then change the font size to 16 point**

7. **Start Word, type and format just the text (not the table) of the memo as shown in Figure B-12, then save the document as LifeWorks Software Memo**

   Format the word Memorandum in Arial 24 point and the text in Times New Roman 12 point.

8. **In Access, click the Web Sales table, click the Copy button 📄 on the Database toolbar, show Word, paste the table after paragraph 2, apply the Table 3D effects 3 AutoFormat, then center the table as shown in Figure B-12**

   Instead of using the Publish It command, you can use the Copy and Paste functions to include an Access table in a Word document. The copied table includes the name of the table as a merged first row.

9. **Copy and paste the line chart and the pie chart from Excel to the memo in Word as shown in Figure B-12, resize the charts where necessary, type your name where indicated in the From: line of the memo, type the date in the Date: line, print a copy, save and close the document, save and close the workbooks in Excel, then exit all programs**

Integration

FIGURE B-12: Completed memo

M E M O R A N D U M

To: Karen Rosen

From: Your Name

Date: Current Date

Re: Web Site Sales

This memo presents information related to the sales generated from the LifeWorks Software Web site during the week of May 7 to 13, 2006. The Web site has been active since January 1 and has already generated total sales of $5,200. In the week of May 7 to 13, the total sales were $321.35.

The table illustrated below displays all the sales generated from the Web site from May 7 to 13, 2006.

Web Sales

ID	Sale Date	Sale Day	Product	Category	Buyer Location	Sale
1	5/7/2006	Sunday	Eat Right	Lifestye	England	$24.95
2	5/8/2006	Monday	Resume Writing	Business	Canada	$19.95
3	5/8/2006	Monday	Astrology Kit	Lifestyle	United States	$24.95
4	5/8/2006	Monday	Eat Right	Lifestyle	England	$25.95
5	5/9/2006	Tuesday	Card Games Plus	Entertainment	United States	$30.95
6	5/10/2006	Wednesday	Astrology Kit	Lifestyle	United States	$24.95
7	5/10/2006	Wednesday	Word Games	Entertainment	Canada	$19.95
8	5/11/2006	Thursday	Typing Tutor	Business	France	$22.95
9	5/12/2006	Friday	Wills & Estates	Business	United States	$24.95
10	5/12/2006	Friday	Cartoon Clips	Entertainment	Australia	$25.95
11	5/12/2006	Friday	Astrology Kit	Lifestyle	Japan	$24.95
12	5/12/2006	Friday	Astrology Kit	Lifestyle	Australia	$24.95
13	5/13/2006	Saturday	Eat Right	Lifestyle	Canada	$25.95

At present, no one product category has dominated the sales. In late May, the company will be designing a new page for inclusion on the MediaLoft Web site. This page will feature the CD ROM software packages included in the Entertainment category. In addition, information about an upcoming sales promotion for Entertainment software will be highlighted on the Web site. Sales of Entertainment software are expected to outstrip the sales of the other categories in June.

Memo to Ms. Karen Rosen: Page 2

Most sales are made on Mondays and Fridays, as shown in the line chart displayed below. Friday is the busiest day. This increase of sales on Fridays confirms recent predictions that most sales are made to people "surfing the web" in their leisure hours.

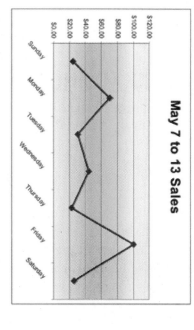

May 7 to 13 Sales

Buyers from all over the world are purchasing products from LifeWorks Software. As a result, LifeWorks Software plans to include French, Japanese, and perhaps German versions of the Web site so as to generate more sales from these countries.

Illustrated below is a pie chart that shows the breakdown of sales by buyer location. At present, the majority of customers are from the United States. However, the number of buyers from Canada and Australia has been steadily increasing.

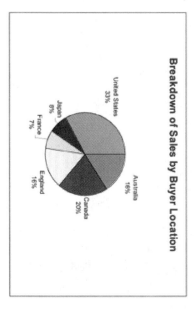

Breakdown of Sales by Buyer Location

▼ INDEPENDENT CHALLENGE 1

Create a two-page company profile for a company of your choice. For example, you could create a company profile for a small computer store you want to expand or a bookkeeping business that you run from your own home. Follow the steps provided to create the data for your company profile, and then publish it in Word, along with a chart you create in Excel.

a. Create a database in the drive and folder where your Data Files are stored called **My Company Profile** that contains information about all the sales made in the past month by your company. Create a table called *Month* **Sales** (for example, December Sales). Assign a category to each sale. For example, the categories for items sold in a computer store could be PCs, Laptops, Accessories, and Software. For ideas, refer to the October Contracts table you created in the Web Visions project. Make sure you also include the price of each item. Answer Yes to create the primary key.

b. Determine the most popular category of items sold, and then create a query table named *Category* **Table** that lists all sales of items in that category.

c. Analyze the query table in Excel to determine the total amount of sales in the most popular category. Format the Excel worksheet attractively for inclusion in the company profile.

d. Analyze the *Month* Sales table in Excel. Create a cylinder chart that shows the total sales of items in each category. Refer to the cylinder chart you created in the Web Visions project for ideas.

e. Switch to Word, create an attractive heading for the company name (use WordArt and insert a picture from the Online Clip Gallery, if you wish), and then write text for your company profile similar to the text included in the Web Visions company profile.

f. Publish the Sales table from Access in the Word profile, and then copy the cylinder chart and worksheet from Excel and paste them into the Word summary.

g. Include your name at the bottom of the Word document, save it as **My Company Profile**, format the company profile attractively, and then print a copy. Save and close all files, and exit all programs.

▼ INDEPENDENT CHALLENGE 2

Create a memo report that provides information about the sales of a particular product line during a specific week, month, or year. Use the memo report you created for LifeWorks Software as your model. The memo report should include a table copied from an Access database. Make sure the table includes the sale date, the description and category of the product, and the sale amount. You may also wish to include the location of the buyers or other relevant information. In addition, the memo report should include a chart that was created in Excel from data included in the Access database. Save all files as **My Memo Report** (they are each given the appropriate extension for the application). Include your name on the memo report in Word, print a copy, then save and close all open files, and exit all programs.

▼ INDEPENDENT CHALLENGE 3

As the owner of Art's Sake, you sell reproductions of paintings by local artists in Vancouver, British Columbia. A potential investor has asked you to prepare a short report about your company. This report includes data copied from an Access database and an Excel workbook. Follow the instructions provided to create the report shown in Figure B-13.

a. In Word, enter and format just the text shown in Figure B-13 (do *not* include the table or chart), then save the document as **Art Sake Report** in the drive and folder where your Data Files are stored. Note that the text is formatted in 12-point Arial and the title in 24-point Bauhaus 93 font (or a similar font), and italics and bold. The two headings are enhanced with the Heading 1 style.

b. Insert the picture file called **Abstract.jpg** from the drive and folder where your Data Files are stored at the top of the report, then size and position it as shown in Figure B-13. (*Hint*: To insert the picture, click Insert on the menu bar, point to Picture, then click From File.) You need to change the layout to Tight and Right.

▼ INDEPENDENT CHALLENGE 3 (CONTINUED)

c. In Access open the file **Art Postcards.mdb** from the drive and folder where your Data Files are stored, sort the records in the Postcards table by Category in ascending order, analyze the table with Excel, and then create a 3-D pie chart that shows the breakdown of postcard sales by category. You need to use the Subtotals function to calculate the total sales of postcards in each category (for example, Abstract, Landscape, etc.). You also need to format the chart and give it a title as shown in Figure B-13. Then copy the pie chart to the Word document as shown in Figure B-13.

d. In Access, select the Price List table, click the OfficeLinks button list arrow, then click Publish It with Microsoft Office Word.

e. Copy the table and paste it into the Word document as shown in Figure B-13, apply the Table Subtle 1 AutoFormat style, then center the table.

f. Type your name at the bottom of the report in Word, print a copy, save and close all files, then exit all programs.

FIGURE B-13: Completed report in Word

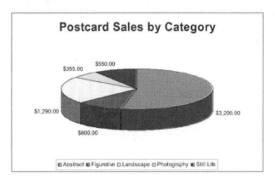

Art's Sake Reproductions

Art Postcard Sales

Art's Sake Reproductions recently began selling postcard reproductions of work by some of its gallery artists. Sales have been brisk, particularly to tourists during the summer months. The pie chart shown below compares the total postcard sales in each of five categories. The top-selling category is abstracts, particularly those by noted local artists such as Merilee Blake and Donald Watson.

Postcard Sales by Category

$550.00
$355.00
$1,290.00
$3,200.00
$600.00

▨ Abstract ▨ Figurative ▨ Landscape ▨ Photography ▨ Still Life

Price List

The price list shown below lists the top ten products sold by Art's Sake Reproductions. Four product categories are represented: Clothing, Posters, Postcards, and Sundries. The Sundries category includes such items as mouse pads, mugs, tote bags, pens, and jigsaw puzzles.

ID	Title	Description	Category	Price
1	Green Horizons	Short-cropped T-shirt	Clothing	$45.00
2	Far Horizons	Mouse pad	Sundry	$15.00
3	Mountain Wall	Mug	Sundry	$6.00
4	Jagged Cliffs	Sweat shirt	Clothing	$55.00
5	Figurations	24" x 36" framed poster	Poster	$60.00
6	Kismet	Mug	Sundry	$7.50
7	Ocean Vistas	Floor puzzle	Sundry	$85.00
8	Dragon's Delight	4" x 6" set of eight	Postcard	$5.00
9	Peak Experience	Mouse pad	Sundry	$22.00
10	Rainforest Chronicle	Sweat shirt	Clothing	$55.00

▼ VISUAL WORKSHOP

Create a database called **Staff Travel** in the drive and folder where your Data Files are stored, then create a table called **Travel Expenses**, as shown in Figure B-14, that includes a primary key. Select the Currency format as the data type for the Expenses field. Analyze the Travel Expenses table in Excel, then create the doughnut chart shown in Figure B-15. Include your name under the chart, save and print the Excel worksheet, then exit both programs.

FIGURE B-14: Travel Expenses table

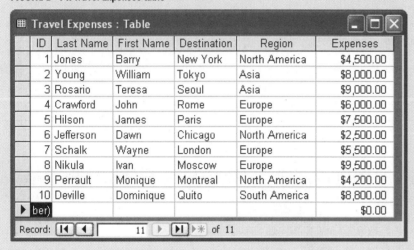

FIGURE B-15: Travel regions chart

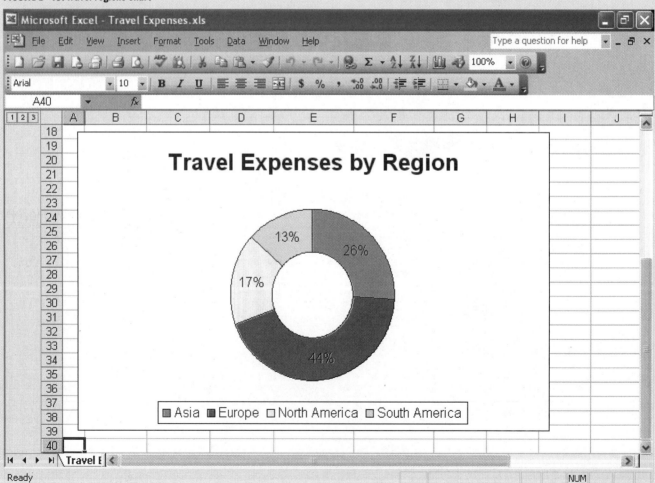

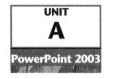

UNIT A
PowerPoint 2003

Getting Started with PowerPoint 2003

OBJECTIVES

Define presentation software
Start PowerPoint 2003
View the PowerPoint window
Use the AutoContent Wizard
View a presentation
Save a presentation
Get Help and research information
Print and close the file, and exit PowerPoint 2003

If you have a SAM user profile, you may have access to hands-on instruction, practice, and assessment of the skills covered in this unit. Log in to your SAM account and go to your assignments page to see what your instructor has assigned.

Microsoft Office PowerPoint 2003 is a computer program that enables you to create visually compelling presentations. With PowerPoint, you can create individual slides and display them as a slide show on your computer, video projector, or even via the Internet. ▓▓▓▓ Maria Abbott is the general sales manager at MediaLoft, a chain of bookstore cafés founded in 1988. MediaLoft stores offer customers the opportunity to purchase books, music, and movies while enjoying a variety of coffees, teas, and freshly baked desserts. As her assistant, Maria needs you to learn the basics of PowerPoint so you can create presentations for the sales department.

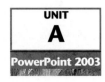

Defining Presentation Software

Presentation software is a computer program you can use to organize and present information and ideas. Whether you are giving a sales pitch or explaining your company's goals and accomplishments, presentation software can help you communicate effectively and professionally. You can use PowerPoint to create presentations, as well as notes for the presenter and handouts for the audience. Table A-1 explains the items you can create using PowerPoint. ▓▓▓▓ Maria wants you to create a presentation that explains a new marketing campaign that the MediaLoft Sales Department is developing. Because you are not that familiar with PowerPoint, you get to work exploring its capabilities. Figure A-1 shows a hand-out you created using a word processor for a recent presentation. Figure A-2 shows how the information might look in PowerPoint.

DETAILS

You can easily complete the following tasks using PowerPoint:

- **Present information in a variety of ways**

  With PowerPoint, you can present information using a variety of methods. For example, you can print hand-out pages or an outline of your presentation for your audience. You can display your presentation as an electronic slide show on a computer. If you are presenting to a large group in a conference room, you can use a video projector. If you want to reach an even wider audience, you can post your presentation so it can be viewed over the Internet.

- **Enter and edit data easily**

  Using PowerPoint, you can enter and edit data quickly and efficiently. When you need to change a part of your presentation, you can use the word processing and outlining capabilities of PowerPoint to edit your content rather than re-create it.

- **Change the appearance of information**

  PowerPoint has many features that can transform the way text, graphics, and slides appear. By exploring some of these capabilities, you discover how easy it is to change the appearance of your presentation.

- **Organize and arrange information**

  Once you start using PowerPoint, you won't have to spend much time making sure your information is correct and in the right order. With PowerPoint, you can quickly and easily rearrange and modify text, graphics, and slides in your presentation.

- **Incorporate information from other sources**

  Often, when you create presentations, you use information from other sources. With PowerPoint, you can import text, graphics, and numerical data from spreadsheet, database, and word processing files such as Microsoft Excel, Microsoft Access, Microsoft Word, and Corel WordPerfect. You can also import graphic images from a variety of sources such as the Internet, image files on a computer, or other graphics programs. Likewise, you can also incorporate changes made to your presentation by others who review it.

- **Show a presentation on any computer that doesn't have PowerPoint installed**

  By using the Package for CD feature, you can copy your presentation and its supporting files to a CD to be viewed on another computer, even if the computer doesn't have PowerPoint installed. The PowerPoint Viewer, which is included on the CD when you package a presentation, displays a presentation as an on-screen slide show on any compatible computer. To package a presentation directly to a CD, your computer must be running Windows XP or later.

FIGURE A-1: Traditional handout

1 Marketing Campaign
  Your Name

2 Market Summary
  • Market: past, present, & future
    – Review changes in market share, leadership, players, market shifts, costs, pricing, competition

3 Product Definition
  • Describe product/service being marketed

4 Competition
  • The competitive landscape
    – Provide an overview of product competitors, their strengths and weaknesses
    – Position each competitor's product against new product

5 Positioning
  • Positioning of product or service
    – Statement that distinctly defines the product in its market and against its competition over time
  • Consumer promise
    – Statement summarizing the benefit of the product or service to the consumer

6 Communication Strategies
  • Messaging by audience
  • Target consumer demographics

7 Packaging & Fulfillment
  • Product packaging
    – Discuss form-factor, pricing, look, strategy
    – Discuss fulfillment issues for items not shipped directly with product
  • COGs
    – Summarize Cost of Goods and high-level Bill of Materials

8 Launch Strategies
  • Launch plan
    – If product is being announced
  • Promotion budget
    – Supply back up material with detailed budget information for review

9 Public Relations
  • Strategy & execution
    – PR strategies
    – PR plan highlights

1

FIGURE A-2: PowerPoint handout

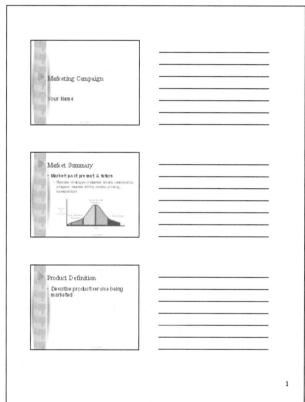

TABLE A-1: Presenting information using PowerPoint

item	use
On-screen presentations	Run a slide show directly from your computer
Web presentations	Broadcast a presentation on the Web or on an intranet that others can view, complete with video and audio
Online meetings	View or work on a presentation with your colleagues in real time
Color overheads	Print PowerPoint slides directly to transparencies on your color printer
Black-and-white overheads	Print PowerPoint slides directly to transparencies on your black-and-white printer
Notes	Print notes that help you remember points about each slide when you speak to a group
Audience handouts	Print handouts with two, three, or six slides on a page
Outline pages	Print the outline of your presentation to highlight the main points

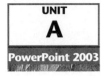
Starting PowerPoint 2003

To start PowerPoint 2003, you must first start Windows. You have to click the Start button on the taskbar, then point to All Programs to display the All Programs menu. Point to Microsoft Office to open the Microsoft Office menu which contains the Microsoft PowerPoint program name and icon. If Microsoft PowerPoint is not in the All Programs menu, it might be in a different location on your computer. If you are using a computer on a network, you might need to use a different starting procedure. ▓▓▓▓ Start PowerPoint to familiarize yourself with the program.

STEPS

1. **Make sure your computer is on and the Windows desktop is visible**
   If any program windows are open, close or minimize them.

2. **Click the Start button [start] on the taskbar, point to All Programs**
   The All Programs menu opens, showing a list of icons and names for all your programs.

3. **Point to Microsoft Office**
   You see the Microsoft Office programs installed on your computer, as shown in Figure A-3. Your screen might look different, depending on which programs are installed on your computer.

   TROUBLE
   If you have trouble finding Microsoft PowerPoint on the Programs menu, check with your instructor or technical support person.

4. **Click Microsoft Office PowerPoint 2003 on the Microsoft Office menu**
   PowerPoint starts, and the PowerPoint window opens, as shown in Figure A-4.

Clues to Use

Creating a PowerPoint shortcut on the desktop

You can make it easier to start PowerPoint by placing a shortcut on the desktop. To create the shortcut, click the Start button [start], then point to All Programs. On the All Programs menu, point to Microsoft Office, point to Microsoft Office PowerPoint, then right-click Microsoft Office PowerPoint 2003. In the shortcut menu that appears, point to Send To, then click Desktop (create shortcut). Windows places a Microsoft PowerPoint shortcut icon on your desktop. In the future, you can start PowerPoint by simply double-clicking this icon, instead of using the Start menu. You can edit or change the name of the shortcut by right-clicking the shortcut icon, clicking Rename on the shortcut menu, and then typing a new name as you would name any item in Windows. If you are working in a computer lab, you may not be allowed to place shortcuts on the desktop. Check with your instructor or technical support person before attempting to add a shortcut.

FIGURE A-3: All Programs menu

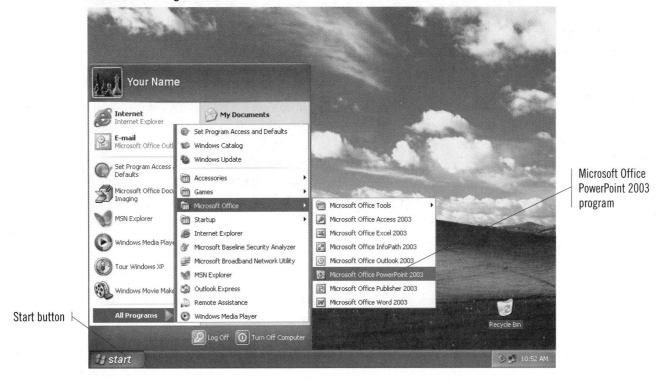

Start button

Microsoft Office PowerPoint 2003 program

FIGURE A-4: PowerPoint window

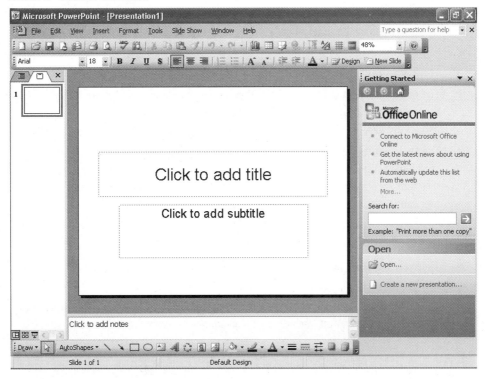

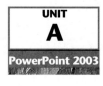

Viewing the PowerPoint Window

When you first start PowerPoint, a blank slide appears in the PowerPoint window. PowerPoint has different **views** that allow you to see your presentation in different forms. By default, the PowerPoint window opens in **Normal view**, which is the primary view that you use to write, edit, and design your presentation. Normal view is divided into three areas called **panes**: the pane on the left contains the Outline and Slides tabs, the Slide pane, and the notes pane. You move around in each pane using the scroll bars. ▓▓▓▓ The PowerPoint window and the specific parts of the Normal view are described below.

DETAILS

Using Figure A-5 as a guide, examine the elements of the PowerPoint window, then find and compare the elements described below:

- The **title bar** contains a program Control Menu button, the program name, the title of the presentation, resizing buttons, and the program Close button.

- The **menu bar** contains the names of the menus you use to choose PowerPoint commands, as well as the Type a question for help box and the Close Window button.

- The **Standard toolbar** contains buttons for commonly used commands, such as copying and pasting. The **Formatting toolbar** contains buttons for the most frequently used formatting commands, such as changing font type and size. The toolbars on your screen may be displayed on one line instead of two. See the Clues to Use for more information on how toolbars are displayed.

- The **Outline tab** displays your presentation text in the form of an outline, without graphics. In this tab, it is easy to move text on or among slides by dragging text to reorder the information.

- The **Slides tab** displays the slides of your presentation as small images, called **thumbnails**. You can quickly navigate through the slides in your presentation by clicking the thumbnails on this tab. You can also add, delete, or rearrange slides using this tab.

- The **Slide pane** displays the current slide in your presentation, including all text and graphics.

- The **notes pane** is used to type notes that reference a slide's content. You can print these notes and refer to them when you make a presentation or print them as handouts and give them to your audience. The notes pane is not visible to the audience when you show a slide presentation in Slide Show view.

- The **task pane** contains sets of hyperlinks for commonly used commands. The commands are grouped into 16 different task panes. The commands include creating new presentations, opening existing presentations, searching for documents, and using the Office Clipboard. You can also perform basic formatting tasks from the task pane such as changing the slide layout, slide design, color scheme, or slide animations of a presentation.

- The **Drawing toolbar**, located at the bottom of the PowerPoint window, contains buttons and menus that let you create lines, shapes, and special effects.

- The **view buttons**, at the bottom of the Outline tab and Slides tab area, allow you to quickly switch between PowerPoint views.

- The **status bar**, located at the bottom of the PowerPoint window, shows messages about what you are doing and seeing in PowerPoint, including which slide you are viewing.

FIGURE A-5: Presentation window in Normal view

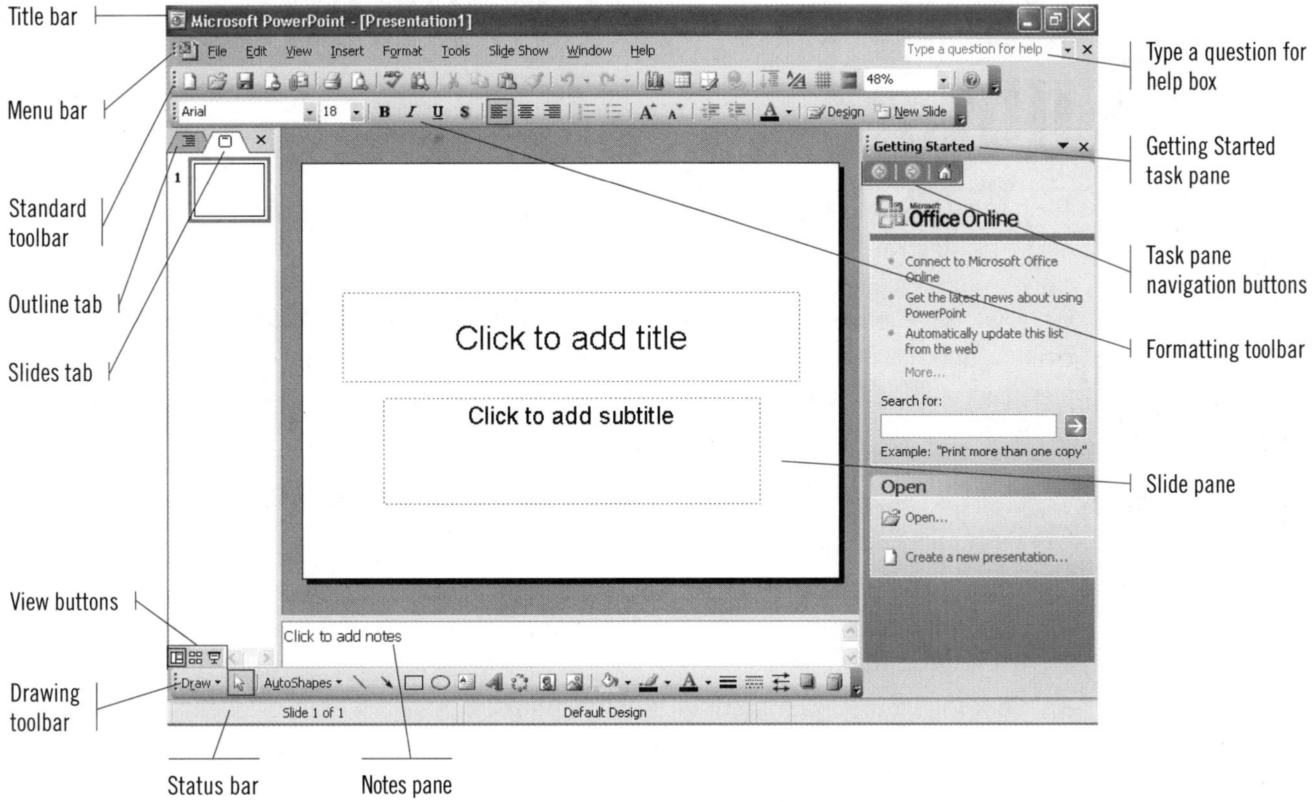

Title bar
Menu bar
Standard toolbar
Outline tab
Slides tab
View buttons
Drawing toolbar
Status bar
Notes pane
Type a question for help box
Getting Started task pane
Task pane navigation buttons
Formatting toolbar
Slide pane
Microsoft PowerPoint - [Presentation1]
Click to add title
Click to add subtitle
Click to add notes

Clues to Use

Toolbars and menus in PowerPoint 2003

PowerPoint 2003 offers personalized toolbars and menus, which modify themselves to your working style. When you use personalized toolbars and menus, the Standard and Formatting toolbars appear on the same row and display only the most frequently used buttons. To use a button that is not visible on a toolbar, click the Toolbar Options button at the end of the toolbar, and then click the button that you want. As you work, PowerPoint adds the buttons you use to the visible toolbars and drops the buttons you haven't used in a while to the Toolbar Options list. Similarly, PowerPoint menus adjust to your work habits, so that the commands you use most often appear on shortened menus. To view additional menu commands, you can either double-click the menu name or click the Expand button (double arrows) at the bottom of a menu.

The lessons in this book assume you have turned off personalized menus and toolbars and are working with all menu commands and toolbar buttons displayed. To turn off personalized toolbars and menus so that you can easily find the commands that are referenced in this book, click Tools on the menu bar, click Customize, select the Show Standard and Formatting toolbars on two rows and Always show full menus check boxes on the Options tab, and then click Close. The Standard and Formatting toolbars appear on separate rows and display all the buttons, and the menus display the complete list of menu commands. (You can also quickly display the toolbars on two rows by clicking either Toolbar Options button and then clicking Show Buttons on Two Rows.)

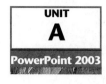

UNIT
A
PowerPoint 2003

Using the AutoContent Wizard

The quickest way to create a presentation is with the AutoContent Wizard. A **wizard** is a series of steps that guides you through a task (in this case, creating a presentation). Using the AutoContent Wizard, you choose a presentation type from the wizard's list of sample presentations. Then you indicate what type of output you want. Next, you type the information for the title slide and the footer. The AutoContent Wizard then creates a presentation with sample text you can use as a guide to help formulate the major points of your presentation. You decide to start your presentation by opening the AutoContent Wizard.

STEPS

QUICK TIP
You can also access the New Presentation task pane by clicking Create a new presentation in the Open section on the Getting Started task pane.

1. **Click the** Other Task Panes list arrow ▼ **in the task pane title bar, then click** New Presentation
   The New Presentation task pane opens.

2. **Point to the** From AutoContent wizard hyperlink **in the New section of the task pane**
   The mouse pointer changes to the Hyperlink pointer 👆. The pointer changes to this shape any time it is positioned over a hyperlink.

3. **Click the** From AutoContent wizard hyperlink
   The AutoContent Wizard dialog box opens, as shown in Figure A-6. The left section of the dialog box outlines the contents of the AutoContent Wizard, and the text in the right section explains the current wizard screen.

4. **Click** Next
   The Presentation type screen appears. This screen contains category buttons and types of presentations. Each presentation type contains suggested text for a particular use. By default, the presentation types in the General category are listed.

5. **Click the** Sales/Marketing **category, click** Marketing Plan **in the list on the right, then click** Next
   The Presentation style screen appears, asking you to choose an output type. The On-screen presentation option is selected by default.

6. **Click** Next, **click in the** Presentation title text box, **then type** Marketing Campaign
   The Presentation options screen requests information that appears on the title slide of the presentation and in the footer at the bottom of each slide. The Date last updated and the Slide number check boxes are selected by default.

7. **Press** [Tab], **then type** Your Name **in the Footer text box**

8. **Click** Next, **then click** Finish
   The AutoContent Wizard opens the presentation based on the Marketing Plan presentation type you chose. Sample text for each slide is listed on the left in the Outline tab, and the title slide appears in the Slide pane on the right side of the screen. Notice that the task pane is no longer visible. The task pane can be easily opened the next time you need it. Compare your screen to Figure A-7.

POWERPOINT A-8 GETTING STARTED WITH POWERPOINT 2003

OFFICE–444

FIGURE A-6: AutoContent Wizard opening screen

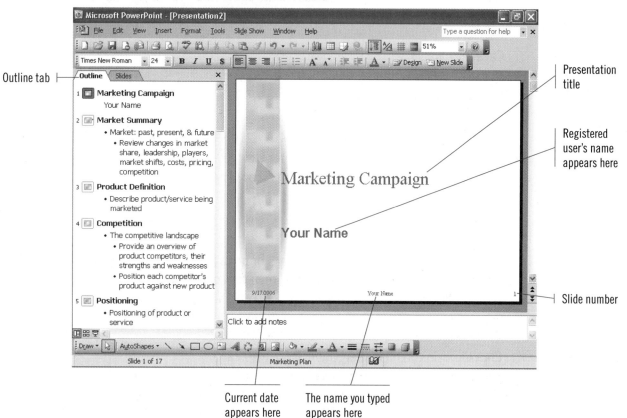

The green box identifies which step you are completing

FIGURE A-7: Presentation created with AutoContent Wizard

Outline tab

Presentation title

Registered user's name appears here

Slide number

Current date appears here

The name you typed appears here

Clues to Use

About wizards and the PowerPoint installation

As you use PowerPoint, you may find that not all AutoContent Wizards are available to you. The wizards that are available depend on your PowerPoint installation. A typical installation of PowerPoint provides you with many wizards, templates, and other features. However, some features may require you to run an install program before you use the feature for the first time. If you find a feature that is not installed, run the install program as directed. In some instances you may be required to insert the Office CD in order to install a feature. If you are working on a networked computer or in a lab, see your technical support person for assistance.

Viewing a Presentation

This lesson introduces you to the four PowerPoint views: Normal view, Slide Sorter view, Slide Show view, and Notes Page view. Each PowerPoint view shows your presentation in a different way and allows you to manipulate your presentation differently. To move easily among most of the PowerPoint views, use the view buttons located at the bottom of the pane containing the Outline and Slides tabs. Table A-2 provides a brief description of the PowerPoint views. 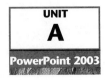 Examine each of the PowerPoint views, starting with Normal view.

STEPS

1. **In the Outline tab, click the small slide icon ▨ next to Slide 4**

   The text for Slide 4 is selected in the Outline tab and Slide 4 appears in the Slide pane as shown in Figure A-8. Notice that the status bar also indicates the number of the slide you are viewing, the total number of slides in the presentation, and the name of the AutoContent wizard you are using.

2. **Click the Previous Slide button ⬆ at the bottom of the vertical scroll bar three times so that Slide 1 (the title slide) appears**

   The scroll box in the vertical scroll bar moves back up the scroll bar. The gray slide icon on the Outline tab indicates which slide is displayed in the Slide pane. As you scroll through the presentation, read the sample text on each slide created by the AutoContent Wizard.

3. **Click the Slides tab**

   Thumbnails of all the slides in your presentation appear on the Slides tab and the Slide pane enlarges.

4. **Click the Slide Sorter View button ▦**

   A thumbnail of each slide in the presentation appears as shown in Figure A-9. You can examine the flow of your slides and drag any slide or group of slides to rearrange the order of the slides in the presentation.

5. **Double-click the first slide in Slide Sorter view**

   The slide appears in Normal view. The Slide pane shows the selected slide.

6. **Click the Slide Show from current slide button ⬚**

   The first slide fills the entire screen. In this view, you can practice running through your slides as they would appear in the slide show.

7. **Press the left mouse button, press [Enter], or press [Spacebar] to advance through the slides one at a time until you see a black slide, then click once more to return to Normal view**

   The black slide at the end of the slide show indicates that the slide show is finished. When you click the black slide (or press [Spacebar] or [Enter]), you automatically return to the slide and view you were in before you ran the slide show, in this case Slide 1 in Normal view.

TROUBLE
If you don't see a menu command, click the Expand button at the bottom of the menu.

8. **Click View on the menu bar, then click Notes Page**

   Notes Page view appears, showing a reduced image of the current slide above a large text box. You can enter text in this box and then print the notes page for your own use to help you remember important points about your presentation. To switch to Notes Page view, you must choose Notes Page from the View menu; there is no Notes Page view button.

FIGURE A-8: Normal view with the Outline tab displayed

Slides tab

Slide icon

Slide Show from current slide button

Slide Sorter View button

Normal View button

Current slide number and total number of slides

Scroll box

Scroll bar

Previous Slide button

AutoContent Wizard presentation type

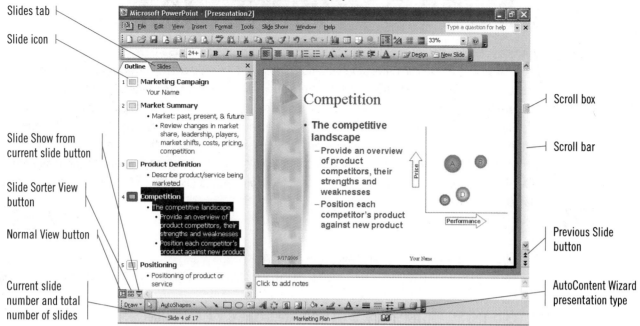

FIGURE A-9: Slide Sorter view

Step 5

Slide Sorter View button

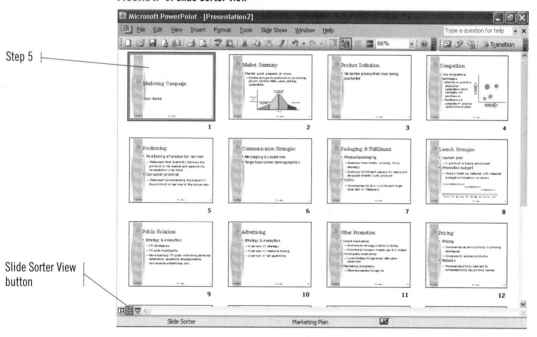

TABLE A-2: PowerPoint views

view name	button	button name	description
Normal	⊞	Normal View	Displays the pane that contains the Outline and Slides tabs, Slide pane, and notes panes at the same time; use this view to work on your presentation's content, layout, and notes concurrently
Slide Sorter	▦	Slide Sorter View	Displays thumbnails of all slides in the order in which they appear in your presentation; use this view to rearrange and add special effects to your slides
Slide Show	▭	Slide Show from current slide	Displays your presentation as an electronic slide show
Notes Page			Displays a reduced image of the current slide above a large text box where you can enter or view notes

PowerPoint 2003

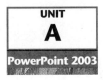

Saving a Presentation

To store your presentation so that you can work on it or view it again at a later time, you must save it as a **file** on a disk. When you first save a presentation, you give it a name, called a **filename**, and determine the location where you want to store the file. After you initially save your presentation, you should then save your presentation periodically as you continue to work so that any changes are saved in the file. As a general rule, it's wise to save your work about every 5 to 10 minutes and before printing. You use either the Save command or the Save As command on the File menu to save your presentation for the first time. When you want to make a copy of an existing presentation using a different name, use the Save As command; otherwise, use the Save command to save your changes to a presentation file. ▰▰▰▰▰ Save your presentation as Marketing Campaign.

STEPS

1. **Click File on the menu bar, then click Save As**

    The Save As dialog box opens, similar to Figure A-10. See Table A-3 for a description of the Save As dialog box button functions.

2. **Click the Save in list arrow, then navigate to the drive and folder where your Data Files are stored**

    A default filename, which PowerPoint creates from the presentation title you entered, appears in the File name text box. If the selected drive or folder contains any PowerPoint files, their filenames appear in the white area in the center of the dialog box.

3. **Click Save**

    Filenames can be up to 255 characters long; you may use lowercase or uppercase letters, symbols, numbers, and spaces. The Save As dialog box closes, and the new filename appears in the title bar at the top of the Presentation window. PowerPoint remembers which view your presentation is in when you save it, so you decide to save the presentation in Normal view instead of Notes Page view.

4. **Click the Normal View button** ▣

    The presentation view changes from Notes Page view to Normal view as shown in Figure A-11.

> **QUICK TIP**
> To save a file quickly, you can press the shortcut key combination [Ctrl][S].

5. **Click the Save button** ▣ **on the Standard toolbar**

    The Save command saves any changes you made to the file to the same location you specified when you used the Save As command. Save your file frequently while working with it to protect your presentation.

Clues to Use

Saving fonts with your presentation

When you create a presentation, it uses the fonts that are installed on your computer. If you need to open the presentation on another computer, the fonts might look different if that computer has a different set of fonts. To preserve the look of your presentation on any computer, you can save, or embed, the fonts in your presentation. Click File on the menu bar, then click Save As. The Save As dialog box opens. Click Tools, click Save Options, then click the Embed TrueType fonts check box in the Save Options dialog box. Click OK to close the Save Options dialog box, then click Save. Now the presentation looks the same on any computer that opens it. Using this option, however, significantly increases the size of your presentation on disk, so only use it when necessary. You can freely embed any TrueType font that comes with Windows. You can embed other TrueType fonts only if they have no license restrictions.

FIGURE A-10: Save As dialog box

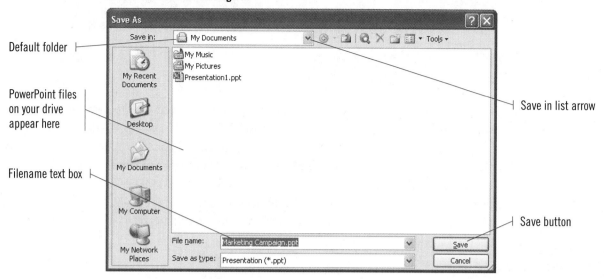

Default folder

PowerPoint files on your drive appear here

Filename text box

Save in list arrow

Save button

FIGURE A-11: Presentation in Normal view

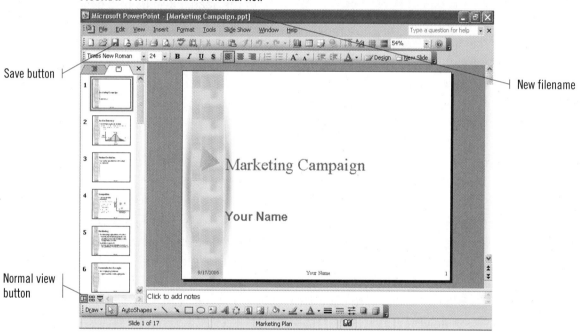

Save button

Normal view button

New filename

TABLE A-3: Save As dialog box button functions

button	button name	used to
	Back	Navigate to the drive or folder previously displayed in the Save in list box
	Up One Level	Navigate to the next highest level in the folder hierarchy
	Search the Web	Connect to the World Wide Web
	Delete	Delete the selected folder or file
	Create New Folder	Create a new folder in the current folder or drive
	Views	Change the way folders and files are viewed in the dialog box
Tools ▾	**Tools**	Open a menu of commands to help you work with selected files and folders

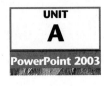

Getting Help and Researching Information

PowerPoint has an extensive Help system that gives you immediate access to program definitions, reference information, and feature explanations. To access Help information, you can type a word, phrase, or question in the Type a question for help box on the menu bar or you can click the Help button on the Standard toolbar. Help information appears in a separate window that you can move and resize. You can also access other resources such as dictionaries, thesauruses, or Web sites to research information on various topics related to PowerPoint. If the information you are looking for does not appear in the Help window, you can rephrase your question and try your search again. You are finished working on your presentation for now and you decide to learn about hyperlinks.

STEPS

TROUBLE

If your search results are not from www.microsoft.com, then you may not be connected to the Internet. Check with your instructor or technical support person for help. If you are unable to connect to the Internet, you will not be able to complete all of the steps in this lesson.

1. **Click in the** Type a question for help box **on the menu bar, type** hyperlinks, **then press** [Enter]
   The Search Results task pane appears showing Help topics related to hyperlinks. See Figure A-12.

2. **If necessary, click the** down scroll arrow **in the Search Results task pane, then click the** About hyperlinks and action buttons **hyperlink in the results list**
   The Microsoft PowerPoint Help window opens and displays information about hyperlinks and action buttons.

3. **Click the** down scroll arrow **on the vertical scroll bar in the Help window to read all of the Help information**
   Notice the hyperlinks (blue words) in the Help text, which you can click to get further information on that particular subject. Two subtopic hyperlinks, which are identified by small blue arrows, are below the Help information. To view information on either of these topics, simply click the topic hyperlink.

4. **Click the** Testing and repairing broken hyperlinks **subtopic, click the down scroll arrow, then read the information**
   Notice that the small blue arrow now points down indicating that the subtopic is displayed.

TROUBLE

A dialog box may open telling you that the Research feature is not installed. Install the Research feature using the Office CD or check with your instructor or technical support person for help.

5. **Click the** Other Task Panes list arrow ▼ **in the task pane title bar, click** Research, **click in the** Search for text box, **type** hyperlinks, **then click the** Start searching button ➡
   The Research task pane displays information found in the default research Web sites and reference books. Figure A-13 shows the Research task pane with the results of the research on the term 'hyperlinks'.

6. **Click the** list arrow **in the Research task pane in the Search for section, then click** All Research Sites
   PowerPoint researches the currently available Web sites for information on hyperlinks and displays the information in the Research task pane. To further help your ability to research topics, PowerPoint allows you to choose which reference books, research Web sites, and other research services you can use when doing research.

7. **Click the** Close button ☒ **in the Microsoft PowerPoint Help window title bar**
   The Help window closes, and your presentation fills the screen again. The Research task pane should still be visible.

8. **Click the** Research options hyperlink **at the bottom of the Research task pane**
   The Research Options dialog box opens. The options in this dialog box allow you to customize the tools that will be used to research information.

9. **Click the** down scroll arrow **in the dialog box to view all of the available options, then click** Cancel

FIGURE A-12: Search Results task pane showing Help topics

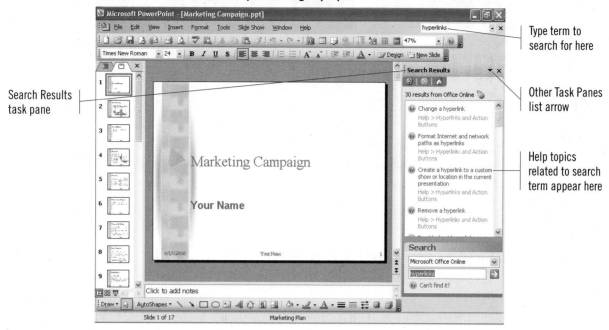

Search Results task pane

Type term to search for here

Other Task Panes list arrow

Help topics related to search term appear here

FIGURE A-13: PowerPoint window showing Research task pane

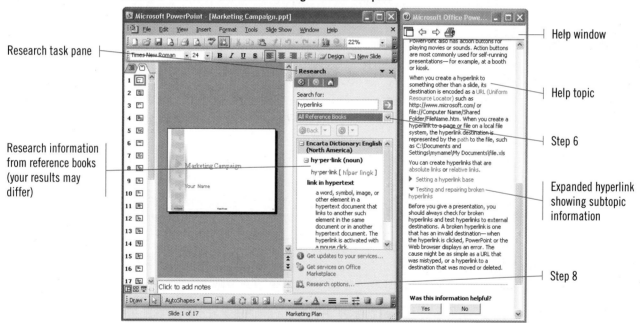

Research task pane

Research information from reference books (your results may differ)

Help window

Help topic

Step 6

Expanded hyperlink showing subtopic information

Step 8

PowerPoint 2003

Clues to Use

Recovering lost presentation files

Sometimes while you are working on a presentation, PowerPoint may freeze, making it impossible to continue working on your presentation, or you may experience a power failure that causes your computer to shut down. If this type of interruption occurs, PowerPoint has a built-in recovery feature that allows you to open and save files that were open during the interruption. When you start PowerPoint again after an interruption, the Document Recovery task pane opens on the left side of your screen, displaying both original and recovered versions of the PowerPoint files that were open. If you're not sure which file to open (original or recovered), it's usually better to open the recovered file because it will have retained the latest information. You can, however, open and review all the versions of the file that was recovered and select the best one to save. Each file listed in the Document Recovery task pane has a list arrow with options that allow you to open the file, save the file, delete the file, or show repairs made to the file.

Printing and Closing the File, and Exiting PowerPoint

You print your presentation when you have completed it or when you want to review your work. Reviewing hard copies of your presentation at different stages gives you an overall perspective of its content and look. When you are finished working on your presentation, even if it is not yet complete, you can close the presentation file and exit PowerPoint. ▰▰▰ You are done working on the presentation for now, so after you save the presentation, you print the slides and notes pages of the presentation so you can review them later; then you close the file and exit PowerPoint.

STEPS

1. **Click File on the menu bar, then click Print**

   The Print dialog box opens. See Figure A-14. In this dialog box, you can specify which slide format you want to print (slides, handouts, notes pages, etc.), the slide range, the number of copies to print, as well as other print options. The default options for the available printer are selected in the dialog box.

2. **In the Print range section in the middle of the dialog box, click the Slides option button to select it, type 4 to print only the fourth slide, then click OK**

   The fourth slide prints. To save paper when you are reviewing your slides, it's a good idea to print in handout format, which lets you print up to nine slides per page.

3. **Click File on the menu bar, then click Print**

   The Print dialog box opens again. The options you choose in the Print dialog box remain there until you close the presentation.

4. **Click the All option button in the Print range section, click the Print what list arrow, click Handouts, click the Slides per page list arrow in the Handouts section, then click 6 if it is not already selected**

5. **Click the Color/grayscale list arrow, click Pure Black and White as shown in Figure A-15, then click OK**

   The presentation prints as handouts that you can give to your audience on three pages. The presentation prints without any gray tones. The pure black-and-white printing option can save printer toner.

6. **Click File on the menu bar, then click Print**

   The Print dialog box opens again.

7. **Click the Print what list arrow, click Outline View, then click OK**

   The outline for each slide in the presentation prints on three pages.

8. **Click File on the menu bar, then click Close**

   If you have made changes to your presentation, a Microsoft PowerPoint alert box opens asking you if you want to save changes you have made to the Marketing Campaign file.

9. **If necessary, click Yes to close the alert box**

10. **Click File on the menu bar, then click Exit**

    The presentation and the PowerPoint program close, and you return to the Windows desktop.

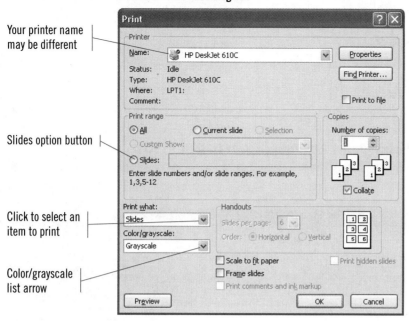

FIGURE A-14: Print dialog box

Your printer name may be different

Slides option button

Click to select an item to print

Color/grayscale list arrow

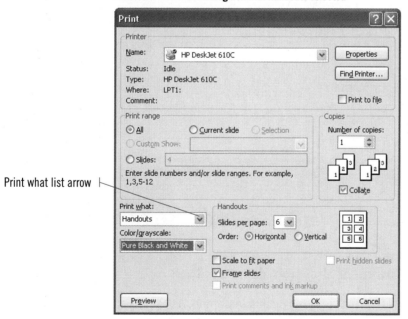

FIGURE A-15: Print dialog box with Handouts selected

Print what list arrow

Clues to Use

Viewing your presentation in grayscale or black and white

Viewing your presentation in pure black and white or in grayscale (using shades of gray) is very useful when you are printing a presentation on a black-and-white printer and you want to make sure your text is readable. To see how your color presentation looks in grayscale or black and white, click the Color/Grayscale button on the Standard toolbar, then click either Grayscale or Pure Black and White. The Grayscale View toolbar appears. You can use the Grayscale View toolbar to select different settings to view your presentation. If you don't like the way an object looks in black and white or grayscale view, you can change its color. Right-click the object, point to Black and White Setting or Grayscale Setting (depending on which view you are in), and choose from the options on the submenu.

Practice

▼ CONCEPTS REVIEW

Label each element of the PowerPoint window shown in Figure A-16.

FIGURE A-16

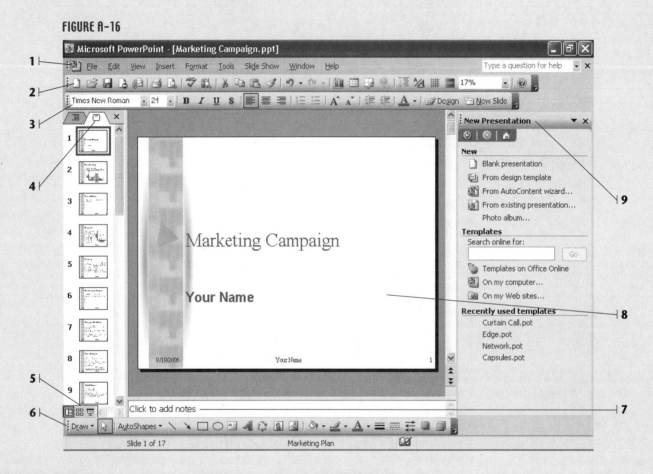

Match each term with the statement that best describes it.

10. Notes pane
11. Slide Sorter view
12. Task pane
13. Normal view
14. Slides tab

a. Displays hyperlinks of common commands
b. Displays the slides of your presentation as thumbnails in Normal view
c. A pane in Normal view that allows you to type notes that reference a slide's content
d. Displays the Outline and Slides tabs, as well as the slide and notes panes
e. A view that shows all your slides as thumbnails

Select the best answer from the list of choices.

15. All of the following are PowerPoint views, *except*:
   a. Slide Sorter view
   b. Notes Page view
   c. Current Page view
   d. Normal view

16. PowerPoint can help you create all of the following, *except*:
   a. A Web presentation
   b. Outline pages
   c. An on-screen presentation
   d. A digital movie

17. The buttons you use to switch between the PowerPoint views are called:
   a. Screen buttons
   b. View buttons
   c. PowerPoint buttons
   d. Toolbar buttons

18. The view that allows you to view your electronic slide show with each slide filling the entire screen is called:
   a. Slide Sorter view
   b. Presentation view
   c. Slide Show view
   d. Electronic view

19. How do you switch to Notes Page view?
   a. Press [Shift] and click in the notes pane.
   b. Click the Notes Page View button.
   c. Click View on the menu bar, then click Notes Page.
   d. All of the above.

20. How do you save changes to your presentation after you have saved it for the first time?
   a. Click Save As on the File menu, select a filename from the list, then assign it a new name.
   b. Click the Save button on the Standard toolbar.
   c. Click Save As on the File menu, then click Save.
   d. Click Save As on the File menu, specify a new location and filename, then click Save.

21. Which wizard helps you create and outline your presentation?
   a. Presentation Wizard
   b. OrgContent Wizard
   c. AutoContent Wizard
   d. Topic Wizard

▼ SKILLS REVIEW

1. Start PowerPoint and view the PowerPoint window.
   a. Identify as many elements of the PowerPoint window as you can without referring to the unit material.
   b. Describe the purpose or function of each element.
   c. For any elements you cannot identify, refer to the unit.

2. Use the AutoContent Wizard.
   a. Start the AutoContent Wizard, then select a presentation category and type. (*Hint*: If you see a message saying you need to install the feature, insert your Office CD in the appropriate drive and click OK. If you are working in a networked computer lab, see your technical support person for assistance. If you are unable to load additional templates, click No as many times as necessary, then select another presentation type.)
   b. Select the output option of your choice.
   c. Enter an appropriate title for the opening slide, enter your name as the footer text, and complete the wizard to show the first slide of the presentation.

3. View a presentation and run a slide show.
   a. View each slide in the presentation to become familiar with its content.
   b. When you are finished, return to Slide 1.
   c. Click the Outline tab and review the presentation contents.
   d. Change to Notes Page view and see if the notes pages in the presentation contain text, then return to Normal view.
   e. Examine the presentation contents in Slide Sorter view.
   f. View all the slides of the presentation in Slide Show view, and end the slide show to return to Slide Sorter view.

4. Save a presentation.
   a. Change to Notes Page view.
   b. Open the Save As dialog box.
   c. Navigate to the drive and folder where your Data Files are stored.
   d. Name your presentation **Practice**.
   e. Click Tools on the menu bar, then click Save Options.
   f. Choose the option to embed the fonts in your presentation, as shown in Figure A-17, then click OK.
   g. Save your file.
   h. Go to a different view than the one you saved your presentation in.
   i. Save the changed presentation.

FIGURE A-17

▼ SKILLS REVIEW (CONTINUED)

5. Get Help and Research Information.

   a. Type creating presentations in the Type a question for help box, then press [Enter].

   b. Click the down scroll arrow in the results list, then click the Create a presentation using a design template hyperlink.

   c. Read the information, then click and read the Tip hyperlink.

   d. Click the Help Window Close button.

   e. Click the Other Task Panes list arrow, then click Research.

   f. Type PowerPoint presentations in the Search for text box.

   g. Click the Search for list arrow, then click All Research Sites.

   h. Read the results that appear.

6. Print and close the file, and exit PowerPoint.

   a. Print slides 2 and 3 as slides in grayscale. (*Hint*: In the Slides text box, type 2-3.)

   b. Print all the slides as handouts, 9 slides per page, in pure black and white.

   c. Print the presentation outline.

   d. Close the file, saving your changes.

   e. Exit PowerPoint.

▼ INDEPENDENT CHALLENGE 1

You own a small photography business where most of your revenue comes from customized portraits for special occasions, such as weddings. In an effort to expand your business and appeal to more consumers, you decide to investigate various ways for you to display and send customer's personal photographs over the Internet. You have recently been using PowerPoint to create marketing presentations and you decide to learn more about PowerPoint's Photo Album feature using PowerPoint Help.

   a. If PowerPoint is not already running, start it.

   b. Use PowerPoint Help to find information on how to publish a photo album to the Web. (*Hint*: Type photo album in the Type a question for help box.)

   c. Write down the steps you followed to get this information, then add your name to the document.

   d. Print the Help window that shows the information you found. (*Hint*: Click the Print button at the top of the Help window.)

Advanced Challenge Exercise

   ■ Use the Research task pane to search for Web sites that relate to photo albums on the Web.

   ■ Click a Web site hyperlink in the Research task pane results list to explore the Web page contents.

   ■ Print the Home page of the Web site you visit.

   ■ Close your Web browser program.

   e. Exit PowerPoint.

PowerPoint 2003

▼ INDEPENDENT CHALLENGE 2

You are in charge of marketing for ArtWorks, Inc., a medium-size company that produces all types of art for corporations to enhance their work environment. The company has a regional sales area that includes areas throughout Western Europe. The president of ArtWorks asks you to plan and create the outline of the PowerPoint presentation he will use to convey a new Internet service that ArtWorks is developing.

    a. If necessary, start PowerPoint.

    b. Start the AutoContent Wizard. (*Hint*: If the task pane is not visible, click View on the menu bar, then click Task Pane.)

    c. On the Presentation type screen, choose the Sales/Marketing category, then choose Product/Services Overview from the list.

    d. Choose the Web presentation output, then assign the presentation an appropriate title, and include your name as the footer text.

    e. Scroll through the outline that the AutoContent Wizard produces. Does it contain the type of information you thought it would?

    f. Plan and take notes on how you would change and add to the sample text created by the wizard. What information do you need to promote ArtWorks to companies?

    g. Switch views. Run through the slide show at least once.

    h. Save your presentation with the name **ArtWorks Online** to the drive and folder where your Data Files are stored.

    i. Print your presentation as handouts (six slides per page).

    j. Close the presentation and exit PowerPoint.

▼ INDEPENDENT CHALLENGE 3

You have recently been promoted to sales manager at Turner Industries. Part of your job is to train sales representatives to go to potential customers and give presentations describing your company's products. Your boss wants you to find an appropriate PowerPoint presentation template that you can use for your next training presentation to recommend strategies to the sales representatives for closing sales. She wants a printout so she can evaluate it.

    a. If necessary, start PowerPoint.

    b. Start the AutoContent Wizard. (*Hint*: If the task pane is not visible, click View on the menu bar, then click Task Pane.)

    c. Examine the available AutoContent Wizards and select one that you could adapt for your presentation. (*Hint*: If you see a message saying you need to install additional templates, insert your Office CD in the appropriate drive and click OK. If you are working in a networked computer lab, see your technical support person for assistance. If you are unable to load additional templates, click No as many times as necessary, then select another presentation type.)

    d. Choose the On-screen presentation type, then enter an appropriate slide title and include your name as the footer text.

    e. Print the presentation as an outline, then print the first slide in pure black and white.

    f. Write a brief memo to your boss describing which wizard you think is most helpful, referring to specific slides in the outline to support your recommendation.

    g. Save the presentation as **Turner Training** to the drive and folder where your Data Files are stored.

    h. Close the presentation and exit PowerPoint.

▼ **INDEPENDENT CHALLENGE 4**

In this unit, you've learned about PowerPoint basics such as how to start PowerPoint, view the PowerPoint window, use the AutoContent Wizard, and run a slide show. There are many Web sites that provide information about how to use PowerPoint more effectively.

Use the Microsoft Web site to access information about the following topic:

- Presentation Tips

a. Connect to the Internet, then go to Microsoft's Web site at www.microsoft.com.

b. In the Search for text box, type **Dale Carnegie Training**, then press [Enter].

c. Locate the hyperlink that provides information on presentation tips from Dale Carnegie Training, then click the hyperlink. See Figure A-18.

d. Print and read the article, then write your name and course identification on the printed document.

Advanced Challenge Exercise

- Create and save a document as **Presentation Tips** to the drive and folder where your Data Files are stored.
- Type your name and course identification at the top of the document.
- The Web article identifies a four-step process for delivering an effective presentation. Using the information in the Web article, identify each of these steps and the most important subpoint. Explain your answers.
- Save your final document, print it, close the document, then exit your word processing program.

e. Exit your Web browser program.

FIGURE A-18

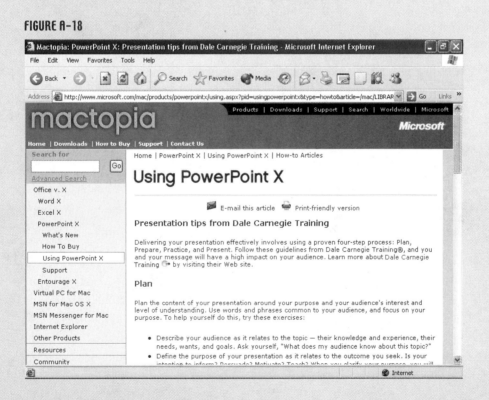

▼ VISUAL WORKSHOP

Create the presentation shown in Figure A-19 using the Project Post-Mortem AutoContent Wizard in the Projects category. Make sure you include your name as the footer. Save the presentation as **Triad** to the drive and folder where your Data Files are stored. Print the slides as handouts, six slides per page, in pure black and white.

FIGURE A-19

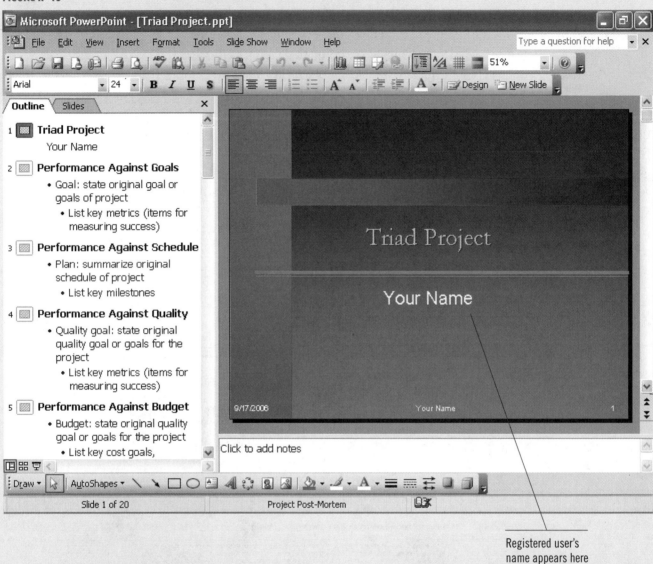

Registered user's name appears here

Creating a Presentation

OBJECTIVES

Plan an effective presentation

Enter slide text

Create a new slide

Enter text in the Outline tab

Add slide headers and footers

Choose a look for a presentation

Check spelling in a presentation

Evaluate a presentation

If you have a SAM user profile, you may have access to hands-on instruction, practice, and assessment of the skills covered in this unit. Log in to your SAM account and go to your assignments page to see what your instructor has assigned.

Now that you are familiar with PowerPoint basics, you are ready to plan and create your own presentation. To do this, you first enter and edit the presentation text, and then you can focus on the design and look of the presentation. PowerPoint helps you accomplish these tasks. You can start with the AutoContent Wizard and then enhance the look of your presentation by selecting a design from a collection of professionally prepared slide designs, called **design templates**. In this unit, you create a presentation using a PowerPoint design template. Maria Abbott, general sales manager at MediaLoft, asks you to prepare a marketing presentation on a new service that MediaLoft is planning to introduce. You begin by planning your presentation.

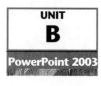

Planning an Effective Presentation

Before you create a presentation using PowerPoint, you need to plan and outline the message you want to communicate and consider how you want the presentation to look. When preparing the outline, you need to keep in mind where you are giving the presentation and who your audience is. It is also important to know what equipment you might need, such as a sound system, computer, or projector. ▆▆▆▆ Use the planning guidelines below to help plan an effective presentation. Figure B-1 illustrates a well thought-out presentation outline.

DETAILS

In planning a presentation, it is important to:

- **Determine the purpose of the presentation**

  When you have a well-defined purpose, developing an outline for your presentation is much easier. You need to present a marketing plan for a new Internet service that MediaLoft is planning to launch later in the year.

- **Determine the message you want to communicate, then give the presentation a meaningful title and outline your message**

  If possible, take time to adequately develop an outline of your presentation content before creating the slides. Start your presentation by defining the new service, describing the competition, and stating the product positioning. See Figure B-1.

- **Determine the audience and the delivery location**

  The presentation audience and delivery location can greatly affect the type of presentation you create. For example, if you had to deliver a presentation to your staff in a small, dimly lit conference room, you may create a very simple presentation with a bright color scheme; however, if you had to deliver a sales presentation to a client in a formal conference room with many windows, you may need to create a very professional-looking presentation with a darker color scheme. You will deliver this presentation in a large conference room to MediaLoft's marketing management team.

- **Determine the type of output—black-and-white or color overhead transparencies, on-screen slide show, or an online broadcast—that best conveys your message, given time constraints and computer hardware availability**

  Because you are speaking in a large conference room to a large group and have access to a computer and projection equipment, you decide that an on-screen slide show is the best output choice for your presentation.

- **Determine a look for your presentation that will help communicate your message**

  You can choose one of the professionally designed templates that come with PowerPoint, modify one of these templates, or create one of your own. You want a simple and artistic template to convey the marketing plan.

- **Determine what additional materials will be useful in the presentation**

  You need to prepare not only the slides themselves but also supplementary materials, including speaker notes and handouts for the audience. You use speaker notes to help remember a few key details, and you pass out handouts for the audience to use as a reference.

1. eMedia
   - Proposed Marketing Plan
   - Your Name
   - August 12, 2006
   - Director of Internet Services

2. Product Definition
   - Internet media provider
     - Music and video
     - Articles and trade papers
     - Historical papers archive
   - On-demand publishing
     - Articles, books, research papers, games, and more...

3. Competition
   - Bookstores
   - Internet services
   - Media services
   - Ratings

4. Product Positioning
   - Licensed media download service provider
   - Interactive service provider
   - Publishing service provider

PowerPoint 2003

Clues to Use

Using templates from the Web

When you create a presentation, you have the option of using one of the design templates supplied with PowerPoint, or you can use a template from another source, such as a Web server or the Template Gallery on the Microsoft Office Web site. To create a presentation using a template from a Web server, start PowerPoint, open the New Presentation task pane, then click the On my Web sites hyperlink under Templates. The New from Templates on my Web Sites dialog box opens. Locate and open the template you want to use, then save it with a new name. To use a template from the Microsoft Office Online Web site, open the New Presentation task pane, then click the Templates on Office Online hyperlink. Your Web browser opens to the Microsoft Office Online Templates Web site. Locate the PowerPoint template you want to use, then click the Download Now button to open and save the template in PowerPoint. The first time you use the Templates Web site, you must install the Microsoft Office Template and MediaControl and accept the license agreement.

Entering Slide Text

Each time you start PowerPoint, a new presentation with a blank title slide appears in Normal view. The title slide has two **text placeholders**—boxes with dashed-line borders—where you enter text. The top text placeholder on the title slide is the **title placeholder**, labeled "Click to add title". The bottom text placeholder on the title slide is the **Subtitle text placeholder**, labeled "Click to add subtitle". To enter text in a placeholder, simply click the placeholder and then type your text. After you enter text in a placeholder, the placeholder becomes a text object. An **object** is any item on a slide that can be manipulated. Objects are the building blocks that make up a presentation slide. ▰▰▰▰ Begin working on your presentation by starting PowerPoint and entering text on the title slide.

STEPS

1. Start PowerPoint

A new presentation appears displaying a blank title slide in Normal view.

2. Move the pointer over the title placeholder labeled "Click to add title" in the Slide pane

The pointer changes to I when you move the pointer over the placeholder. In PowerPoint, the pointer often changes shape, depending on the task you are trying to accomplish.

3. Click the title placeholder in the Slide pane

The **insertion point**, a blinking vertical line, indicates where your text appears when you type in the title placeholder. A **selection box**, the slanted line border, appears around the title placeholder, indicating that it is selected and ready to accept text. See Figure B-2.

> **TROUBLE**
> If you press a wrong key, press [Backspace] to erase the character.

4. Type eMedia

PowerPoint center-aligns the title text within the title placeholder, which is now a text object. Notice that text appears on the slide thumbnail in the slides tab.

5. Click the subtitle text placeholder in the Slide pane

A wavy red line may appear under the word "eMedia" in the title text object indicating that the automatic spellchecking feature in PowerPoint is active. If it doesn't appear on your screen, it may mean that the automatic spellchecking feature is turned off.

6. Type Proposed Marketing Plan, then press [Enter]

The insertion point moves to the next line in the Subtitle text object.

7. Type Your Name, press [Enter], type August 12, 2006, press [Enter], then type Director of Internet Services

Notice that the AutoFit Options button ⬌ appears near the text object. The AutoFit Options button on your screen indicates that PowerPoint has automatically decreased the size of all the text in the text object to fit in the text object.

8. Click the Autofit Options button ⬌, then click Stop Fitting Text to This Placeholder on the shortcut menu

The text in the Subtitle text box changes back to its original size.

> **TROUBLE**
> If the insertion point is blinking in a blank line after completing this step, press [Backspace] one more time.

9. Position I to the right of 2006, drag to select the entire line of text, press [Backspace], then click outside the main text object in a blank area of the slide

The text and the line the text was on are deleted and the Autofit Options button closes, as shown in Figure B-3. Clicking a blank area of the slide deselects all selected objects on the slide.

10. Click the Save button 🖬 on the Standard toolbar, then save your presentation as eMediaB to the drive and folder where your Data Files are stored

FIGURE B-2: Slide with selected title text placeholder

Selection box

Title text placeholder

Insertion point

Subtitle text placeholder

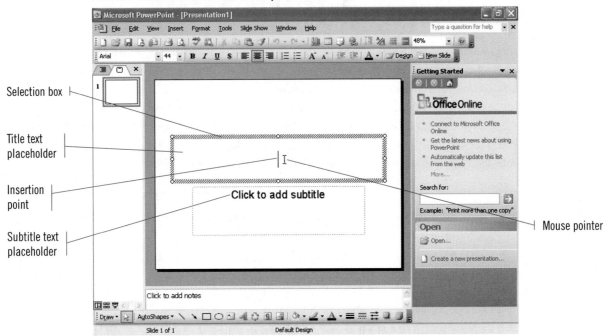

Mouse pointer

FIGURE B-3: Title slide with text

Red wavy line indicates automatic spellchecking is on

Subtitle text is centered in the text box

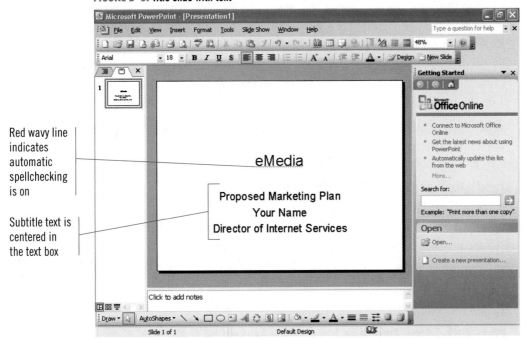

Clues to Use

Using Speech Recognition

Speech recognition technology lets you enter text and issue commands in PowerPoint by talking into a standard microphone connected to your computer. It is an Office-wide program that you must install and set up before you can use it. To set up Speech Recognition, start Microsoft Word, click Tools on the menu bar, then click Speech. You might be prompted to install the Speech Recognition files using the Office CD. Once you have installed the Speech Recognition files, the Speech Recognition component is available in all Office programs, including PowerPoint. To begin

using Speech Recognition, you first need to train your computer to understand how you speak by using a Training Wizard. A Training Wizard is a series of paragraphs that you read into your computer's microphone. These training sessions teach the Speech module to recognize your voice. They also teach you the speed and level of clarity with which you need to speak so that the program can understand you. Training sessions improve the performance of the Speech Recognition module. If you don't use the training sessions, the Speech Recognition module may be inaccurate.

Creating a New Slide

To help you create a new slide easily, PowerPoint offers 27 predesigned slide layouts. A **slide layout** determines how all of the elements on a slide are arranged. Slide layouts include a variety of placeholder arrangements for different objects, including text, clip art, tables, charts, diagrams, and media clips. Layouts are organized by type in the following categories: text layouts, content layouts, text and content layouts, and other layouts. You have already used the Title Slide layout in the previous lesson. Table B-1 describes some of the placeholders you'll find in PowerPoint's slide layouts. To continue developing the presentation, you create a slide that defines the new service MediaLoft is developing.

STEPS

QUICK TIP

You can also insert a new slide from the Slide Layout task pane: point to the slide layout you want, click the slide layout list arrow, then click Insert New Slide.

1. **Click the** New Slide button **on the Formatting toolbar**

   A new blank slide (now the current slide) appears as the second slide in your presentation and the Slide Layout task pane opens, as shown in Figure B-4. The new slide in the Slide pane contains a title placeholder and a **body text placeholder** for a bulleted list. Notice that the status bar indicates Slide 2 of 2 and that the Slides tab now contains two slide thumbnails. The Slide Layout task pane identifies the different PowerPoint slide layouts that you can use in your presentation. A dark border appears around the Title and Text slide layout identifying it as the currently applied layout for the slide. You can easily change the current slide's layout by clicking a slide layout icon in the Slide Layout task pane.

2. **Point to the** Title and 2-Column Text layout **in the Slide Layout task pane**

   When you place your pointer over a slide layout icon, a selection list arrow appears. You can click the list arrow to choose options for applying the layout. After a brief moment, a ScreenTip also appears that identifies the slide layout by name.

3. **Click the** Title and 2-Column Text layout **in the Slide Layout task pane**

   A slide layout with two text placeholders replaces the Title and Text slide layout for the current slide.

TROUBLE

When AutoCorrect is active, if you mistype a common word, PowerPoint automatically corrects it when you press [Spacebar] or [Enter]. You know PowerPoint has automatically corrected a word when you point to a word and a small rectangle appears under the word. To see a list of common typing errors that PowerPoint corrects automatically, click Tools on the menu bar, then click AutoCorrect Options.

4. **Type** Product Definition, **then click the** left body text placeholder **in the Slide pane**

   The text you type appears in the title placeholder, and the insertion point appears next to a bullet in the left body text placeholder.

5. **Type** Internet media provider, **then press** [Enter]

   A new first-level bullet automatically appears when you press [Enter].

6. **Press** [Tab]

   The new first-level bullet indents and becomes a second-level bullet.

7. **Type** Music and video, **press** [Enter], **type** Articles and trade papers, **press** [Enter], **then type** Historical papers archive

   The left text object now has four bulleted points.

8. **Press** [Ctrl][Enter], **then type** On-demand publishing

   Pressing [Ctrl][Enter] moves the insertion point to the next text placeholder on the slide. Because this is a two-column layout, the insertion point moves to the other body text placeholder on the slide.

9. **Press** [Enter], **click the** Increase Indent button **on the Formatting toolbar, enter the four second-level bulleted items shown in Figure B-5, click in a blank area of the slide, then click the** Save button **on the Standard toolbar**

   The Increase Indent button indents the first-level bullet, which changes it to a second-level bullet. Clicking the Save button saves all of the changes to the file. Compare your screen with Figure B-5.

FIGURE B-4: New blank slide in Normal view

New slide thumbnail added to Slides tab

Body text placeholder

Total number of slides

Current slide number

New Slide button

Slide Layout task pane may appear differently on your screen

Title and 2-column Text layout

Current slide layout

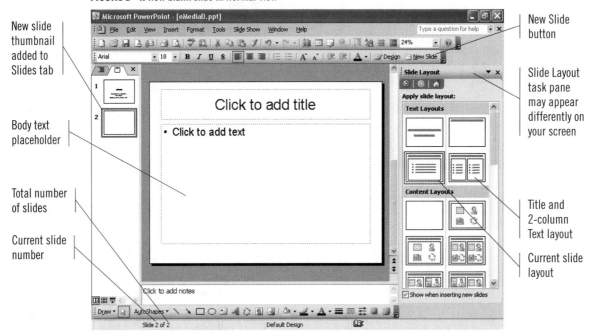

FIGURE B-5: New slide with Title and 2-Column Text slide layout

Save button

First-level bullet

Second-level bullet

Two text objects based on the slide layout

Type this text to complete Step 9

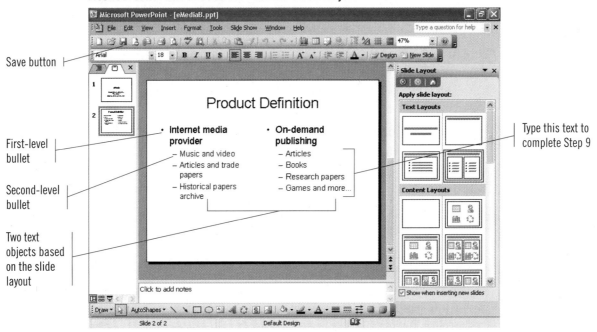

TABLE B-1: Slide Layout placeholders

placeholder	symbol	description
Bulleted List		Inserts a short list of related points
Clip Art		Inserts a picture from the Clip Organizer
Chart		Inserts a chart created with Microsoft Graph
Diagram or Organization Chart		Inserts a diagram or organizational chart
Table		Inserts a table
Media Clip		Inserts a music, sound, or video clip
Content		Inserts objects such as a table, a chart, clip art, a picture, a diagram or organizational chart, or a media clip

PowerPoint 2003

Entering Text in the Outline Tab

You can enter presentation text by typing directly on the slide, as you've learned already, or, if you'd rather focus on the presentation text without worrying about the layout, you can enter it in the Outline tab. As in a regular outline, the headings, or titles, appear first; beneath the titles, the subpoints, or body text, appear. Body text appears as one or more lines of bulleted text indented under a title. ▰▰▱▱▱▱ You switch to the Outline tab to enter body text for two more slides.

STEPS

1. **Click the Outline tab to the left of the Slide pane**

   The Outline tab enlarges to display the text that is on your slides. The slide icon for Slide 2 is highlighted, indicating that it's selected. Notice the numbers 1 and 2 that appear to the left of each of the first-level bullets for Slide 2, indicating that there are two body text objects on the slide.

2. **Point to the Title and Text layout in the Slide Layout task pane, click the list arrow, then click Insert New Slide**

   A new slide, Slide 3, with the Title and Text layout appears as the current slide below Slide 2. A selected slide icon ▣ appears next to the slide number in the Outline tab when you add a new slide. See Figure B-6. Text that you enter next to a slide icon becomes the title for that slide.

3. **Click to the right of the Slide 3 slide icon in the Outline tab, type Competition, press [Enter], then press [Tab]**

   A new slide is inserted when you press [Enter], but because you want to enter body text for the slide you just created, you press Tab, which indents this line to make it part of Slide 3.

4. **Type Bookstoes, press [Enter], type E-sites, press [Enter], type Media services, press [Enter], type Ratings, then press [Enter]**

   Make sure you typed "Bookstoes" without the "r" as specified in the step.

5. **Press [Shift][Tab]**

   The bullet that was created when you pressed [Enter] changes to a new slide icon.

6. **Type Product Positioning, press [Ctrl][Enter], type Licensed media download provider, press [Enter], type Publishing service provider, press [Enter], type Interactive service provider, then press [Ctrl][Enter]**

   Pressing [Ctrl][Enter] while the cursor is in the title text object moves the cursor into the body text object. Pressing [Ctrl][Enter] while the cursor is in the body text object creates a new slide with the same layout as the previous slide. Two of the bulleted points you just typed for Slide 4 are out of order, and you don't need the new Slide 5 you just created.

7. **Click the Undo button ↺ on the Standard toolbar**

   Clicking the Undo button undoes the previous action. Slide 5 is deleted and the insertion point moves back up to the last bullet in Slide 4.

8. **Position the pointer to the left of the last bullet in Slide 4 in the Outline tab**

   The pointer changes to ✛.

9. **Drag the mouse up until the pointer changes to ↕ and a horizontal indicator line appears above the second bullet point in Slide 4, then release the mouse button**

   The third bullet point moves up one line in the outline and trades places with the second bullet point, as shown in Figure B-7.

10. **Click the Slides tab, click the Slide 2 thumbnail in the Slides tab, then save your work**

    Slide 2 of 4 should appear in the status bar.

FIGURE B-6: Normal view with Outline tab open

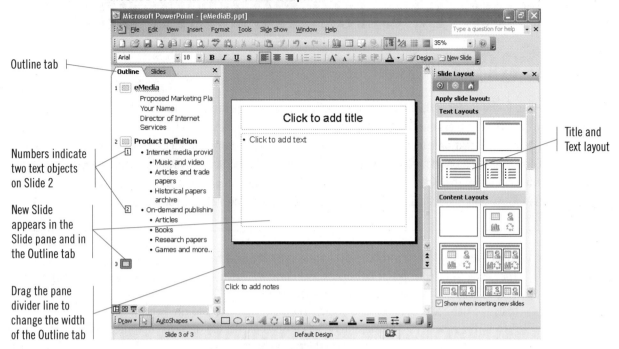

Outline tab

Numbers indicate two text objects on Slide 2

New Slide appears in the Slide pane and in the Outline tab

Drag the pane divider line to change the width of the Outline tab

Title and Text layout

FIGURE B-7: Bulleted item moved up in the Outline tab

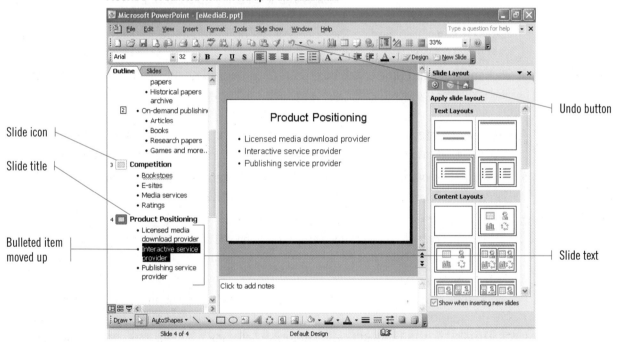

Slide icon

Slide title

Bulleted item moved up

Undo button

Slide text

Clues to Use

What do I do if I see a lightbulb on a slide?

If you are showing the Office Assistant, you may see a yellow light-bulb in your presentation window. The lightbulb is part of the PowerPoint Help system and it can mean several things. First, the Office Assistant might have a suggestion for an appropriate piece of clip art for that slide. Second, the Office Assistant might have a helpful tip based on the task you are performing. This is known as a context-sensitive tip. Third, the Office Assistant might have detected a style, such as a word in the slide title that should be capitalized, which is inconsistent with preset style guidelines. When you see a lightbulb, you can click it, read the dialog balloon, and click the option you prefer, or you can ignore it. If the Office Assistant is hidden or turned off, the lightbulb does not appear.

PowerPoint 2003

Adding Slide Headers and Footers

Header and footer text, such as your company or product name, the slide number, and the date, can give your slides a professional look and make it easier for your audience to follow your presentation. On slides, you can add text only to the footer; however, notes or handouts can include both header and footer text. Footer information that you apply to the slides of your presentation is visible in the PowerPoint views and when you print the slides. Notes and handouts header and footer text is visible when you print notes pages, handouts, and the outline. ![icon] You add footer text to the slides of your presentation.

STEPS

1. **Click** View **on the menu bar, then click** Header and Footer
   The Header and Footer dialog box opens, as shown in Figure B-8. The Header and Footer dialog box has two tabs: a Slide tab and a Notes and Handouts tab. The Slide tab is selected. There are three types of footer text, Date and time, Slide number, and Footer. The Date and time and the Footer check boxes are selected by default. The rectangles at the bottom of the Preview box identify the default position and status of the three types of footer text on the slides. Two of the rectangles at the bottom of the Preview box have dark borders.

2. **Click the** Date and time check box **to deselect it**
   The date and time suboptions are no longer available and the far-left rectangle at the bottom of the Preview box has a light border. The middle rectangle identifies where the Footer text—the only check box still selected—will appear on the slide. The rectangle on the right shows where the slide number will appear if you select that check box.

3. **Click the** Date and time check box, **then click the** Update automatically option button
   Now every time you view the slide show or print the slides in this presentation, the current date appears in the footer.

4. **Click the** Update automatically list arrow, **then click the** fourth option **in the list**
   The date format changes to display the Month spelled out, the date number, and four-digit year.

5. **Click the** Slide number check box, **click in the** Footer text box, **then type** Your Name
   The Preview box now shows that all three footer placeholders are selected.

6. **Click the** Don't show on title slide check box
   Selecting this check box prevents the footer information you entered in the Header and Footer dialog box from appearing on the title slide. Compare your screen to Figure B-9.

7. **Click** Apply to All
   The dialog box closes and the footer information is applied to all of the slides in your presentation except the title slide. You can click the Apply button to apply footer information to just one slide in the presentation if you want.

8. **Click the** Slide 1 thumbnail **in the Slides tab, click** View **on the menu bar, then click** Header and Footer
   The Header and Footer dialog box opens, displaying all of the options that you specified for the presentation. You want to show your company slogan in the footer on the title slide.

9. **Click the** Date and time check box, **the** Slide number check box, **and the** Don't show on title slide check box **to deselect them, then select the text in the Footer text box**

10. **Type** "All Media...All the Time", **click** Apply, **then save your work**
    Only the text in the Footer text box appears on the title slide. Clicking Apply applies the footer information to just the current slide.

FIGURE B-8: Header and Footer dialog box

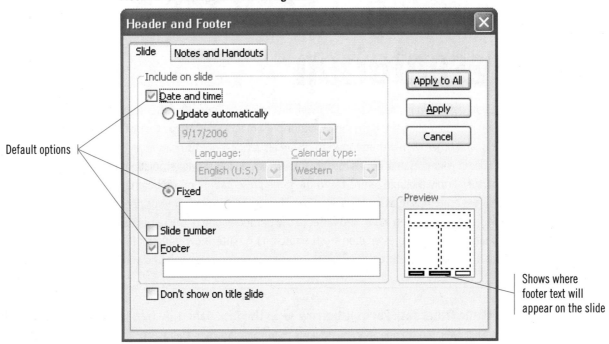

Default options

Shows where footer text will appear on the slide

FIGURE B-9: Completed Header and Footer dialog box

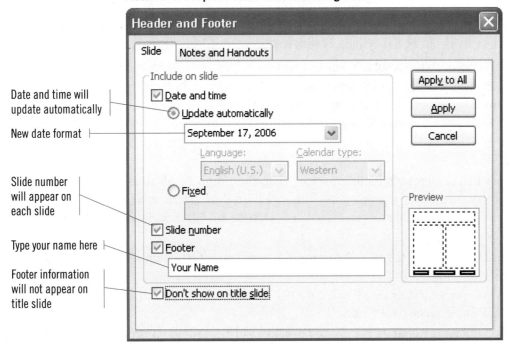

Date and time will update automatically

New date format

Slide number will appear on each slide

Type your name here

Footer information will not appear on title slide

Clues to Use

Entering and printing notes

You can add notes to your slides when there are certain facts you want to remember during a presentation or when there is information you want to hand out to your audience. Notes do not appear on the slides when you run a slide show. Use the Notes pane in Normal view or Notes Page view to enter notes for your slides. To enter text notes on a slide, click in the Notes pane, then type. If you want to insert graphics as notes, you must use Notes Page view. To open

Notes Page view, click View on the menu bar, then click Notes Page. You can print your notes by clicking the Print what list arrow and then clicking Notes Pages in the Print dialog box. The notes page can be a good handout to give your audience to use during the presentation and then after as a reminder. If you don't enter any notes in the Notes pane, and print the notes pages, the slides print as thumbnails with blank lines to the right of the thumbnails to handwrite notes.

Choosing a Look for a Presentation

To help you design your presentation, PowerPoint provides a number of design templates so you can have professional help creating the right look for your presentation. A **design template** has borders, colors, text attributes, and other elements arranged to create a specific look. You can apply a design template to one or all the slides in your presentation. In most cases, you would apply one template to an entire presentation; you can, however, apply multiple templates to the same presentation, or a different template on each slide. You can use a design template as is, or you can modify any element to suit your needs. Unless you have training in graphic design, it is often easier and faster to use or modify one of the templates supplied with PowerPoint, rather than design your presentation from scratch. No matter how you create your presentation, you can save it as a template for future use. You decide to use an existing PowerPoint template.

STEPS

QUICK TIP

You can click the Slide Design button ☑ Design on the Formatting toolbar to open the Slide Design task pane.

1. **Click the Other Task Panes list arrow ▼ in the task pane title bar, then click Slide Design**

   The Slide Design task pane appears, similarly to the one shown in Figure B-10. This task pane is split into sections: the hyperlinks that open sub task panes are at the top of the pane; the Used in This Presentation section, which identifies the templates currently applied to the presentation (in this case, the Default Design template); the Recently Used section, which identifies up to four templates you have applied recently (this section does not appear on your screen if you have not used any other templates); and the Available For Use section, which lists all of the standard PowerPoint design templates that you can apply to a presentation.

QUICK TIP

If you know what design template you want to use for a new presentation, you can apply it before you enter the presentation content. Open a new blank presentation, open the Slide Design task pane, then apply the template.

2. **Scroll down to the Available For Use section of the Slide Design task pane, then place your pointer over the Capsules template (tenth row, second column)**

   A ScreenTip identifies the template, and a selection list arrow appears next to the Capsules template icon. The list arrow provides options for you to choose from when applying design templates. To determine how a design template looks on your presentation, you need to apply it. You can apply as many templates as you want until you find one that you like.

3. **Click the Capsules template list arrow, then click Apply to All Slides**

   The Capsules template is applied to all the slides. Notice the new slide background color, the new graphic elements, new fonts, and the new slide text color. You decide that this template doesn't work well with the presentation content.

4. **Click the Network template list arrow (eleventh row, first column), then click Apply to Selected Slides**

   The Network template is applied to just the title slide of the presentation. This design template doesn't fit with the presentation content either.

QUICK TIP

One way to apply multiple templates to the same presentation is to click the Slide Sorter View button, select a slide or a group of slides, then click the template.

5. **Click the Edge template list arrow (eleventh row, second column), then click Apply to All Slides**

   This simple design template looks good with the presentation content and fits the MediaLoft company image.

6. **Click the Next Slide button ▼ three times**

   Preview all the slides in the presentation to see how they look.

7. **Click the Previous Slide button ▲ two times to return to Slide 2**

   Compare your screen to Figure B-11.

8. **Save your changes**

FIGURE B-10: Normal view with Slide Design task pane open

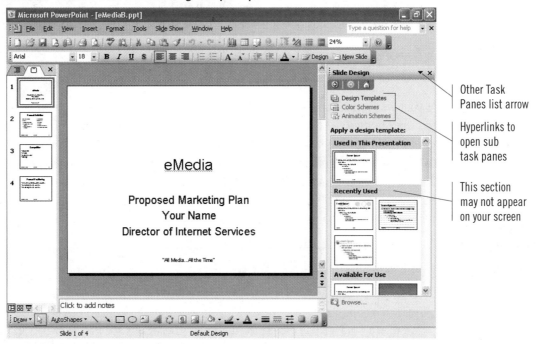

Other Task Panes list arrow

Hyperlinks to open sub task panes

This section may not appear on your screen

FIGURE B-11: Presentation with Edge template design applied

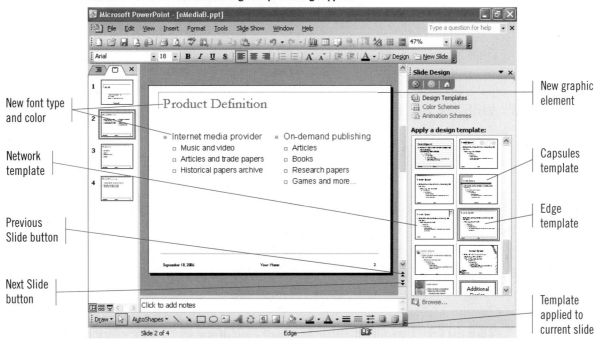

New font type and color

Network template

Previous Slide button

Next Slide button

New graphic element

Capsules template

Edge template

Template applied to current slide

Clues to Use

Using design templates

You are not limited to using the templates PowerPoint provides; you can also modify a PowerPoint template or even create your own. For example, you might want to use your company's color as a slide background or incorporate your company's logo on every slide. If you modify an existing template, you can keep, change, or delete any color, graphic, or font. To create a new template, click Blank Presentation on the New Presentation task pane. Add the design elements to the slide to create the look you want for the presentation.

Open the Save As dialog box, click the Save as type list arrow, choose Design Template, name your template, then click Save. PowerPoint automatically adds the file extension .pot to the filename, saves the template to the Templates folder, and adds it to the Slide Design task pane so that you can use your customized template as a basis for all future presentations. To apply a template that you created to an existing presentation, open the presentation, then choose the template in the Slide Design task pane.

Checking Spelling in a Presentation

As your work nears completion, you need to review and proofread your presentation thoroughly for errors. You can use the spellchecking feature in PowerPoint to check for and correct spelling errors. This feature compares the spelling of all the words in your presentation against the words contained in its electronic dictionary. You still must proofread your presentation for punctuation, grammar, and word-usage errors because the spellchecker recognizes only misspelled words, not misused words. For example, the spellchecker would not identify "The test" as an error, even if you had intended to type "The best." 🔲🔲🔲 You're finished adding and changing text in the presentation, so you can now check the spelling in the presentation.

STEPS

TROUBLE
If your spellchecker doesn't find the word "eMedia," then a previous user may have accidentally added it to the custom dictionary. Skip Steps 1 and 2 and continue with the lesson.

1. **Click the Slide 1 thumbnail in the Slides tab, then click the Spelling button 📝 on the Standard toolbar**

   PowerPoint begins to check the spelling in your entire presentation. When PowerPoint finds a misspelled word or a word it doesn't recognize, the Spelling dialog box opens, as shown in Figure B-12. For an explanation of the commands available in the Spelling dialog box, see Table B-2. In this case, PowerPoint does not recognize "eMedia" on Slide 1. It suggests that you replace it with the word "media". You want the word to remain as you typed it.

2. **Click Ignore All**

   Clicking Ignore All tells the spellchecker not to stop at and question any more occurrences of this word in this presentation. The next word the spellchecker identifies as an error is the word "Bookstoes" in the body text object on Slide 3. In the Suggestions list box, the spellchecker suggests "Bookstores."

QUICK TIP
The spellchecker does not check the text in inserted pictures or objects.

3. **Verify that Bookstores is selected in the Suggestions list box, then click Change**

   If PowerPoint finds any other words it does not recognize, either change them or ignore them. When the spellchecker finishes checking your presentation, the Spelling dialog box closes, and an alert box opens with a message that the spelling check is complete.

4. **Click OK**

   The alert box closes. You are satisfied with the presentation so far and you decide to print it.

TROUBLE
If your preview window does not show the slide in color it is because you have selected a black and white printer.

5. **Click the Print Preview button 🔳 on the Standard toolbar**

   The Print Preview window opens, displaying the presentation's title slide as shown in Figure B-13.

6. **Make sure Slides is selected in the Print What list box, click the Options list arrow on the Print Preview toolbar, then click Frame Slides**

   The slides of your presentation print with a frame around each page.

7. **Click the Print button 🖨 Print... on the Print Preview toolbar, click OK in the Print dialog box, click the Close Preview button Close on the Print Preview toolbar, then save your presentation**

Clues to Use

Checking spelling as you type

PowerPoint checks your spelling as you type. If you type a word that is not in the electronic dictionary, a wavy red line appears under it. To correct an error, right-click the misspelled word, then review the suggestions, which appear in the shortcut menu. You can select a suggestion, add the word you typed to your custom dictionary, or ignore it.

To turn off automatic spellchecking, click Tools on the menu bar, then click Options to open the Options dialog box. Click the Spelling and Style tab, and in the Spelling section, click the Check spelling as you type check box to deselect it. To temporarily hide the wavy red lines, click the Hide all spelling errors check box to select it.

FIGURE B-12: Spelling dialog box

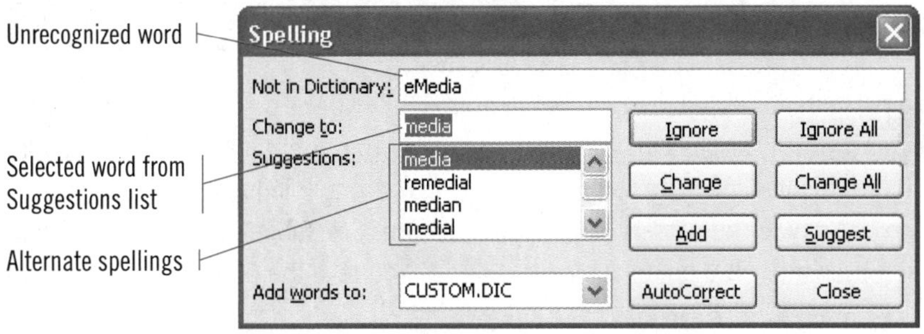
Unrecognized word
Selected word from Suggestions list
Alternate spellings
Spelling
Not in Dictionary: eMedia
Change to: media
Suggestions:
media
remedial
median
medial
Ignore
Ignore All
Change
Change All
Add
Suggest
Add words to: CUSTOM.DIC
AutoCorrect
Close

FIGURE B-13: Print Preview window

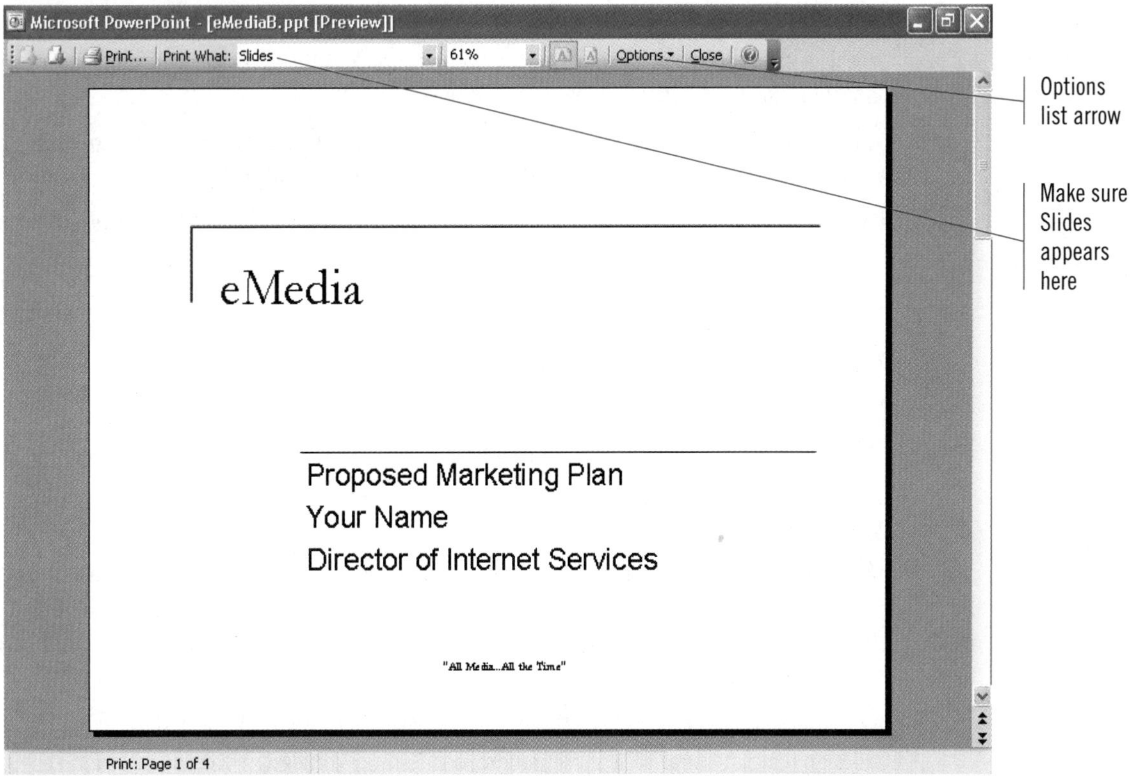
Microsoft PowerPoint - [eMediaB.ppt [Preview]]
Print... Print What: Slides
61%
Options
Close
Options list arrow
Make sure Slides appears here
eMedia
Proposed Marketing Plan
Your Name
Director of Internet Services
"All Media...All the Time"
Print: Page 1 of 4

TABLE B-2: Spelling dialog box commands

command	description
Ignore/Ignore All	Continues spellchecking without making any changes to the identified word (or all occurrences of the identified word)
Change/Change All	Changes the identified word (or all occurrences) to the suggested word
Add	Adds the identified word to your custom dictionary; spellchecker will not flag it again
Suggest	Suggests an alternative spelling for the identified word
AutoCorrect	Adds the suggested word as an AutoCorrect entry for the highlighted word
Add words to	Lets you choose a custom dictionary where you store words you often use but that are not part of the PowerPoint dictionary

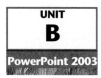

Evaluating a Presentation

As you create a presentation, keep in mind that good design involves preparation. An effective presentation is both focused and visually appealing—easy for the speaker to present and easy for the audience to understand. The visual elements (colors, graphics, and text) can strongly influence the audience's attention and interest and can determine the success of your presentation. See Table B-3 for general information on the impact a visual presentation has on an audience. ▓▓▓▓ You take the time to evaluate your presentation's effectiveness.

STEPS

1. **Click the** Slide Show button ☞, **then press** [Enter] **to move through the slide show**

2. **When you are finished viewing the slide show, click the** Slide Sorter View button ⊞
   You decide that Slide 4 should come before Slide 3.

3. **Drag** Slide 4 **between Slides 2 and 3, then release the mouse button**
   The thin black line that moved with the pointer indicates the slide's new position. The final presentation is shown in Slide Sorter view. Compare your screen to Figure B-14.

4. **When you are finished evaluating your presentation according to the guidelines below, save your changes, then close the presentation and exit PowerPoint**
   Figure B-15 shows a poorly designed slide. Contrast this slide with your eMedia presentation as you review the following guidelines.

DETAILS

When evaluating a presentation, it is important to:

- **Keep your message focused**
  Don't put everything you plan to say on your presentation slides. Keep the audience anticipating further explanations to the key points shown in the presentation.

- **Keep your text concise**
  Limit each slide to six words per line and six lines per slide. Use lists and symbols to help prioritize your points visually. Your presentation text provides only the highlights; use notes to give more detailed information. Your presentation focuses attention on the key issues and you supplement the information with further explanation and details during your presentation.

- **Keep the design simple, easy to read, and appropriate for the content**
  A design template makes the presentation consistent. If you design your own layout, keep it simple and use design elements sparingly. Use similar design elements consistently throughout the presentation; otherwise, your audience may get confused. You used a simple design template; the horizontal lines give the presentation a somewhat artistic look, which is appropriate for a casual professional presentation.

- **Choose attractive colors that make the slide easy to read**
  Use contrasting colors for slide background and text to make the text readable. If you are giving an on-screen presentation, you can use almost any combination of colors that look good together.

- **Choose fonts and styles that are easy to read and emphasize important text**
  As a general rule, use no more than two fonts in a presentation and vary the font size, using nothing smaller than 24 points. Use bold and italic attributes selectively.

- **Use visuals to help communicate the message of your presentation**
  Commonly used visuals include clip art, photographs, charts, worksheets, tables, and movies. Whenever possible, replace text with a visual, but be careful not to overcrowd your slides. White space on your slides is OK!

FIGURE B-14: The final presentation in Slide Sorter view

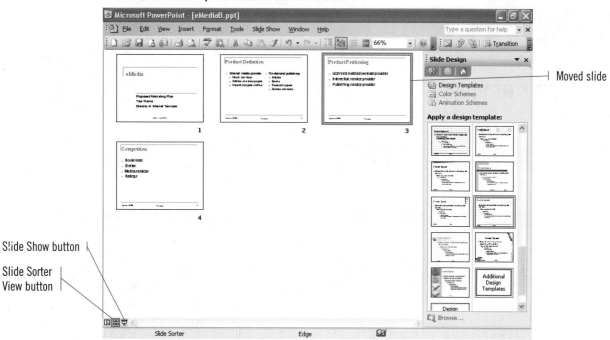

Moved slide

Slide Show button

Slide Sorter View button

FIGURE B-15: A poorly designed slide in Normal view

Background color does not fit other slide elements

Too many words used

Too many fonts used

Font size too small

Design template does not fit content

Object serves no purpose

Poor graphic choice

Color does not complement slide color

Drawn objects serve no purpose

TABLE B-3: Audience impact from a visual presentation

impact	description
Visual reception	Most people receive up to 75% of all environmental stimuli through the human sense of sight
Learning	Up to 90% of what an audience learns comes from visual and audio messages
Retention	Combining visual messages with verbal messages can increase memory retention by as much as 30%
Presentation goals	You are twice as likely to achieve your communication objectives using a visual presentation
Meeting length	You are likely to decrease the average meeting length by 25% when you use visual presentation

Source: Presenters Online, www.presentersonline.com

Practice

▼ CONCEPTS REVIEW

Label each element of the PowerPoint window shown in Figure B-16.

FIGURE B-16

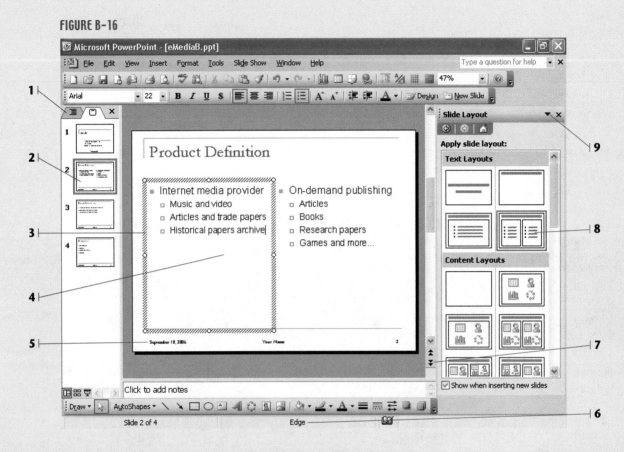

Match each term with the statement that best describes it.

10. **Text placeholder**
11. **Slide layout**
12. **Selection box**
13. **Design template**
14. **Slide icon**
15. **Insertion point**

a. A specific design, format, and color scheme that is applied to all the slides in a presentation
b. Indicates where your text will appear when you type in a text object
c. Determines how all of the elements on a slide are arranged
d. The slanted line border that appears around a text placeholder, indicating that it is ready to accept text
e. A box with a dashed border in which you can type text
f. In Outline view, the symbol that represents a slide

Select the best answer from the list of choices.

16. **According to the unit, which of the following is *not* a guideline for planning a presentation?**
    a. Determine the purpose of the presentation.
    b. Determine what you want to produce when the presentation is finished.
    c. Determine which type of output you need to best convey your message.
    d. Determine who else can give the final presentation.

17. **Other than the Slide pane, where else can you enter slide text?**
    a. Outline tab
    b. Print Preview
    c. Notes Page view
    d. Slides tab

18. **Which of the following statements is *not* true?**
    a. You can customize any PowerPoint template.
    b. The spellchecker identifies "there" as misspelled if the correct word for the context is "their".
    c. Speaker notes do not appear during the slide show.
    d. PowerPoint has many colorful templates from which to choose.

19. **When you evaluate your presentation, you should make sure it follows which of the following criteria?**
    a. The slides should include every piece of information to be presented so the audience can read it.
    b. The slides should use as many colors as possible to hold the audience's attention.
    c. Many different typefaces make the slides more interesting.
    d. The message should be clearly outlined without a lot of extra words.

20. **What is the definition of a slide layout?**
    a. A slide layout automatically applies all the objects you can use on a slide.
    b. A slide layout determines how all the elements on a slide are arranged.
    c. A slide layout applies a different template to the presentation.
    d. A slide layout puts all your slides in order.

21. **When the spellchecker identifies a word as misspelled, which of the following is *not* a choice?**
    a. To ignore this occurrence of the error
    b. To change the misspelled word to the correct spelling
    c. To have the spellchecker automatically correct all the errors it finds
    d. To ignore all occurrences of the error in the presentation

22. **When you type text in a text placeholder, it becomes:**
    a. A label.
    b. A title.
    c. A selection box.
    d. A text object.

▼ SKILLS REVIEW

1. **Enter slide text.**
   a. Start PowerPoint if necessary.
   b. In the Slide pane in Normal view, enter the text **Product Marketing** in the title placeholder.
   c. In the main text placeholder, enter **Rueben Agarpao**.
   d. On the next line of the placeholder, enter **Manager**.
   e. On the next line of the placeholder, enter **April 14, 2006**.
   f. Deselect the text object.
   g. Save the presentation as **RouterJet Tests** to the drive and folder where your Data Files are stored.

2. Create new slides.

a. Create a new slide.

b. Review the text in Table B-4, then select the appropriate slide layout.

c. Enter the text from Table B-4 into the new slide.

d. Create a new bulleted list slide using the Slide Layout task pane.

e. Enter the text from Table B-5 into the new slide.

f. Save your changes.

3. Enter text in the Outline tab.

a. Open the Outline tab.

b. Create a new bulleted list slide after the last one.

c. Enter the text from Table B-6 into the new slide.

d. Move the third bullet point in the second indent level to the second position.

e. Switch back to the Slides tab.

f. Save your changes.

4. Add slide headers and footers.

a. Open the Header and Footer dialog box.

b. Type today's date into the Fixed text box.

c. Add the slide number to the footer.

d. Type your name in the Footer text box.

e. Apply the footer to all of the slides.

f. Open the Header and Footer dialog box again, then click the Notes and Handouts tab.

g. Enter today's date in the Fixed text box.

h. Type the name of your class in the Header text box.

i. Type your name in the Footer text box.

j. Apply the header and footer information to all the notes and handouts.

k. Save your changes.

5. Choose a look for a presentation.

a. Open the Slide Design task pane.

b. Locate the Profile template, then apply it to all the slides.

c. Move to Slide 1.

d. Locate the Pixel template, then apply it to Slide 1.

e. Save your changes.

6. Check spelling in a presentation.

a. Perform a spelling check on the document and change any misspelled words. Ignore any words that are correctly spelled but that the spellchecker doesn't recognize.

b. Save your changes.

7. Evaluate a presentation.

a. View Slide 1 in the Slide Show view, then move through the slide show.

b. Evaluate the presentation using the points described in the lesson as criteria.

c. Preview your presentation.

d. Print the outline of the presentation.

e. Print the slides of your presentation in grayscale with a frame around each slide.

f. Save your changes, close the presentation, and exit PowerPoint.

TABLE B-4

text object	text to insert
Slide title	RouterJet Project Tests - Rueben
First indent level	Focus: Component System
Second indent level	User access components
	Security components
	Network components
	System components
First indent level	Data Files and Report
Second indent level	Compile component data files
	Define component interface parameters
	Write function data report

TABLE B-5

text object	text to insert
Slide title	RouterJet Project Tests - Jeremy
First indent level	Focus: Network Integration
Second indent level	Server codes and routes
	File transfer
	Data conversion
	Platform functionality ratings

TABLE B-6

text object	text to insert
Slide title	RouterJet Project Tests - Nura
First indent level	Focus: Software QA
Second indent level	User access testing
	Software compatibility testing
	Platform testing

▼ INDEPENDENT CHALLENGE 1

You have been asked to give a one-day course at a local adult education center. The course is called "Personal Computing for the Slightly Anxious Beginner" and is intended for adults who have never used a computer. One of your responsibilities is to create presentation slides that outline the course materials.

Plan and create presentation slides that outline the course material for the students. Create slides for the course introduction, course description, course text, grading policies, and a detailed syllabus. Create your own course material, but assume the following: the school has a computer lab with personal computers running Microsoft Windows software; each student has a computer; the prospective students are intimidated by computers but want to learn; and the course is on a Saturday from 9 a.m. to 5 p.m., with a one-hour lunch break.

a. Write a short paragraph that explains the results you want to see, the information you need, and the type of message you want to communicate.

b. Write an outline of your presentation. Indicate which content should go on each of the slides. Remember that your audience has never used computers before and needs computer terms defined.

c. Start PowerPoint and create the presentation by entering the title slide text.

d. Create the required slides as well as an ending slide that summarizes your presentation.

Advanced Challenge Exercise

- Open the Notes Page view.
- To at least three slides, add notes that you want to remember when you give the class.
- Print the Notes Page view for the presentation.

e. Check the spelling in the presentation.

f. Save the presentation as **Computer Class 101** to the drive and folder where your Data Files are stored.

g. View the presentation in Slide Show view.

h. Add your name as a footer on the notes and handouts, print handouts (six slides per page), and then print the presentation outline.

i. Save your changes, close your presentation, then exit PowerPoint.

▼ INDEPENDENT CHALLENGE 2

You are the training director for Catch Up, Ltd., a German company in Berlin that coordinates special events, including corporate functions, weddings, and private parties. You regularly train groups of temporary employees that you can call on as coordinators, kitchen and wait staff, and coat checkers for specific events. The company trains 10 to 15 new workers each month for the peak season between May and September. One of your responsibilities is to orient new temporary employees at the next training session.

Plan and create presentation slides that outline your employee orientation. Create slides for the introduction, agenda, company history, dress requirements, principles for interacting successfully with guests, and safety requirements. Create your own presentation and company material, but assume the following: Catch Up, Ltd. is owned by Jan Negd-Sorenson; the new employee training class lasts four hours, and your orientation lasts 15 minutes; the training director's presentation lasts 15 minutes; and the dress code requires uniforms, supplied by Catch Up, Ltd. (white for daytime events, black and white for evening events).

a. Think about the results you want to see, the information you need, and the message you want to communicate.

b. Write a presentation outline. What content should go on the slides?

c. Start PowerPoint and create the presentation by entering the slide text for all your slides.

d. Create a slide that summarizes your presentation, then add an appropriate design template.

e. Create an ending slide with the following information:

Catch Up, Ltd.

Gubener Strasse 765, 10243 Berlin

(Berlin-Friedrichshain)

TEL.: 393795, FAX: 39375719

f. Check the spelling in the presentation.

g. Save the presentation as Catch Up Training to the drive and folder where your Data Files are stored.

h. View the slide show, then view the slides in Slide Sorter view. Evaluate your presentation; make any changes necessary so that the final version is focused, clear, concise, and readable.

i. Add your name as a footer on the notes and handouts, print the presentation as handouts (two slides per page), then print the presentation outline.

j. Save your changes, close your presentation, then exit PowerPoint.

▼ INDEPENDENT CHALLENGE 3

You are an independent distributor of natural foods in Albuquerque, New Mexico. Your business, All Natural Foods, has grown progressively since its inception eight years ago, but sales and profits have leveled off over the last nine months. In an effort to stimulate growth, you decide to acquire two major natural food dealers, which would allow All Natural Foods to expand its territory into surrounding states. Use PowerPoint to develop a presentation that you can use to gain a financial backer for the acquisition.

a. Start PowerPoint. Choose the Maple design template. Enter Growth Plan as the main title on the title slide, and All Natural Foods as the subtitle.

b. Save the presentation as Growth Plan Proposal to the drive and folder where your Data Files are stored.

c. Add five more slides with the following titles: Slide 2–Background; Slide 3–Current Situation; Slide 4–Acquisition Goals; Slide 5–Our Management Team; Slide 6–Funding Required.

d. Enter text into the text placeholders of the slides. Use both the Slide pane and the Outline tab to enter text.

e. Check the spelling in the presentation.

f. View the presentation as a slide show, then view the slides in Slide Sorter view.

g. Add your name as a footer on the notes and handouts, save your changes, then print handouts (six slides per page).

h. Close your presentation, then exit PowerPoint.

Advanced Challenge Exercise

- Create a new slide at the end of the presentation. Enter concluding text on the slide, summarizing the main points of the presentation.
- Apply at least one design template to the presentation.
- Evaluate your presentation using the points identified in the Evaluating a Presentation lesson. Use a word processor to write a short paragraph explaining how your presentation met the goals for proper presentation development.
- Make any changes you feel are necessary, then identify the changes and explain your reasoning in a word processing document.
- Save the presentation as Growth Plan Proposal 2 to the drive and folder where your Data Files are stored.
- Print the presentation outline, close your presentation, then exit PowerPoint.

▼ INDEPENDENT CHALLENGE 4

One of the best things about PowerPoint is the flexibility you have in creating your presentations, but that same flexibility can result in slides that may appear cluttered, unorganized, and hard to read. Unit B introduced you to some concepts that you can use to help create good presentations using PowerPoint. Use the Web to research more guidelines and tips on creating effective presentations.

Plan and create a presentation that explains these tips to an audience of beginning PowerPoint users. The information you find on the Web should include the following topics:

- Message organization
- Text arrangement and amount
- Slide layout and design
- Presentation development
- Room layout and delivery
- Equipment

a. Connect to the Internet, then use your favorite search engine to locate Web sites that have information on presentations. Use the keywords **presentation tips** to conduct your search.

b. Review at least two Web sites that contain information about presentation tips and guidelines.

c. Start PowerPoint. Title the presentation **Presentation Tips**.

d. Create a presentation with at least five slides. Each slide should contain one main tip with supporting information about that tip.

e. Add a final slide titled **Presentation Tip URLs**. List the Web site addresses—the URLs—from which you obtained the information you used in your presentation.

f. Apply an appropriate design template.

g. Save the presentation as **Presentation Info** to the drive and folder where your Data Files are stored.

h. Add your name as a footer to the slides, notes, and handouts, check the spelling in the presentation, then view the final presentation as a slide show.

i. View your presentation in Slide Sorter view and evaluate it. Make any changes necessary so that the final version is focused, clear, concise, and readable.

j. Save your final presentation, print the slides as handouts (two per page), then close the presentation and exit PowerPoint.

Create the marketing presentation shown in Figures B-17 and B-18. Add today's date as the date on the title slide. Save the presentation as **Trade Proposal** to the drive and folder where your Data Files are stored. Review your slides in Slide Show view, add your name as a footer to the slides, notes, and handouts. Print the first slide of your presentation as a slide, then print the outline. Save your changes, close the presentation, and exit PowerPoint.

FIGURE B-17

FIGURE B-18

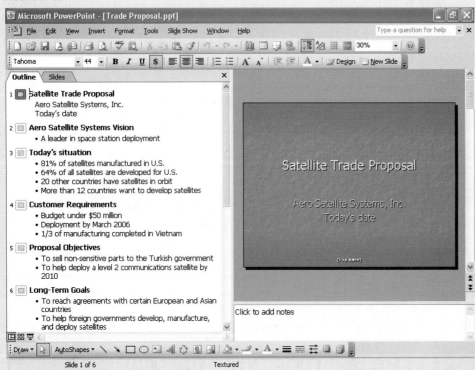

UNIT
C
PowerPoint 2003

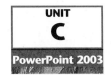

Modifying a Presentation

OBJECTIVES

- Open an existing presentation
- Draw and modify an object
- Edit drawn objects
- Align and group objects
- Add and arrange text
- Format text
- Import text from Microsoft Word
- Customize the color scheme and background

SAM

If you have a SAM user profile, you may have access to hands-on instruction, practice, and assessment of the skills covered in this unit. Log in to your SAM accont and go to your assignments page to see what your instructor has assigned.

After you create the basic outline of your presentation and enter text, you need to add images to your slides to help you communicate your message effectively. In this unit, you open an existing presentation; draw and modify objects; add, arrange, and format text; and work with the color scheme. You continue your work on the eMedia marketing presentation by drawing and modifying objects from the AutoShapes menu. You then edit the text and change the color scheme to create a professional look for the presentation.

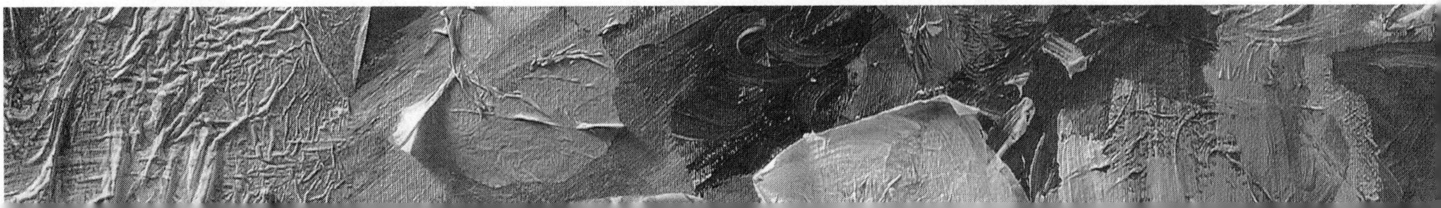

Opening an Existing Presentation

Sometimes the easiest way to create a new presentation is by changing an existing one. Revising a presentation means that you do not have to re-create slides that already exist and that you can use them again. You simply open the file you want to change, then use the Save As command to save a copy of the file with a new name. Whenever you open an existing presentation in this book, you will save a copy of it with a new name—this keeps the original file intact. Saving a copy does not affect the original file. ▰▰▰▰ You are ready to add some visual elements to your presentation, so you open the presentation you have been working on and save it with a new name.

STEPS

QUICK TIP

To open the file without opening a copy, click the Open hyperlink under Open in the Getting Started task pane, or click the Open button 🗁 on the Standard toolbar.

1. **Start PowerPoint, then click the** Create a new presentation **hyperlink in the Open section in the Getting Started task pane**
   The New Presentation task pane opens.

2. **Click the** From existing presentation **hyperlink in the New section in the New Presentation task pane**
   The New from Existing Presentation dialog box opens.

3. **Click the** Look in list arrow, **locate the drive and folder where your Data Files are stored, click the** Views button list arrow ▦ ˇ **on the dialog box toolbar, then click** Preview
   A list of your Data Files appears in the dialog box.

4. **If it is not selected, click** PPT C-1.ppt
   The first slide of the selected presentation appears in the preview box on the right side of the dialog box. See Figure C-1.

5. **Click** Create New
   A copy of the PPT C-1.ppt presentation file opens in Normal view. The presentation title bar displays the temporary filename "Presentation2".

QUICK TIP

If the file is not yet named, you can click the Save button 🖫 to open the Save As dialog box.

6. **Click** File **on the menu bar, then click** Save As
   The Save As dialog box opens.

7. **Make sure the Save in list box shows the drive and folder where your Data Files are stored, verify that the current filename in the File name text box is selected, then type** eMediaC

8. **Click** Save **to close the Save As dialog box and save the file**
   The file is saved with the name eMediaC.

TROUBLE

If you have another PowerPoint presentation open and it appears next to this presentation, close it, then repeat Step 9.

9. **Click the** Slide Design button 🖼 **on the Formatting toolbar, click** Window **on the menu bar, then click** Arrange All
   See Figure C-2. You can work with the task pane opened or closed. Many of the figures in this book show only the window that contains the Slide and notes panes and the Slides and Outline tabs.

FIGURE C-1: New from Existing Presentation dialog box

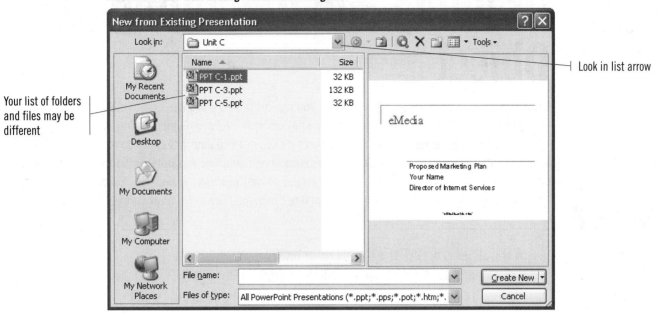

Your list of folders and files may be different

Look in list arrow

FIGURE C-2: First slide of the eMedia presentation

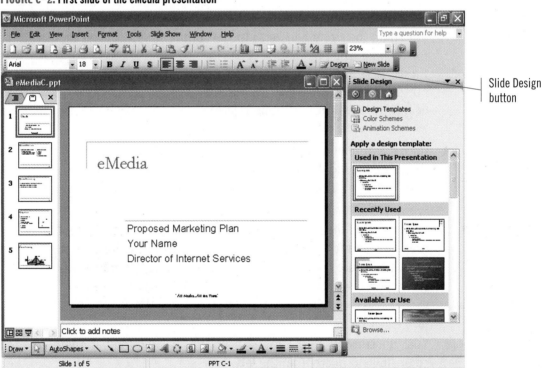

Slide Design button

Clues to Use

Setting permissions

In PowerPoint 2003, you can set specific access permissions for people who review or edit your work, so you have better control over your content. For example, you may want to give a user permission to edit or change your presentation but not allow them to print it. You can also restrict a user by permitting them to view the presentation, without the ability to edit or print the presentation, or you can give the user full access or control of the presentation. To set user access permissions, click the Permission button on the Standard toolbar. To use this feature, you have to first install the Windows Rights Management software.

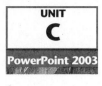

Drawing and Modifying an Object

Using the drawing commands in PowerPoint, you can draw lines and shapes, and insert objects to enhance your presentation. The objects that you create or insert with the PowerPoint drawing tools can be modified to meet your design needs. The graphic attributes that you can change include fill color, line color, line style, shadow, and 3-D effects. To add drawn objects to your slides, use the buttons on the Drawing toolbar, which is typically docked at the bottom of the screen above the status bar. ░░░░░ You decide to draw more objects on Slide 4 of your presentation to complete the graphic elements on the slide.

STEPS

1. **In the Slides tab, click the Slide 4 thumbnail**

   Slide 4, titled "Competition", appears in the Slide pane.

2. **Press and hold [Shift], click the body text object, then release [Shift]**

   A dotted selection box with small circles called **sizing handles** appears around the text object. If you click a text object without pressing [Shift], a selection box composed of slanted lines appears, indicating that the object is active and ready to accept text, but it is not selected. When an object is selected, you can change its size, shape, or attributes by dragging one of the sizing handles.

   > **TROUBLE**
   > If you are not satisfied with the size of the text object, resize it again.

3. **Position the pointer over the right, middle sizing handle, the pointer changes to ↔, then drag the sizing handle to the left until the vertical line aligns with the top and bottom middle sizing handles**

   The text object is about half its original size, as shown in Figure C-3. When you position the pointer over a sizing handle, it changes to ↔. It points in different directions depending on which sizing handle it is positioned over. When you drag a sizing handle, the pointer changes to ┼, and a dotted outline appears, representing the size of the text object.

4. **Click the AutoShapes button `AutoShapes ▾` on the Drawing toolbar, point to Block Arrows, then click the Right Arrow button ⇨ (first row, first column)**

   After you select a shape from the AutoShapes menu and move the pointer over the slide, the pointer changes to ┼.

   > **TROUBLE**
   > If your arrow object is not approximately the same size as the one shown in Figure C-4, press [Shift] and drag one of the corner sizing handles to resize the object.

5. **Position ┼ in the blank area of the slide to the right of the text object and below the graph, press and hold [Shift], drag down and to the right to create an arrow object, as shown in Figure C-4, release [Shift], then release the mouse button**

   When you release the mouse button, an arrow object appears on the slide, filled with the default color and outlined with the default line style. Pressing [Shift] while you create the object maintains the object's proportions as you change its size.

6. **Click the Line Color list arrow ▨▾ on the Drawing toolbar, then point to the dark green color (fourth square from the left)**

   A ScreenTip appears identifying this color as the Follow Title Text Scheme Color.

7. **Click the dark green color**

   PowerPoint applies the green color to the selected arrow object's outline.

8. **Click the Fill Color list arrow ▨▾ on the Drawing toolbar, then click the white color (first square on the left, the Follow Background Scheme Color)**

   PowerPoint fills the selected arrow object with white.

9. **Click the Save button 🖫 on the Standard toolbar to save your changes**

FIGURE C-3: Resizing a text object

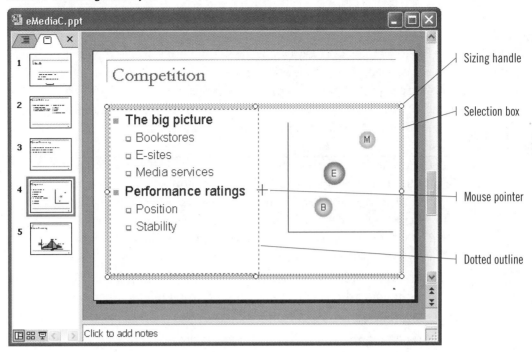

FIGURE C-4: Arrow object on slide

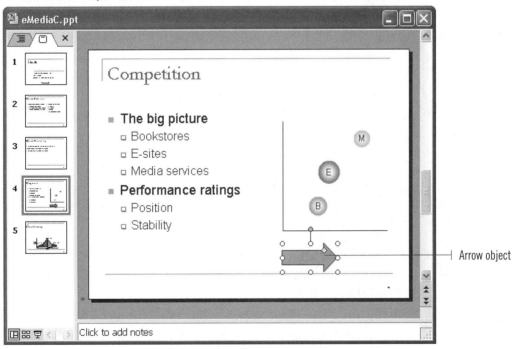

Clues to Use

Understanding PowerPoint objects

In PowerPoint, you often work with multiple objects on the same slide. These may be text objects or graphic objects, such as drawn objects, clip art, or charts. To help you organize objects on a slide, you can align, group, and stack the objects using the Align or Distribute, Group, and Order commands on the Draw menu on the Drawing toolbar. When you align objects, you place their edges (or their centers) on the same plane. For example, you might want to align two squares vertically (one above the other) so that their left edges are in a straight vertical line. When you group objects, you combine two or more objects into one object. It's often helpful to group objects into one when you have finished positioning them on the slide. When you stack objects, you determine their order, that is, which ones are in front and which are in back. You can use the stacking order of objects to overlap them to create different effects.

Editing Drawn Objects

In PowerPoint, you can easily change the size and shape of objects on a slide. You can alter the appearance of any object by dragging the sizing handles to adjust its dimensions. You can add text to most PowerPoint objects and you can move or copy objects. You want two arrows on Slide 4 that are the same shape and size. You first change the shape of the arrow object you've already drawn, and then you make a copy of it. Finally, you rotate one arrow to complete the graphic element.

STEPS

1. **Click the arrow object to select it, if it is not already selected**
   In addition to sizing handles, two other handles appear on the selected object. You use the **adjustment handle**—a small yellow diamond—to change the appearance of an object. The adjustment handle appears next to the most prominent feature of the object, like the head of an arrow in this case. You use the **rotate handle**—a small green circle—to rotate the object.

   TROUBLE
   If you have trouble aligning the object in this step, press and hold [Alt] to turn off the snap to grid feature, then drag the object.

2. **Press and hold [Shift], drag the right, middle sizing handle on the arrow object to the right approximately ½", release [Shift], then release the mouse button**

3. **Position the pointer over the middle of the selected arrow object so that it changes to ⟱, then drag the arrow object so that the arrow aligns with the horizontal axis of the chart as shown in Figure C-5**
   A dotted outline appears as you move the arrow object to help you position it. PowerPoint uses a hidden grid to align objects; it forces objects to "snap" to the grid lines. Make any adjustments to the arrow object position.

   QUICK TIP
   Rulers can help you align objects. To display the rulers, position the pointer in a blank area of the slide, right-click, then click Ruler on the shortcut menu.

4. **Position ⟱ over the arrow object, then press and hold [Ctrl]**
   The pointer changes to ⟱, indicating that PowerPoint makes a copy of the arrow object when you drag the mouse.

5. **Holding [Ctrl], drag the arrow object to the left until the dotted lines indicate that the arrow object copy is in a blank area of the slide, release [Ctrl], then release the mouse button**
   An identical copy of the arrow object appears on the slide.

6. **Type Price**
   The text appears in the center of the selected arrow object. The text is now part of the object, so if you move or rotate the object, the text moves with it.

   QUICK TIP
   You can also use the Rotate or Flip commands on the Draw button on the Drawing toolbar to rotate or flip objects 90 degrees.

7. **Position the pointer over the rotate handle of the selected arrow object so that it changes to ↻, then drag the rotate handle counterclockwise until the arrow head is pointing straight up**
   If you need to make any adjustments to the arrow object, drag the rotate handle again. Compare your screen with Figure C-6.

8. **Click the other arrow object, type Performance, then click in a blank area of the slide**
   Clicking a blank area of the slide deselects all objects that are selected.

9. **Click the Save button 💾 on the Standard toolbar to save your changes**

FIGURE C-5: Slide showing resized arrow object

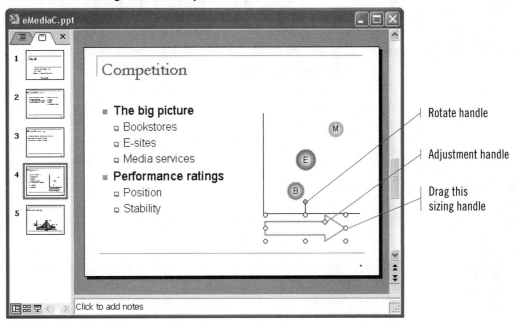

FIGURE C-6: Slide showing duplicated arrow object

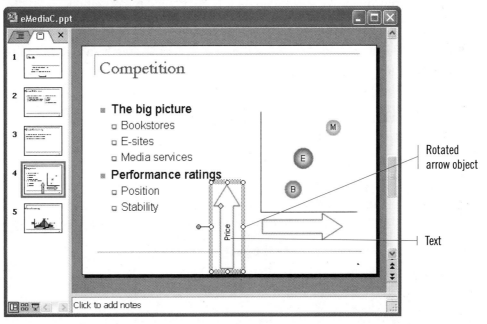

Clues to Use

More ways to change objects

You can layer objects over one another by changing their stacking order, or you can change the appearance of an object by making it three-dimensional or by applying a shadow effect. To change the stacking order of an object, select the object, click the Draw button on the Drawing toolbar, point to Order, then click one of the menu commands shown in Figure C-7. To make an object three-dimensional, select it, click the 3-D Style button ▣ on the Drawing toolbar, then click one of the buttons on the shortcut menu shown in Figure C-8. To add a shadow to an object, select it, click the Shadow Style button ▣ on the Drawing toolbar, then click one of the buttons on the shortcut menu shown in Figure C-9.

FIGURE C-7: Order menu

- Bring to Front
- Send to Back
- Bring Forward
- Send Backward

FIGURE C-8: 3-D Style menu

FIGURE C-9: Shadow Style menu

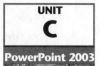

Aligning and Grouping Objects

After you create objects, modify their appearance, and edit their size and shape, you can position them on the slide, align them, distribute them, and then group them. The Align command arranges objects relative to each other by snapping the selected objects to a hidden grid of evenly spaced vertical and horizontal lines. The Distribute command evenly distributes the space horizontally or vertically between selected objects. The Group command groups objects into one object, which makes retaining their relative position easy while editing and moving them. ▰▰▰▰ You are ready to position and group the arrow objects on Slide 4 and then align and distribute some other objects with which you have been working.

STEPS

1. **Right-click a blank area of the slide, then click** Grid and Guides **on the shortcut menu**
   The Grid and Guides dialog box opens.

2. **Click the** Display drawing guides on screen check box, **then click** OK
   The PowerPoint guides appear as dotted lines on the slide. (The dotted lines may be very faint on your screen.) The guides intersect at the center of the slide. They help you position the arrow object.

3. **Position** ⬚ **over the** vertical guide **in a blank area of the slide, press and hold the mouse button until the pointer changes to a guide measurement, then drag the guide to the right until the guide measurement box reads approximately** 1.00

4. **Position** ⬚ **over the** Price arrow object, **then drag it so that the right edge of the selection box touches the vertical guide as shown in Figure C-10**
   The arrow object attaches or "snaps" to the vertical guide.

5. **With the Price arrow object selected, press and hold** [Shift], **click the** Performance arrow object, **then release** [Shift]
   The two objects are now selected.

6. **Click the** Draw button [Draw ▾] **on the Drawing toolbar, then click** Group
   The arrow objects group to form one object without losing their individual attributes. Notice the sizing handles and rotate handle now appear on the outer edge of the grouped object, not around each individual object.

7. **In the Slides tab, click the** Slide 5 thumbnail, **press and hold** [Shift], **click each of the** five graph object shapes, **then release** [Shift]
   The five graph object shapes are selected.

8. **Click** [Draw ▾], **then point to** Align or Distribute
   A menu of alignment and distribution options appears. The top three options align objects vertically; the next three options align objects horizontally; and the last three options evenly distribute the space between objects.

9. **Click** Align Bottom, **click** [Draw ▾], **point to** Align or Distribute, **click** Distribute Horizontally, **then click a blank area of the slide**
   The graph objects are now aligned horizontally along their bottom edges and are distributed evenly so that the space between each object is equal. Compare your screen with Figure C-11.

10. **Right-click a blank area of the slide, click** Grid and Guides **on the shortcut menu, click the** Display drawing guides on screen check box, **click** OK, **then click the** Save button [💾] **on the Standard toolbar to save your changes**
    The guides are no longer displayed on the slide.

FIGURE C-10: Repositioned arrow object

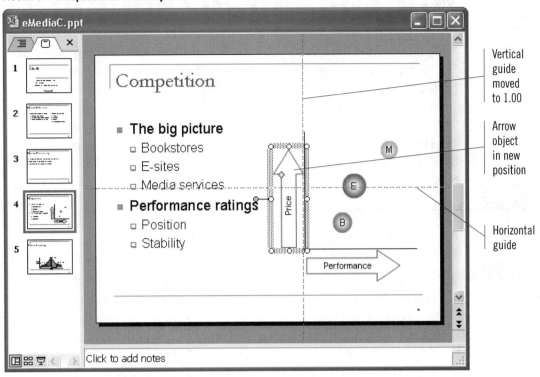

Vertical guide moved to 1.00

Arrow object in new position

Horizontal guide

FIGURE C-11: Aligned and distributed graph objects

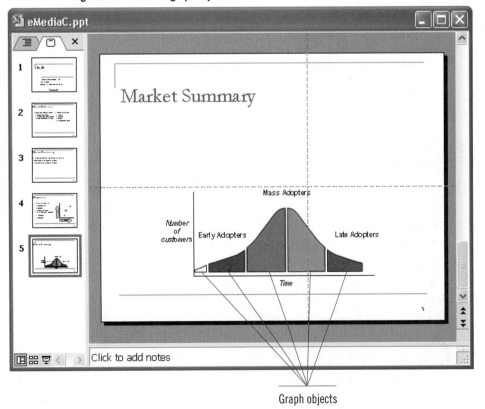

Graph objects

PowerPoint 2003

Adding and Arranging Text

Using the advanced text-editing capabilities of PowerPoint, you can easily type, insert, or rearrange text. The PowerPoint slide layouts allow you to enter text in prearranged text placeholders. If these text placeholders don't provide the flexibility you need, you can use the Text Box button on the Drawing toolbar to create your own text objects. With the Text Box button, you can create two types of text objects: a text label, used for a small phrase where text doesn't automatically wrap to the next line inside the box; and a word processing box, used for a sentence or paragraph where the text wraps inside the boundaries of the box. ▓▓▓▓ You decide that Slide 5 needs a little more information to make it complete. Use the Text Box button to create a word processing box to enter information about the graph chart that is on the slide.

STEPS

1. **Click the Text Box button** 🔲 **on the Drawing toolbar**
   The pointer changes to ↓.

2. **Position ↓ near the left side of the slide, above the top of the chart, then drag down and toward the right side of the slide about an inch and a half to create a word processing box**
   Your screen should look similar to Figure C-12. When you begin dragging, an outline of the text object appears, indicating how large a text object you are drawing. After you release the mouse button, an insertion point appears inside the text object, ready to accept text.

   QUICK TIP
   To create a text label in which text doesn't wrap, click 🔲, position ↓ where you want to place the text, then click once and enter the text.

3. **Type Changes in market, costs, share, pricing, and competition**
   Notice that the text object increases in size as your text wraps inside the text object. There is a mistake in the text. It should read "market share".

4. **Double-click the word share to select it**

5. **Position the pointer on top of the selected word and press and hold the mouse button**
   The pointer changes to 🔼.

6. **Drag the word share to the right of the word market in the text object, then release the mouse button**
   A dotted insertion line appears as you drag, indicating where PowerPoint places the word when you release the mouse button. The word "share" moves next to the word "market". Moving the word "share" leaves an extra comma, which you need to delete.

   QUICK TIP
   You also can use the Cut and Paste buttons on the Standard toolbar or the Cut and Paste commands on the Edit menu to move a word.

7. **Position Ⅰ to the right of one of the commas after the word "costs", then press [Backspace]**
   One of the commas is deleted.

8. **Drag the right-middle sizing handle of the text object to the right until the word "costs" moves to the top line of the text object, position 🔼 over the text object border, then drag it to the center of the slide**
   Your screen should look similar to Figure C-13.

9. **Click a blank area of the slide outside the text object, then click the Save button 🔲 on the Standard toolbar to save your changes**

FIGURE C-12: Word processing box ready to accept text

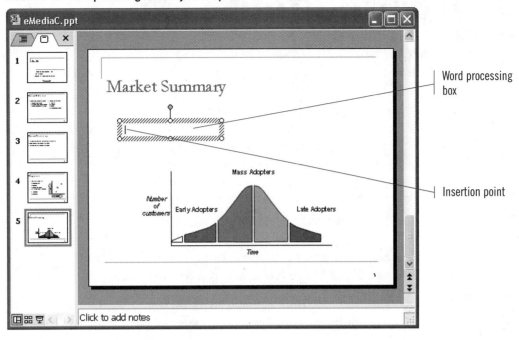

Word processing box

Insertion point

FIGURE C-13: Text added to the word processing box

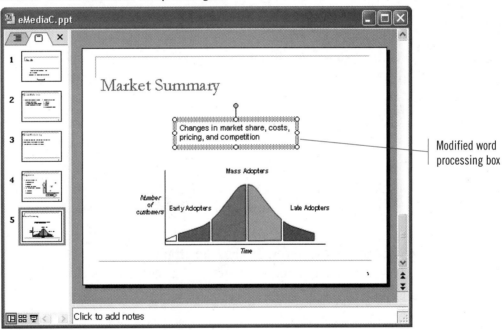

Modified word processing box

Clues to Use

Review a presentation

You can send a copy of a presentation over the Internet to others for them to review, edit, and add comments. To send your presentation out for review, you can use Microsoft Outlook, which automatically tracks changes made by reviewers, or you can use any other compatible e-mail program. To send a presentation to reviewers using Outlook, click File on the menu bar, point to Send To, then click Mail Recipient (for Review). Outlook opens and automatically creates a "Review Request" e-mail with the PowerPoint presentation attached to it for you to send to reviewers. Reviewers can use any version of PowerPoint to review, edit, and comment on their copy of your presentation. Once a reviewer is finished with the presentation and sends it back to you, you can combine their changes and comments with your original presentation using the PowerPoint Compare and Merge Presentations feature. When you do this, the Revisions task pane opens with commands that allow you to accept or reject reviewers' changes.

Formatting Text

Once you have entered and arranged the text in your presentation, you can modify the way the text looks to emphasize your message. Important text needs to be highlighted in some way to distinguish it from other text or objects on the slide. Less important information does not need to be emphasized. For example, if you have two text objects on the same slide, you could draw attention to one text object by changing its color or size. To change the way text looks, you need to select it, then choose a Formatting command. In this lesson, you use some of the commands on the Formatting and Drawing toolbars to change the way the new text object looks on Slide 5.

STEPS

1. On Slide 5, press [Shift], then click the new text object

The entire text object is selected. Any changes you make affect all the text in the selected text object. Changing the text's size and appearance helps emphasize it. When a text object is already selected because you have been entering text in it, you can select the entire text object by clicking on its border with ⁺⇖.

> **QUICK TIP**
>
> You can also click the Font Size list arrow 18 ▾ on the Formatting toolbar, then click the font size you want from the list.

2. Click the Increase Font Size button [A˄] on the Formatting toolbar twice

The text increases in size to 24 points. The size of the font is listed in the Font Size text box on the Formatting toolbar.

3. Click the Italic button [*I*] on the Formatting toolbar

The text changes from normal to italic text. The Italic and Bold buttons are toggle buttons, which you click to turn the attribute on or off.

> **QUICK TIP**
>
> The Font Color button can also be found on the Drawing toolbar.

4. Click the Font Color list arrow [A ▾] on the Formatting toolbar

The Font Color menu appears, showing the eight colors used in the current presentation and the More Colors command, which lets you choose additional colors.

5. Click More Colors to open the Colors dialog box, then click the teal cell in the upper-left corner of the color hexagon, second from the left, as shown in Figure C-14

The Current color and the New color appear in the box in the lower-right corner of the dialog box.

6. Click OK

The text in the text object changes to teal, and the teal color is added as the ninth color in the set of colors used in the presentation.

7. Click the Font list arrow on the Formatting toolbar

A list of available fonts opens with Arial, the font used in the text object, selected in the list.

8. Click the down scroll arrow, then click Times New Roman

The Times New Roman font replaces the original font in the text object.

9. Click the Center button [≡] on the Formatting toolbar, then resize the text object so that the word "costs" is on the top line in the text object

The text is aligned in the center of the text object and is contained on two lines.

10. Drag the text object so it is centered over the chart, click a blank area of the slide outside the text object to deselect it, then click the Save button [💾] on the Standard toolbar

Compare your screen to Figure C-15.

FIGURE C-14: Colors dialog box

Select this color

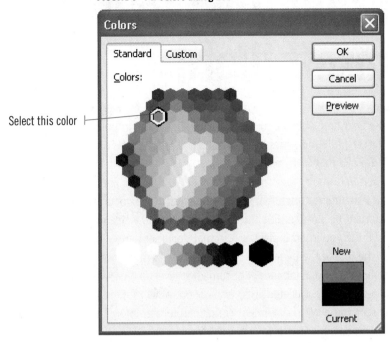

FIGURE C-15: Slide showing formatted text object

Formatted text

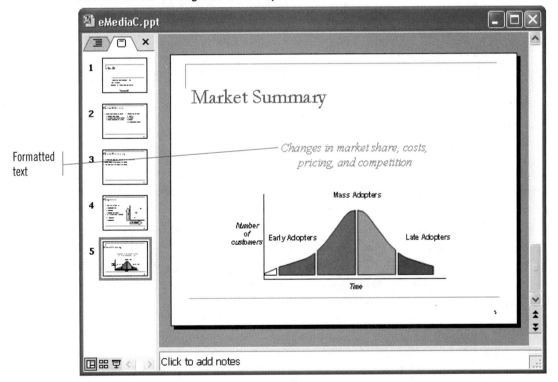

Clues to Use

Replacing text and attributes

As you review your presentation, you may decide to replace certain words throughout the entire presentation. You can automatically modify words, sentences, text case, and periods. To replace specific words or sentences, click Edit on the menu bar, then click Replace. To automatically add or remove periods from title or body text and to automatically change the case of title or body text, click Tools on the menu bar, click Options, click the Spelling and Style tab, then click Style Options to open the Style Options dialog box. Specify the options you want on the Case and End Punctuation tab. The options on the Visual Clarity tab in the Style Options dialog box control the legibility of bulleted text items on the slides.

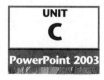

Importing Text from Microsoft Word

PowerPoint makes it easy to insert information from other sources, such as Microsoft Word, into a presentation. If you have an existing Word document or outline, you can import it into PowerPoint to create a new presentation or insert additional slides in an existing presentation. Documents saved in Microsoft Word format (.doc), Rich Text Format (.rtf), plain text format (.txt), and HTML format (.htm) can be inserted into a presentation. When you import a Microsoft Word or a Rich Text Format document into a presentation, PowerPoint creates an outline structure based on the styles in the document. For example, a Heading 1 style in the Word document becomes a slide title in PowerPoint and a Heading 2 style becomes the first level of text in a bulleted list. If you insert a plain text format document into a presentation, PowerPoint creates an outline based on the tabs at the beginning of the document's paragraphs. Paragraphs without tabs become slide titles; paragraphs with one tab indent become first-level text in bulleted lists; paragraphs with two tabs become second-level text in bulleted lists; and so on. ▄▄▄▄▄ One of your colleagues from the Sales Department has sent you a Word document containing further information that you need for your presentation. You insert this document into your presentation.

1. **Click the Outline tab, then click the up scroll arrow in the Outline tab until the Slide 4 slide title appears**

2. **Click the Slide 4 icon** 🔲

   Slide 4 appears in the Slide pane. Each time you click a slide icon in the Outline tab, the slide title and text are highlighted indicating the slide is selected. Before you insert information into a presentation, you must first designate where you want the information to be placed. In this case, the Word document is inserted after Slide 4, the selected slide.

3. **Click Insert on the menu bar, then click Slides from Outline**

   The Insert Outline dialog box opens.

4. **Locate the Word document PPT C-2.doc in the drive and folder where your Data Files are stored, then click Insert**

   Three new slides (5, 6, and 7) are added to the presentation. See Figure C-16. Slide 5 is selected showing you where the information from the Word document begins.

5. **Read the text for the new Slide 5 in the Slide pane, click the down scroll arrow in the Outline tab until the Slide 8 icon is displayed, click the Slide 6 icon 🔲 in the Outline tab, then review the text on that slide**

   Slide 6 is selected; you can see the text for Slide 7 in the Outline tab.

6. **Click the Slides tab, then click the Slide 7 thumbnail**

   After reviewing the text on this slide, you realize that someone else is covering this information in another presentation.

7. **Right-click the Slide 7 thumbnail, then click Delete Slide on the shortcut menu**

   Slide 7 is deleted from the presentation. The last slide in the presentation, Market Summary, now appears in the Slide pane. Compare your screen to Figure C-17.

8. **Click the Save button 🔲 on the Standard toolbar to save your changes**

FIGURE C-16: Outline tab showing imported text

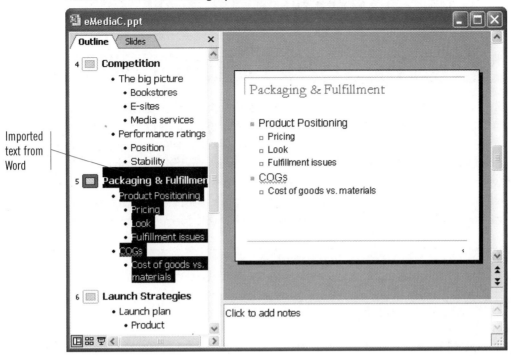

Imported text from Word

FIGURE C-17: Presentation after deleting slide

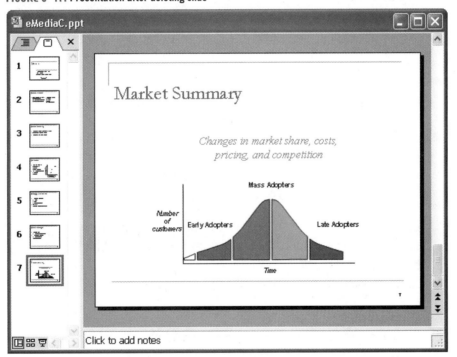

Clues to Use

Inserting slides from other presentations

To insert slides into the current presentation, click Insert on the menu bar, then click Slides from Files. Click Browse in the Slide Finder dialog box, then locate the presentation from which you want to copy slides. In the Select slides section, select the slide(s) you want to insert, click Insert, then click Close. The new slides automatically take on the design of the current presentation. If both presentations are open, you can copy the slides from one presentation to another. Change the view of each presentation to Slide Sorter view, select the desired slides, then copy and paste them (or use drag and drop) into the desired presentation. You can then rearrange the slides in Slide Sorter view if necessary.

Customizing the Color Scheme and Background

Every PowerPoint presentation has a **color scheme**, a set of eight coordinated colors that determine the colors for the slide elements in your presentation: slide background, text and lines, shadows, title text, fills, accents, and hyperlinks. The design template that is applied to a presentation determines its color scheme. See Table C-1 for a description of the slide color scheme elements. The **background** is the area behind the text and graphics. Every design template in PowerPoint—even the blank presentation template—has a color scheme that you can use or modify. You can change the background color and appearance independently of changing the color scheme. ▦▦▦▦ You change the color scheme and modify the background of the presentation.

STEPS

1. **Click the** Color Schemes hyperlink **in the Slide Design task pane**

   The current, or default, color scheme is selected with a blue border as shown in Figure C-18. Additional color schemes designed specifically for the applied design template (in this case, the Edge template) are also shown.

2. **Click the** color scheme icon **in the fourth row, second column in the Slide Design task pane**

   The new color scheme is applied to all the slides in the presentation. In this case, the new color scheme changes the color of the slide graphics and title text, but the bulleted text and background remain the same.

3. **Click** Format **on the menu bar, then click** Background

   The Background dialog box opens.

4. **In the Background fill section, click the** list arrow **below the preview of the slide, click** Fill Effects, **then click the** Gradient tab, **if it is not already selected**

5. **Click the** One color option button **in the Colors section, click the** Color 1 list arrow, **then click the** olive green color **(the Follow Accent Scheme Color)**

   The green color fills the Color 1 list arrow and the four variant colors preview in the Variants section, showing that the background is shaded with green.

6. **Drag the** Brightness scroll box **all the way to the right (toward Light) in the Colors section, click the** Diagonal down option button **in the Shading Styles section, then click the** lower-left variant

   The four variant previews change shading. Compare your screen to Figure C-19.

7. **Click** OK, **then click** Apply to All

   The slide background is now shaded from green to white and then green again.

8. **Click the** Slide Sorter View button ▦, **click the** Zoom list arrow **on the Standard toolbar, then click** 50%

   The final presentation appears in Slide Sorter view. Compare your screen to Figure C-20.

9. **Add your name as a footer on the notes and handouts, print the slides as handouts (4 slides per page), click the** Save button ▦, **close the presentation, then exit PowerPoint**

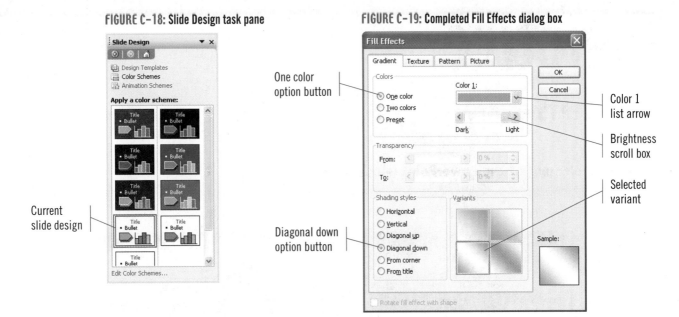

FIGURE C-18: Slide Design task pane

Current slide design

One color option button

Color 1 list arrow

Brightness scroll box

Selected variant

Diagonal down option button

FIGURE C-19: Completed Fill Effects dialog box

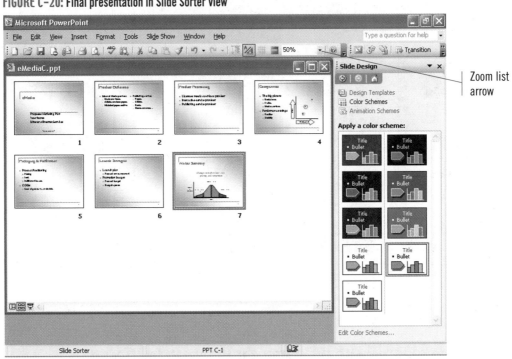

FIGURE C-20: Final presentation in Slide Sorter view

Zoom list arrow

TABLE C-1: Color scheme elements

scheme element	description
Background color	Color of the slide's canvas or background
Text and lines color	Used for text and drawn lines; contrasts with the background color
Shadows color	Color of the shadow of the text or other object; generally a darker shade of the background color
Title text color	Used for slide title; like the text and line colors, contrasts with the background color
Fills color	Contrasts with both the background and the text and line colors
Accent colors	Colors used for other objects on slides, such as bullets
Accent and hyperlink colors	Colors used for accent objects and for hyperlinks you insert
Accent and followed hyperlink color	Color used for accent objects and for hyperlinks after they have been clicked

PowerPoint 2003

Practice

▼ CONCEPTS REVIEW

Label each element of the PowerPoint window shown in Figure C-21.

FIGURE C-21

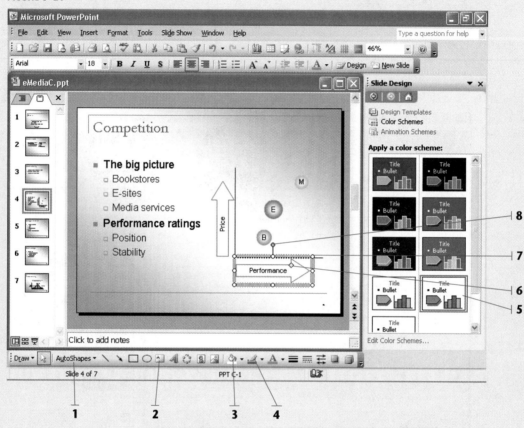

Match each term or button with the statement that best describes it.

9. Sizing handle

10. Guide

11. Text label

12. Color scheme

13. Background

a. A text object for a word or small phrase

b. A dotted line that helps you position objects

c. The area behind the text and graphics of a slide

d. Used to change the size and shape of an object

e. A set of eight coordinated colors

Select the best answer from the list of choices.

14. What is the easiest way to line objects along their tops on a slide?

a. Group the objects together

b. Use PowerPoint anchor lines

c. Place the objects on the edge of the slide

d. Use the Align Top command

15. What does *not* happen when you group objects?

a. Sizing handles appear around the grouped object.

b. Objects are grouped together as a single object.

c. Objects lose their individual characteristics.

d. The grouped objects have a rotate handle.

16. What is *not* true about guides?

a. You can drag a guide off the slide to delete it.

b. A PowerPoint guide is a dotted line.

c. Slides can have only one vertical and one horizontal guide.

d. You can press [Ctrl] and drag a guide to create a new one.

17. What is *not* true about a presentation color scheme?

a. Every presentation has a color scheme.

b. There are eight colors to every color scheme.

c. You can't change the background color without changing the color scheme.

d. The color scheme determines the colors of a slide.

18. How do you change the size of a PowerPoint object?

a. Click the Resize button.

b. Drag a sizing handle.

c. Drag the rotate handle.

d. You can't change the size of a PowerPoint object.

19. What would you use to position objects at a specific place on a slide?

a. PowerPoint lines

b. PowerPoint anchor lines

c. PowerPoint placeholders

d. PowerPoint guides and rulers

20. PowerPoint objects can be:

a. Grouped and aligned.

b. Converted to pictures.

c. Distributed evenly.

d. Both A and C.

21. What is a slide background?

a. The slide grid

b. The area behind text and graphics

c. A picture

d. The pasteboard off the slide

22. What does the adjustment handle do?

a. Changes the angle adjustment of an object

b. Changes the appearance of an object

c. Adjusts the position of an object

d. Adjusts the size of an object

▼ SKILLS REVIEW

1. Open an existing presentation.

   a. Start PowerPoint.

   b. Open the file **PPT C-3.ppt** from the drive and folder where your Data Files are stored.

   c. Save it as **Product Report.ppt** to the drive and folder where your Data Files are stored.

2. Draw and modify an object.

FIGURE C-22

   a. Click Slide 4 in the Slides tab, insert the Left-Right-Up Arrow AutoShape from the Block Arrows category on the AutoShapes menu to the blank area on the slide.

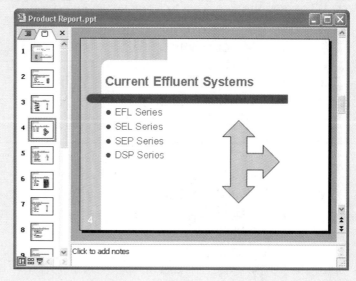

   b. Open the Line Color menu, click More Line Colors, then click the black color cell in the Colors dialog box to make the line color black.

   c. Change the fill color to light green (the Follow Accent Scheme Color).

   d. Rotate the arrow object so that the middle arrowhead points to the right. (*Hint*: 90° to the right.)

   e. Use the arrows' sizing handles to adjust the size of the object until it matches Figure C-22.

   f. Move the arrow object on the slide so that it is in the center of the blank space on the slide.

   g. Deselect the arrow object, then save your changes.

3. Edit drawn objects.

   a. Select Slide 9, resize the arrow object so it is about ½" shorter. (*Hint*: You might want to resize the bulleted list text object so it does not interfere with your work.)

   b. Drag the arrow object next to the left side of the box.

   c. Use the adjustment handle to lengthen the arrow object's head about ¼", then insert the text **Satisfaction**. Enlarge the arrow object so that all the text fits inside it, if necessary.

   d. Make two copies of the arrow object and arrange them to the left of the first one so that they are pointing in succession toward the box.

   e. Drag to select the word **Satisfaction** on the middle arrow object, then type the word **Growth**.

   f. Replace the word **Satisfaction** on the left arrow object with the word **Products**.

   g. Insert the word **Success** in the cube object.

   h. Change the text font for each of the objects to Arial italic. Enlarge the cube as necessary so the word **Success** fits in it.

   i. Save your changes.

FIGURE C-23

4. Align and group objects.

   a. Align the middles of the four objects, then horizontally distribute the objects.

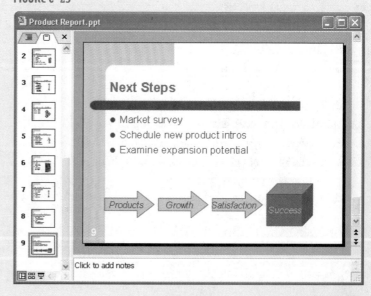

   b. Group the arrow objects and the cube together.

   c. Display the guides, then move the vertical guide left so the box displays 4.17; move the horizontal guide down to display 3.08.

   d. Align the grouped object so its lower-left sizing handle snaps to where the guides intersect. (*Hint*: If your object does not snap to the guides, open the Grid and Guides dialog box, and make sure the Snap objects to grid check box is checked.)

   e. Hide the guides, then save your changes. Compare your screen with Figure C-23.

5. Add and arrange text.

   a. Add the text **Next steps** as a fourth item to the body text box on Slide 2.

   b. Near the bottom of the slide, below the graphic, create a word processing box about 3" wide, and in it enter the text: **The Future of Water Systems and Pumps**.

   c. Drag the word **Pumps** to the right of the word **Water**.

   d. Delete the word **and** and then the letter **s** on the word Pumps. The text object should now read, The Future of Water Pump Systems.

   e. Adjust the size of the text object to fit the text, then move the text object so that it is directly under the graphic.

   f. Save your changes.

6. Format text.

   a. Select the text object so that formatting commands apply to all the text in the object.

   b. Change the font color to the dark green color (the Follow Title Text Scheme Color), increase the font size to 24 points, then, if necessary, resize the word processing box so the text fits on one line.

   c. Change the text style to Italic, then align the words to the center of the text object.

   d. Click Slide 9 in the Slides tab, select the text in the cube, then change the font color to a light fluorescent green. (*Hint*: Use the Colors dialog box.)

   e. Click Slide 1 in the Slides tab, select the top title text font (Hildebrand Water Systems), then change the font size to 44.

   f. Deselect the text object, then save your changes.

7. Import text from Microsoft Word.

   a. Click Slide 9 in the Slides tab.

   b. Import the Word file PPT C-4.doc. Check the formatting of each of the three new slides—slides 10, 11, and 12.

   c. In the Slides tab, drag Slide 8 below Slide 11.

   d. In the Slides tab, delete Slide 9, Market Surveys.

   e. Save your changes.

8. Customize the color scheme and background.

   a. Open the Slide Design task pane and click the Color Schemes hyperlink.

   b. Apply the top right color scheme in the list to all the slides.

   c. Open the Background dialog box, then open the Fill Effects dialog box.

   d. On the Gradient tab, select the One color option, click the Color 1 list arrow, then click the yellow color.

   e. Drag the Brightness scroll box almost all the way to the right, select the From corner shading style and the lower-right variant.

   f. Apply this background to all slides.

   g. Add your name as a footer to the notes and handouts.

   h. Save your changes, then print the slides as handouts (4 slides per page).

   i. Close the file and exit PowerPoint.

▼ INDEPENDENT CHALLENGE 1

In this unit, you learned that when you work with multiple objects on a PowerPoint slide, there are ways to arrange them so your information appears neat and well organized. Using a word processing program, write a summary explaining how to perform each of these tasks in PowerPoint. Make sure you explain what happens to the objects when you perform these tasks. Also explain *why* you would perform these tasks.

a. Start your word processor, open a new document, then save the file as **Arranging Objects** to the drive and folder where your Data Files are stored.

b. Explain the six different ways to align objects.

c. Explain what the Distribute command does.

d. Explain the concept of grouping objects.

e. Add your name as the first line in the document, save your changes, print the document, close the document, then exit the word processor.

▼ INDEPENDENT CHALLENGE 2

You work for Language Systems, a major producer of language-teaching CD-ROMs with accompanying instructional books. Twice a year the company holds title meetings to determine the new title list for the following production term and to decide which current CD titles need to be revised. As the director of acquisitions, you chair the September Title Meeting and present the basic material for discussion.

a. Start PowerPoint, open the file PPT C-5.ppt from the drive and folder where your Data Files are stored, and save it as **2006 Title Meeting**.

b. Add an appropriate design template to the presentation.

c. After Slide 6, Insert the Word outline PPT C-6.doc that contains different product titles.

d. Examine all of the slides in the presentation and apply italic formatting to all product and book titles.

e. Format the text so that the most important information is the most prominent.

f. Add appropriate shapes that emphasize the most important parts of the slide content. Format the objects using color and shading. Use the Align or Distribute and Group commands to organize your shapes.

Advanced Challenge Exercise

■ Using the AutoShapes menu, draw a shape from the Block Arrows menu, then apply 3-D Style 12 to the object using the 3-D Styles button.

■ Format at least one object with Shadow Style 2 using the Shadow Styles button on the Drawing toolbar.

g. Spell check, view the final slide show, and evaluate your presentation. Make any necessary changes.

h. Add your name as footer text on the notes and handouts, save the presentation, print the slides as handouts, close the file, and exit PowerPoint.

▼ INDEPENDENT CHALLENGE 3

The Learning Company is dedicated to the design and development of instructional software that helps college students learn software applications. You need to design four new logos for the company that incorporate the new company slogan: Software is a snap! The marketing group will decide which of the four designs looks best. Create your own presentation slides, but assume that the company colors are blue and green.

a. Sketch your logos and slogan designs on a piece of paper. What text and graphics do you need for the slides?

b. Start PowerPoint, create a new blank presentation, and save it as **Software Learning** to the drive and folder where your Data Files are stored.

c. Create four different company logos, each one on a separate slide. Use the shapes on the AutoShapes menu, and enter the company slogan using the Text tool. (*Hint*: Use the Title only layout.) The logo and the marketing slogan should match each other in tone, size, and color; and the logo objects should be grouped together to make it easier for other employees to copy and paste.

d. Format the fill color, line color, and fonts appropriately using the commands on the Formatting and Drawing toolbars.

Advanced Challenge Exercise

■ Create at least one arrow object using the Arrow button and one line object using the Line button on the Drawing toolbar.

■ Use the Line Style button and Dash Style button on the Drawing toolbar to format objects.

■ Format an arrow object with the Arrow Style button on the Drawing toolbar.

e. Spell check, view the final slide show, and evaluate your presentation.

f. Add your name as footer text, save the presentation, print the slides and notes pages (if any), close the file, and exit PowerPoint.

▼ INDEPENDENT CHALLENGE 4

Your company is planning to offer 401(k) retirement plans to all its employees. The Human Resources Department has asked you to construct and deliver a brief presentation about 401(k) plans to employees. To find the necessary information for the presentation, you decide to use the Web. The information you find on the Web should answer the following questions:

- What is a 401(k) plan?
- How does a 401(k) plan work?
- How much can I contribute to my 401(k) plan at work?
- When do I have to start taking money from my 401(k) account?
- Is there a penalty for early withdrawal?

a. Connect to the Internet, then use a search engine to locate Web sites that have information on 401(k) plans.

b. Review at least two Web sites that contain information about 401(k) plans. Print the Home pages of the Web sites you use to gather data for your presentation.

c. Start PowerPoint. On the title slide, title the presentation **401(k) Plans: What Employees Need to Know**. The presentation should contain at least five slides, including the title slide. Refer to the bulleted list above as you create your content.

d. Save the presentation as **401k Plans** to the drive and folder where your Data Files are stored.

e. Apply a design template to the presentation, then customize the slide background.

f. Use text formatting as necessary to make text visible and help emphasize important points.

g. At least one slide should contain an object from the AutoShapes menu. Customize the object's size and color.

h. Add your name as a footer to the slides, spell check the presentation, and view the final presentation.

i. Save the final version of the presentation, print the slides, then close the file, and exit PowerPoint.

Create a one-slide presentation for SASLtd, a London-based company, that looks like the one shown in Figure C-24. Use a text box for each group heading. Group the objects in the lower-right logo. (*Hint*: The top-left rectangle object uses an option from the 3-D menu.) If you don't have the exact fonts, use something similar. Add your name as footer on the slide, save the presentation as **SASLtd** to the drive and folder where your Data Files are stored, then print the slide.

FIGURE C-24

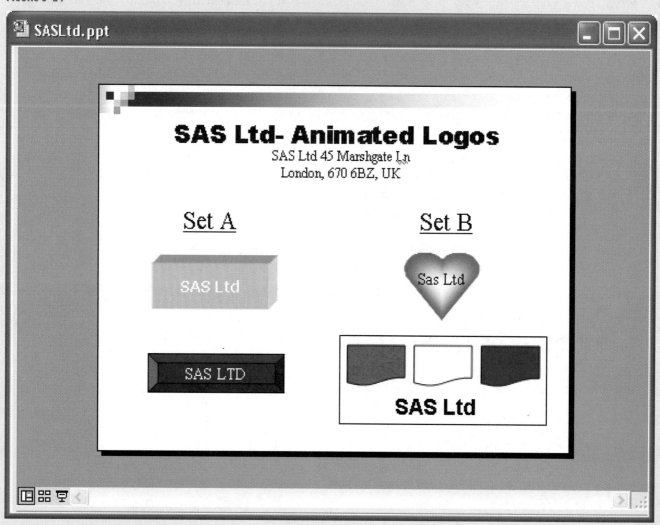

Enhancing a Presentation

OBJECTIVES

Insert clip art
Insert, crop, and scale a picture
Embed a chart
Enter and edit data in the datasheet
Format a chart
Create tables in PowerPoint
Use slide show commands
Set slide show timings and transitions
Set slide animation effects

If you have a SAM user profile, you may have access to hands-on instruction, practice, and assessment of the skills covered in this unit. Log in to your SAM account and go to your assignments page to see what your instructor has assigned.

After completing the content of your presentation, you can supplement your slide text with clip art, photographs, charts, and other visual elements that help communicate your message and keep your presentation visually interesting. In this unit, you learn how to insert three of the most common visual elements: a clip art image, a picture, and a chart. These objects are created in other programs. After you add the objects, you rehearse the slide show and add special effects. You made changes to the eMedia presentation based on feedback from colleagues. Now you want to revise the presentation to make it easier to understand and more interesting to watch.

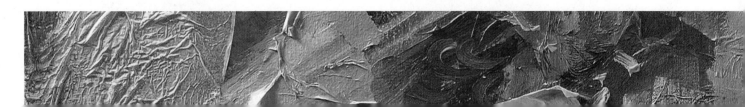

Inserting Clip Art

PowerPoint has ready access to many professionally designed images, called **clip art**, that you can place in your presentation. Using clip art is the easiest and fastest way to enhance a presentation. In Microsoft Office, clip art and other media files, including photographs, movies, and sounds, are stored in a file index system called the Microsoft Clip Organizer. The Clip Organizer sorts the clip art into groups, including My Collections, Office Collections, and Web Collections. The Office Collections group holds all the media files that come with Microsoft Office. You can customize the Clip Organizer by adding clips to a collection, moving clips from one collection to another, or creating a new collection. As with drawing objects, you can modify clip art images by changing their shape, size, fill, or shading. Clip art is available from many sources outside the Clip Organizer, including the Microsoft Office Online Web site and collections on CD-ROMs. 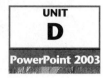 Add a picture from the Clip Organizer to one of the slides and then adjust its size and placement.

STEPS

1. **Start PowerPoint, open the presentation** PPT D-1.ppt **from the drive and folder where your Data Files are stored, save it as** eMediaD, **click** View **on the menu bar, click** Task Pane, **click** Window **on the menu bar, then click** Arrange All

2. **Click** Slide 8 **in the Slides tab, then click the** Insert Clip Art button 🖼 **on the Drawing toolbar**
   The Clip Art task pane opens. Each clip in the Clip Organizer is identified by descriptive keywords. At the top of the task pane in the Search for text box, you enter a keyword to search for clips that meet that description. You can search for a clip in a specific collection or in all collections. You can search for a clip that is a specific media type, such as clip art, photographs, movies, or sounds. At the bottom of the task pane, you can click one of the hyperlinks to organize clips, locate other pieces of clip art at the Office Online Web site, or read tips on how to find clip art.

3. **Select any text in the** Search for text box, **type** plans, **then click** Go
   PowerPoint searches for clips identified by the keyword "plans".

4. **Scroll down in the Clip Art task pane, then click the** clip art thumbnail **shown in Figure D-1**
   The clip art object appears in the center of the slide and the Picture toolbar opens. If you don't have the clip art picture shown in Figure D-1 in your Clip Organizer, select a similar picture.

5. **Place the pointer over the** lower-right sizing handle, **then drag the** handle **down and to the right about ½"**
   The clip art object proportionally increases in size.

6. **Click the** Line Style button ≡ **on the Picture toolbar, then click the** 6pt solid line style
   The clip art now has a 6-point border. It appears to be framed.

7. **Drag the** clip art object **to the right of the text object as shown in Figure D-2**
   The new clip art object appears next to the text object. Compare your screen to Figure D-2.

8. **Click a blank area of the slide, then click the** Save button 🖫 **on the Standard toolbar to save your changes**

FIGURE D-1: Screen showing Clip Art task pane

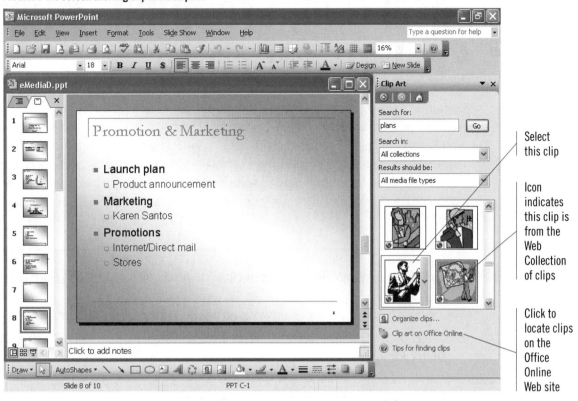

Select this clip

Icon indicates this clip is from the Web Collection of clips

Click to locate clips on the Office Online Web site

FIGURE D-2: Slide with clip art object resized and repositioned

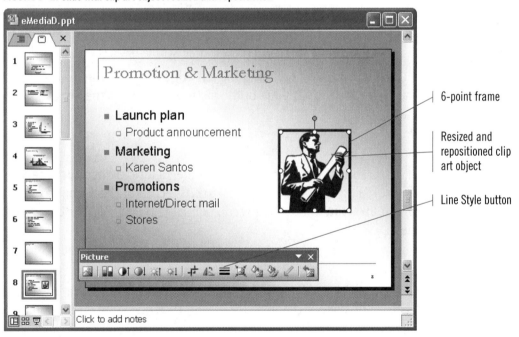

6-point frame

Resized and repositioned clip art object

Line Style button

Clues to Use

Find more clips online

If you can't find the clips you need in the Clip Organizer, you can easily download and use clips from the Clip Art and Media Web page in the Microsoft Office Online Web site. To get clips from the Clip Art and Media Web page, click the Clip art on Office Online hyperlink at the bottom of the Clip Art task pane. This will launch your Web browser and automatically connect you to the Microsoft Office Online Web site. You can search the site by keyword or browse by media type category. Each clip you download is automatically inserted into the Clip Organizer Web Collections folder and appears in the Clip Art task pane.

Inserting, Cropping, and Scaling a Picture

A picture in PowerPoint is a scanned photograph, a piece of line art, clip art, or other artwork that is created in another program and inserted into a PowerPoint presentation. You can insert 18 types of pictures. As with other PowerPoint objects, you can move or resize an inserted picture. You can also crop pictures. **Cropping** a picture means to hide a portion of the picture. Although you can easily change a picture's size by dragging a corner sizing handle, you can also **scale** it to change its size by a specific percentage. ▓▓▓▓▓ In this lesson, you insert a picture that has previously been saved to a file, and then you crop and scale it and adjust its background.

STEPS

1. **Click Slide 6 in the Slides tab, then click the Insert Picture button 🖻 on the Drawing toolbar**

   The Insert Picture dialog box opens. By default, the My Pictures folder is selected.

2. **Select the file PPT D-2.bmp from the drive and folder where your Data Files are stored, then click Insert**

   The picture appears in the center of the slide, and the Picture toolbar opens.

3. **Drag the picture to the right of the text object**

   The picture would fit better on the slide if it didn't show the boxes on the left side of the picture.

4. **Click the Crop button 🔁 on the Picture toolbar, then place the pointer over the left-middle sizing handle of the picture**

   The pointer changes to ⊣. When the Crop button is active, the sizing handles appear as straight black lines.

5. **Press and hold [Alt], then drag the left edge of the picture to the right until the dotted line indicating the left edge of the picture has cut out the boxes, as shown in Figure D-3, then click 🔁**

   Pressing [Alt] while dragging or drawing an object in PowerPoint overrides the automatic snap-to-grid setting. Now the picture needs to be enlarged and positioned into place.

6. **Click the Format Picture button 🖼 on the Picture toolbar, click the Size tab in the Format Picture dialog box, make sure the Lock aspect ratio check box has a check mark, click the Height up arrow in the Scale section until the Height and Width percentages reach 175%, then click OK**

   When you are scaling a picture and Lock aspect ratio is selected, the ratio of height to width remains the same. The white background is distracting.

7. **With the picture still selected, click the Set Transparent Color button ✎ on the Picture toolbar, the pointer changes to ✐, then click the white background in the picture**

   The white background is no longer visible, and the picture contrasts well with the background.

8. **Drag the picture to center it in the blank area to the right of the text object on the slide, click a blank area on the slide to deselect it, then save your changes**

   See Figure D-4.

FIGURE D-3: Using the cropping pointer to crop a picture

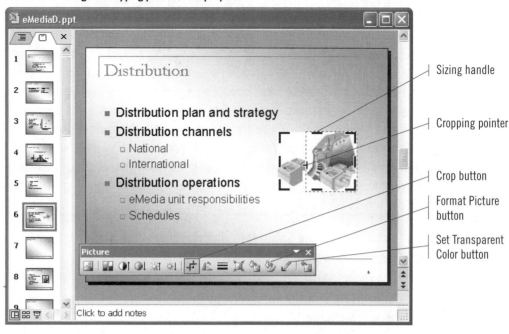

Sizing handle

Cropping pointer

Crop button

Format Picture button

Set Transparent Color button

FIGURE D-4: Cropped and resized picture

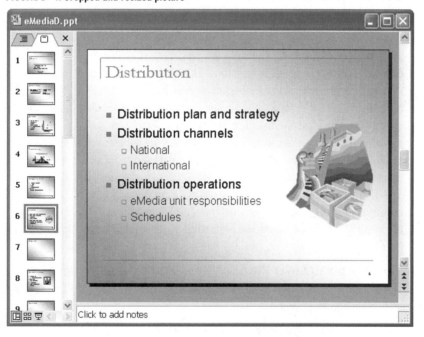

Clues to Use

Using graphics in PowerPoint

You can insert pictures with a variety of graphics file **formats**, or file types, in PowerPoint. Most of the clip art that comes with PowerPoint is in Windows metafile format and has the .wmf file extension. You can change the colors in a .wmf graphic object by selecting it, then clicking the Recolor Picture button 🖼 on the Picture toolbar. You can then replace each color in the graphic with another color. A graphic in .wmf format can be ungrouped into its separate PowerPoint objects, then edited with any of the PowerPoint drawing tools. You cannot recolor or ungroup pictures (files with the .bmp or .tif extension). The clip art you inserted in the last lesson is in .wmf format, and the picture you inserted in this lesson is in .bmp format.

You can also save PowerPoint slides as graphics and later use them in other presentations, in graphics programs, and on Web pages. Display the slide you want to save, then click Save As from the File menu. In the Save As dialog box, click the Save as type list arrow, and scroll to the desired graphics format. Name the file, click OK, then click the desired option when the alert box appears asking if you want to save all the slides or only the current slide.

PowerPoint 2003

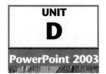

Embedding a Chart

Often, the best way to communicate information is with a visual aid such as a chart. PowerPoint comes with a program called **Microsoft Graph** that you can use to create charts for your slides. A **chart** is the graphical representation of numerical data. Every chart has a corresponding **datasheet** that contains the numerical data displayed by the chart. Table D-1 lists the chart types available in Microsoft Graph. When you insert a chart object into PowerPoint, you are actually embedding it. **Embedding** an object means that the object becomes part of the PowerPoint file, but you can double-click on the embedded object to display the tools of the program in which the object was created. If you modify the embedded object, the original object file does not change. ⬛⬛⬛ You embed a chart on Slide 9 that shows the potential revenue of the eMedia product.

STEPS

1. **Click** Slide 9 **in the Slides tab, click the** Other Task Panes list arrow ▼ **on the task pane title bar, then click** Slide Layout

   The Slide Layout task pane opens with the Title and Text layout selected.

2. **Click the** Title and Content layout thumbnail **in the Content Layouts section of the Slide Layout task pane**

   Remember to use the ScreenTips to help locate the correct slide layout. A content placeholder appears on the slide. Six buttons are in the middle of the placeholder. Each of these buttons represents a different object, such as a table, picture, or chart, which you can apply to your slide.

   > **QUICK TIP**
   > You can also add a chart to a slide by clicking the Insert Chart button 📊 on the Standard toolbar.

3. **Click the** Insert Chart button 📊 **in the content placeholder**

   Microsoft Graph opens and embeds a default datasheet and chart into the slide, as shown in Figure D-5. The datasheet consists of rows and columns. The intersection of a row and a column is called a **cell**. Cells are referred to by their row and column location; for example, the cell at the intersection of column A and row 1 is called cell A1. Cells along the left column and top row of the datasheet typically contain **data labels** that identify the data in a column or row; for example, "East" and "1st Qtr" are data labels. Cells below and to the right of the data labels contain the data values that are represented in the chart. Each column and row of data in the datasheet is called a **data series**. Each data series has corresponding **data series markers** in the chart, which are graphical representations such as bars, columns, or pie wedges. The gray boxes along the left side of the datasheet are called **row headings** and the gray boxes along the top of the datasheet are called **column headings**. Notice that the PowerPoint Standard and Formatting toolbars have been replaced with the Microsoft Graph Standard and Formatting toolbars, and the menu bar has changed to include Microsoft Graph commands.

   > **QUICK TIP**
   > When Data and Chart are on the menu bar, you are working in Graph. Click outside the chart object to return to PowerPoint.

4. **Move the pointer over the datasheet**

   The pointer changes to ✛. Cell A1 is the **active cell**, which means that it is selected. The active cell has a thick black border around it.

5. **Click cell** B3, **which contains the value 46.9**

   Cell B3 is now the active cell.

6. **Click a blank area on the slide to exit Graph, then click again to deselect the chart object**

   The chart closes and the PowerPoint menu bar and toolbars appear.

7. **Save your changes**

FIGURE D-5: Microsoft Graph datasheet and chart in PowerPoint

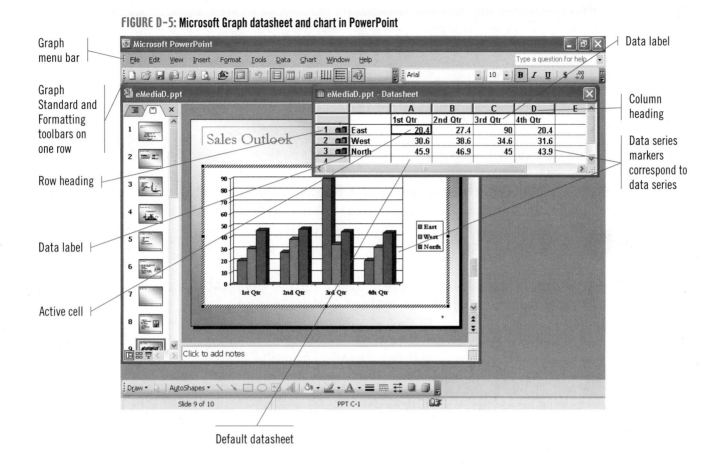

Graph menu bar

Graph Standard and Formatting toolbars on one row

Row heading

Data label

Active cell

Data label

Column heading

Data series markers correspond to data series

Default datasheet

TABLE D-1: Microsoft Graph chart types

chart type	looks like	use to
Column		Track values over time or across categories
Bar		Compare values in categories or over time
Line		Track values over time
Pie		Compare individual values to the whole
XY (Scatter)		Compare pairs of values
Area		Show contribution of each data series to the total over time
Doughnut		Compare individual values to the whole with multiple series
Radar		Show changes in values in relation to a center point
Surface		Show value trends across two dimensions
Bubble		Indicate relative size of data points
Stock		Show stock market information or scientific data
Cylinder		
Cone		Track values over time or across categories
Pyramid		

Entering and Editing Data in the Datasheet

After you embed the default chart into your presentation, you need to replace the data labels and numeric data with the correct information. If you have data in a spreadsheet or other source, you can import it into Microsoft Graph; otherwise you can type your own information into the datasheet. As you enter data in the cells or make changes to data labels in the datasheet, the chart automatically changes to reflect the new entries. ▰▰▱▱▱ You have been asked to create a chart showing the projected revenue figures for the first year of eMedia operation.

STEPS

1. **Double-click the chart on Slide 9, then, if necessary, drag the Datasheet title bar to move the datasheet to the upper-right corner of the Slide pane**

   The chart is selected and the datasheet opens. The column data labels representing the quarters are correct, but the row data labels need adjusting, and the numeric data needs to be replaced with eMedia's projected quarterly sales figures for the Media and Publishing divisions.

2. **Click the East row label, type Media, then press [Enter]**

   After you press [Enter], the data label in Row 2 becomes selected. Pressing [Enter] in the datasheet moves the active cell down one cell; pressing [Tab] in the datasheet moves the active cell to the right one cell.

3. **Type Publish, then press [Tab]**

   Cell A2 becomes active. Notice in the chart, behind the datasheet, that the data labels you typed are now in the legend to the right of the chart. The information in Row 3 of the datasheet is not needed.

4. **Click the row heading for Row 3, then press [Delete]**

   Clicking the row heading for Row 3 selects the entire row. The default information in Row 3 of the datasheet is deleted and the columns in the chart adjust accordingly. The quarters appear along the horizontal axis, the values appear along the vertical axis in the chart.

5. **Click cell A1, type 17,000, press [Enter], type 14,500, press [Tab], then press [▲] to move to cell B1**

   Notice that the height of each column in the chart, as well as the values along the vertical axis, adjust to reflect the numbers you typed. The vertical axis is also called the **Value axis**. The horizontal axis is called the **Category axis**.

6. **Enter the rest of the numbers shown in Figure D-6 to complete the datasheet, then press [Enter]**

   The chart currently shows the columns grouped by quarter, and the legend represents the rows in the datasheet. The icons in the row headings indicate that the row labels appear in the legend. It would be more effective if the column data appeared in the legend so you could compare quarterly earnings for each eMedia product.

7. **Click the By Column button ▦ on the Standard toolbar**

   The division labels are now on the Category axis of the chart, and the quarters are listed in the legend. The groups of data markers (the columns) now represent the projected revenue for each product by quarter. Notice that the small column chart icons that used to be in the row headings in the datasheet have now moved to the column headings, indicating that the series are now in columns.

8. **Click a blank area on the slide, click again to deselect the chart object, compare your chart to Figure D-7, then save the presentation**

   The datasheet closes, allowing you to see your entire chart. This chart layout clearly shows eMedia's projected revenue for the first year it's in operation.

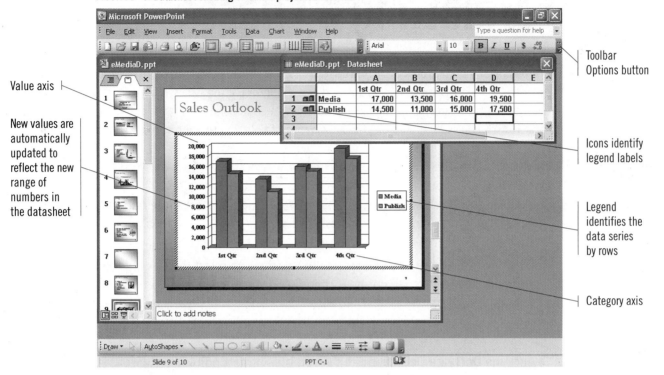

Value axis

New values are automatically updated to reflect the new range of numbers in the datasheet

Toolbar Options button

Icons identify legend labels

Legend identifies the data series by rows

Category axis

FIGURE D-7: Chart showing data grouped by division

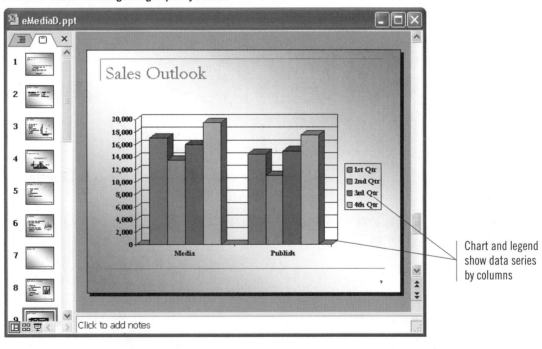

Chart and legend show data series by columns

PowerPoint 2003

Clues to Use

Series in Rows vs. Series in Columns

If you have difficulty visualizing the difference between the Series in Rows and the Series in Columns commands on the Data menu, think about what is represented in the legend. **Series in Rows** means that the information in the datasheet rows will be on the Value or vertical axis and is the information shown in the legend, and the column labels will be on the Category or horizontal axis.

Series in Columns means that the information in the columns becomes the information shown on the Value axis and in the legend, and the row labels will be on the horizontal or Category axis. Microsoft Graph places a small chart icon representing the chart type on the axis items that are currently represented by the chart series items, for example, bars, columns, or lines.

Formatting a Chart

Microsoft Graph lets you change the appearance of the chart to emphasize certain aspects of the information you are presenting. You can change the chart type (for example pie, column, bar, or line), create titles, format the chart labels, move the legend, add arrows, or format the data series markers. Like other objects in PowerPoint, you can change the fill color, pattern, line style and color, and style of most elements in a chart. 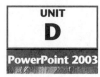 You want to improve the appearance of your chart by formatting the Value and Category axes and by inserting a title.

STEPS

1. **Double-click the chart to open Microsoft Graph, then click the Close button ☒ in the Datasheet window to close the datasheet**

   The Microsoft Graph menu and toolbars remain at the top of the window.

2. **Click one of the revenue numbers on the Value axis to select the axis, then click the Currency Style button $ on the Formatting toolbar**

   Before you can format any object on the chart, you need to select it. The numbers on the Value axis appear with dollar signs and two decimal places. You don't need to show the two decimal places because all the values are whole numbers.

TROUBLE

If you don't see $ or .00 →.0 on the Formatting toolbar, click a Toolbar Options button on a toolbar to locate buttons that are not visible on your toolbar.

3. **Click the Decrease Decimal button .00 →.0 on the Formatting toolbar twice**

   The numbers on the Value axis now have dollar signs and show only whole numbers. See Figure D-8. The division names on the Category axis would be easier to see if they were larger.

4. **Click one of the division names on the Category axis, click the Font Size list arrow 18 ▾ on the Formatting toolbar, then click 20**

   The font size changes from 18 points to 20 points for both labels on the Category axis. The chart would be easier to read if it had a title and axis labels.

5. **Click Chart on the menu bar, click Chart Options, then click the Titles tab, if it is not already selected**

   The Chart Options dialog box opens. You can change the chart title, axes, gridlines, legend, data labels, and the data table.

6. **Click in the Chart title text box, then type eMedia Projected Revenue**

   The preview box shows you how the chart looks with the title.

7. **Press [Tab] twice to move the insertion point to the Value (Z) axis text box, then type Revenue**

   In a 3-D chart, the Value axis is called the Z-axis, and the depth axis, which you don't usually work with, is the Y-axis. You decide to move the legend to the bottom of the chart.

8. **Click the Legend tab, click the Bottom option button, then click OK**

   The legend moves to the bottom of the chart, and the new chart title and axis title appear on the chart. The axis title would look better and take up less space if it were rotated 90 degrees.

9. **Right-click the Revenue label on the Value axis, click Format Axis Title, click the Alignment tab, drag the red diamond in the Orientation section counterclockwise to a vertical position so that the spin box reads 90 degrees, click OK, then click a blank area of the slide**

   Graph closes and the PowerPoint toolbars and menu bar appear.

10. **Drag the chart to the center of the slide, click a blank area of the slide, then save your changes**

    Compare your screen to Figure D-9.

FIGURE D-8: Chart showing applied Currency style to data

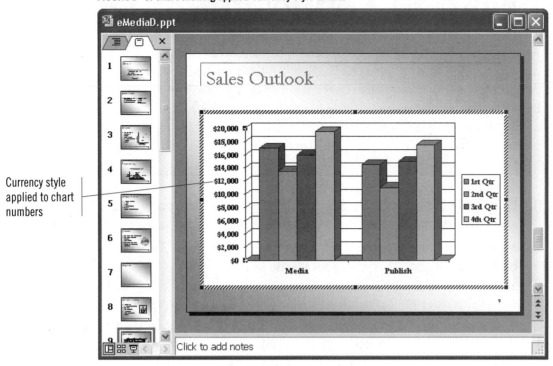

Currency style applied to chart numbers

FIGURE D-9: Slide showing formatted chart

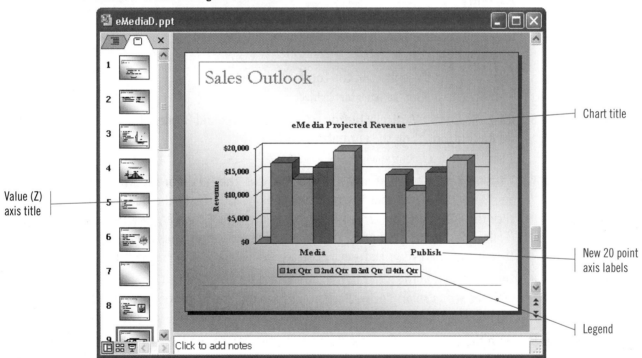

Chart title

Value (Z) axis title

New 20 point axis labels

Legend

Clues to Use

Customizing data series in charts

You can easily customize the look of any chart in Microsoft Graph. Click the chart to select it, then double-click any data series element (a column, for example) to open the Format Data Series dialog box. Use the tabs to change the element's fill color, border, shape, or data label. You can even use the same fill effects you apply to a presentation background. In 3-D charts, you can change the chart depth as well as the distances between series.

Creating Tables in PowerPoint

As you create your PowerPoint presentation, you may need to organize information into rows and columns. A table is ideal for this type of information. There are three ways to create a table in PowerPoint, you can click the Insert Table button on the Standard toolbar, the Table command on the Insert menu, or the Table icon on any of the content slide layouts. Once you have created a table, you can use the buttons on the Tables and Borders toolbar or on the Formatting toolbar to format the table to best present the information. ▓▓▓▓ You decide to create a table describing eMedia's different pricing plans.

STEPS

1. **Click** Slide 7 **in the Slides tab, then click the** Insert Table button 🔲 **on the Standard toolbar**
   A grid appears that allows you to specify the number of columns and rows you want in your table.

TROUBLE
If the Tables and Borders toolbar does not open, click View on the menu bar, point to Toolbars, then click Tables and Borders. If the toolbar obscures part of the table, drag it out of the way.

2. **Move your pointer over the grid to select a** 3 × 3 cell area **("3 × 3 Table" appears at the bottom of the grid), then click your mouse button**
   A table with three columns and three rows appears on the slide, and the Tables and Borders toolbar opens. The table has nine cells. The first cell in the table is selected and ready to accept text.

3. **Type** Basic, **press** [Tab], **type** Standard, **press** [Tab], **type** Premium, **then press** [Tab]
   The text you typed appears in the top three cells of the table. Pressing [Tab] moves the insertion point to the next cell. Pressing [Enter] moves the insertion point to the next line in the cell.

4. **Enter the rest of the table information shown in Figure D-10, do not press** [Tab] **after the last entry**
   Pressing [Tab] when the insertion point is in the cell in the last column and last row in a table creates a new row and places the insertion point in the cell in the first column of that row. The table would look better if it were formatted.

5. **Drag to select the entries in the top row of the table**
   The text in the first row becomes highlighted.

QUICK TIP
You can change the height or width of any table cell by dragging its top or side borders.

6. **Click the** Center Vertically button 🔲 **on the Tables and Borders toolbar, then click the** Center button ▤ **on the Formatting toolbar**
   The text is centered horizontally and vertically.

7. **With the text in the first row still selected, click the** Fill Color list arrow 🔲 **on the Tables and Borders toolbar, click the** red color **(Follow Title Text Scheme Color) in the first row, click the** Font Color list arrow 🔲 **on the Formatting toolbar, click the** white color **(Follow Background Scheme Color) in the first row, then click a blank area of the slide**
   The cells in the top row are filled with the color red and the font color for the text in the cells is white.

8. **Select the text in the other two rows, vertically center the text, then fill these two rows with the white color (Follow Background Scheme Color) in the first row of the Fill Color list**
   The table would look better if the last two rows were a little farther away from the cell edges.

QUICK TIP
You can use the Format Table dialog box to apply a diagonal line through any table cell. Click the Borders tab, then click a diagonal line button.

9. **With the bottom two rows still selected, click** Format **on the menu bar, click** Table, **click the** Text Box tab, **click the** Left up arrow **until it reads** .25, **click** OK, **click a blank area of the slide, then save the presentation**
   The Tables and Borders toolbar closes and the table is no longer selected. Compare your screen with Figure D-11.

FIGURE D-10: The new table before formatting

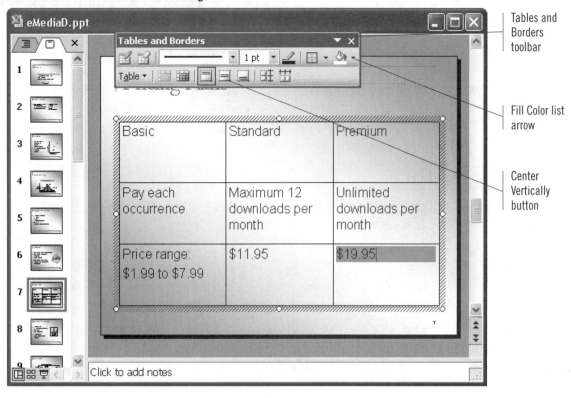

Tables and Borders toolbar

Fill Color list arrow

Center Vertically button

FIGURE D-11: Formatted table

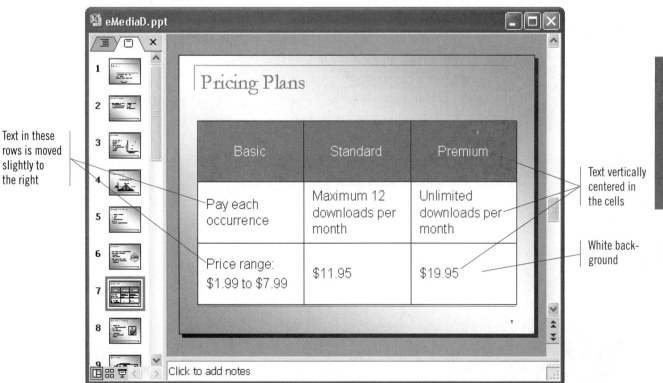

Text in these rows is moved slightly to the right

Text vertically centered in the cells

White background

PowerPoint 2003

Using Slide Show Commands

With PowerPoint, you can show a presentation on any compatible computer using Slide Show view. As you've seen, Slide Show view fills your computer screen with the slides of your presentation, showing them one at a time, similarly to how a slide projector shows slides. Once your presentation is in Slide Show view, you can use a number of slide show options to tailor the show. For example, you can draw on, or **annotate**, slides or jump to a specific slide. ▰▰▰▰ You run the slide show of your presentation and practice using some of the custom slide show options to make your presentation more effective.

STEPS

1. **Click Slide 1 in the Slides tab, then click the Slide Show from current slide button** 🖳
   The first slide of the presentation fills the screen.

2. **Press [Spacebar]**
   Slide 2 appears on the screen. Pressing [Spacebar] or clicking the left mouse button is the easiest way to move through a slide show. Another way is to use the keys listed in Table D-2. You can also use the Slide Show shortcut menu for on-screen navigation during a slide show.

3. **Right-click anywhere on the screen, point to Go to Slide on the shortcut menu, then click 6 Distribution**
   The slide show jumps to Slide 6. You can highlight or emphasize major points in your presentation by annotating the slide during a slide show using one of PowerPoint's annotation tools.

   > **QUICK TIP**
   > The Slide Show menu buttons are transparent and will change to match the background color on the slide.

4. **Move the mouse across the screen to display the Slide Show toolbar, click the Pen Options menu button** ✏️, **then click Highlighter**
   The pointer changes to ▯.

   > **QUICK TIP**
   > You have the option of saving annotations you create while in Slide Show view when you end or quit the slide show.

5. **Drag** ▯ **to highlight the words National, International, and Schedules**
   Compare your screen to Figure D-12. While the annotation tool is visible, mouse clicks do not advance the slide show; however, you can still move to the next slide by pressing [Spacebar] or [Enter].

6. **Click** ✏️ **on the Slide Show toolbar, click Erase All Ink on Slide, then press [Ctrl][A]**
   The annotations on Slide 6 are erased and the pointer returns to ⬚.

7. **Click the Slide Show menu button** ▭ **on the Slide Show toolbar, point to Go to Slide, then click 9 Sales Outlook on the menu**
   Slide 9 appears.

   > **QUICK TIP**
   > If you know the slide number of a slide you want to jump to during a slide show, type the number, then press [Enter].

8. **Press [Home], then click the left mouse button, press [Spacebar], or press [Enter] to advance through the slide show**
   After the black slide that indicates the end of the slide show appears, the next click ends the slide show and returns you to Normal view.

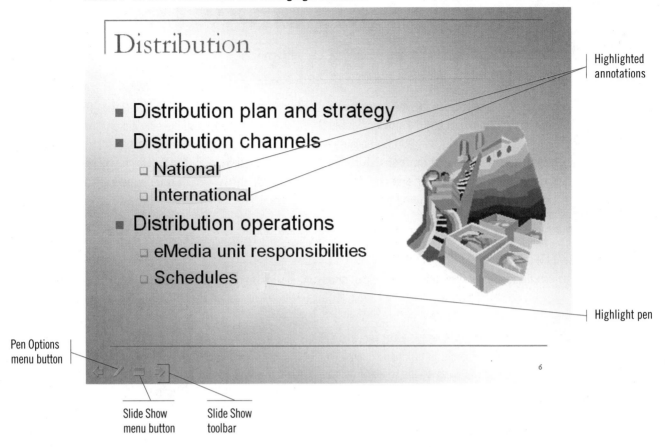

TABLE D-2: Basic Slide Show keyboard controls

control	description
[Enter], [Spacebar], [PgDn], [N], [down arrow key], or [right arrow key]	Advances to the next slide
[E]	Erases the annotation drawing
[Home], [End]	Moves to the first or last slide in the slide show
[H]	Displays a hidden slide
[up arrow key] or [PgUp]	Returns to the previous slide
[W]	Changes the screen to white; press again to return
[S]	Pauses the slide show; press again to continue
[B]	Changes the screen to black; press again to return
[Ctrl][M]	Shows or hides annotations on the slide
[Ctrl][A]	Changes pointer to ⤢
[Esc]	Stops the slide show

PowerPoint 2003

Setting Slide Show Timings and Transitions

In a slide show, you can specify when and how each slide appears on the screen. You can set the **slide timing**, which is the amount of time a slide is visible on the screen. Each slide can have a different slide timing. Setting the right slide timing is important because it determines how long you have to discuss the material on each slide. You can also set **slide transitions**, which are the special visual and audio effects you apply to a slide that determine how it moves in and out of view during the slide show. ▰▰▰ You decide to set a 10 second slide timing for each slide and to set transitions for all the slides.

STEPS

1. **Click the** Slide Sorter View button ⊞

   Slide Sorter view shows a thumbnail of the slides in your presentation. The number of slides you see on your screen depends on the current zoom setting in the Zoom box on the Standard toolbar. Notice that the Slide Sorter toolbar appears next to the Standard toolbar.

   > **TROUBLE**
   >
   > If you don't see 🖼️, click a Toolbar Options button ⌄ on the Slide Sorter toolbar to locate buttons that are not visible on your toolbar.

2. **Click the** Slide Transition button 🖼️ **on the Slide Sorter toolbar**

   The Slide Transition task pane opens. The list box at the top of the task pane contains the slide transitions that you can apply to the slides of your presentation. Use the Modify transition section to change the speed of slide transitions. You can also add a sound to a slide so that it plays during a slide show. Use the Advance slide section to determine how slides progress during a slide show—either manually or with a slide timing.

3. **Make sure the** On mouse click check box **is selected in the Advance slide section, click the** Automatically after check box **to select it, drag to select the number in the Automatically after text box, type** 10, **then click** Apply to All Slides

   The timing between slides is 10 seconds which appears under each slide in Slide Sorter view. When you run the slide show, each slide will remain on the screen for 10 seconds. You can override a slide's timing and speed up the slide show by pressing [Spacebar], [Enter], or clicking the left mouse button.

   > **QUICK TIP**
   >
   > Click the transition icon under any slide to see its transition play.

4. **Scroll down the list of transitions at the top of the task pane, click** Wheel Clockwise, 8 Spokes, **then click** Apply to All Slides

   All of the slides now have the Wheel Clockwise transition applied to them as indicated by the transition icon under each slide. You can apply a transition to one slide or to all of the slides in your presentation. The selected slide, Slide 1, displays the slide transition immediately after you apply the transition to all the slides. See Figure D-13. The slide transition would have more impact if it were slowed down.

5. **Click the** Speed list arrow **in the Modify transition section in the task pane, click** Medium, **then click** Apply to All Slides

6. **Scroll down the Slide Sorter view pane, click** Slide 10, **click the** Sound list arrow **in the Modify transition section in the task pane, scroll down the list, then click** Chime

   The sound plays when you apply the sound to the slide. The sound will now play when Slide 10 appears during the slide show.

   > **QUICK TIP**
   >
   > To end a slide show, press [Esc] or click End Show on the Slide Show menu.

7. **Press** [Home], **click the** Slide Show button **in the Slide Transition task pane, then watch the slide show advance automatically**

8. **When you hear the chime and see the black slide at the end of the slide show, press** [Spacebar]

   The slide show ends and returns to Slide Sorter view with Slide 1 selected.

FIGURE D-13: Screen showing Slide Transition task pane

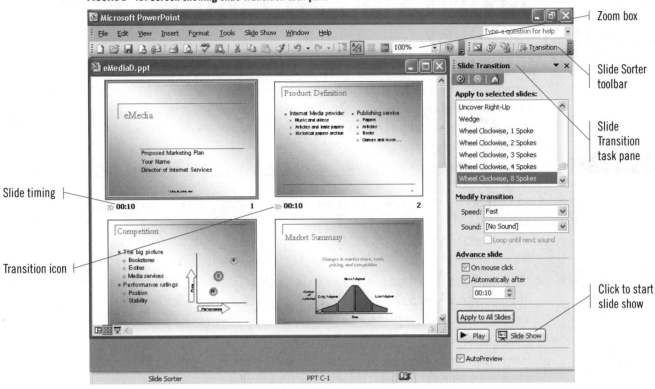

Zoom box

Slide Sorter toolbar

Slide Transition task pane

Slide timing

Transition icon

Click to start slide show

Clues to Use

Rehearsing slide show timing

You can set different slide timings for each slide. For example, you can have the title slide appear for 20 seconds, the second slide for 3 minutes, and so on. You can set timings by clicking the Rehearse Timings button [icon] on the Slide Sorter toolbar or by choosing the Rehearse Timings command on the Slide Show menu. The Rehearsal toolbar shown in Figure D-14 opens. It contains buttons to pause between slides and to advance to the next slide. After opening the Rehearsal toolbar, practice giving your presentation. PowerPoint keeps track of how long each slide appears and sets the timing accordingly. You can view your rehearsed timings in Slide Sorter view. The next time you run the slide show, you can use the timings you rehearsed.

FIGURE D-14: Rehearsal toolbar

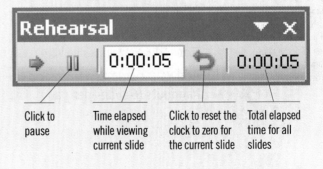

Click to pause

Time elapsed while viewing current slide

Click to reset the clock to zero for the current slide

Total elapsed time for all slides

Setting Slide Animation Effects

Animation effects let you control how the graphics and main points in your presentation appear on the screen during a slide show. You can animate text, images, or even individual chart elements, or you can add sound effects. You can set custom animation effects or use one of the PowerPoint animation schemes. An **animation scheme** is a set of predefined visual effects for the slide transition, title text, and bullet text of a slide. ⟪▨▨▨⟫ You want to animate the text and graphics of several slides in your presentation using PowerPoint animation schemes.

STEPS

1. **In Slide Sorter view, click Slide 2, press and hold [Ctrl], click Slides 3, 5, 6, and 8, then release [Ctrl]**

   All of the selected slides have bulleted lists on them. The bullets can be animated to appear one at a time during a slide show.

   > **QUICK TIP**
   > Keep in mind that the animation effects you choose give a certain "flavor" to your presentation. They can be serious and business-like or humorous. Choose appropriate effects for your presentation content and audience.

2. **Click the Other Task Panes list arrow ▼, click Slide Design – Animation Schemes, scroll down the Apply to selected slides list to the Exciting section, then click Neutron**

   Each of the selected slides previews the Neutron animation scheme.

3. **Click Slide 1, click the Slide Show button on the Slide Design – Animation Schemes task pane, then press [Esc] when you see the black slide**

   The Neutron animation scheme is displayed on the selected slides. You can also animate objects on a slide by setting custom animations. To set custom animation effects, the slide you want to animate must be in Slide view.

4. **Double-click Slide 3 in Slide Sorter view, click Slide Show on the menu bar, then click Custom Animation**

   The Custom Animation task pane opens. Objects that are already animated appear in the Custom Animation task pane list in the order in which they will be animated. **Animation tags** on the slide label the order in which elements are animated during a slide show.

   > **QUICK TIP**
   > If you want the parts of a grouped object to animate individually, then you must ungroup them first.

5. **Click the grouped arrow object on the slide to select it, then click the Add Effect button in the Custom Animation task pane**

   A menu of animation effects appears.

6. **Point to Entrance, then click More Effects**

   The Add Entrance Effect dialog box opens. All of the effects in this dialog box allow an object to enter the slide using a special effect.

   > **QUICK TIP**
   > To change the order in which objects are animated on the slide, select the object you want to change in the Custom Animation list in the task pane, then click the appropriate Re-Order arrow below the list.

7. **Scroll down to the Exciting section, click Pinwheel, then click OK**

   The arrow object now has the pinwheel effect applied to it as shown in Figure D-15.

8. **Run the Slide Show from Slide 1**

   The special effects make the presentation more interesting to view.

9. **Click the Slide Sorter View button 🔳, click the Zoom list arrow on the Standard toolbar, then click 50%**

   Figure D-16 shows the completed presentation in Slide Sorter view at 50% zoom.

10. **Add your name as a footer on the notes and handouts, save your presentation, print it as handouts (6 slides per page), then close the presentation and exit PowerPoint**

FIGURE D-15: Screen with Custom Animation task pane open

Animation tag

Animation tag for grouped arrow object

Graphic represents Neutron animation path

Custom Animation list

Pinwheel effect added to arrow object

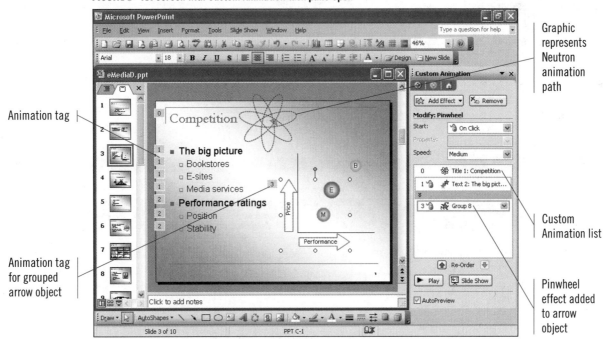

FIGURE D-16: Completed presentation in Slide Sorter view

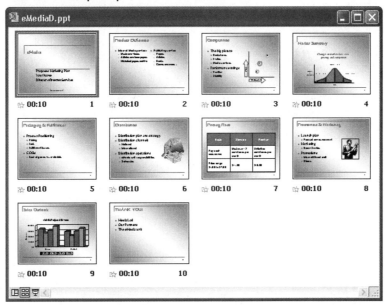

Clues to Use

Presentation checklist

You should always rehearse your slide show. If possible, rehearse your presentation in the room and with the computer that you will use. Use the following checklist to prepare for the slide show:

- Is **PowerPoint** or **PowerPoint Viewer** installed on the computer?
- Is your **presentation file** on the hard drive of the computer you will be using? Try putting a shortcut for the file on the desktop. Do you have a backup copy of your presentation file on a floppy disk?
- Is the **projection device** working correctly? Can the slides be seen from the back of the room?

- Do you know how to control **room lighting** so that the audience can see both your slides and their handouts and notes? You may want to designate someone to control the lights if the controls are not close to you.
- Will the **computer** be situated so you can advance and annotate the slides yourself? If not, designate someone to advance them for you.
- Do you have enough copies of your **handouts**? Bring extras. Decide when to hand them out, or whether you prefer to have them waiting at the audience members' seats when they enter.

Practice

▼ CONCEPTS REVIEW

Label each element of the PowerPoint window shown in Figure D-17.

FIGURE D-17

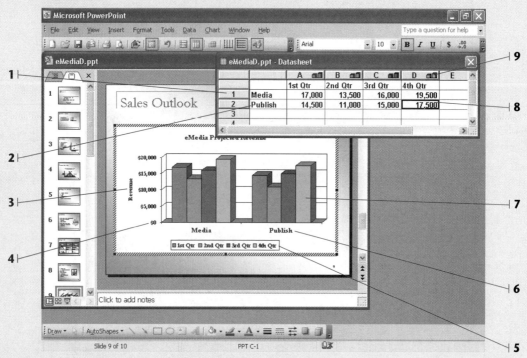

Match each term with the statement that best describes it.

10. Annotate
11. Data series markers
12. Crop
13. Datasheet
14. Chart
15. Animation scheme

a. Graphical representations of numerical data
b. A set of predefined visual effects
c. A graphical representation of numerical data
d. Where the numerical data is stored for a chart
e. To hide a portion of a picture
f. To draw on a slide during a slide show

Select the best answer from the list of choices.

16. **When you want an object to become a part of a PowerPoint file you:**
    a. Annotate the object.
    b. Embed the object.
    c. Crop the object.
    d. Scale the object.

17. **Professionally designed images that you can place in your presentation are called:**
    a. Thumbnails.
    b. Pictures.
    c. Clip art.
    d. AutoShapes.

18. **Cropping is essentially the same as:**
    a. Hiding.
    b. Deleting.
    c. Resizing.
    d. Scaling.

19. **What are you doing when you drag a sizing handle of an object?**
    a. Moving
    b. Scaling
    c. Hiding
    d. Deleting

20. What does pressing [Alt] while dragging an object's sizing handle do?

a. Overrides the automatic snap-to-grid setting

c. Deletes that portion of the object

b. Constrains the proportions of the object

d. Scales the object larger or smaller

21. What is a chart in PowerPoint?

a. A datasheet that contains numerical data

c. A graphical representation of numerical data

b. A table you create with the Diagram button

d. An organizational chart

22. Where is the numerical data for a chart found?

a. The data series markers

c. The chart

b. The slide

d. The datasheet

23. Which axis is the vertical axis?

a. Value axis

c. Legend axis

b. Category axis

d. Horizontal axis

▼ SKILLS REVIEW

1. Insert clip art.

a. Open the presentation PPT D-3.ppt from the drive and folder where your Data Files are stored, then save it as **Year End Report**.

b. Go to Slide 2, search for clip art using the keyword CD, then insert the clip on the slide.

c. On the Picture tab of the Format Picture dialog box, click the Color list arrow, then click Grayscale.

d. Drag the graphic so the top of the graphic aligns with the body text box and is centered in the blank area on the right of the slide, then save your changes.

2. Insert, crop, and scale a picture.

a. Go to Slide 6 and insert the picture file PPT D-4.jpg.

b. Crop about ¾" off the top of the picture.

c. Drag the picture so its top is aligned with the top line of text.

d. Scale the picture to 65%, then using the Color button on the picture toolbar change the picture to grayscale.

e. Reposition the graphic, then save your changes.

3. Embed a chart.

a. Go to Slide 3, 2005 CD Sales by Quarter, and apply the Title and Content layout.

b. Start Microsoft Graph.

c. Deselect the chart object and save your changes.

4. Enter and edit data in the datasheet.

a. Open Graph again.

b. Enter the information shown in Table D-4 into the datasheet.

c. Delete any unused rows of default data.

d. Place the data series in columns.

e. Save your changes.

TABLE D-4

	1st Qtr	2nd Qtr	3rd Qtr	4th Qtr
East Div.	405	340	390	320
West Div.	280	320	380	250

5. Format a chart.

a. Close the datasheet but leave Graph running.

b. Change the region names font on the Category axis to 20 point and regular font style (no bold).

c. Apply the Currency Style with no decimals to the values on the Value axis.

d. Insert the chart title **Division Sales**.

e. Add the title **Thousands** to the Value axis, then change the alignment of this label to vertical.

f. Change the legend text font to 16-point Arial font and regular font style (no bold).

g. Exit Graph and save your changes.

6. Create a table.

a. Insert a new slide after Slide 2 using the Title and Content slide layout.

b. Add the slide title **CD Sales by Type**.

c. Click the Insert Table button in the placeholder, then insert a table with two columns and five rows.

d. Enter **Type** in the first cell and **Sales** in the second cell in the first row.

e. In the first column, enter the following: **Rock**, **Rap**, **New Age**, and **Country**.

    f. In the second column, enter sales figures: **20,000**, **35,000**, **55,650**, and **80,000** for each CD type.

    g. Format the table using fills, horizontal and vertical alignment, and other features.

    h. Save your changes.

7. Use slide show commands.

    a. Begin the slide show at Slide 1, then proceed through the slide show to Slide 3.

    b. On Slide 3, use the Ballpoint pen to draw straight-line annotations under each type of music.

    c. Erase the pen annotations, then change the pointer back to an arrow.

    d. Go to 5 Summary slide using the Slide Show menu button on the Slide Show toolbar, then using the Highlighter, high-light all of the points on the slide.

    e. Press [End] to move to the last slide. Don't save any changes.

    f. Return to Normal view.

8. Set slide show timings and transitions.

    a. Switch to Slide Sorter view, then open the Slide Transition task pane.

    b. Specify that all slides should advance after eight seconds.

    c. Apply the Newsflash transition effect to all slides.

    d. View the slide show to verify the transitions are correct, then save your changes.

9. Set slide animation effects.

    a. Switch to Normal view, then open the Custom Animation task pane.

    b. Switch to Slide 5, apply the (Entrance) Fly In animation effect to the bulleted list.

    c. Go to Slide 2, apply the (Emphasis) Shimmer animation effect to the text object. (*Hint*: Look in the Moderate section after clicking More effects.)

    d. Apply the (Exit) Faded Zoom animation effect to the graphic on Slide 2. (*Hint*: Look in the Subtle section after click-ing More effects.)

    e. Run the slide show from the beginning to check the animation effects.

    f. Add your name as a footer to the notes and handouts, then print the presentation as handouts (4 slides per page).

    g. Save your changes, close the presentation, and exit PowerPoint.

▼ INDEPENDENT CHALLENGE 1

You are a financial management consultant for Northwest Investments, located in Tacoma, Washington. One of your responsi-bilities is to create standardized presentations on different financial investments for use on the company Web site. In this chal-lenge, you enhance the look of the slides by adding and formatting objects and adding animation effects and transitions.

    a. Open the file PPT D-5.ppt from the drive and folder where your Data Files are stored, and save it as **Web Seminar1**.

    b. Add your name as the footer on all slides and handouts.

    c. Apply the Title and Chart layout to Slide 6, and enter the data in Table D-5 into the datasheet.

    d. Format the chart. Add titles as necessary.

TABLE D-5

	1 year	3 year	5 year	10 year
Bonds	4.2%	5.2%	7.9%	9.4%
Stocks	4.5%	6.3%	9.8%	10.6%
Mutual Funds	6.1%	6.3%	7.4%	8.1%

Advanced Challenge Exercise

    ■ Double-click one of the 10 year data series markers to select the data series.

    ■ On the Data Labels tab, click the Series name check box.

    ■ On the Patterns tab, click the red color in the Area section.

    e. Add an appropriate clip art item to Slide 2, then format as necessary.

    f. On Slide 4, use the Align and Group commands to organize the shapes.

    g. Spell check the presentation, then save it.

    h. View the slide show, evaluate your presentation, and add a template of your choice. Make changes if necessary.

    i. Set animation effects, slide transitions, and slide timings, keeping in mind that your audience includes potential investors who need the information you are presenting to make decisions about where to put their hard-earned money.

    j. View the slide show again.

    k. Print the slides as handouts (6 slides per page), then close the presentation, and exit PowerPoint.

▼ INDEPENDENT CHALLENGE 2

You are the manager of the Indiana University Student Employment Office. Work-study students staff the office; new students start every semester. Create a presentation that you can use to train them.

a. Plan and create the slide presentation. As you plan your outline, make sure you include slides that will help explain to the work-study staff the main features of the office, including its employment database, library of company directories, seminars on employment search strategies, interviewing techniques, and resume development, as well as its student consulting and resume bulk-mailing services. Add more slides with more content if you wish.

b. Use an appropriate design template.

c. Add clip art and photographs available in the Clip Organizer to help create visual interest.

d. Save the presentation as **Indiana USEO** to the drive and folder where your Data Files are stored. View the slide show and evaluate the contents of your presentation. Make any necessary adjustments.

e. Add transitions, special effects, and timings to the presentation. Remember that your audience is university students who need to assimilate a lot of information in order to perform well in their new jobs. View the slide show again to evaluate the effects you added.

f. Add your name as a footer to slides and handouts. Spell check, save, and print the presentation as handouts (4 slides per page).

g. Close the presentation and exit PowerPoint.

▼ INDEPENDENT CHALLENGE 3

You are the managing development engineer at SportDesign, Inc, an international sports product design company located in Ottawa, Ontario, Canada. SportDesign designs and manufactures items such as bike helmets, bike racks, and kayak paddles, and markets these items primarily to countries in North America and Western Europe. You need to create a quarterly presentation that outlines the progress of the company's newest technologies, and present it.

a. Plan and create a slide show presentation that includes two new technologies.

b. Use an appropriate design template.

c. Add one chart and one table in the presentation that shows details (such as performance results, testing criteria, etc.) about the new technologies.

d. Include at least two slides that explain how the new technologies will appeal specifically to individual countries in the European and North American markets.

e. Set slide transitions, animation effects, and slide timings. View the slide show to evaluate the effects you added.

Advanced Challenge Exercise

- Click the Rehearse Timings button on the Slide Sorter toolbar.
- Set slide timings for each slide in the presentation.
- Save new slide timings.

f. Add your name as a footer to the handouts. Save the presentation as **SportDesign** to the drive and folder where your Data Files are stored.

g. Print the presentation as handouts (4 slides per page), then close the presentation and exit PowerPoint.

▼ INDEPENDENT CHALLENGE 4

You work for IRAssets, a small retirement investment firm. You have been asked to complete a retirement investing presentation started by your boss. Most of the information has already been entered into the PowerPoint presentation; you just need to add a template and a table to complete the presentation. To find the data for the table, you need to use the Web to locate certain information.

You'll need to find the following information on the Web:

- Data for a table that compares the traditional IRA with the Roth IRA.
- Data for a table that compares at least two other retirement plans.

▼ INDEPENDENT CHALLENGE 4 (CONTINUED)

a. Open the file PPT D-6.ppt from the drive and folder where your Data Files are stored and save it as **Retirement**.

b. Connect to the Internet, then use a search engine to locate Web sites that have information on retirement plans.

c. Review at least two Web sites that contain information about retirement plans. Print the Home pages of the Web sites you use to gather data for your presentation.

d. Apply the Title and Table layout to Slide 7, then enter the data you found that compares the IRA retirement plans.

e. Apply the Title and Table layout to Slide 8, then enter the data you found that compares the other retirement plans.

f. Apply a template to the presentation, then customize the slide background and the color scheme.

g. Format the Autoshape objects on Slides 4 and 5.

h. Use text formatting to help emphasize important points, then add your name as a footer to the handouts.

i. Add slide transitions, slide timings, and animation effects.

j. Spell check the presentation, view the slide show, save the final version, then print the handouts.

k. Close the presentation and exit PowerPoint.

▼ VISUAL WORKSHOP

Create a slide with a chart that looks like the slide in Figure D-18. Add your name as a footer on the slide. Save the presentation as **2006 Expenses** to the drive and folder where your Data Files are stored.

FIGURE D-18

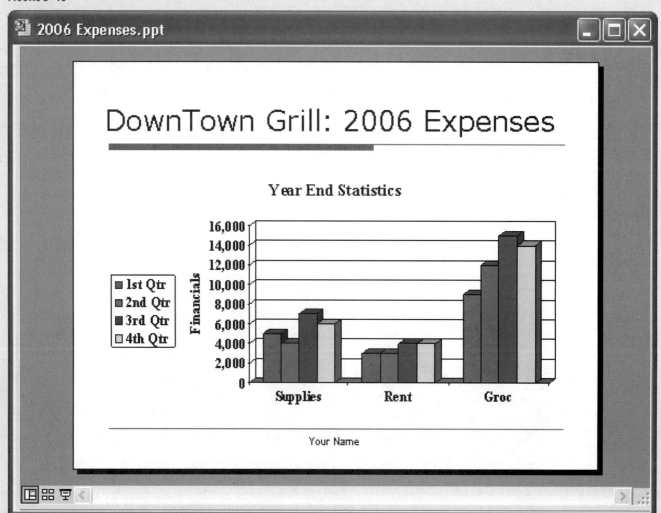

Integrating Word, Excel, Access, and PowerPoint

OBJECTIVES

You can integrate elements created in Word, Excel, and Access to produce PowerPoint presentations that cover a broad spectrum of company activities. For example, you may have information about your customers and products stored in an Access database, financial information stored in Excel workbooks, and sales literature stored in Word. You can communicate this information in the form of a PowerPoint presentation that viewers can easily understand. The PowerPoint slide show feature provides you with a flexible medium in which to bring together information from a variety of sources. By creating links between PowerPoint and the source programs, you can also keep the presentation up to date and ready to go at a moment's notice. ▂▂▂ Maria Abbott, MediaLoft's general sales manager, frequently puts together sales presentations that include data from Access, Excel, and Word. She asks you to explore how linking and embedding are used to add objects to a PowerPoint presentation, and then how to include objects from all three applications in a sales presentation and a lecture presentation created in PowerPoint.

Identifying Integration Opportunities

You can add objects to the slides in your PowerPoint presentation in two ways. First, you can **embed** objects such as charts or tables, and second, you can **link** them. An object can be an Excel workbook or a table in a Word document. Data can be text that you select in a document, or it can be selected values from a worksheet. Suppose you paste an Excel chart into a PowerPoint file called Sales Presentation.ppt. In this case, the file called Sales Presentation.ppt is the **destination file** and PowerPoint is the **destination program**. Maria asks you to explore embedding and linking in more detail so that you can include objects from other Office applications in a PowerPoint presentation.

DETAILS

Microsoft Office applications can be used together to:

- **Embed objects**

  You can choose to embed objects in a PowerPoint presentation. To embed an object in a PowerPoint presentation, you use the Object command on the Insert menu, or you use the Copy command in the source program and the Paste or Paste Special command in PowerPoint. Although there is no link to the source file when you embed an object, you can still edit the embedded object using its source program. Once embedded, an object becomes a part of the PowerPoint file. As a result, the file size of the PowerPoint presentation increases relative to the file size of the embedded object.

- **Link objects**

  When you link an object to a PowerPoint slide, a representation or picture of the object is placed on the slide instead of the actual object. This representation of the object is connected, or linked, to the original file. The object is still stored in the source file, unlike an embedded object, which is stored directly on a slide. Any changes you make to a linked object's source file are reflected in the linked object. You can open the source file and make changes to the linked object as long as you have access to the source program (either installed on your computer or over a network), and to the source file. To link an object to a PowerPoint presentation, you use the Object command on the Insert menu, and then click the Link to file check box in the Object dialog box. You can also copy the object in its source program, click the Paste Special command on the Edit menu in the destination file, and then click the Paste link option button in the Paste Special dialog box. The differences between embedding and linking are summarized in Table C-1.

- **Edit embedded objects**

  To edit an embedded object, you double-click the object. The source program starts, and the menu and toolbars of the source program appear. Changes made to an embedded object in its source program are reflected in the destination file, but these modifications do not affect the original object in the source file because an embedded object has no link to its source file. Suppose, for example, that you've embedded an Excel worksheet on a slide in a PowerPoint presentation. You then decide that you need to add together some of the values in the worksheet. You double-click the object to open it in Excel, use AutoSum in Excel to add the required values, and then click outside the object to return to the PowerPoint slide. See Figure C-1.

- **Edit linked objects**

  To edit a linked object, you can double-click the object to open the source file in its source program, and then make your changes. You can also make changes to the object in the source program. The changes made to a linked file are reflected in both the source file and in the linked object in the destination file. See Figure C-2.

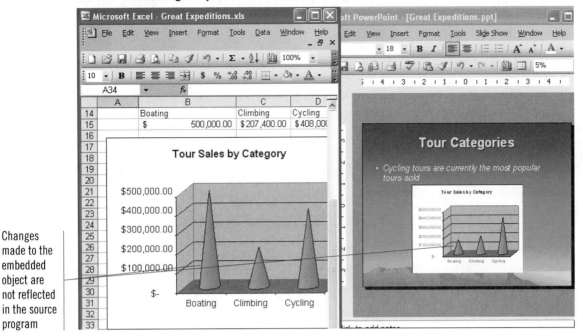

FIGURE C-1: Embedding an object on a PowerPoint slide

Changes made to the embedded object are not reflected in the source program

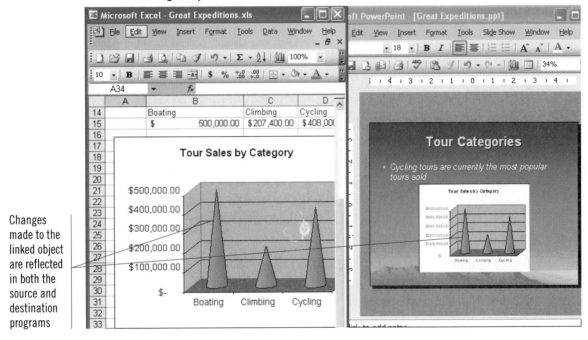

FIGURE C-2: Linking an object on a PowerPoint slide

Changes made to the linked object are reflected in both the source and destination programs

TABLE C-1: Embedding vs. linking

action	situation
Embed	You are the only user of an object, and you want the object to be a part of your presentation.
Embed	You want to access the object in its source program, even if the source file is not available.
Embed	You want to update the object manually while working in PowerPoint.
Link	You always want your object to have the latest information.
Link	The object's source file is shared on a network or where other users have access to the file and can change it.
Link	You want to keep your presentation file size small.

INTEGRATING WORD, EXCEL, ACCESS, AND POWERPOINT INTEGRATION C-3

UNIT
C
Integration

Project 1: Sales Presentation for Great Expeditions

MediaLoft's Seattle store wants to work with a local tour company called Great Expeditions to sponsor a series of travel lectures. As MediaLoft's general sales manager, Maria Abbott receives sales data from Great Expeditions. She asks you to put together an on-screen PowerPoint presentation that highlights the most popular tours and communicates the company's new marketing plan. You start by creating source materials for the presentation in Access and Excel.

ACTIVITY

Creating the Source Materials

STEPS

You need to create the Tours table in Access, then copy the table to Excel and create the two charts.

1. **Start Access, create a blank database using the New File task pane, go to the drive and folder where your Data Files are stored, type Great Expeditions in the File name box, then click Create**

> **QUICK TIP**
> You can create the primary key in Design View, or wait until prompted.

2. **Create the table in Design View, then enter the field names and select the appropriate data types as shown in Figure C-3**

3. **Click the View button 🔲, click Yes to save the table, name it Tours, click OK, click Yes to create a primary key if necessary, then enter the records for the Tours table and adjust column widths, as shown in Figure C-4**

4. **Close and save the Tours table, click Tours in the Great Expeditions Database window if necessary, then click the Copy button 🗐 on the Database toolbar**

> **QUICK TIP**
> When you use the Analyze It with Microsoft Excel function to transfer data from Access to Excel, you merely move the Access data to Excel so that you can use Excel tools to analyze the data.

5. **Start Excel, close the Getting Started task pane, click Edit on the menu bar, click Paste Special, click the Paste link option button, click OK to accept the default Microsoft Excel 8.0 Format, click an empty cell to deselect the table, then save the workbook as Great Expeditions in the drive and folder where your Data Files are stored**

   You use the Copy and Paste Special commands to link the Access table with the new workbook in Excel.

6. **Click cell G1, type Total, click cell G2, type =E2*F2, press [Enter], copy the formula down the column to cell G11, click the Currency Style button 💲 on the Formatting toolbar, click cell G12, then double-click the AutoSum button Σ on the Standard toolbar**

   You should see $516,500.00 in cell G12.

7. **Widen columns as required, click cell B14, type Boating, press [Tab], type Climbing in cell C14, press [Tab], type Cycling in cell D14, click cell B15, type the formula =G2+G3+G6, then press [Enter] to display the total for Boating tour sales**

8. **As shown in Figure C-5, enter the formulas required to calculate the total tour sales for the Climbing tours and the Cycling tours, then use the Chart Wizard to create a Cone chart from cells B14 to D15**

   In Step 3 of the wizard, enter the Chart title and deselect the Show legend check box. Position and size the chart as shown in Figure C-5. The formulas in cells B15 to D15 ensure that the chart is automatically updated when you change values in the Tours table in Access.

9. **Enter the tour locations and formulas in cells F14 to H15 as shown in Figure C-5, create a pie chart from the data, then save the workbook**

   Include a chart title, the legend, and the percentages. Your pie chart should appear as shown in Figure C-5.

FIGURE C-3: Design View of the Tours table

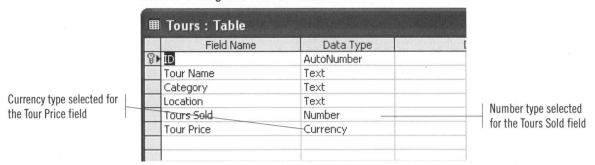

Currency type selected for the Tour Price field

Number type selected for the Tours Sold field

FIGURE C-4: Records for the Tours table

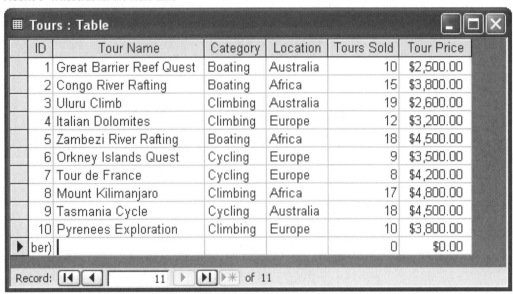

FIGURE C-5: Completed cone and pie charts

Formula for cell B15: =G2+G3+G6

Formula for cell C15: =G4+G5+G9+G11

Formula for cell D15: =G7+G8+G10

Formula for cell F15: =G2+G4+G10

Formula for cell H15: =G5+G7+G8+G11

Formula for cell G15: =G3+G6+G9

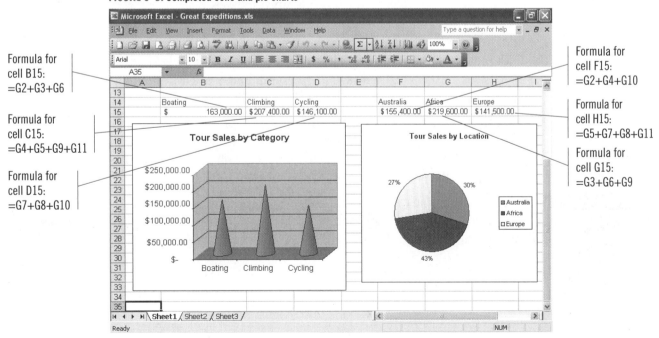

UNIT
C

Integration

ACTIVITY **Creating the Presentation**

You've created the source materials required for your presentation. Now you need to use Word to create an outline of your presentation. You will then send the outline to PowerPoint, where you will apply a PowerPoint design.

STEPS

1. **Start** Word, **then click the** Outline View button ▤ **in the lower-left corner of the document window**

2. **Type** Great Expeditions, **press** [Enter], **press** [Tab], **type** Sales Presentation, **press** [Enter], **type** Your Name, **press** [Enter], **then save the document as** Great Expeditions **in the drive and folder where your Data Files are stored**

3. **Press** [Shift][Tab], **type** Sales Mission, **press** [Enter], **press** [Tab], **type the text for the remaining slides, as shown in Figure C-6, then check the spelling**

   Remember to press [Tab] to indent the outline and [Shift][Tab] to move the cursor to the next level up in the outline. Don't worry if your text formatting is different from Figure C-6.

4. **Save the document, click** File **on the menu bar, click** Send To, **then click** Microsoft Office PowerPoint

   The outline appears in PowerPoint in Normal view. Each top-level outline heading is on its own slide.

TROUBLE
You may need to scroll to see the Mountain Top design template.

5. **Click the** Slide Design button ☑ Design **on the Formatting toolbar, click the** Mountain Top **slide design in the Apply a design template section of the task pane, click** Color Schemes **at the top of the Slide Design task pane, click the** color scheme with the medium blue background **(third row, second column), then close the Slide Design task pane**

6. **Click** View **on the menu bar, point to** Master, **click** Slide Master, **click the** Master title style placeholder, **click the** Bold button **B** **on the Formatting toolbar, click the** Second level placeholder, **click the** Font Color button list arrow **A ▾** **on the Formatting toolbar, select the** light blue color **near the middle of the color selections, then click** Close Master View **on the Slide Master View toolbar**

7. **Click** Format **on the menu bar, click** Slide Layout, **click the** Title Slide text layout, **close the Slide Layout task pane, then save the presentation as** Great Expeditions **in the drive and folder where your Data Files are stored**

8. **Click** Slide 3 **in the Slide pane, click the** Excel program button **on the taskbar, click a white area of the** cone chart, **click the** Copy button **on the Standard toolbar, click the** PowerPoint program button **on the taskbar, click** Edit **on the menu bar, click** Paste Special, **click the** Paste link option button, **then click** OK

TROUBLE
Depending on how you move and size the chart, your values may change to show increments of $100,000 instead of $50,000.

9. **Click** Format **on the menu bar, click** Slide Layout, **apply the** Title and Text over Content **slide layout in the Text and Content Layouts section, close the Slide Layout task pane, then size and position the cone chart, as shown in Figure C-7**

FIGURE C-6: Outline of the Great Expeditions sales presentation

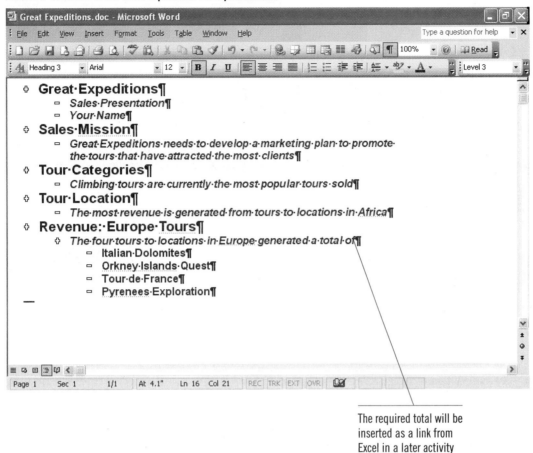

The required total will be inserted as a link from Excel in a later activity

FIGURE C-7: Cone chart on Slide 3

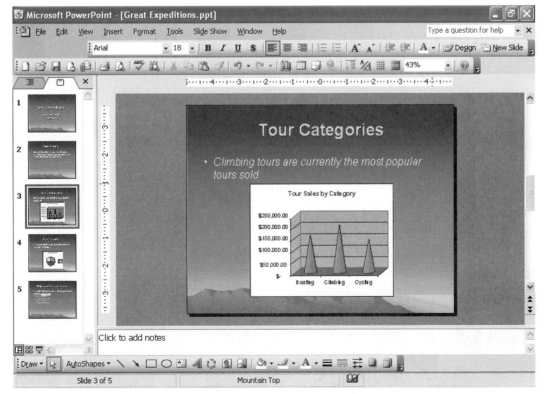

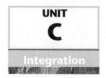

UNIT
C

Integration

Updating the Presentation

After copying the pie chart from Excel and pasting it as a link on Slide 4, you need to copy the total number of tours sold to Europe, and paste it as a link on Slide 5 of the presentation. Finally, you open the Tours table in Access, change the number of tours sold in response to new information received, and then update the links to the charts in PowerPoint. The linked object on Slide 5 is also updated.

STEPS

1. Copy the pie chart from Excel, paste it as a link onto Slide 4 in PowerPoint, apply the Title and Text over Content slide layout, then resize and position the pie chart, as shown in Figure C-8

2. Switch to Excel, click cell H15 (which contains the total revenue from tours in Europe), click the Copy button on the Standard toolbar, switch to PowerPoint, show Slide 5, click after of, press [Spacebar] once, click Edit on the menu bar, click Paste Special, click Paste link, then click OK

TROUBLE

If necessary, select the Title and Text slide layout before repositioning the object.

3. With the Excel object selected, click the Fill Color button list arrow on the Drawing toolbar, click the white color, then as shown in Figure C-9, size and position the Excel object and increase the width of the text box

   The Excel object shows the amount $141,500.00, which represents the total revenue generated from tours to locations in Europe.

4. Click the Access program button on the taskbar, open the Tours table, then enter new values for the Tours Sold column, as shown in Table C-2

5. Close the Tours table, switch to Excel, click Edit on the menu bar, click Links, click Update Values, click Close, switch to PowerPoint, click Edit on the menu bar, click Links, click the first link listed, click Update Now, click on and update the remaining two links, click Close, then verify that the Excel object is now $349,400.00

6. View Slide 3, verify that the Cycling cone has increased, select Climbing in the bullet text, then type Cycling

   The bullet text now reads, "Cycling tours are currently the most popular tours sold."

7. Show Slide 4, select Africa, then type Europe

8. Click File on the menu bar, click Print, click the Print what list arrow, click Handouts, click the Slides per page list arrow, click 6, then click OK

9. Save and close the presentation, then save and close the files in Access, Excel, and Word

---

Clues to Use

Reestablishing links

To reestablish links, you should start with the program that does not contain links and then open the remaining files in the order in which they are linked. For this presentation, the order of files is Access, Excel, and PowerPoint.

FIGURE C-8: Pie chart on slide 4

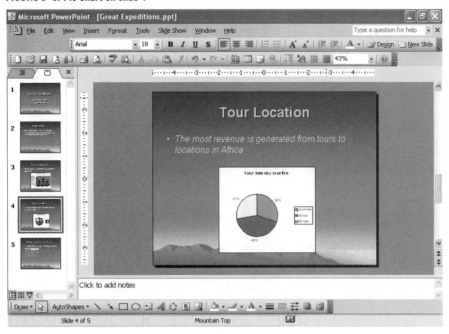

FIGURE C-9: Excel object sized and positioned on Slide 5

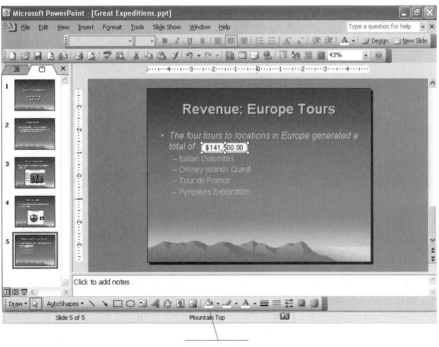

Fill Color button

TABLE C-2: New information for the Tours table

Orkney Islands Quest	30
Tour de France	40
Tasmania Cycle	30

INTEGRATING WORD, EXCEL, ACCESS, AND POWERPOINT INTEGRATION C-9

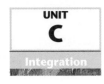

Project 2: Career Options Lecture Presentation

Cape Cod Business College has asked to rent space at the Boston MediaLoft to present a short lecture about the career options that potential students can expect after graduating from the college. As the assistant to the general sales manager at MediaLoft, you have volunteered to create the presentation from information provided by the college.

ACTIVITY

Creating the Source Materials and Presentation

STEPS

You first work in Access and Excel to create source materials that will be used in the Career Options presentation.

1. **Create an Access database called** Careers, **create a table, enter the fields in Design View, include a primary key, enter the records in Datasheet View, as shown in Figure C-10, adjust column widths, then name the table** Employment

2. **Close the table, click** Employment, **click the** Copy button 📋, **switch to a new blank document in Excel, paste the table as a link in the worksheet using** Microsoft Excel 8.0 Format, **adjust column widths, then save the workbook as** Careers

3. **Select cells** C2 to F6, **then click the** AutoSum button Σ **on the Standard toolbar**

4. **Select cells** C1 to E1, **press and hold [Ctrl], select cells** C6 to E6, **click the** Chart Wizard button 📊, **click** Pie, **click the** second Chart subtype **in the top row (the 3-D pie), then click** Next

5. **Click** Next, **click the** Legend tab, **click the** Bottom option button, **click** Finish, **click** Chart **on the menu bar, click** 3-D View, **select the contents of the Elevation text box if necessary, type** 40, **click** Apply, **click** Close, **increase the chart size as shown in Figure C-11, then save the workbook**

6. **Right-click the** pie chart, **click** Format Chart Area, **click the** Patterns tab **if necessary, click the** None option button **in the Area section of the dialog box, then click** OK

   When you copy the chart to the PowerPoint presentation, the white chart background is replaced by the background color of the PowerPoint slide.

7. **Open a blank presentation in PowerPoint, close the task pane if necessary, click the** Outline tab, **enter slide titles and text required for the presentation, as shown in Figure C-12, check the spelling, then save the presentation as** Careers

   You can drag the Outline pane to increase its width, as shown in Figure C-12.

8. **Click the** Slide Design button 📝 Design **on the Formatting toolbar, select the** Network **design, click** Format **on the menu bar, click** Background, **click the** Background fill list arrow, **then click** Fill Effects

9. **Click the** Gradient tab **if necessary, click the** Preset option button, **click the** Preset colors list arrow, **select** Daybreak **from the list of Preset colors, click** OK, **click** Apply to All, **close the Slide Design task pane, then save the presentation**

   You can modify any of PowerPoint's preset design schemes in many ways to produce a variety of interesting looks.

FIGURE C-10: Employment table

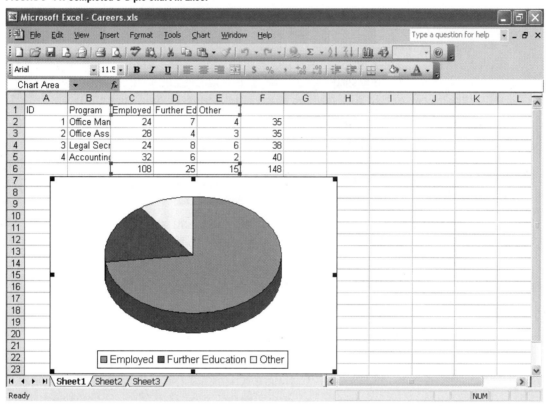

Select the Number data type for the Employed, Further Education, and Other fields

FIGURE C-11: Completed 3-D pie chart in Excel

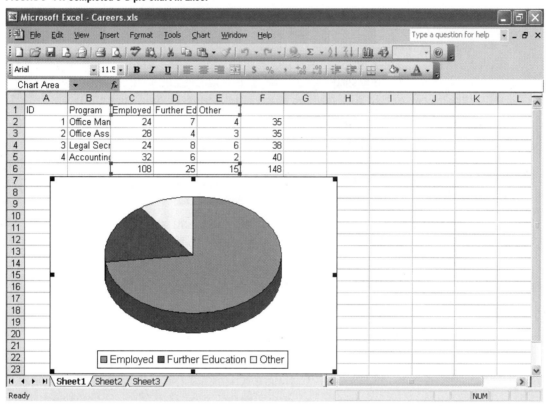

FIGURE C-12: Career Options Presentation outline

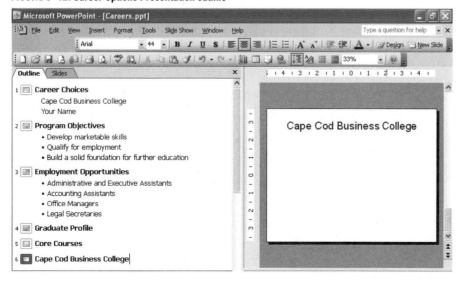

INTEGRATING WORD, EXCEL, ACCESS, AND POWERPOINT INTEGRATION C-11

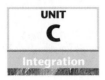

Adding Excel and Word Objects to the

ACTIVITY

Presentation

STEPS

You need to copy and modify the Excel chart, then add a table to Slide 5 and a WordArt object to Slide 6.

1. **Switch to Excel, click the** pie chart **if necessary, click the** Copy button 🔳, **switch to PowerPoint, view** Slide 4: Graduate Profile, **open the** Slide Layout task pane **if necessary, apply the** Title Only slide layout **from the Text Layouts section, click** Edit **on the menu bar, click** Paste Special, **click the** Paste link option button, **then click** OK

2. **With the chart still selected, click** Format **on the menu bar, click** Object, **click the** Picture tab, **click** Recolor, **click the** Fills option button, **click the** list arrow **next to the light blue color (you may need to scroll down), click the** yellow-green color **(the fifth color box), change the maroon slice to the** green color **(the sixth color box), click** OK, **click** OK, **then size and position the chart as shown in Figure C-13**

3. **View** Slide 5: Core Courses, **click** Insert **on the menu bar, click** Object, **click the** Create from file option button, **click** Browse, **navigate to the drive and folder where your Data Files are stored, double-click** INT C-1.doc, **then click** OK

   You embedded the table as an object in the PowerPoint file. If you wanted to change the data in the table, you could double-click the table from the PowerPoint slide and edit it using Word features. The original table stored as a Word document would not change.

4. **Size and position the table on Slide 5 as shown in Figure C-14**

5. **View** Slide 6: Cape Cod Business College, **apply the** Title Only **slide layout, click the** Insert WordArt button ◢ **on the Drawing toolbar, click the** second style in the second row, **click** OK, **type** Make Career Choices, **press** [Enter], **type** That Make Sense, **select the** Tahoma **font or a font of your choice, then click** OK

6. **Click the** Shadow Style button ⬛ **on the Drawing toolbar, click** Shadow Style 1, **then size and position the object as shown in Figure C-15**

7. **Open the** Employment table **in Access, reduce the number of Employed Accounting Assistants to** 10 **and increase the number of students in the Office Manager program who went on to Further Education to** 25, **then close the table**

8. **Switch to Excel, click** Edit **on the menu bar, click** Links, **click** Update Values, **then click** Close

9. **Print a sheet of PowerPoint handouts (six slides to the page), save and close the files in PowerPoint, Access, and Excel, then close all of the applications**

FIGURE C-13: Completed 3-D pie chart

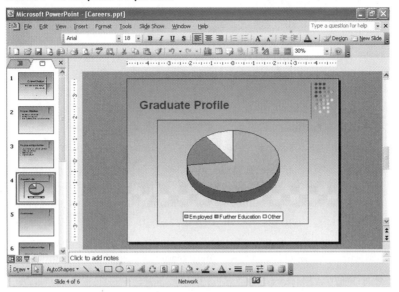

FIGURE C-14: Word table sized and positioned

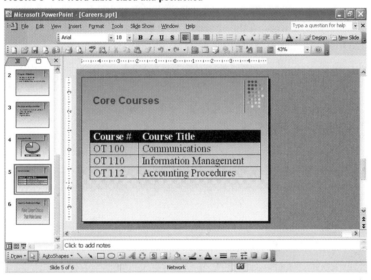

FIGURE C-15: WordArt object

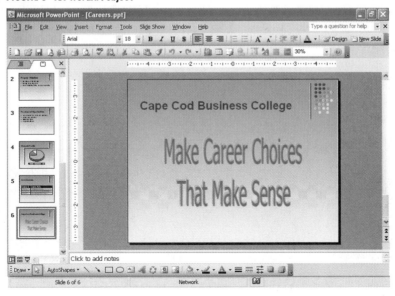

▼ INDEPENDENT CHALLENGE 1

Create an on-screen presentation of eight to 10 slides that highlights sales information and recommends marketing strategies for a company or organization of your choice. For example, you could create a presentation for a theme park that shows the revenues from 10 rides and then offers marketing suggestions for attracting more customers to the two most popular rides. Follow the steps provided to create a table in Access, charts in Excel, an outline in Word, and the presentation in PowerPoint.

    a. Start Access, create a database called **My Company Sales**, and create a table consisting of at least four fields and 10 records. Call the table *Product* **table**. Include fields in the table that you can use in charts. For example, a table for the Rides presentation could include the following fields: Ride Name, Category (for example, Extreme, Mild, Kiddie), Number of Riders, and Ride Cost.

    b. Copy the table and paste it as a link into Excel, and then save the workbook as **My Company Sales**. Create two charts that illustrate sales information about your company. For example, you could create a pie chart that shows the break-down of rides by category and a column or bar chart that demonstrates the revenue from each of the 10 rides listed in the Access table.

    c. In Word, create a new document, switch to Outline view, create the headings and subheadings for your presentation, then save it as **My Company Sales**. Refer to the presentation you created for Project 1 for ideas. Make sure to include your name in the presentation outline. Send the completed outline to PowerPoint.

    d. Apply the slide design of your choice to the presentation, and then select a new color scheme for the design.

    e. Switch to Slide Master view, and modify the appearance of the text in the placeholders.

    f. In Normal view, paste the charts as links on the appropriate slides, and format them as necessary to make them readable and attractive. Save the presentation as **My Company Sales**.

    g. Change some values in the Access table, update the charts in Excel and PowerPoint, print the presentation slides as handouts (nine slides to the page), then save and close all files.

▼ INDEPENDENT CHALLENGE 2

Create a presentation that informs an audience about a specific college course. Imagine that your audience is people interested in taking the course. Your presentation needs to inform them about the course and encourage them to enroll. If you wish, adapt the presentation you created for the Career Options project to suit the needs of a course of your choice.

    a. Create a table in Access that lists certain statistics regarding the course. For example, you could list three or four years of classes (for example, 2003, 2004, 2005) and then specify the average grade in each of three categories of evaluation (for example, Exams, Assignments, and Presentations). Save the table as **Statistics** and save the database as **My Course**.

    b. Copy the Access table to Excel as a link, save the file as **My Course**, and create one or two charts from the data.

    c. Create the presentation outline in PowerPoint and save the file as **My Course**. Make sure to include your name on the first slide. Include at least eight slides in your presentation. The information you present should inform your audience about the course and encourage their participation. Plan one or two slides for your Excel charts and one slide for a Word table. Save the Word document in which you create the table as **My Course**. Include a WordArt object on the last slide of the presentation.

    d. Change some values in the Access table, update the charts in Excel and PowerPoint, print a copy of your presentation as a handout with nine slides to a page, then save and close all files.

▼ INDEPENDENT CHALLENGE 3

Your supervisor has asked you to create a presentation that informs your coworkers at Midwest Bank about a company fitness program and encourages them to participate. Follow the instructions provided to create and then modify the presentation that you plan to give to your coworkers.

    a. In Access, create a database called **Fitness**, then create the Fitness Classes table shown in Figure C-16. Select the AutoNumber data type for the ID field and the Number data type for the Participants field.

b. In Word, create the table shown in Figure C-17, then save the document as **Fitness**. Note that the Table Contemporary AutoFormat is applied, and the font size of all the text is 16-point.

c. In PowerPoint, create the presentation shown in Figure C-18, then save it as **Fitness**. Create the chart in Excel from data copied from the Fitness Classes table in Access and pasted as a link. In Excel, you need to calculate the data required for the chart and then save the workbook as **Fitness**. Insert the Word table on Slide 5. Apply the Parchment preset background in the Gradient tab of the Fill Effects dialog box to all the slides. In Slide Master view, change the font in the Master Title Style placeholder to Comic Sans MS and bold. Search for **couples exercising** to find the clip art picture shown on Slide 6. (*Hint:* You need to be online to find this clip art. If you aren't online, use a picture of your choice.) In Access, change the number of participants in the Medium Step Aerobics classes to 75. Update the Excel and PowerPoint files if necessary.

d. Print the slides in your presentation as a handout of three slides to one page.

e. Close all open files and exit all applications.

FIGURE C-16: Fitness Classes table in Access

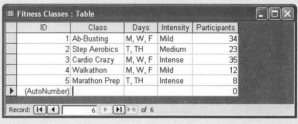

FIGURE C-17: Rewards table in Word

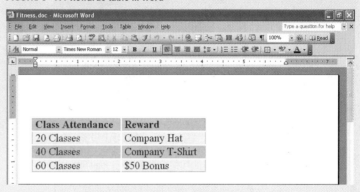

FIGURE C-18: Fitness Program presentation in Slide Sorter view

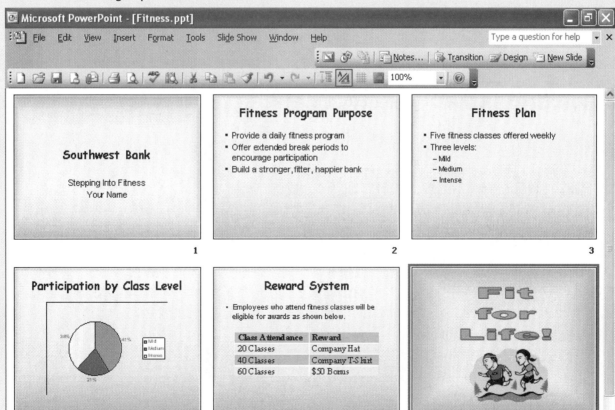

INTEGRATING WORD, EXCEL, ACCESS, AND POWERPOINT INTEGRATION C-15

▼ VISUAL WORKSHOP

For a course on tourism in France, you have decided to create a presentation that focuses on popular hotels in various locations from Paris to Nice. One of the slides in the presentation will be a pie chart that shows the breakdown of hotel guests by location. Create the Hotels table in an Access database called **Hotels**, as shown in Figure C-19, and include a primary key. Copy the table and paste it as a link into Excel, then create a pie chart that shows the number of guests at each location (for example, Arles, Nice, etc.). Start PowerPoint, select the Title Only slide layout, then copy the pie chart and paste it as a link onto the first slide. Add a title to the slide, apply the Digital Dots slide design, select the light gray color scheme, and then insert the clip art image. (*Hint*: Search for **France**. Your clip art may vary.) Switch to Access, change the number of guests who stayed at the Hotel Champs de Mars in Paris to 600, switch to Excel, update the link so that the Paris slice increases to 53%, switch to PowerPoint, compare the slide to Figure C-20, then put **Your Name** in the slide footer. (*Hint*: Use the Header and Footer command on the View menu.) Print a copy of the slide. Save the PowerPoint and Excel files as **Hotels**, then close the files and exit all applications.

FIGURE C-19: Hotels table

FIGURE C-20: Completed slide

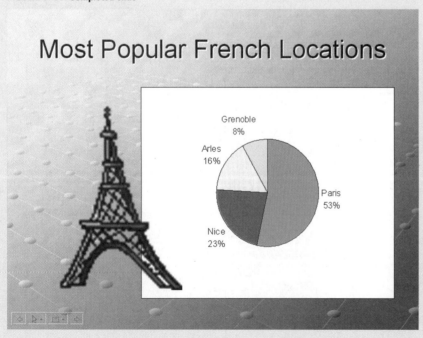

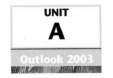

Getting Started with Outlook 2003

OBJECTIVES

Understand e-mail
Start Outlook 2003
View the Outlook 2003 window
Add a contact to the Address Book
Create and send a new message
Reply to and forward messages
Send a message with an attachment
Create a distribution list
Send a message to a distribution list

If you have a SAM user profile, you may have access to hands-on instruction, practice, and assessment of the skills covered in this unit. Log in to your SAM account and go to your assignments page to see what your instructor has assigned.

Microsoft Office Outlook 2003 is an integrated desktop information management program that lets you manage your personal and business information and communicate with others. Using Outlook, you can manage your e-mail, appointments, contacts, tasks, notes, and files. In this unit, you will learn how to use the e-mail features of Outlook. You are a marketing assistant at MediaLoft, a chain of bookstore cafés that sells books, CDs, and movies. MediaLoft wants to create a new series of designs for shopping bags and packaging based on its logo. Your manager, Alice Wegman, has asked you to organize a meeting of design and sales professionals to review the suggested design changes. You will use Outlook 2003 to communicate with the team and Alice.

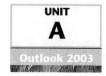

Understanding E-mail

E-mail software lets you send and receive electronic messages, or **e-mail**, over a network, within an intranet, and through the Internet. A **computer network** is the hardware and software that makes it possible for two or more computers to share information and resources. An **intranet** is a computer network that connects computers in a local area only, such as computers in a company's office. The **Internet** is a network of connected computers and computer networks located around the world. Figure A-1 illustrates how e-mail messages can travel over a network. ◄▅▅▅ MediaLoft employees use e-mail to communicate with each other and with clients because it is fast, reliable, and easy.

DETAILS

The benefits of using e-mail include:

- **Provides a convenient and efficient way to communicate**

  E-mail is an effective way to communicate with coworkers or colleagues who are located in different places. You can send and receive messages whenever you wish. Unlike communication by telephone, recipients do not have to be at their computers at the same time that you send a message to receive it. E-mail uses **store-and-forward technology**: messages are *stored* on a service provider's computer until a recipient logs on to a computer and requests his or her messages. At that time, the messages are *forwarded* to the recipient's computer.

- **Allows you to send large amounts of information**

  Your messages can be as long as you wish, and you can also attach a file (such as a spreadsheet, image, or word-processing document) to a message.

- **Lets you communicate with several people at once**

  You can create your own electronic address book that stores the names and e-mail addresses of the people with whom you frequently communicate. You can then send the same message to multiple individuals at one time.

- **Ensures delivery of information**

  With Outlook, you have the option of receiving a notification message when a recipient receives and reads your e-mail, if you and the recipient of the message are connected to the same network. If you are away and unable to access e-mail because of a vacation or other plans, you can also set up an automatic message so senders are alerted to the fact that you might not receive your mail for a specified time period.

- **Lets you communicate from a remote place**

  If you have an Internet connection and communications software, you can connect your computer at home to the computers at your office. This gives you the flexibility to send and receive messages when you are not at the office. You can also sign up with an ISP (Internet service provider) and send e-mail to people on the Internet. You can connect to the Internet using a telephone line or other, faster technologies including satellite, DSL (Digital Subscriber Line), cable, ISDN (Integrated Services Digital Network), T1, or T3.

- **Provides a record of communications**

  You can organize the messages you send and receive in a way that best suits your working style. Organizing your saved messages lets you keep a record of communications, which can be very valuable in managing a project or business. You can also flag messages to give an instant visual cue that distinguishes those messages that require immediate attention from those that can wait.

- **Allows you to store information**

  You can store e-mail messages in folders and refer to them again in the future. Unlike paper mail, which can be lost or damaged, e-mail is safely stored on your computer. Just like any other files you store on your computer, make sure you regularly back up the drive where your Outlook files are stored.

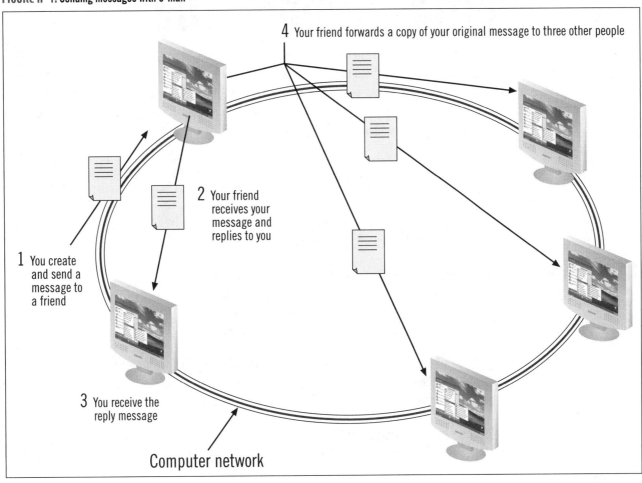

4 Your friend forwards a copy of your original message to three other people

2 Your friend receives your message and replies to you

1 You create and send a message to a friend

3 You receive the reply message

Computer network

Clues to Use

Electronic mail etiquette

When you compose a message, take extra care in what you say and how you say it. The recipient of your message doesn't have the benefit of seeing your body language or hearing the tone of your voice to interpret what you are saying. For example, using all capital letters in the text of a message is the e-mail equivalent of shouting and is not appropriate. Carefully consider the content of your message before you send it, and don't send confidential or sensitive material.

Remember, once you send a message, you might not be able to prevent it from being delivered. If your e-mail account is a company account, it's a good idea to learn whether your company permits the sending of personal messages. All messages you send have been legally interpreted as property of the company for which you work, so don't assume that your messages are private.

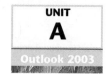

Starting Outlook 2003

Before you can create, send, or read messages, you must start Outlook. Depending on how your e-mail system is set up, you may be prompted to choose a profile during the startup process. A **profile** is a set of information used to identify individual e-mail users. Profiles allow more than one user to have individual e-mail accounts on the same computer and are common in classroom environments. ▰▰ You need to start Outlook in order to send an e-mail message to Alice.

STEPS

1. **Click the** Start button ▱ start **on the taskbar, point to** All Programs, **then point to** Microsoft Office

   Outlook is in the Microsoft Office submenu on the All Programs menu. See Figure A-2. You can also click the Launch Microsoft Outlook icon ▱ on the Quick Launch toolbar to start Outlook.

TROUBLE

If the Choose Profile dialog box opens, click the Profile Name list arrow to select your profile, then click OK. If you don't know which profile to use, or if you have not created a profile and cannot start Outlook, ask your technical support person for assistance.

2. **Click** Microsoft Office Outlook 2003

   Outlook starts and displays one of its many views. Outlook has eight modules: Mail, Calendar, Contacts, Tasks, Notes, Folder List, Shortcuts, and Journal. Your installation may be set up to start in Outlook Today, or possibly in Outlook Mail with the Navigation Pane displayed.

3. **Click the** Mail icon ▱ **in the Outlook Navigation Pane if it is not already selected**

   The Outlook window shows Mail selected. Depending on the settings on your computer, the icons in the Navigation Pane may include text or be stacked vertically rather than placed horizontally.

4. **Click** Inbox **in the Navigation Pane**

   Refer to Figure A-3. The **Inbox** folder is the folder in Outlook that stores all incoming e-mail messages.

TROUBLE

If there is no check mark next to one or both of these items, click the item on the View menu to display it in the Outlook Window.

5. **Click** View **on the menu bar**

   The View menu should show a check mark next to Navigation Pane and Status Bar.

6. **Point to** Reading Pane **on the View menu, then click** Right **to select it if it isn't already selected**

   The View menu closes. Your screen should look like Figure A-3.

FIGURE A-2: Starting Outlook 2003

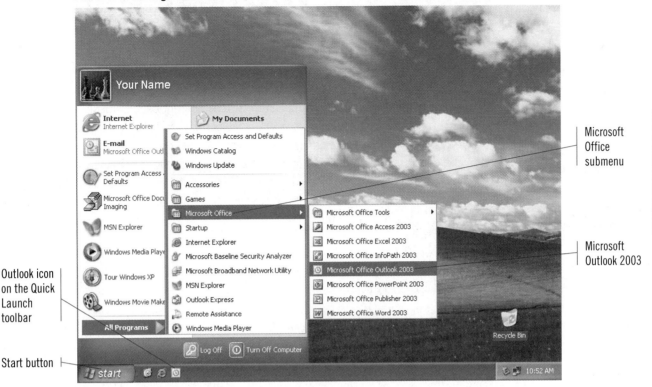

Outlook icon on the Quick Launch toolbar

Start button

Microsoft Office submenu

Microsoft Outlook 2003

FIGURE A-3: Outlook Mail

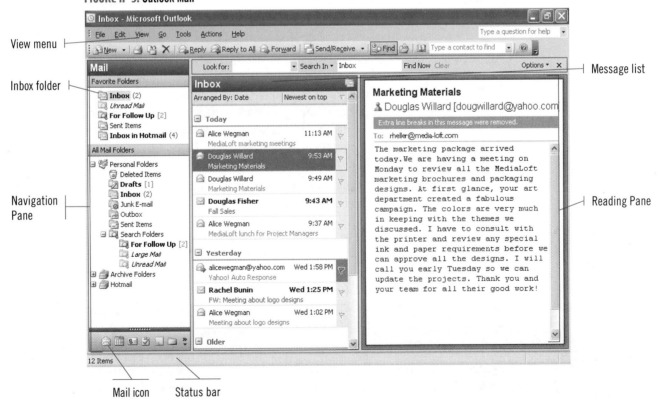

View menu

Inbox folder

Navigation Pane

Mail icon   Status bar

Message list

Reading Pane

GETTING STARTED WITH OUTLOOK   OUTLOOK A-5

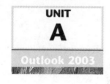
Viewing the Outlook 2003 Window

Outlook is a personal information manager. Outlook uses several types of basic elements, called **items**, to store information. These include appointments, contacts, tasks, journal entries, notes, and documents. You will use Outlook to manage e-mail. To begin to understand the many features of Outlook, and how to use Outlook to send and receive e-mail, you need to understand how each part of the Outlook window works. Figure A-4 shows the Outlook Mail window with the Inbox displayed. ▓▓▓▓▓ A new message has arrived for Ruth from Alice, a design specialist. Read the details in this lesson to learn about the various elements of the window.

DETAILS

- At the top of the window, the **title bar** contains the name of the open Outlook folder you are viewing, in this case it is the Inbox folder, and the name of the program is Microsoft Outlook. When you double-click an e-mail message to open it in a new window, the subject of the message appears in the title bar.

- The **menu bar** (as in all Windows programs) contains the names of the menus. Clicking a menu name on the menu bar displays a list of related commands.

- The **Standard toolbar** contains buttons that give you quick access to the most frequently used commands, such as New Mail Message, Reply, Forward, Print, Find, and Delete. You can also access your Address Book from the Standard toolbar by clicking the Address Book button or by entering a contact name in the Find a Contact text box. Outlook searches for the contact, then displays the contact window for that person.

QUICK TIP
The Navigation Pane can be customized to display some or all of the icons with text.

- The **Navigation Pane** displays the folders you can use to organize your e-mail. **Favorite Folders** are those folders you use most often, so they are readily accessible in the Navigation Pane. In Figure A-4, the Inbox folder is currently open. To open a different folder, you simply click the folder icon. When you click a folder, the contents of the folder are displayed to the right of the Navigation Pane in the Message list. The bottom of the Navigation Pane provides icons for navigating to Mail, Calendar, Contacts, Tasks, Notes, Journal, Shortcuts, and Folders.

- The **Inbox folder** contains all the messages that are sent to you. New messages always arrive in the Inbox. The **Outbox** stores any unsent messages that you write. Once you click the Send button, messages are no longer in the Outbox and may be copied to the Sent Items folder. By default, a copy of each e-mail that you send is stored in the **Sent Items** folder. The **Search Folders** are a tool for organizing your e-mail; instead of actually containing messages, these folders provide shortcuts to messages based on criteria you specify. The **Deleted Items folder** contains messages you have deleted. Deleted Items are available until you specifically empty the Deleted Items folder through a series of menu commands.

QUICK TIP
If you are using Hotmail or another Web-based e-mail provider, you may have a separate Inbox in the Folders list.

- When the Inbox folder is open, the **Inbox** shows a list of message headers for the e-mails you have received. Each **message header** identifies the sender of the message, the subject, the date and time the message was received, and the size of the message. Message headers of unread messages appear in boldface. The number of unread messages in a folder appears in parentheses to the right of the folder in the Navigation Pane. Outlook groups and organizes the messages in the Inbox and other folders. By default, messages are arranged by date with the newest message on top. You can click Arranged by to change the grouping to the other options, which include Conversation, From, To, Size, Subject, Type, Flag, Attachments, E-mail Account, Importance, and Categories.

- **Message header icons** appear in message headers, identifying the attributes of the message. For example, an icon that looks like a closed envelope indicates that the message has not been read. See Table A-1 for a description of some of the icons that may appear next to a message.

- The **Reading Pane** provides a vertical window in which you can preview the selected e-mail message. You use the Reading Pane to read and scroll through messages without opening them in a new window. You double-click a message to open it in a new window.

- The **status bar** at the bottom of the window indicates the total number of messages that the open folder contains, as well as the number of messages that have not been read.

FIGURE A-4: The Outlook Mail window

Title bar

Menu bar

Standard toolbar

Messages arranged by date

Two unread messages

Outlook 2003

Folders

Navigation Pane

Reading Pane

Drag to display buttons with text

Navigation Pane buttons

Status bar

Unread message icon

Read Message icon

Message header

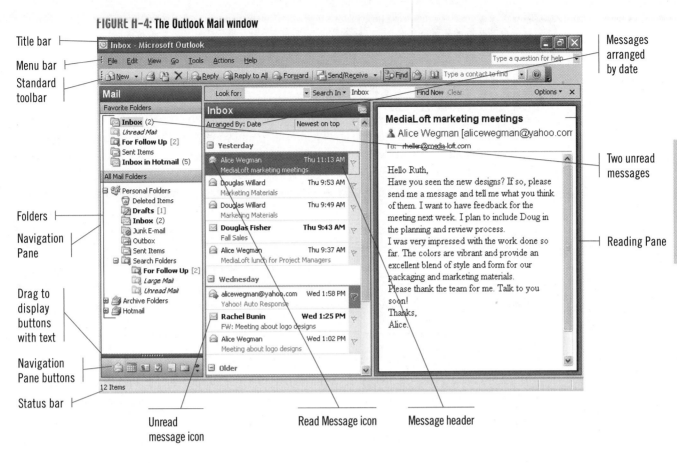

TABLE A-1: Message header icons

icon	description
	High-priority message
	Low-priority message
	Unread message
	Read message
	Forwarded message
	Replied to message
	Message has an attachment
	Flagged message (flag can be red, blue, yellow, green, orange, or purple)
	Flag on message is complete

Adding a Contact to the Address Book

You can add the names and e-mail addresses of people to whom you frequently send e-mail messages to the Address Book in Outlook. Outlook refers to your Address Book entries as "contacts," and places them in a folder called Contacts. When you create a new contact, you type the person's full name and e-mail address. You are given the option of entering additional information about that person, including his or her personal and business mailing address, telephone number, mobile phone number, Web page, Instant Message address, and even a picture. Adding a contact to your Address Book saves you from having to type someone's e-mail address each time you want to send a message. It also reduces the chance that your message will not be delivered because you typed the e-mail address incorrectly. ░░░░ Since you'll be corresponding with Alice frequently, you create a contact for her in your Address Book. You also decide to create contacts for Ruth Heller and Ramon Valdez, MediaLoft colleagues, since they will eventually be involved in the logo design project.

STEPS

QUICK TIP

The Address Book is also available if you click Tools on the menu bar, then click Address Book.

1. **Click the Address Book button 📖 on the Standard toolbar**

   The Address Book opens. The Address Book shown in Figure A-5 does not contain any contacts. The Address Book on your screen may already have entries.

2. **Click the New Entry button 🗐 on the Address Book toolbar**

   The New Entry dialog box opens. The default settings are to add a New Contact as the entry type and to put the entry in the Contacts folder.

3. **Make sure New Contact is selected, then click OK**

   The Untitled Contact window opens, as shown in Figure A-6. The General and Details tabs in the Contact window contain fields into which you can enter information about each contact. The General tab, which displays the basic contact information, is displayed by default.

QUICK TIP

Click the Full Name button in the Contact window to open the Check Full Name dialog box and create a contact with a Title, First name, Middle name, Last name, and Suffix.

4. **Type Alice Wegman in the Full Name text box, click the E-mail text box, type alicewegman@yahoo.com, then press [Tab]**

   Outlook recognizes Alice as the first name and Wegman as the last name, as entered in the Full Name text box. If Outlook had been unsure of the name because of a nontraditional entry, such as just one name, the Check Full Name dialog box would have opened to give you an opportunity to verify the entry. Alice's name and e-mail address appear in the Display as text box, as shown in Figure A-7. You can edit the Display as text box to change the way a name is displayed in the message header of an e-mail message.

5. **Click the Save and Close button 🗐 Save and Close on the Contact window Standard toolbar**

   Alice Wegman is added as a new contact in the Address Book.

6. **Click 🗐 on the Address Book toolbar, then click OK**

   A new Untitled Contact window opens.

7. **Type Ruth Heller in the Full Name text box, type your e-mail address in the E-mail text box, then click 🗐 Save and Close**

   Ruth Heller is added to the Address Book with your e-mail address.

8. **Click 🗐 on the Address Book toolbar, click OK, type Ramon Valdez in the Full Name text box, type your e-mail address in the E-mail text box, click 🗐 Save and Close, click the Add this as a new contact anyway option button in the Duplicate Contact Detected dialog box, then click OK**

   Ramon Valdez is also added to your Address Book.

9. **Click the Close button on the Address Book window title bar**

   The Address Book closes and you return to the Inbox.

FIGURE A-5: Address Book

New Entry button

Address Book
toolbar

Names from Contacts
will be listed here

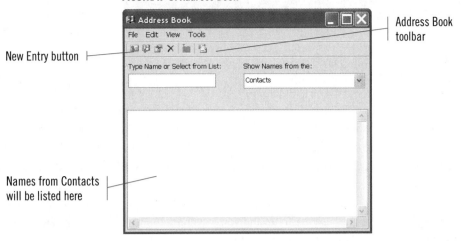

FIGURE A-6: Untitled Contact Window

Contact window
Standard toolbar

Full Name text box

E-mail text box

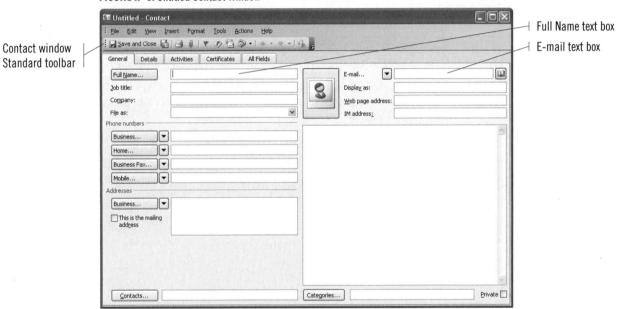

FIGURE A-7: Alice Wegman Contact window

Alice Wegman in
title bar

Full Name button

Shows how address
is displayed in
message header

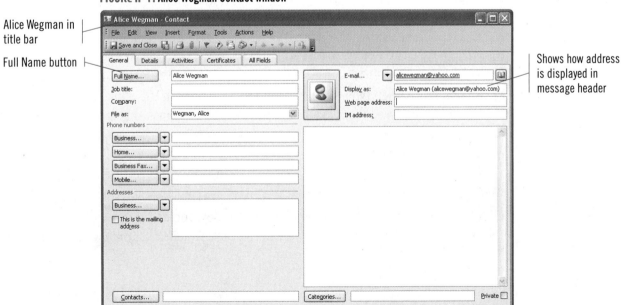

Outlook 2003

Creating and Sending New Messages

When you create an e-mail message, you must indicate to whom you are sending the message and specify any other people who should receive a copy. You also need to enter a meaningful subject for the message to give its recipients an idea of its content. You write the text of your message in the message body. After you create the message, you then send it. Outlook 2003 uses Microsoft Word as the default text editor, which means that you have access to the same text-formatting features in Outlook that you use when you create Word documents. You can change the color of text or use different fonts in your message, you can create a bulleted list within your e-mail message, and you can check the spelling of your message easily. 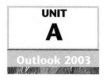 You are ready to write and send a message to Alice and Ramon about an upcoming meeting. You've already invited an international marketing expert, Doug Willard, to the meeting. You also send him a copy of the message to remind him about it.

STEPS

1. **Click the New Mail Message button 🔲 New on the Standard toolbar**

   A new Untitled Message window opens, as shown in Figure A-8. You can type the recipient's e-mail address in the To text box, or click the To button to select a contact from the Select Names dialog box.

2. **Click the To button 🔲 To...**

   The Select Names dialog box opens, listing names from the Contacts folder of the Address Book. You can see the three entries that you added to the Contacts folder.

> **QUICK TIP**
> You can add more than one contact to the list of Message Recipients at the same time by clicking the first contact, pressing [CTRL], clicking the rest of the contacts, then clicking the To button.

3. **Double-click Alice Wegman in the Name list**

   The Display As name for Alice Wegman (her full name followed by her e-mail address) is placed in the list of Message Recipients, in the To text box.

4. **Click Ramon Valdez in the Name list, then click the Bcc button in the Message Recipients list**

   The Select Names dialog box looks like Figure A-9.

5. **Click OK**

   The Select Names dialog box closes. You can send e-mail to recipients even if they are not already in your Address Book by typing an e-mail address directly in the Message window.

6. **Click the Cc text box in the Untitled Message window, then type dougwillard@yahoo.com**

   Cc stands for courtesy copy. **Courtesy copies** are typically sent to message recipients who need to be aware of the correspondence between the sender and the recipients. **Bcc**, or **blind courtesy copy**, is used when the sender does not want to reveal who he or she has sent courtesy copies to. Message headers include the Display As names and e-mail addresses of To and Cc recipients, but not of Bcc recipients.

7. **Press [Tab] twice, then type Meeting about logo designs in the Subject text box**

   The Subject text box should be a brief statement that indicates the purpose of your message.

8. **Press [Tab] to place the insertion point in the message body, then type the body of the message, as shown in Figure A-10**

   The message is complete. The subject appears in the title bar of the Message window. You can see that the Word spelling feature has identified the word "MediaLoft" as a possible spelling error.

9. **Click the Send button 🔲 Send on the Message window toolbar**

   The message is sent, the Message window closes, and Outlook stores a copy of the message in your Sent Items folder.

FIGURE A-8: Untitled Message window

Button appears if more than one e-mail account is set up

To button

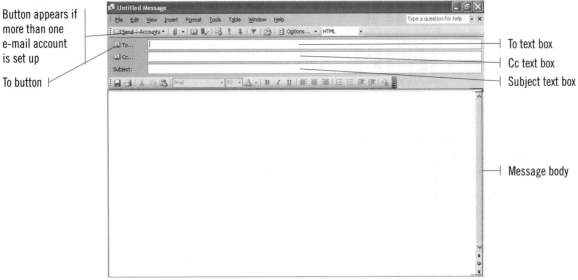

To text box

Cc text box

Subject text box

Message body

FIGURE A-9: Select Names dialog box

Names in the Contacts folder

Message recipients list

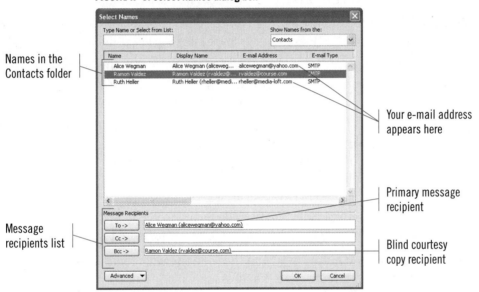

Your e-mail address appears here

Primary message recipient

Blind courtesy copy recipient

FIGURE A-10: Creating a message

Subject in title bar

Message window toolbar

Message recipients

Message body

Subject text box

E-mail toolbar

Replying to and Forwarding Messages

To read a message that arrives in your Inbox, you can select it, then preview it in the Reading Pane. To open the message in its own window, you can double-click the message header, or right-click the message header, then click Open from the shortcut menu. After reading a message, you can delete it, move it to another folder, flag it for follow-up, or keep it in your Inbox. You can also send a response back to the sender of the message. Clicking the Reply button on the Standard toolbar automatically addresses the e-mail to the original sender and includes the text of the original sender's message in the message body. You can also forward a message that you have received to another person by clicking the Forward button. 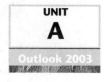 Alice responds that she will be unavailable. You reply to her and forward her message to Doug, to let him know the meeting is off for now.

STEPS

TROUBLE
If you are using Web-based e-mail, you may have to click a different Inbox folder in the Favorites section or in the All Mail Folders section.

1. **Click the Send/Receive button** ⊟Send/Receive **on the Standard toolbar**
   Outlook checks for any messages in the Outbox that need to be sent and delivers messages to your Inbox.

2. **Click the Inbox folder in the Favorite Folders section of the Navigation Pane**
   A message from Alice Wegman appears in the Inbox window, as shown in Figure A-11.

3. **Click the message from alicewegman@yahoo.com in the Inbox to select it**
   Alice's message appears in the Reading Pane. Alice is out of the office and has set up an automatic response through her e-mail service. Your original message is quoted below the automatic response message.

TROUBLE
Yahoo! mail only sends one Auto Response to each sender. If you send more than one message to Alice's e-mail address from the same e-mail address, you will only get one Yahoo! Auto Response message back.

4. **Double-click the message from alicewegman@yahoo.com, then click the Reply button** ⊜Reply
   A new Message window for replying opens. The message is addressed back to Alice. The subject line is preceded by "RE:", indicating that the message is a reply. Information about the original message appears in the Message window above the original message from Alice. The insertion point is at the top of the message body.

5. **Type I will call you next week to reschedule.**
   See Figure A-12. You are now ready to send your reply back to Alice.

6. **Click the Send button** ⊟Send **on the Message window toolbar, then click the Message window Close button to close the message**
   The message is sent and a copy of it is stored in your Sent Items folder. The Mail window displays the messages in the Inbox. The Replied to Message icon ⊜ appears next to the original message from alicewegman@yahoo.com, indicating that you have replied to the message.

QUICK TIP
You can reply simultaneously to the sender of an e-mail message and everyone to whom the original message was sent by clicking the Reply to All button on the Standard toolbar.

7. **Click the message from alicewegman@yahoo.com in the Inbox, then click the Forward button** ⊜Forward **on the Standard toolbar**
   A new Message window for forwarding Alice's message opens. The subject line is preceded by "FW:", indicating that the message is a forwarded message. There are no addresses in the To or Cc boxes yet.

8. **Type dougwillard@yahoo.com in the To text box, then press [Enter]**
   You are forwarding a copy of Alice's message to Doug Willard. AutoComplete fills in an address as you type when it recognizes it as unique. You can press Enter to accept the address you want after AutoComplete suggests it.

9. **Click the top of the message body, type Doug, I have to cancel the meeting for now. I will call you next week., click** ⊟Send, **then click** ⊟Send/Receive
   The message is sent to Doug, and a copy of it is stored in your Sent Items folder. The Forwarded Message icon ⊜ now appears next to the message in the Inbox.

10. **Click the Flag icon for the message from alicewegman@yahoo.com**
    The flag turns red. The message is marked for follow-up so you know you still have to arrange the meeting. The number next to the For Follow Up folder in the Favorites Folder list has increased by one.

FIGURE A-11: Inbox with message from Alice

Messages in the Inbox organized by date

Inbox folder in Favorite Folders section

All mail folders

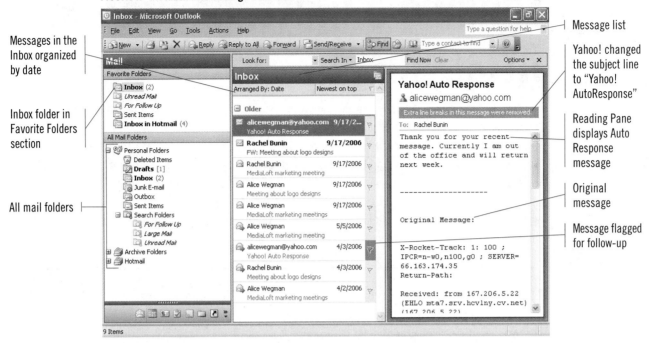

Message list

Yahoo! changed the subject line to "Yahoo! AutoResponse"

Reading Pane displays Auto Response message

Original message

Message flagged for follow-up

Outlook 2003

9 Items

FIGURE A-12: Replying to a message

Subject includes RE: prefix

Your reply message to Alice

Details of message from Alice

Alice's Auto Response message

Your original message to Alice

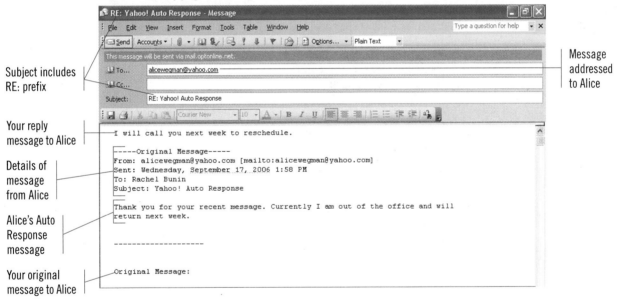

Message addressed to Alice

Clues to Use

Flagging messages

If you use e-mail for business, school, or personal communication, you will find that you receive many e-mail messages. Some can be read and discarded. Others require additional attention or follow-up. Organizing your e-mail can help you keep up with the many messages you are likely to receive. Quick Flags can assist you in your effort to manage your e-mail. If you click the flag icon next to the message, it is marked by default with a red Quick Flag. However, you can use flags of multiple colors to mark messages for different categories of follow-up. Flags are available in red, blue, yellow, green, orange, or purple. To apply a flag, click Actions on the menu bar, point to Follow Up, then click the colored flag you want to use to categorize the message. You can also right-click the message, then point to Follow Up to apply a flag. To select from a list of flag actions and specify a due date in the Flag for Follow Up dialog box, right-click a message, point to Follow Up, then click Add Reminder. The For Follow Up folder always contains an up-to-date list of all Quick Flagged messages in every folder in your mailbox.

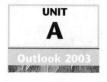
Sending a Message with an Attachment

In addition to composing a message by typing in the Message window to send an e-mail message to a coworker or friend, you can **attach** a file to an e-mail message. For example, in an office environment, employees can attach Word or Excel documents to e-mail messages so that other employees can open them, make changes to them, and then return them to the original sender or forward them. You can attach any type of computer file to an e-mail message, including pictures, video clips, and audio clips. The recipient needs the appropriate software in order to open an attachment. You have received some design samples for the logos. You would like Alice to review these when she returns to the office. You send her an e-mail message and attach two image files to the message.

STEPS

1. **Click the** New Mail Message button 📧 New **on the Standard toolbar**
   A new Untitled Message window opens.

TROUBLE
If you have other contacts that begin with "Ali," continue typing Alice's name until Outlook recognizes your entry.

2. **Type** Ali **in the To text box, then press** Enter
   Outlook recognizes the first three letters of the Alice Wegman contact and fills in the rest of her e-mail address.

3. **Press** [Tab] **twice, then type** Logo Samples **in the Subject text box**
   The subject indicates the topic of the e-mail message.

4. **Click the** Insert File button 📎 **on the Message window toolbar**
   The Insert File dialog box opens. Files are shown in List view, but you can use Thumbnails view to see what the files you are going to attach look like.

5. **Click the** Views button list arrow 📅 ▾, **click** Thumbnails, **click the** Look in list arrow, **then locate the drive and folder where your Data Files are stored, as shown in Figure A-13**
   There are three Data Files for this unit; logo1.jpg and logo2.jpg are the image files that you want to send to Alice.

6. **Click** logo1.jpg, **press and hold** [Shift], **click** logo2.jpg, **then click** Insert
   The logo1.jpg and logo2.jpg files appear in the Attach text box, as shown in Figure A-14. The icon next to each filename indicates that each is an image file, and the numbers in parentheses next to the filenames specify the size of each file.

7. **Click the** Attachment Options button 📎 Attachment Options... **to open the Attachment Options task pane, if necessary**
   The Attachment Options task pane opens on the right side of the window.

TROUBLE
Attachments such as video clips or picture files may be too large in file size for some e-mail systems to handle.

8. **Verify that** Don't resize, send originals **appears in the Picture options section of the Attachment Options task pane, then click the** Close button **in the Attachment Options task pane**
   You don't want to resize the logo because you want Alice to see the exact design. If you were sending a large file, you might consider resizing the picture to facilitate delivery.

9. **Click the** message body, **type** Alice, I am attaching two sample designs., **then click the** Send button 📧 Send **on the Message window toolbar**
   The message, along with the two image files, is sent, and a copy of the message is stored in your Sent Items folder.

FIGURE A-13: Insert File dialog box

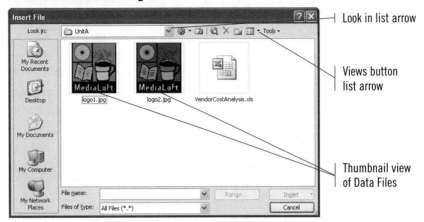

Look in list arrow

Views button list arrow

Thumbnail view of Data Files

FIGURE A-14: Attaching a file

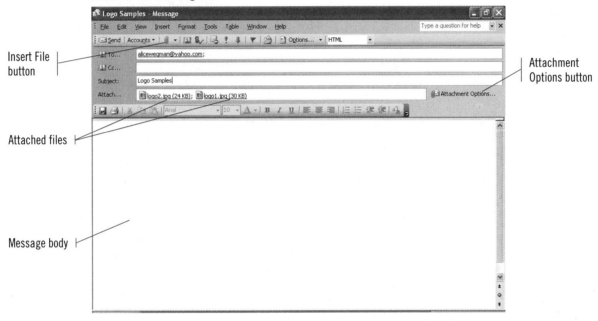

Insert File button

Attached files

Message body

Attachment Options button

Clues to Use

Options when sending messages

In Outlook, there are several options that affect how messages are delivered. To change these options, click the Options button on the Message window toolbar to open the Message Options dialog box shown in Figure A-15. You can, for example, assign a level of importance and a level of sensitivity so that the reader can prioritize messages. You can also encrypt the message for privacy. If both the Sender and Recipient are using Outlook, you can add Voting buttons to your message for recipients to use in responding. In addition, when you want to know when a message has been received or read, you can select the Request a delivery receipt for this message check box or the Request a read receipt for this message check box. You can also specify a future date for delivering a message, if the timing of the message is important. Lastly, if you want replies to your message to be sent to a different e-mail address than your own, you can click the Have replies sent to check box and then specify a new destination address for replies.

FIGURE A-15: Message Options dialog box

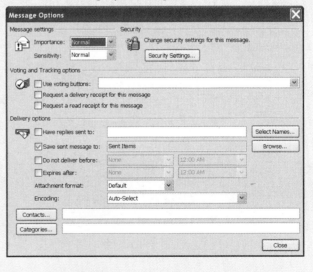

Creating a Distribution List

When using Outlook to communicate with friends or coworkers, you may find that you need to send messages to the same group of people on a regular basis. If your Contacts folder contains many contacts, it can be time consuming to scroll through all the names to select the ones you want, and you might forget to include someone in an important message. Fortunately, Outlook provides an easy way to group your contacts. You can create a **distribution list**, which is a collection of contacts to whom you want to send the same messages. For example, if you send messages reminding your staff of a weekly meeting, you can create a distribution list called "Team" that contains the names of your staff. When you want to send a message to everyone on the team, you simply select Team from the Select Names dialog box, instead of selecting each user's name individually. When created, distribution lists are automatically added to the Contacts folder. You will be sending a lot of information about the logo design project to Alice, Ramon, and Ruth. You decide to create a distribution list containing their e-mail addresses. You name the distribution list "Design Team."

STEPS

1. **Click the** Address Book button 📖 **on the Standard toolbar, then click the** New Entry button 🖼 **on the Address Book toolbar**

   The New Entry dialog box opens. You can choose New Contact or a New Distribution List from the New Entry dialog box.

2. **Click** New Distribution List, **then verify that** Contacts **appears in the Put this entry In the text box, as shown in Figure A-16**

   The new distribution list will be placed in the Contacts folder, along with your other contacts.

3. **Click** OK

   The Untitled Distribution List window opens. The Members tab is selected.

4. **Type** Design Team **in the Name text box, as shown in Figure A-17, then click the** Select Members button

   The Select Members dialog box opens. It displays the contacts in your Contacts folder, alphabetically by the first name. From this list, you select the names to include in the distribution list.

QUICK TIP

If the names in the Select Members dialog box you want are contiguous, click the first name, press and hold [Shift], then click the last name to select all the names in the list.

5. **Click** Alice Wegman, **press and hold** [Ctrl], **click** Ramon Valdez, **click** Ruth Heller, **then release** [Ctrl]

   Your Select Members dialog box should look similar to Figure A-18. Using [Ctrl] lets you select noncontiguous (nontouching) names in the list.

6. **Click the** Members button

   The three names appear in the Add to distribution list Members text box. Names are separated by semicolons.

7. **Click** OK

   The Design Team Distribution List dialog box is complete. You can easily see who will get mail that is sent to the Design Team distribution list, and you can add new members or remove members. You could also click the Notes tab to write information to help describe the purpose of the list.

8. **Click the** Save and Close button 🖫 Save and Close **on the Distribution List window Standard toolbar**

   The Design Team distribution list appears alphabetically in the Address Book, as shown in Figure A-19. A Distribution List icon precedes the name of each distribution list.

9. **Close the Address Book**

   The Address Book closes, and you return to the Outlook Inbox.

FIGURE A-16: New Entry dialog box

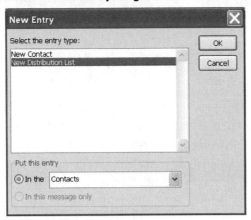

FIGURE A-17: Untitled Distribution List window

Name of distribution list —|

Select Members button —|

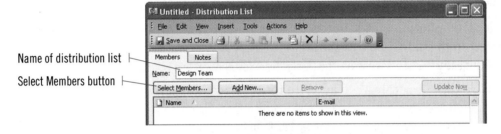

FIGURE A-18: Select Members dialog box

Selected contacts —|

Members button —|

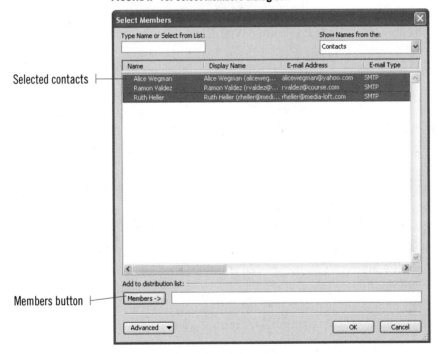

FIGURE A-19: Design Team distribution list in Address Book

Distribution List icon —|

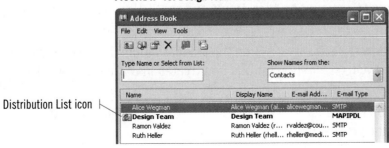

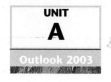
Sending a Message to a Distribution List

Distribution lists make it possible for you to send a message to the same group, without having to select each contact in the group. Once a distribution list is created, you can add new members to it or delete members from it, as necessary. If you change information about a contact who is part of a distribution list, the distribution list is automatically updated. ████ A new meeting for the whole design team has been scheduled. You want to send the agenda for the meeting to everyone who will be attending. You compose a message and send it to the Design Team distribution list.

1. **Click the** New Mail Message button ⧆ New **on the Standard toolbar**

2. **Click the** To button ⧆ To... **in the Message window, then type** d **in the Type Name or Select from List text box, as shown in Figure A-20**
   The first entry that starts with "d", the Design Team distribution list, is highlighted.

3. **Double-click** Design Team **to add it to the Message Recipients list, then click** OK
   The Select Names dialog box closes. The Design Team distribution list is added to the To text box in the Message window. The Expand button next to the Design Team name gives you the option of expanding the list. If you expand the list, it replaces the list name with the members of the list. You cannot collapse an expanded list.

4. **Type** Design meeting agenda **in the Subject text box, press** [Tab], **type** 9am–10am: Review design samples, **press** [Enter], **type** 10am–11:30am: Review vendor proposals, **then press** [Enter]
   Your screen should resemble Figure A-21. When you send this message, it will go to all the members on the Design Team distribution list.

5. **Type your first and last name below the meeting agenda in the message body, click** File **on the menu bar, click** Print, **verify the settings in the Print dialog box, then click** OK
   You plan to tape the printed agenda to your bulletin board in your office.

6. **Click the** Send button ⧆ Send **in the Message window, click the** Send/Receive button ⧆ Send/Receive **on the Standard toolbar, then click the** Inbox folder **in the Navigation Pane**
   The message is sent to the distribution list. You received your copy. It is important to know how to clear out your Inbox and the various folders in Outlook. You need to delete the messages created in this unit.

7. **Click the** first message **you received in the Inbox, press and hold** [Ctrl], **click** each message **received in the Inbox as you completed this unit, then click the** Delete button ✕ **on the Standard toolbar**
   The messages in the Inbox are now in the Deleted Items folder. You can access messages in the Deleted Items folder as long as it has not been emptied. Every message you sent as you completed this unit was saved in the Sent Items folder.

8. **Click the** Sent Items folder **in the Favorite Folders section of the Navigation Pane, select all the messages you sent to Alice, Doug, and the Design Team, then click** ✕
   The messages in the Sent Items folder are placed in the Deleted Items folder.

9. **Click the** Address Book button ⧆ **on the Standard toolbar, press and hold** [Ctrl], **click each contact and distribution list that you created in this unit, click** ✕, **then close the Address Book**

10. **Click** Tools **on the menu bar, click** Empty "Deleted Items" Folder, **click** Yes, **click** File **on the menu bar, then click** Exit **to exit Outlook**

FIGURE A-20: Selecting the distribution list

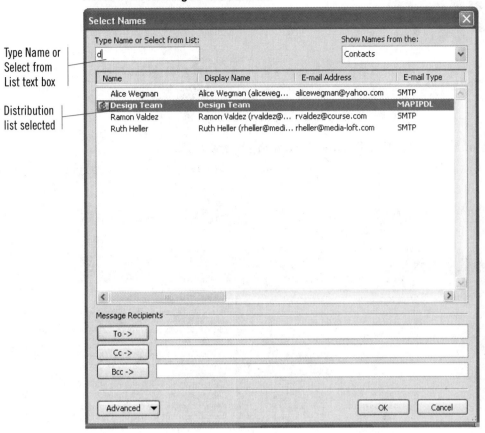

Type Name or Select from List text box

Distribution list selected

FIGURE A-21: Message addressed to Design Team

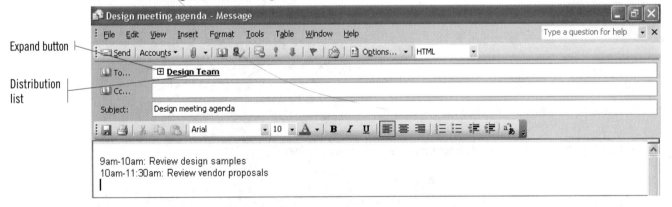

Expand button

Distribution list

Clues to Use

What is Microsoft Outlook Express?

Microsoft Outlook Express is a program that you can use to exchange e-mail and join newsgroups. It comes with Windows XP. It focuses primarily on e-mail, so it does not have the other modules of Outlook. However, after you learn how to use the e-mail capabilities of Outlook, you could apply those skills to Outlook Express.

Practice

▼ CONCEPTS REVIEW

Label the elements of the Outlook window shown in Figure A-22.

FIGURE A-22

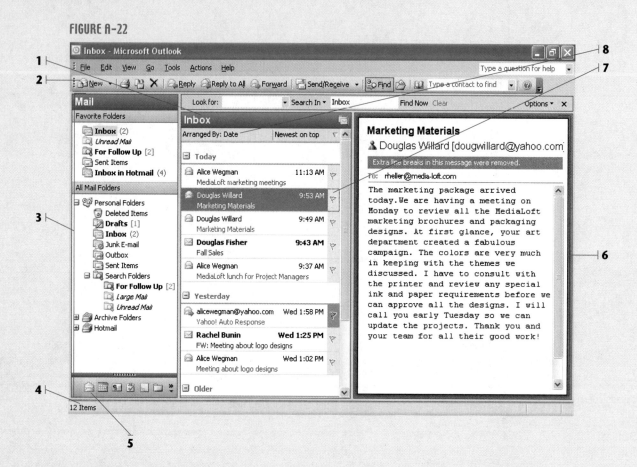

Match each term with the statement that best describes it.

9. E-mail
10. Attachment
11. Reading Pane
12. Distribution list
13. Inbox
14. Contacts folder

a. Stores names and e-mail addresses
b. A list of contacts that are grouped together and given a descriptive name
c. A computer file that is sent along with an e-mail message
d. Messages that are sent and received over a computer network
e. Contains messages you have received
f. Area used to preview a message

Select the best answer from the list of choices.

15. You can open the Mail window in Outlook by clicking:
   a. [icon].
   b. [icon].
   c. [icon].
   d. [icon].

16. When you select a message in the Inbox and then click [X] **, the message:**
   a. Is moved to the Sent Items folder.
   b. Is moved to the Deleted Items folder.
   c. Is deleted.
   d. Is flagged for follow-up.

17. Which of the following is *not* a message header icon?
   a. [icon]
   b. [icon]
   c. [icon]
   d. [icon]

18. To read a message that arrives in your Inbox, you:
   a. Click View on the menu bar, then click Read.
   b. Double-click the message.
   c. Click the Read button on the Standard toolbar.
   d. Flag the message to read.

19. To send an attachment with your e-mail message, you:
   a. Click Insert on the menu bar, then click Attachment.
   b. Click Insert on the menu bar, point to type, then click the File button.
   c. Click the Insert File button.
   d. You can't attach files to messages.

20. When you forward a selected message to another person, the e-mail addresses for the original recipients of the message:
   a. Appear in the To text box.
   b. Do not appear in any text box.
   c. Appear in the Cc text box.
   d. Appear in the To text box and the Cc text box.

21. To create a new message, you:
   a. Click the Inbox button.
   b. Click the Create button.
   c. Click the New Mail Message button.
   d. Click the Send button.

22. To send the same message to multiple recipients, which of the following is *not* an option?
   a. Selecting multiple names from the Contacts folder in the Select Names dialog box
   b. Dragging the message to each of the recipient names
   c. Creating a distribution list containing the names of the recipients
   d. Entering multiple names in the To text box

▼ SKILLS REVIEW

1. Start Outlook and view the Outlook 2003 window.
   a. Start Outlook.
   b. Choose a profile if you are prompted to during the startup of Outlook.
   c. Click the Mail icon on the Navigation Pane.

   d. Click the Inbox folder.

   e. Locate the following items: menu bar, title bar, status bar, Reading Pane, Standard toolbar, and Navigation Pane.

2. **Add a contact to the Address Book.**

   a. Open the Address Book.

   b. Open the New Entry dialog box.

   c. Create a new contact with the Full Name **Martha Sevigny** and the e-mail address **martha_sevigny@yahoo.com**.

   d. Save and close the new contact.

   e. Close the Address Book.

3. **Create and Send new messages.**

   a. Open a New Mail Message window.

   b. Click the To button.

   c. Verify that Contacts appears in the Show Names from the text box.

   d. Add Martha Sevigny as the primary recipient.

   e. Close the Select Names dialog box.

   f. Enter **alicewegman@yahoo.com** as a courtesy copy recipient.

   g. Type **Lunch on Wednesday** as the Subject of the message.

   h. In the message body, type: **Martha, I will be near your office on Wednesday. Can you meet me for lunch? I would also like to invite Alice Wegman.**

   i. Send the message.

4. **Reply to and Forward messages.**

   a. Click the Send/Receive button on the Standard toolbar.

   b. Display the contents of the Inbox folder.

   c. Read the message from Martha in the Reading Pane.

   d. Click the Reply button on the Standard toolbar.

   e. In the message body, type **Martha, I look forward to hearing about your vacation.**, then send the message.

   f. Forward the message you received from Martha to **alicewegman@yahoo.com**.

   g. In the top of the forwarded message body, type **Alice, Martha has responded below that she cannot make our lunch meeting. We'll reschedule lunch for another time.**

   h. Send the message.

5. **Send a message with an attachment.**

   a. Open a new mail message.

   b. Open the Address Book, then select Martha Sevigny as the message recipient.

   c. Enter **Cost analysis** as the Subject of the message.

   d. In the message body, type: **Martha, here is the cost analysis you requested. Let me know which vendor you want to hire.**

   e. Open the Insert File dialog box.

   f. Locate the drive and folder where your Data Files are stored. Change the view to Icons.

   g. Attach the file VendorCostAnalysis.xls to the message.

   h. Send the message.

6. **Create a distribution list.**

   a. Create three new contacts in the Address Book. You can use your own e-mail address and/or those of your friends.

   b. Open the Address Book.

   c. Create a new distribution list and name it **Development Team**.

   d. Select at least three contacts to be included in the distribution list.

   e. Save and close the distribution list.

   f. Close the Address Book.

7. Send a message to a distribution list.

   a. Create a new mail message.

   b. Enter the Development Team distribution list as the primary recipients of the message.

   c. Enter Summer Picnic as the Subject of the message.

   d. In the message body, type: Please plan to attend the annual company picnic. It will be the second Saturday in July.

   e. Send the message.

8. Delete items.

   a. Delete all of the messages in the Inbox folder from this exercise.

   b. Delete all of the messages in the Sent Items folder from this exercise.

   c. Delete all of the contacts and the distribution list you added to the Address Book in this exercise.

   d. Empty the Deleted Items folder.

   e. Exit Outlook.

▼ INDEPENDENT CHALLENGE 1

You are a member of a planning board in your town. You have been appointed as the chairperson of the committee to investigate a proposal for rezoning a four-block area of downtown as open space. You decide to use Outlook to communicate with the other members of the committee as well as with the local newspaper, the town council, and the mayor. Since you'll also be corresponding with the planning board frequently, you create a distribution list of its members.

   a. Start Outlook.

   b. Open the Address Book and add yourself as well as five other new contacts to the Address Book. Use the names and e-mail addresses of classmates or friends.

   c. Create a distribution list called Planning Board.

   d. Add four of the contacts to the distribution list. Be sure to include yourself on the list.

   e. Create a new message and address it to the Planning Board distribution list.

   f. Type Open Space Proposal - Public Hearing as the Subject of the message.

   g. In the message body, type There will be a public hearing on Monday at 7:00 p.m. We should prepare our presentations and contact the local newspaper to be sure they cover the story.

   h. Press [Enter] and then type your name.

   i. Send the message, then click the Send/Receive button. Depending on the speed and type of Internet connection you are using, you may need to click the Send/Receive button again, after waiting a few moments, if you do not receive the e-mail in your Inbox the first time you click the Send/Receive button.

   j. Open the message in the Inbox, flag it with a red follow-up flag, then print it.

Advanced Challenge Exercise

   ■ Forward the message to the person you did not include in the distribution list.

   ■ Use the Message Options dialog box to specify that the message has High Importance.

   ■ In the message body, type: Forgot to include you in this mailing! Please read the message, hope you can be there.

   ■ Send the message.

   k. Delete all of the messages in the Inbox folder related to this Independent Challenge.

   l. Delete all of the messages in the Sent Items folder related to this Independent Challenge.

   m. Delete the distribution list and the contacts that you added to the Address Book in this Independent Challenge.

   n. Empty the Deleted Items folder.

   o. Exit Outlook.

▼ INDEPENDENT CHALLENGE 2

You are planning a study trip to Europe with a group from the university. You have to send e-mail messages with an attachment as you organize this trip.

   a. Log onto the Internet and use your favorite search engine to find a Web site about Copenhagen, Denmark. Do not close your browser window.

   b. Start Outlook, then create a new message and address it to a friend, family member, or classmate.

   c. Enter your e-mail address in the Cc text box.

   d. Type Trip to Copenhagen in the Subject text box.

   e. Start your word processor and write two facts that you learned about Copenhagen from your Web research. Conclude the document with a personal note about why you want to participate in a study program in Denmark. Save the document file to the drive and folder where your Data Files are stored, using a filename you will remember.

   f. Type a short note to the recipient of the message, telling him or her that you thought they would like to learn these facts about Copenhagen, and that you are looking forward to seeing many new sites and learning about the culture of Scandinavia during your trip abroad.

   g. Attach the word processing document to the message.

   h. Send the message, then click the Send/Receive button. Depending on the speed and type of Internet connection you are using, you may need to click the Send/Receive button again, after waiting a few moments, if you do not receive a response e-mail the first time you click the Send/Receive button.

   i. Print a copy of the message.

Advanced Challenge Exercise

   ■ Click the Internet Explorer button on the taskbar to view the Web site about Copenhagen. Locate a picture on the Web site. If this site does not have a picture, find another Web site that does.

   ■ Right-click the picture, then click E-mail Picture on the shortcut menu. Click OK if a dialog box opens asking if you want to make the pictures smaller.

   ■ When a new Message window opens, enter your e-mail address in the To box, then write a brief message in the body of the message.

   ■ Send the message, then read the message and view the picture when it arrives in your Inbox.

   j. Delete all of the messages received for this Independent Challenge from your Inbox.

   k. Delete all of the messages sent for this Independent Challenge from the Sent Items folder.

   l. Empty the Deleted Items folder.

   m. Exit Outlook.

Managing Information Using Outlook

OBJECTIVES

Organize your contacts

Manage your appointments and tasks

Use the Journal and Notes

If you have a SAM user profile, you may have access to hands-on instruction, practice, and assessment of the skills covered in this unit. Log in to your SAM account and go to your assignments page to see what your instructor has assigned.

To effectively use Microsoft Office Outlook 2003 in managing your business and personal information, it is important to know not only how to send and receive e-mail, but also how to use the additional modules in Outlook. Outlook integrates several tools, including Mail, Calendar, Contacts, Tasks, Notes, and Journal to provide you with a uniquely comprehensive information manager. ▨▨▨ Now that you know how to manage your e-mail, you will learn how Outlook acts as a comprehensive desktop information manager to help you organize all aspects of your business and personal information.

Organizing Your Contacts

Contacts in Microsoft Outlook enables you to manage all your business and personal contact information. Contacts is a robust address database. When you create a contact for a person with whom you want to communicate, you store general and detailed information in fields in the Contacts folder. Each field, such as first name, last name, or phone number, stores specific information. Once you create a contact, you can use Contacts to quickly locate a phone number, make a call, send a meeting request, send a task request, or e-mail a message. You can sort, group, and filter contacts by any field of information. You can also easily share contacts within your business or personal community. To open Contacts, click the **Contacts icon** 🖼 in the Navigation Pane.

DETAILS

Review the following features of Contacts:

TROUBLE

If you do not enter a first and last name, the Check Full Name dialog box opens, allowing you to enter the full name for the contact, including title, first name, middle name, last name, and suffix, if appropriate.

• **To add a contact:** Click the **New Contact button** 🖼 New on the toolbar to open the Untitled Contact window. You enter information for a new contact in each field. Type the contact's name in the Name text box.

You can store up to three addresses in the Address text box. Choose Business, Home, or Other from the Address list, then type the address in the Address text box. If Outlook can't identify an appropriate street, city, state/province, postal code, and country/region, the Check Address dialog box opens for you to verify the information.

Click the **Details tab** to enter a contact's detailed information, including the contact's department or office, profession, the assistant's or manager's name, the contact's birthday, anniversary, or even the contact's nickname. Figure AP-1 shows the General tab in a completed contact window.

After you complete the Full Name text box, you can click the **File as list arrow** in the Contact window to choose from several File as options. Outlook allows you to file each contact under any name format that you choose, including by first name, last name, a company name, or company or job title. You can view your contacts in the Outlook window in a variety of ways by clicking an option button in the Current View section of the Navigation Pane. View options include: Address Cards, Detailed Address Cards, Phone List, By Company, By Category, By Location, and By Follow-Up Flag. See Figure AP-2.

QUICK TIP

You can also place a call by clicking the AutoDialer button 🖼 on the Contact window Standard toolbar.

• **To call a contact:** If you have a modem connected to a telephone line, you can set up your computer for automatic phone dialing and dial a contact telephone number. To call a contact, click **Actions** on the menu bar, click **Call Contact**, click the phone number you want to call, then click **Start Call**. After Outlook has dialed the phone number, pick up the phone handset and have the conversation. To end the conversation, click **End Call** and then hang up the phone.

• **To track e-mail, tasks, phone calls, appointments, and documents relating to a specific contact:** When you create a new Outlook item, such as a task, appointment, or note, you can link it to the contact or contacts to which it relates. You can also link files you create in other Office programs to a contact. Click the **Activities tab** in the Contact window to view the e-mail sent to or from a contact.

• **Send contact information over the Internet: VCards** are the Internet standard for creating and sharing virtual business cards. To send a vCard to someone via e-mail, click the contact you want to send as a vCard, click **Actions** on the menu bar, then click **Forward as vCard**. You can also include your vCard with your e-mail signature.

• **Create a mailing list:** By filtering the Contacts list, you create a subset of your Contacts folder. You then use the filtered list to begin a mail merge from Outlook. When you **filter** a list, you search for only specific information—for example, only those contacts that live in New Jersey. Using this filtered list, you use Outlook to create a variety of merged documents in Word, such as form letters or mailing labels. You can also use a filtered list and mail merge to send bulk e-mail messages or faxes to your contacts. Click the **Customize Current View link** in the Navigation Pane to open the Customize View dialog box. Click **Filter** to open the Filter dialog box, then specify the filter criteria. Once you have filtered the contacts you want for the merge, click **Tools** on the menu bar, then click **Mail Merge** to start the merge. Complete the Mail Merge Contacts dialog box to specify the contacts, fields, and document file to use, and to designate merge options such as document type and whether you want to merge to a new document, a printer, or e-mail.

FIGURE AP-1: A completed contact

General tab

Details tab displays additional fields

Click to open Check Full Name dialog box

Click to display or enter Home or Other address

How contact will appear on To: line of message

Image of contact

File as list arrow

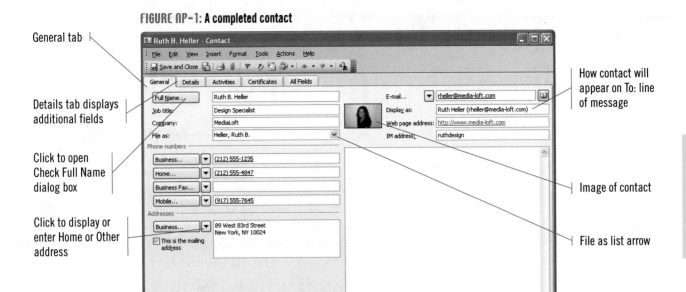

FIGURE AP-2: Contacts in Detailed Address Cards view

New Contact button

Contact window Standard toolbar

Contacts Navigation Pane

Contacts icon

Number of Contacts

Distribution List

Letter buttons to navigate to contacts

Detailed Address Card

Customize Current View link

AutoDialer button

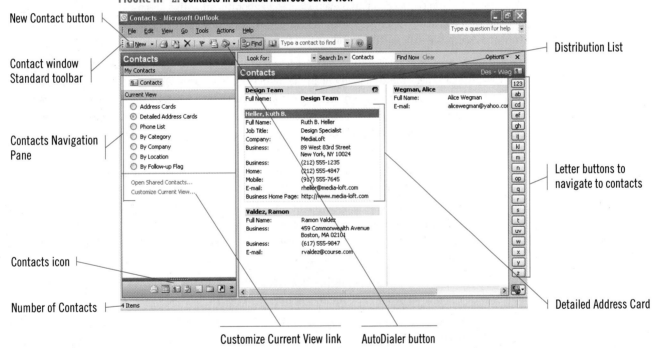

Clues to Use

Using Categories

You use categories in Outlook to tag items so you can track and organize them by specific criteria. A **category** is a keyword or phrase. Outlook provides a list of categories in the Master Category List organized into general categories such as Business, Personal, Phone Calls, Hot Contacts, Holiday Cards, and Status. To assign a category to a contact, click the Categories button at the bottom of the contact window, then check the box next to the appropriate category. You can add your own categories or delete existing categories. You can assign a contact to as many categories as you need. You can filter or sort by category. If you click the By Category option button in the Current View of the Navigation Pane, you can see your contacts grouped by category. You can assign any item in Outlook, such as a task, a meeting, or a note, to any category or to many categories.

Managing Your Appointments and Tasks

The Calendar and Tasks in Microsoft Outlook provide convenient, effective means to manage your appointments and to-do list. **Calendar** is the electronic equivalent of your desk calendar, while **Tasks** is an electronic to-do list. Calendar defines an **appointment** as an activity that does not involve inviting other people or scheduling resources, a **meeting** as an activity you invite people to or reserve resources for, and an **event** as an activity that lasts 24 hours or longer. You can specify the subject and location of the activity, and its start and end times. You can also ensure that you do not forget the activity by having Outlook sound a reminder prior to the start of the activity. Outlook notifies you if the activity conflicts with, or is adjacent to, another scheduled activity. You can view any period of time in Calendar. For example, you can look at and plan activities for next month or even next year. To review your appointments, meetings, and events, click the **Calendar icon** 📅 in the Navigation Pane. The Calendar for a work week is shown in Figure AP-3.

DETAILS

Review the following features of Calendar and Tasks:

- **To create a new appointment:** Click the **New Appointment button** 📅 New on the Standard toolbar. You specify the subject, location, and even label the appointment with a specific color to make the type of appointment apparent visually, as shown in Figure AP-4. Recurring appointments are entered once, and then you set a recurrence pattern. The appointments that recur are marked by a special indicator.

- **To schedule a meeting:** Click the New list arrow on the Standard toolbar, then click **Meeting Request**. The Calendar can check the availability of all the invitees and resources. Once you select a meeting time and location, you can send invitations in meeting requests by entering contact names in the To text box, then clicking the **Send button** Send. If an invitee accepts the invitation, Outlook posts the meeting automatically to the invitee's calendar. If you share calendars through a network, you can click the **Open a Shared Calendar link** in the Navigation Pane to view the calendars of your colleagues.

- **To view your activities:** You can choose to view Calendar by day, week, or month, and you can use the **Date Navigator** to quickly view specific dates. Dates displayed in boldface on the Date Navigator indicate days on which you have scheduled appointments. In the Day, Work Week, or Week views in Calendar, a color bar to the left of the entry identifies the meeting or appointment as Free, Tentative, Busy, or Out of the Office. You can turn on the Reading Pane so that when viewing the Calendar, if you click a meeting or appointment, the details appear in the Reading Pane.

- **To publish a Calendar over the Web:** Click **File** on the menu bar, then click **Save as Web Page**. The Calendar can then be shared over an intranet or over the Internet.

- **To manage your business and personal to-do list:** Click the **Tasks icon** 📋 in the Navigation Pane. Figure AP-5 shows the Tasks in Simple List view. To create a new task, click the **New Task button** 📋 New on the Standard toolbar to open the New Task window. You can also quickly enter a task by typing the task directly in the task list. You can sort your tasks in several different ways by clicking a column header in the task list, including sorting your tasks by subject, by status, by priority, or by due date. You can mark your progress on tasks by percentage complete, and you can have Outlook create status summary reports in e-mail messages, and then send the summary to anyone on the update list. To assign tasks to another person and have Outlook automatically update you on the status of the task completion, click **Actions** on the menu bar, then click **New Task Request**.

- **To coordinate your tasks and your appointments:** The task list from Tasks can be displayed in the **TaskPad** in Calendar. To view the TaskPad in Calendar, click **View** on the menu bar, then click **TaskPad**. It appears to the right of the Calendar below the Date Navigator. Click **View** on the menu bar, then click **TaskPad View** to specify which tasks are displayed and how they are organized in the TaskPad. To schedule time to complete a task, simply drag a task from the TaskPad to a time block in the Calendar. Any changes you make to a task are reflected in both the TaskPad in Calendar and the task list in Tasks.

FIGURE AP-3: Calendar

Go to Today button

Recurring indicator

Reminder indicator

Time marked Out of Office

Time marked Tentative

Calendar showing work week

All-day event

Date Navigator

Displayed Week

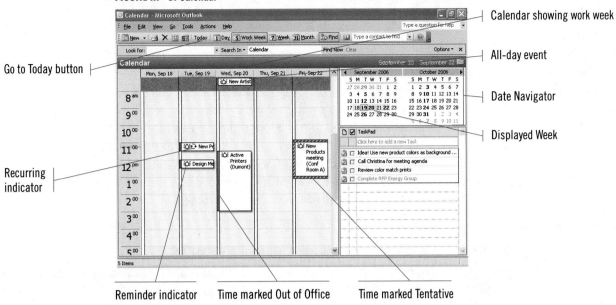

FIGURE AP-4: New appointment

Appointment details

Show as busy in Calendar

Linked Contact

Label color options

Click to open Categories dialog box

Assigned category

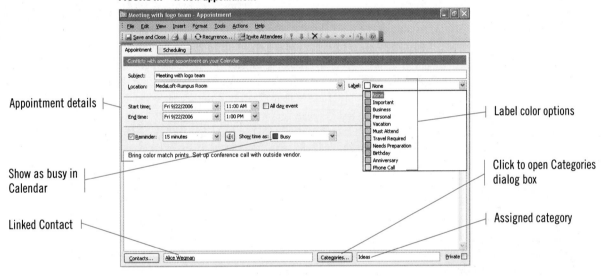

FIGURE AP-5: Tasks - Simple List view

New Task button

Current View options

Tasks icon

Type new task here

Completed task

Task list

Click to insert check mark when task is complete

Overdue task

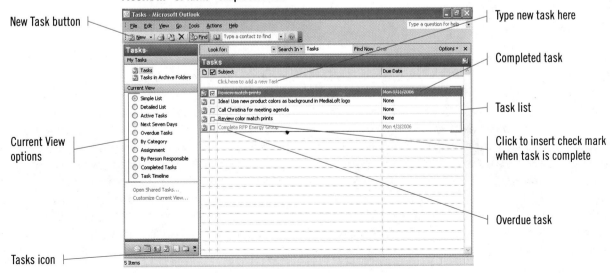

Using the Notes and Journal

Notes in Microsoft Outlook are the electronic version of the sticky notes you would buy at your local stationery store. Notes provide a convenient way to quickly jot down a reminder or an idea. Notes include all the organizing and grouping features of the other items, including being able to assign categories, contacts, or even colors. You can also forward a note to share an idea with a colleague. The **Journal** is a way to provide a trail of your activities. If you turn the Journal on, you can see a timeline of any calls, messages, appointments, or tasks, and it also tracks all documents, spreadsheets, databases, presentations, or any Office file that you specify. Note that e-mail is tracked on the Activities tab of each contact rather than in the Journal, and it is tracked regardless of whether or not Journal is on. Open the contact, then click the Activities tab to view any e-mail received from or sent to a contact.

DETAILS

Review the following features of the Journal and Notes:

- **To quickly write down an idea or a note concerning a contact, an appointment, or a task:** Click the **Notes icon** 🔲 in the Navigation Pane, then click the **New Note button** 🔲 New on the Standard toolbar to open a new note. You type the note directly in the Note window. Begin the note with a meaningful phrase so that the Notes list appears with meaningful titles. Click the **Note icon** 🗒 in the upper-left corner of the Note window to open a menu you can use to color-code each note, to assign a category or contact, and to forward or print the note. Notes are date and time stamped at the time they are created.

- **To work with Notes:** Figure AP-6 shows the Notes window. The Navigation Pane provides many options for viewing the Notes. You can use the views to help organize the reminders or ideas. If you want to turn a note into an appointment or meeting, you drag the note from the Notes window to the Calendar icon in the Navigation Pane. A New Appointment window opens with the details from the note filled in the appropriate fields. If you drag the note to the Tasks icon in the Navigation Pane, a New Task window opens and you can specify a due date and other Task details.

- **To turn on the Journal:** Click **Go** on the menu bar, then click **Journal**. When you turn on the Journal, you specify the Journal options, such as which items to track, in the Journal Options dialog box, shown in Figure AP-7. If the Journal is already on, click **Tools** on the menu bar, click **Options**, then click **Journal Options** to open the Journal Options dialog box. The Journal is displayed as a timeline on your screen. Any activities that have been specified to be tracked appear for each day as icons. You can scroll through the Journal to get an overview of your activities. You can sort or group the activities in the Journal. If you want to recall an event, the Journal is a great tool; you can see any documents that may have been created on a specific day. The Journal folder contains shortcuts to the activities that have been recorded. Click the icon to view the item.

- **To add an existing document to the Journal:** The Journal may not have been on when you created a spreadsheet or document that you want to be recorded in the Journal. Use Windows Explorer or the desktop to locate the file or item you want to record, then drag the item to the Journal and select the options you want for the entry.

Clues to Use

Using Outlook Today

The **Outlook Today page**, as shown in Figure AP-8, provides a preview of your day at a glance. It is the electronic version of your daily planner book and provides a snapshot view of the current activities, tasks, contacts, notes, and messages in the Outlook folders. To view Outlook Today, click the **Shortcuts icon** 🔲 on the Navigation pane, then click the **Outlook Today link**. (Outlook Today may also be the default view when you open Outlook.) Outlook Today shows your appointments over a range of time in the Calendar section. It also displays your tasks in one convenient place. Click the check box to the left of a task on the Outlook Today page to indicate you've completed it. In addition, Outlook Today displays how many messages are in your Inbox, Outbox, and Drafts folders. To view detailed information on any item in Outlook Today, click the task, appointment, meeting, or folder. Click the **Customize Outlook Today link** to customize the information that appears in Outlook Today to fit your personal style and work habits. You can choose to show from one to seven days of appointments in the Calendar section; you can sort your tasks in Outlook Today by Importance, Due Date, Creation Time, or Start Date, and in ascending or descending order; you can add or delete folders from the Messages folder list; and you can pick a different visual appearance for Outlook Today from an available list.

FIGURE AP-6: Notes

New Note button

Click to change icons to list or small icons

Icons view

Customize Current View link

Color-coded notes as large icons

Notes icon

First lines of note help identify the note

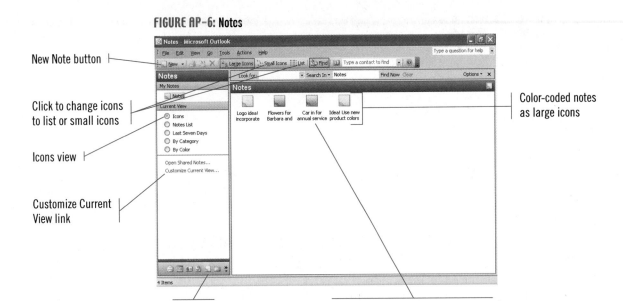

FIGURE AP-7: Journal Options dialog box

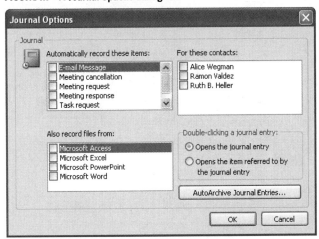

FIGURE AP-8: Outlook Today page

Appointments for today

Expanded buttons with text

Today's date

Customize Outlook Today link

Overdue task in red

E-mail messages

Things to do

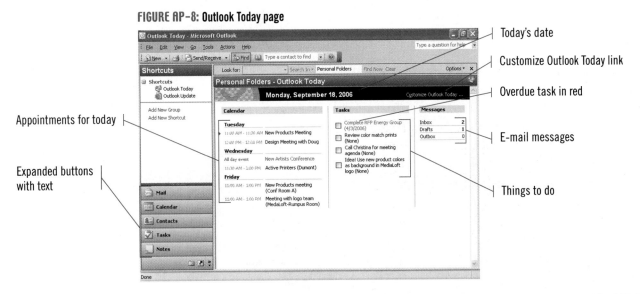

Practice

▼ CONCEPTS REVIEW

Label the elements of the Calendar window shown in Figure AP-9.

FIGURE AP-9

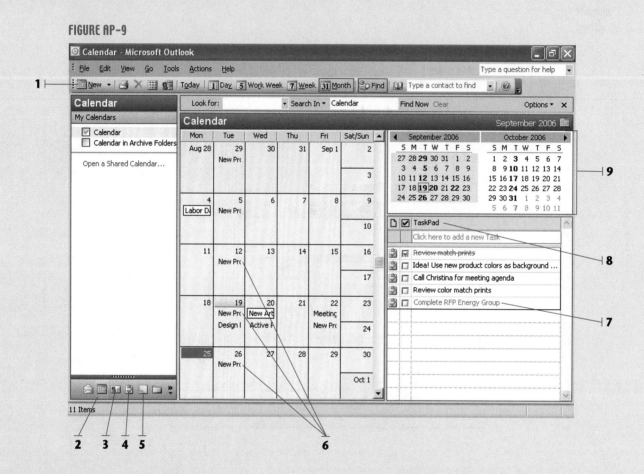

Select the best answer from the list of choices.

10. Which of the following is _not_ available in Outlook?
   a. Mail   **b.** Notes   **c.** Calendar   **d.** Planner

11. To schedule your appointments, meetings, and events, you use:
   a. Tasks.   **b.** Notes.   **c.** Contacts.   **d.** Calendar.

12. To manage your business and personal to-do list you use:
   a. Tasks.   **b.** Journal.   **c.** Contacts.   **d.** Calendar.

13. To track appointments, documents, and activities, you use:
   a. Tasks.   **b.** Journal.   **c.** Contacts.   **d.** Calendar.

Glossary

Absolute cell reference A cell reference that contains a dollar sign before the column letter and/or row number to indicate the absolute, or fixed, contents of specific cells. For example, the formula $A$1+$B$1 calculates only the sum of these specific cells no matter where the formula is copied in the workbook.

Access database file All of the objects (tables, queries, forms, reports, macros, modules) created in an Access database are stored in one file with an .mdb extension.

Active cell A selected cell in a Graph datasheet or an Excel worksheet.

Address bar A toolbar that typically appears below the Standard Buttons toolbar; it displays the address of the Web page currently open.

Address book A collection of usernames and e-mail addresses you can access to quickly address an e-mail message.

Adjustment handle A small yellow diamond that changes the appearance of an object's most prominent feature.

Align To place objects' edges or centers on the same plane.

Alignment Commands used in Form or Report Design View to either left-, center-, or right-align a value within its control, or to align the top, bottom, right, or left edge of the control with respect to other controls. (Access)

Alignment The placement of cell contents; for example, left, center, or right. (Excel)

Alignment The position of text in a document relative to the margins. (Word)

AND criteria Criteria placed in the same row of the query design grid. All criteria on the same row must be true for a record to appear on the resulting datasheet.

Animation scheme A set of predefined visual effects for a slide transition, title text, and bullet text of the slides in a PowerPoint presentation.

Animation tag Identifies the order in which objects are animated on a slide during a slide show.

Annotate A freehand drawing on the screen made by using the Annotation tool. You can annotate only in Slide Show view.

Application *See* Program.

Appointment In Calendar, a scheduled activity that does not involve inviting other people or scheduling resources.

Area chart A line chart in which each area is given a solid color or pattern to emphasize the relationship between the pieces of charted information.

Argument Information that a function needs to calculate an answer. In an expression, multiple arguments are separated by commas. All of the arguments are enclosed in parentheses; for example, =SUM(A1:B1).

Argument ScreenTip The yellow box that appears as you build a function. As you build the function using different elements, the box displays these elements. You can click each element to display its online help.

Arithmetic operator Plus (+), minus (-), multiply (*), divide (/), or exponentiation (^) character used in a mathematical calculation.

Ascending order A sequence in which information is placed in alphabetical order or arranged from smallest number to largest number.

Asterisk Wildcard character that represents any group of characters.

Attachment A file, such as a Word document, graphic image, or Excel spreadsheet, that is sent with an e-mail message.

Attribute The styling features such as bold, italics, and underlining that can be applied to cell contents.

AutoCalculate value Value displayed in the status bar that represents the sum of values in the selected range.

AutoComplete A feature that automatically completes entries based on other entries in the same column. (Excel)

AutoComplete A feature that automatically suggests text to insert. (Word)

AutoContent Wizard A wizard that helps you get a presentation started by supplying a sample outline and a design template. (Word)

AutoCorrect A feature that automatically detects and corrects typing errors, minor spelling errors, and capitalization, and inserts certain typographical symbols as you type.

AutoFill A feature that creates a series of text entries or numbers when a range is selected using the fill handle.

AutoFill Options button Allows you to specify what you want to fill and whether or not you want to include formatting.

AutoFit A feature that automatically adjusts the width of a column to accommodate its widest entry when the boundary to the right of the column selector is double-clicked.

AutoForm Tool to quickly create a form that displays all of the fields of the selected record source.

AutoFormat Preset schemes that can be applied to format a range instantly. Excel comes with 16 AutoFormats that include colors, fonts, and numeric formatting.

Automatic page break A page break that is inserted automatically at the bottom of a page.

AutoNumber A field data type in which Access enters a sequential integer for each record added into the datasheet. Numbers cannot be reused even if the record is deleted.

AutoSum A feature that automatically creates totals using the SUM function when you click the AutoSum button.

AutoText A feature that stores frequently used text and graphics so they can be easily inserted into a document.

Avg function Built-in Access function used to calculate the average of the values in a given field.

Background The area behind the text and graphics on a slide.

Background color The color applied to the background of a cell.

Bar chart A chart that shows information as a series of horizontal bars.

Bcc Stands for blind courtesy copy; is used when the sender does not want to reveal who he or she has sent courtesy copies to.

Blind courtesy copy *See* Bcc.

.bmp The abbreviation for the bitmap graphics file format.

Body text Subpoints or bullet points on a slide under the slide title.

Body text placeholder A reserved box on a slide for main points.

Bold Formatting applied to text to make it thicker and darker.

Border A line that can be added above, below, or to the sides of a paragraph, text, or table cell; a line that divides the columns and rows of a table. (Word)

Border The edge of a cell, an area of a worksheet, or a selected object; you can change its color or line style. (Excel)

Bound control A control used in either a form or report to display data from the underlying record source; also used to edit and enter new data in a form.

Bound object frame A bound control used to show OLE data such as a picture on a form or report.

Browser A program designed to help you view the text, graphic images, and multimedia on the Web.

Browser window The specific area where the current Web page appears.

Bullet A small graphic symbol, usually a round or square dot, often used to identify items in a list.

Business productivity software Programs, such as word processors, spreadsheets, and databases, that businesses use to accomplish daily tasks and become more productive.

Calculated control A control that uses information from existing controls to calculate new data such as subtotals, dates, or page numbers; used in either a form or report.

Calculated field A field created in Query Design View that results from an expression of existing fields, Access functions, and arithmetic operators. For example, the entry Profit: [RetailPrice]-[WholesalePrice] in the field cell of the query design grid creates a calculated field called Profit that is the difference between the values in the RetailPrice and WholesalePrice fields.

Calculation A new value that is created by entering an expression in a text box on a form or report.

Calendar The scheduling component within Outlook that stores appointments, meetings, and scheduled events; it is the electronic equivalent of a daily desk calendar.

Caption A field property used to override the technical field name with an easy-to-read caption entry when the field name appears on datasheets, forms, and reports.

Category A keyword or phrase used to organize and group items in Outlook.

Category axis Also known as the x-axis or horizontal axis in a 2-dimensional chart.

Cc Stands for courtesy copy; typically sent to message recipients who need to be aware of the correspondence between the sender and the recipients.

Cell The box formed by the intersection of a table row and table column. (Word)

Cell The intersection of a column and row in a worksheet, datasheet, or table. (Excel)

Cell address The location of a cell expressed by the column and row coordinates; the cell address of the cell in column A, row 1, is A1.

Cell pointer A highlighted rectangle around a cell that indicates the active cell.

Cell reference The address or name that identifies a cell's position in a worksheet; it consists of a letter that identifies the cell's column and a number that identifies its row; for example, cell B3. Cell references in worksheets can be used in formulas and are relative or absolute.

Center Alignment in which an item is centered between the margins.

Character spacing Formatting that changes the width or scale of characters, expands or condenses the amount of space between characters, raises or lowers characters relative to the line of text, and adjusts kerning (the space between standard combinations of letters).

Character style A named set of character format settings that can be applied to text to format it all at once.

Chart A graphic representation of worksheet or datasheet information. Types include 2-D and 3-D column, bar, pie, area, and line charts.

Chart sheet A separate sheet that contains only a chart linked to worksheet data.

Chart Wizard A series of dialog boxes that helps you create or modify a chart. (Excel)

Chart Wizard A wizard that steps you through the process of creating charts within forms and reports. (Access)

Check box Bound control used to display "yes" or "no" answers for a field. If the box is "checked" it indicates "yes" information in a form or report.

Click and Type A feature that allows you to automatically apply the necessary paragraph formatting to a table, graphic, or text when you insert the item in a blank area of a document in Print Layout or Web Layout view.

Click and type pointer A pointer used to move the insertion point and automatically apply the paragraph formatting necessary to insert text at that location in the document.

Clip A media file, such as a graphic, photograph, sound, movie, or animation, that can be inserted into a document.

Clip art A graphic images such as a corporate logo, picture, or photo that can be inserted into documents, presentations, Web pages, spreadsheets, and other Office files.

Clip Organizer A library of art, pictures, sounds, video clips, and animations that all Office applications share.

Clipboard A temporary storage area for items that are cut or copied from any Office file and are available for pasting. *See* Office Clipboard and System Clipboard.

Clipboard task pane A task pane that shows the contents of the Office Clipboard; contains options for copying and pasting items.

Color scheme The set of eight coordinated colors that make up a PowerPoint presentation; a color scheme assigns colors for text, lines, objects, and background. You can change the color scheme in any presentation at any time.

Column break A break that forces text following the break to begin at the top of the next column.

Column chart The default chart type in Excel, which displays information as a series of vertical columns.

Column heading Gray boxes along the top of a datasheet. (Access)

Column heading The gray box containing the letter above the column in a worksheet. (Excel)

Column headings Part of the e-mail window that identifies sections of the message header. (Outlook)

Combination chart Combines a column and line chart to compare data requiring different scales of measure.

Combo box A bound control used to display a list of possible entries for a field in which you can also type an entry from the keyboard. It is a "combination" of the list box and text box controls.

Command button An unbound control used to provide an easy way to initiate an action or run a macro.

Command Button Wizard A wizard that steps you through the process of creating a command button.

Comments A feature that makes it possible to communicate with teammates using typed notes that are embedded in a document.

Compact on Close Feature found on the General tab of the Options dialog box which compacts and repairs your database each time you close it.

Compacting Rearranging the data and objects on the storage medium so space formerly occupied by deleted objects is eliminated. Compacting a database doesn't change the data, but reduces the overall size of the database.

Comparison operators Characters such as > and < that allow you to find or filter data based on specific criteria.

Compatibility The ability of documents created in different programs to easily exchange and share information.

Complex formula An equation that uses more than one type of arithmetic operator.

Computer network The hardware and software that make it possible for two or more computers to share information and resources.

Conditional format A cell format that is based on the cell's value or the outcome of a formula.

Contacts The Outlook component that enables you to manage all your business and personal contact information.

Contacts folder A folder that stores all the e-mail addresses and personal information for your contacts.

Control Any element on a form or report such as a label, text box, line, or combo box. Controls can be bound, unbound, or calculated.

Control menu box A box in the upper-left corner of a window used to resize or close a window.

Copy To place a copy of an item on the Clipboard without removing it from a document.

Courtesy copy *See* Cc.

Criteria Entries (rules and limiting conditions) that determine which records are displayed when finding or filtering records in a datasheet or form, or when building a query.

Crop To hide part of a picture or object using the Cropping tool.

Currency A field data type used for monetary values.

Current record box *See* Record selector box.

Current record symbol A black triangle symbol that appears in the record selector box to the left of the record that has the focus in either a datasheet or a form.

Cut To remove an item from a document and place it on the Clipboard.

Cut and paste To move text or graphics using the Cut and Paste commands.

DAP *See* page.

Data The unique information you enter into the fields of the records.

Data access page (DAP) *See* page.

Data label Information that identifies the data in a column or row in a datasheet.

Data marker A graphical representation of a data point, such as a bar or column.

Data point Individual piece of data plotted in a chart.

Data series A column or row in a datasheet. Also, the selected range in a worksheet that Excel converts into a graphic and displays as a chart.

Data series marker A graphical representation of a data series, such as a bar or column.

Data source The file that contains unique data for each individual recipient in a merge.

Data type A required property for each field that defines the type of data that can be entered in each field. Valid data types include AutoNumber, Text, Number, Currency, Date/Time, OLE Object, and Memo.

Database A collection of related information, such as a list of employees. Also, a collection of tables associated with a general topic (for example, sales of products to customers).

Database management system A program that organizes data and allows you to link multiple groups of information.

Database toolbar Toolbar that contains buttons for common tasks that affect the entire database or are common to all database objects.

Database window The window that includes common elements such as the Access title bar, menu bar, and toolbar.

Database window toolbar Toolbar that contains buttons used to open, modify, create, delete, and view objects.

Database Wizard An Access wizard that creates a sample database file for a general purpose such as inventory control, event tracking, or expenses. The objects created by the Database Wizard can be used and modified.

Datasheet A spreadsheet-like grid that displays fields as columns and records as rows. (Access)

Datasheet The component of a chart that contains the numerical data displayed in a chart. (Excel)

Datasheet View A view that lists the records of the object in a datasheet. Table, query, and most form objects have a Datasheet View.

Date function Built-in Access function used to display the current date on a form or report.

Date Navigator A feature in Calendar that allows you to quickly view a specific day, week, or month by clicking the day or month.

Date/Time A field data type used for date and time data.

Delete To permanently remove an item from a document.

Deleted Items folder The folder that contains messages you have deleted. Empty the Deleted Items folder to permanently remove the items from your computer.

Design grid *See* Query design grid.

Design template Predesigned slide design with formatting and color schemes that you can apply to an open presentation.

Design View A view in which the structure of the object can be manipulated. Every Access object has a Design View.

Destination file The file that receives the copied information. For example, a query table created in Access, the source file, can be copied to and edited in a Word document, an Excel worksheet, or a PowerPoint presentation, the destination file.

Detail section The section of a form or report that contains the controls that are printed for each record in the underlying query or table.

Dialog box A window that opens when a program needs more information to carry out a command.

Distribution list A collection of contacts to whom you regularly send the same messages.

Document The electronic file you create using Word.

Document properties Details about a file, such as author name or the date the file was created, that are used to organize and search for files.

Document window The workspace in the program window that displays the current document.

Domain name The common name given to a Web site. Most pages begin with "www" (which identifies that the page is on the World Wide Web), followed by a dot, or period, and then the Web site's domain name.

Drag and drop To move text or a graphic by dragging it to a new location using the mouse.

Drag-and-drop technique Method in which you drag the contents of selected cells to a new location.

Drawing toolbar A toolbar that contains buttons that let you create lines, shapes, and special effects.

Drop cap A large dropped initial capital letter that is often used to set off the first paragraph of an article.

Dummy column/row Blank column or row included at the end of a range that enables a formula to adjust when columns or rows are added or deleted.

Dynamic Data Exchange (DDE) link The connection between the source file and the destination file when an object is pasted as a link into the destination file.

Edit mode The mode in which Access assumes you are trying to edit a particular field, so keystrokes such as [Ctrl][End], [Ctrl][Home], [↑], and [↓] move the insertion point within the field.

Edit record symbol A pencil symbol that appears in the record selector box to the left of the record that is currently being edited in either a datasheet or a form.

Electronic spreadsheet A computer program that performs calculations on data and organizes information into worksheets. A worksheet is divided into columns and rows, which form individual cells.

E-mail Electronic mail messages that are sent over a network and the Internet.

E-mail software A program that lets you send and receive electronic messages over a network and the Internet.

Embedded chart A chart displayed as an object in a worksheet.

Embedded object An object that maintains a link to the source program, but not to the source file. When you double-click an embedded object, the source program opens and you can edit the object. The source file that the object originally represented does not change

Emoticons Simple keyboard characters that are used to express an emotion or mood, such as :) for a smiling face, or :(for a sad face.

Event In Calendar, an activity that lasts 24 hours or longer.

Exploding pie slice A slice of a pie chart that has been pulled away from the whole pie to add emphasis.

Expression A combination of values, functions, and operators that calculates a single value. Access expressions start with an equal sign and are placed in a text box in either Form Design View or Report Design View.

Favorite Folders Those folders you use most often, so they are readily accessible in the Navigation Pane.

Favorites list A list of your own frequently visited Web pages. When you find a Web page you want to revisit, add the site address to the Favorites list, then access the site by clicking a link rather than having to type the URL.

Field A code that serves as a placeholder for data that changes in a document, such as a page number. (Word)

Field The smallest piece of information in a database such as the customer's name, city, or phone number. (Access)

Field list A list of the available fields in the table or query that it represents.

Field names The names given to each field in Table Design or Table Datasheet View.

Field Properties pane The lower half of Table Design View that shows you the properties for the currently selected field.

Field property *See* Properties.

Field selector The button to the left of a field in Table Design View that indicates which field is currently selected. Also the thin gray bar above each field in the query grid.

Field Size A field property that determines the largest number that can be entered in a field (for Number or Currency fields) or the number of characters that can be entered in a field (for Text fields).

File An electronic collection of information that has a unique name, distinguishing it from other files.

File format A file type, such as .bmp, .jpg, or .gif.

Filename The name given to a document when it is saved.

Fill color The cell background color.

Fill handle A small square in the lower-right corner of the active cell used to copy cell contents.

Filter A temporary view of a subset of records. A filter can be saved as a query object if you wish to apply the same filter later without re-creating it.

Filter (verb) To search for information based on specific criteria.

Filter window A window that appears when you click the Filter By Form button when viewing data in a datasheet or in a form window. The Filter window allows you to define the filter criteria.

Find A command used to locate specific data within a field.

First line indent A type of indent in which the first line of a paragraph is indented more than the subsequent lines.

Fit (Print option) An option that automatically adjusts a preview to display all pages in a report.

Floating graphic A graphic to which text wrapping has been applied, making the graphic independent of text and able to be moved anywhere on a page.

Focus The property that indicates which field would be edited if you were to start typing.

Folder A subdivision of a disk that works like a filing system to help you organize files.

Font The typeface or design of a set of characters (letters, numbers, symbols, and punctuation marks).

Font effect Font formatting that applies a special effect to text, such as a shadow, an outline, small caps, or superscript.

Font size The size of characters, measured in units called points (pts).

Footer Information, such as text, a page number, or a graphic, that appears at the bottom of every page in a document or a section.

Foreign key field In a one-to-many relationship between two tables, the foreign key field is the field in the "many" table that links the table to the primary key field in the "one" table.

Form An Access object that provides an easy-to-use data entry screen that generally shows only one record at a time.

Form Design toolbar When working in Form Design View, the toolbar that appears with buttons that help you modify a form's controls.

Form Design View The view of a form in which you add, delete, and modify the form's properties, sections, and controls.

Form Footer A section that appears at the bottom of the screen in Form View for each record, but prints only once at the end of all records when the form is printed.

Form Header A section that appears at the top of the screen in Form View for each record, but prints only once at the top of all records when the form is printed.

Form View View of a form object that displays data from the underlying recordset and allows you to enter and update data.

Form Wizard An Access wizard that helps you create a form.

Format The appearance of text and numbers, including color, font, attributes, borders, and shading. *See also* Number format.

Format Painter A feature used to copy the format settings applied to the selected text or cell to other text or cells you want to format the same way.

Formatting Enhancing the appearance of the information through font, size, and color changes.

Formatting marks Nonprinting characters that appear on screen to indicate the ends of paragraphs, tabs, and other formatting elements.

Formatting toolbar A toolbar that contains buttons for frequently used formatting commands.

Formula A set of instructions used to perform numeric calculations (adding, multiplying, averaging, etc.).

Formula bar The area below the menu bar and above the Excel workspace where you enter and edit data in a worksheet cell. The formula bar becomes active when you start typing or editing cell data. It includes the Enter button and the Cancel button.

Formula prefix An arithmetic symbol, such as the equal sign (=), used to start a formula.

Full screen view A view that shows only the document window on screen.

Function A special, predefined formula that provides a shortcut for a commonly used calculation, for example, SUM or COUNT.

Getting Started task pane A task pane that contains shortcuts for opening documents, for creating new documents, and for accessing information on the Microsoft Web site.

.gif The abbreviation for the graphics interchange format file.

Glossary terms Words in the Help system that are shown as blue hyperlinks and display the word's definition when clicked.

Go button Used along with the Address bar to help you search for Web sites about a particular topic. Enter a keyword or phrase in the Address bar, then click the Go button to activate the search; a list of related Web sites opens in a search results Web page.

Graphic image *See* Image.

Grid Evenly spaced horizontal and vertical lines that appear on a slide when it is being created to help place objects. Lines do not appear when slide is shown or printed.

Gridlines Horizontal and/or vertical lines within a chart that make the chart easier to read.

Group (n) A collection of objects.

Group (v) To combine multiple objects into one object.

Group Footer A section of the report that contains controls that print once at the end of each group of records.

Group Header A section of the report that contains controls that print once at the beginning of each group of records.

Grouping To sort records in a particular order, plus provide a section before and after each group of records.

Grouping records In a report, to sort records based on the contents of a field, plus provide a group header section that precedes the group of records and provide a group footer section that follows the group of records.

Groups bar Located just below the Objects bar in the database window, the Groups bar displays the Favorites and any user-created groups, which in turn contain shortcuts to objects. Groups are used to organize the database objects into logical sets.

Groups button Button on the Groups bar that expands or collapses that section of the database window.

Gutter Extra space left for a binding at the top, left, or inside margin of a document.

Handles *See* Sizing handles.

Hanging indent A type of indent in which the second and subsequent lines of a paragraph are indented more than the first.

Hard page break *See* Manual page break.

Header Information, such as text, a page number, or a graphic, that appears at the top of every page in a document or a section.

Help system A utility that gives you immediate access to definitions, steps, explanations, and useful tips.

Highlighting Transparent color that can be applied to text to call attention to it.

Home page The Web page that opens every time you start a browser. The term "home page" also applies to the main page that opens when you first go to a Web site.

Horizontal ruler A ruler that appears at the top of the document window in Print Layout, Normal, and Web Layout view.

Hyperlink A field data type that stores World Wide Web addresses. A hyperlink can also be a control on a form that when clicked, opens another database object, external file, or external Web page. (Access)

Hyperlink Text that, when clicked, opens another file, a Web page on the World Wide Web, or an e-mail client such as Microsoft Office Outlook. A hyperlink can also take you to a different section in the current file.

Hypertext Markup Language (HTML) The formatting language used to create Web pages.

I-beam pointer The pointer used to move the insertion point and select text.

Image A nontextual piece of information such as a picture, piece of clip art, drawn object, or graph. Because images are graphical (and not numbers or letters), they are sometimes referred to as graphical images.

Image control A control used to store a single piece of clip art, a photo, or a logo on a form or report.

Inbox The folder that contains incoming messages.

Indent The space between the edge of a line of text or a paragraph and the margin.

Indent marker A marker on the horizontal ruler that shows the indent settings for the active paragraph.

Inline graphic A graphic that is part of a line of text.

Input Information that produces desired results, or output, in a worksheet.

Insertion point A blinking vertical line that indicates where the next character will appear when text is entered in a text placeholder. (PowerPoint)

Insertion point The blinking vertical line that appears in the formula bar or in a cell during editing. (Excel)

Insertion point The blinking vertical line that shows where text will appear when you type in a document. (Word)

Integration The ability to use information across multiple programs. For example, you can include a chart created in Excel in a document created in Word.

Internet A communications system that connects computers and computer networks located around the world using telephone lines, cables, satellites, and other telecommunications media.

Internet Explorer The browser that is part of the Microsoft Windows operating system.

Intranet A computer network that connects computers in a specific area only, such as the computers in a company's office. An intranet can be accessed internally or through a remote location.

Is Not Null Criterion that finds all records in which any entry has been made in the field.

Is Null Criterion that finds all records in which no entry has been made in the field.

Italic Formatting applied to text to make the characters slant to the right.

Item In Outlook, a basic element that stores information, such as an appointment, contact, task, journal entry, note, or document.

Journal A component in Outlook that provides a trail of your activities. If you turn the Journal on, you can see a timeline of any calls, messages, appointments, or tasks, and it also tracks all documents, spreadsheets, databases, presentations, or any Office file that you specify.

Justify Alignment in which an item is flush with both the left and right margins.

Key field *See* Primary key field.

Key field combination Two or more fields that as a group contain unique information for each record.

Key field symbol *See* Key symbol.

Key symbol In Table Design View, the symbol that appears as a miniature key in the field indicator box to the left of the field name. It identifies the field that contains unique information for each record.

Keyboard shortcut A combination of keys or a function key that can be pressed to perform a command.

Keyword A representative word on which the Help system can search to find information on your area of interest.

Keyword Criteria or word related to the topic for which you are searching. (World Wide Web)

Label An unbound control that displays static text on forms and reports. (Access)

Label Descriptive text or other information that identifies the rows and columns of a worksheet. Labels are not included in calculations. (Excel)

Label prefix A character, such as the apostrophe, that identifies an entry as a label and controls the way it appears in the cell.

Landscape orientation A print setting that positions the file on the page so the page is wider than it is tall.

Left function Access function that returns a specified number of characters, starting with the left side of a value in a Text field.

Left indent A type of indent in which the left edge of a paragraph is moved in from the left margin.

Left-align Alignment in which the item or paragraph is flush with the left margin.

Legend A key explaining how information is represented by colors or patterns in a chart.

Line chart A graph of data that is mapped by a series of lines. Line charts show changes in data or categories of data over time and can be used to document trends.

Line control An unbound control used to draw lines on a form or report that divides it into logical groupings.

Line spacing The amount of space between lines of text.

Link A connection to the original file. For example, when you link an object to a PowerPoint slide, a representation, or picture, of the object is placed on the slide instead of the actual object. This representation of the object is connected, or linked, to the original file. Changes made to the source file are reflected in the linked object.

Link *See* Hyperlink.

Linked object An object that maintains a connection to the source file so that the object is updated when the data in the source file changes.

Links bar A place to store and display links to Web pages that you use often. You can add a link to the Links bar by dragging the Internet Explorer icon that precedes the URL in the Address bar to the Links bar.

List box A bound control that displays a list of possible choices for the user. Used mainly on forms.

List style A named set of format settings, such as indents and outline numbering, that can be applied to a list to format it all at once.

Logical view The datasheet of a query is sometimes called a logical view of the data because it is not a copy of the data, but rather, a selected view of data from the underlying tables.

Lookup Wizard A wizard used in Table Design View that allows one field to "look up" values from another table or entered list. For example, you might use the Lookup Wizard to specify that the CustomerNumber field in the Sales table display the CustomerName field entry from the Customers table.

Macro An Access object that stores a collection of keystrokes or commands such as those for printing several reports in a row or providing a toolbar when a form opens.

Mail Merge The process of combining the addresses in Outlook with a document in Word to create a mass mailing of personalized letters using the Contacts. Contacts can be filtered on Categories to create a subset of contacts for the merge.

Main document The document that contains the standard text, which is the text that remains the same for each recipient in a merge.

Manual page break A page break inserted to force the text following the break to begin at the top of the next page.

Margin The blank area between the edge of the text and the edge of a page.

Media Player A software program that allows you to play sound files and view media files such as live or prerecorded video and graphic images.

Meeting In Calendar, an activity you invite people to or reserve resources for.

Memo A field data type used for lengthy text such as comments or notes. It can hold up to 64,000 characters of information.

Menu bar The bar below the title bar that contains the names of menus, that when clicked, open menus from which you choose program commands. Menu bars can change depending on the view.

Merge The process of combining data from a data source such as an Access database with a document created in Word. The data could consist of the names, addresses, and other information about a company's customers, contacts, and suppliers. The document in Word could be a form letter. You can merge data from the database with a form letter to create a series of individually addressed form letters.

Message header The area at the top of a message that identifies the sender of the message, the subject, the date and time the message was received, and the size of the message. Message headers include the Display As names and e-mail addresses of To and Cc recipients, but not of Bcc recipients.

Message header icon Icon that appears in a message header that identifies an attribute of the message.

Microsoft Graph The program that creates a datasheet and chart to graphically depict numerical information in PowerPoint.

Microsoft Outlook Express A program that comes with Windows XP that focuses primarily on e-mail, and does not have the other modules of Outlook. You can use it to exchange e-mail and join newsgroups.

Minor gridlines Gridlines that show the values between the tick marks.

Mirror margins Margins used in documents with facing pages, where the inside and outside margins are mirror images of each other.

Mixed reference A formula containing both a relative and absolute reference.

Mode indicator A box located in the lower-left corner of the status bar that informs you of a program's status. For example, when Excel is performing a task, the word "Wait" appears.

Module An Access object that stores Visual Basic programming code that extends the functions of automated Access processes.

Moving border The dashed line that appears around a cell or range that is copied to the Clipboard.

Name box The left-most area in the formula bar that shows the cell reference or name of the active cell. For example, A1 refers to cell A1 of the active worksheet. You can also display a list of names in a workbook using the Name list arrow.

Name property Property of a text box that gives the text box a meaningful name.

Named range A range of cells given a meaningful name; it retains its name when moved and can be referenced in a formula.

Navigation buttons Buttons in the lower-left corner of a datasheet or form that allow you to quickly navigate between the records in the underlying object as well as add a new record.

Navigation mode A mode in which Access assumes that you are trying to move between the fields and records of the datasheet (rather than edit a specific field's contents), so keystrokes such as [Ctrl][Home] and [Ctrl][End] move you to the first and last field of the datasheet.

Navigation pane Displays the folders used to organize e-mail. Also includes customizable button icons for Mail, Calendar, Contacts, Tasks, Notes, Folder list, Shortcuts, and the Journal.

Navigation toolbar Toolbar at the lower-left corner of Datasheet View, Form View, or a Web page that helps you navigate between records.

Negative indent A type of indent in which the left edge of a paragraph is moved to the left of the left margin.

New Record button Button you click to add records to a database.

Normal view A presentation view that divides the presentation window into three sections: Slides or Outline tab, Slide pane, and notes pane. (PowerPoint)

Normal view A view that shows a document without margins, headers and footers, or graphics. (Word)

Notes The component in Outlook used to write a short reminder, idea or note concerning an appointment or task; it is an electronic version of the popular colored paper sticky notes.

Notes folder The folder that stores the Notes you have created in Outlook.

Notes Page view A presentation view that displays a reduced image of the current slide above a large text box where you can type notes.

Notes pane The area in Normal view that shows speaker notes for the current slide; also in Notes Page view, the area below the slide image that contains speaker notes.

Number A field data type used for numeric information used in calculations, such as quantities.

Number format A format applied to values to express numeric concepts, such as currency, date, and percentage.

Object A chart or graphic image that can be moved and resized and that contains handles when selected. (Excel)

Object A table, query, form, report, page, macro, or module in an Access database. (Access)

Object An item you place or draw on a slide that can be manipulated. Objects are drawn lines and shapes, text, clip art, imported pictures, and embedded objects. (PowerPoint)

Object buttons Buttons on the Objects bar that provide access to the different types of objects (tables, queries, forms, reports, macros, modules) in the current database.

Objects bar In the opening database window, the toolbar that presents the seven Access objects and groups.

Objects button Button on the Objects bar that expands or collapses that section of the database window.

Office Assistant An animated character that offers tips and provides access to the program's Help system.

Office Clipboard A temporary storage area shared by all Office programs that can be used to cut, copy and paste multiple items within and between Office programs. The Office Clipboard can hold up to 24 items collected from any Office program. *See also* Clipboard task pane and System Clipboard.

OLE Object A field data type that stores pointers that tie files, such as pictures, sound clips, or spreadsheets, created in other programs to a record.

One-to-many line The line that appears in the Relationships window and shows which field is duplicated between two tables to serve as the linking field. The one-to-many line displays a "1" next to the field that serves as the "one" side of the relationship and displays an infinity symbol next to the field that serves as the "many" side of the relationship when referential integrity is specified for the relationship. Also called the one-to-many join line.

One-to-many relationship The relationship between two tables in an Access database in which a common field links the tables together. The linking field is usually the primary key field in the "one" table of the relationship and the foreign key field in the "many" table of the relationship.

Online collaboration The ability to share information over the Internet.

Open To use one of the methods for opening a document to retrieve it and display it in the document window.

Option button A bound control used to display a limited list of mutually exclusive choices for a field such as "female" or "male" for a gender field in a form or report.

Option group A bound control placed on a form that is used to group together several option buttons that provide a limited number of values for a field.

OR criteria Criteria placed on different rows of the query design grid. A record will appear in the resulting datasheet if any of the criteria is true for any single row.

Order of precedence The order in which Excel calculates parts of a formula: (1) exponents, (2) multiplication and division, and (3) addition and subtraction.

Outbox The folder that contains messages you have sent, but which Outlook has not yet delivered.

Outdent *See* Negative indent.

Outline tab The section in Normal view that displays your presentation text in the form of an outline, without graphics.

Outline view A view that shows the headings of a document organized as an outline.

Outlook Today page A customizable view within Outlook that provides a preview of your day's tasks, appointments, and messages at a glance.

Output The end result of a worksheet.

Overtype mode A feature that allows you to overwrite existing text as you type.

Page An Access object that creates Web pages from Access objects as well as provides Web page connectivity features to an Access database. Also called data access page (DAP).

Page Footer A section of a form or report that contains controls that print once at the bottom of each page.

Page function Built-in Access function used to display the current page number on a report.

Page Header A section of a form or report that contains controls that print once at the top of each page. On the first page of the report, the Page Header section prints below the Report Header section.

Pane A section of the PowerPoint window, such as the Slide or Notes pane.

Paragraph spacing The amount of space between paragraphs.

Paragraph style A named set of paragraph and character format settings that can be applied to a paragraph to format it all at once.

Paste To insert items stored on the Clipboard into a document.

Paste Function A series of dialog boxes that helps you build functions; it lists and describes all Excel functions.

Personal information manager (PIM) A program that includes tools, such as a scheduler and a contact manager, that help you manage a typical business day.

Personalized menus/toolbars The menus and toolbars that modify themselves to reflect those features that you use most often.

Pie chart A circular chart that represents data as slices of a pie. A pie chart is useful for showing the relationship of parts to a whole; pie slices can be extracted for emphasis. *See also* Exploding pie slice.

PivotTable An arrangement of data that uses one field as a column heading, another as a row heading, and summarizes a third field, typically a Number field, in the body.

PivotTable Wizard Form creation tool that provides a series of steps to create a summarized arrangement of data in a PivotTable arrangement.

Pixel One pixel is the measurement of one picture element on the screen.

Placeholder A dashed line box where you place text or objects.

Plot area The area inside the horizontal and vertical chart axes.

Point A unit of measure used for fonts and row height. One inch equals 72 points, or a point is equal to ½ of an inch.

Pointing method Specifying formula cell references by selecting the desired cell with the mouse instead of typing its cell reference; it eliminates typing errors. Also known as Pointing.

Portrait orientation A print setting that positions the document on the page so the page is taller than it is wide.

Pound sign Wildcard that stands for a single-number digit (#).

PowerPoint Viewer A special application designed to run a PowerPoint slide show on any compatible computer that does not have PowerPoint installed.

PowerPoint window A window that contains the running PowerPoint application. The PowerPoint window includes the PowerPoint menus, toolbars, and Presentation window.

Presentation graphics A program that is used to develop slides and hand outs for a visual presentation.

Presentation software A software program used to organize and present information.

Preview A view of the worksheet exactly as it will appear on paper.

Primary key field A field that contains unique information for each record. A primary key field cannot contain a null entry.

Primary sort field In a query grid, the leftmost field that includes sort criteria. It determines the order in which the records will appear and can be specified "ascending" or "descending."

Print Layout view A view that shows a document as it will look on a printed page.

Print Preview A view of a file as it will appear when printed.

Profile A set of information used to identify individual e-mail users.

Program Task-oriented software (such as Excel or Word) that enables you to perform a certain type of task such as data calculation or word processing.

Properties Characteristics that further define the field (if field properties), control (if control properties), section (if section properties), or object (if object properties).

Property sheet A window that displays an exhaustive list of properties for the chosen control, section, or object within the Form Design View or Report Design View.

Publish To post Web pages on an intranet or the Web so people can access the pages through a browser.

Query An Access object that provides a spreadsheet-like view of the data, similar to that in tables. It may provide the user with a subset of fields and/or records from one or more tables. Queries are created when the user has a "question" about the data in the database.

Query design grid The bottom pane of the Query Design View window in which you specify the fields, sort order, and limiting criteria for the query.

Query Design View The window in which you develop queries by specifying the fields, sort order, and limiting criteria that determine which fields and records are displayed in the resulting datasheet.

Query grid *See* Query design grid.

Question mark Wildcard character that stands for any single character.

Range A selected group of adjacent cells.

Range finder A feature that outlines an equation's arguments in blue and green.

Range format A format applied to a selected range in a worksheet.

Raw data *See* Data.

Reading Layout view A view that shows a document so that it is easy to read and annotate.

Reading pane The pane of the Inbox that allows you to read and scroll through your messages without opening them. Can be displayed on the right or bottom of the Outlook window.

Record A group of related fields, such as all demographic information for one customer.

Record number box *See* Specific record box.

Record selector box The small square to the left of a record in a datasheet that marks the current record or the edit record symbol when the record has the focus or is being edited.

Record Source In a form or report, the property that determines which table or query object contains the fields and records that the form or report will display. It is the most important property of the form or report object. A bound control on a form or report also has a Record Source property. In this case, the Record Source property identifies the field to which the control is bound.

Recordset The value of the Record Source property.

Rectangle control An unbound control used to draw rectangles on the form that divide the other form controls into logical groupings.

Related Links Search results that appear as a list of links to related Web sites.

Relational database A database in which more than one table, such as the customer, sales, and inventory tables, can share information. The term "relational database" means the tables are linked or "related" with a common field of information. An Access database is relational.

Relational database software Software such as Access that is used to manage data organized in a relational database.

Relative cell reference A type of cell reference used to indicate a relative position in the worksheet. It allows you to copy and move formulas from one area to another of the same dimensions. Excel automatically changes the column and row numbers to reflect the new position. Also known as Relative reference.

Report An Access object that creates a professional printout of data that may contain such enhancements as headers, footers, and calculations on groups of records.

Report Design View View of a report in which you add, delete, and edit the report's properties, sections, and controls.

Report Footer On a report, a section that contains controls that print once at the end of the last page of the report.

Report Header On a report, a section that contains controls that print once at the top of the first page of the report.

Report section properties Properties that determine what information appears in different report sections and how it is formatted.

Report Wizard An Access wizard that helps you create a report.

Right indent A type of indent in which the right edge of a paragraph is moved in from the right margin.

Right-align Alignment in which an item is flush with the right margin.

Rotate handle A green circular handle at the top of a selected object that you can drag to rotate the selected object upside-down, sideways, or to any angle in between.

Row heading The gray box containing the row number to the left of the row.

Row height The vertical dimension of a cell.

Row selector The small square to the left of a field in Table Design View or the Tab Order dialog box.

Rulers Vertical and horizontal guides that appear in Form and Report Design View to help you position controls.

Sans serif font A font (such as Arial) whose characters do not include serifs, which are small strokes at the ends of letters.

Save To store a file permanently on a disk or to overwrite the copy of a file that is stored on a disk with the changes made to the file.

Save As Command used to save a file for the first time or to create a new file with a different filename, leaving the original file intact.

Scale To change the size of a graphic to a specific percentage of its original size.

ScreenTip A descriptive message that appears when you point to a toolbar button.

Scroll To use the scroll bars or arrow keys to display different parts of a window.

Scroll arrows The arrows at the ends of the scroll bars that are clicked to scroll a document one line at a time.

Scroll bars The bars on the right edge (vertical scroll bar) and bottom edge (horizontal scroll bar) of the document window that are used to display different parts of the document in the document window.

Scroll box The box in the scroll bars that can be dragged to scroll a document or web page.

Search Companion Enables you to search in two ways: it can provide a list of links similar in content or topic to the Web page you are currently viewing; or you can use the Search Companion text box to search for information based on keywords. When in use, it appears in the left pane of the browser window.

Search engine A special Web site that searches the Internet for Web sites based on key words or phrases that you enter and then provides you with a list of links to related Web sites.

Search Folders A tool for organizing your e-mail; instead of actually containing messages, these folders provide shortcuts to messages based on criteria you specify.

Secondary sort field In a query grid, the second field from the left that includes sort criteria. It determines the order in which the records will appear if there is a "tie" on the primary sort field. (For example, the primary sort field might be the State field. If two records both contained the data "IA" in that field, the secondary sort field, which might be the City field, would determine the order of the IA records in the resulting datasheet.)

Section A location of a form or report that contains controls. The section in which a control is placed determines where and how often the control prints. (Access)

Section A portion of a document that is separated from the rest of the document by section breaks. (Word)

Section break A formatting mark inserted to divide a document into sections.

Select To click or highlight an item in order to perform some action on it.

Selection box A slanted line border that appears around a text object or placeholder, indicating that it is ready to accept text.

Sent Items folder The folder that contains messages you have sent.

Series in Columns The information in the columns of a datasheet that are on the Value axis; the row labels are on the Category axis.

Series in Rows The information in the datasheet rows that are on the Value axis; the column labels are the Category axis.

Series of labels Preprogrammed series, such as days of the week and months of the year. They are formed by typing the first word of the series, then dragging the fill handle to select and fill the desired range of cells.

Serif font A font (such as Times New Roman) whose characters include serifs, which are small strokes at the ends of letters.

Shading A background color or pattern that can be applied to text, tables, or graphics.

Sheet A term used for a worksheet.

Sheet tab A description at the bottom of each worksheet that identifies it in a workbook. In an open workbook, move to a worksheet by clicking its sheet tab. Also known as Worksheet tab.

Sheet tab scrolling buttons Buttons that enable you to move among sheets within a workbook.

Shortcut key *See* Keyboard shortcut.

Sizing handles The small circles that appear around a selected object. Dragging a handle resizes the object.

Slide A "page" in an on-screen display in a visual presentation.

Slide layout This determines how all of the elements on a slide are arranged, including text and content placeholders.

Slide pane The section of Normal view that contains the current slide.

Slide show An on-screen display of consecutive images in a presentation.

Slide Show view A view that shows a presentation as an electronic slide show; each slide fills the screen.

Slide Sorter view A view that displays a thumbnail of all slides in the order in which they appear in your presentation; used to rearrange slides and add special effects.

Slide timing The amount of time a slide is visible on the screen during a slide show.

Slide transition The special effect that moves one slide off the screen and the next slide on the screen during a slide show. Each slide can have its own transition effect.

Slides tab The section in Normal View that displays the slides of your presentation as small thumbnails.

Smart tag A purple dotted line that appears under text that Word identifies as a date, name, address, or place.

Smart Tag Actions button The button that appears when you point to a smart tag.

Soft page break *See* Automatic page break.

Sort Reorder records in either ascending or descending order based on the values of a particular field.

Source document Original paper document, such as an employment application or medical history form, upon which data is recorded.

Source file The file from which information is copied.

Specific record box Part of a box in the lower-left corner in Datasheet view and Form view of the Navigation buttons and which indicates the current record number. You can click in the specific record box, then type a record number to quickly move to that record. Also called the current record box or record number box.

Spreadsheet A program used to analyze data, perform calculations, and create charts.

Standard Buttons toolbar Toolbar with buttons for common options, such as stopping the loading of a Web page, moving from one Web page to another, printing Web pages, and searching for information on the Internet.

Standard toolbar The toolbar containing the buttons that perform some of the most commonly used commands such as Cut, Copy, Paste, Save, Open, and Print.

Status bar The bar at the bottom of the Access window that provides informational messages and other status information (such as whether the Num Lock is active). (Access)

Status bar The bar at the bottom of the Excel window that provides information about various keys, commands, and processes. (Excel)

Status bar The bar at the bottom of the Outlook window that provides information such as the total number of messages that the open folder contains, the number of those messages that have not been read, and whether or not a filter is applied. (Outlook)

Status bar The bar at the bottom of the PowerPoint window that contains messages about what you are doing and seeing in PowerPoint, such as the current slide number or a description of a command or button. (PowerPoint)

Status bar The bar at the bottom of the Word program window that shows the vertical position, section, and page number of the insertion point, the total number of pages in a document, and the on/off status of several Word features. (Word)

Status bar Located below the browser window, it performs three main functions: 1) displays information about your the connection progress when a new Web page is loading, 2) notifies you when you connect to another Web site, and 3) identifies the percentage of information transferred from the Web server to your browser. The status bar also displays the Web addresses of any link on the Web page when you move your mouse pointer over it. (Internet Explorer)

Status indicator Logo that appears on the right side of the menu bar; is animated while a new Web page loads.

Store-and-forward technology A computer-based communication system in which the senders and recipients don't have to be on their computers at the same time to communicate.

Style A named collection of character and paragraph formats that are stored together and can be applied to text to format it quickly.

Subscript A font effect in which text is formatted in a smaller font size and placed below the line of text.

Subtitle text placeholder A box on the title slide reserved for subpoint text.

Suite A group of programs supplied together for purchase; designed so that information can be easily transferred among the programs.

SUM The most frequently used function, this adds columns or rows of cells.

Superscript A font effect in which text is formatted in a smaller font size and placed above the line of text.

Symbols Special characters that can be inserted into a document using the Symbol command.

System Clipboard A clipboard that stores only the last item cut or copied from a document. *See* Clipboard and Office Clipboard.

Tab *See* Tab stop.

Tab control An unbound control used to create a three-dimensional aspect to a form so that other controls can be organized and shown in Form View by clicking the "tabs."

Tab leaders Lines that appear in front of tabbed text.

Tab order The sequence in which the controls on the form receive the focus when the user presses [Tab] or [Enter] in Form view.

Tab stop A location on the horizontal ruler that indicates where to align text.

Table A collection of records for a single subject, such as all of the customer records. (Excel)

Table A grid made up of rows and columns of cells that you can fill with text and graphics. (Word)

Table An object that is a collection of records for a single subject, such as an inventory of products. (Access)

Table Datasheet toolbar The toolbar that appears when you are viewing a table's datasheet.

Table Design View The view in which you can add, delete, or modify fields and their associated properties.

Table style A named set of table format settings that can be applied to a table to format it all at once.

Table Wizard An interactive tool used to create a new table from a list of sample tables and sample fields.

Task Pad An area in Calendar that displays your task list.

Task pane An area located on the right side of the screen in each program that lets you complete common tasks.

Task pane list arrow Lets you switch between different task panes.

Tasks The component within Outlook that works as an electronic to-do list. You can view tasks, mark your progress on tasks, assign tasks to colleagues, and track completion.

Tasks folder The folder that stores your business and personal to-do list.

Template A formatted document that contains placeholder text you can replace with your own text.

Template A file saved with a special format that lets you open a new file based on an existing workbook's design and/or content. (Excel)

Text A field data type that allows text information or combinations of text and numbers such as a street address. By default, it is 50 characters but can be changed. The maximum length of a text field is 255 characters.

Text annotations Labels added to a chart to draw attention to a particular area.

Text box A common control used on forms and reports to display data bound to an underlying field. A text box can also show calculated controls such as subtotals and dates. (Access)

Text box Any text you create using the Text Box button. A word processing box and a text label are both examples of a text box.

Text color The color applied to text.

Text label A text box you create using the Text Box button, where the text does not automatically wrap inside the box.

Text placeholder A box with a dashed-line border and text that you replace with your own text.

Thumbnail A small image of a slide. Thumbnails are visible on the Slides tab and in Slide Sorter view.

Tick marks Notations of a scale of measure on a chart axis.

Timing *See* Slide timing.

Title The first line or heading on a slide.

Title bar The bar at the top of the program window that indicates the program name and the name of the current file, web page or open folder.

Title placeholder A box on a slide reserved for the title of a presentation or slide.

Title slide The first slide in a presentation.

Toggle button A bound control used to indicate "yes" or "no" answers for a field. If the button is "pressed" it displays "yes" information. (Access)

Toggle button A button that turns a feature on and off.

Toolbar A bar that contains buttons that you can click to perform commands.

Toolbar Options button A button you click on a toolbar to view toolbar buttons not currently visible.

Toolbox toolbar The toolbar that has common controls that you can add to a report or form when working in Report Design View or Form Design View.

Top-level domain In a Web page address, it tells you the type of site you are visiting, such as com for commerce, edu for educational, gov for government, or org for nonprofit organization.

Tracking A feature that keeps a record of edits and shows the edits others make in a document.

Truncate To shorten the display of cell information because a cell is too wide.

Type a question for help box Area on the menu bar in which you can query the Help system by typing a question.

Unbound control A control that does not change from record to record and exists only to clarify or enhance the appearance of the form, using elements such as labels, lines, and clip art.

Unbound object frame An unbound control that is used to display clip art, a sound clip, or other multimedia content and that doesn't change as you navigate from record to record on a form or report.

Undo To reverse a change by using the Undo button or command.

Undo button Button that allows you to undo your last action.

Uniform Resource Locator (URL) The Web page's address; appears in the Address bar after you open (or load) the page.

Value axis Also known as the y-axis (or vertical axis) in a 2-dimensional chart, this area often contains numerical values that help you interpret the magnitude of chart elements.

Values Numbers, formulas, or functions used in calculations.

Vcards The Internet standard for creating and sharing virtual business cards.

Vertical alignment The position of text in a document relative to the top and bottom margins.

Vertical ruler A ruler that appears on the left side of the document window in Print Layout view.

Vertical scroll bar Used to move the current page up or down in the window to view the parts of the page that are not visible.

View A way of displaying a file in the application window; each view provides features useful for editing and formatting different types of documents.

View buttons Buttons to the left of the horizontal scroll bar that are used to change views.

Web browser (browser) Software program used to access and display Web pages. You must use a browser such as Microsoft Internet Explorer, Opera, or Netscape Navigator, to view Web pages that are on the Web.

Web Layout view A view that shows a document as it will look when viewed with a Web browser.

Web page Document that contains text, graphics, and/or sound, saved in HTML format and published to the World Wide Web for viewing through a browser.

Web site A group of Web pages focused on a particular subject or business.

What-if analysis A decision-making feature in which data is changed and formulas based on it are automatically recalculated.

Wildcards Special characters used in criteria to find, filter, and query data. The asterisk (*) stands for any group of characters. For example, the criteria I* in a State field criterion cell would find all records where the state entry was IA, ID, IL, IN, or Iowa. The question mark (?) wildcard stands for only one character.

Window A rectangular area of the screen where you view and work on the open file.

Wizard An interactive set of dialog boxes that guides you through a task.

.wmf The abbreviation for the Windows metafile file format, which is the format of some clip art.

Word processing box A text box you create using the Text Box button, where the text automatically wraps inside the box.

Word processing program A software program that includes tools for entering, editing, and formatting text and graphics.

Word program window The window that contains the Word program elements, including the document window, toolbars, menu bar, and status bar.

WordArt A drawing object that contains text formatted with special shapes, patterns, and orientations.

Word-wrap A feature that automatically moves the insertion point to the next line as you type.

Workbook A collection of related worksheets contained within a single file.

Worksheet An area within the electronic spreadsheet that contains columns and rows that form individual cells. A worksheet contains 256 columns by 65,536 rows.

Worksheet tab *See* Sheet tab.

Worksheet window Includes the tools that enable you to create and work with worksheets.

World Wide Web (Web) A part of the Internet that brings text, graphics, and multimedia information to your desktop. It contains linked Web pages.

X-axis The horizontal axis in a chart; because it often shows data categories, such as months, it is also called the category axis.

X-axis label A label describing a chart's x-axis.

XY (scatter) chart Compares trends over uneven time or measurement intervals; used in scientific and engineering disciplines for trend spotting and extrapolation.

Y-axis The vertical axis in a chart; because it often shows numerical values in a 2-dimensional chart, it is also called the value axis.

Y-axis label A label describing the y-axis of a chart.

Yes/No A field data type that stores only one of two values, "Yes" or "No."

Zoom A feature that enables you to focus on a larger or smaller part of the worksheet in Print Preview.

Zoom pointers Mouse pointers displayed in Print Preview that allow you to change the zoom magnification of a printout.

Index